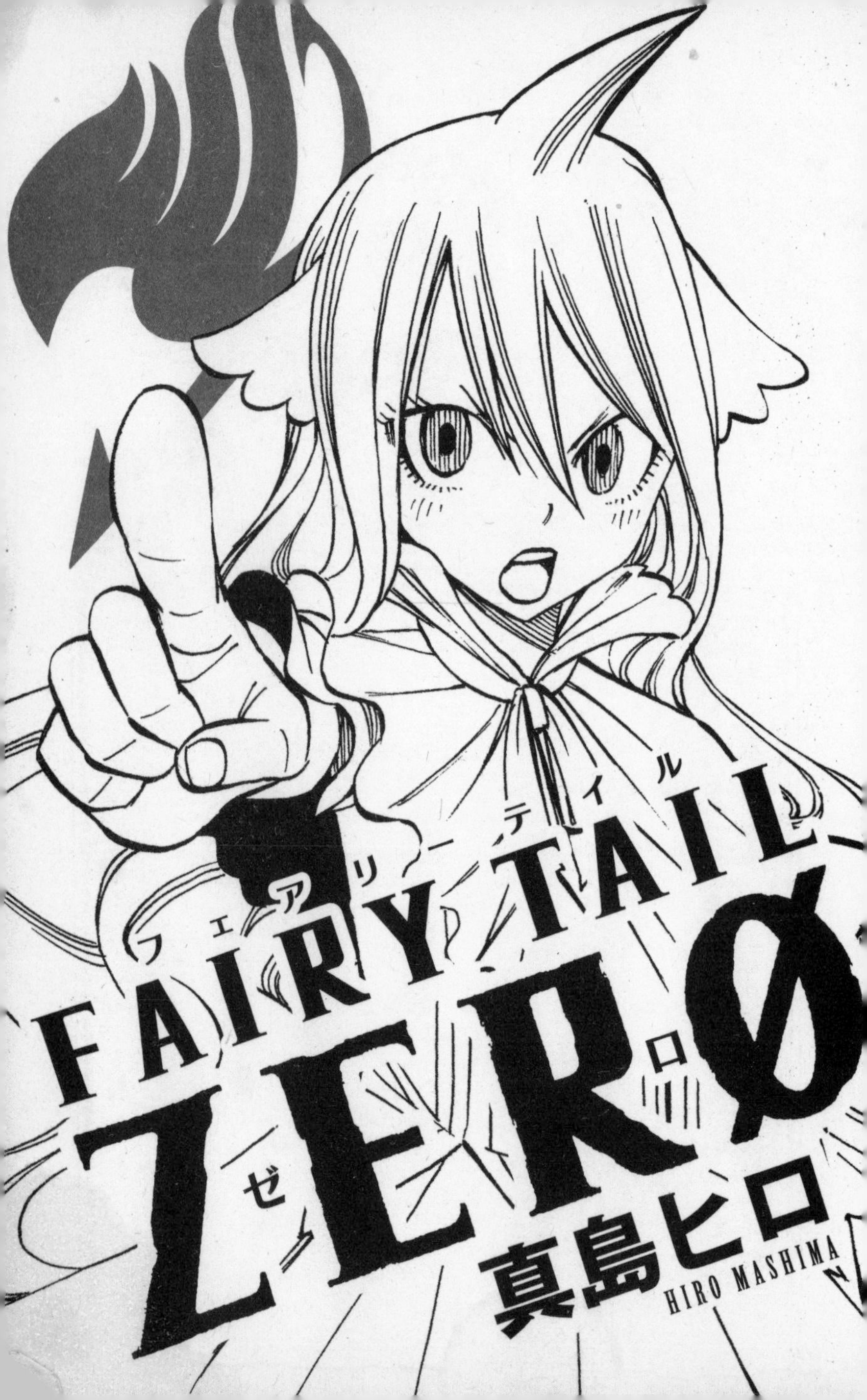
フェアリーテイル
FAIRY TAIL
ゼロ
ZERØ
真島ヒロ
HIRO MASHIMA

フェアリーテイル
FAIRY TAIL ZERØ

ゼ

CONTENTS

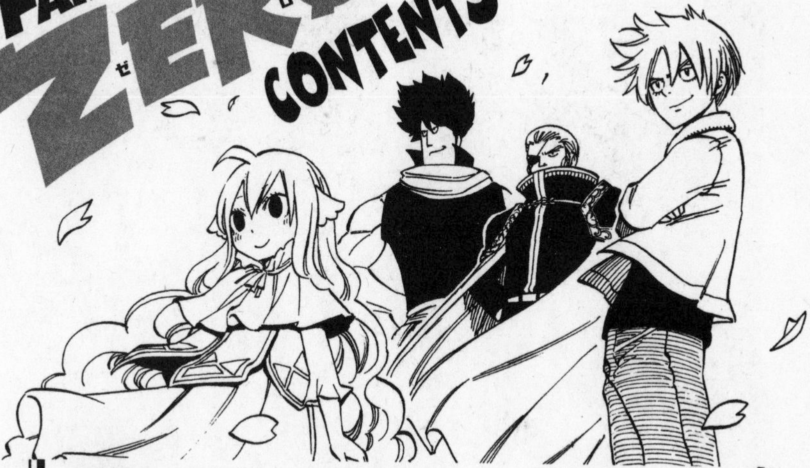

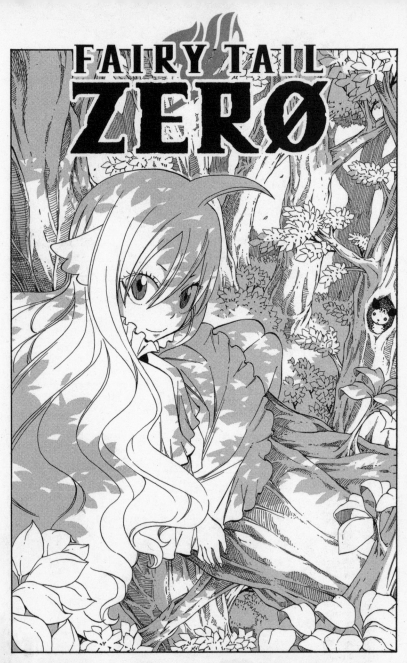

FAIRY TAIL ZERØ

Chapter 1: The Fairies in My Heart

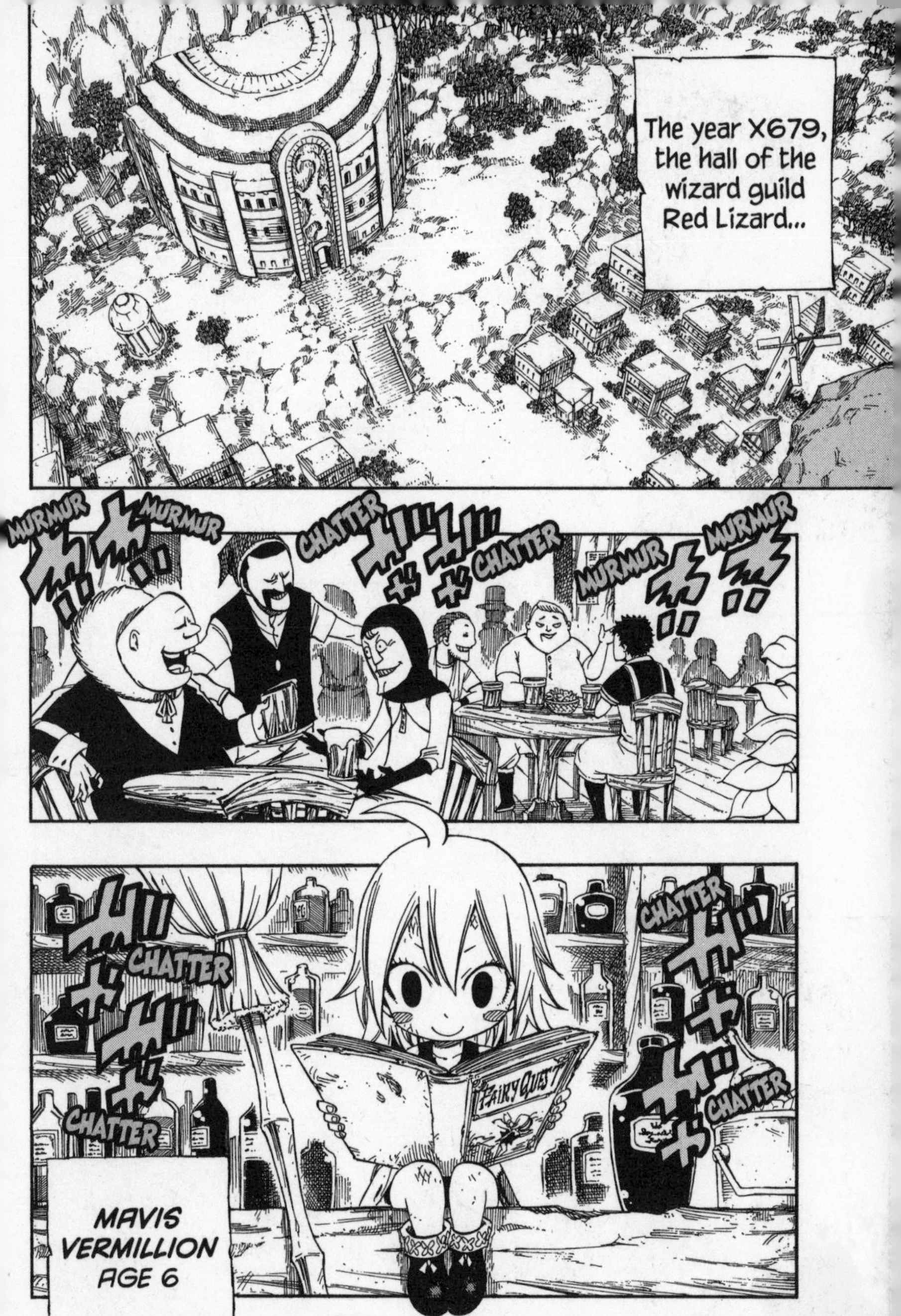
The year X679, the hall of the wizard guild Red Lizard...
MURMUR
MURMUR
CHATTER
CHATTER
MURMUR
MURMUR
CHATTER
CHATTER
CHATTER
CHATTER
MAVIS VERMILLION AGE 6

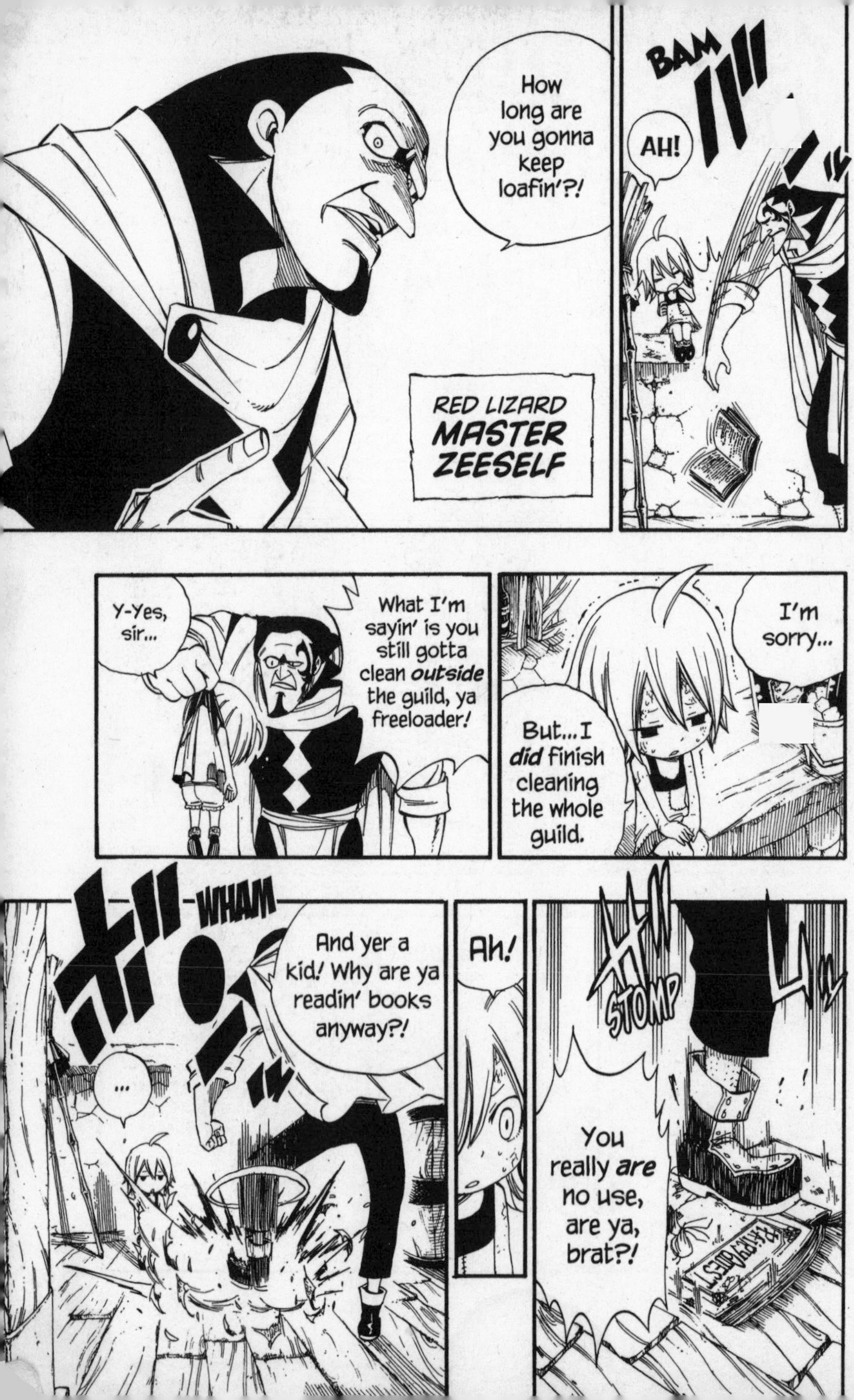
BAM
AH!
How long are you gonna keep loafin'?!
RED LIZARD MASTER ZEESELF
I'm sorry...
But...I *did* finish cleaning the whole guild.
What I'm sayin' is you still gotta clean *outside* the guild, ya freeloader!
Y-Yes, sir...
STOMP
You really *are* no use, are ya, brat?!
Ah!
WHAM
And yer a kid! Why are ya readin' books anyway?!
...

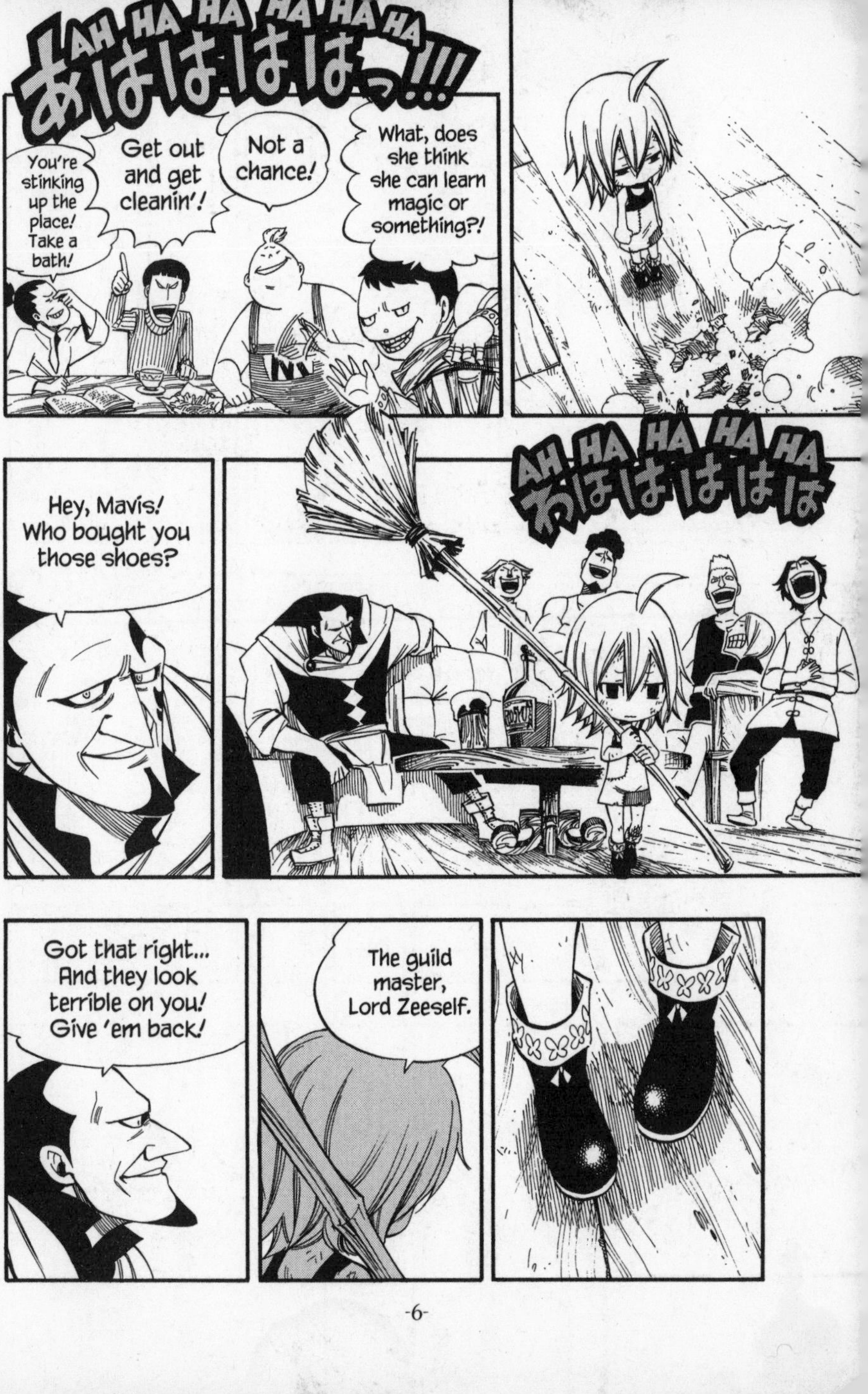
AH HA HA HA HA HA
あははははっ!!!
What, does she think she can learn magic or something?!
Not a chance!
Get out and get cleanin'!
You're stinking up the place! Take a bath!
AH HA HA HA HA HA
おははははは
Hey, Mavis! Who bought you those shoes?
The guild master, Lord Zeeself.
Got that right... And they look terrible on you! Give 'em back!

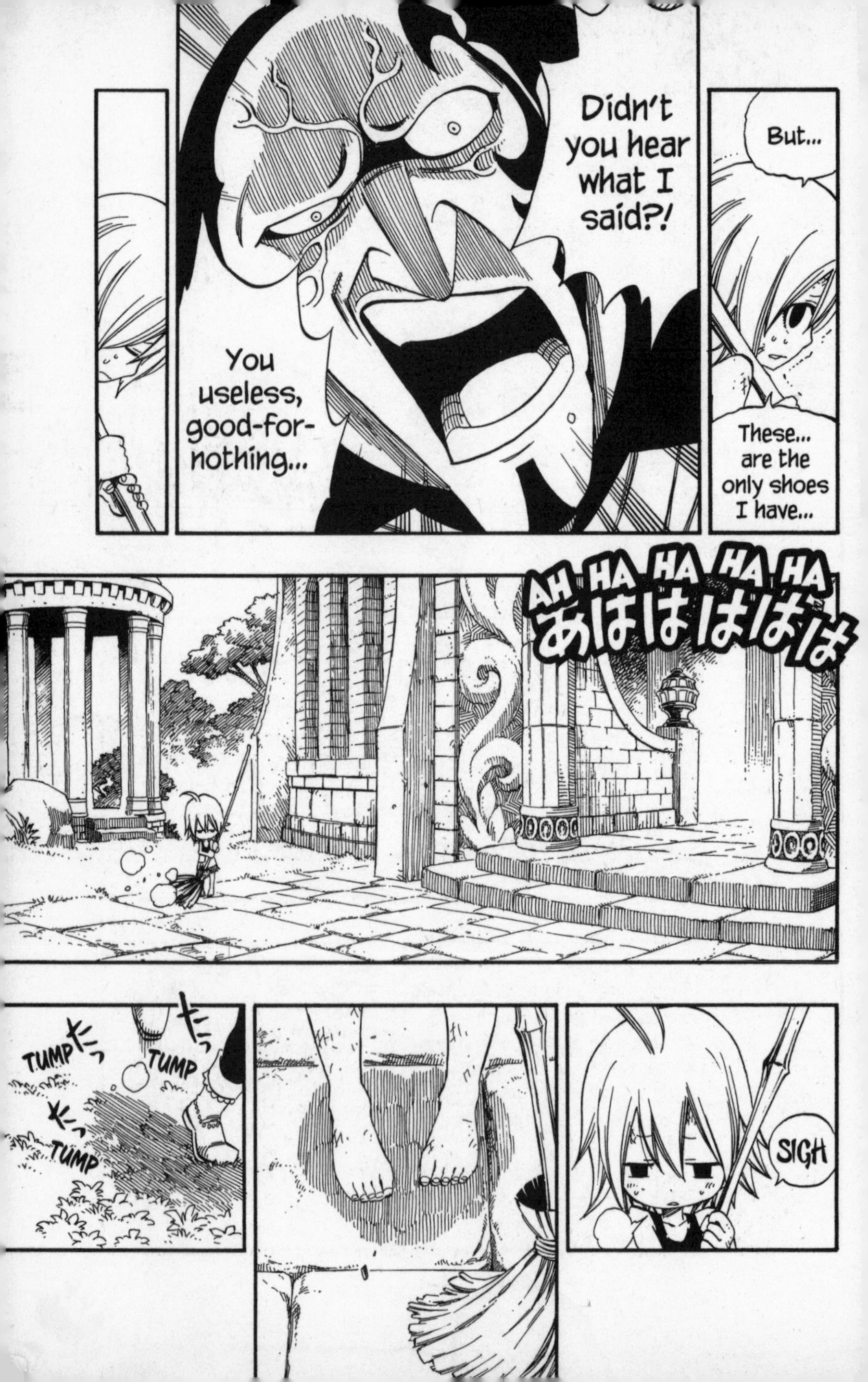
But...
These... are the only shoes I have...
Didn't you hear what I said?!
You useless, good-for-nothing...
AH HA HA HA HA
あははははは
SIGH
TUMP
TUMP
TUMP

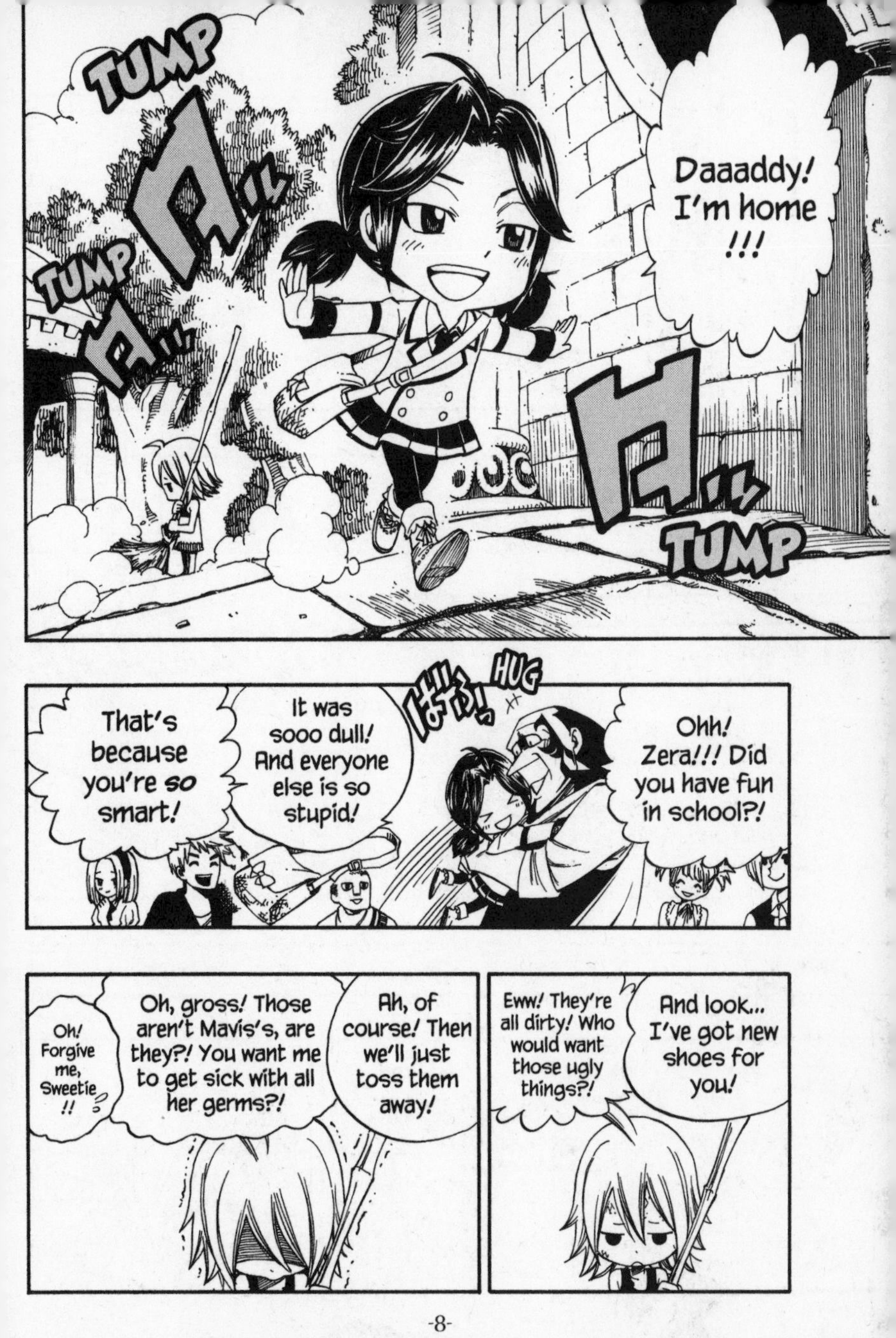
Daaaddy! I'm home !!!
TUMP
TUMP
TUMP
Ohh! Zera!!! Did you have fun in school?!
HUG
It was sooo dull! And everyone else is so stupid!
That's because you're *so* smart!
And look... I've got new shoes for you!
Eww! They're all dirty! Who would want those ugly things?!
Ah, of course! Then we'll just toss them away!
Oh, gross! Those aren't Mavis's, are they?! You want me to get sick with all her germs?!
Oh! Forgive me, Sweetie !!

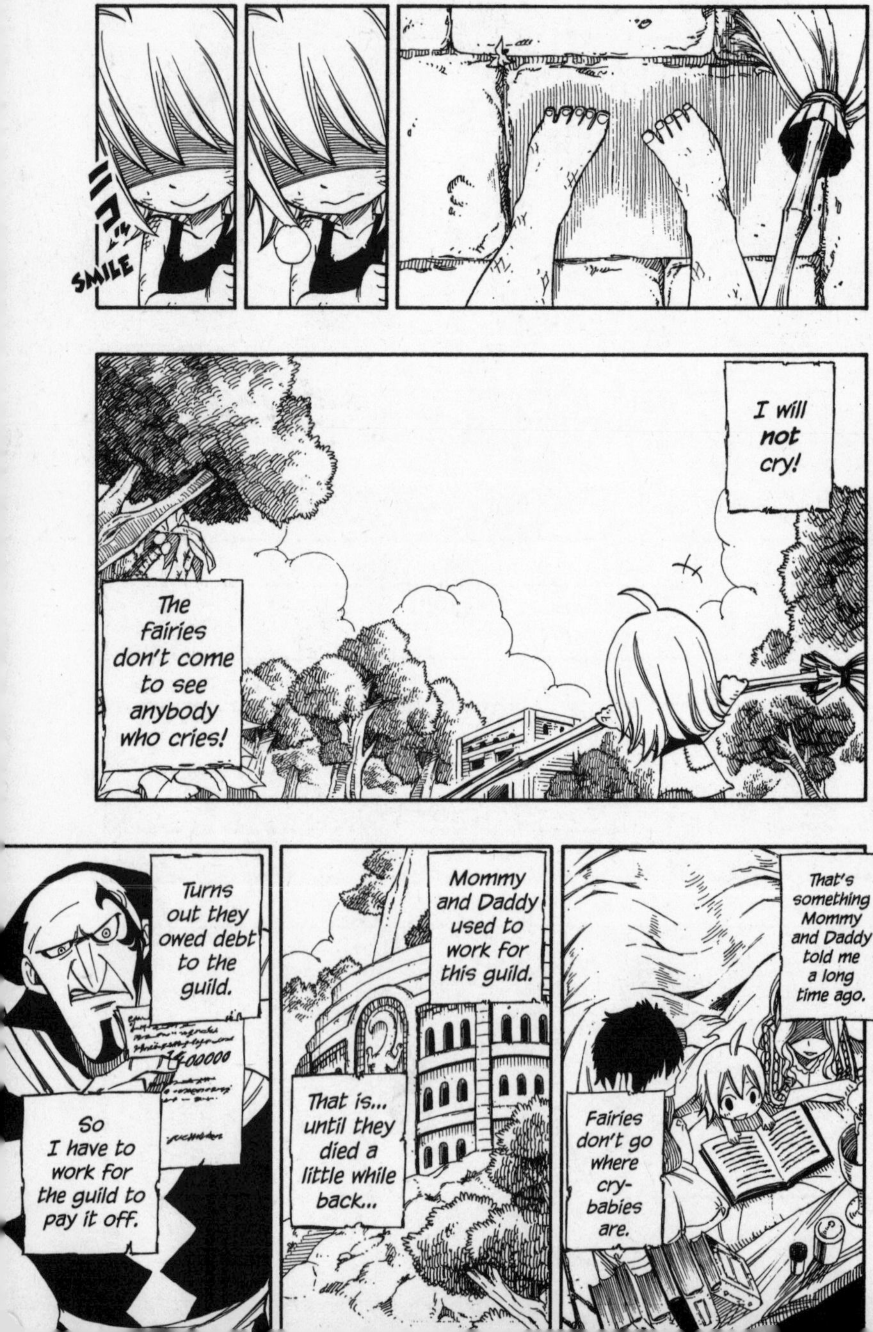
SMILE
I will not cry!
The fairies don't come to see anybody who cries!
That's something Mommy and Daddy told me a long time ago.
Fairies don't go where cry-babies are.
Mommy and Daddy used to work for this guild.
That is... until they died a little while back...
Turns out they owed debt to the guild.
So I have to work for the guild to pay it off.

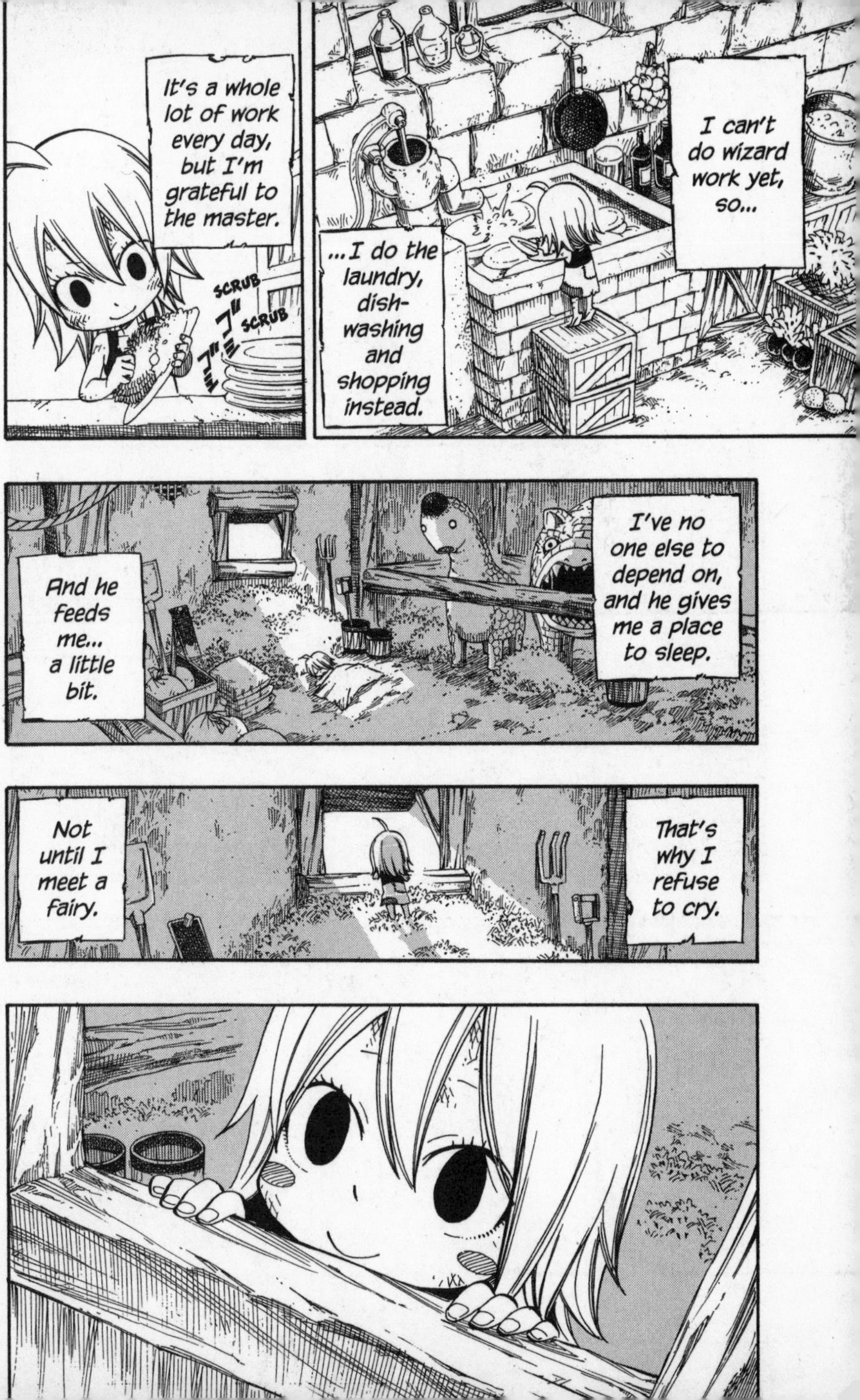
I can't do wizard work yet, so...
...I do the laundry, dish-washing and shopping instead.
It's a whole lot of work every day, but I'm grateful to the master.
SCRUB
SCRUB
I've no one else to depend on, and he gives me a place to sleep.
And he feeds me... a little bit.
That's why I refuse to cry.
Not until I meet a fairy.

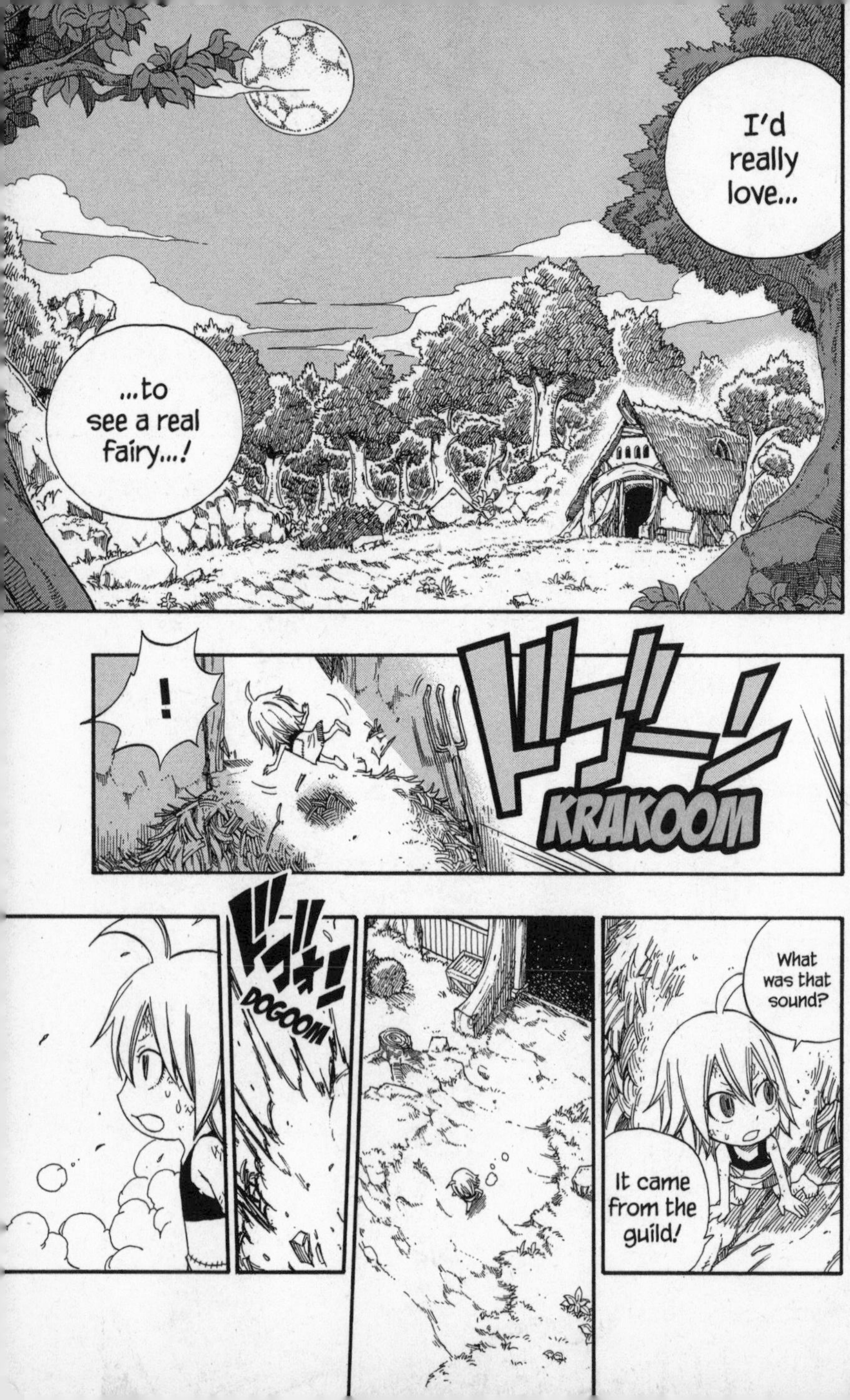
I'd really love...
...to see a real fairy...!
KRAKOOM
!
What was that sound?
It came from the guild!
DOGOOM

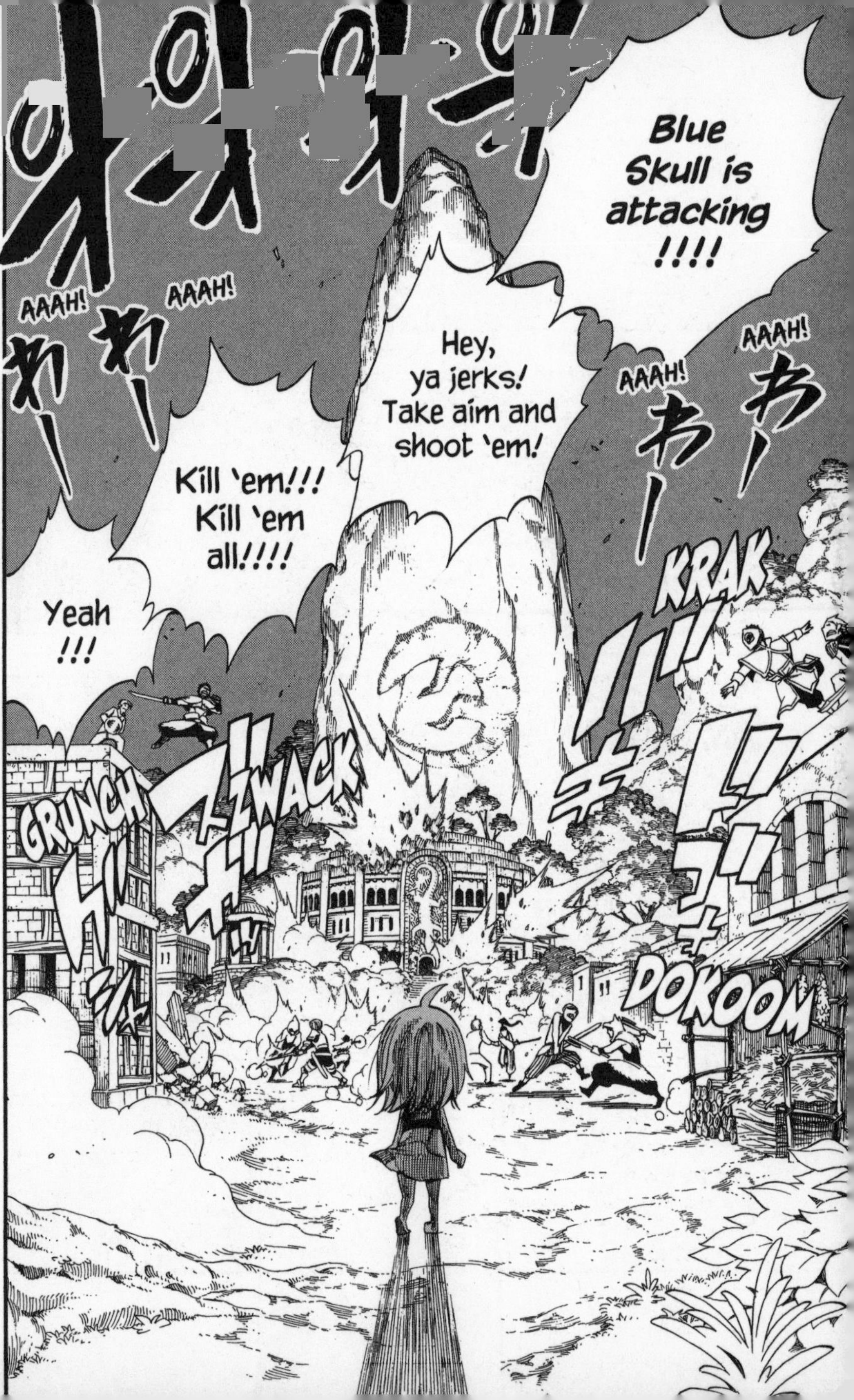
Blue Skull is attacking !!!!
AAAH!
AAAH!
Hey, ya jerks! Take aim and shoot 'em!
Kill 'em!!! Kill 'em all!!!!
AAAH!
AAAH!
Yeah !!!
KRAK
DOKOOM
ZWACK
GRUNCH

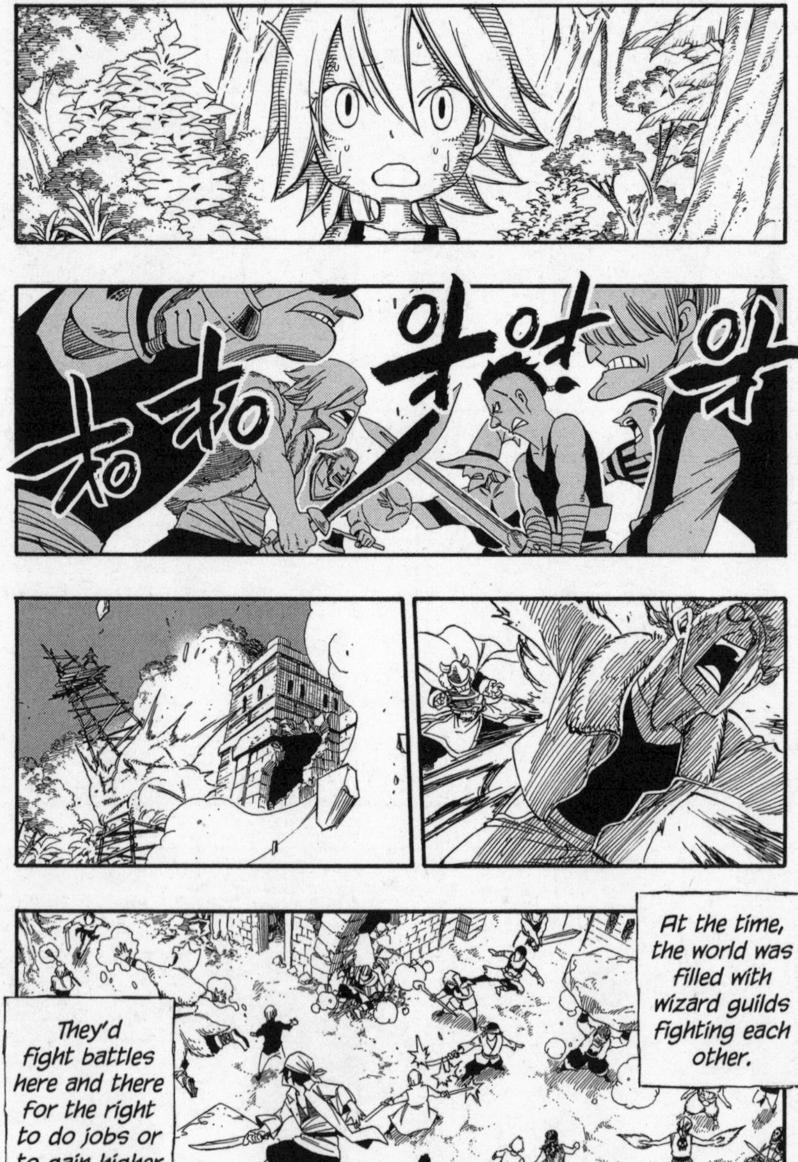
At the time, the world was filled with wizard guilds fighting each other.
They'd fight battles here and there for the right to do jobs or to gain higher status.

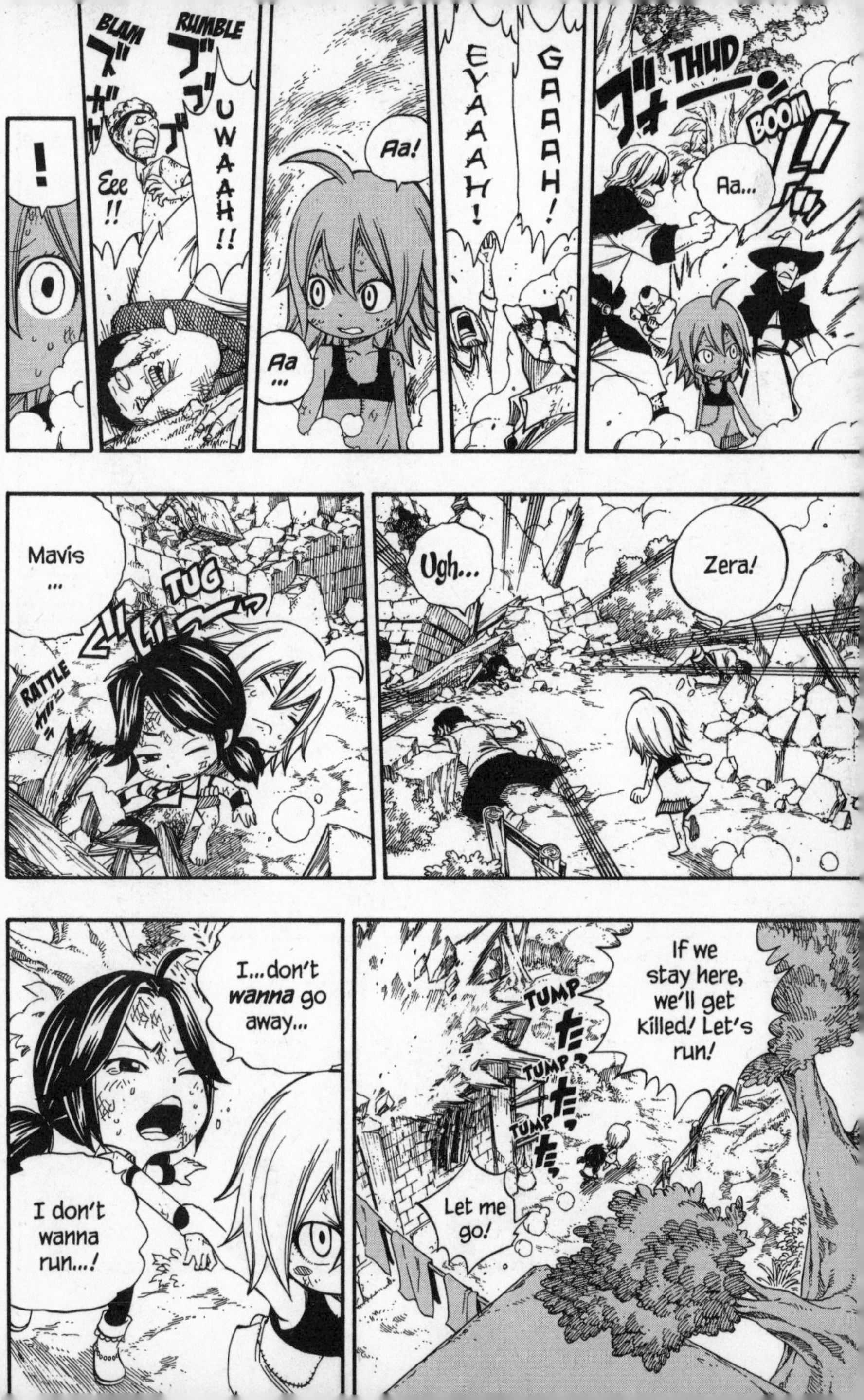
THUD
BOOM
Aa...
GAAAAH!
EYAAAAH!
Aa!
Aa...
RUMBLE
BLAM
UWAAH!!
Eee!!
!
Zera!
Ugh...
Mavis...
TUG
RATTLE
If we stay here, we'll get killed! Let's run!
TUMP
TUMP
TUMP
Let me go!
I...don't *wanna* go away...
I don't wanna run...!

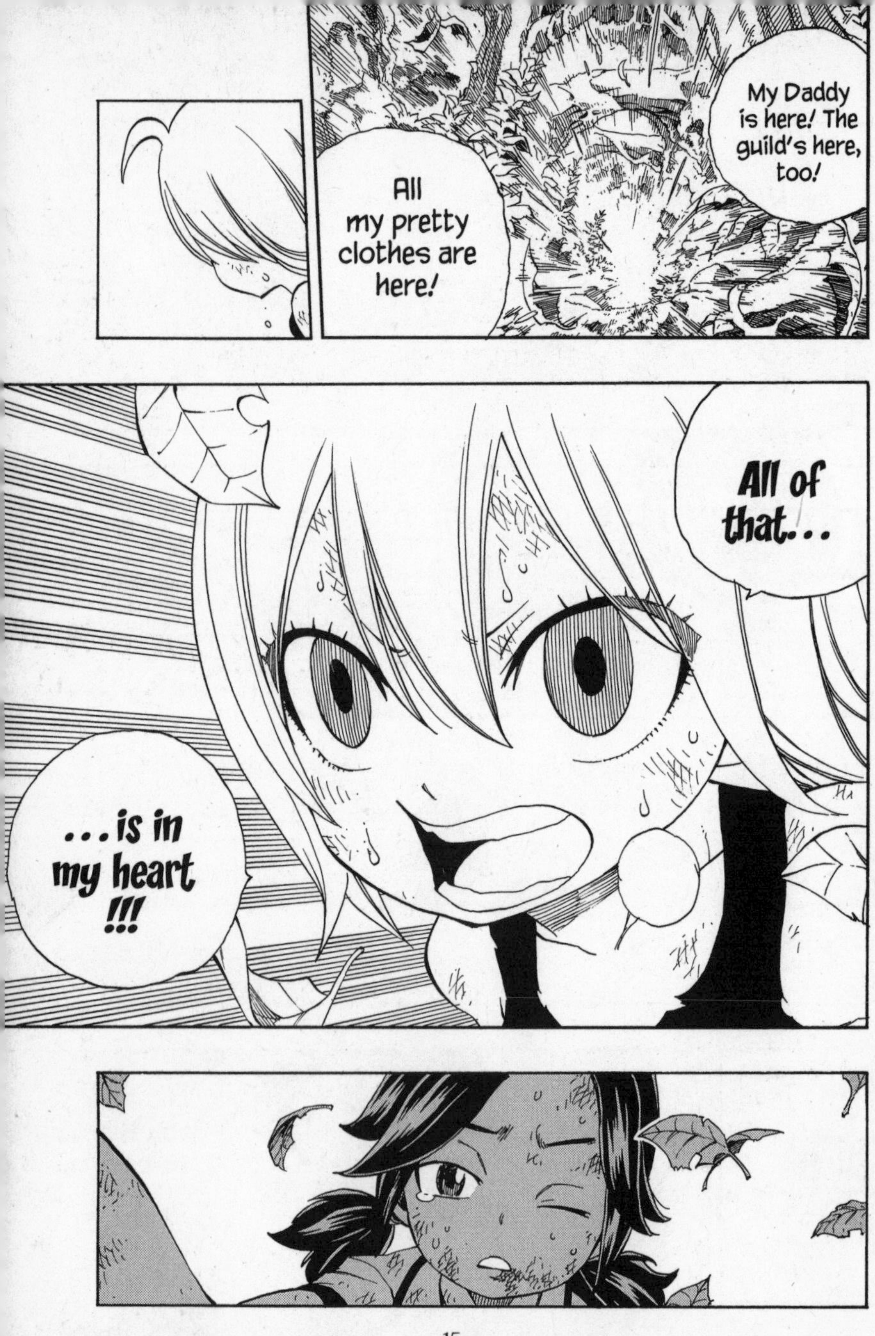
My Daddy is here! The guild's here, too!
All my pretty clothes are here!
All of that...
...is in my heart !!!

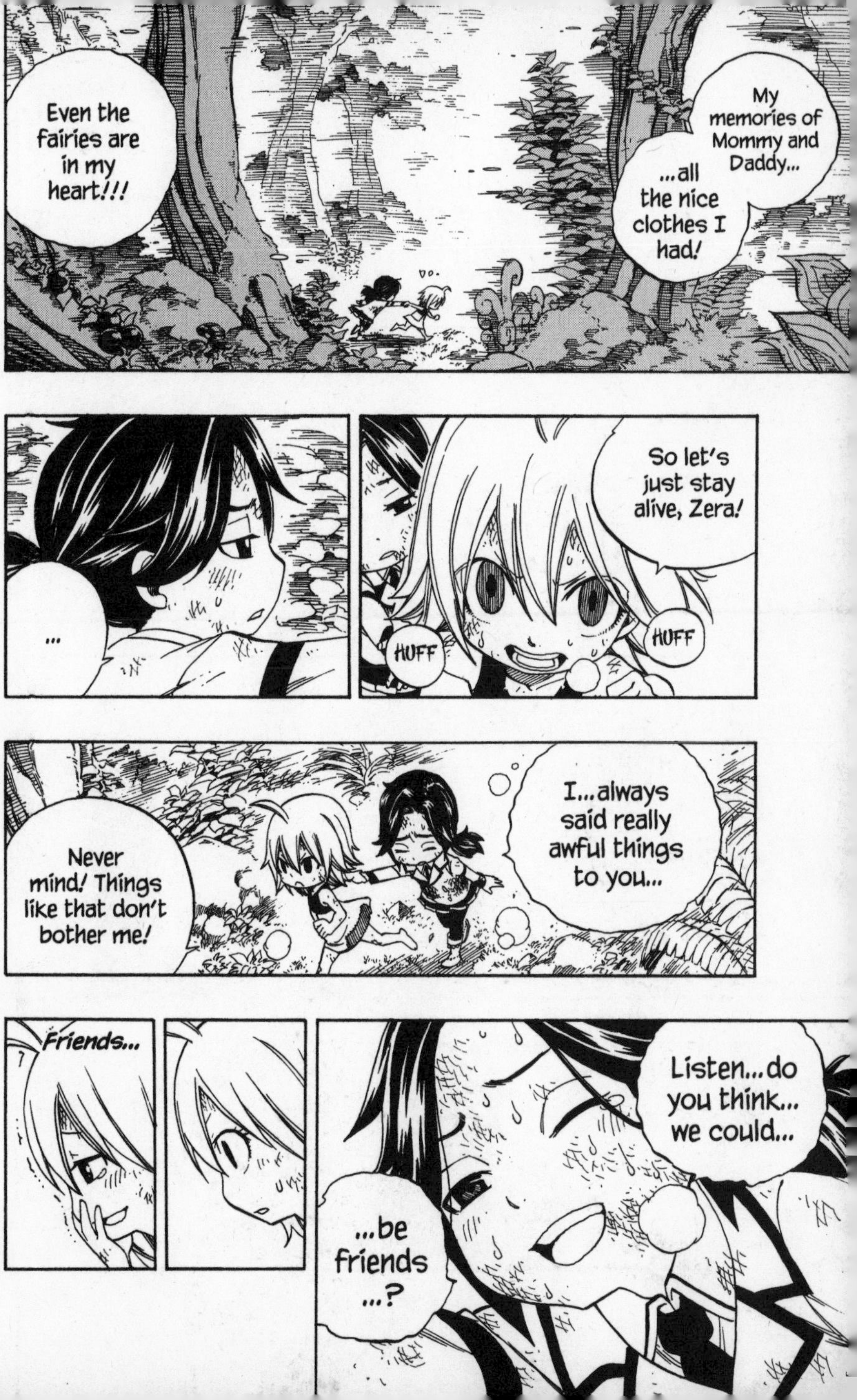
My memories of Mommy and Daddy...
...all the nice clothes I had!
Even the fairies are in my heart!!!
So let's just stay alive, Zera!
HUFF
HUFF
...
I...always said really awful things to you...
Never mind! Things like that don't bother me!
Listen...do you think... we could...
...be friends ...?
Friends...

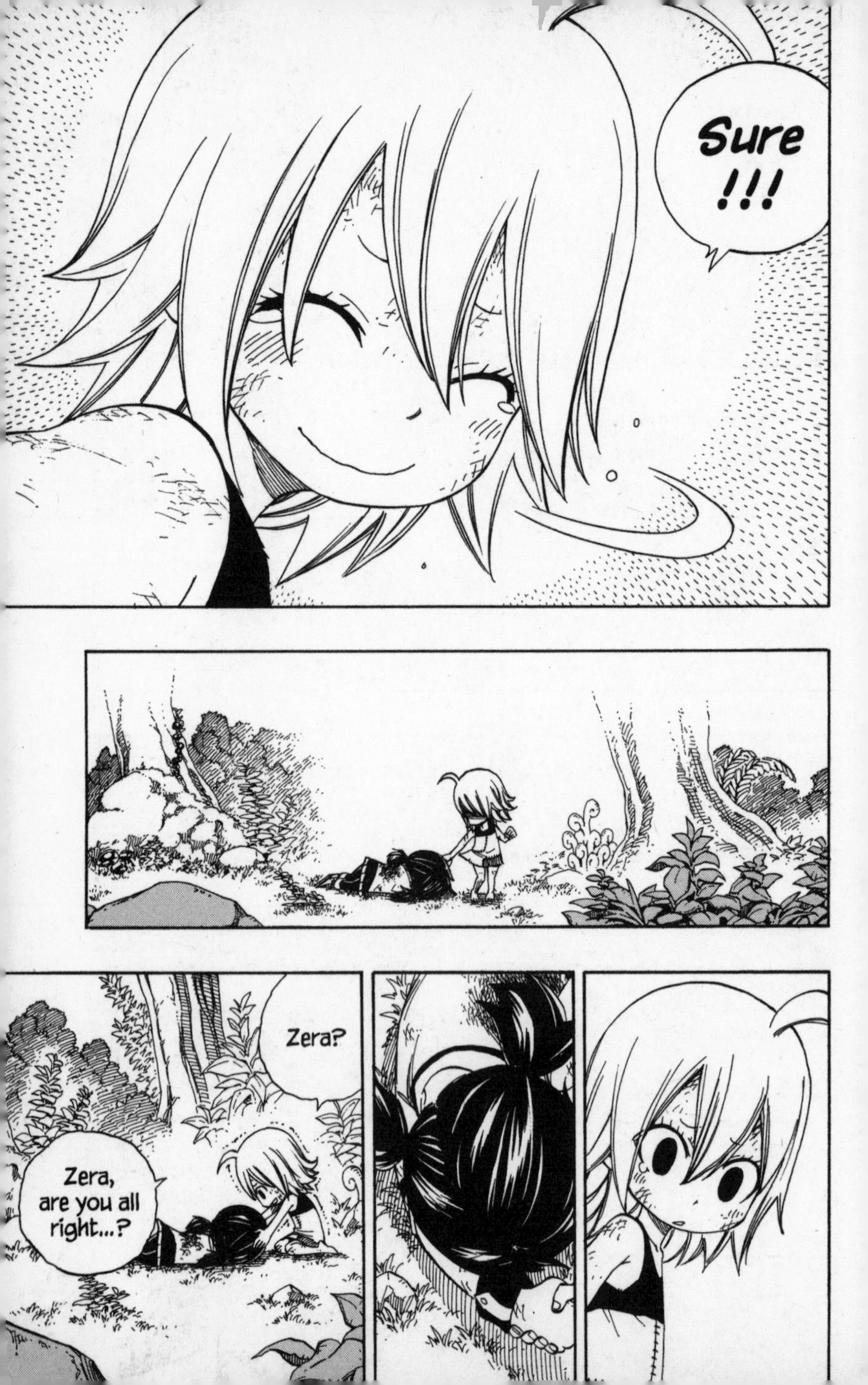
Sure !!!
Zera?
Zera, are you all right...?

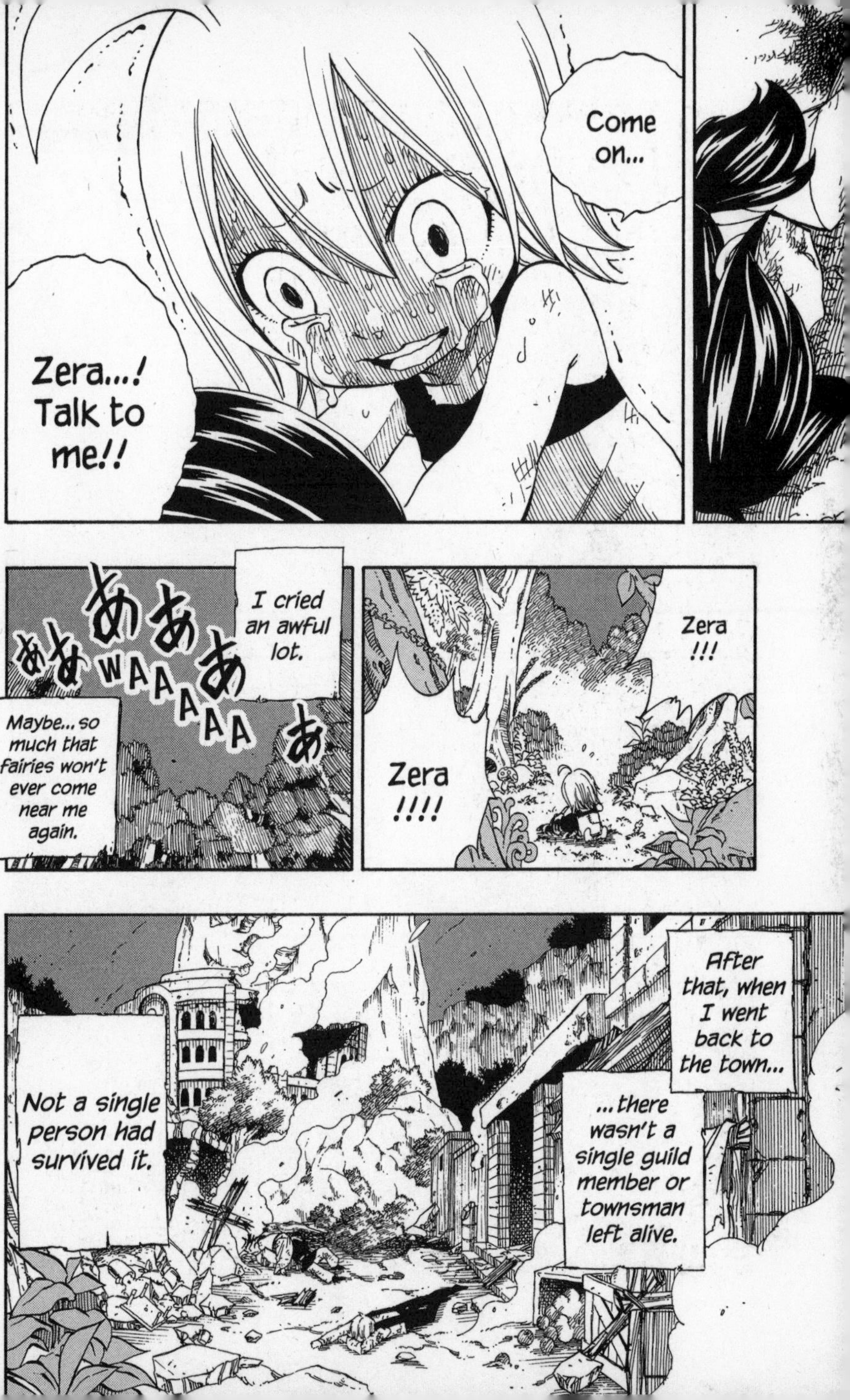
Come on...
Zera...! Talk to me!!
Zera !!!
Zera !!!!
I cried an awful lot.
WAAAAAA
Maybe... so much that fairies won't ever come near me again.
After that, when I went back to the town...
...there wasn't a single guild member or townsman left alive.
Not a single person had survived it.

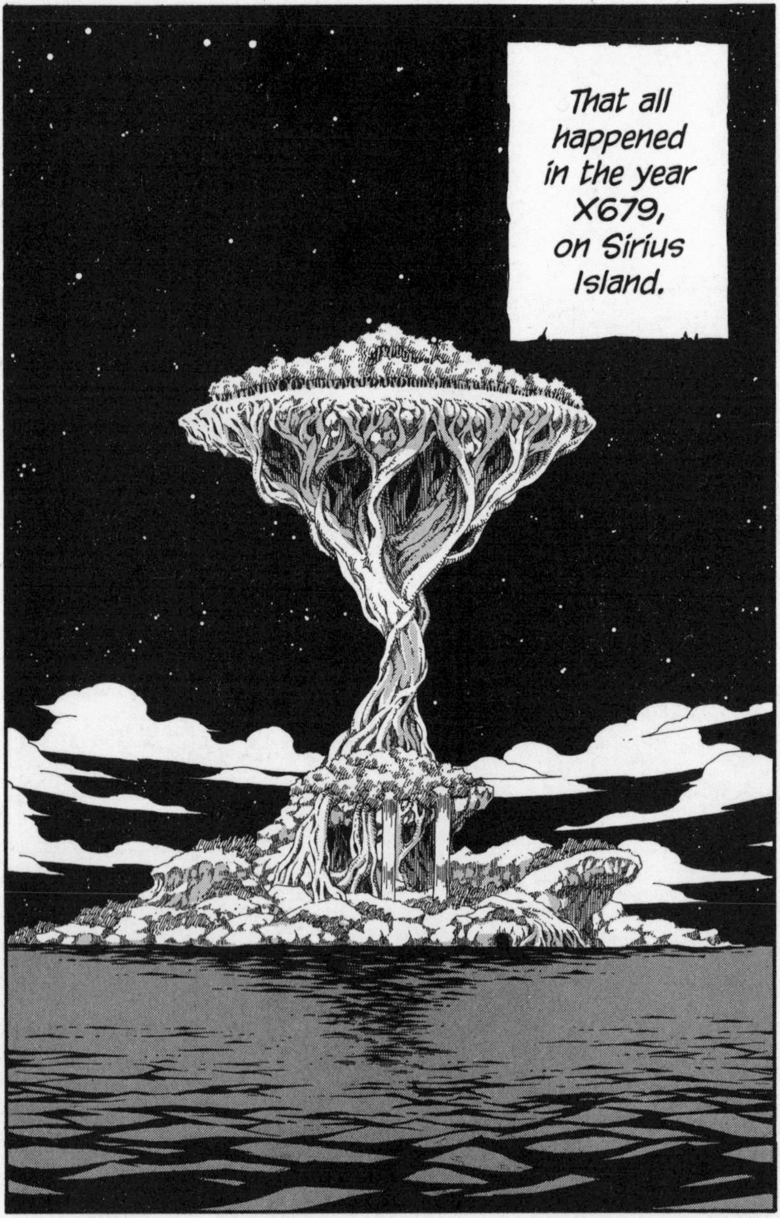
That all happened in the year X679, on Sirius Island.

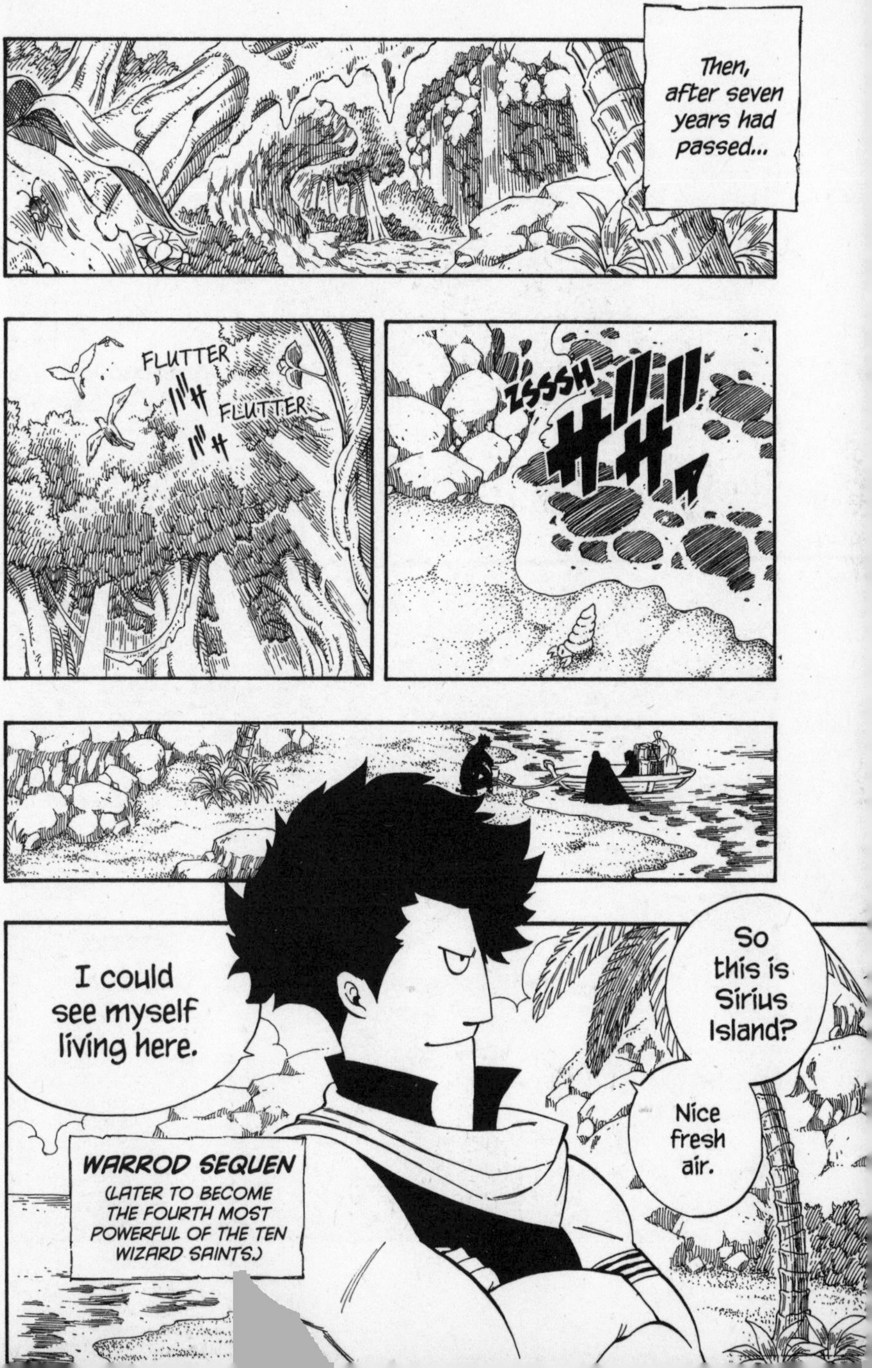
Then, after seven years had passed...
ZSSSH
FLUTTER
FLUTTER
So this is Sirius Island?
Nice fresh air.
I could see myself living here.
WARROD SEQUEN
(LATER TO BECOME THE FOURTH MOST POWERFUL OF THE TEN WIZARD SAINTS.)

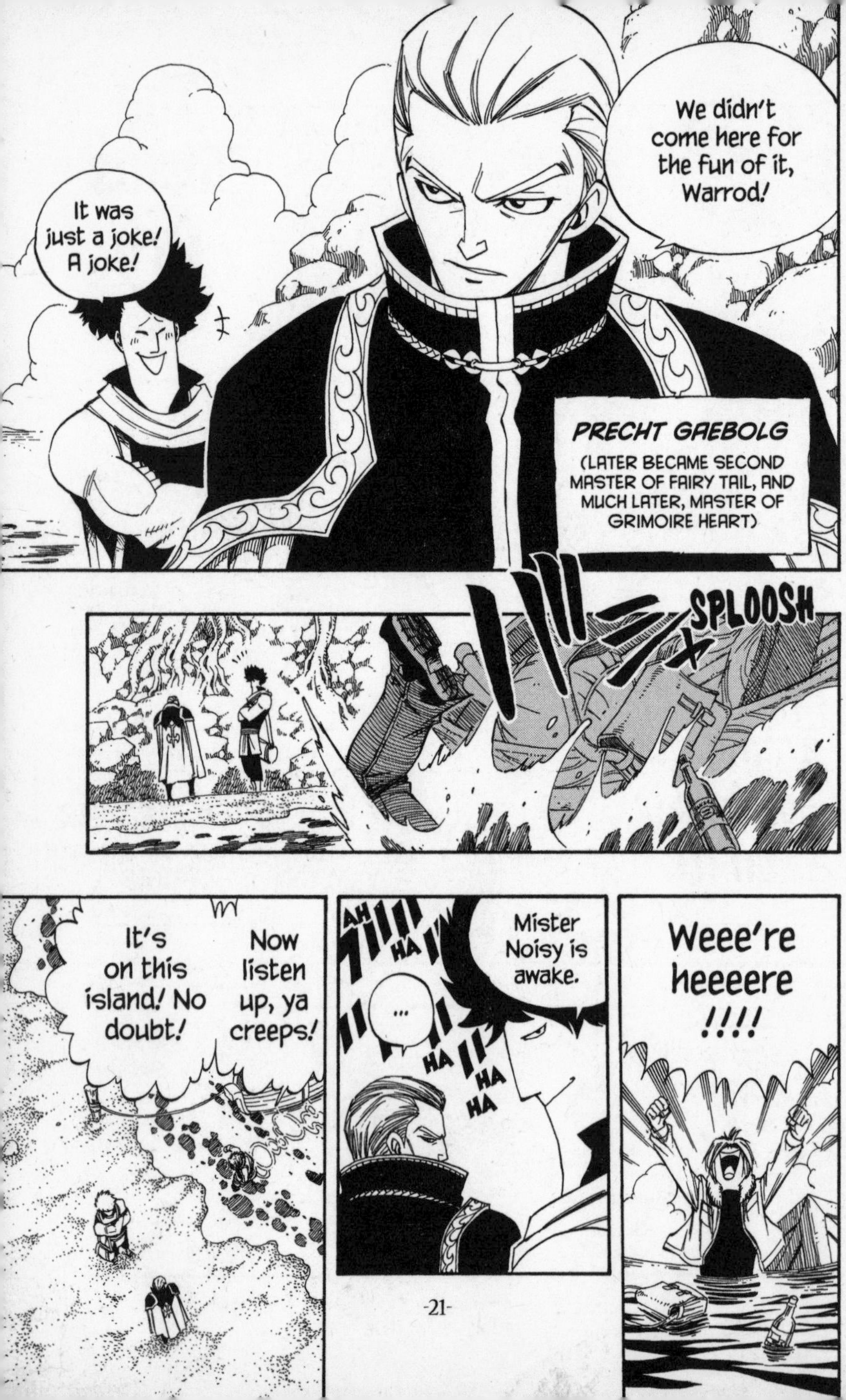

We didn't come here for the fun of it, Warrod!
PRECHT GAEBOLG
(LATER BECAME SECOND MASTER OF FAIRY TAIL, AND MUCH LATER, MASTER OF GRIMOIRE HEART)
It was just a joke! A joke!
SPLOOSH
Weee're heeeere !!!!
Mister Noisy is awake.
AH HA HA HA HA HA
...
Now listen up, ya creeps!
It's on this island! No doubt!

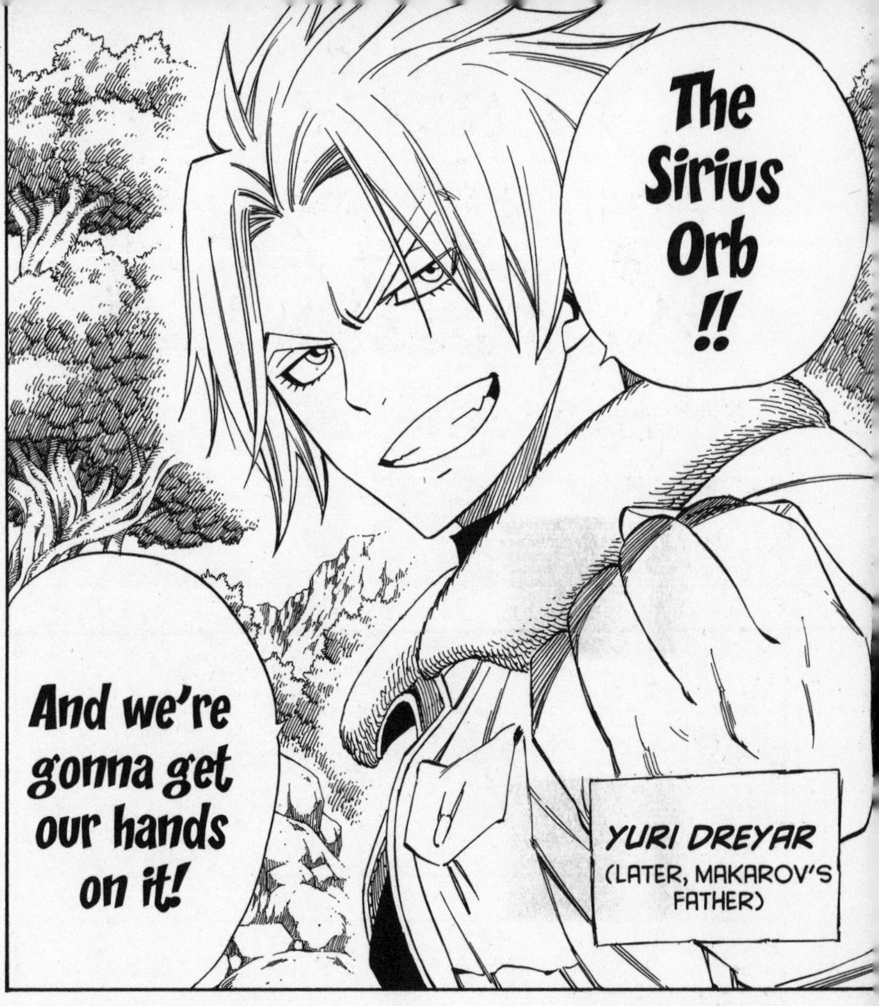
The Sirius Orb!!
And we're gonna get our hands on it!
YURI DREYAR (LATER, MAKAROV'S FATHER)

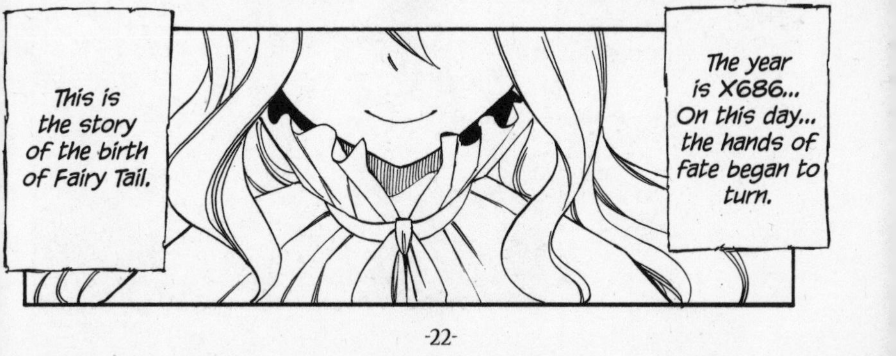
The year is X686... On this day... the hands of fate began to turn.
This is the story of the birth of Fairy Tail.

FAIRY TAIL ZERØ

Chapter 2: The Truth Game

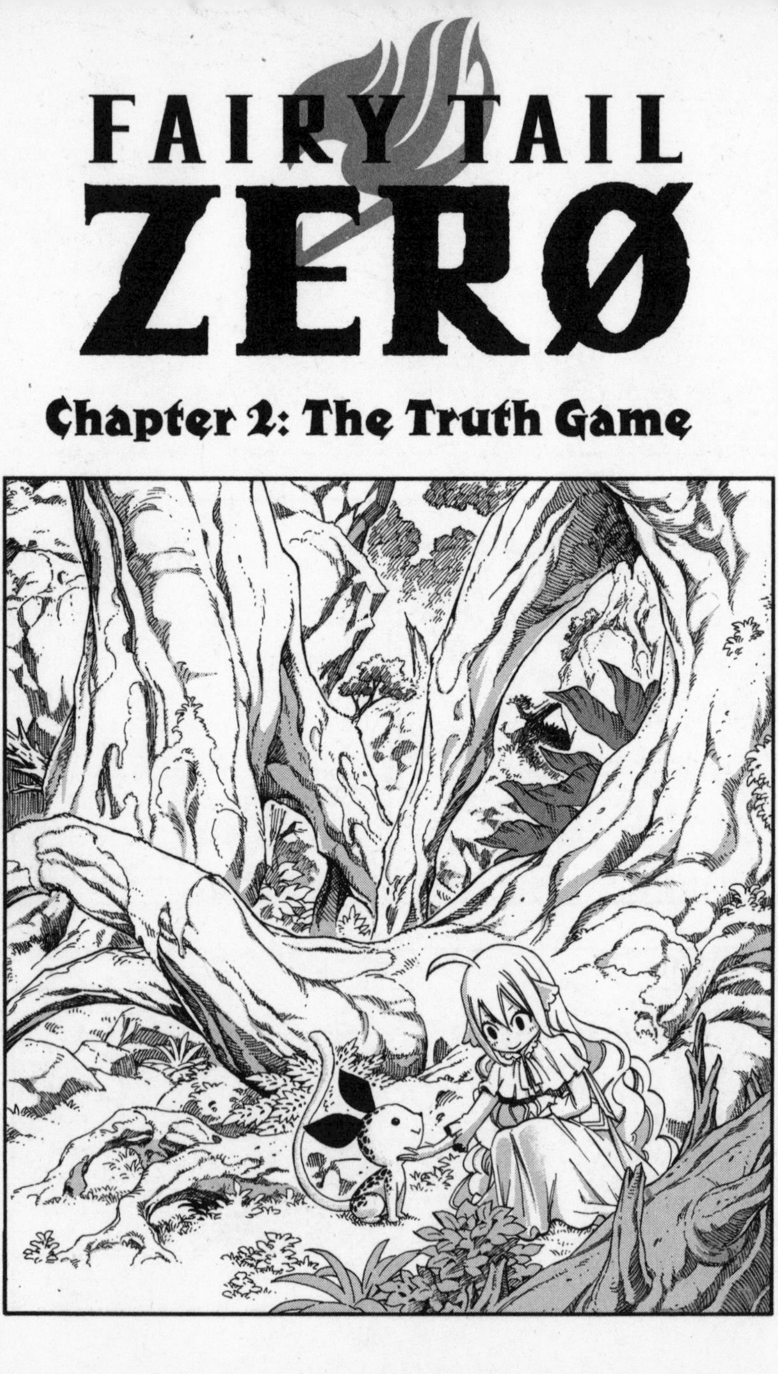

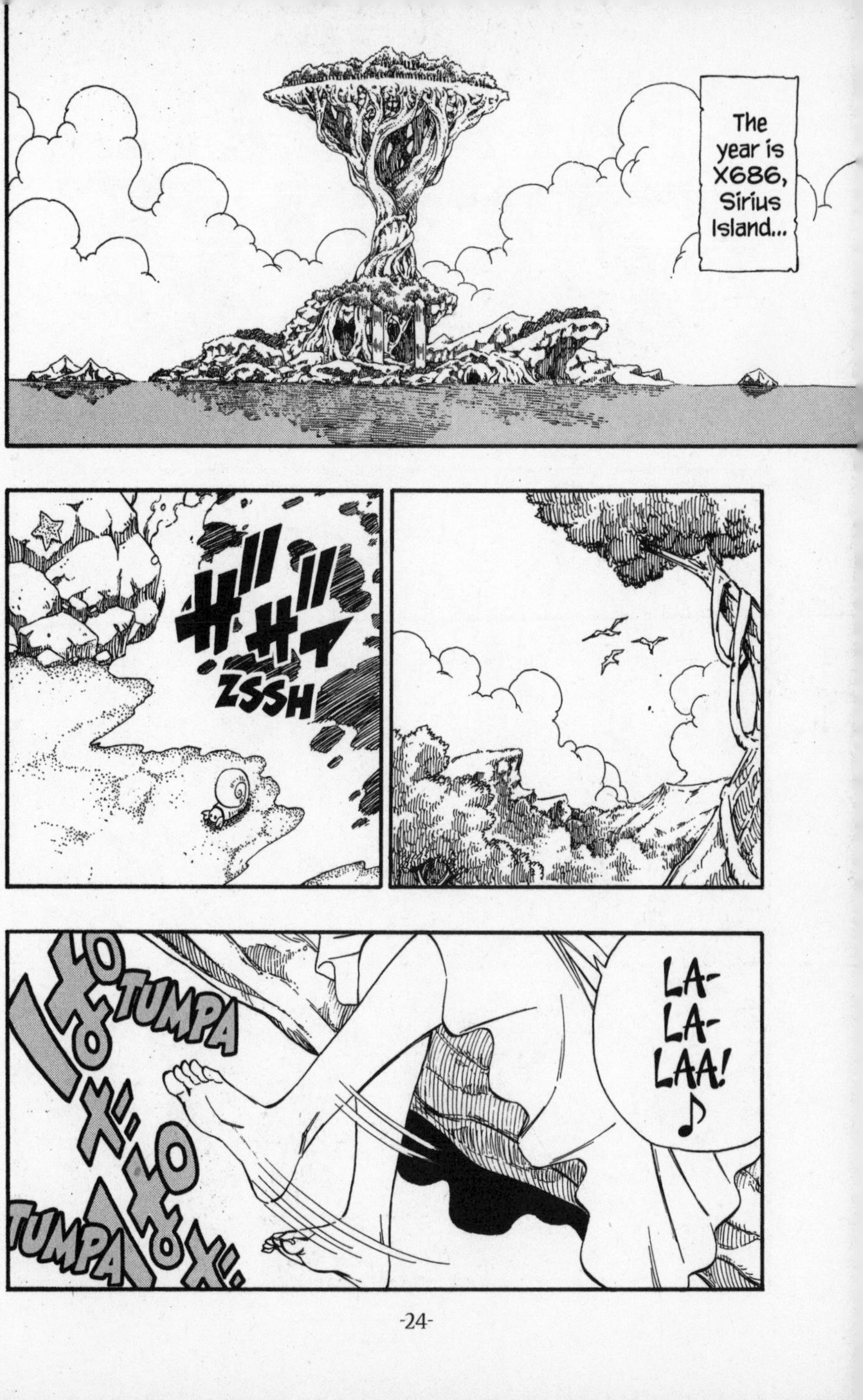
The year is X686, Sirius Island...
ZSSH
LA-LA-LAA! ♪
TUMPA
TUMPA

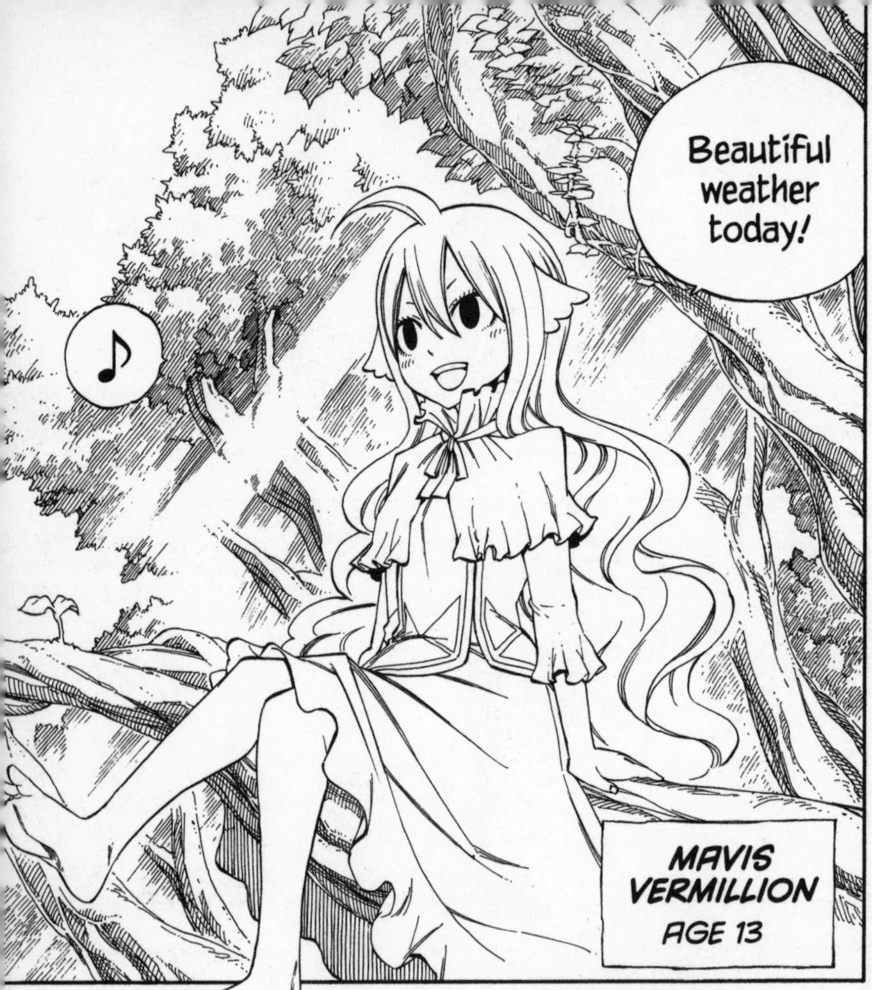
Beautiful weather today!
♪
MAVIS VERMILLION
AGE 13
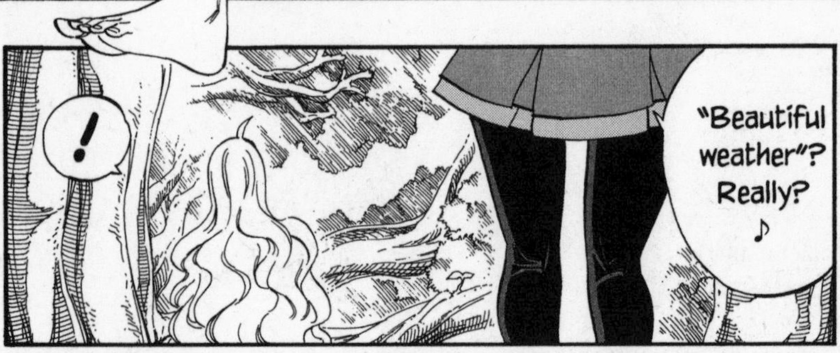
"Beautiful weather"? Really? ♪
!

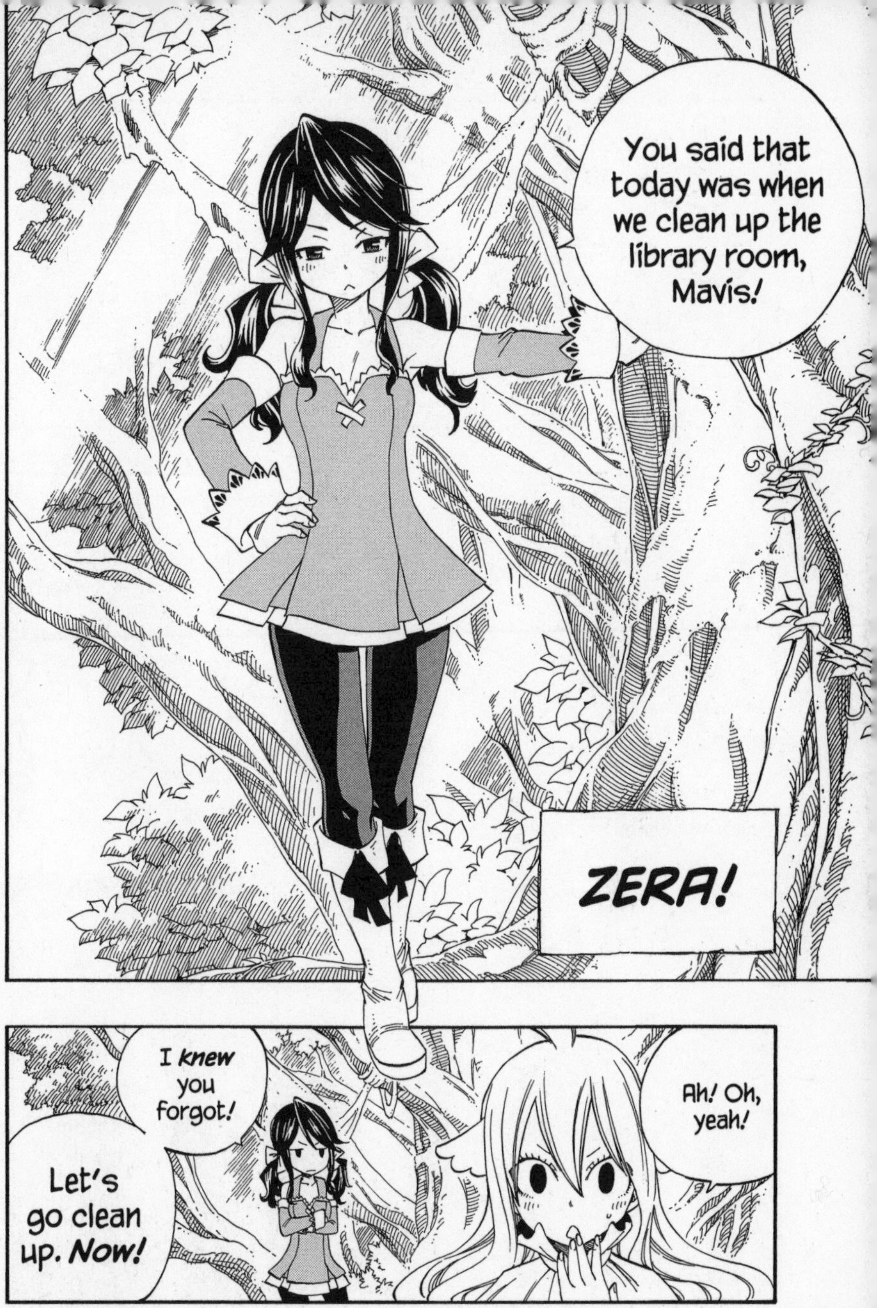
You said that today was when we clean up the library room, Mavis!
ZERA!
Ah! Oh, yeah!
I *knew* you forgot!
Let's go clean up. *Now!*

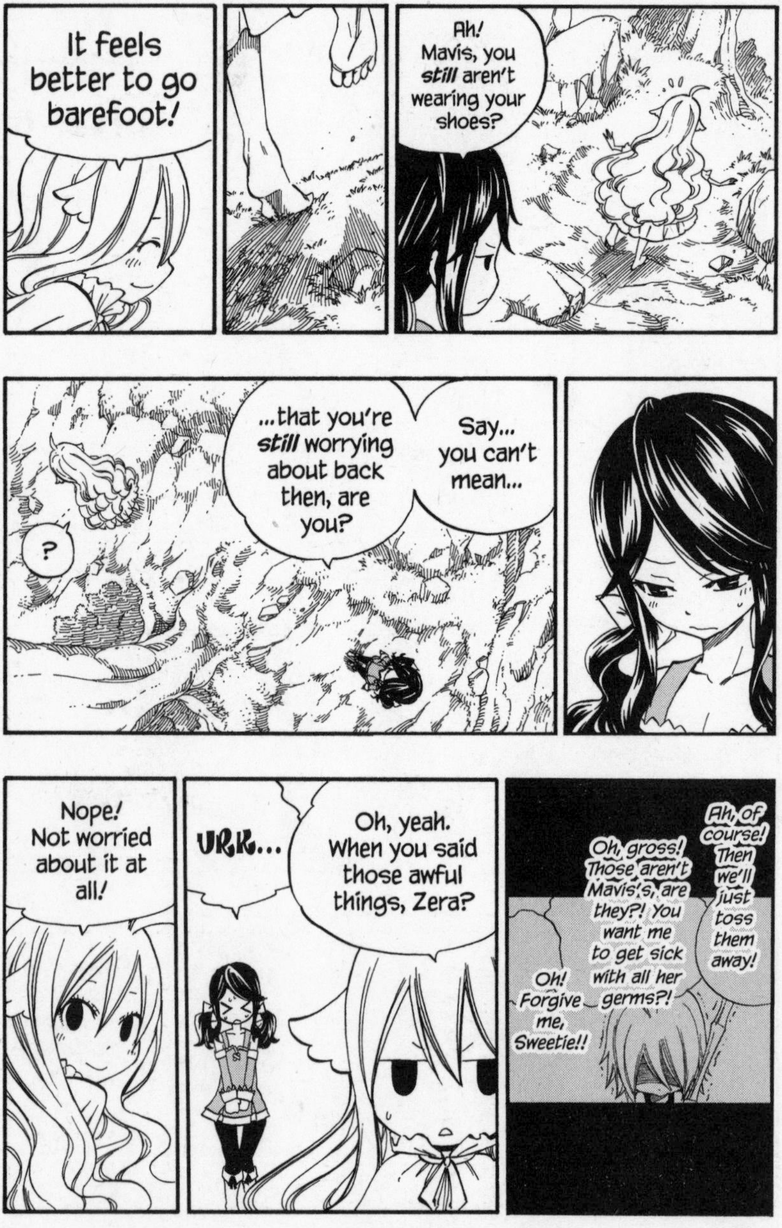
Ah! Mavis, you *still* aren't wearing your shoes?
It feels better to go barefoot!
Say... you can't mean...
...that you're *still* worrying about back then, are you?
?
Ah, of course! Then we'll just toss them away!
Oh, gross! Those aren't Mavis's, are they?! You want me to get sick with all her germs?!
Oh! Forgive me, Sweetie!!
Oh, yeah. When you said those awful things, Zera?
URK...
Nope! Not worried about it at all!

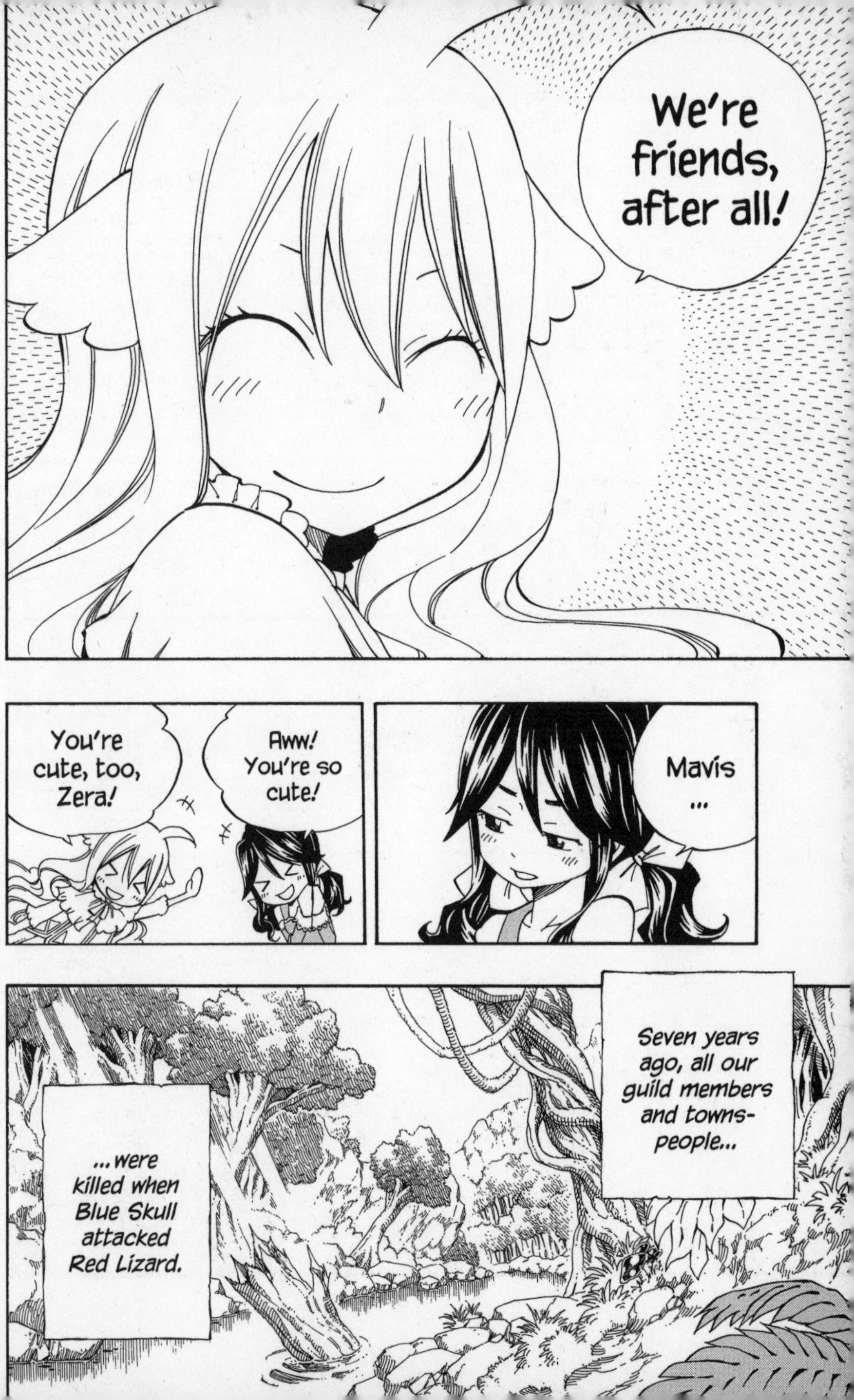
We're friends, after all!
Mavis ...
Aww! You're so cute!
You're cute, too, Zera!
Seven years ago, all our guild members and towns-people...
...were killed when Blue Skull attacked Red Lizard.

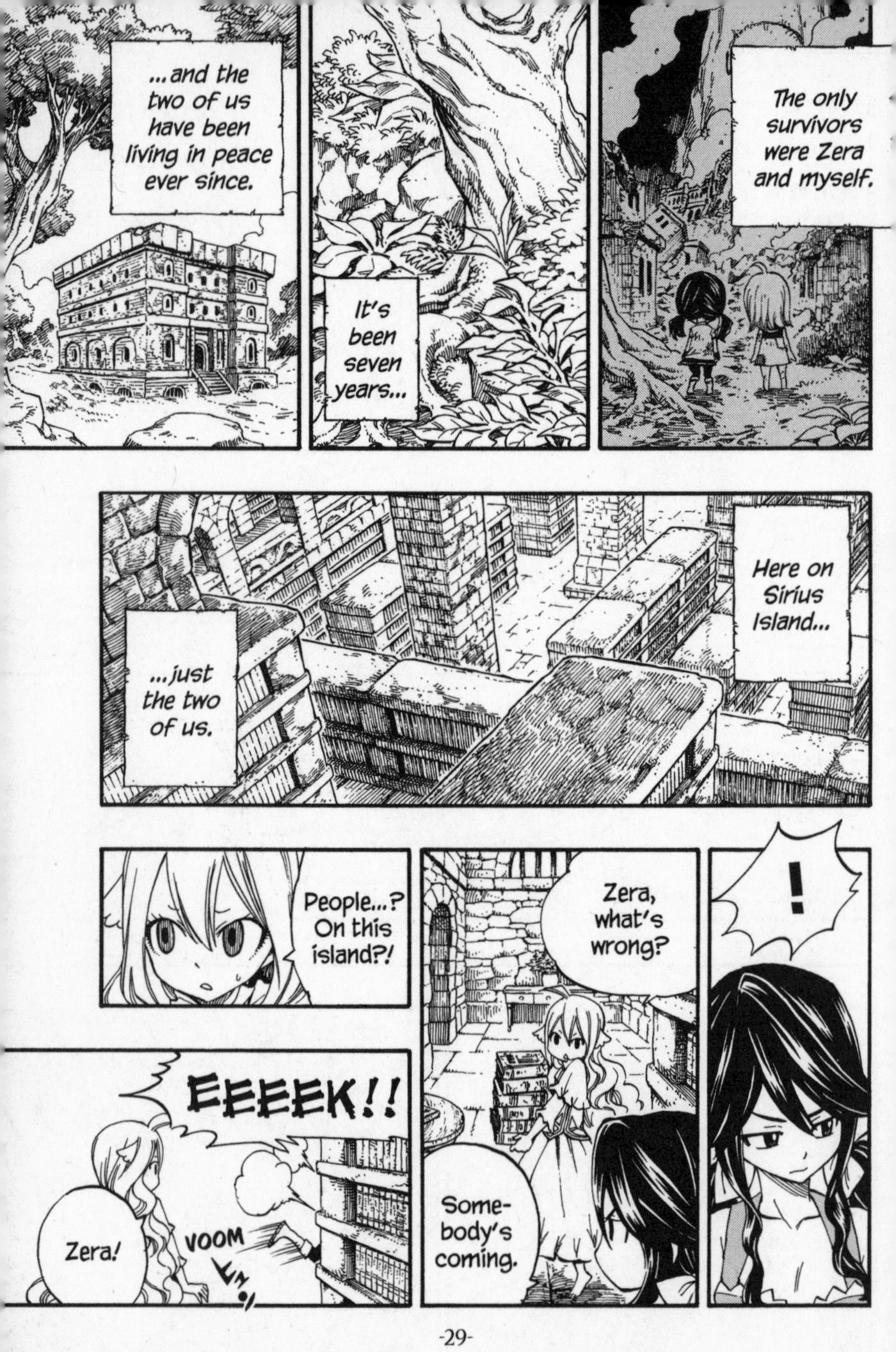
The only survivors were Zera and myself.
It's been seven years...
...and the two of us have been living in peace ever since.
Here on Sirius Island...
...just the two of us.
!
Zera, what's wrong?
Some-body's coming.
People...? On this island?!
EEEEK!!
VOOM
Zera!

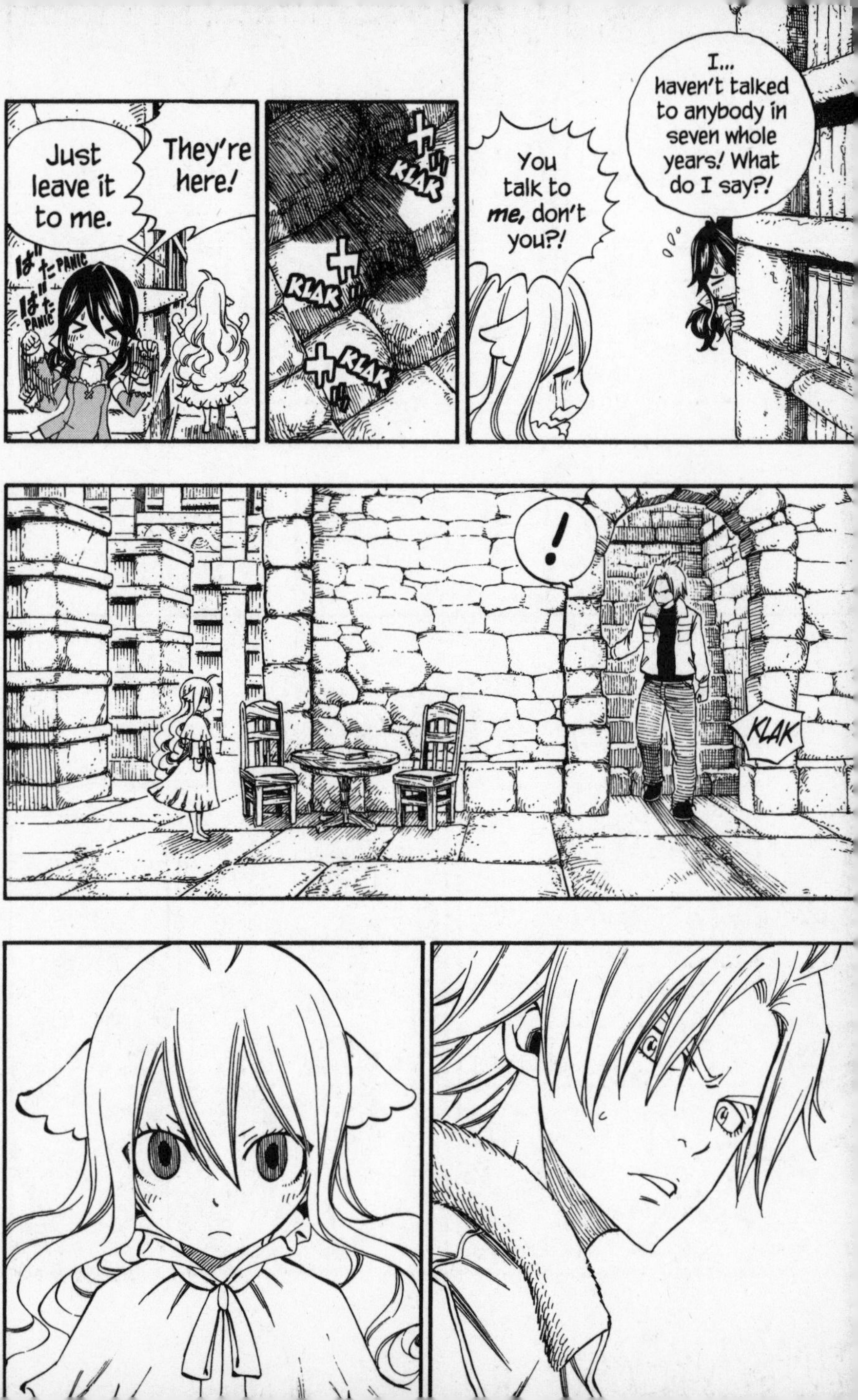
I... haven't talked to anybody in seven whole years! What do I say?!
You talk to *me,* don't you?!
KLAK
KLAK
KLAK
They're here!
Just leave it to me.
ばた PANIC
ばた PANIC
!
KLAK

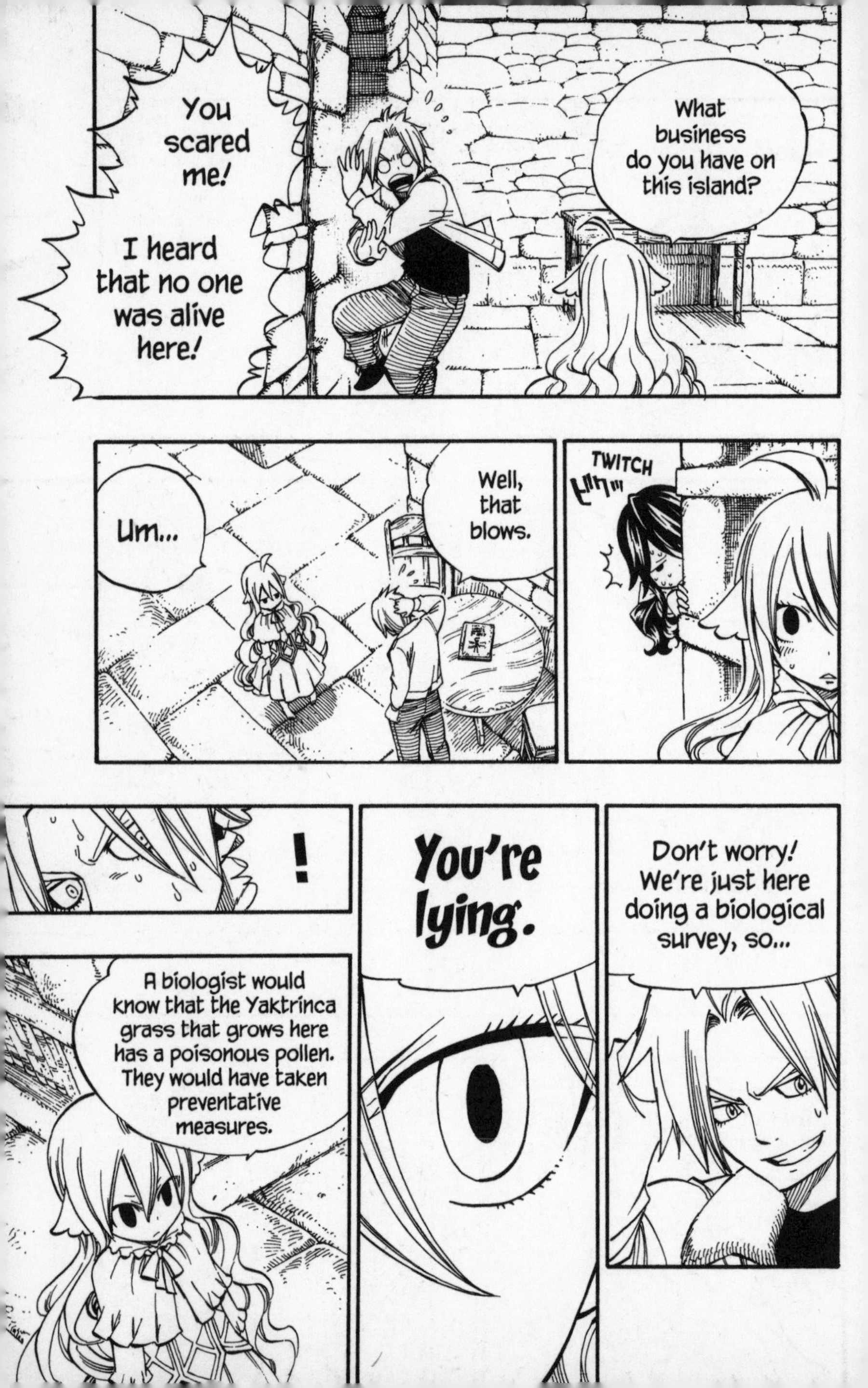
What business do you have on this island?
You scared me!
I heard that no one was alive here!
TWITCH
Well, that blows.
Um...
Don't worry! We're just here doing a biological survey, so...
You're lying.
!
A biologist would know that the Yaktrinca grass that grows here has a poisonous pollen. They would have taken preventative measures.

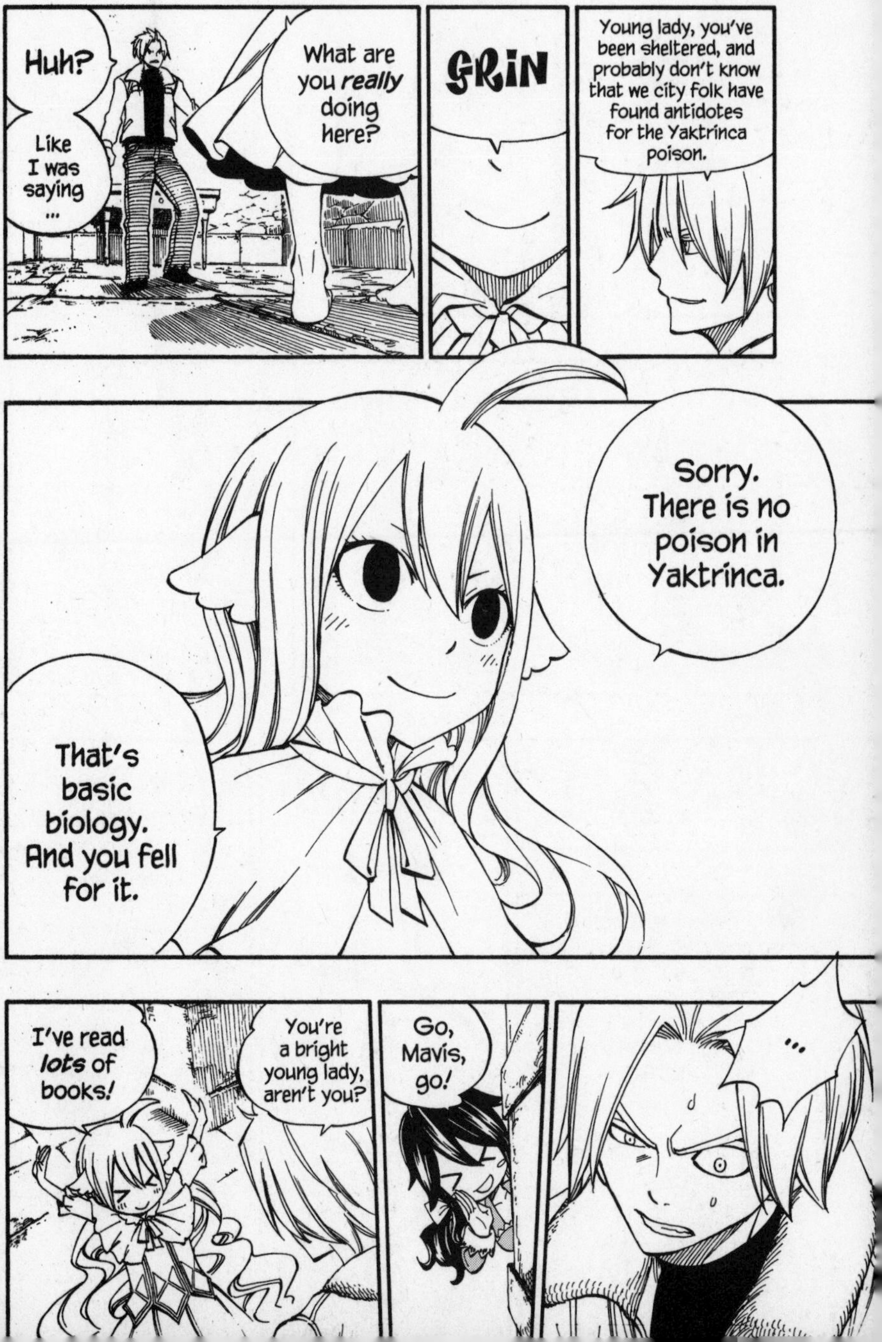
Young lady, you've been sheltered, and probably don't know that we city folk have found antidotes for the Yaktrinca poison.
GRIN
What are you *really* doing here?
Huh?
Like I was saying ...
Sorry. There is no poison in Yaktrinca.
That's basic biology. And you fell for it.
...
Go, Mavis, go!
You're a bright young lady, aren't you?
I've read *lots* of books!

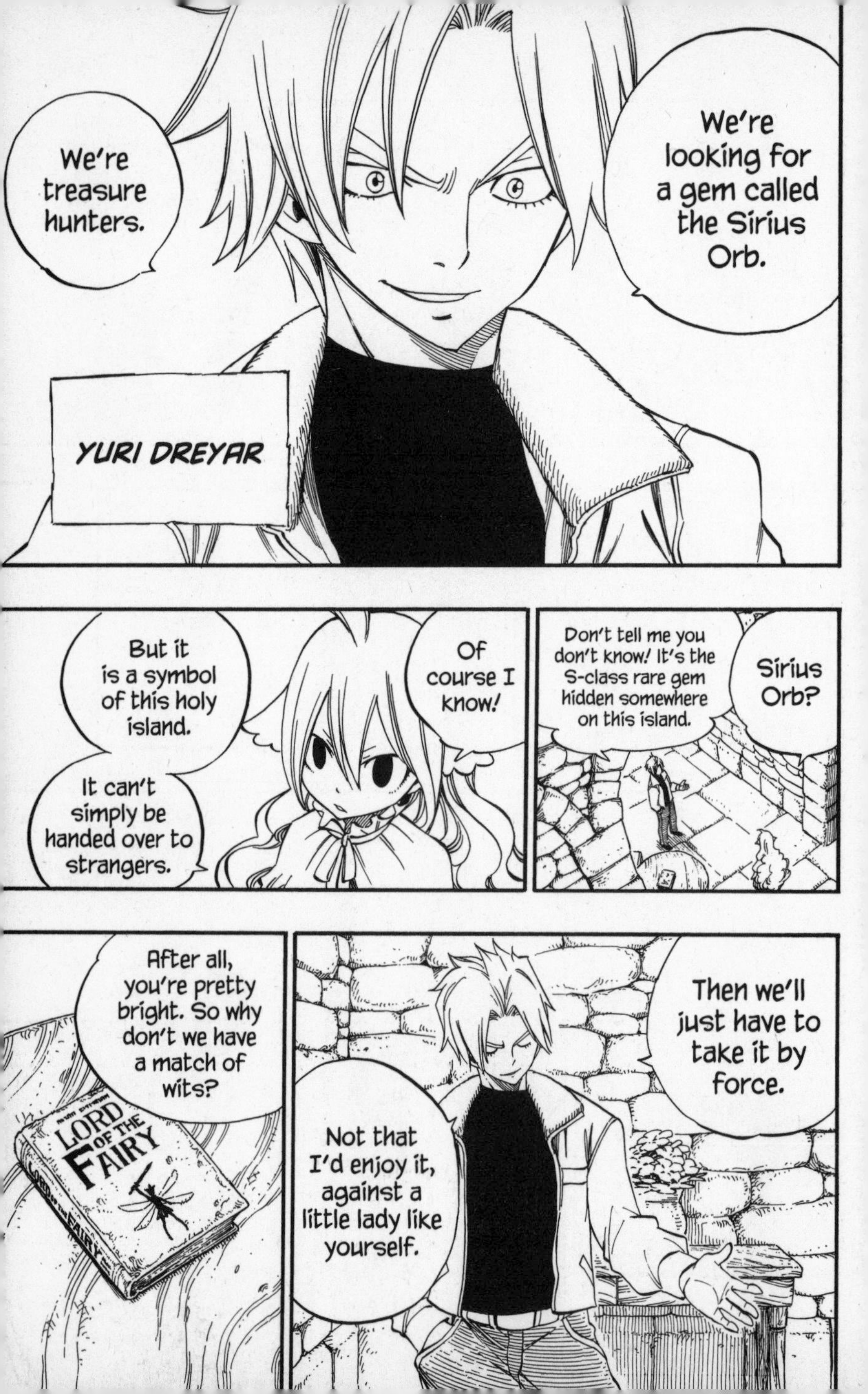
We're looking for a gem called the Sirius Orb.
We're treasure hunters.
YURI DREYAR
Sirius Orb?
Don't tell me you don't know! It's the S-class rare gem hidden somewhere on this island.
Of course I know!
But it is a symbol of this holy island.
It can't simply be handed over to strangers.
Then we'll just have to take it by force.
Not that I'd enjoy it, against a little lady like yourself.
After all, you're pretty bright. So why don't we have a match of wits?
LORD OF THE FAIRY

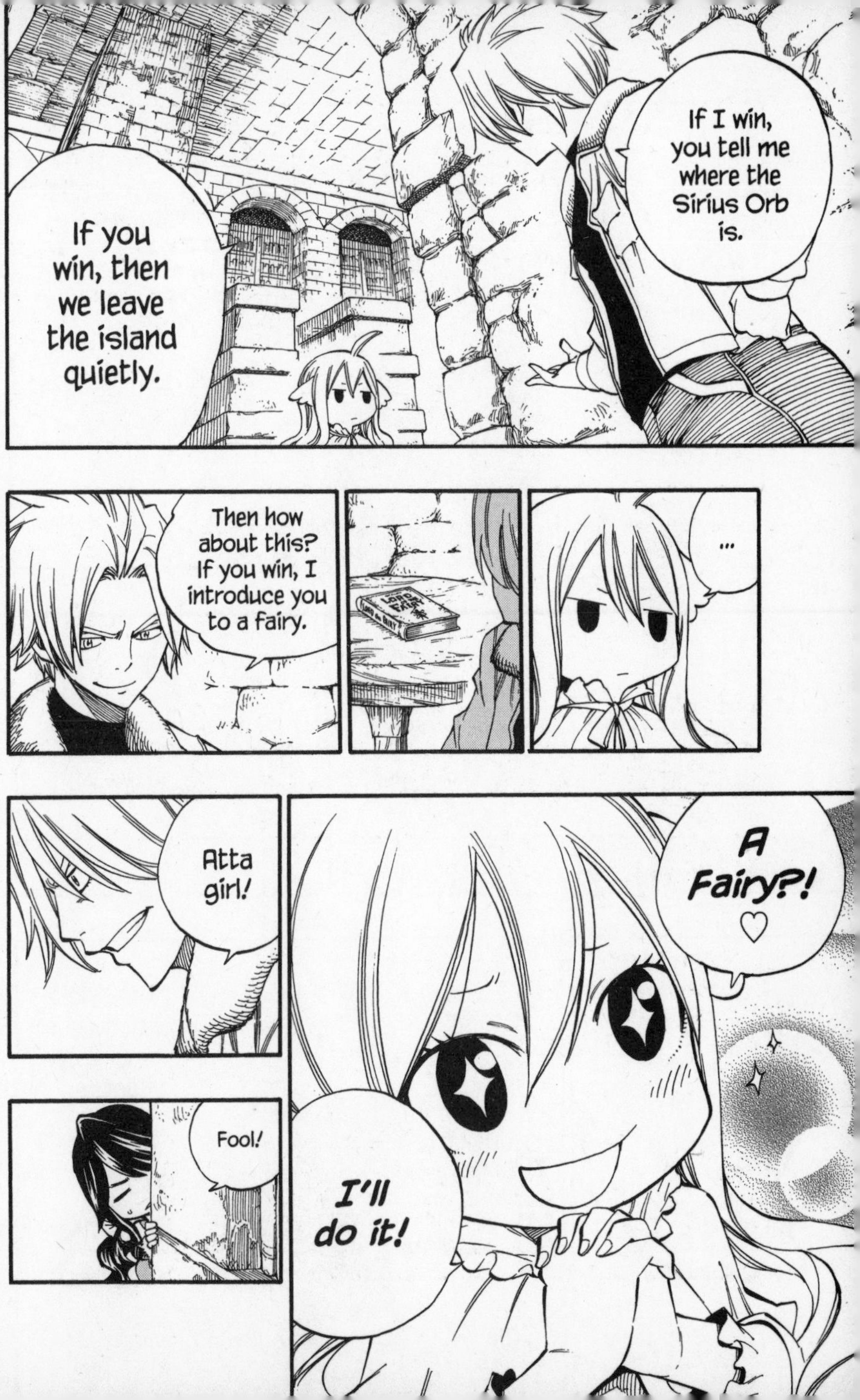
If I win, you tell me where the Sirius Orb is.
If you win, then we leave the island quietly.
...
Then how about this? If you win, I introduce you to a fairy.
A Fairy?! ♡
I'll do it!
Atta girl!
Fool!

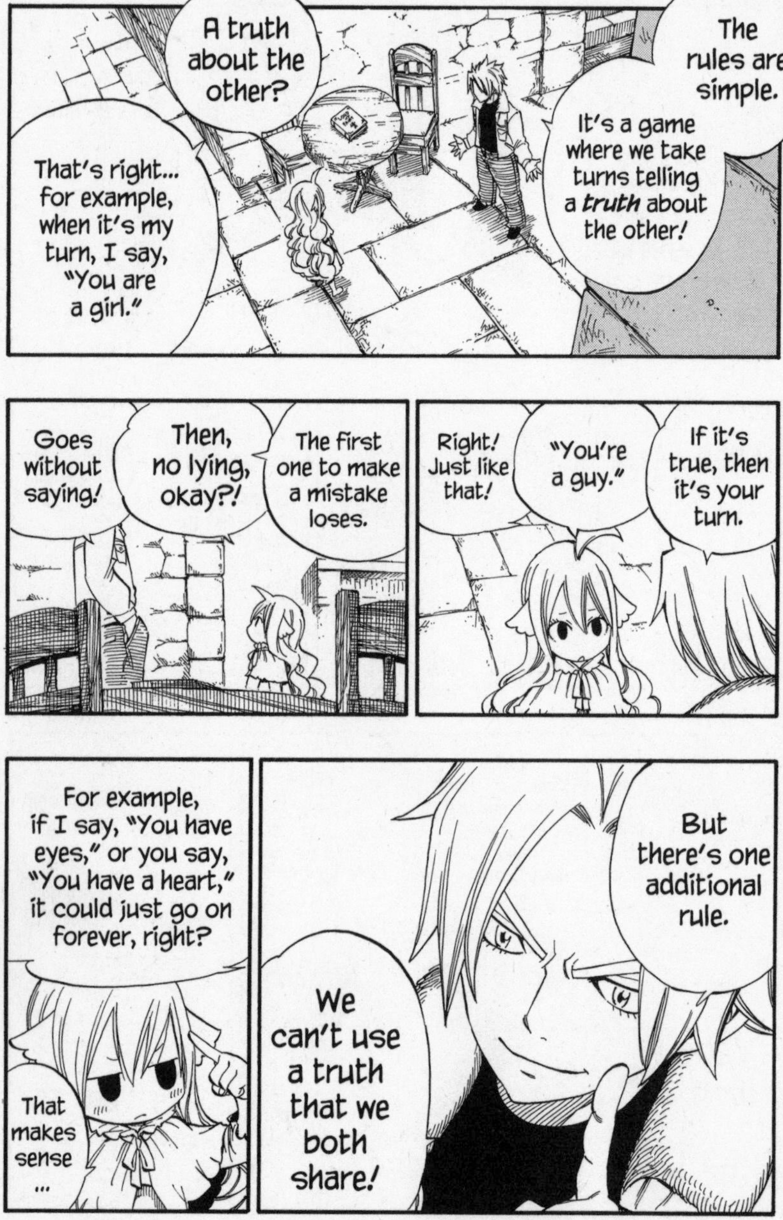
The rules are simple.
It's a game where we take turns telling a *truth* about the other!
A truth about the other?
That's right... for example, when it's my turn, I say, "You are a girl."
If it's true, then it's your turn.
"You're a guy."
Right! Just like that!
The first one to make a mistake loses.
Then, no lying, okay?!
Goes without saying!
But there's one additional rule.
We can't use a truth that we both share!
For example, if I say, "You have eyes," or you say, "You have a heart," it could just go on forever, right?
That makes sense ...

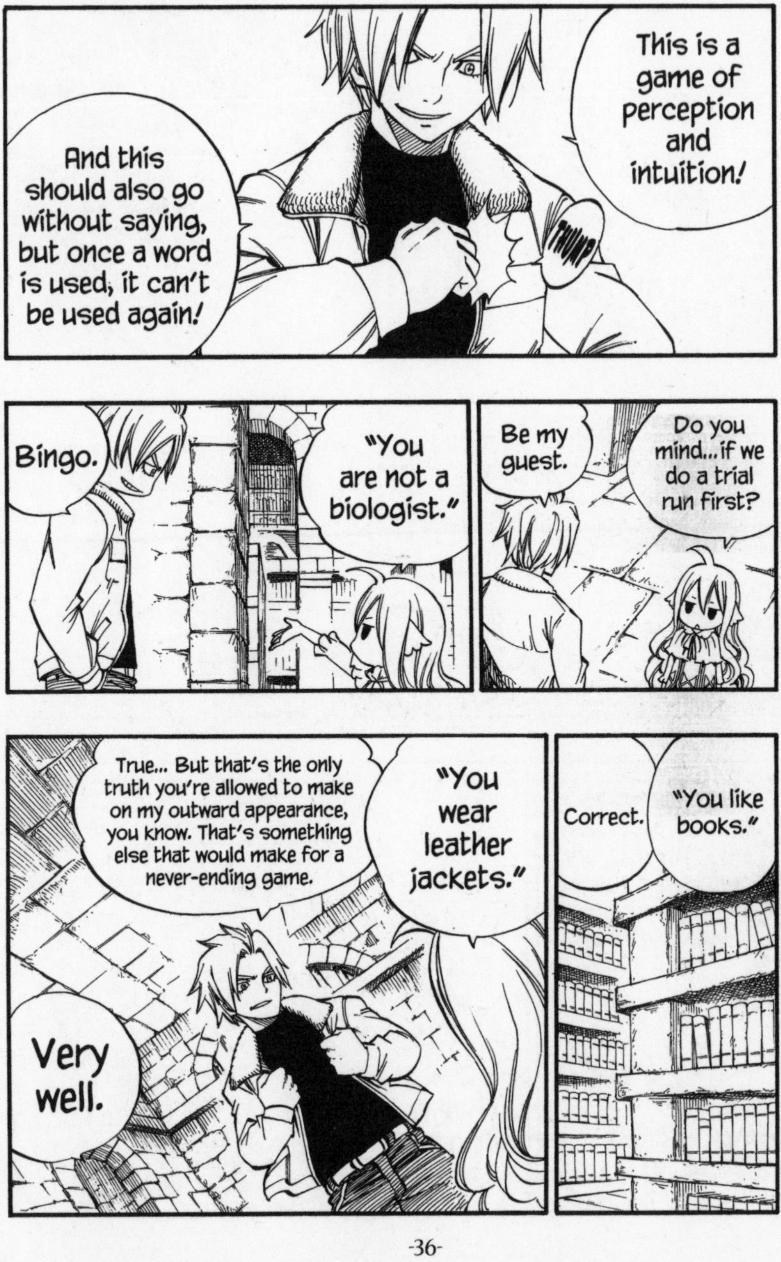
This is a game of perception and intuition!
THUMP
And this should also go without saying, but once a word is used, it can't be used again!
Do you mind...if we do a trial run first?
Be my guest.
"You are not a biologist."
Bingo.
"You like books."
Correct.
"You wear leather jackets."
True... But that's the only truth you're allowed to make on my outward appearance, you know. That's something else that would make for a never-ending game.
Very well.

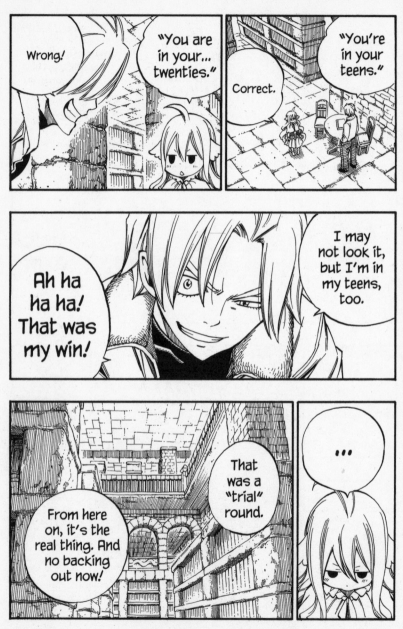

"You're in your teens."
Correct.
"You are in your... twenties."
Wrong!
I may not look it, but I'm in my teens, too.
Ah ha ha ha! That was my win!
...
That was a "trial" round.
From here on, it's the real thing. And no backing out now!

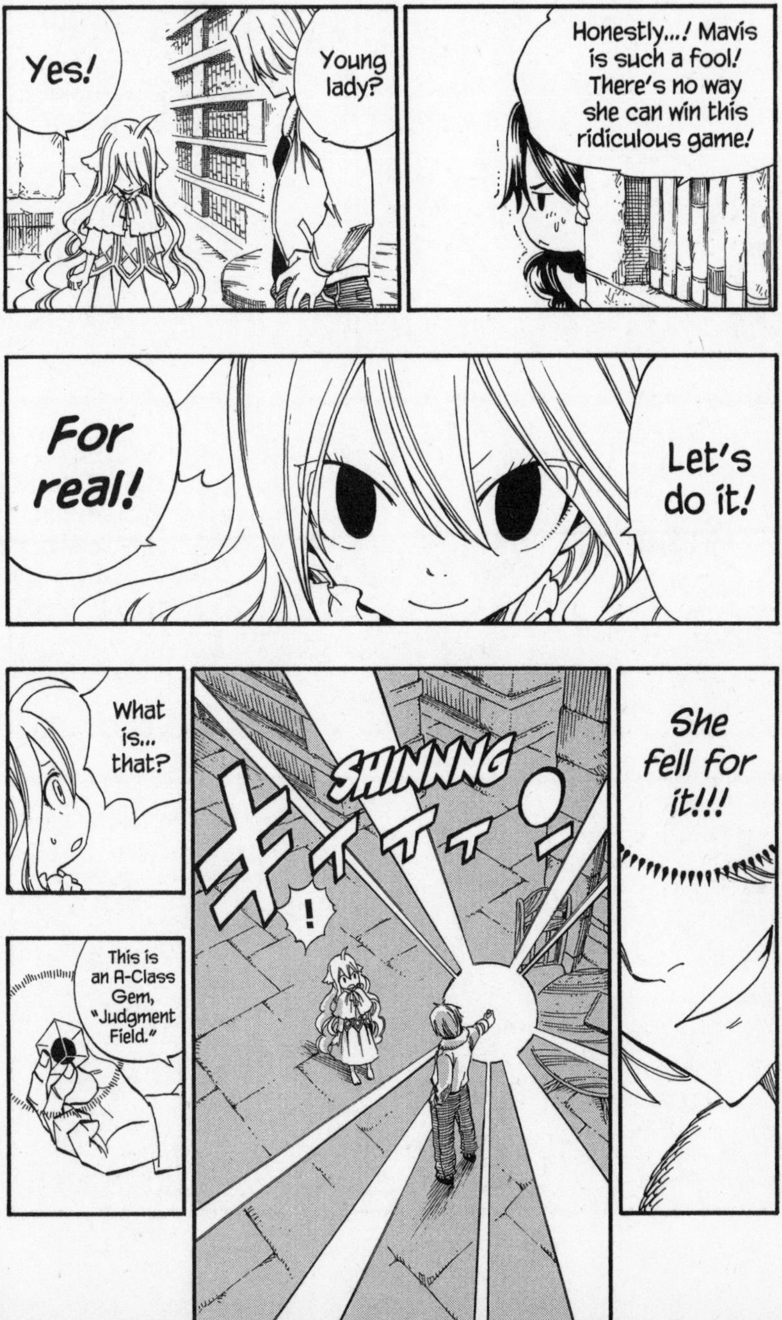
Honestly...! Mavis is such a fool! There's no way she can win this ridiculous game!
Young lady?
Yes!
Let's do it!
For real!
She fell for it!!!
SHINNNG
!
What is... that?
This is an A-Class Gem, "Judgment Field."

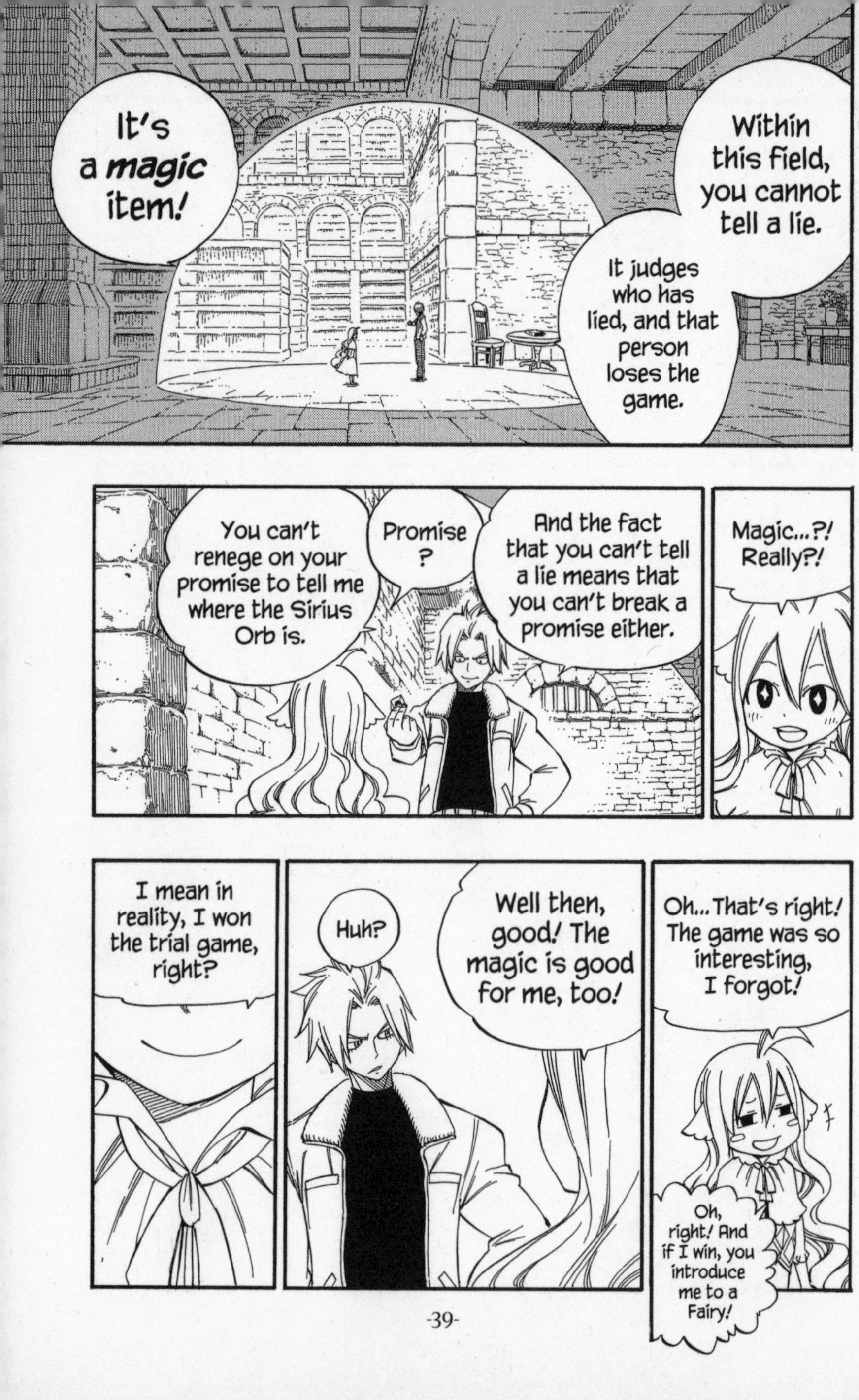
Within this field, you cannot tell a lie.
It's a *magic* item!
It judges who has lied, and that person loses the game.
Magic...?! Really?!
And the fact that you can't tell a lie means that you can't break a promise either.
Promise ?
You can't renege on your promise to tell me where the Sirius Orb is.
Oh... That's right! The game was so interesting, I forgot!
Oh, right! And if I win, you introduce me to a Fairy!
Well then, good! The magic is good for me, too!
Huh?
I mean in reality, I won the trial game, right?

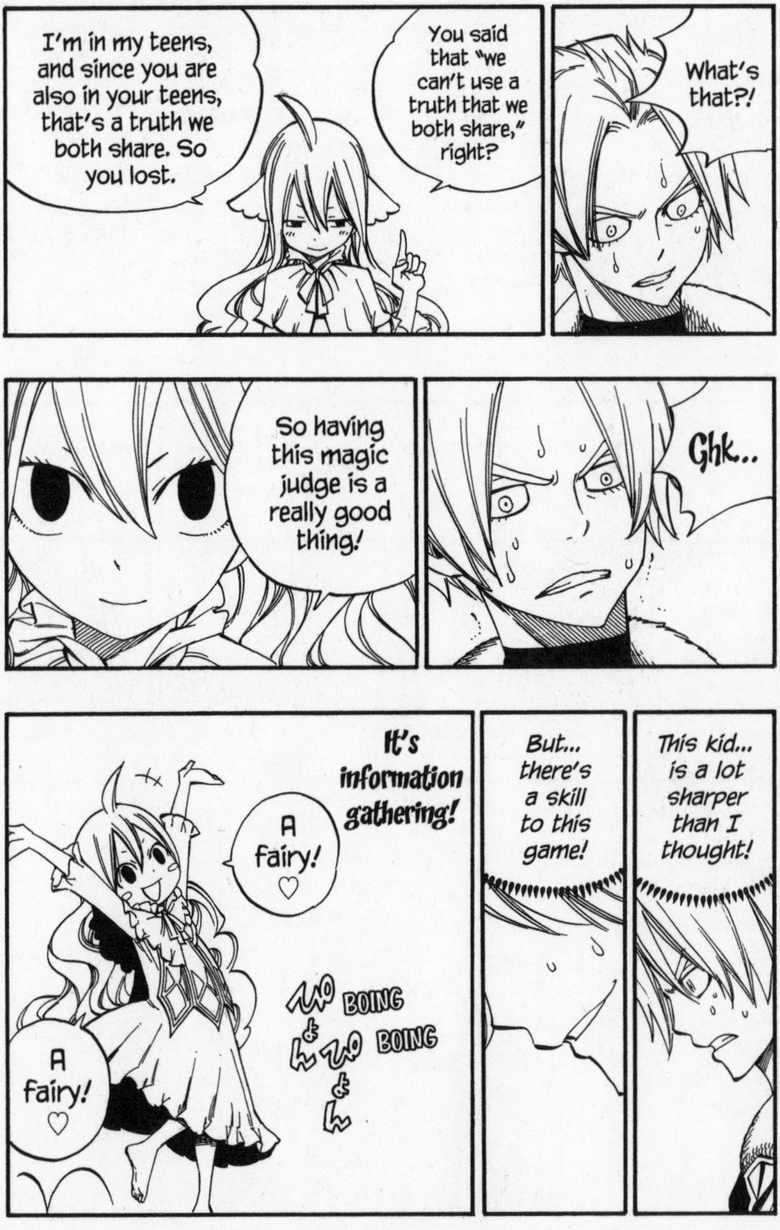

What's that?!
You said that "we can't use a truth that we both share," right?
I'm in my teens, and since you are also in your teens, that's a truth we both share. So you lost.
Ghk...
So having this magic judge is a really good thing!
This kid... is a lot sharper than I thought!
But... there's a skill to this game!
It's information gathering!
A fairy! ♡
BOING
BOING
A fairy! ♡

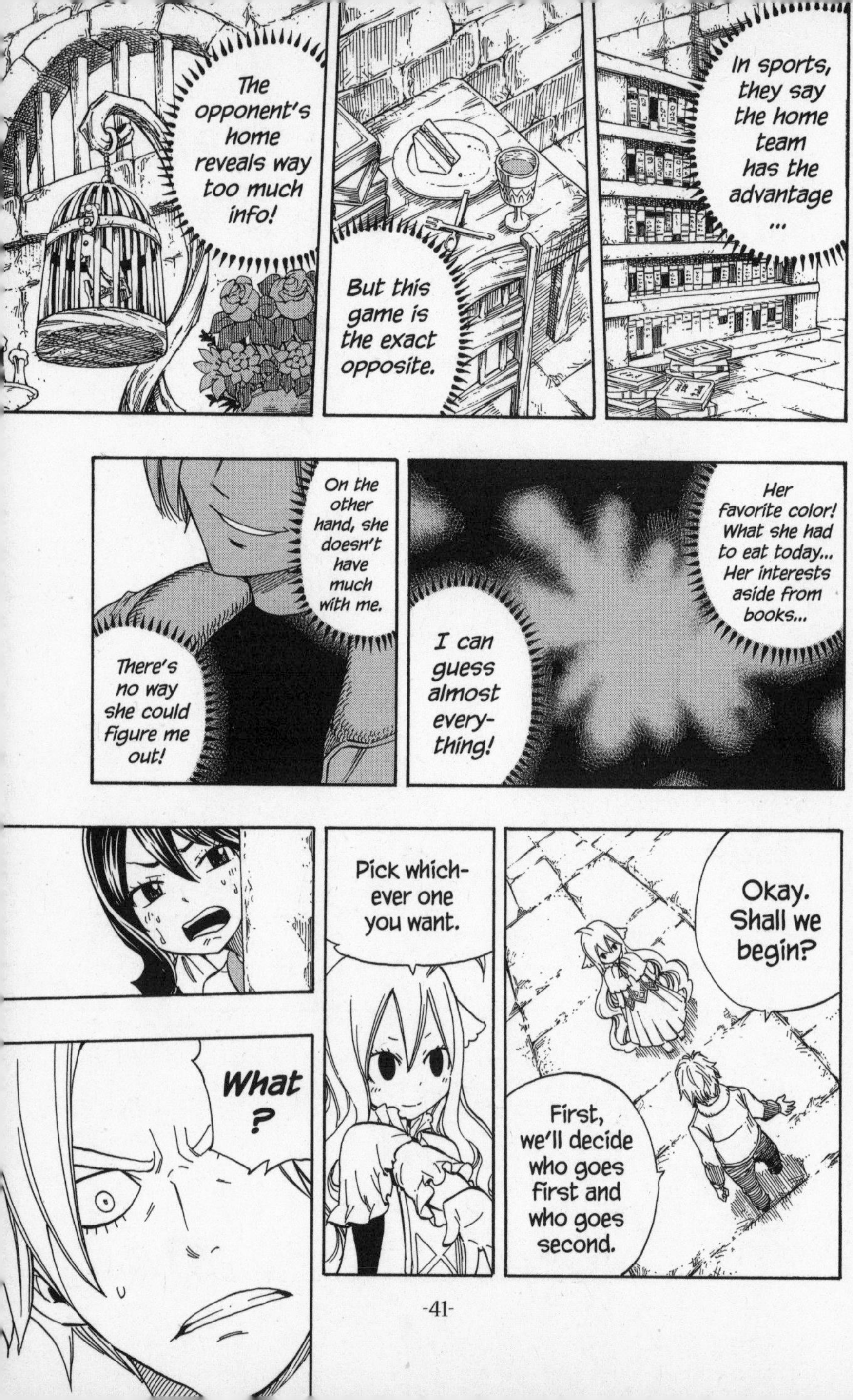
In sports, they say the home team has the advantage ...
But this game is the exact opposite.
The opponent's home reveals way too much info!
Her favorite color! What she had to eat today... Her interests aside from books...
I can guess almost every-thing!
On the other hand, she doesn't have much with me.
There's no way she could figure me out!
Okay. Shall we begin?
First, we'll decide who goes first and who goes second.
Pick which-ever one you want.
What ?

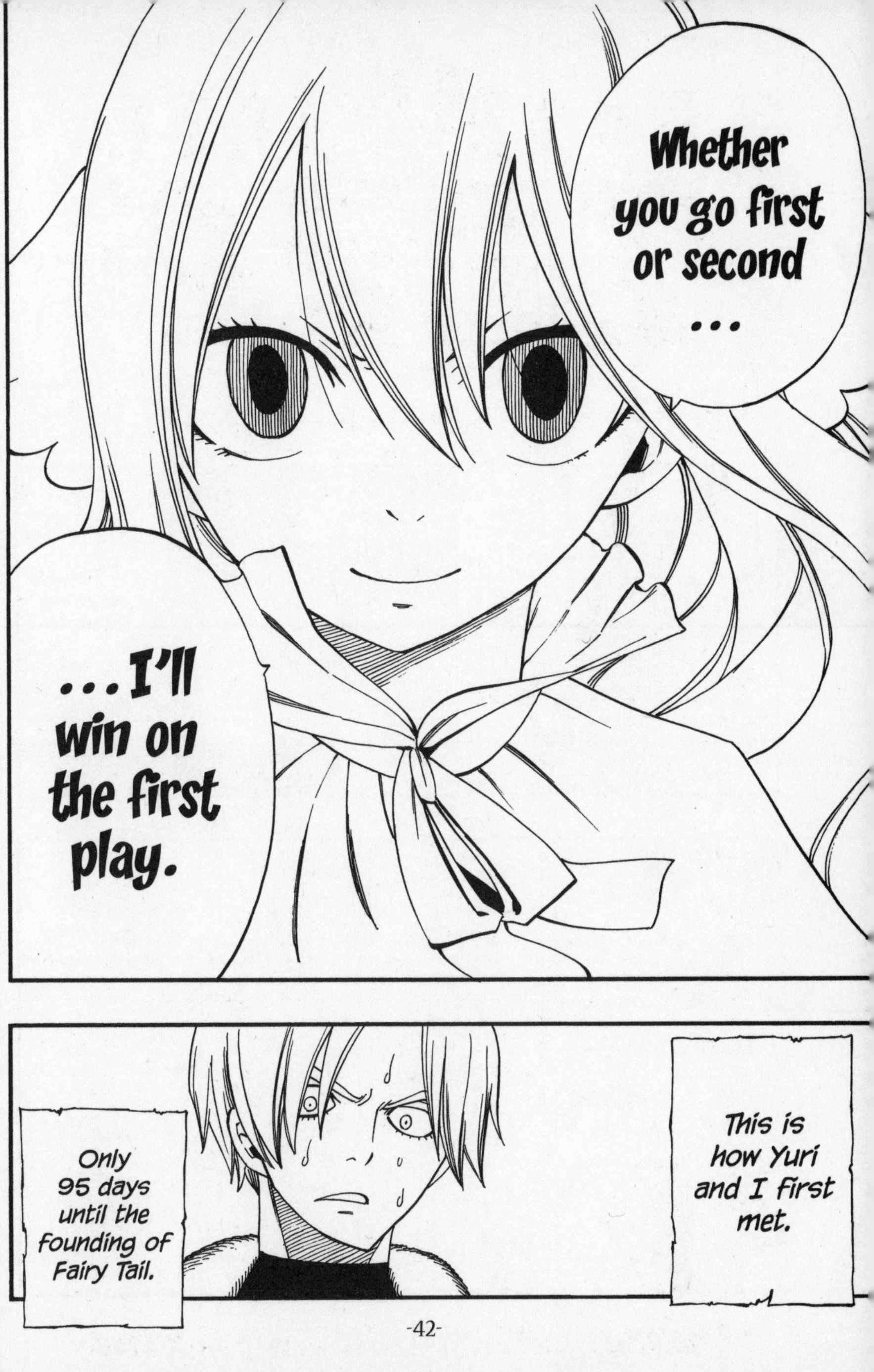
Whether you go first or second ...
...I'll win on the first play.
This is how Yuri and I first met.
Only 95 days until the founding of Fairy Tail.

FAIRY TAIL ZERØ

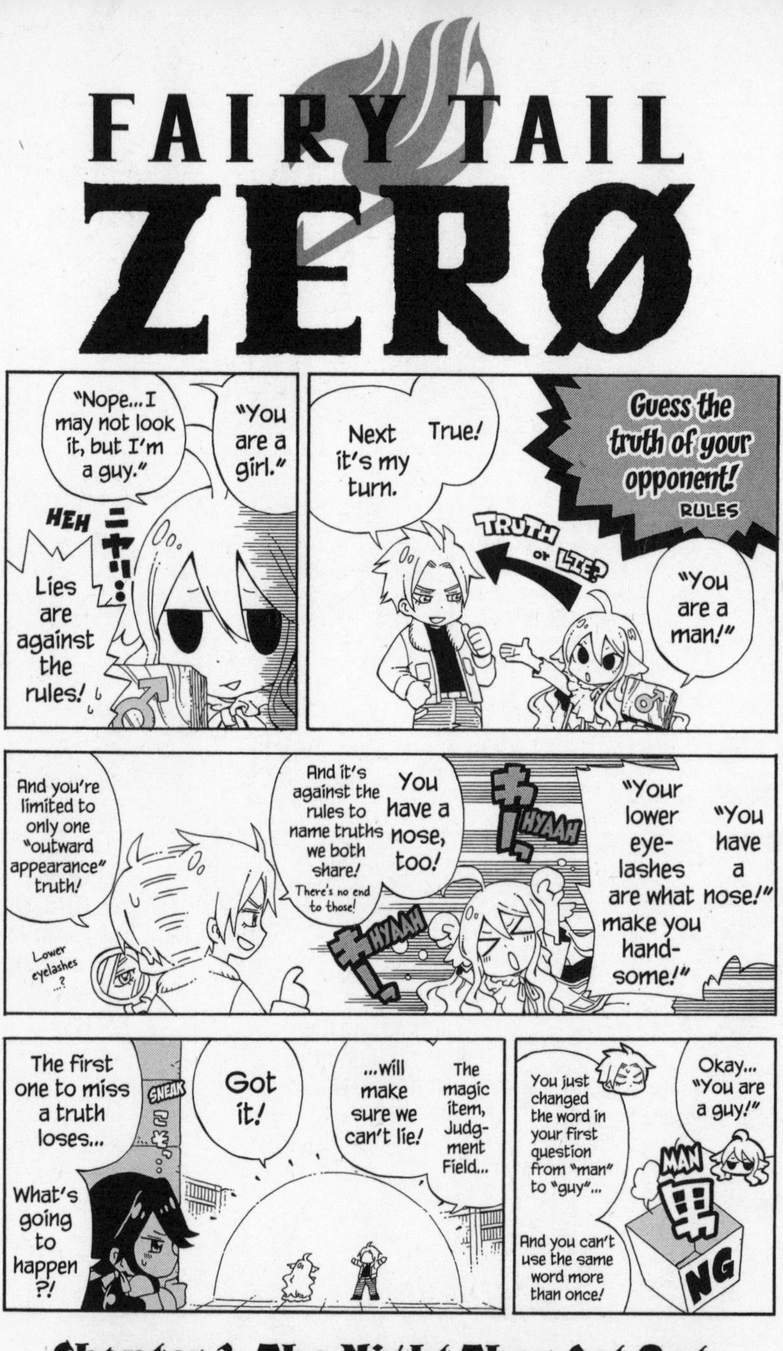
Guess the truth of your opponent!
RULES
"You are a man!"
TRUTH or LIE?
True!
Next it's my turn.
"You are a girl."
"Nope...I may not look it, but I'm a guy."
HEH
Lies are against the rules!
"You have a nose!"
"Your lower eye-lashes are what make you hand-some!"
HYAAH
HYAAH
You have a nose, too!
And it's against the rules to name truths we both share!
There's no end to those!
And you're limited to only one "outward appearance" truth!
Lower eyelashes ...?
Okay... "You are a guy!"
You just changed the word in your first question from "man" to "guy"...
MAN
NG
And you can't use the same word more than once!
The magic item, Judg-ment Field...
...will make sure we can't lie!
Got it!
The first one to miss a truth loses...
SNEAK
What's going to happen ?!

Chapter 3: The Night They Set Out

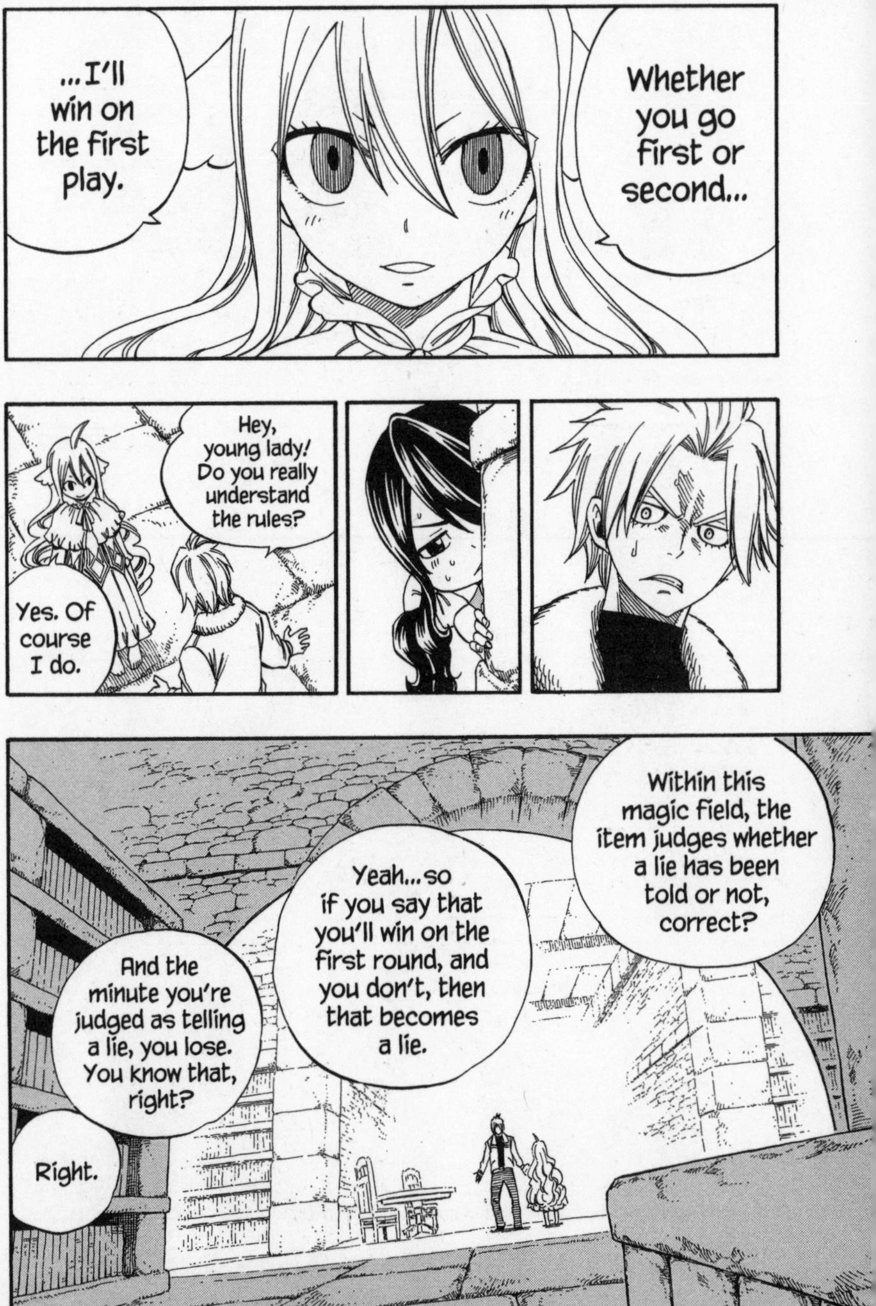
Whether you go first or second...
...I'll win on the first play.
Hey, young lady! Do you really understand the rules?
Yes. Of course I do.
Within this magic field, the item judges whether a lie has been told or not, correct?
Yeah...so if you say that you'll win on the first round, and you don't, then that becomes a lie.
And the minute you're judged as telling a lie, you lose. You know that, right?
Right.

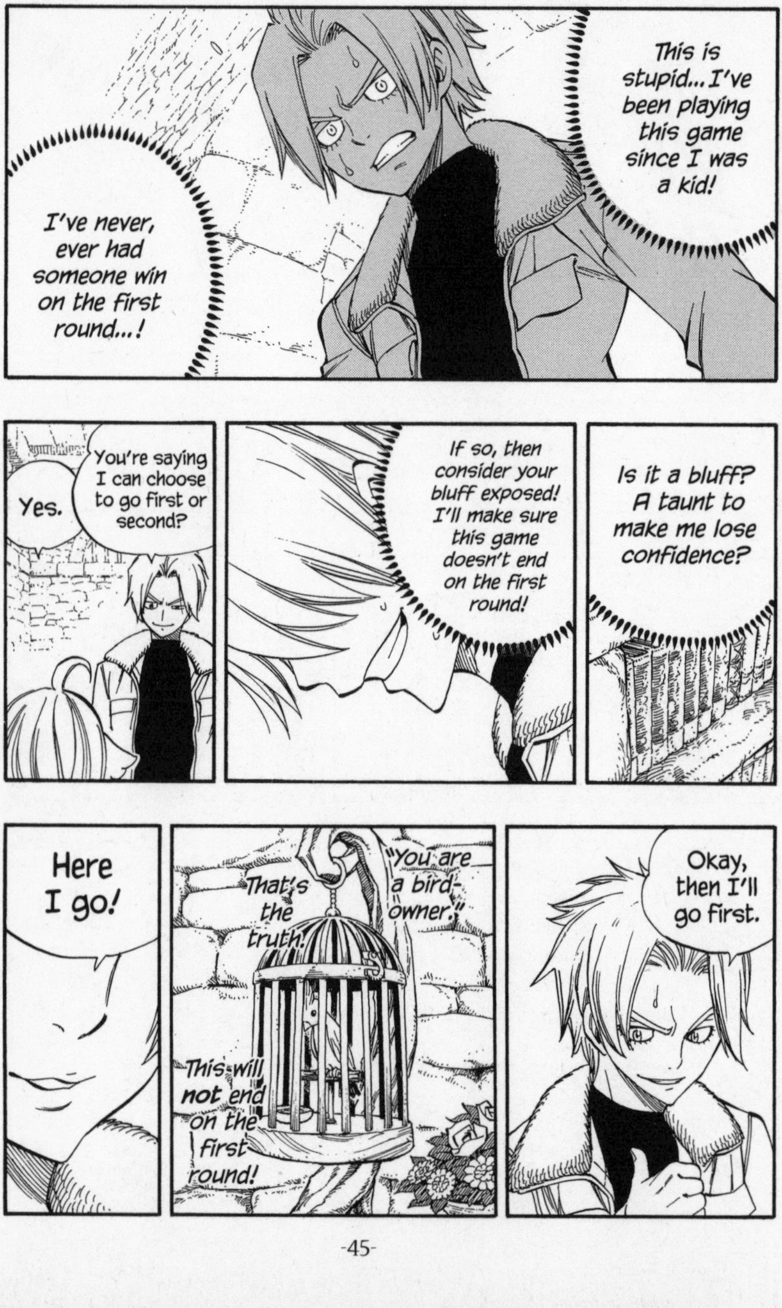
This is stupid...I've been playing this game since I was a kid!
I've never, ever had someone win on the first round...!
Is it a bluff? A taunt to make me lose confidence?
If so, then consider your bluff exposed! I'll make sure this game doesn't end on the first round!
You're saying I can choose to go first or second?
Yes.
Okay, then I'll go first.
"You are a bird-owner."
That's the truth.
This will **not** end on the first round!
Here I go!

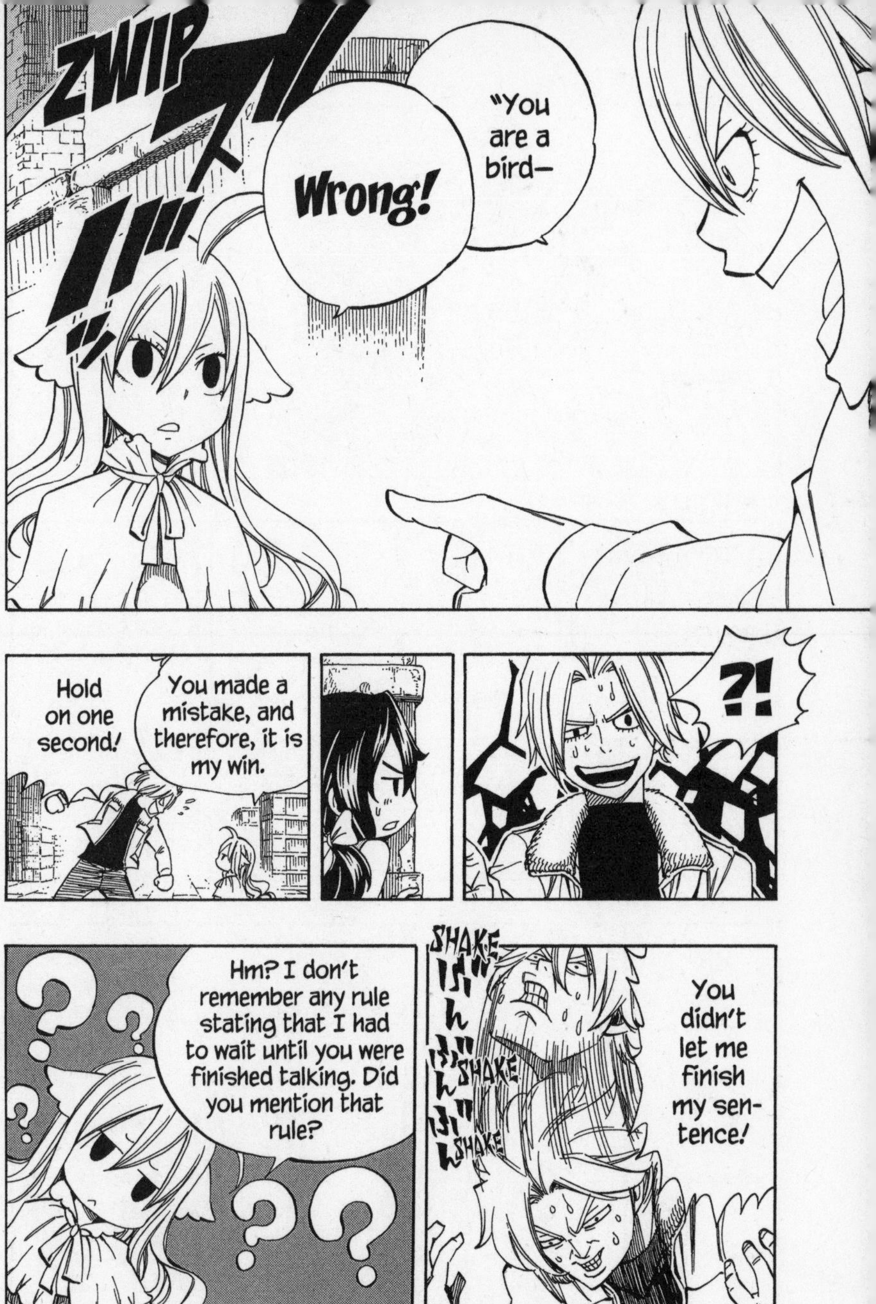
“You are a bird—
Wrong!
ZWIP
?!
You made a mistake, and therefore, it is my win.
Hold on one second!
You didn't let me finish my sentence!
SHAKE
SHAKE
SHAKE
Hm? I don't remember any rule stating that I had to wait until you were finished talking. Did you mention that rule?

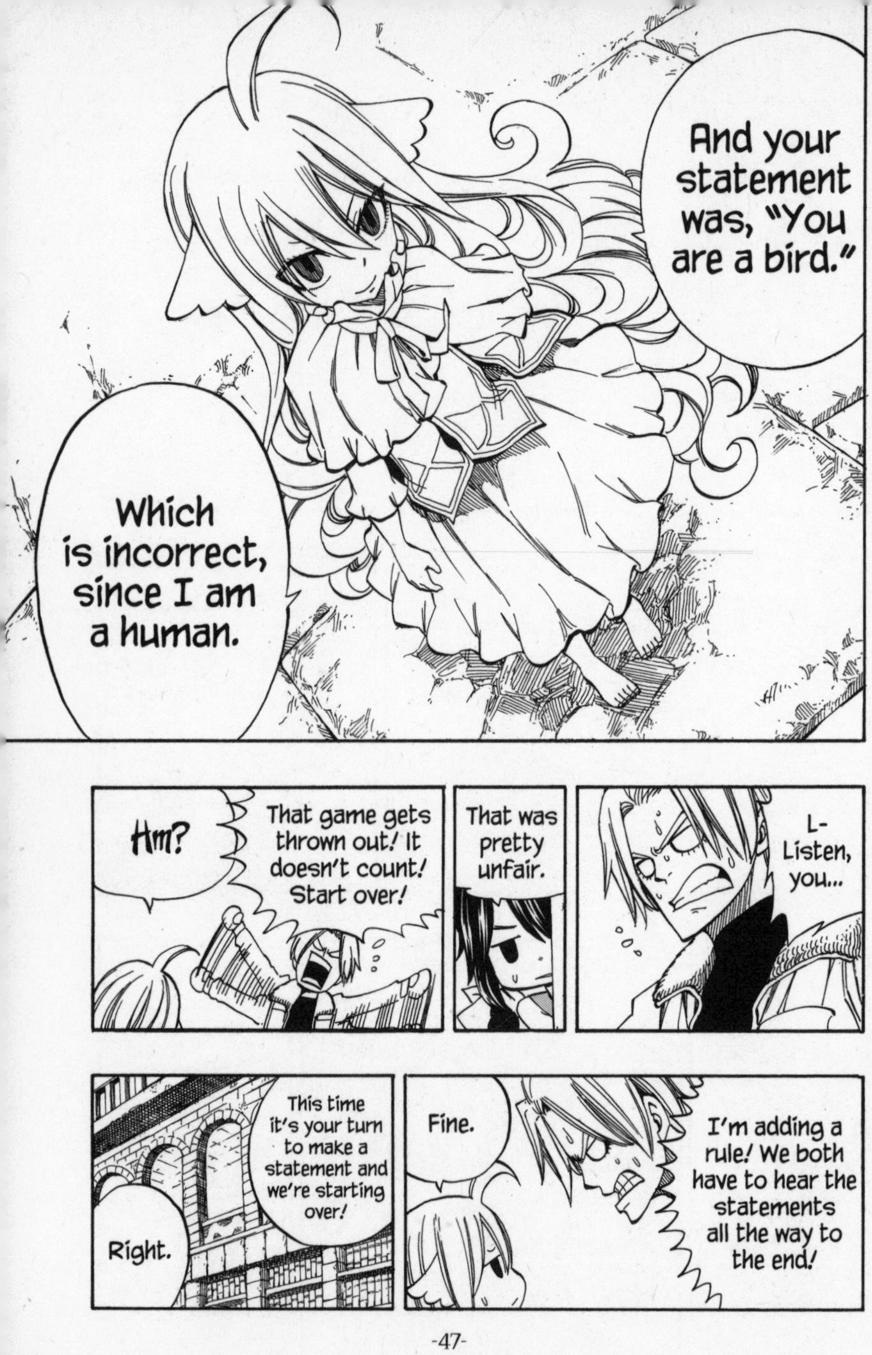
And your statement was, "You are a bird."
Which is incorrect, since I am a human.
L- Listen, you...
That was pretty unfair.
That game gets thrown out! It doesn't count! Start over!
Hm?
I'm adding a rule! We both have to hear the statements all the way to the end!
Fine.
This time it's your turn to make a statement and we're starting over!
Right.

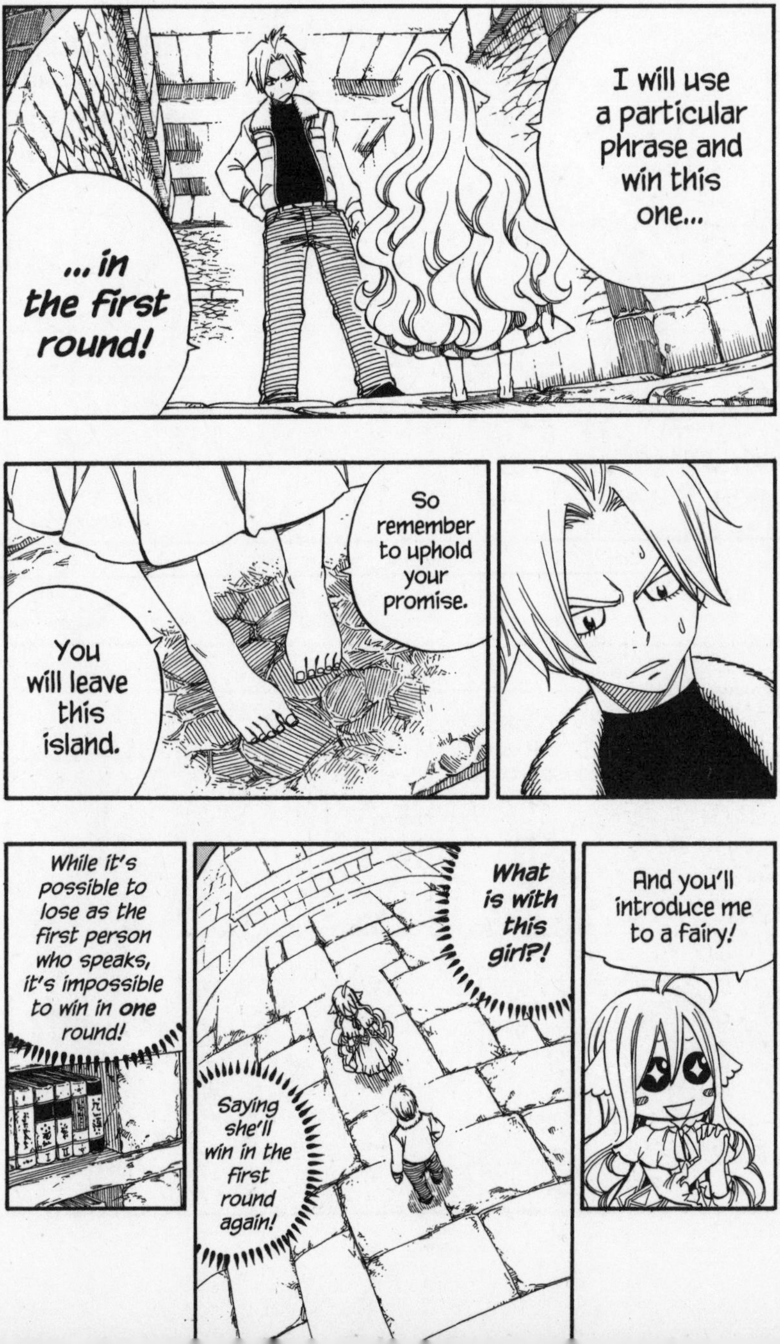

I will use a particular phrase and win this one...
...in the first round!
So remember to uphold your promise.
You will leave this island.
And you'll introduce me to a fairy!
What is with this girl?!
Saying she'll win in the first round again!
While it's possible to lose as the first person who speaks, it's impossible to win in one round!

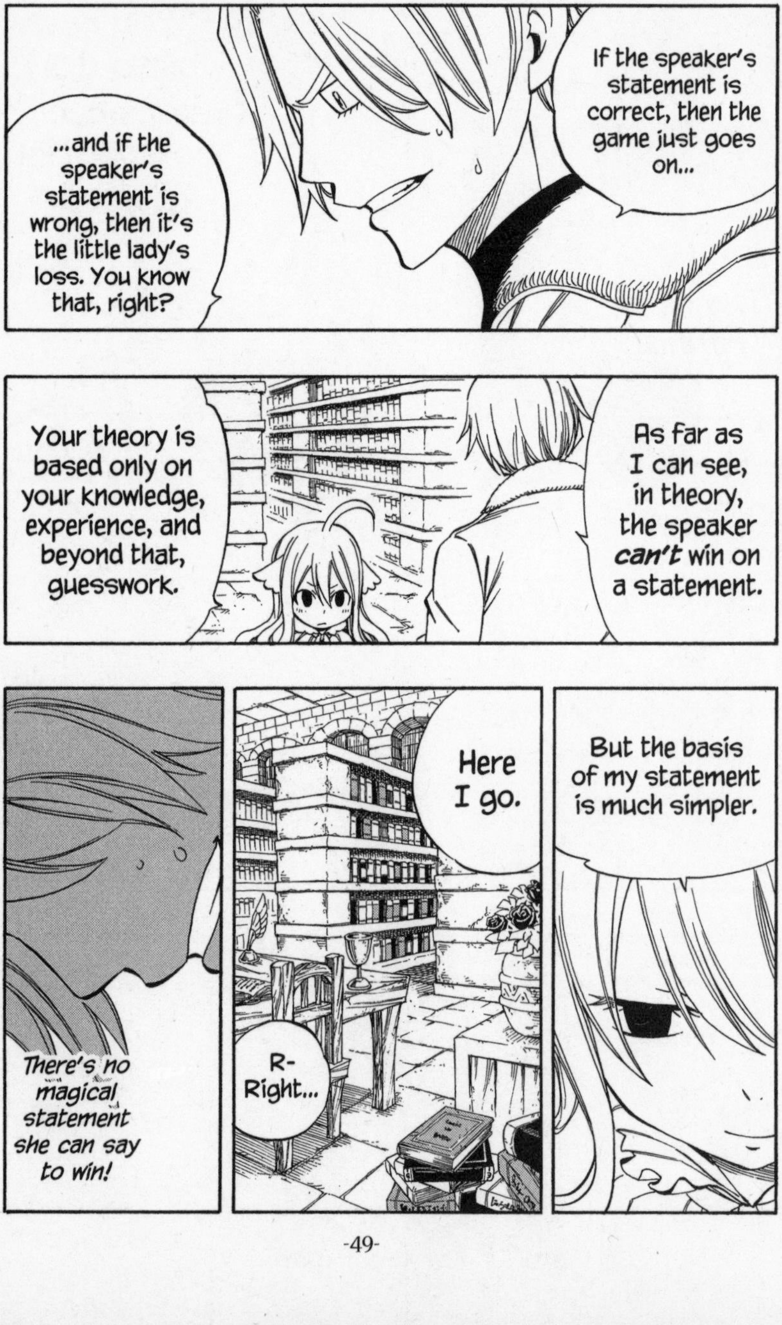
If the speaker's statement is correct, then the game just goes on...
...and if the speaker's statement is wrong, then it's the little lady's loss. You know that, right?
As far as I can see, in theory, the speaker *can't* win on a statement.
Your theory is based only on your knowledge, experience, and beyond that, guesswork.
But the basis of my statement is much simpler.
Here I go.
R- Right...
There's no magical statement she can say to win!

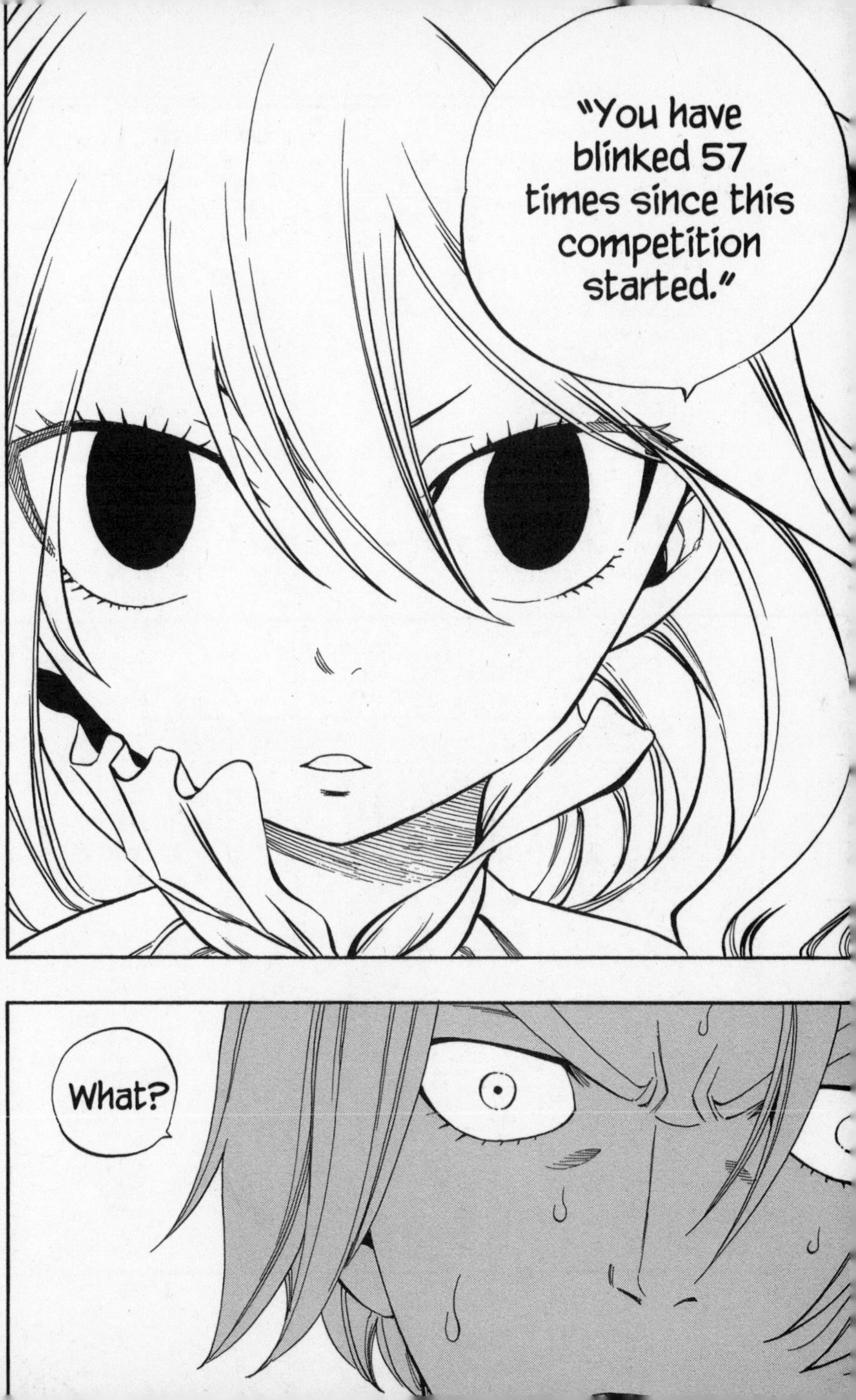
"You have blinked 57 times since this competition started."
What?

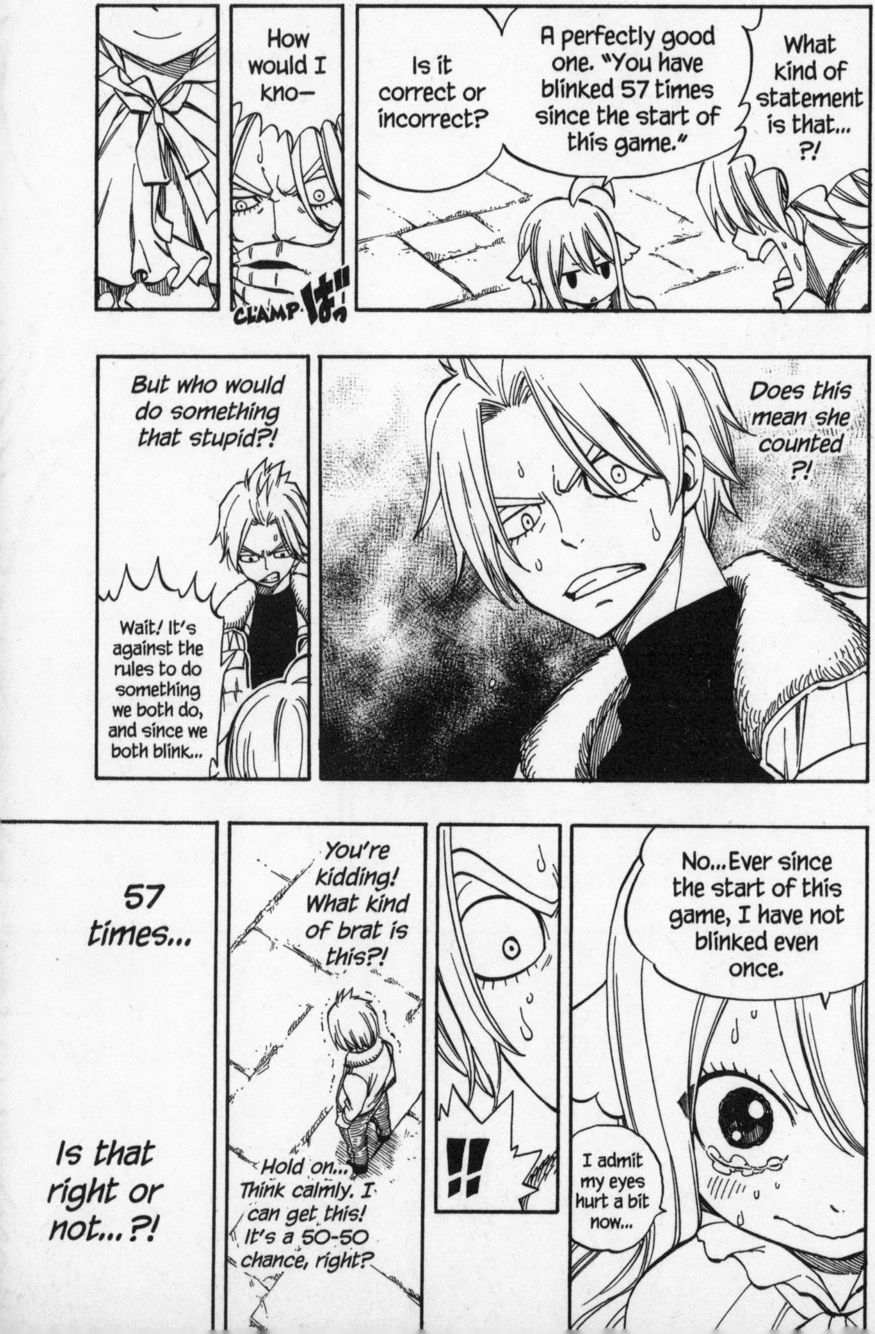
What kind of statement is that...?!
A perfectly good one. "You have blinked 57 times since the start of this game."
Is it correct or incorrect?
How would I kno—
CLAMP
ぱっ
Does this mean she counted?!
But who would do something that stupid?!
Wait! It's against the rules to do something we both do, and since we both blink...
No... Ever since the start of this game, I have not blinked even once.
I admit my eyes hurt a bit now...
!!
You're kidding! What kind of brat is this?!
Hold on... Think calmly. I can get this! It's a 50-50 chance, right?
57 times...
Is that right or not...?!

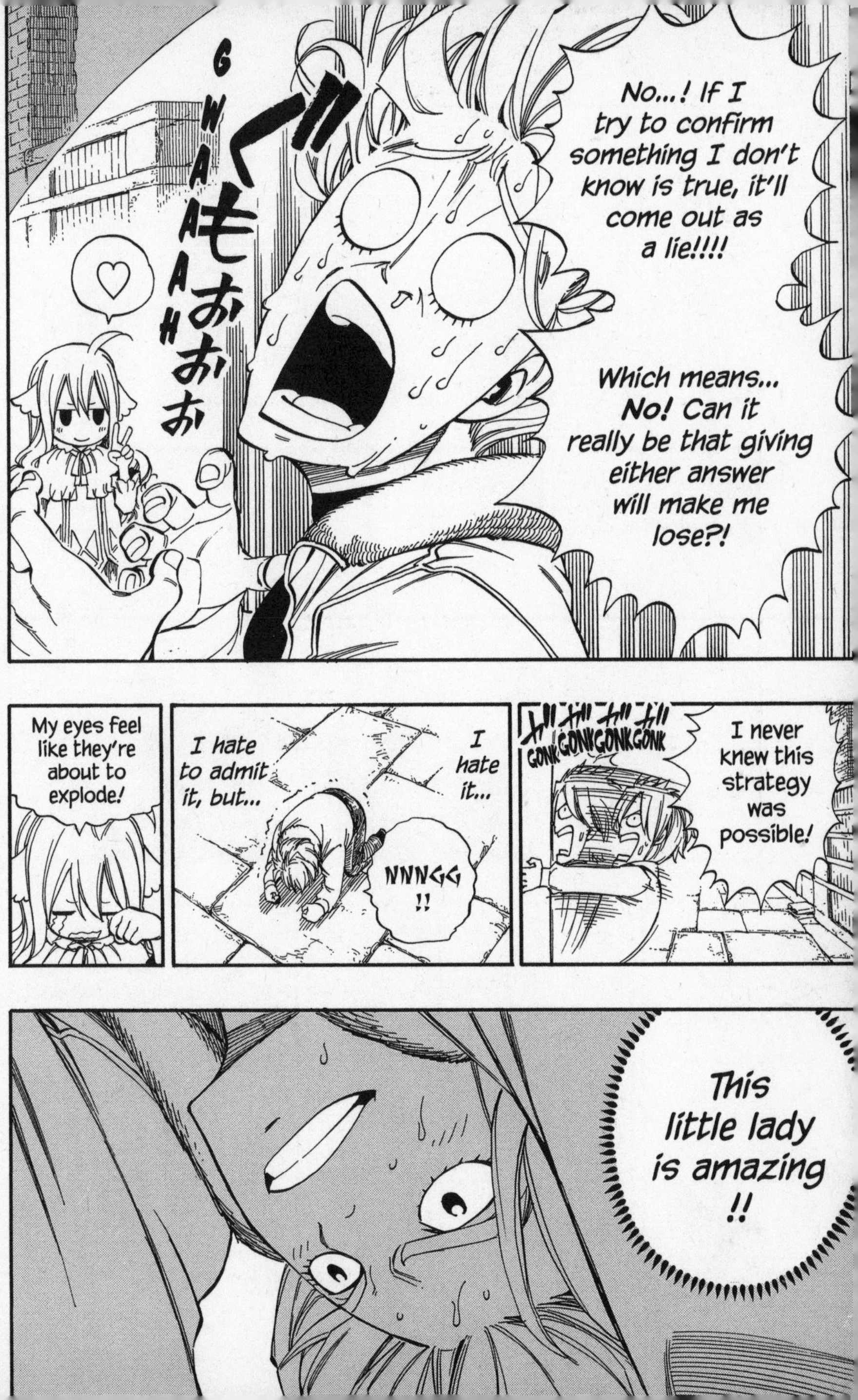
No...! If I try to confirm something I don't know is true, it'll come out as a lie!!!!
Which means... No! Can it really be that giving either answer will make me lose?!
GWAAAAH
くもおおお
♡
I never knew this strategy was possible!
GONK GONK GONK GONK
I hate it...
I hate to admit it, but...
NNNGG !!
My eyes feel like they're about to explode!
This little lady is amazing !!

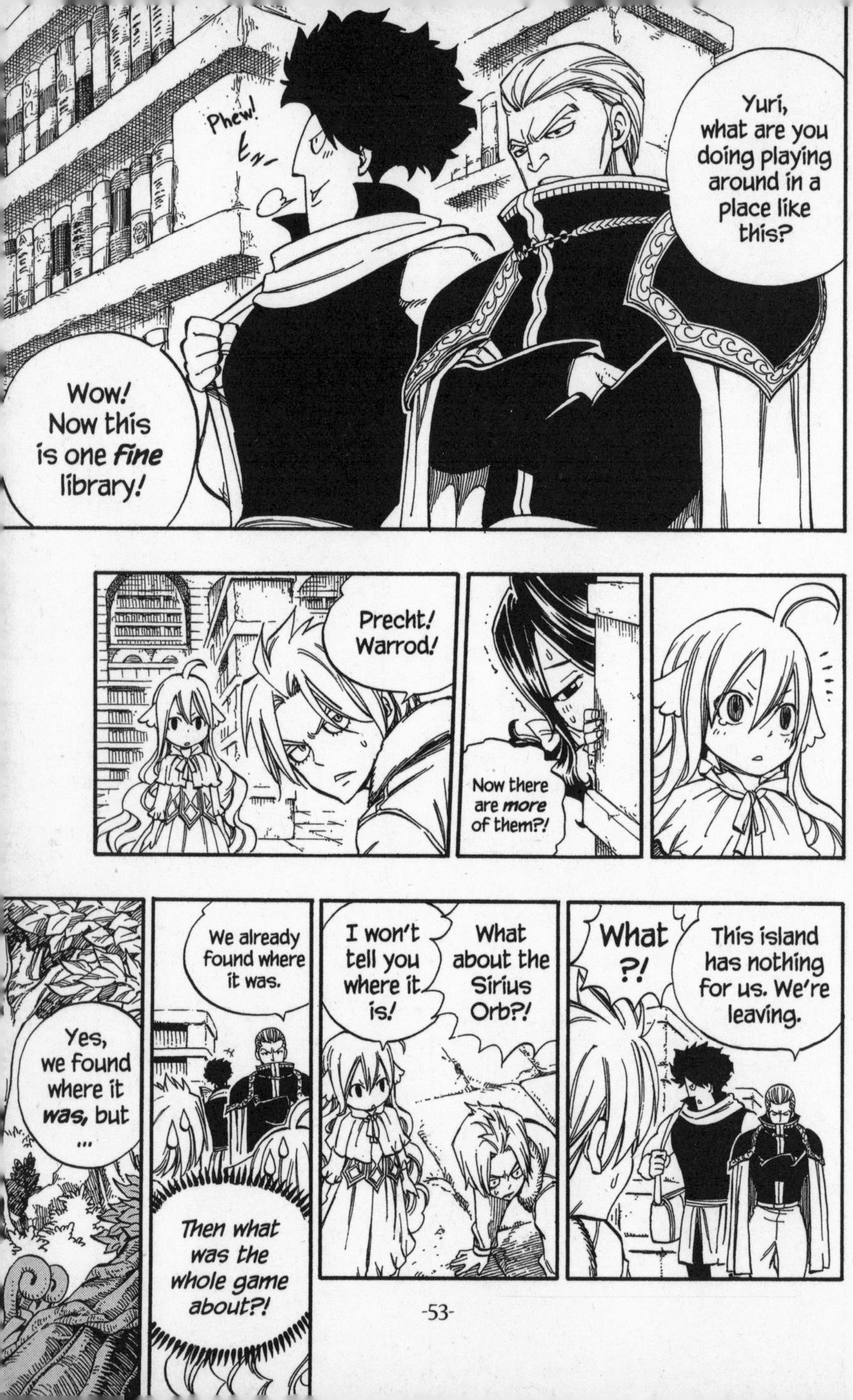
Yuri, what are you doing playing around in a place like this?
Phew!
Wow! Now this is one *fine* library!
Now there are *more* of them?!
Precht! Warrod!
This island has nothing for us. We're leaving.
What ?!
What about the Sirius Orb?!
I won't tell you where it is!
We already found where it was.
Then what was the whole game about?!
Yes, we found where it *was*, but ...

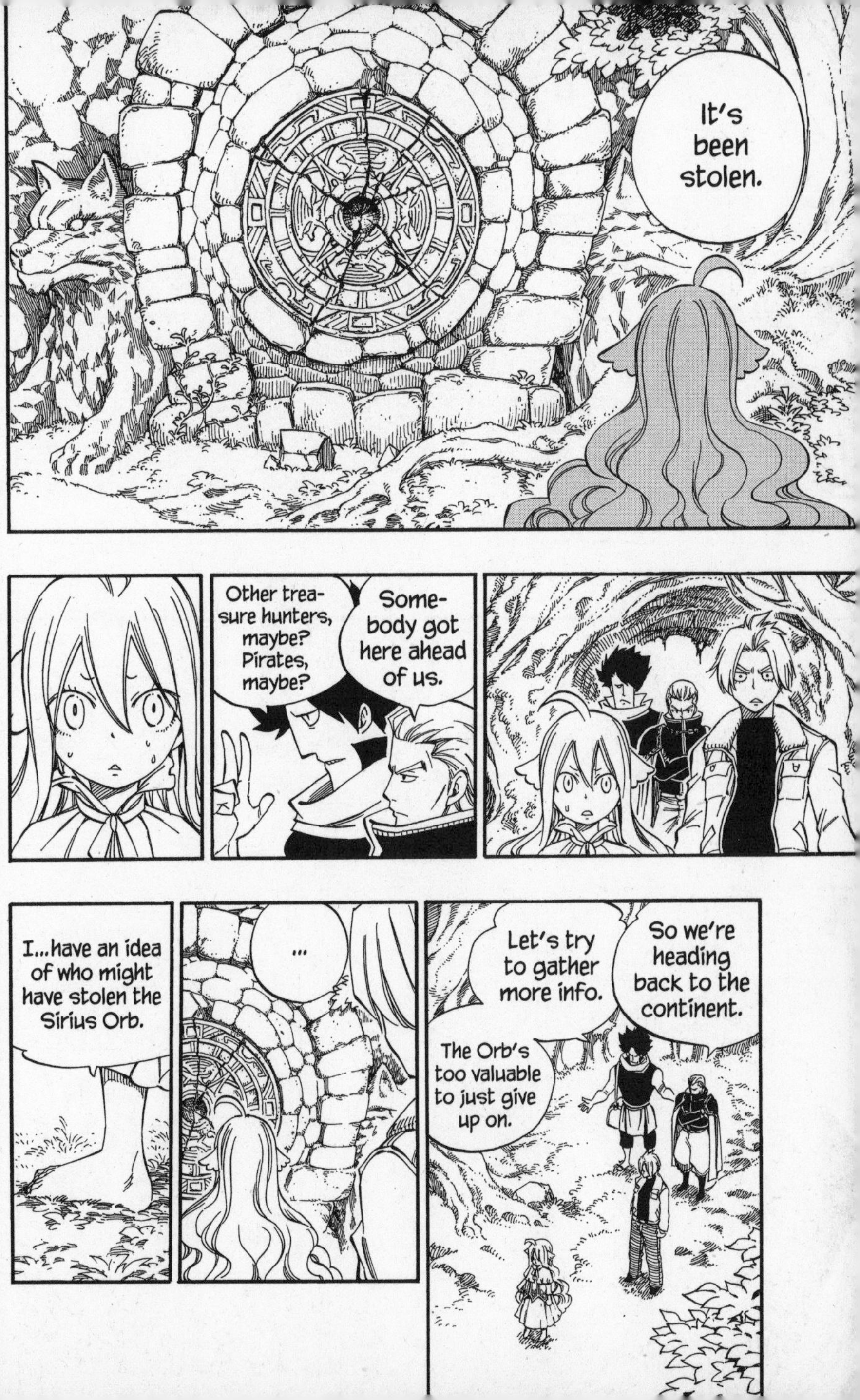
It's been stolen.
Somebody got here ahead of us.
Other treasure hunters, maybe? Pirates, maybe?
So we're heading back to the continent.
Let's try to gather more info.
The Orb's too valuable to just give up on.
...
I...have an idea of who might have stolen the Sirius Orb.

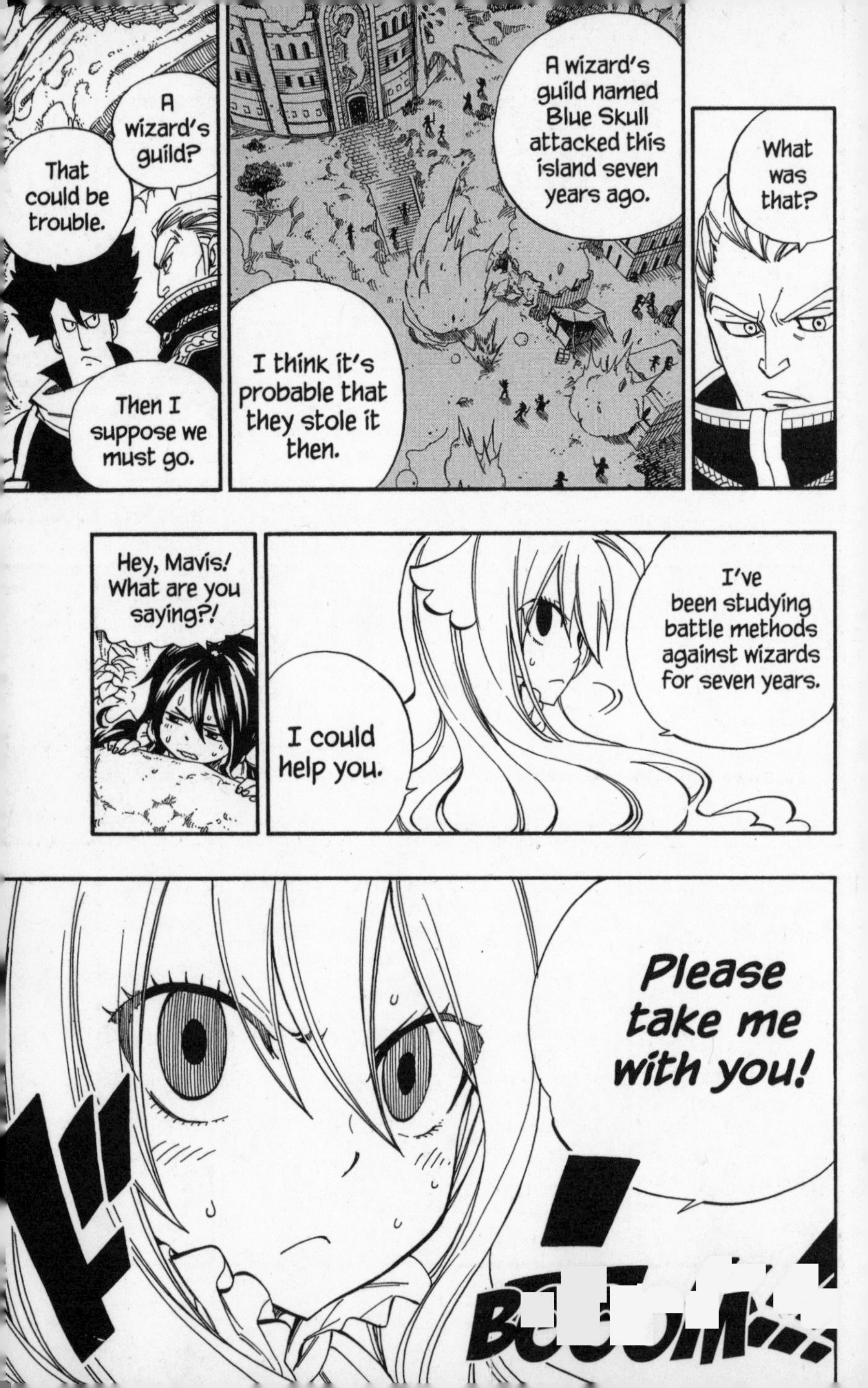
What was that?
A wizard's guild named Blue Skull attacked this island seven years ago.
I think it's probable that they stole it then.
A wizard's guild?
That could be trouble.
Then I suppose we must go.
I've been studying battle methods against wizards for seven years.
I could help you.
Hey, Mavis! What are you saying?!
Please take me with you!

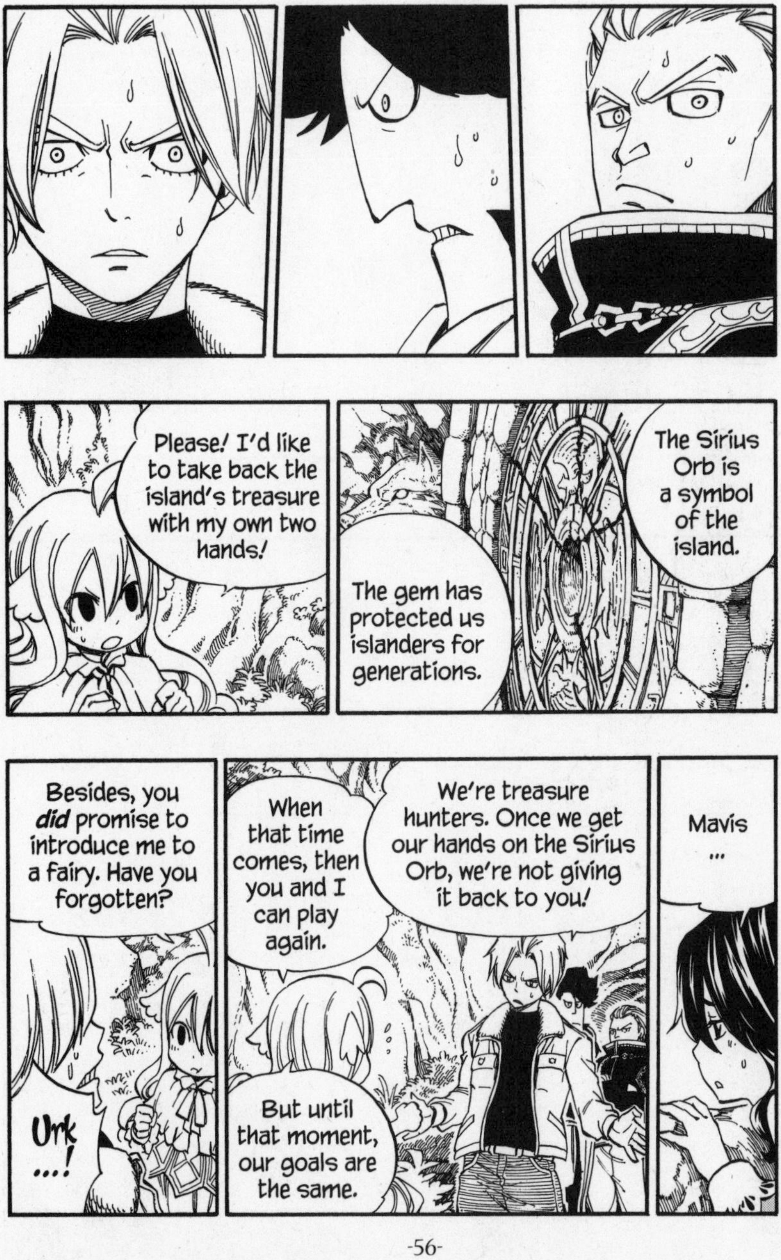
The Sirius Orb is a symbol of the island.
The gem has protected us islanders for generations.
Please! I'd like to take back the island's treasure with my own two hands!
Mavis ...
We're treasure hunters. Once we get our hands on the Sirius Orb, we're not giving it back to you!
When that time comes, then you and I can play again.
But until that moment, our goals are the same.
Besides, you *did* promise to introduce me to a fairy. Have you forgotten?
Urk ...!

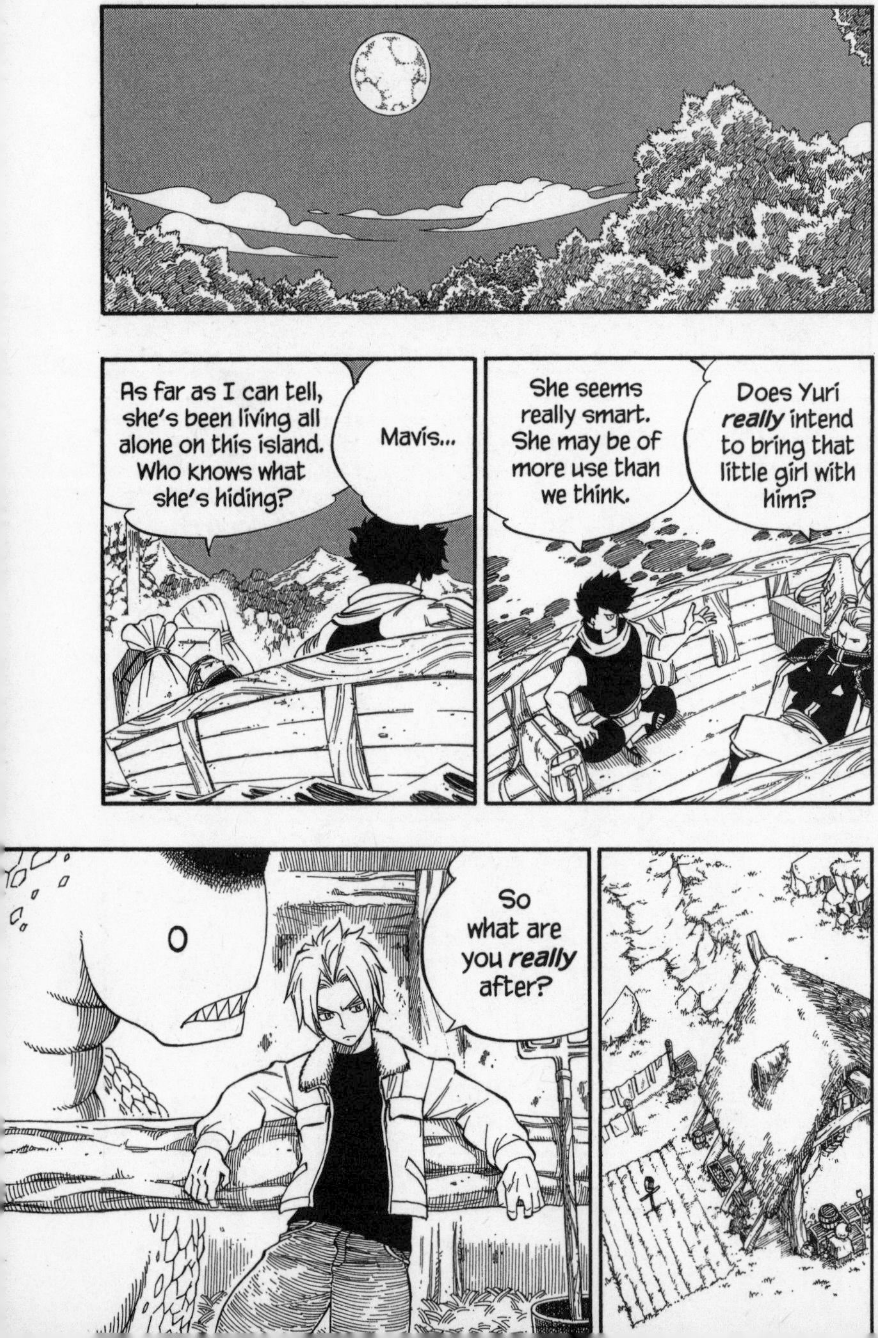
Does Yuri *really* intend to bring that little girl with him?
She seems really smart. She may be of more use than we think.
Mavis...
As far as I can tell, she's been living all alone on this island. Who knows what she's hiding?
So what are you *really* after?

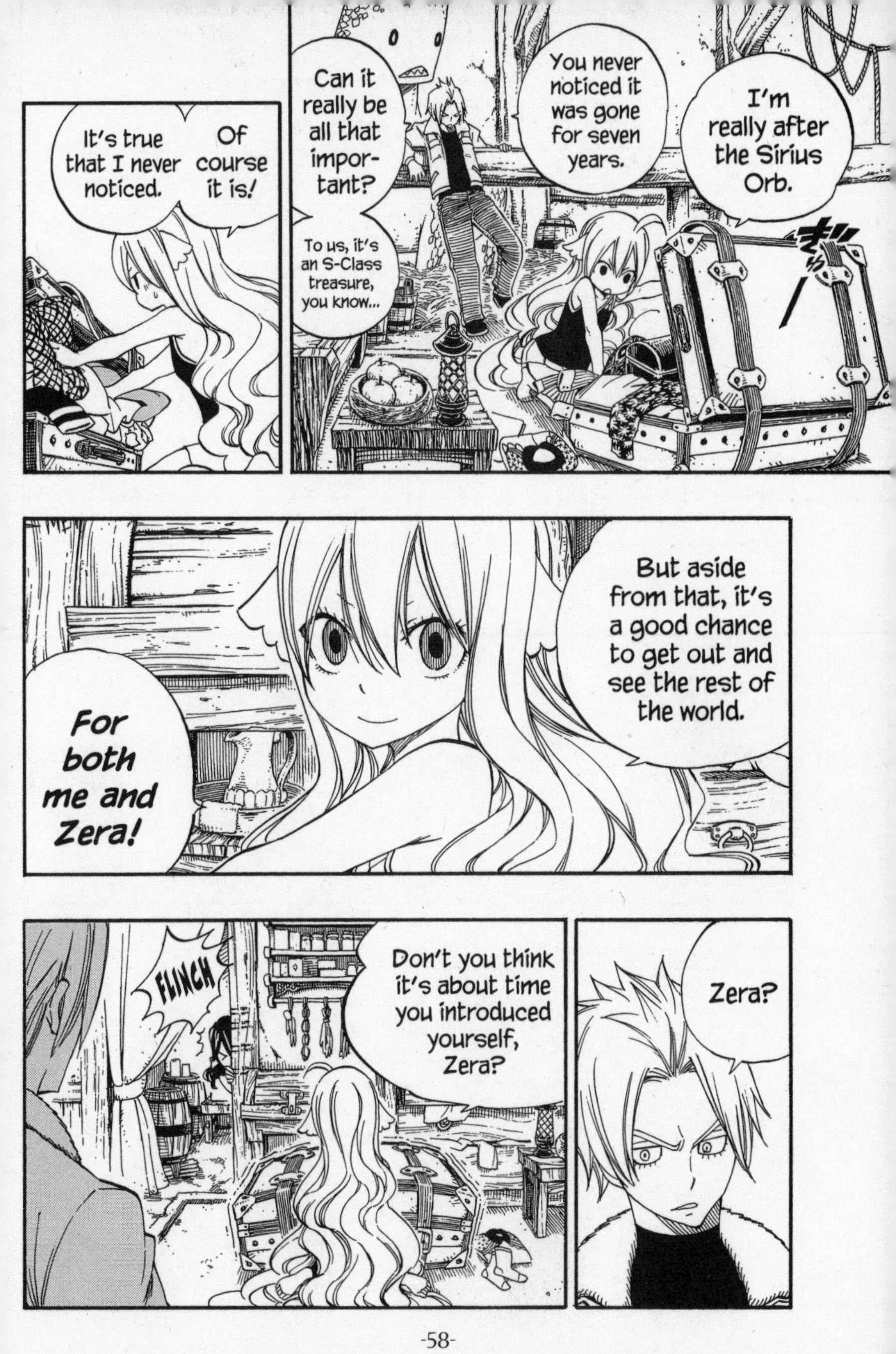
I'm really after the Sirius Orb.
You never noticed it was gone for seven years.
Can it really be all that important?
To us, it's an S-Class treasure, you know...
Of course it is!
It's true that I never noticed.
But aside from that, it's a good chance to get out and see the rest of the world.
For both me and Zera!
Zera?
Don't you think it's about time you introduced yourself, Zera?
FLINCH

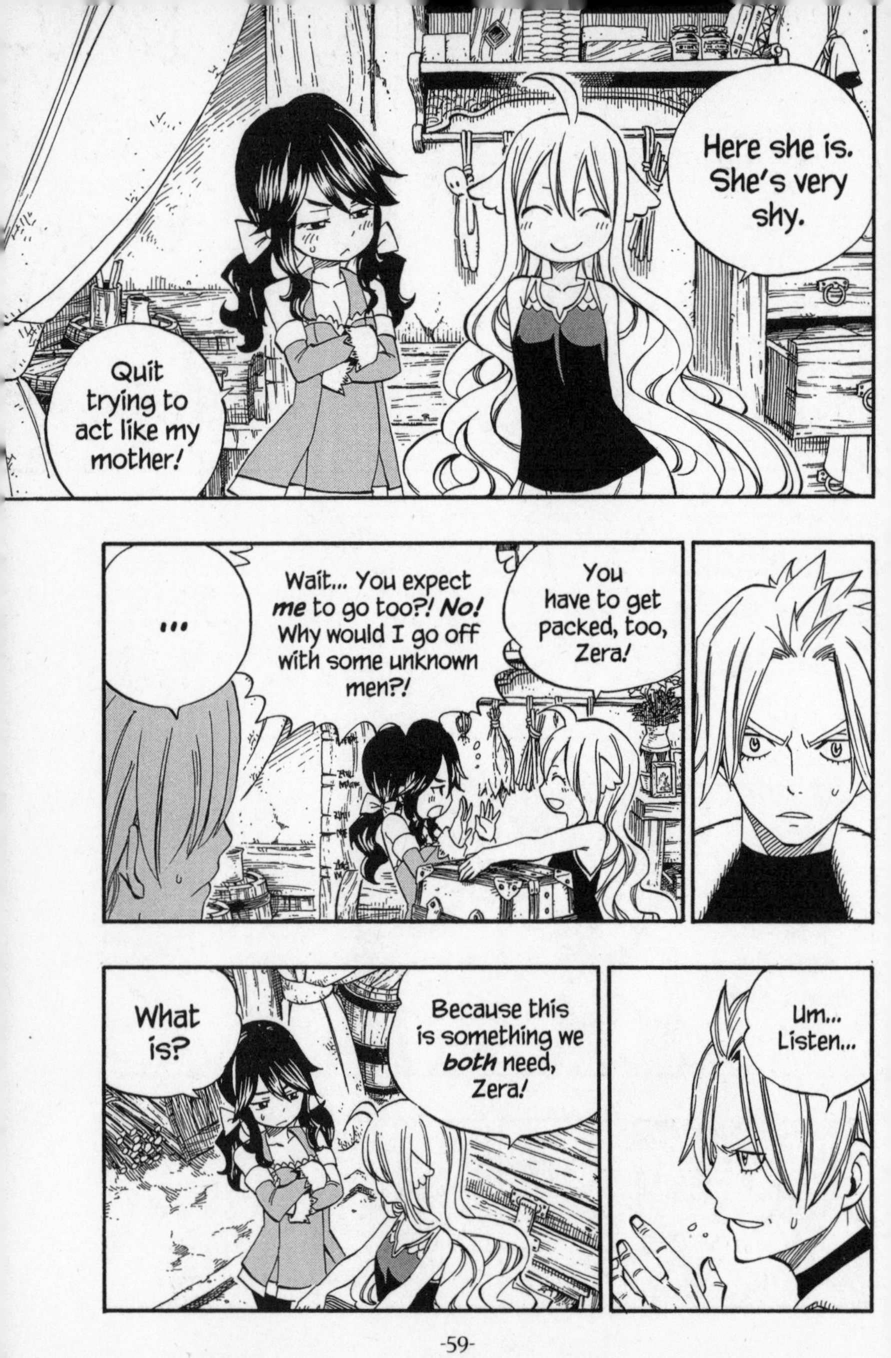
Here she is. She's very shy.
Quit trying to act like my mother!
You have to get packed, too, Zera!
Wait... You expect *me* to go too?! ***No!*** Why would I go off with some unknown men?!
...
Um... Listen...
Because this is something we ***both*** need, Zera!
What is?

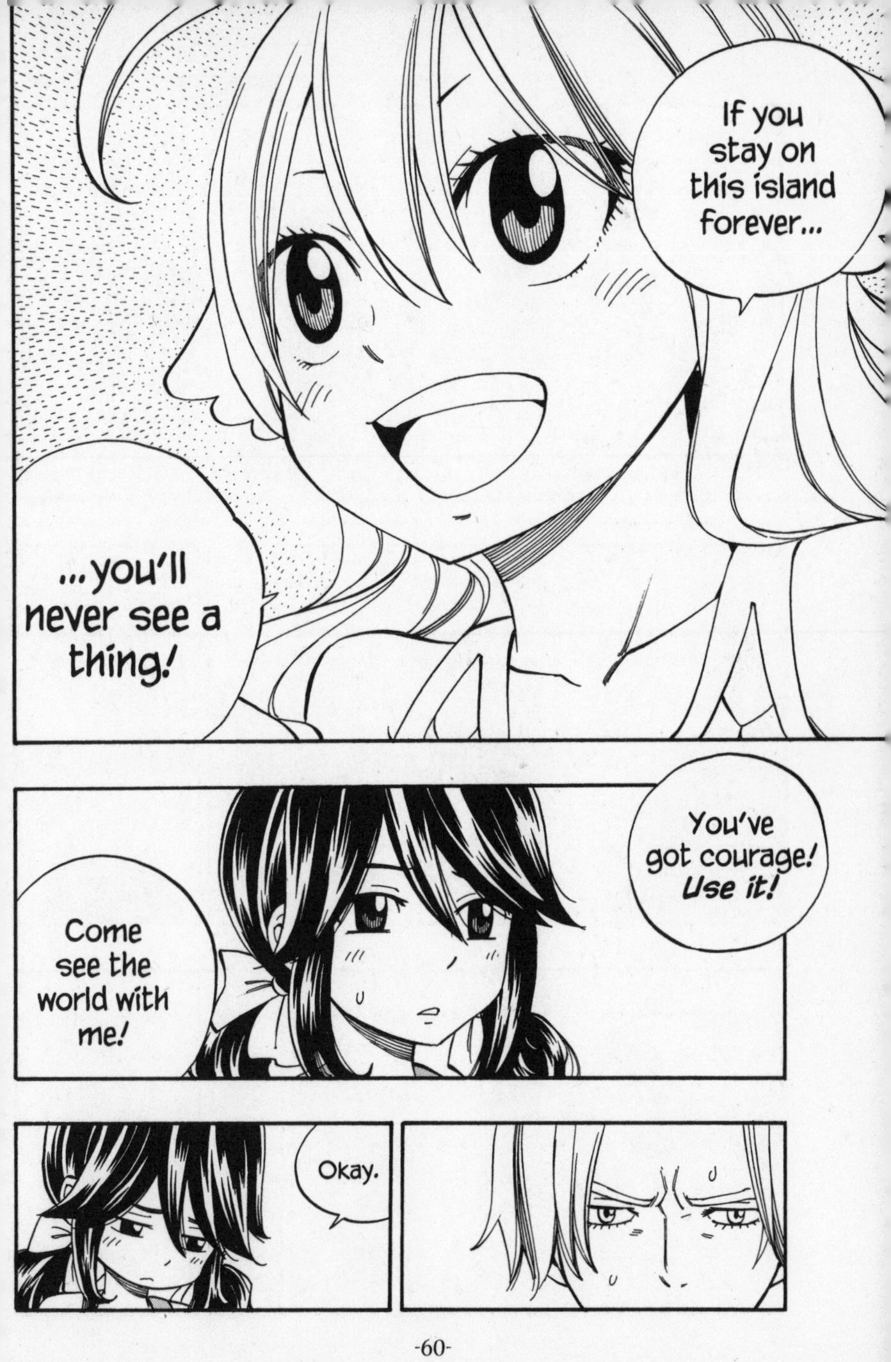
If you stay on this island forever...
...you'll never see a thing!
You've got courage! *Use it!*
Come see the world with me!
Okay.

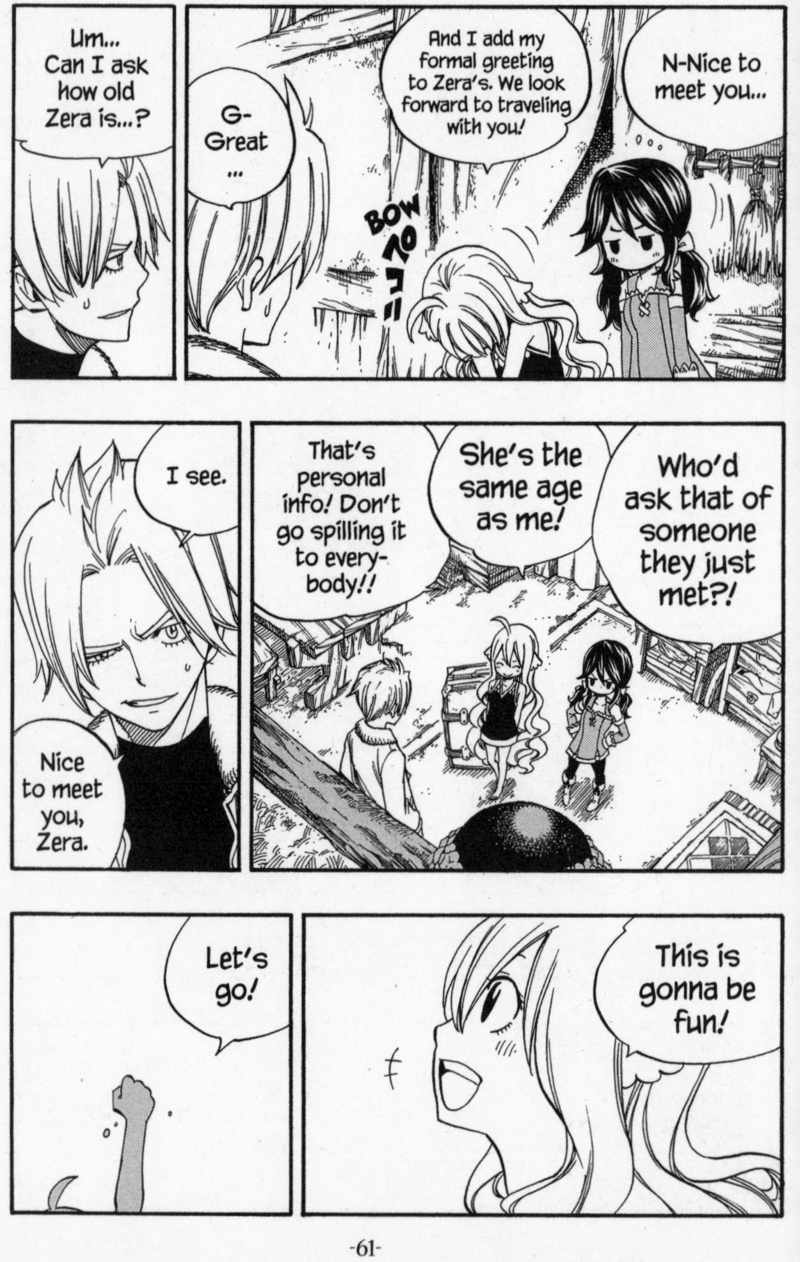
N-Nice to meet you...
And I add my formal greeting to Zera's. We look forward to traveling with you!
BOW
G-Great...
Um... Can I ask how old Zera is...?
Who'd ask that of someone they just met?!
She's the same age as me!
That's personal info! Don't go spilling it to every-body!!
I see.
Nice to meet you, Zera.
This is gonna be fun!
Let's go!

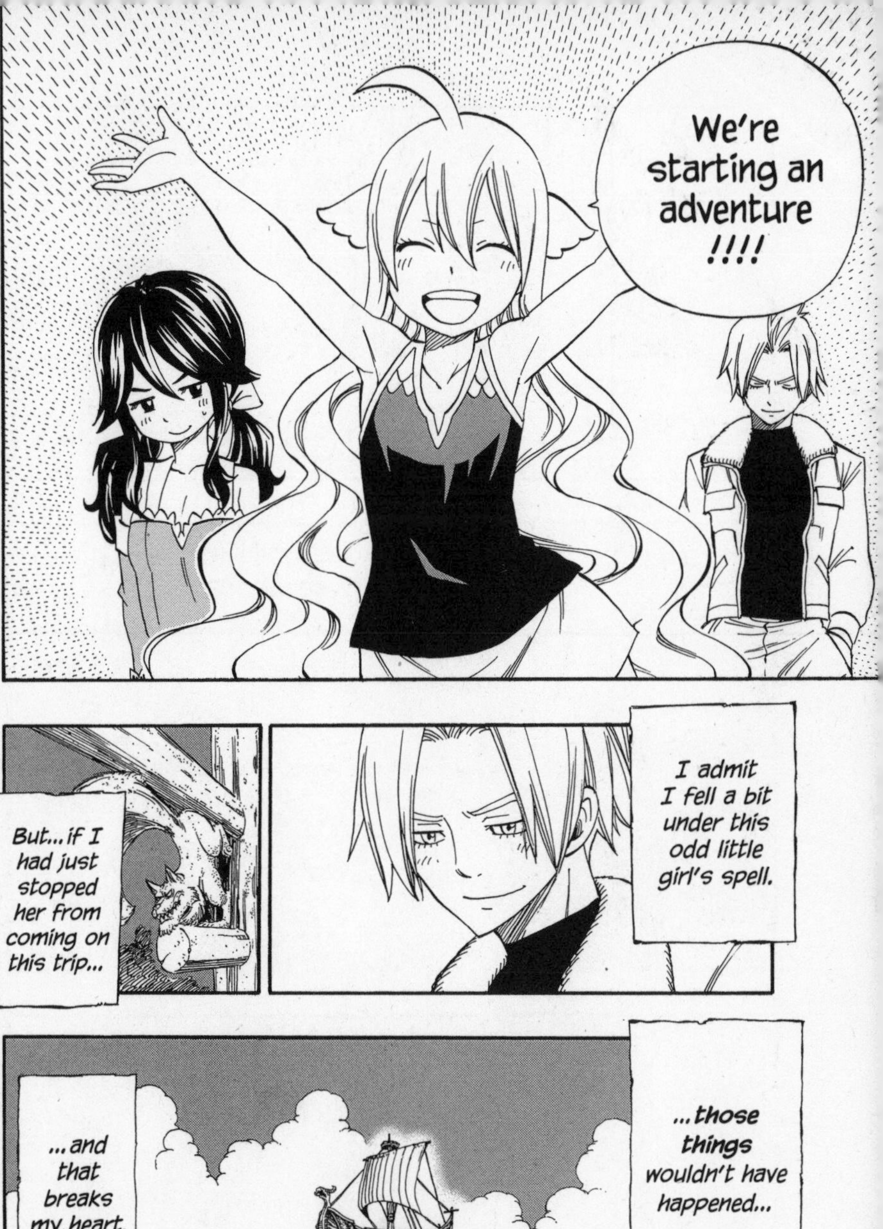

We're starting an adventure !!!!
I admit I fell a bit under this odd little girl's spell.
But...if I had just stopped her from coming on this trip...
...those things wouldn't have happened...
...and that breaks my heart.

FAIRY TAIL ZERØ

Chapter 4: Dancing with Blades

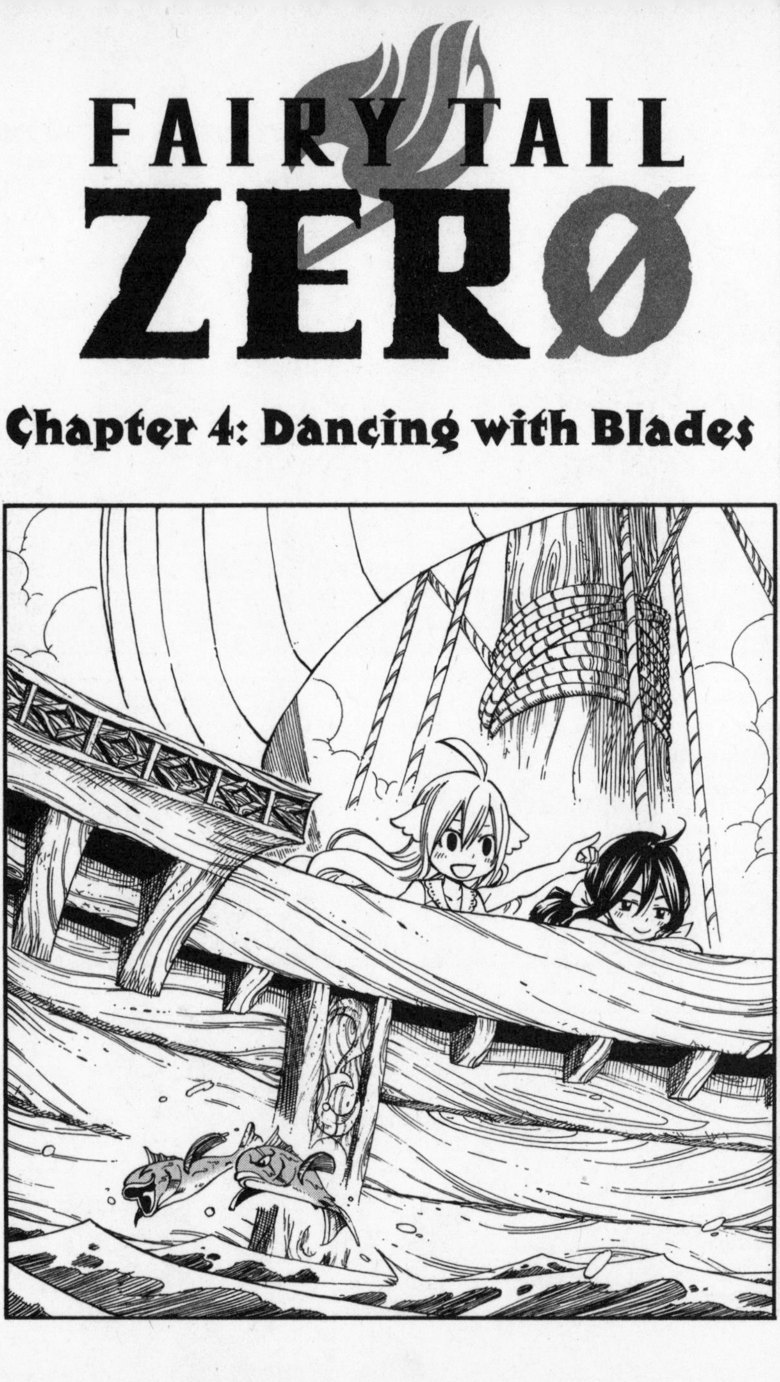

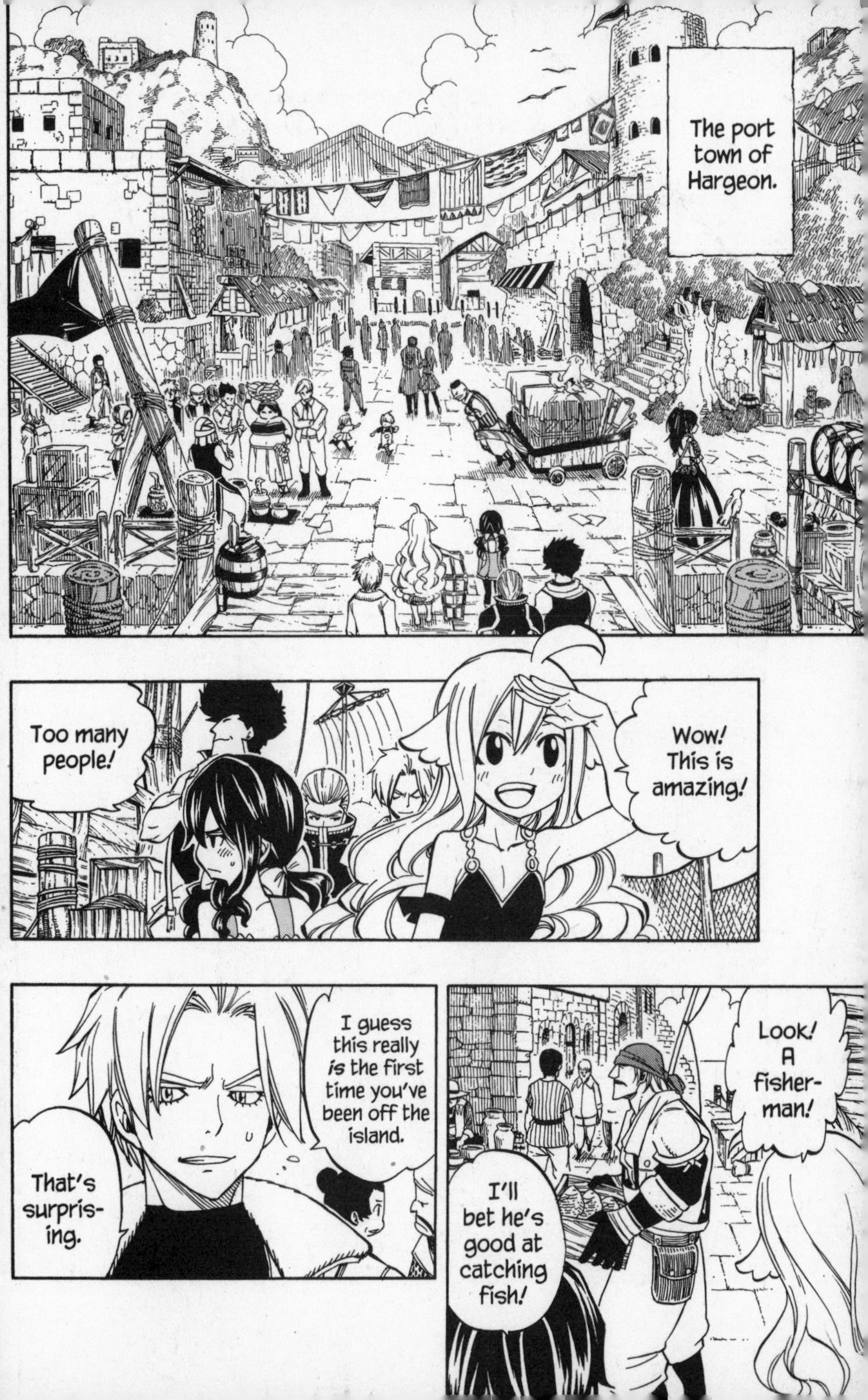
The port town of Hargeon.
Wow! This is amazing!
Too many people!
Look! A fisher-man!
I'll bet he's good at catching fish!
I guess this really *is* the first time you've been off the island.
That's surpris-ing.

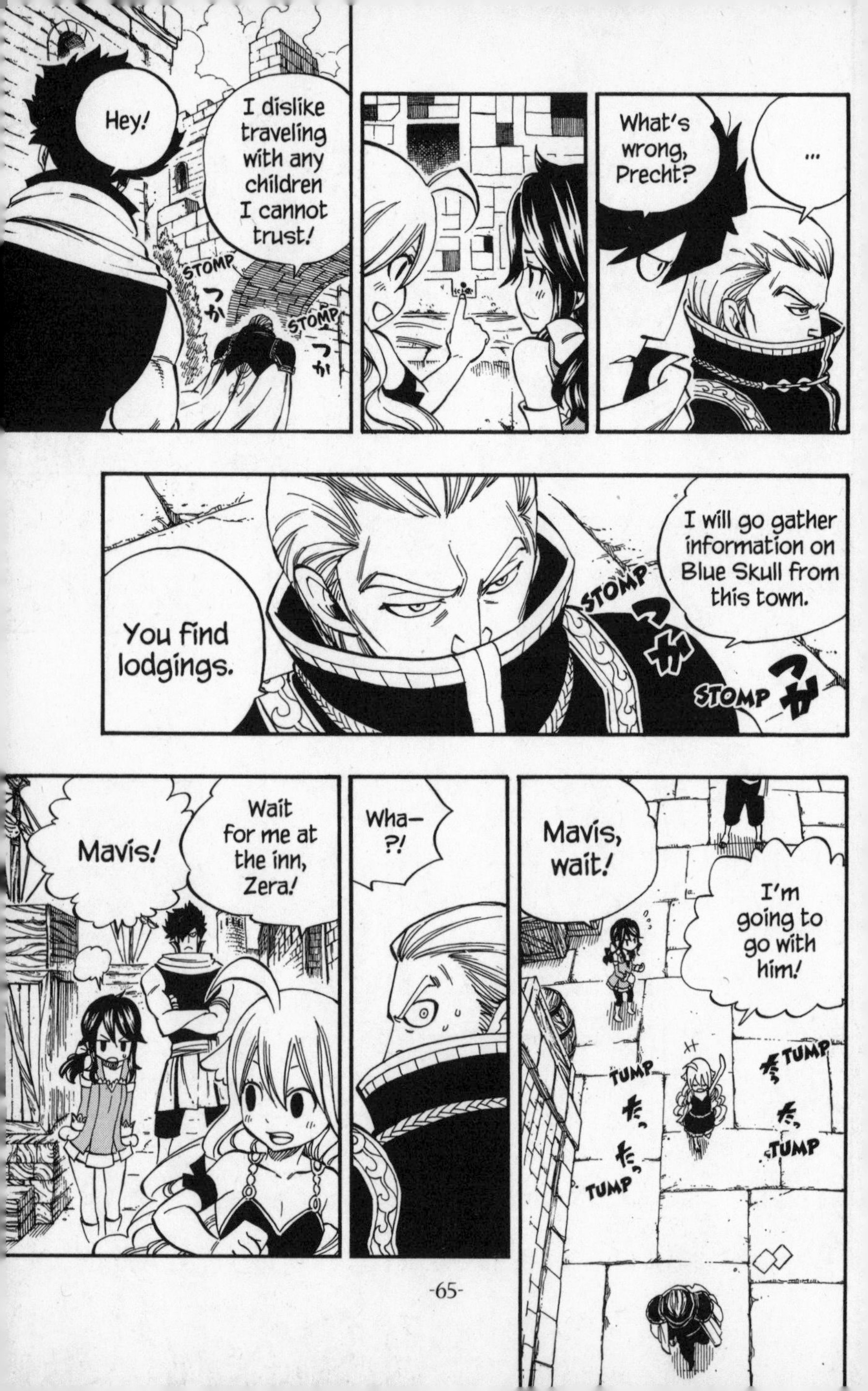
...
What's wrong, Precht?
I dislike traveling with any children I cannot trust!
Hey!
STOMP
つか
STOMP
つか
I will go gather information on Blue Skull from this town.
STOMP
つか
STOMP
つか
You find lodgings.
I'm going to go with him!
Mavis, wait!
TUMP
たっ
TUMP
たっ
TUMP
たっ
TUMP
たっ
Wha– ?!
Wait for me at the inn, Zera!
Mavis!

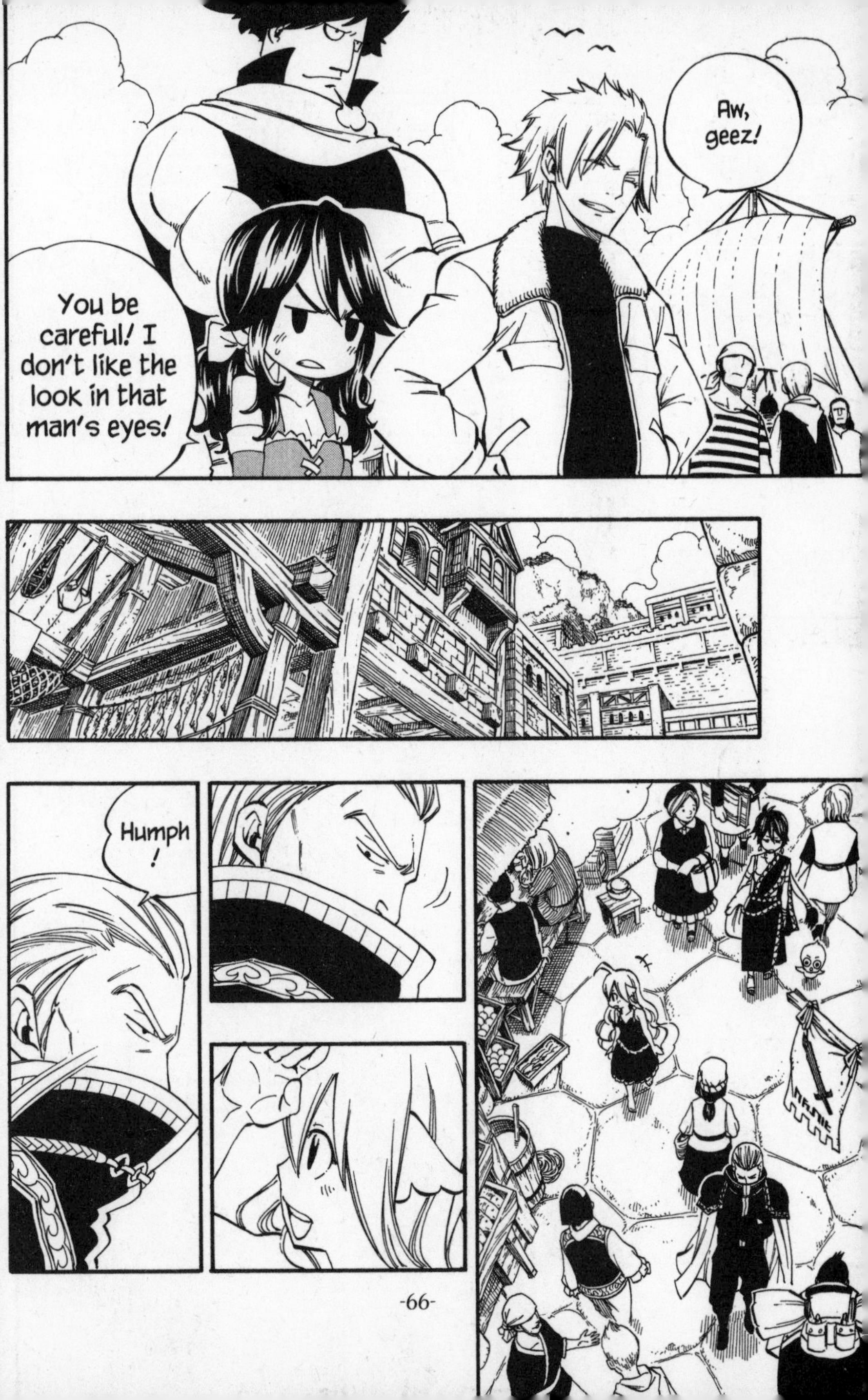
Aw, geez!
You be careful! I don't like the look in that man's eyes!
Humph!

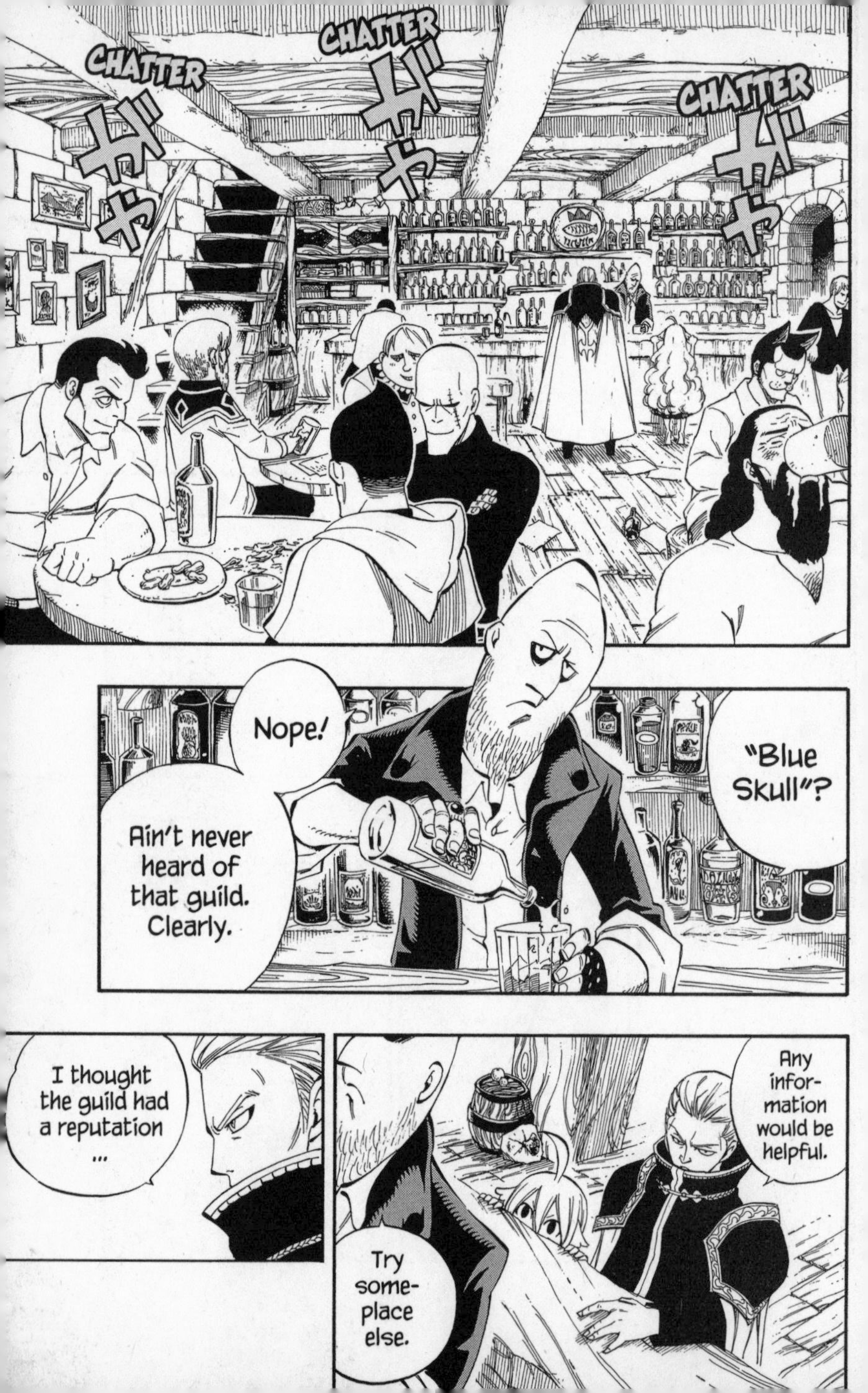
CHATTER
CHATTER
CHATTER
"Blue Skull"?
Nope!
Ain't never heard of that guild. Clearly.
Any information would be helpful.
Try someplace else.
I thought the guild had a reputation ...

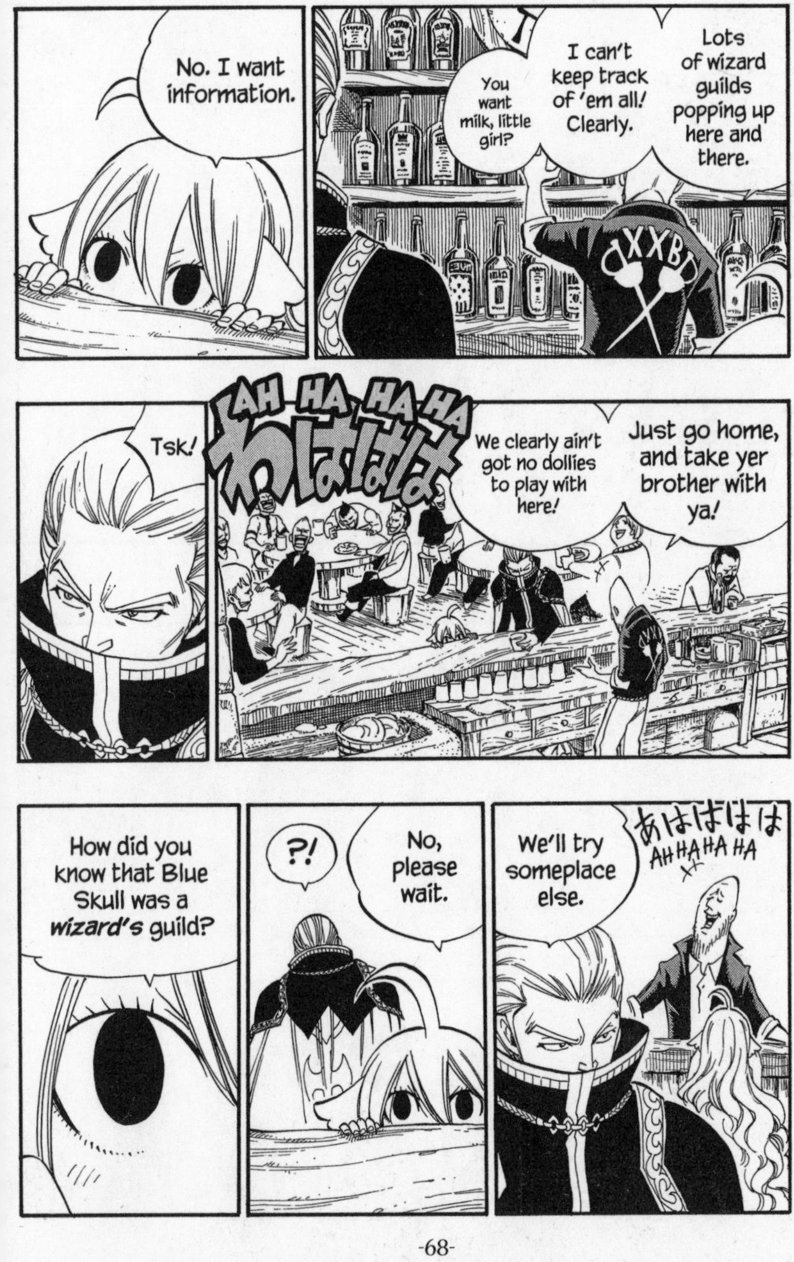
Lots of wizard guilds popping up here and there.
I can't keep track of 'em all! Clearly.
You want milk, little girl?
No. I want information.
Just go home, and take yer brother with ya!
We clearly ain't got no dollies to play with here!
わははは
AH HA HA HA
Tsk!
あははははは
AH HA HA HA
We'll try someplace else.
No, please wait.
?!
How did you know that Blue Skull was a *wizard's* guild?

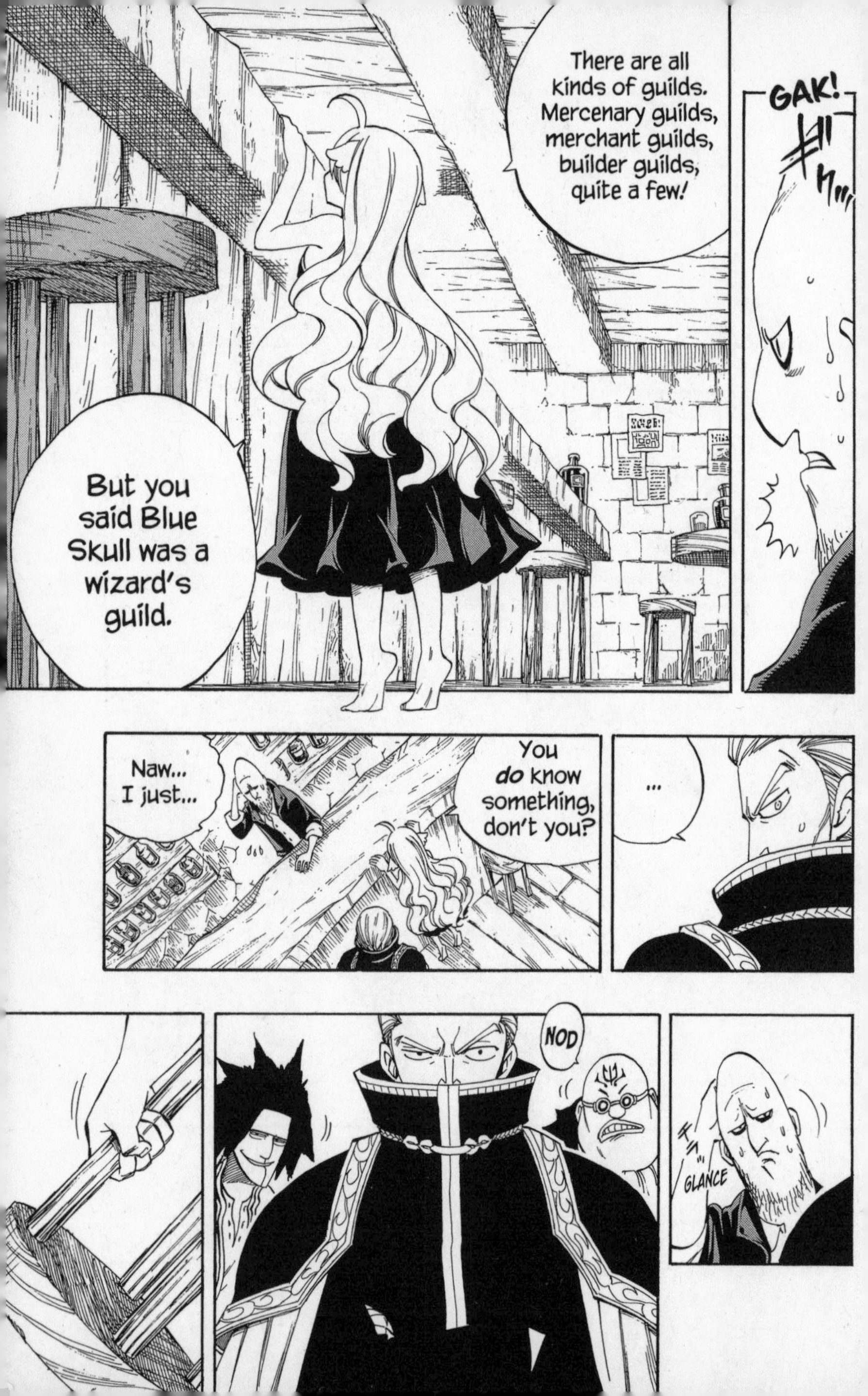
GAK!
There are all kinds of guilds. Mercenary guilds, merchant guilds, builder guilds, quite a few!
But you said Blue Skull was a wizard's guild.
...
You *do* know something, don't you?
Naw... I just...
GLANCE
NOD

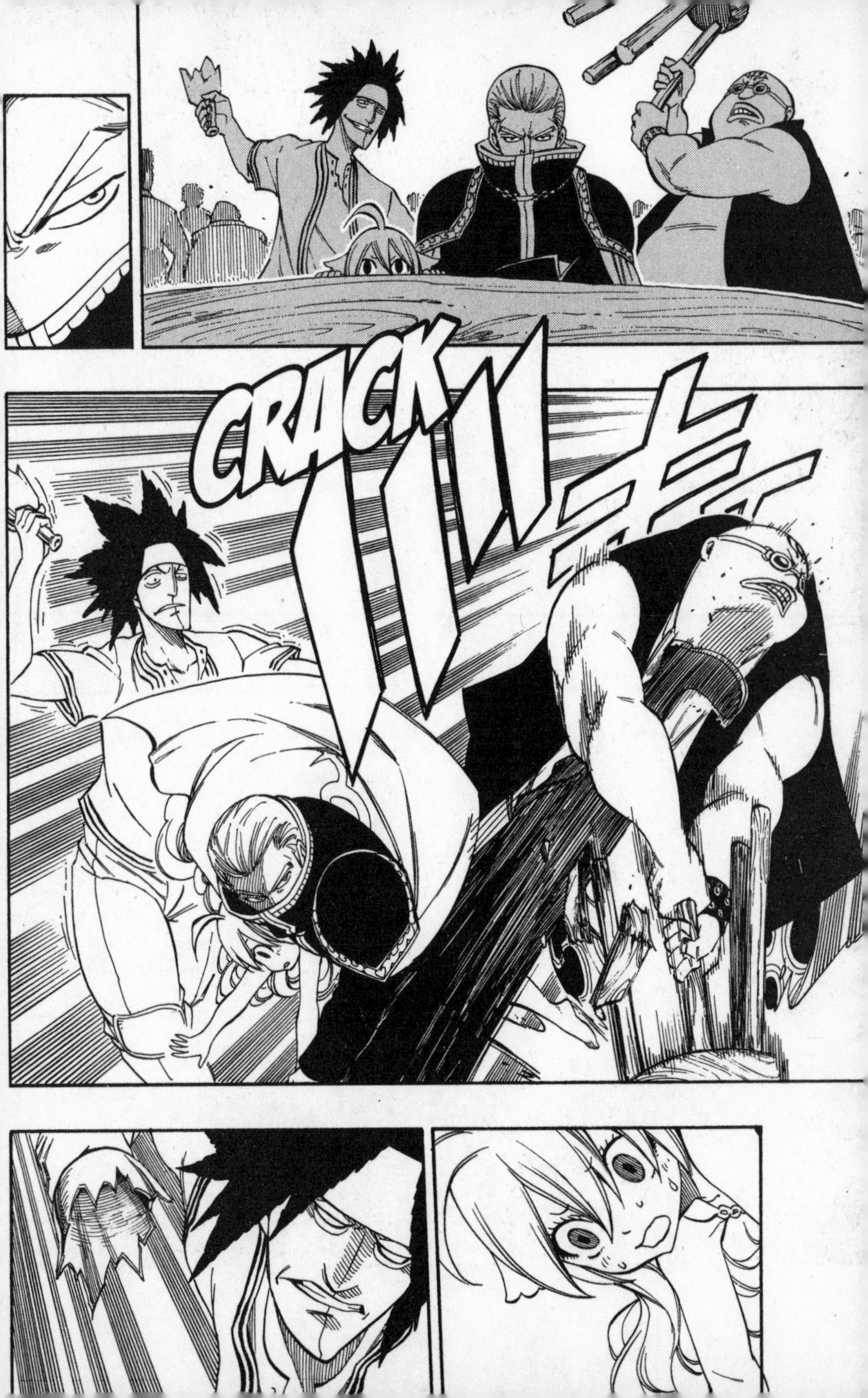
CRACK

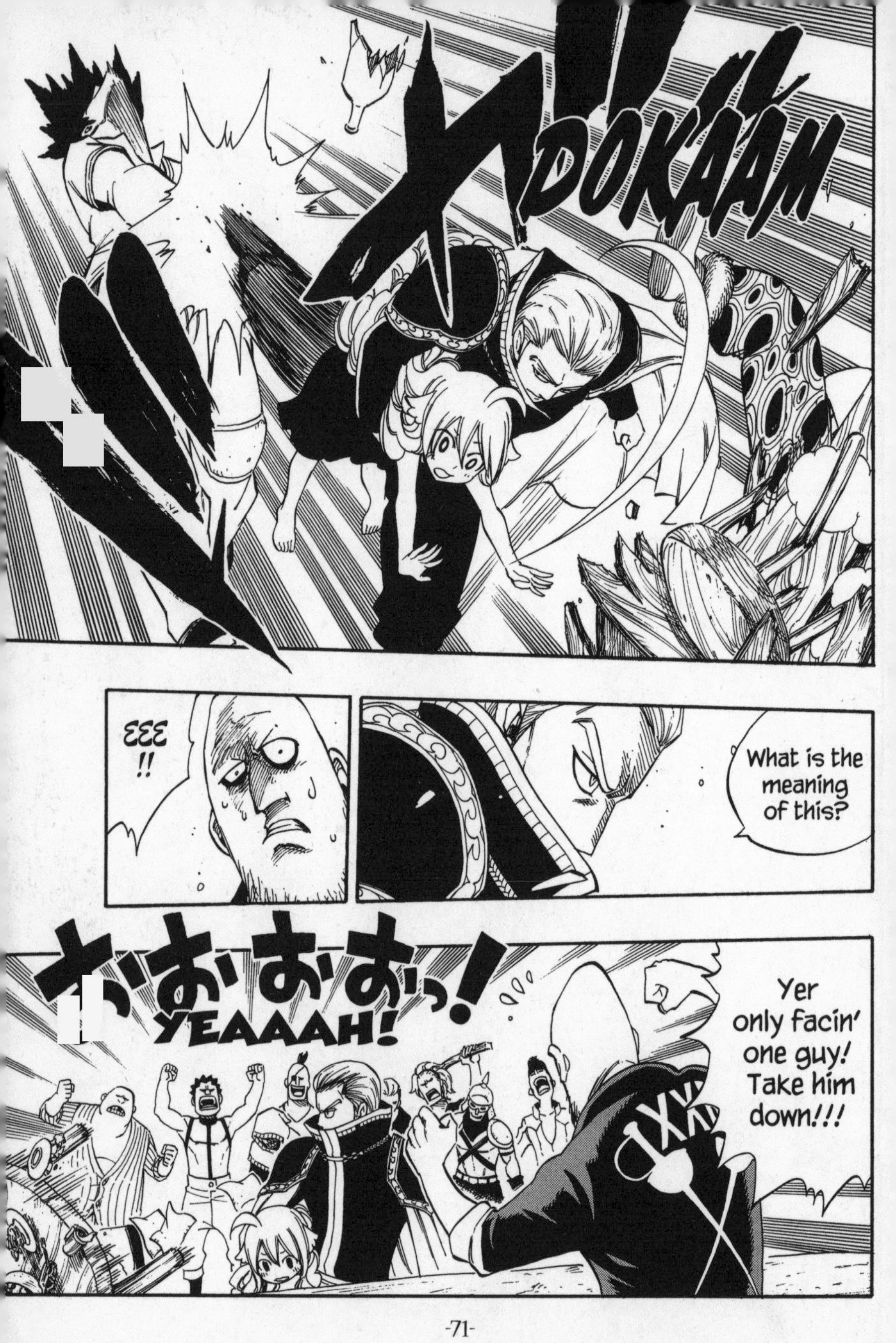
DOKAAAN
What is the meaning of this?
EEE!!
Yer only facin' one guy! Take him down!!!
YEAAAH!

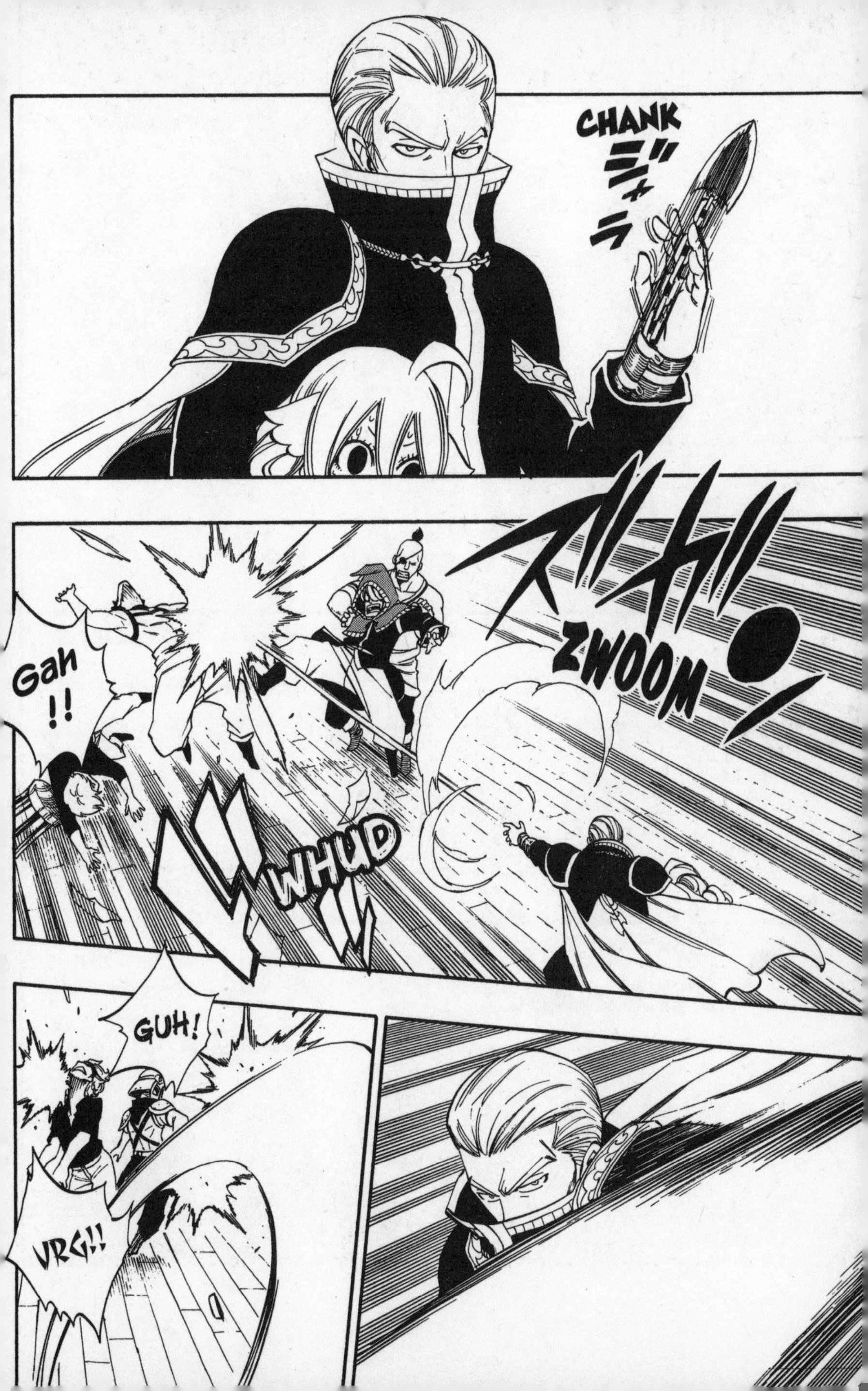
CHANK
ジャラ
ZWOOM
Gah!!
WHUD
GUH!
VRG!!

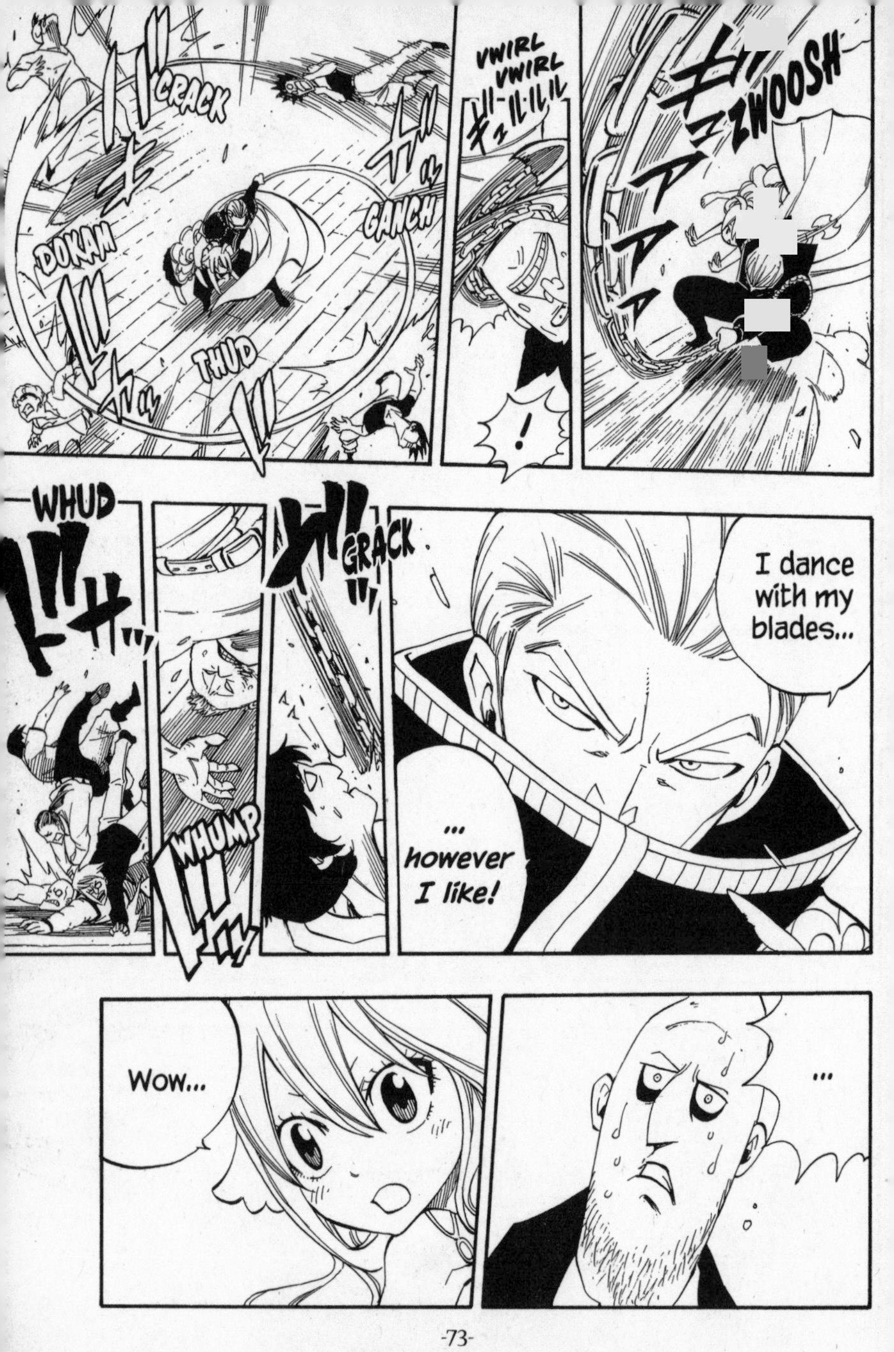
ZWOOSH
VWIRL
VWIRL
!
CRACK
GANCH
DOKAM
THUD
I dance with my blades...
... however I like!
GRACK
WHUMP
WHUD
...
Wow...

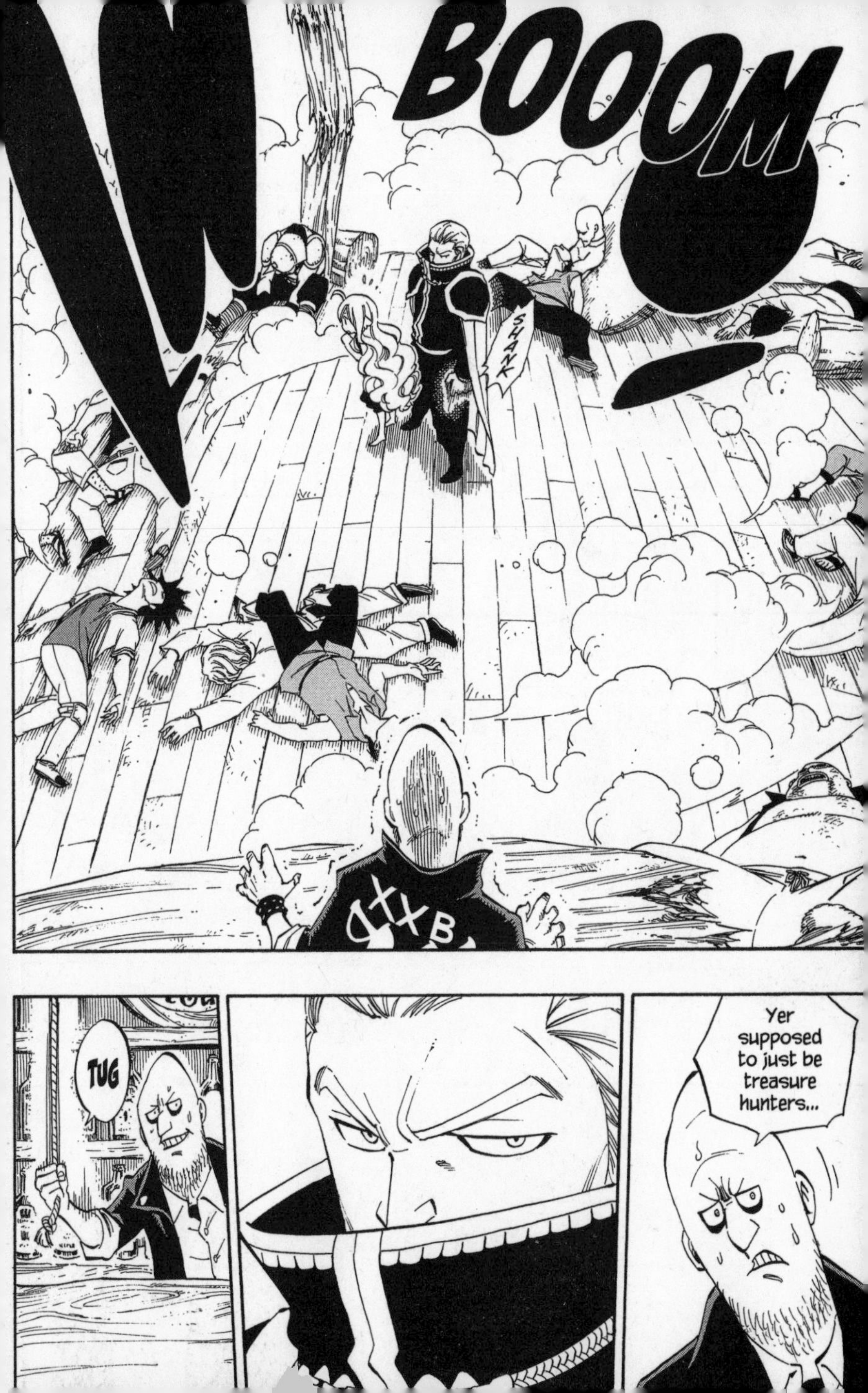
BOOOM
SHANK
Yer supposed to just be treasure hunters...
TUG

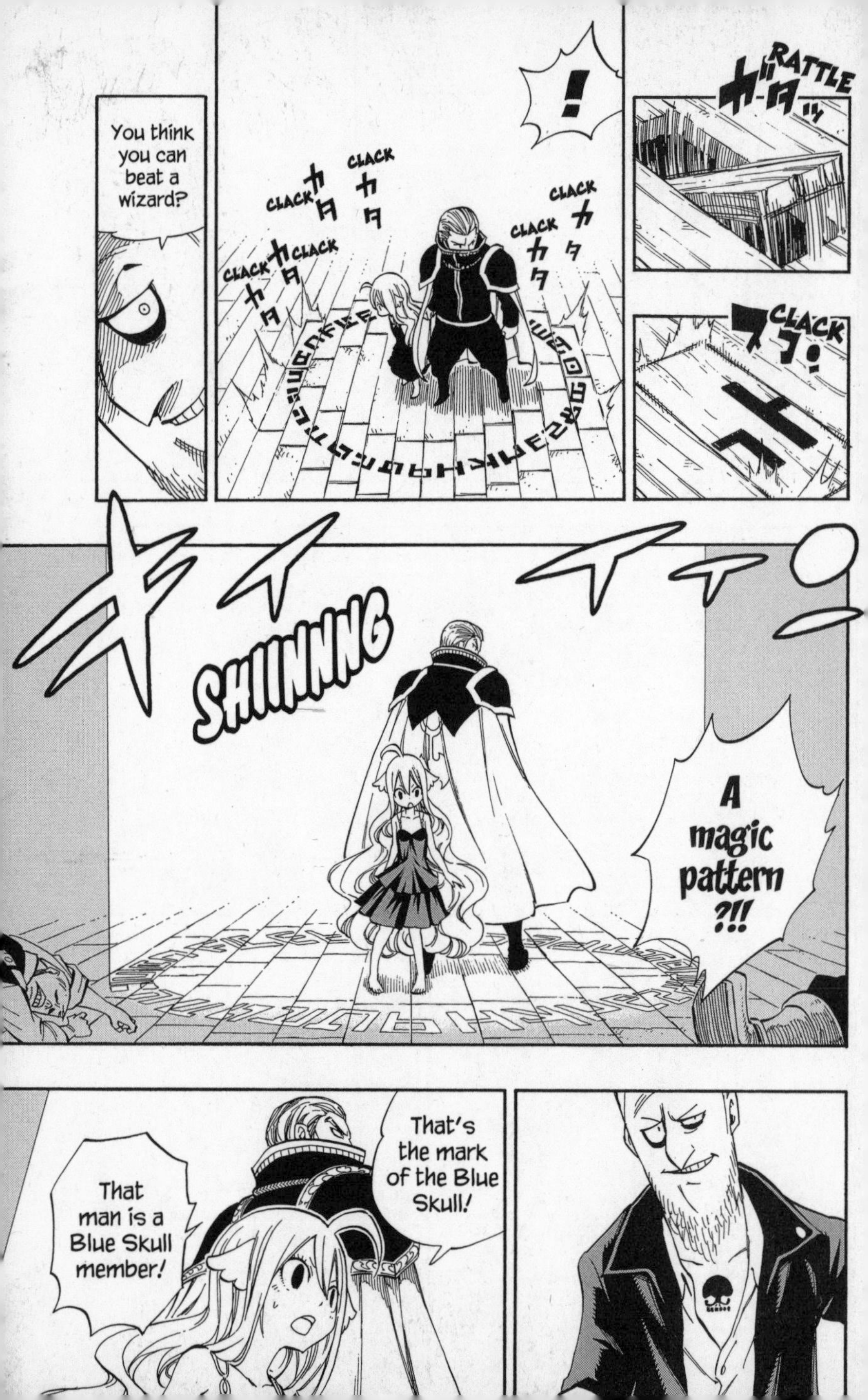
RATTLE
CLACK
!
CLACK
CLACK
CLACK
CLACK
CLACK
CLACK
You think you can beat a wizard?
SHIINNNG
A magic pattern?!!
That's the mark of the Blue Skull!
That man is a Blue Skull member!

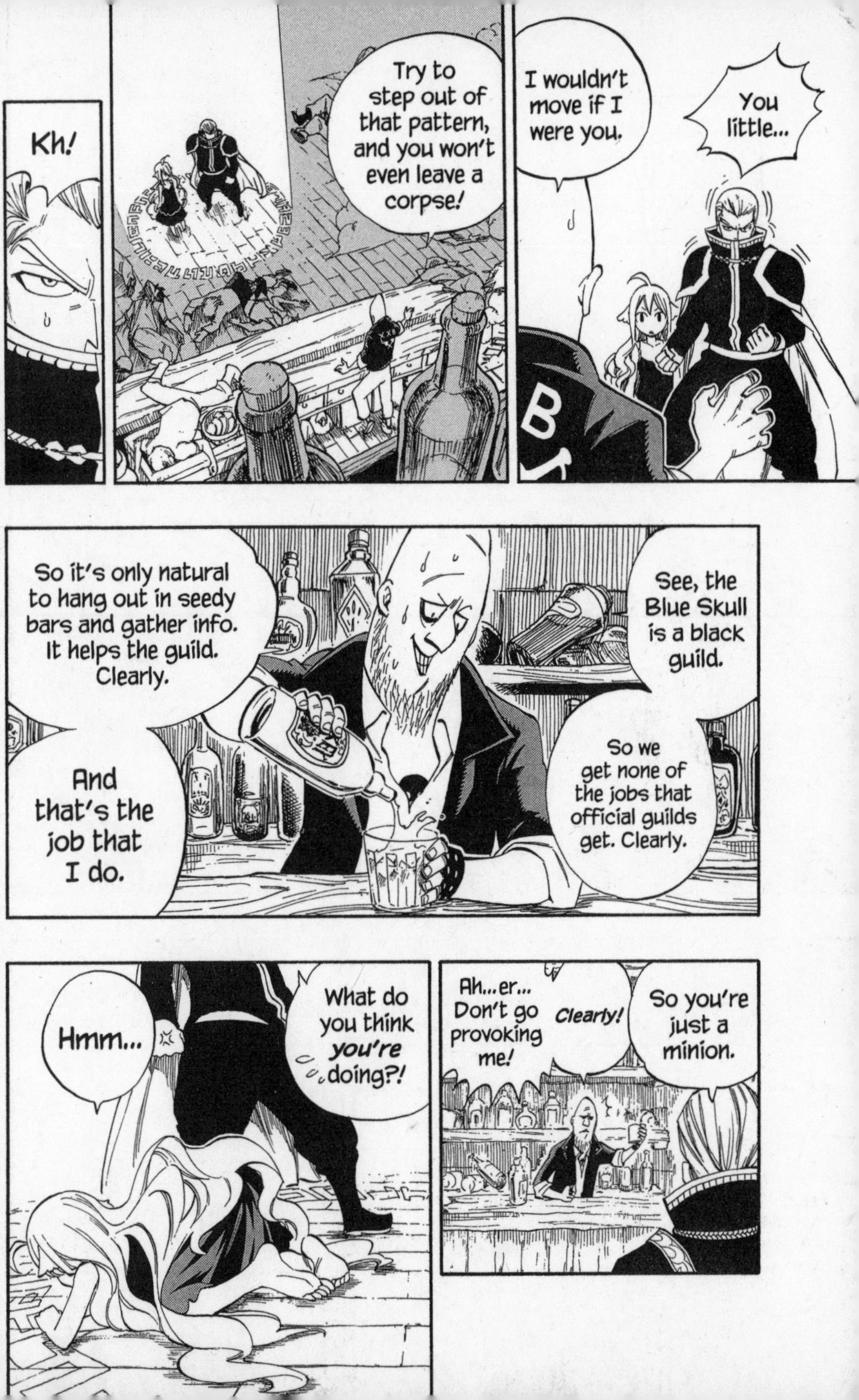
You little...
I wouldn't move if I were you.
Try to step out of that pattern, and you won't even leave a corpse!
Kh!
See, the Blue Skull is a black guild.
So we get none of the jobs that official guilds get. Clearly.
So it's only natural to hang out in seedy bars and gather info. It helps the guild. Clearly.
And that's the job that I do.
So you're just a minion.
Clearly!
Ah...er... Don't go provoking me!
What do you think *you're* doing?!
Hmm...

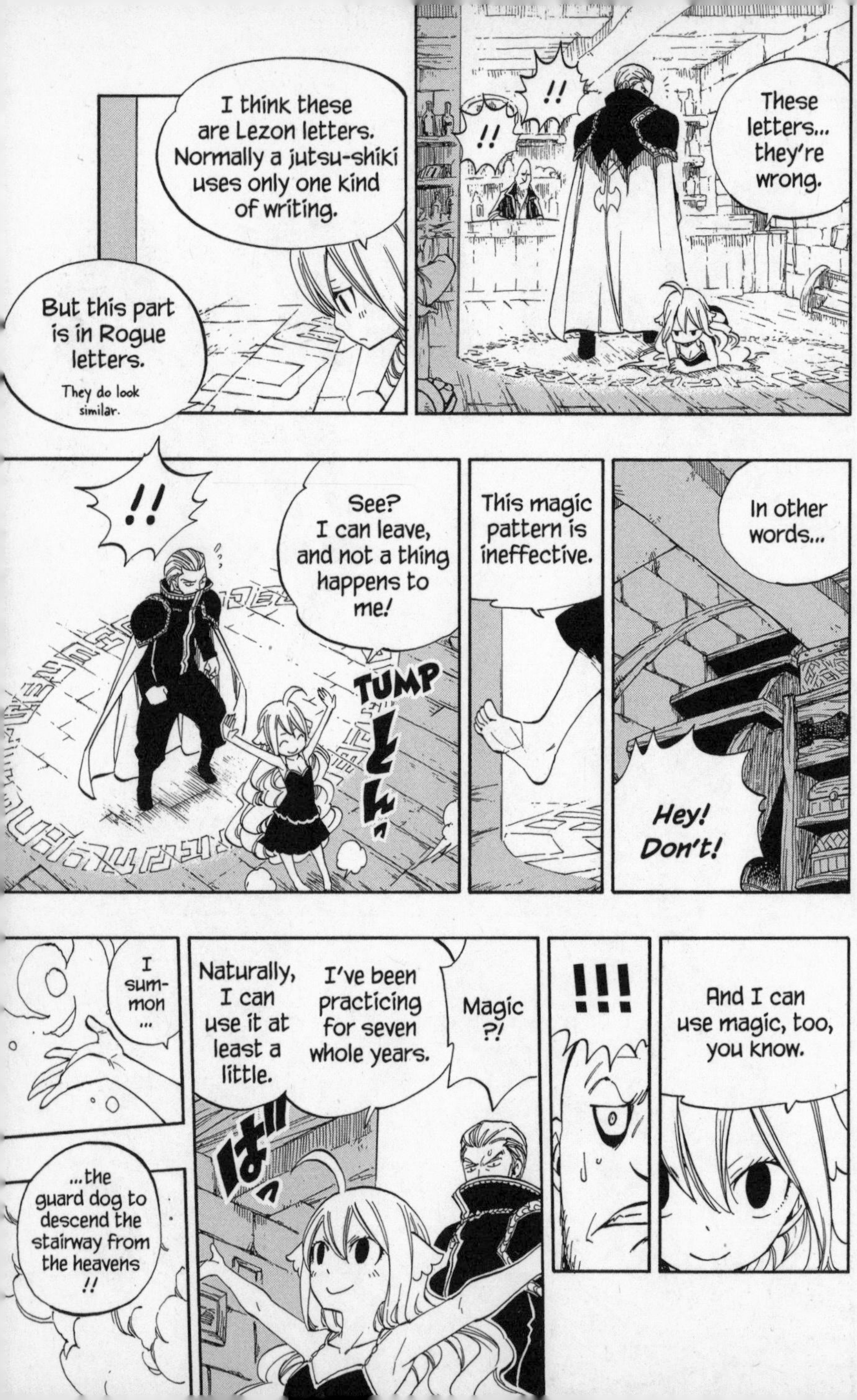
These letters... they're wrong.
!!
!!
I think these are Lezon letters. Normally a jutsu-shiki uses only one kind of writing.
But this part is in Rogue letters.
They do look similar.
In other words...
Hey! Don't!
This magic pattern is ineffective.
See? I can leave, and not a thing happens to me!
!!
TUMP
とん
And I can use magic, too, you know.
!!!
Magic ?!
I've been practicing for seven whole years.
Naturally, I can use it at least a little.
は
I summon...
...the guard dog to descend the stairway from the heavens !!

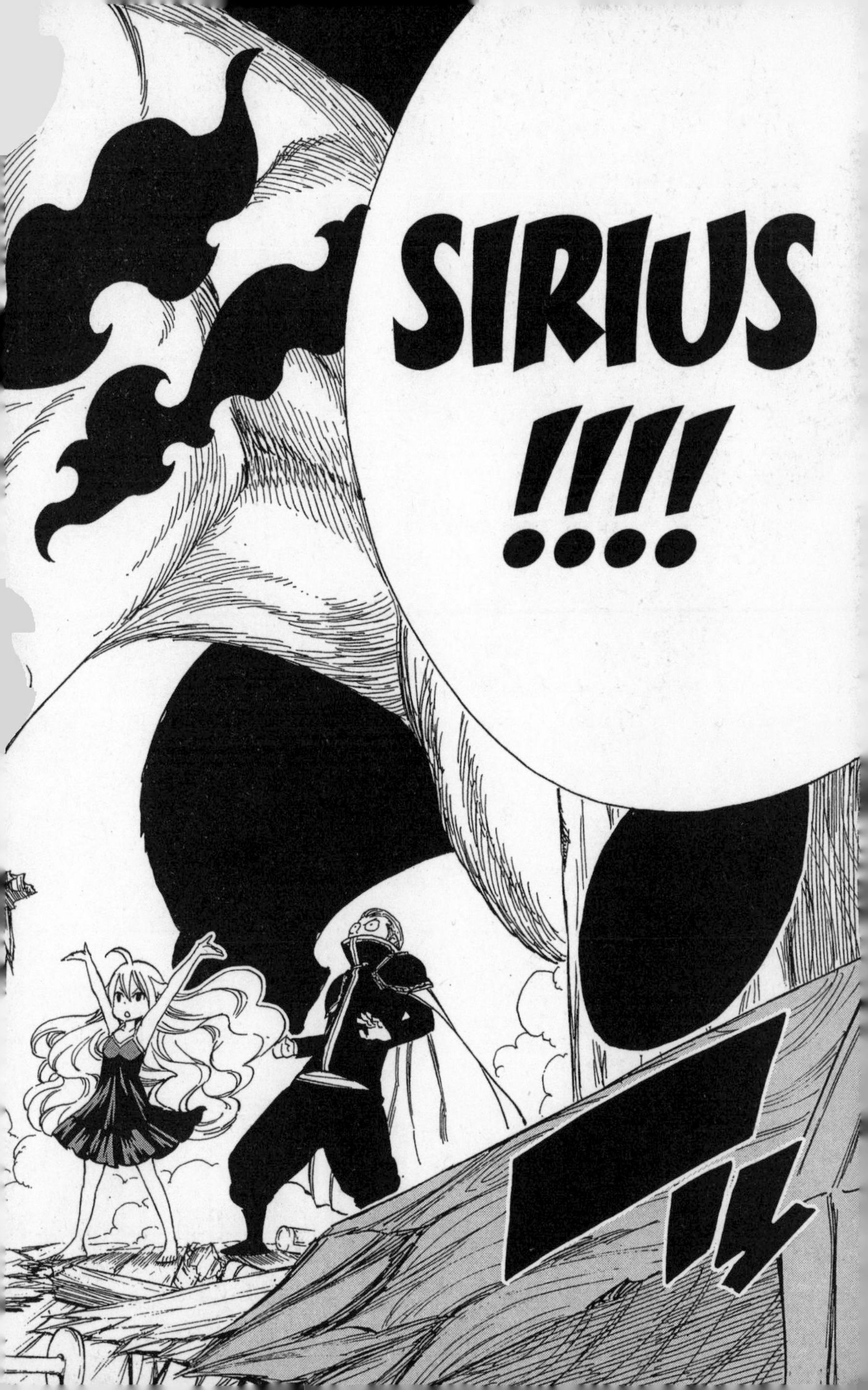
SIRIUS !!!!

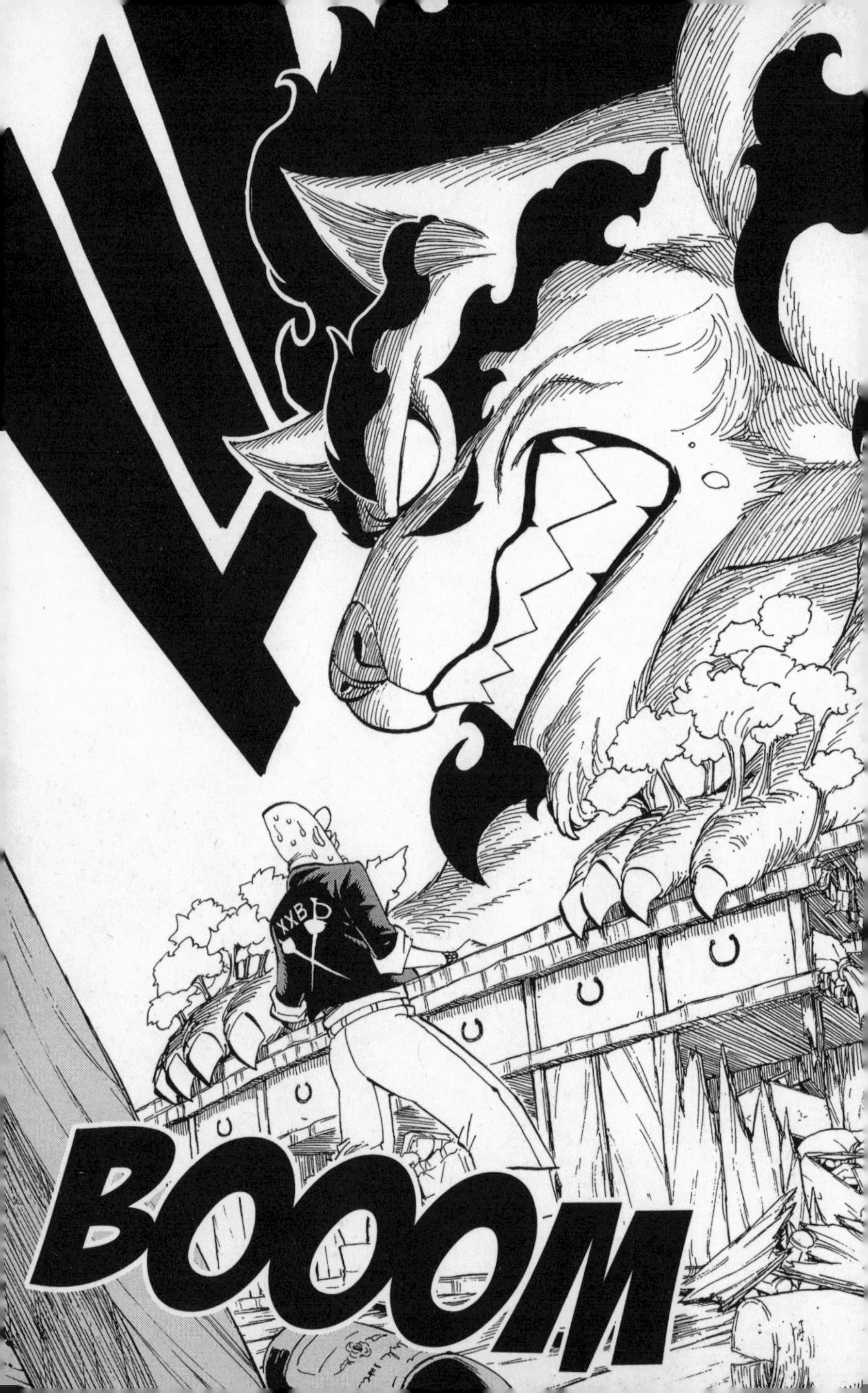
BOOOM

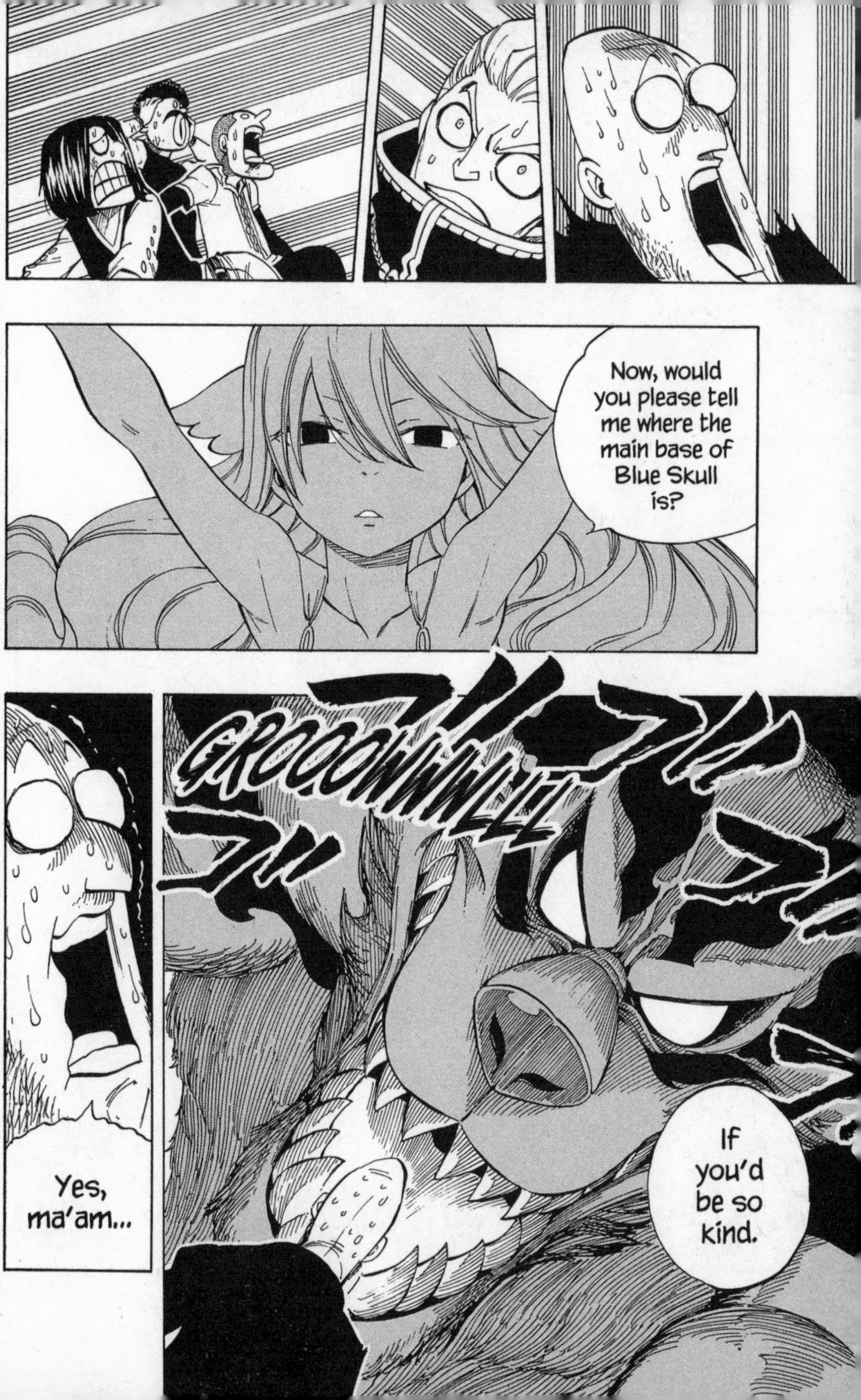
Now, would you please tell me where the main base of Blue Skull is?
GROOOWWLLL
If you'd be so kind.
Yes, ma'am...

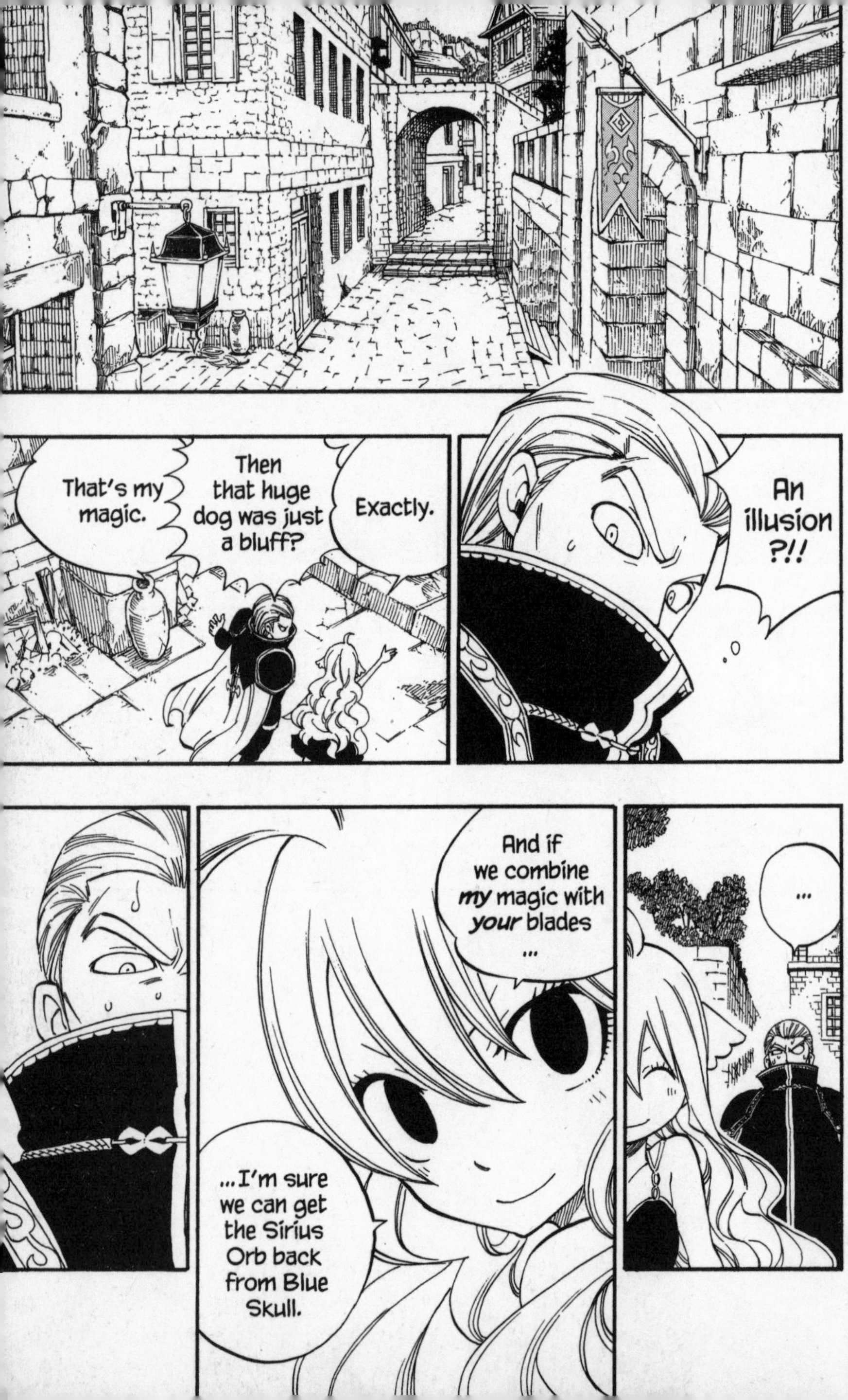
An illusion ?!!
Exactly.
Then that huge dog was just a bluff?
That's my magic.
...
And if we combine *my* magic with *your* blades ...
...I'm sure we can get the Sirius Orb back from Blue Skull.

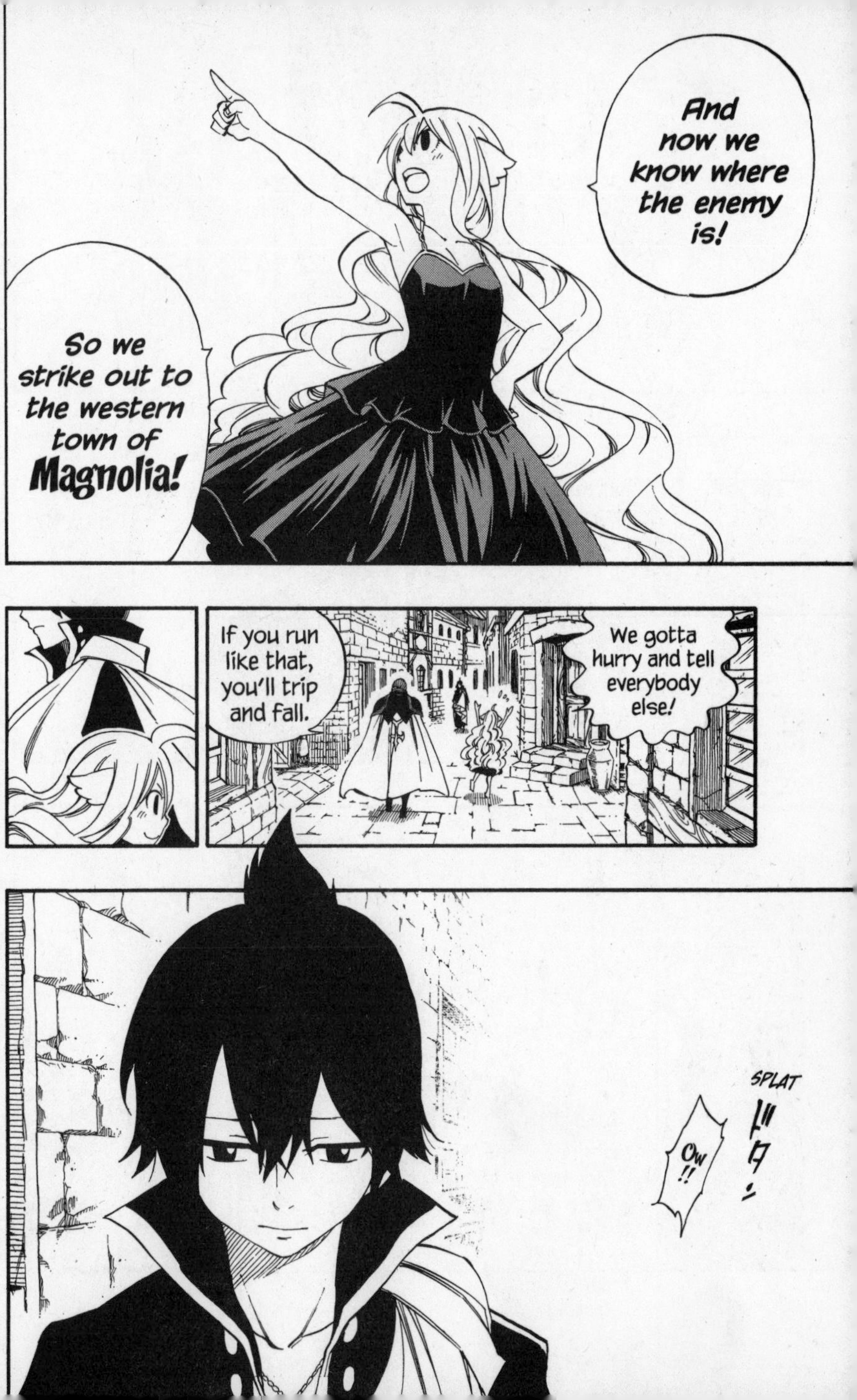
And now we know where the enemy is!
So we strike out to the western town of Magnolia!
We gotta hurry and tell everybody else!
If you run like that, you'll trip and fall.
SPLAT
Ow!!

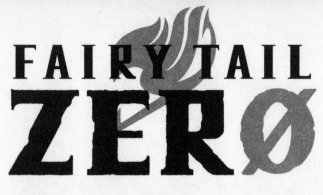

FAIRY TAIL ZERØ

Chapter 5: Moonlit Lake

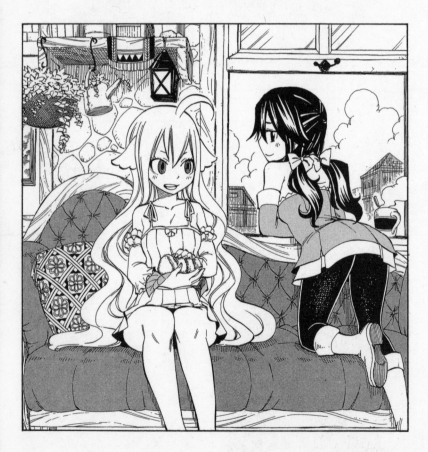

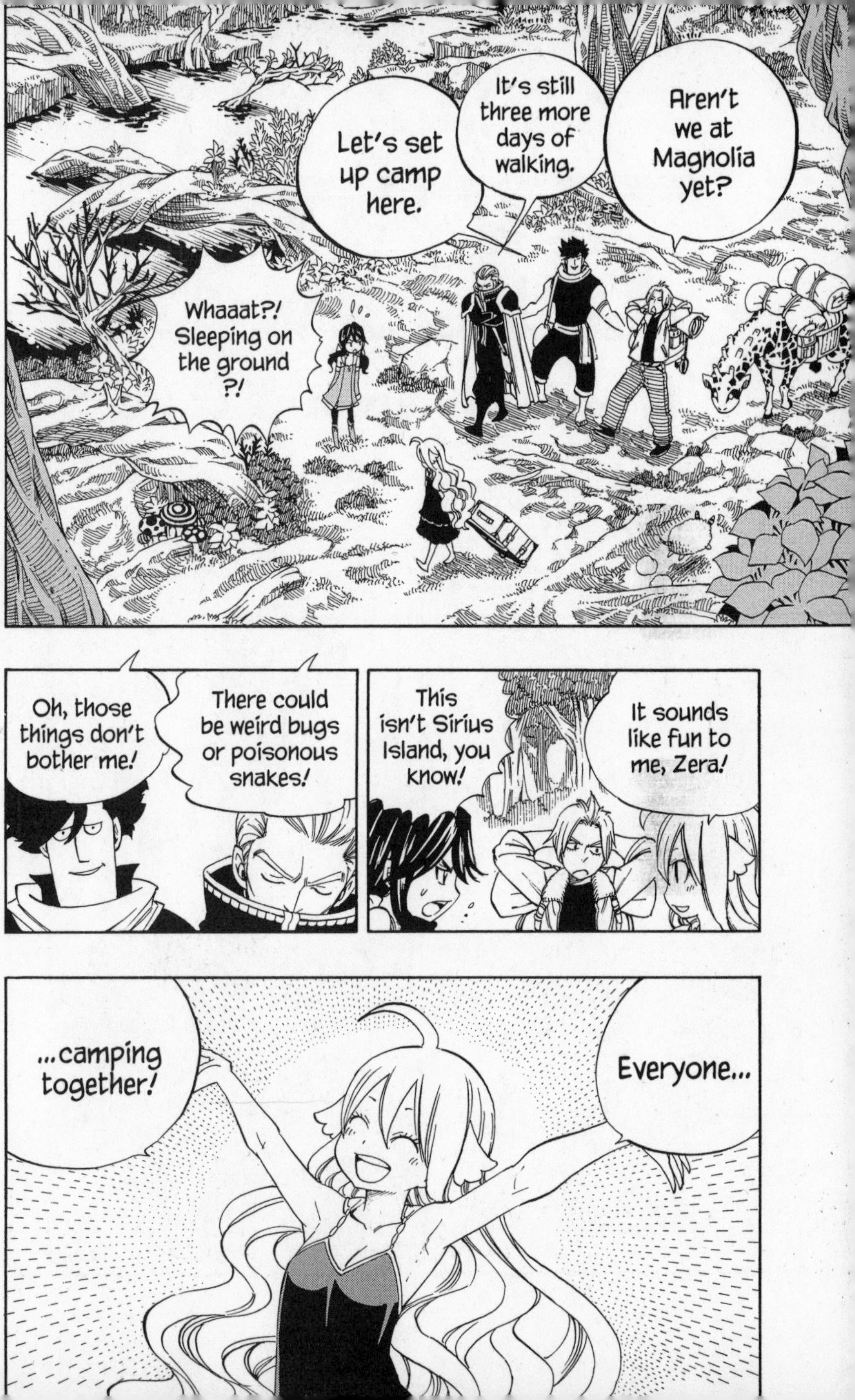
Aren't we at Magnolia yet?
It's still three more days of walking.
Let's set up camp here.
Whaaat?! Sleeping on the ground?!
It sounds like fun to me, Zera!
This isn't Sirius Island, you know!
There could be weird bugs or poisonous snakes!
Oh, those things don't bother me!
Everyone...
...camping together!

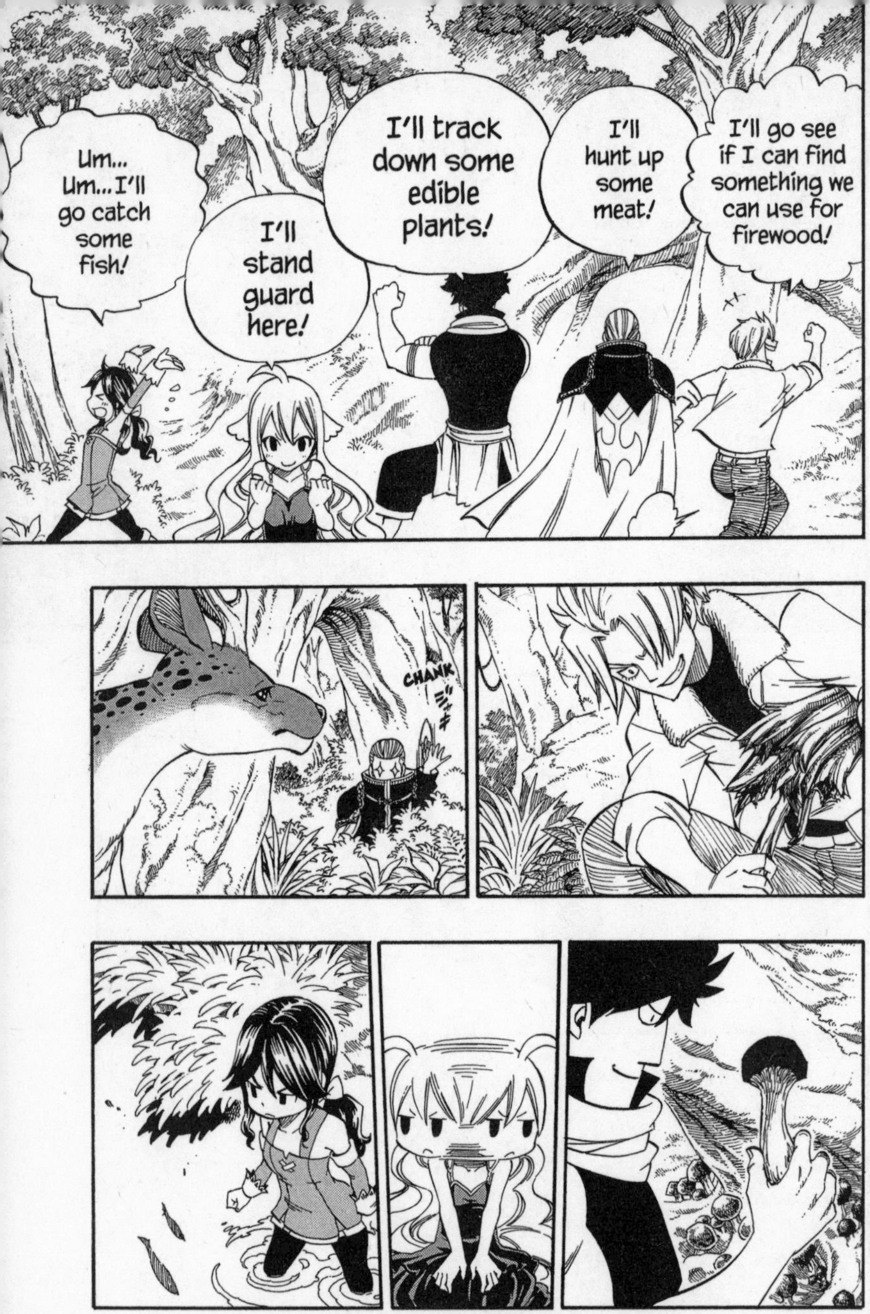
I'll go see if I can find something we can use for firewood!
I'll hunt up some meat!
I'll track down some edible plants!
I'll stand guard here!
Um... Um...I'll go catch some fish!
CHANK
ジャキ

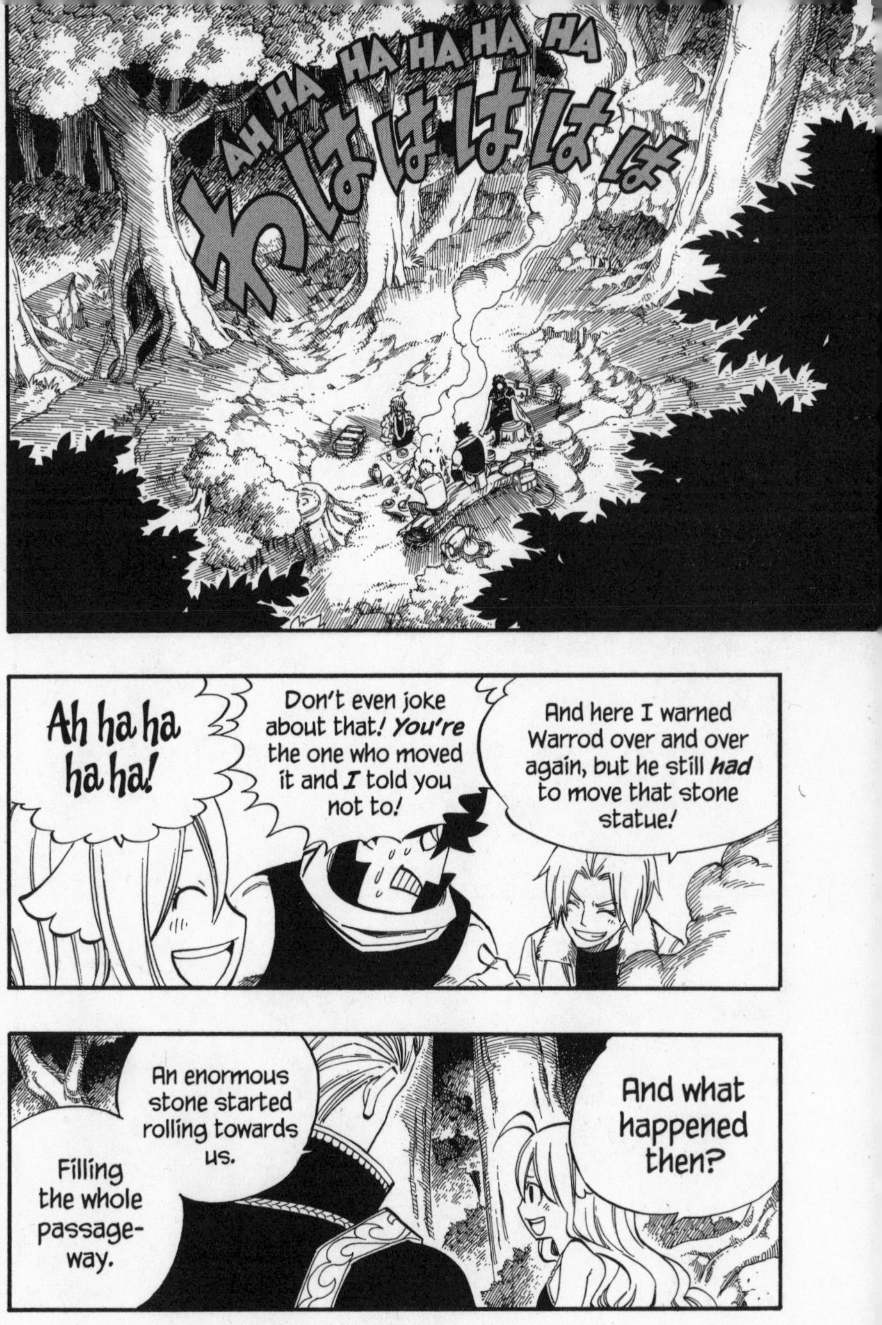
AH HA HA HA HA HA
わははははは
And here I warned Warrod over and over again, but he still *had* to move that stone statue!
Don't even joke about that! *You're* the one who moved it and *I* told you not to!
Ah ha ha ha ha!
And what happened then?
An enormous stone started rolling towards us.
Filling the whole passage-way.

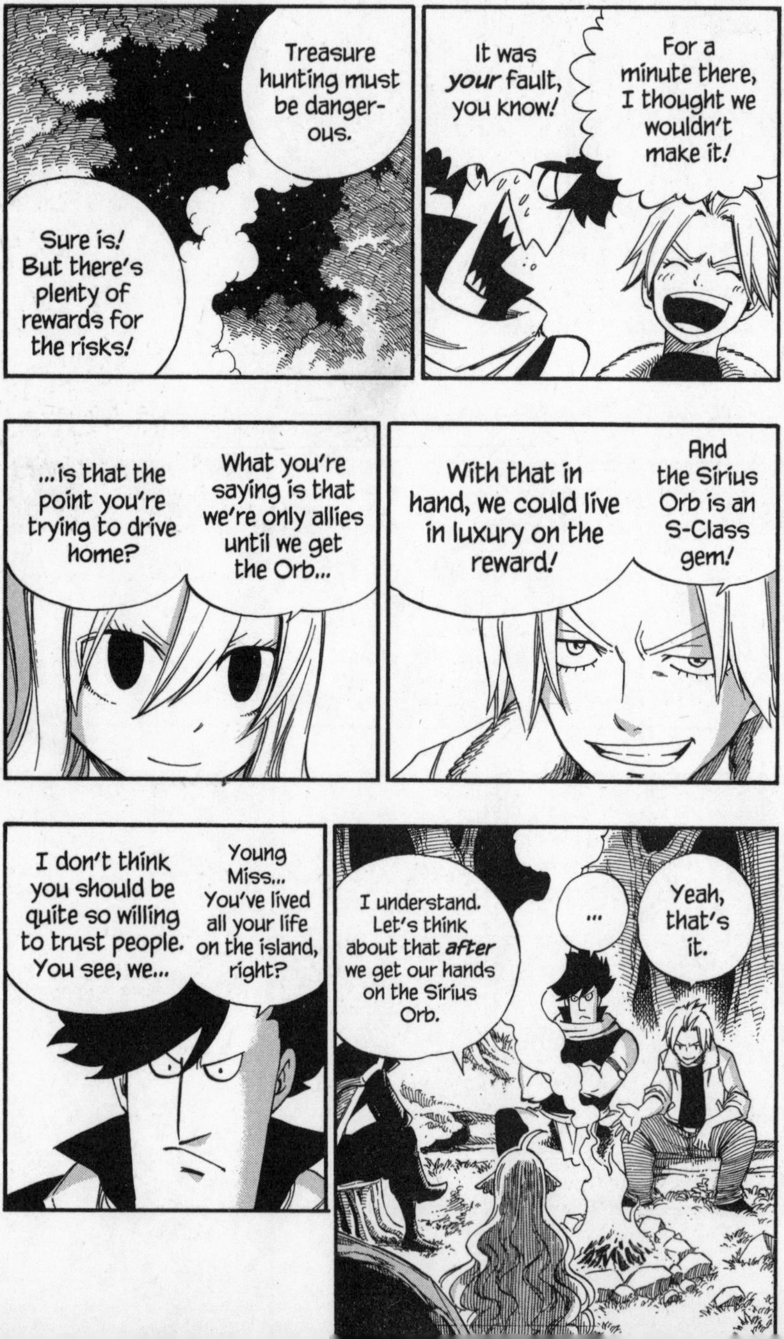
For a minute there, I thought we wouldn't make it!
It was *your* fault, you know!
Treasure hunting must be danger-ous.
Sure is! But there's plenty of rewards for the risks!
And the Sirius Orb is an S-Class gem!
With that in hand, we could live in luxury on the reward!
What you're saying is that we're only allies until we get the Orb...
...is that the point you're trying to drive home?
Yeah, that's it.
...
I understand. Let's think about that *after* we get our hands on the Sirius Orb.
Young Miss... You've lived all your life on the island, right?
I don't think you should be quite so willing to trust people. You see, we...

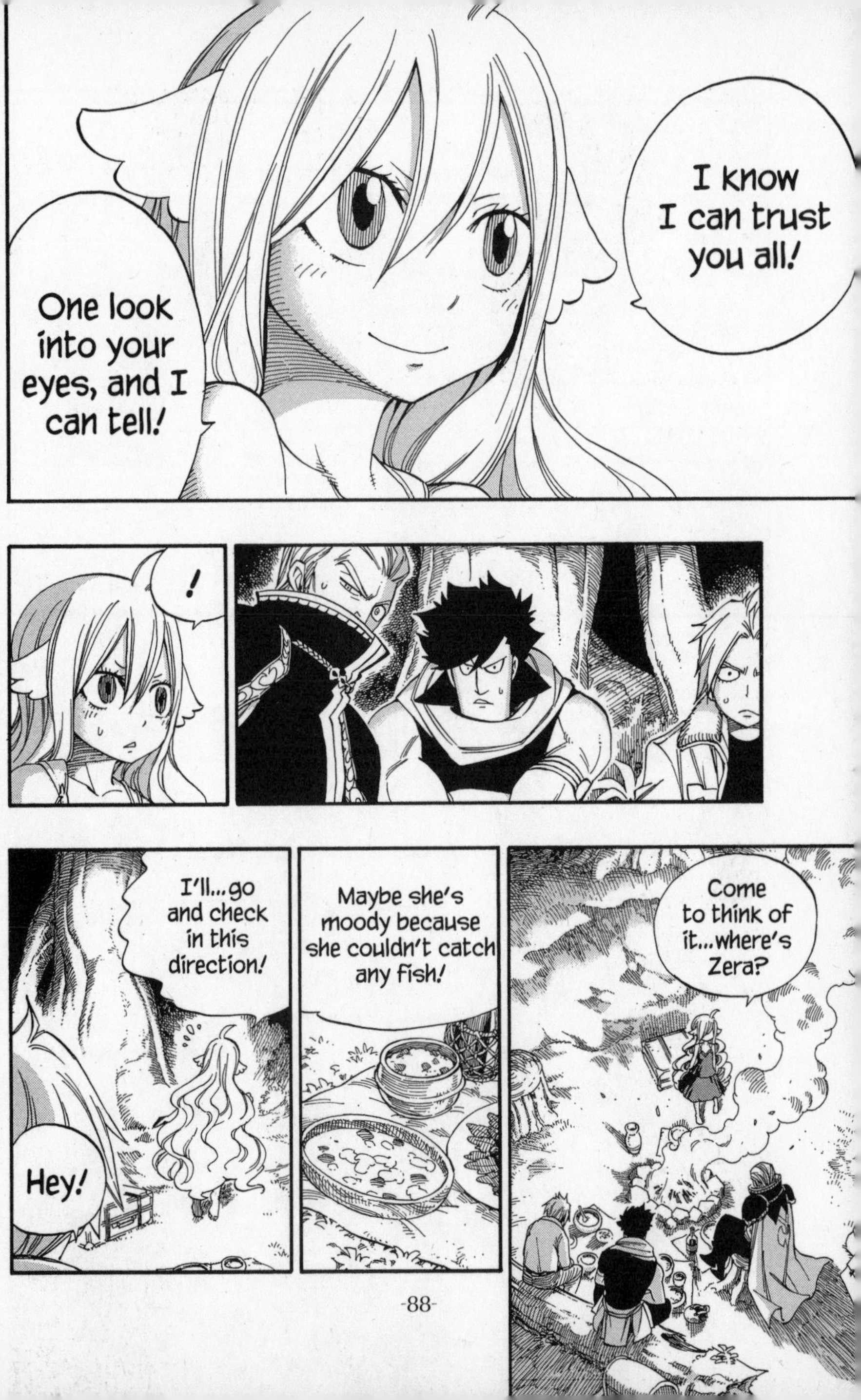
I know I can trust you all!
One look into your eyes, and I can tell!
!
Come to think of it...where's Zera?
Maybe she's moody because she couldn't catch any fish!
I'll...go and check in this direction!
Hey!

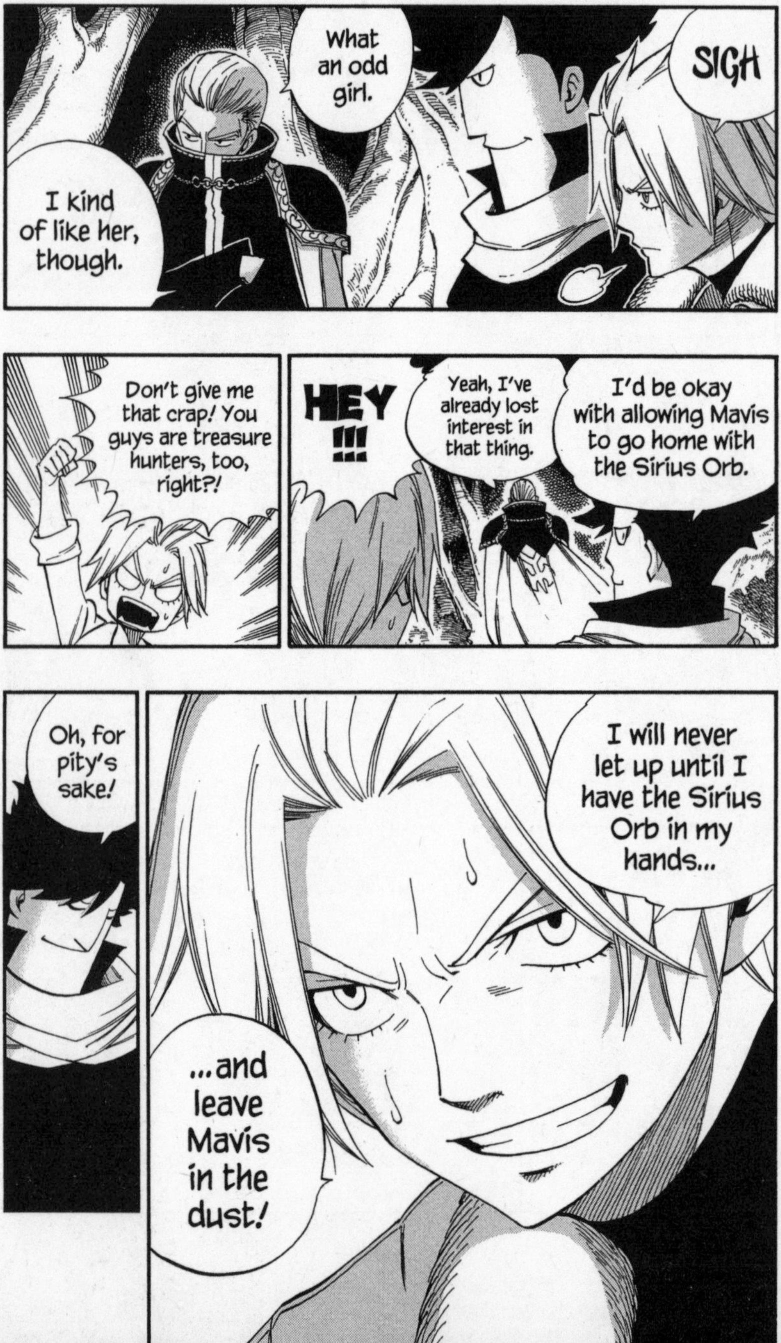
SIGH
What an odd girl.
I kind of like her, though.
I'd be okay with allowing Mavis to go home with the Sirius Orb.
Yeah, I've already lost interest in that thing.
HEY !!!
Don't give me that crap! You guys are treasure hunters, too, right?!
I will never let up until I have the Sirius Orb in my hands...
...and leave Mavis in the dust!
Oh, for pity's sake!

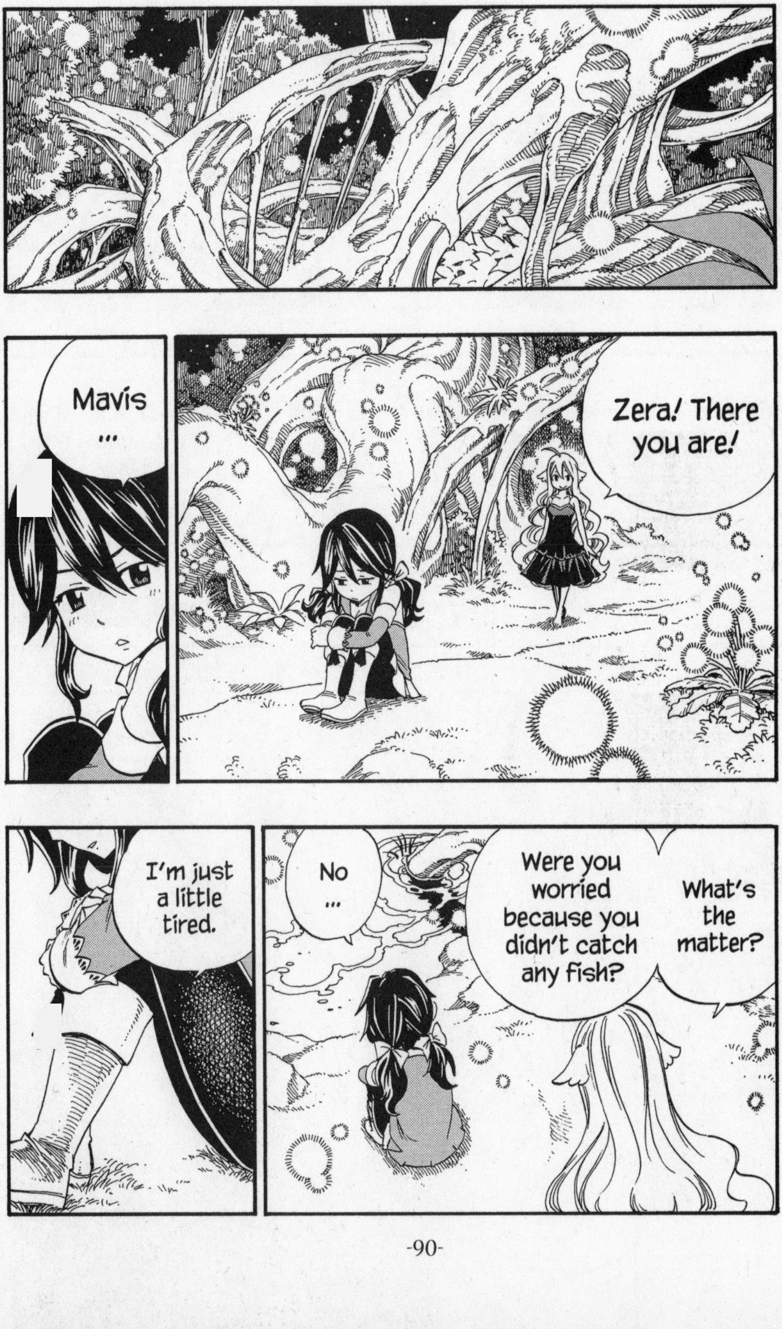
Zera! There you are!
Mavis ...
What's the matter?
Were you worried because you didn't catch any fish?
No ...
I'm just a little tired.

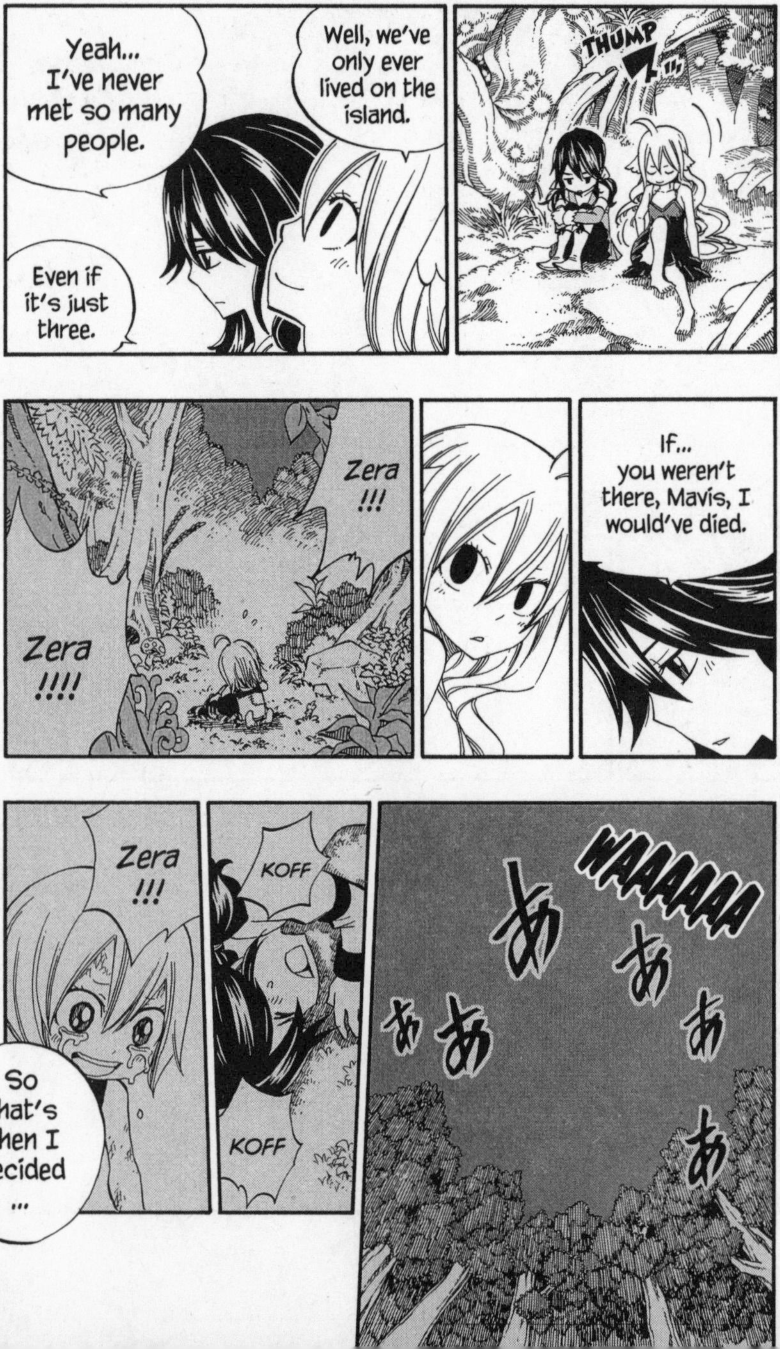
THUMP
Well, we've only ever lived on the island.
Yeah... I've never met so many people.
Even if it's just three.
If... you weren't there, Mavis, I would've died.
Zera !!!
Zera !!!!
WAAAAAA
あああああああ
KOFF
KOFF
Zera !!!
So that's when I decided ...

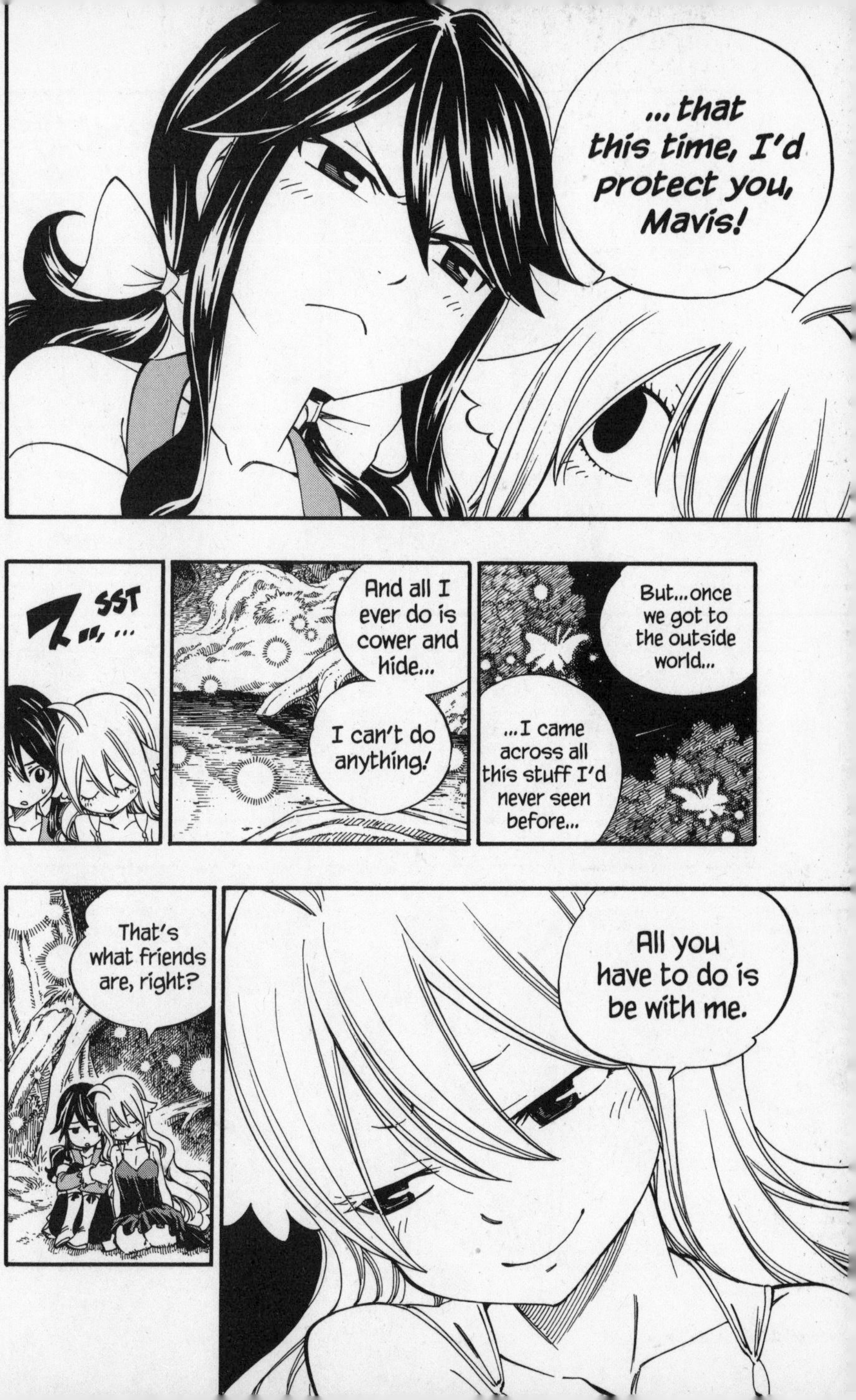
...that this time, I'd protect you, Mavis!
But...once we got to the outside world...
...I came across all this stuff I'd never seen before...
And all I ever do is cower and hide...
I can't do anything!
Z...SST...
All you have to do is be with me.
That's what friends are, right?

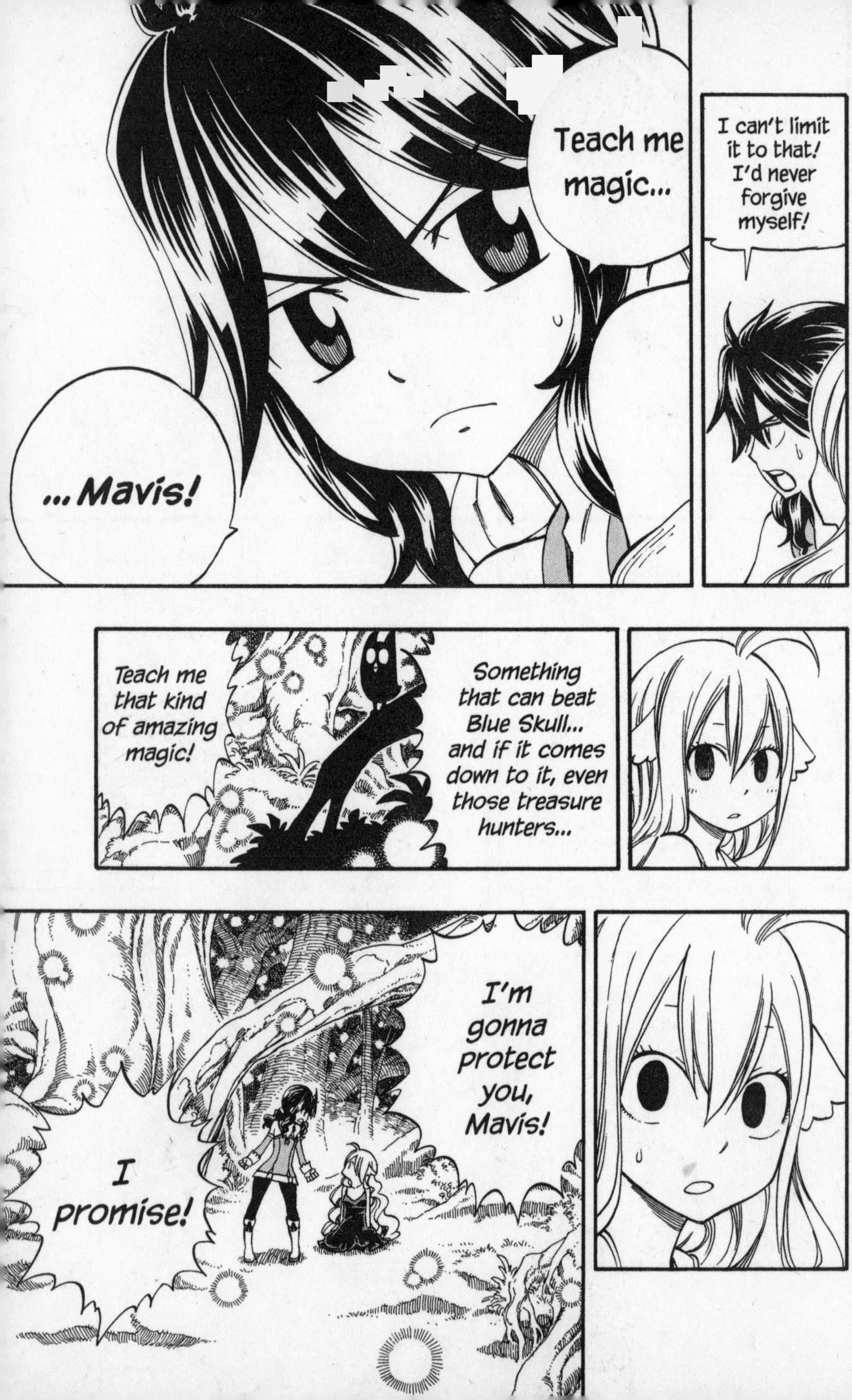
I can't limit it to that! I'd never forgive myself!
Teach me magic...
...Mavis!
Something that can beat Blue Skull... and if it comes down to it, even those treasure hunters...
Teach me that kind of amazing magic!
I'm gonna protect you, Mavis!
I promise!

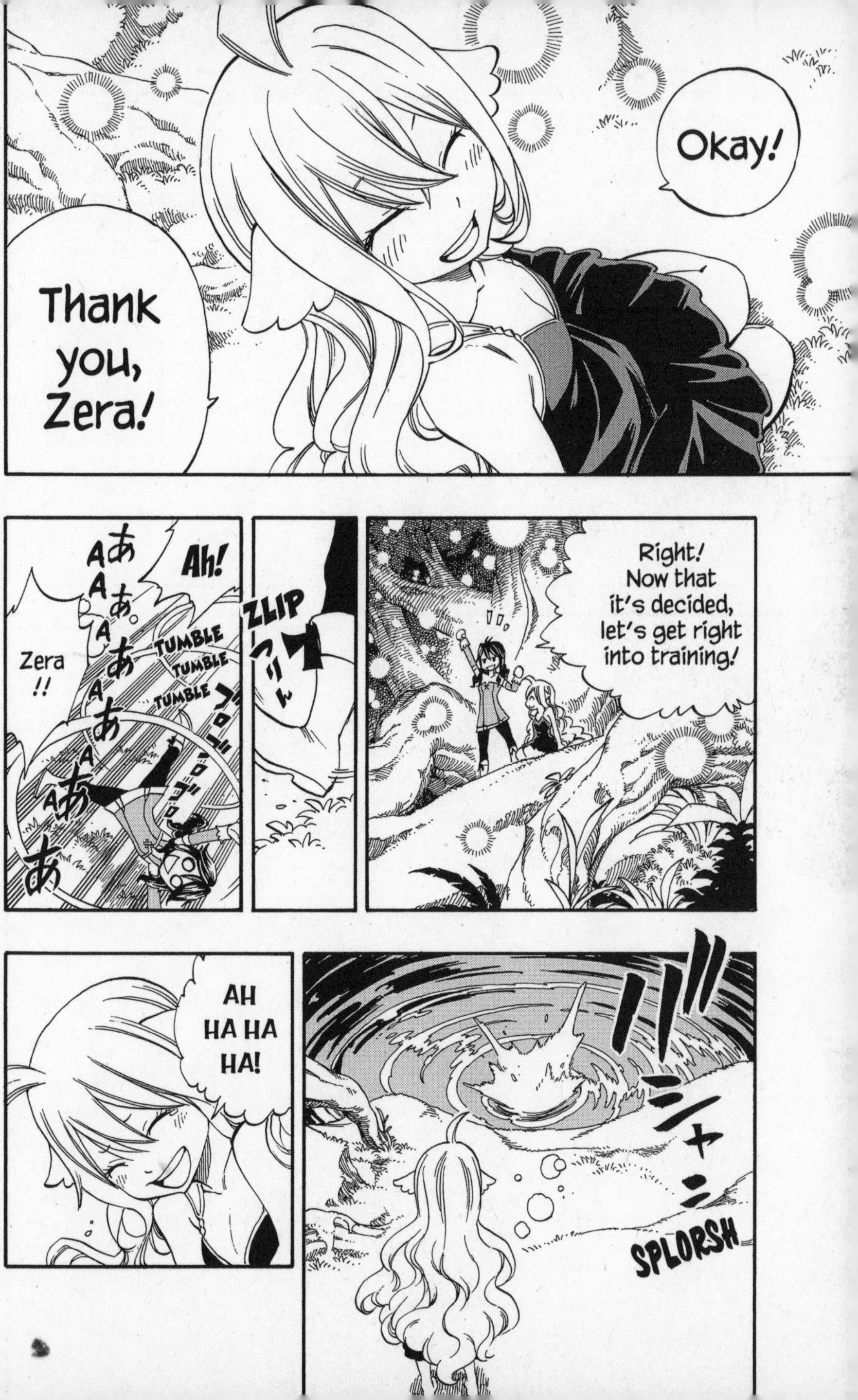

Okay!
Thank you, Zera!
Right! Now that it's decided, let's get right into training!
ZLIP
Ah!
AAAAAAA
TUMBLE
TUMBLE
TUMBLE
Zera!!
SPLORSH
AH HA HA HA!

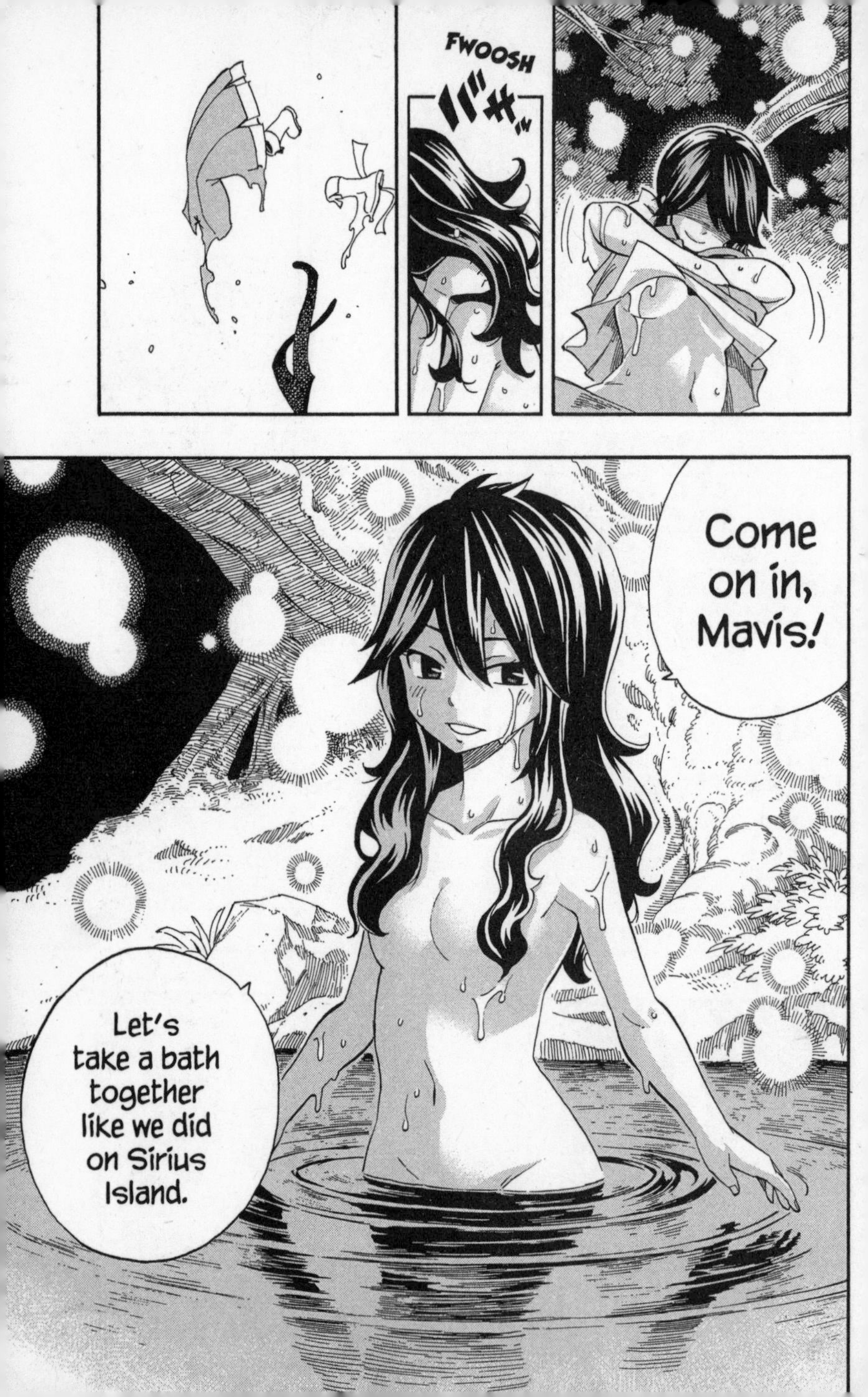
FWOOSH
Come on in, Mavis!
Let's take a bath together like we did on Sirius Island.

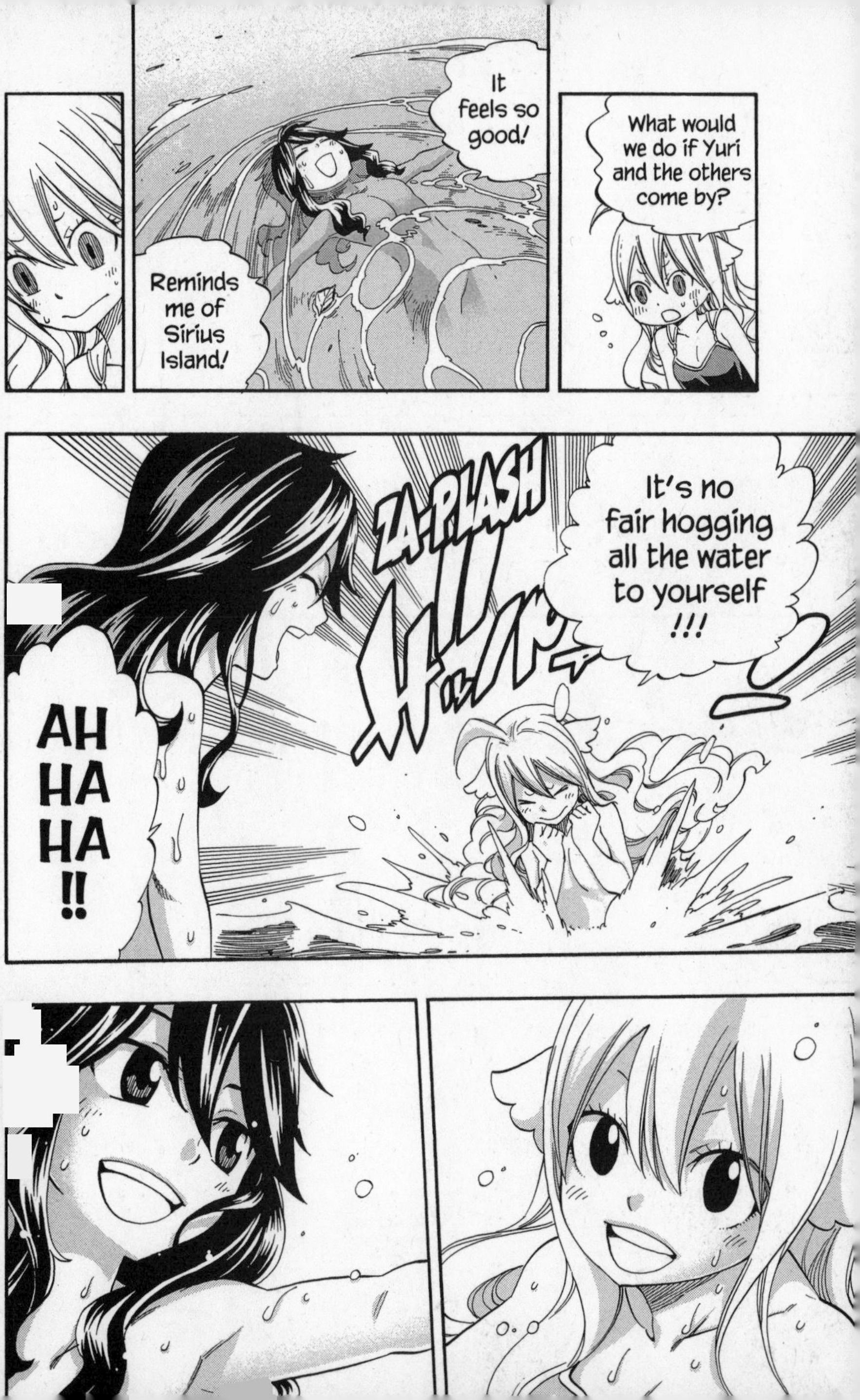
What would we do if Yuri and the others come by?
It feels so good!
Reminds me of Sirius Island!
It's no fair hogging all the water to yourself!!!
ZA-PLASH
AH HA HA!!

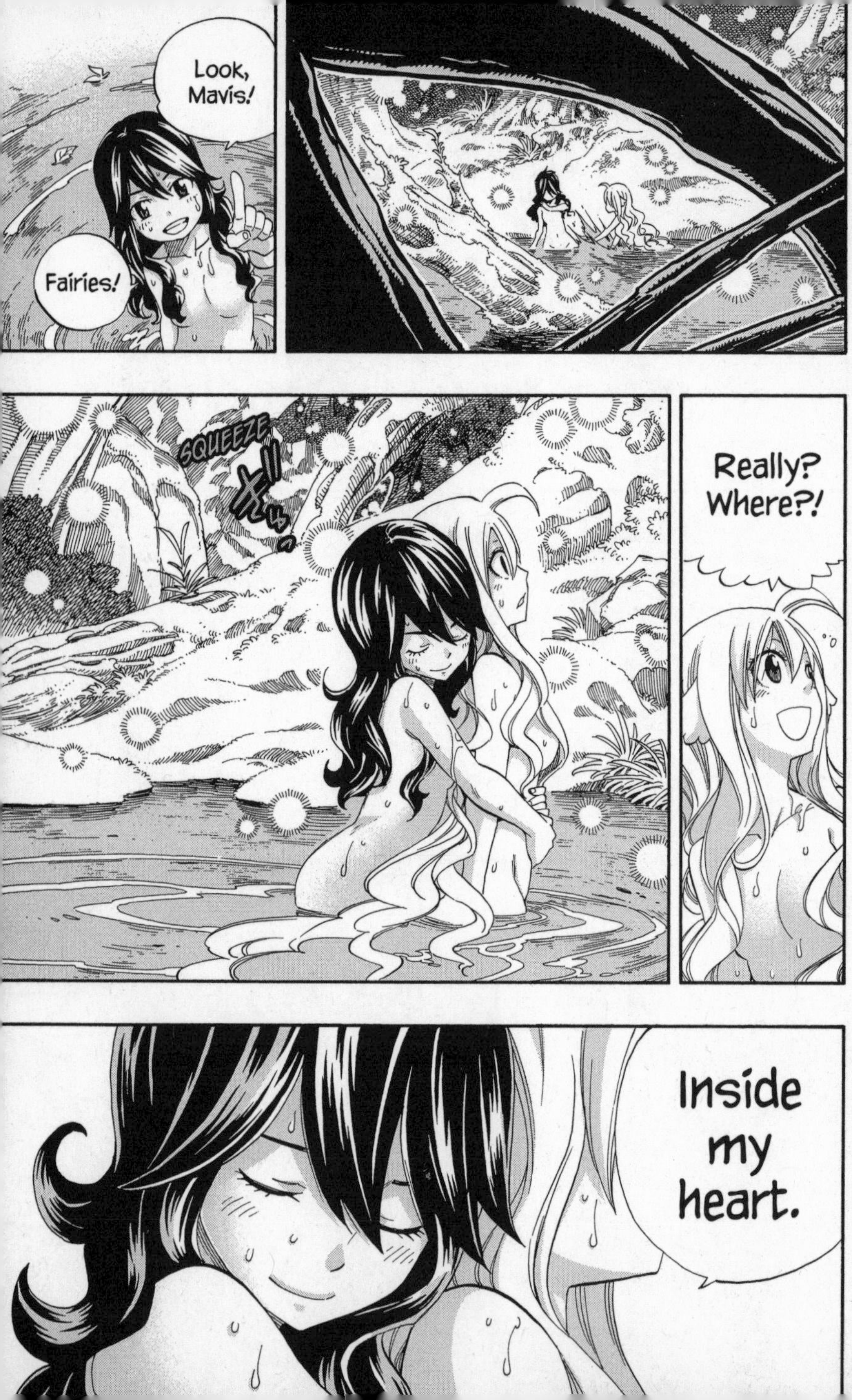
Look, Mavis!
Fairies!
Really? Where?!
SQUEEZE
Inside my heart.

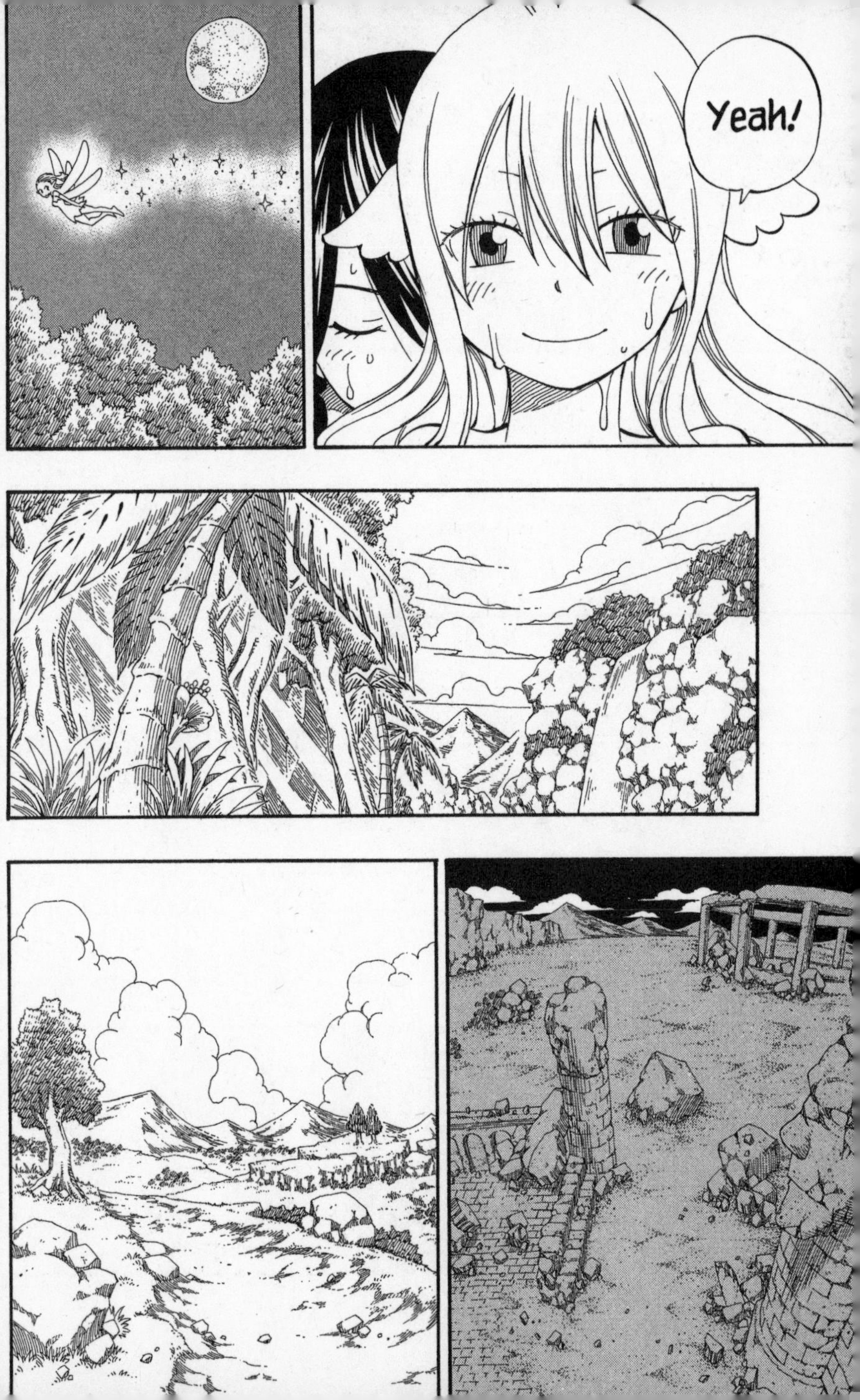
Yeah!

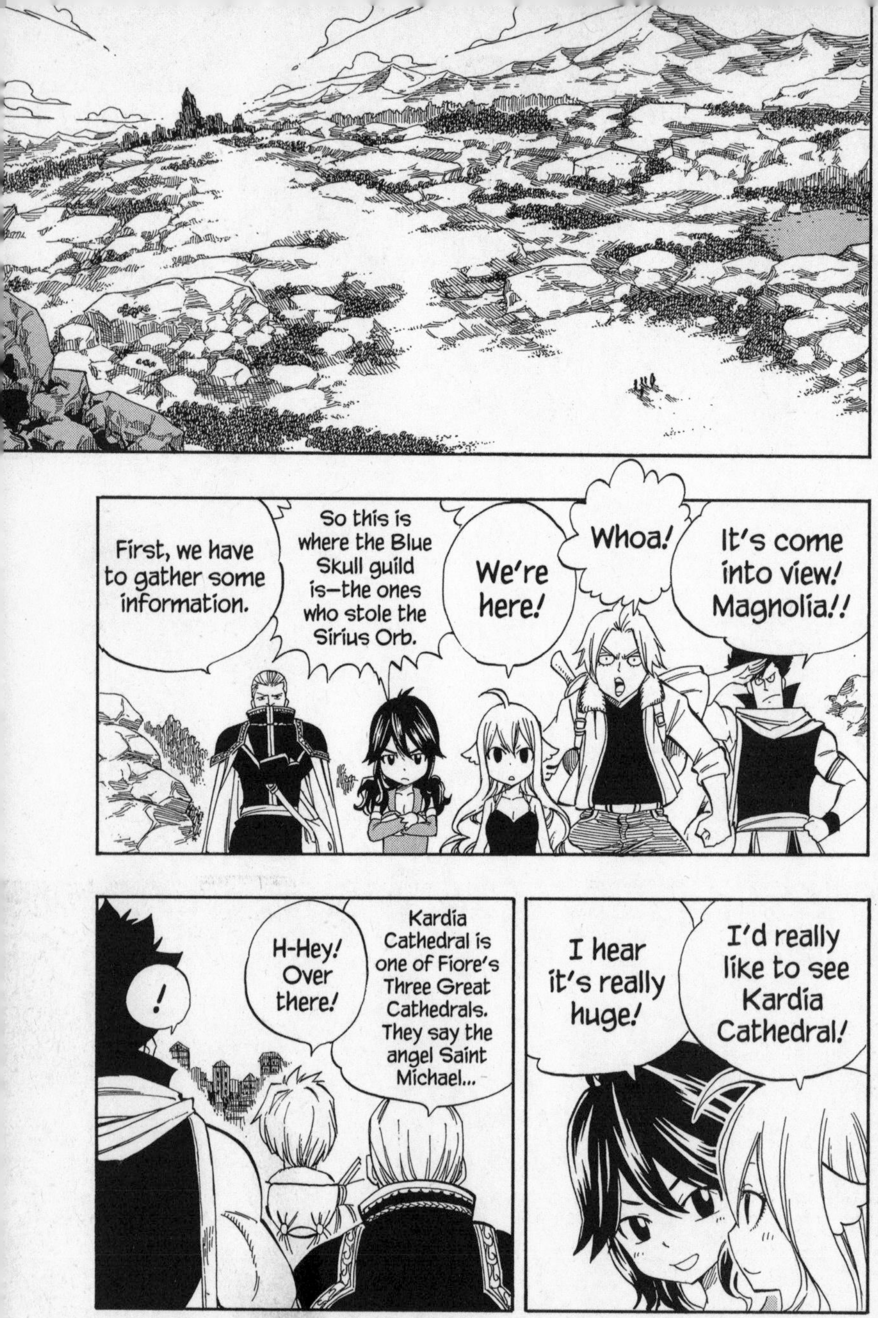

It's come into view! Magnolia!!
Whoa!
We're here!
So this is where the Blue Skull guild is—the ones who stole the Sirius Orb.
First, we have to gather some information.
I'd really like to see Kardia Cathedral!
I hear it's really huge!
Kardia Cathedral is one of Fiore's Three Great Cathedrals. They say the angel Saint Michael...
H-Hey! Over there!
!

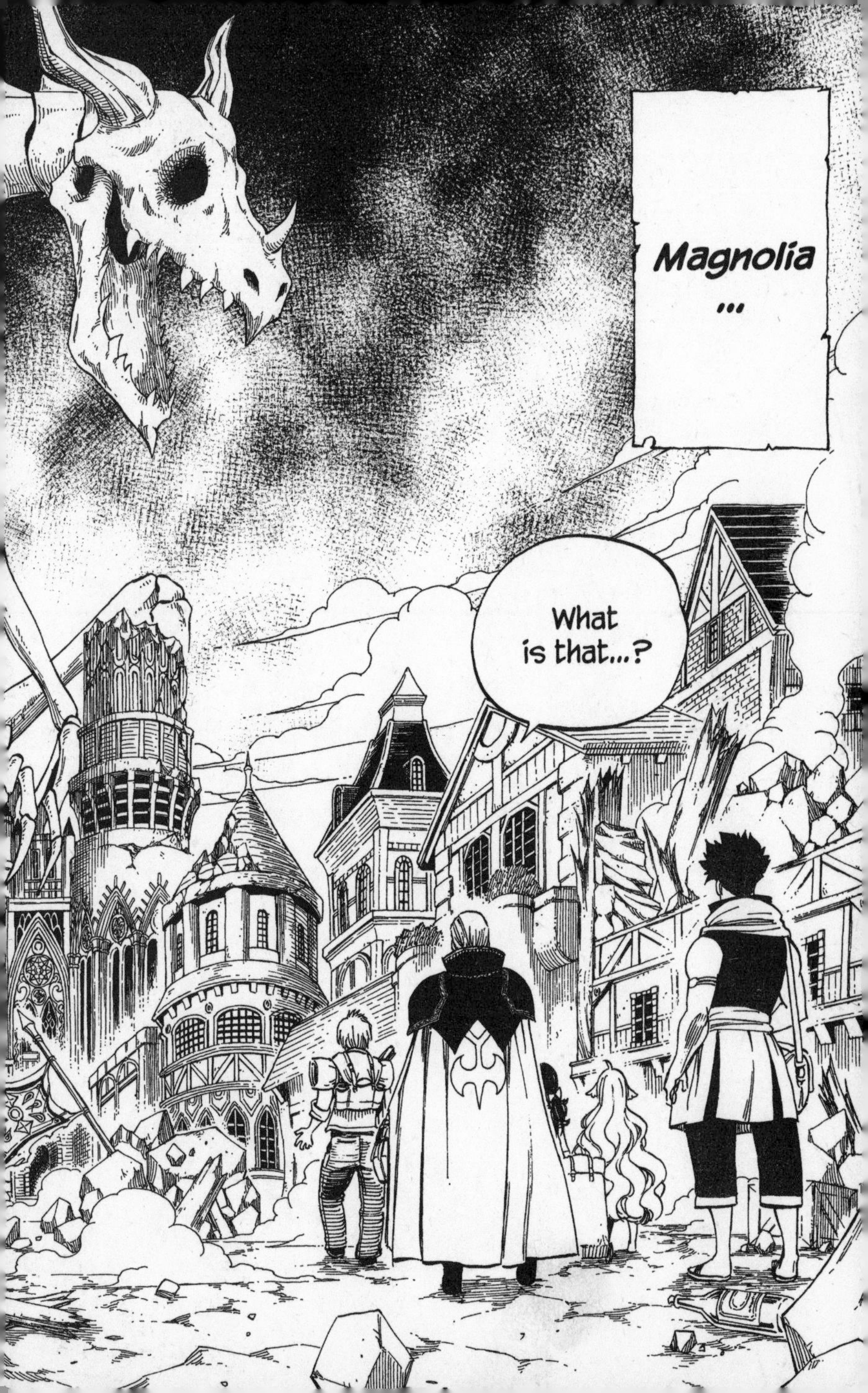
Magnolia
...
What is that...?

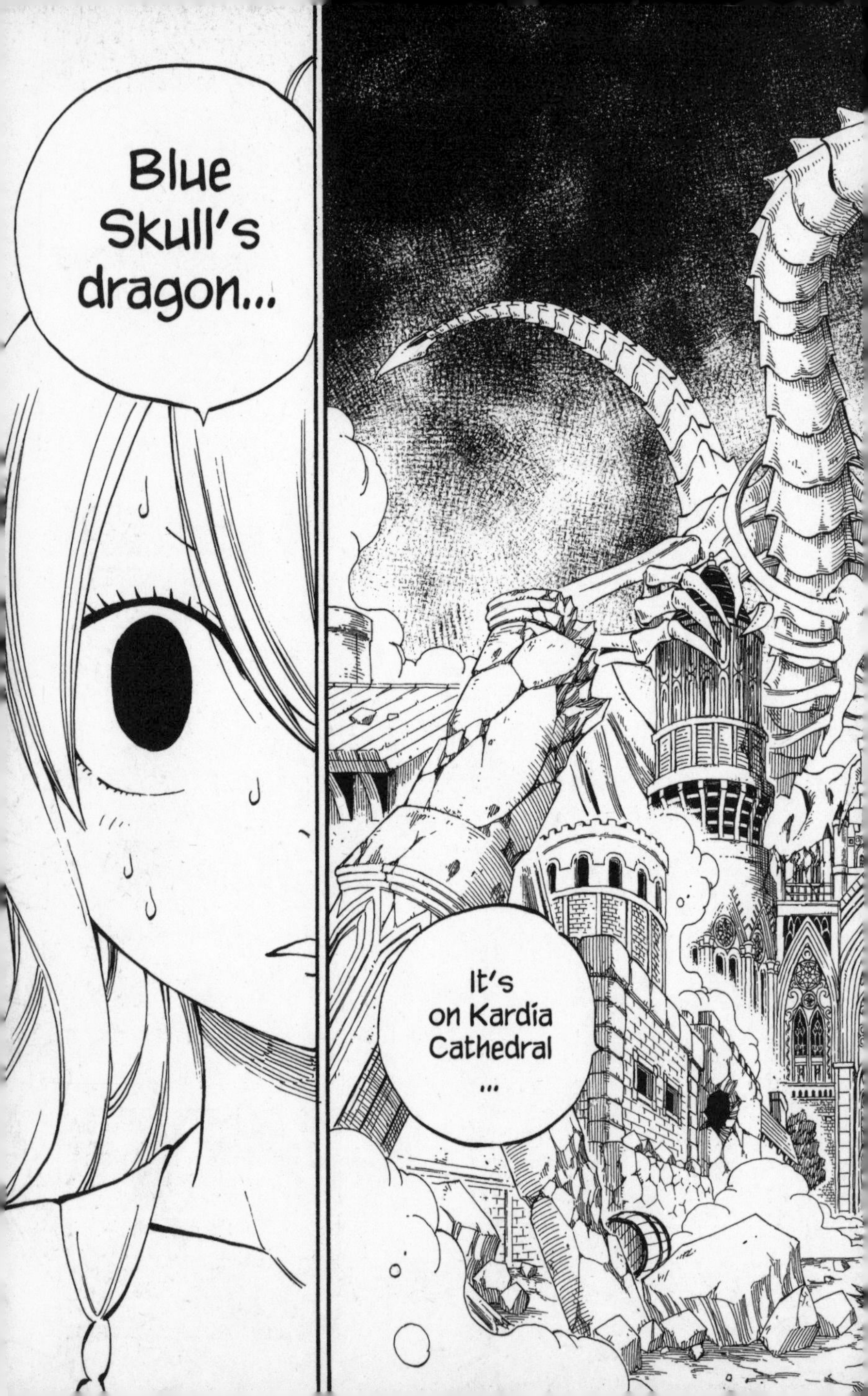
It's on Kardia Cathedral ...
Blue Skull's dragon...

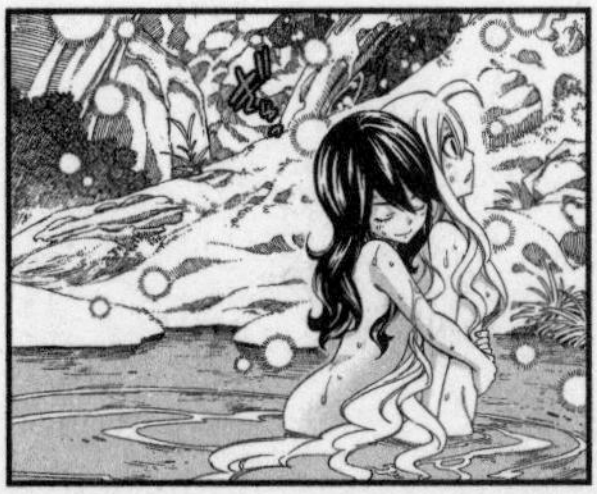

FAIRY TAIL ZERØ

Chapter 6: Blue Skull

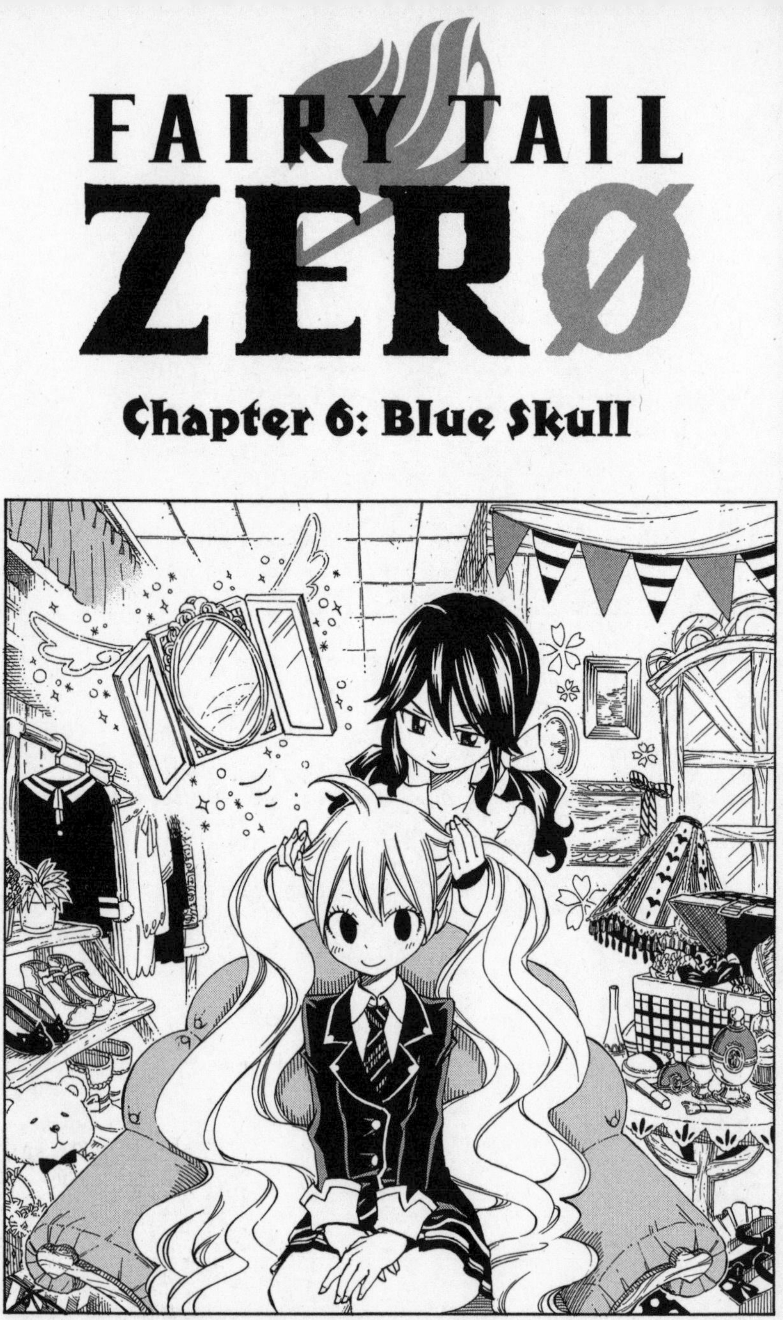

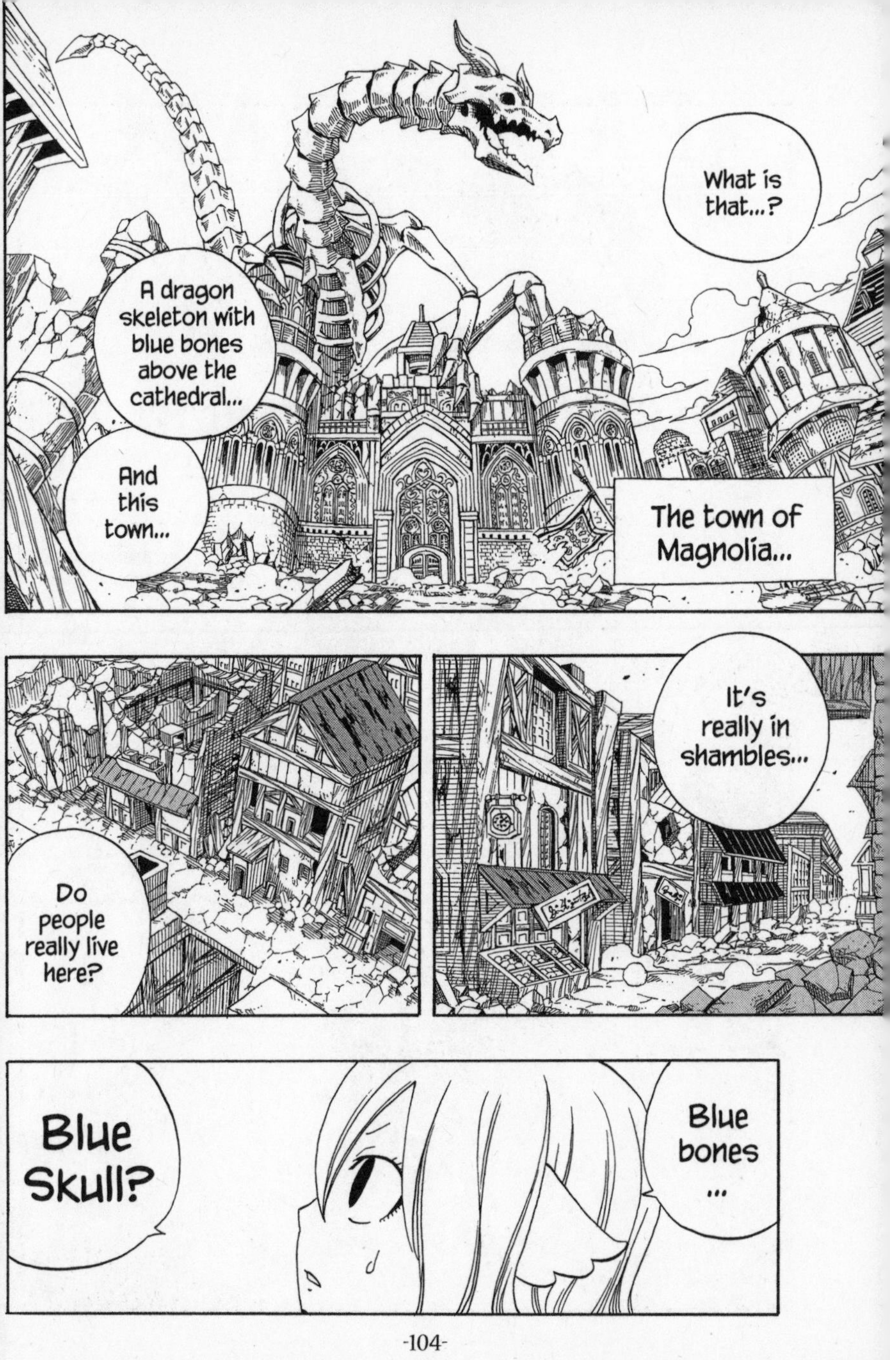
What is that...?
A dragon skeleton with blue bones above the cathedral...
And this town...
The town of Magnolia...
It's really in shambles...
Do people really live here?
Blue bones ...
Blue Skull?

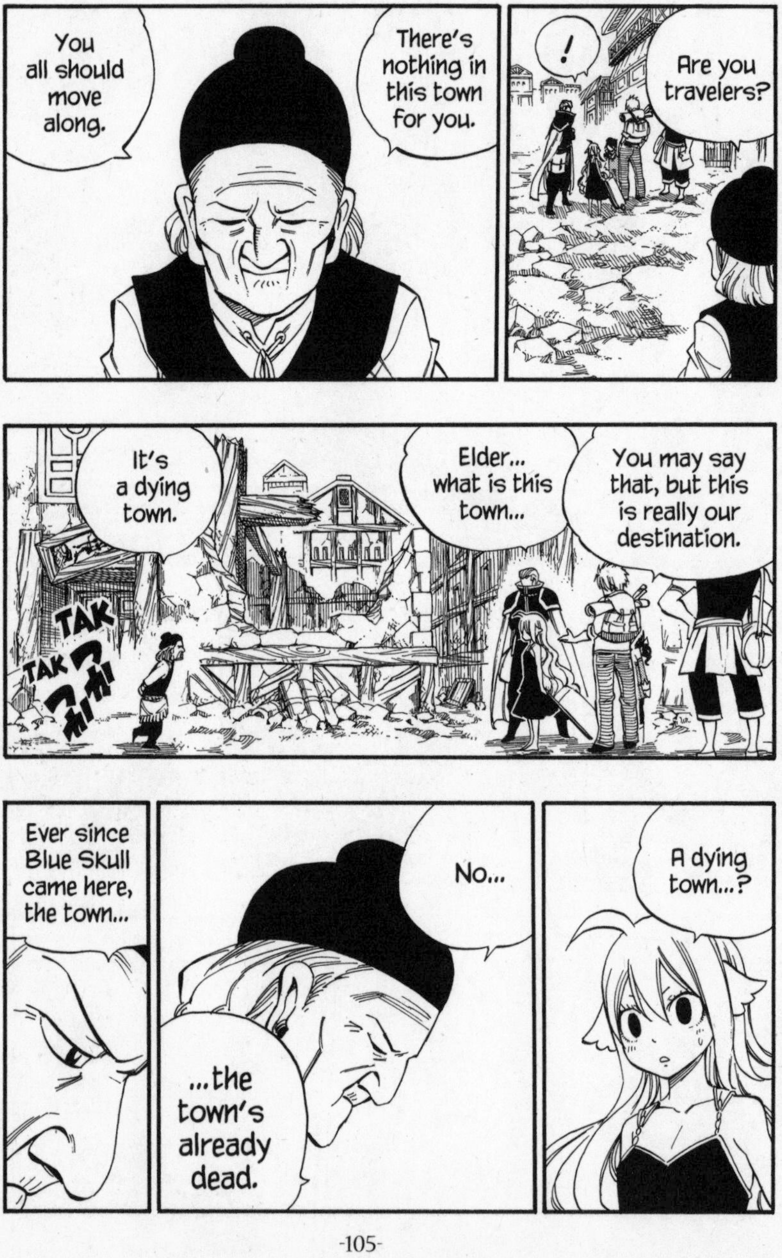
!
Are you travelers?
There's nothing in this town for you.
You all should move along.
You may say that, but this is really our destination.
Elder... what is this town...
It's a dying town.
TAK TAK
つかつか
A dying town...?
No...
...the town's already dead.
Ever since Blue Skull came here, the town...

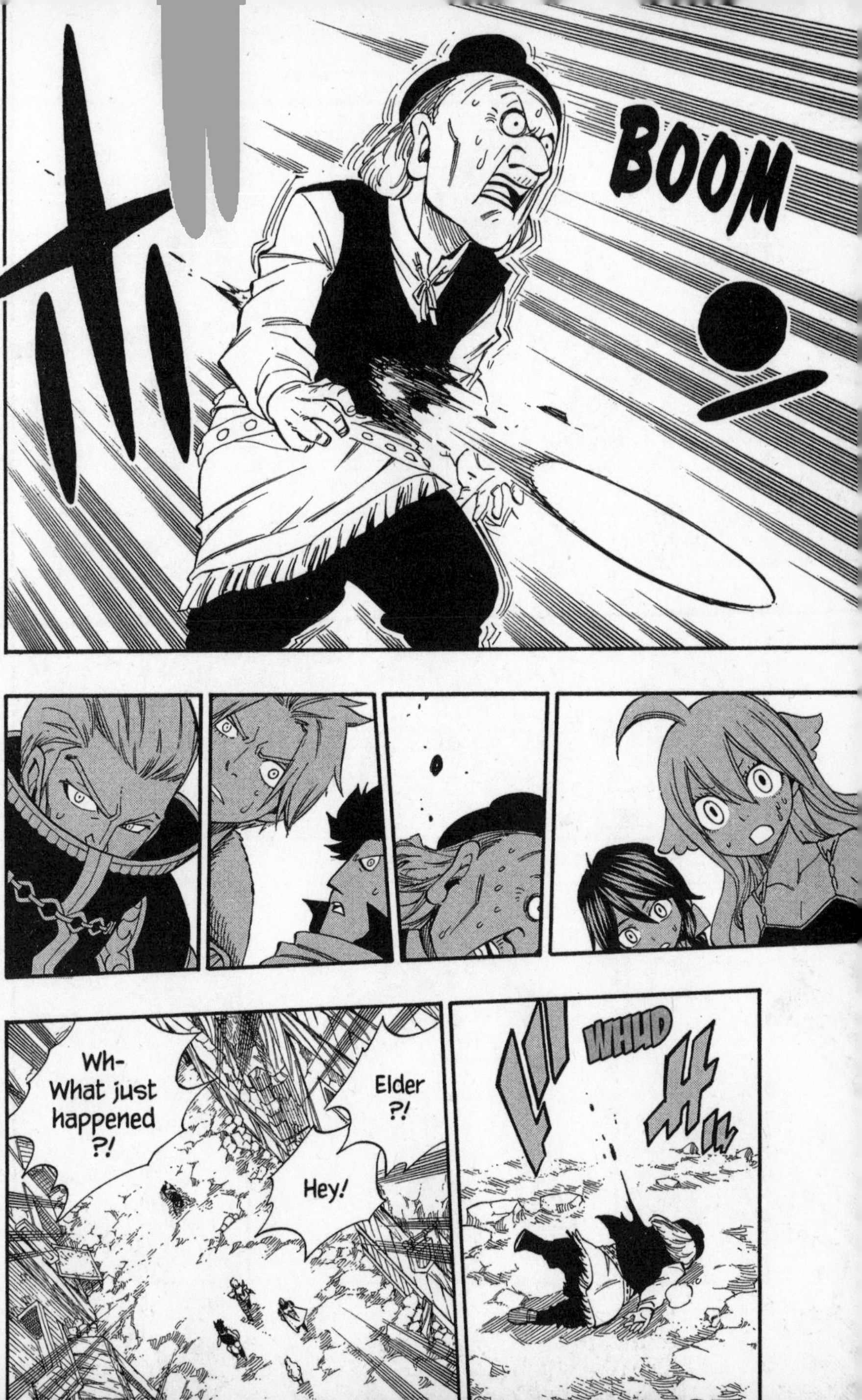
BOOM
WHUD
Elder ?!
Wh- What just happened ?!
Hey!

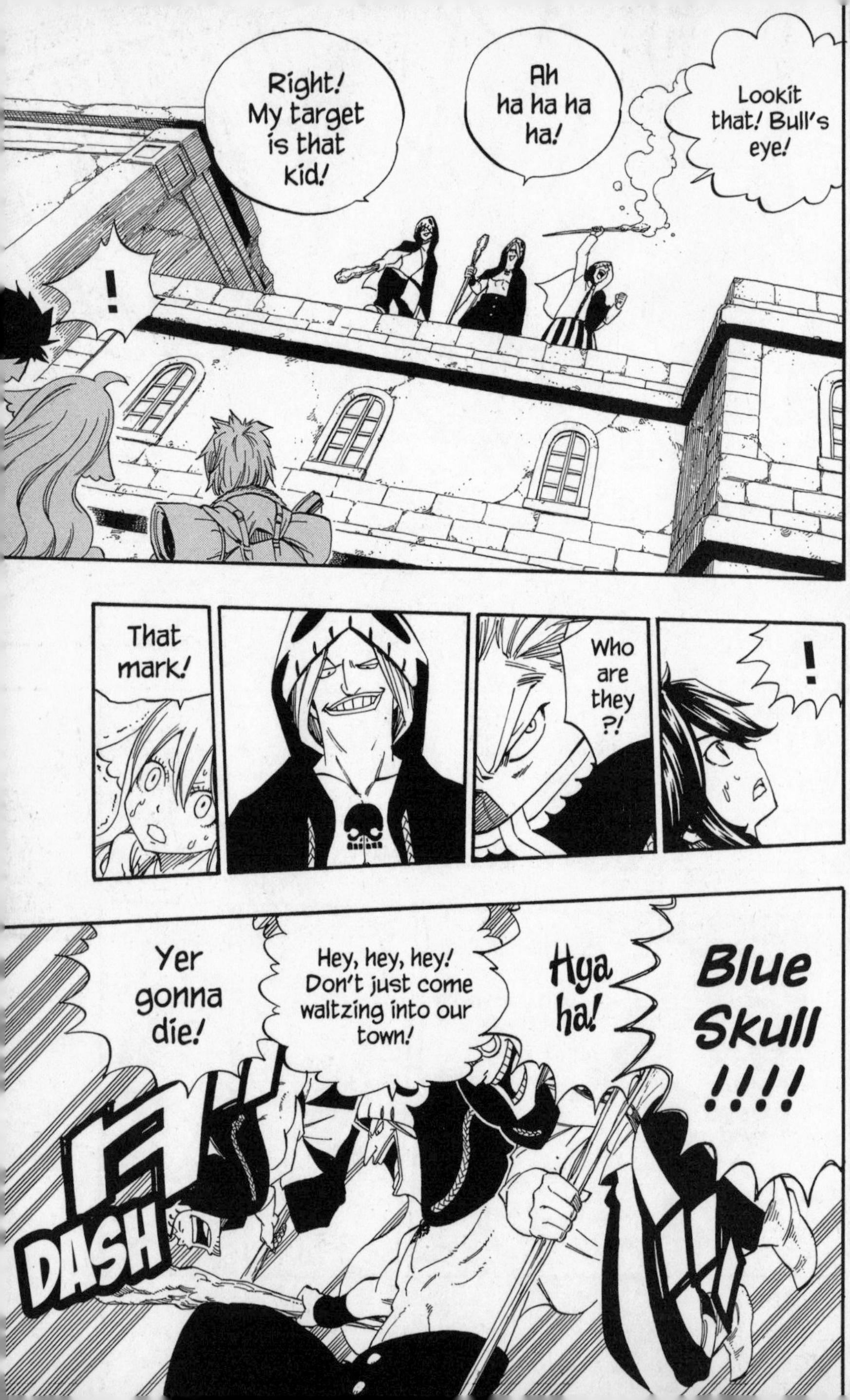
Lookit that! Bull's eye!
Ah ha ha ha ha!
Right! My target is that kid!
!
!
Who are they?!
That mark!
Blue Skull!!!!
Hya ha!
Hey, hey, hey! Don't just come waltzing into our town!
Yer gonna die!
DASH

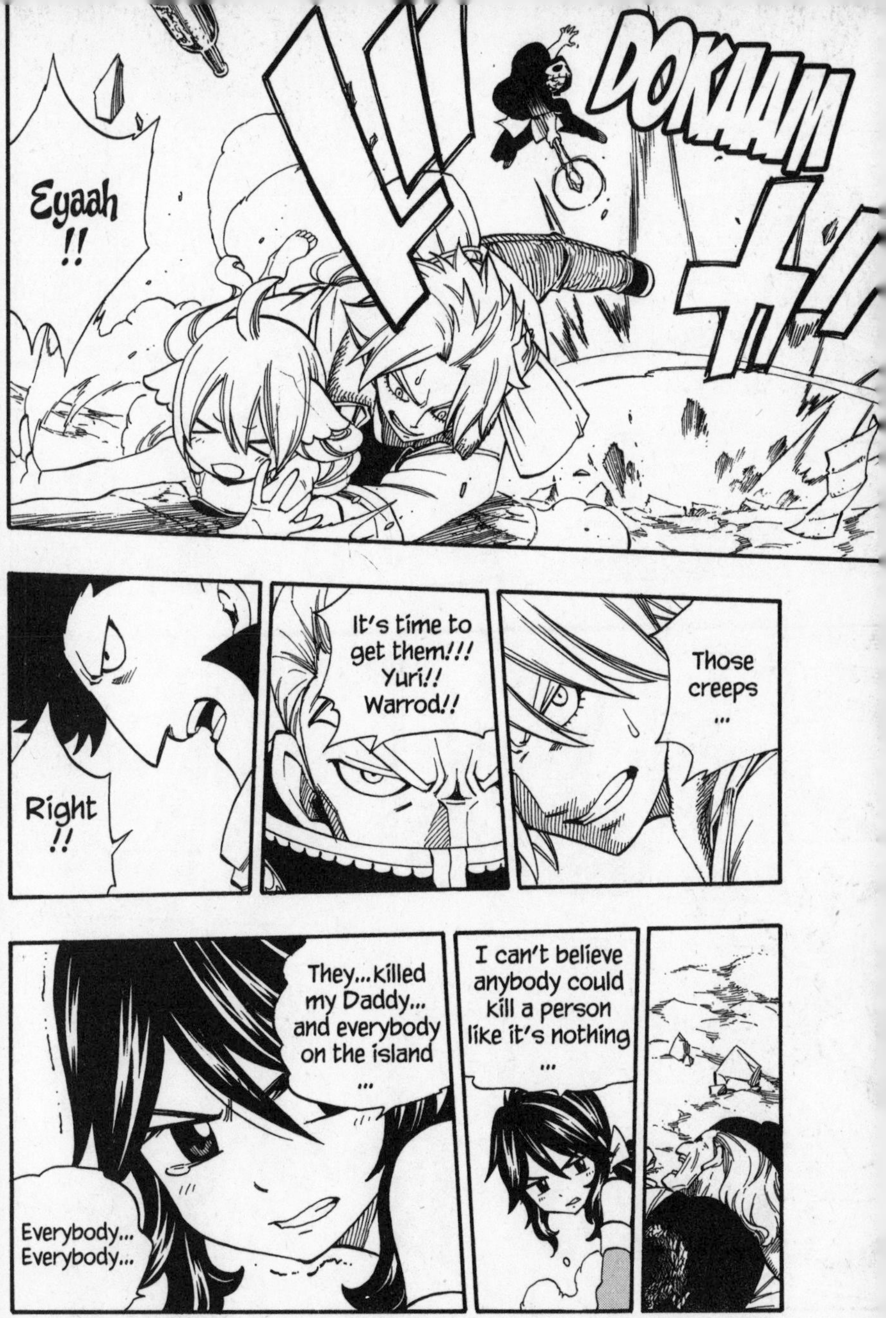
DOKAAN
Eyaah!!
Those creeps ...
It's time to get them!!! Yuri!! Warrod!!
Right!!
I can't believe anybody could kill a person like it's nothing ...
They...killed my Daddy... and everybody on the island ...
Everybody... Everybody...

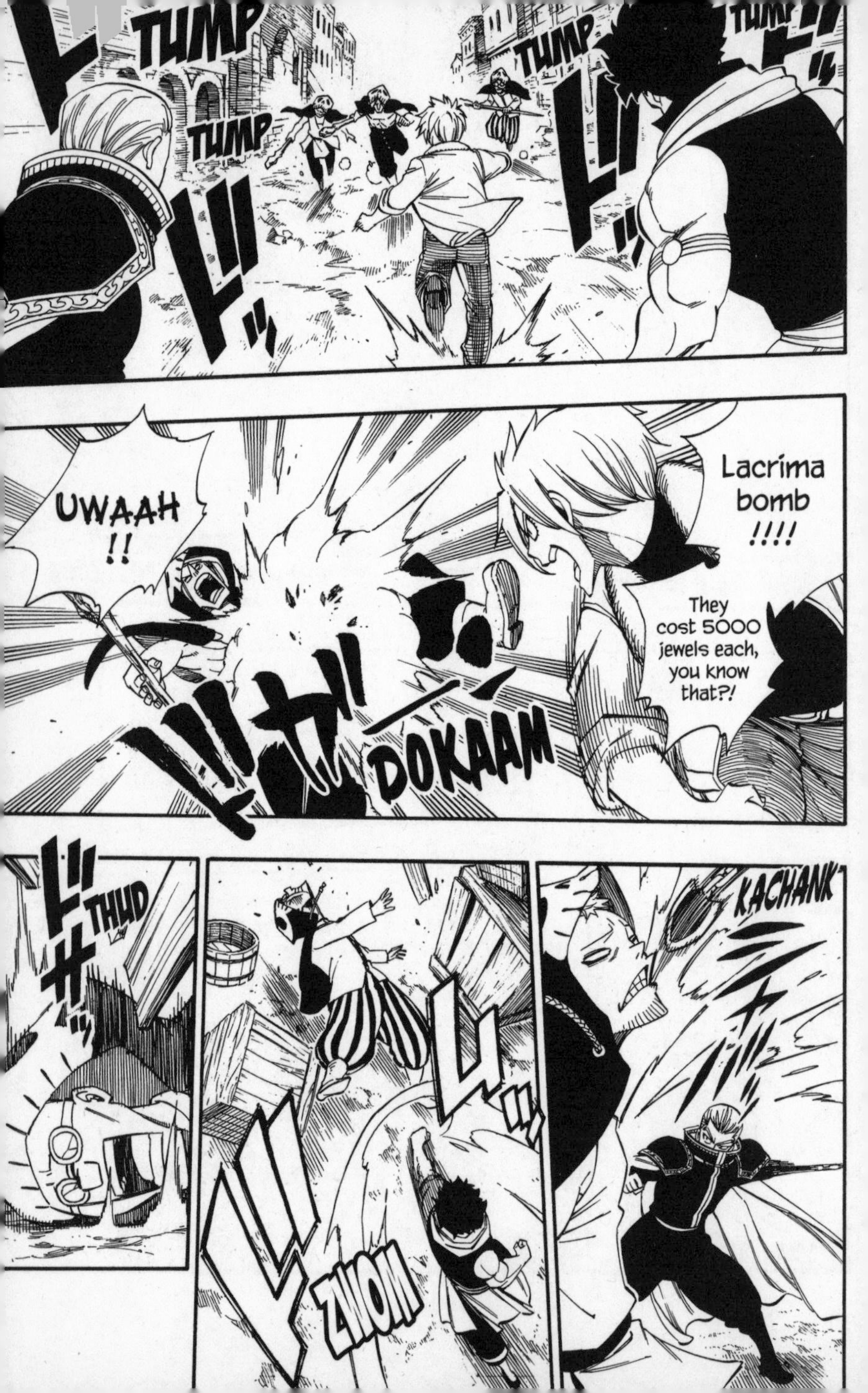
TUMP
TUMP
TUMP
TUMP
Lacrima bomb !!!!
They cost 5000 jewels each, you know that?!
UWAAH !!
DOKAAM
KACHANK
ZWOM
THUD

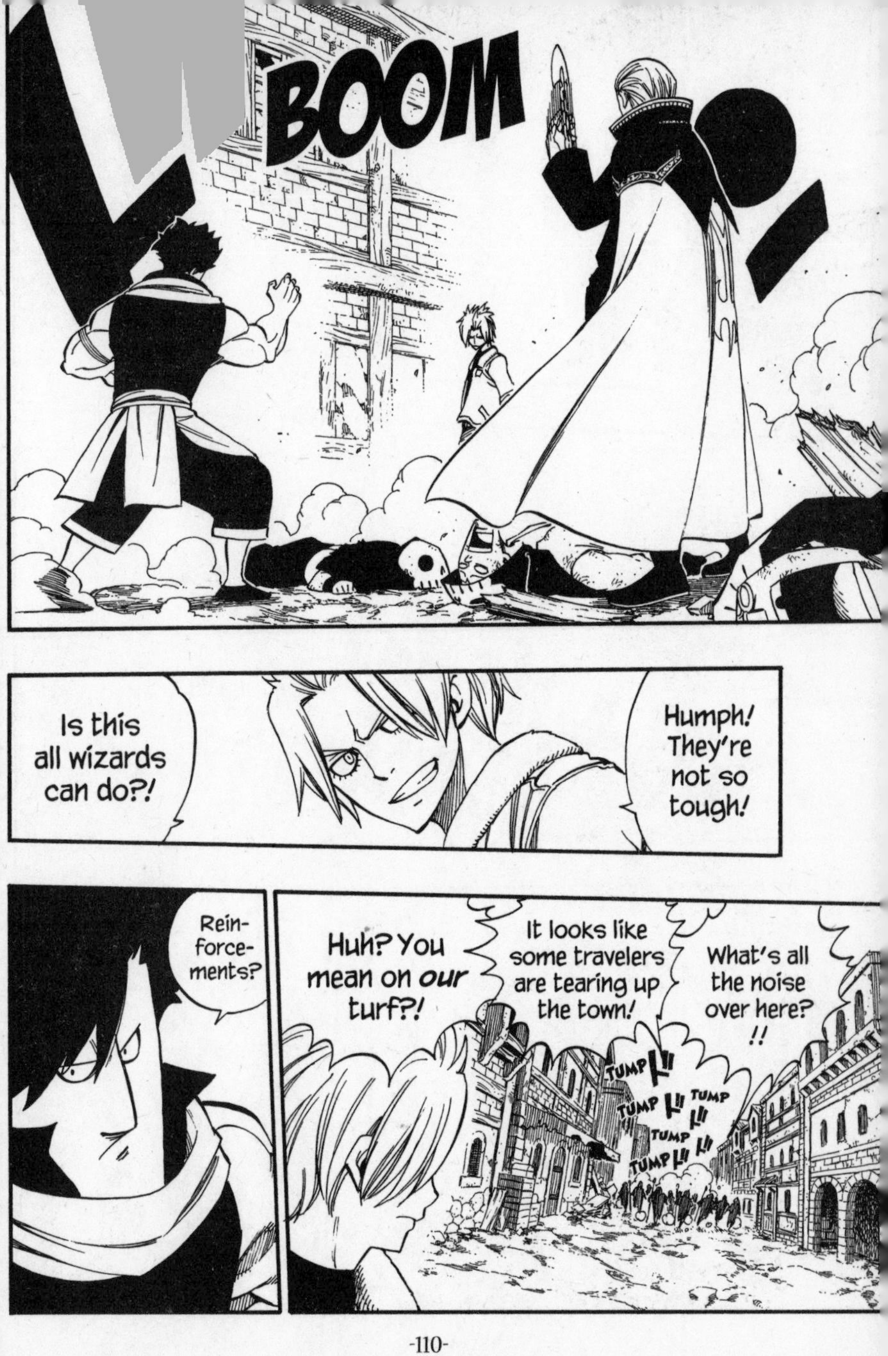
BOOM
Humph! They're not so tough!
Is this all wizards can do?!
What's all the noise over here? !!
It looks like some travelers are tearing up the town!
Huh? You mean on *our* turf?!
TUMP
TUMP
TUMP
TUMP
TUMP
Rein-force-ments?

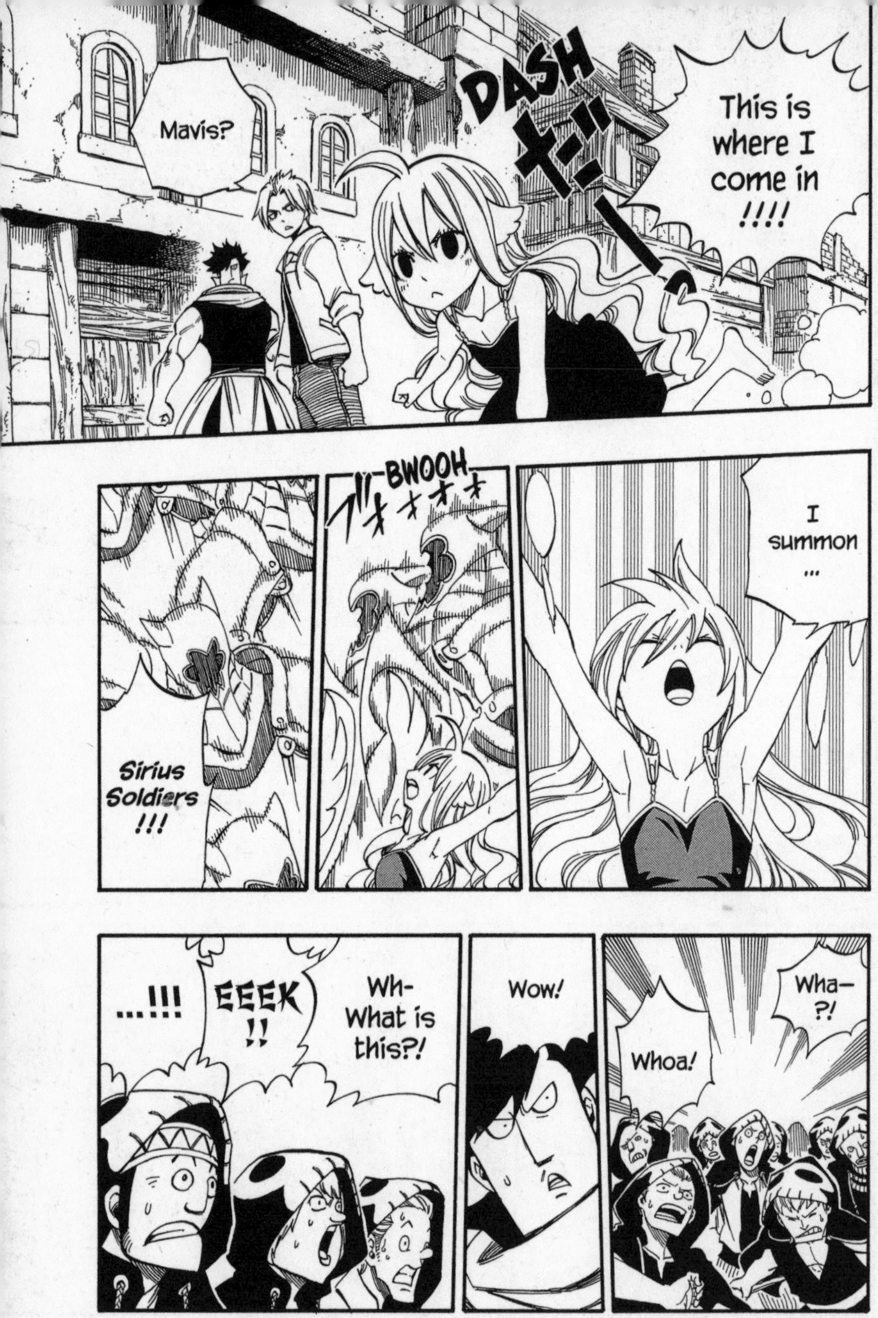
This is where I come in !!!!
DASH
Mavis?
I summon ...
BWOOH
Sirius Soldiers !!!
Wha-?!
Whoa!
Wow!
Wh- What is this?!
EEEK !!
...!!!

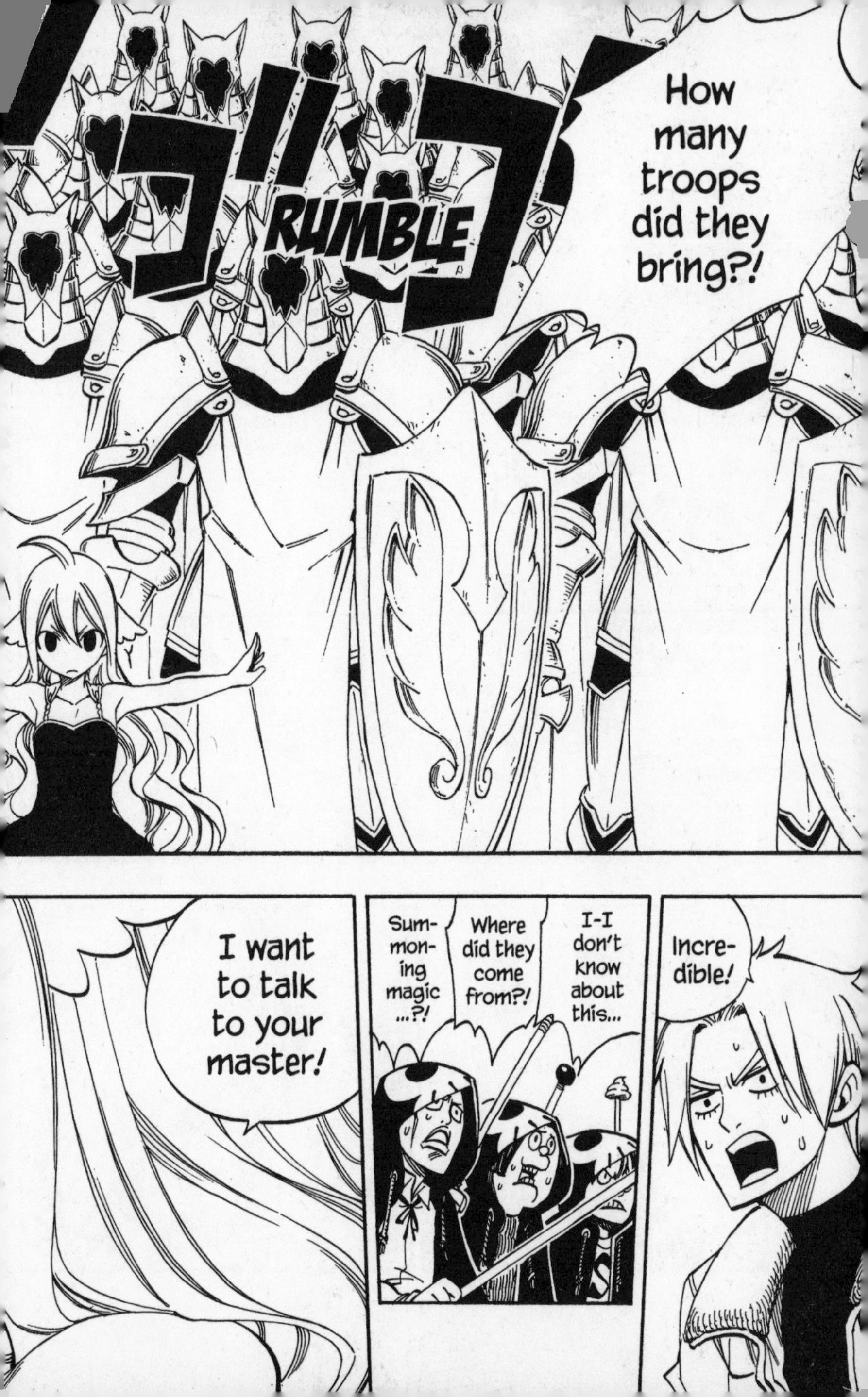
How many troops did they bring?!
RUMBLE
Incredible!
I-I don't know about this...
Where did they come from?!
Summoning magic...?!
I want to talk to your master!

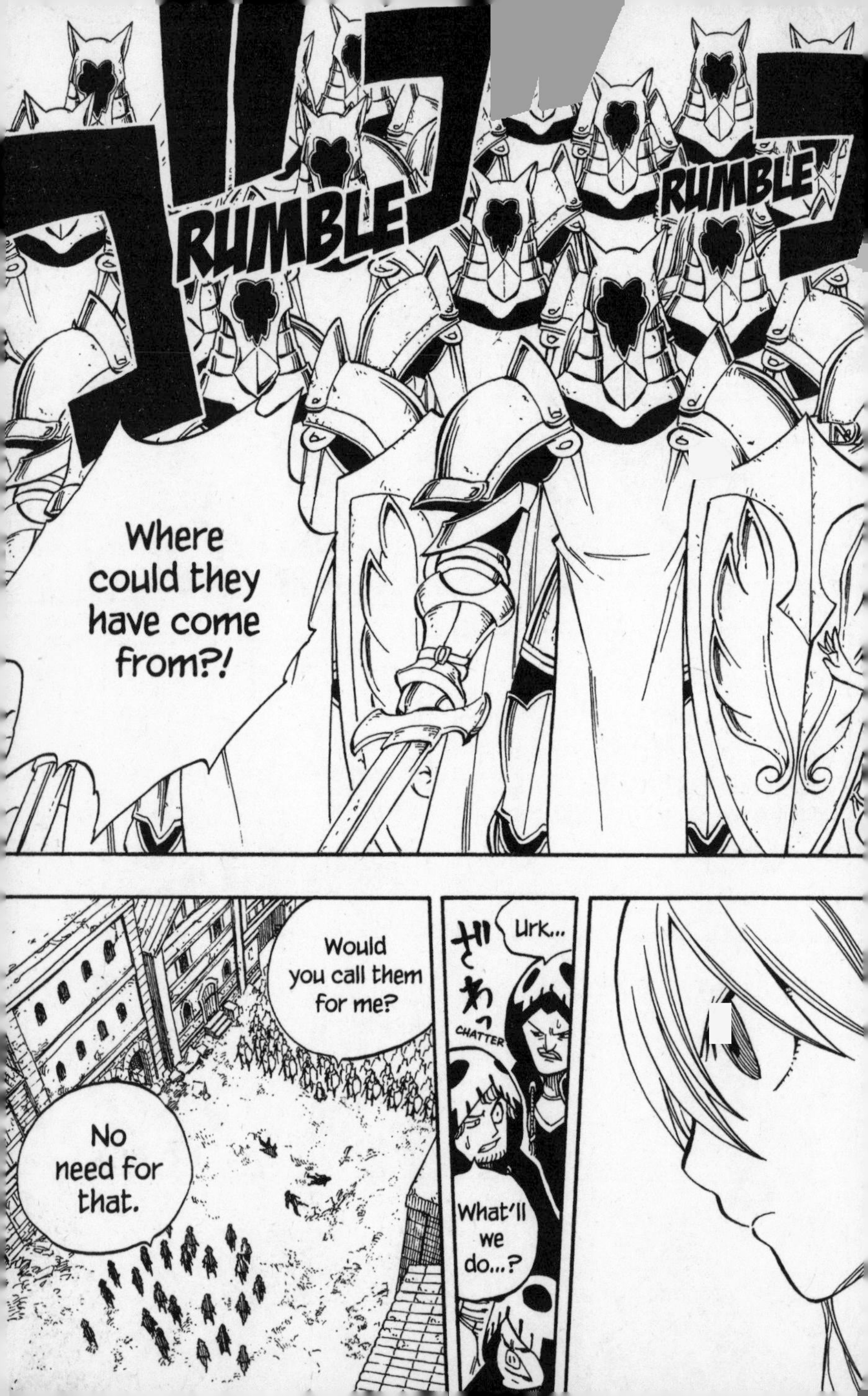
RUMBLE
RUMBLE
Where could they have come from?!
Urk...
ざわっ
CHATTER
What'll we do...?
Would you call them for me?
No need for that.

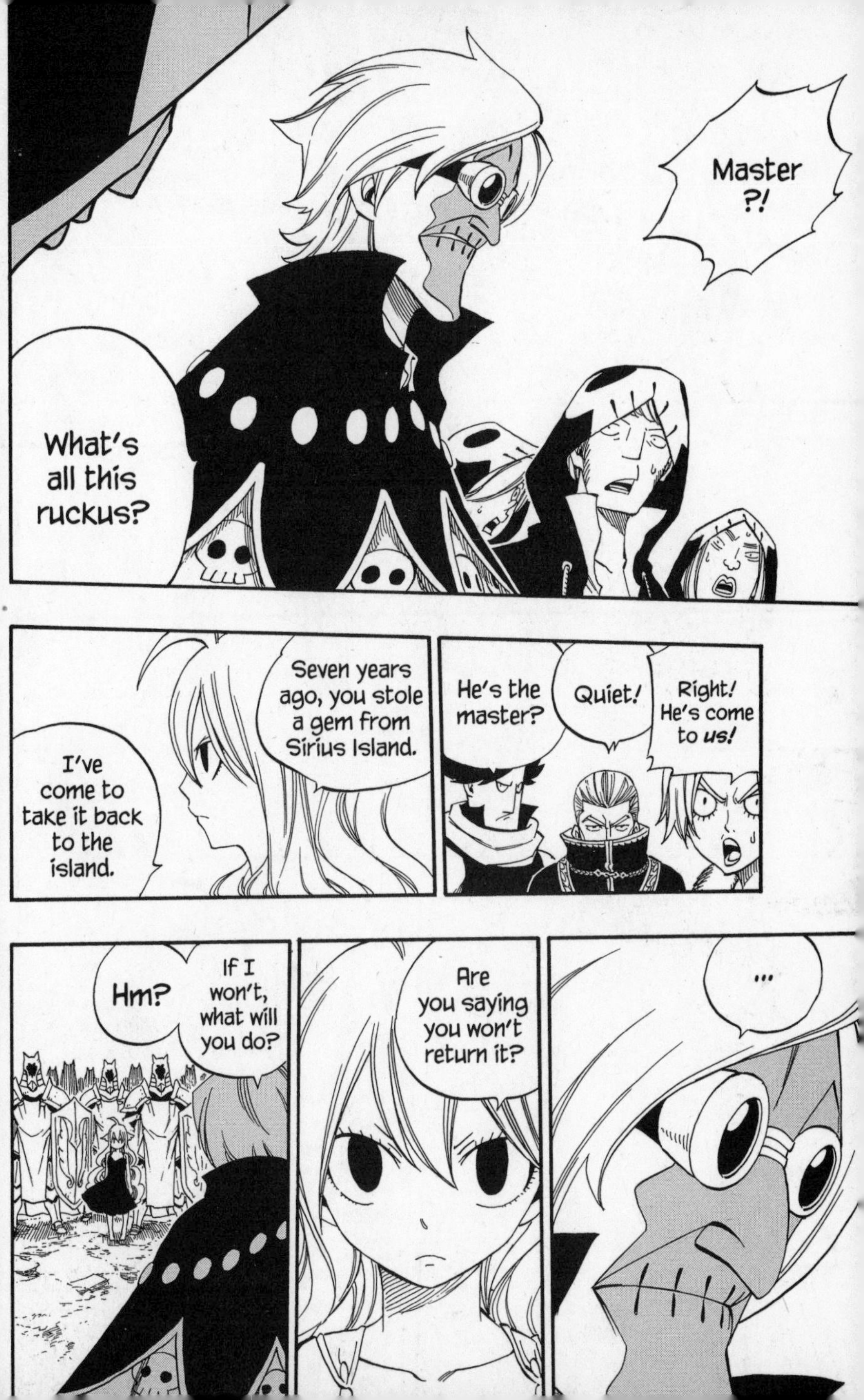
Master ?!
What's all this ruckus?
Right! He's come to *us*!
Quiet!
He's the master?
Seven years ago, you stole a gem from Sirius Island.
I've come to take it back to the island.
...
Are you saying you won't return it?
If I won't, what will you do?
Hm?

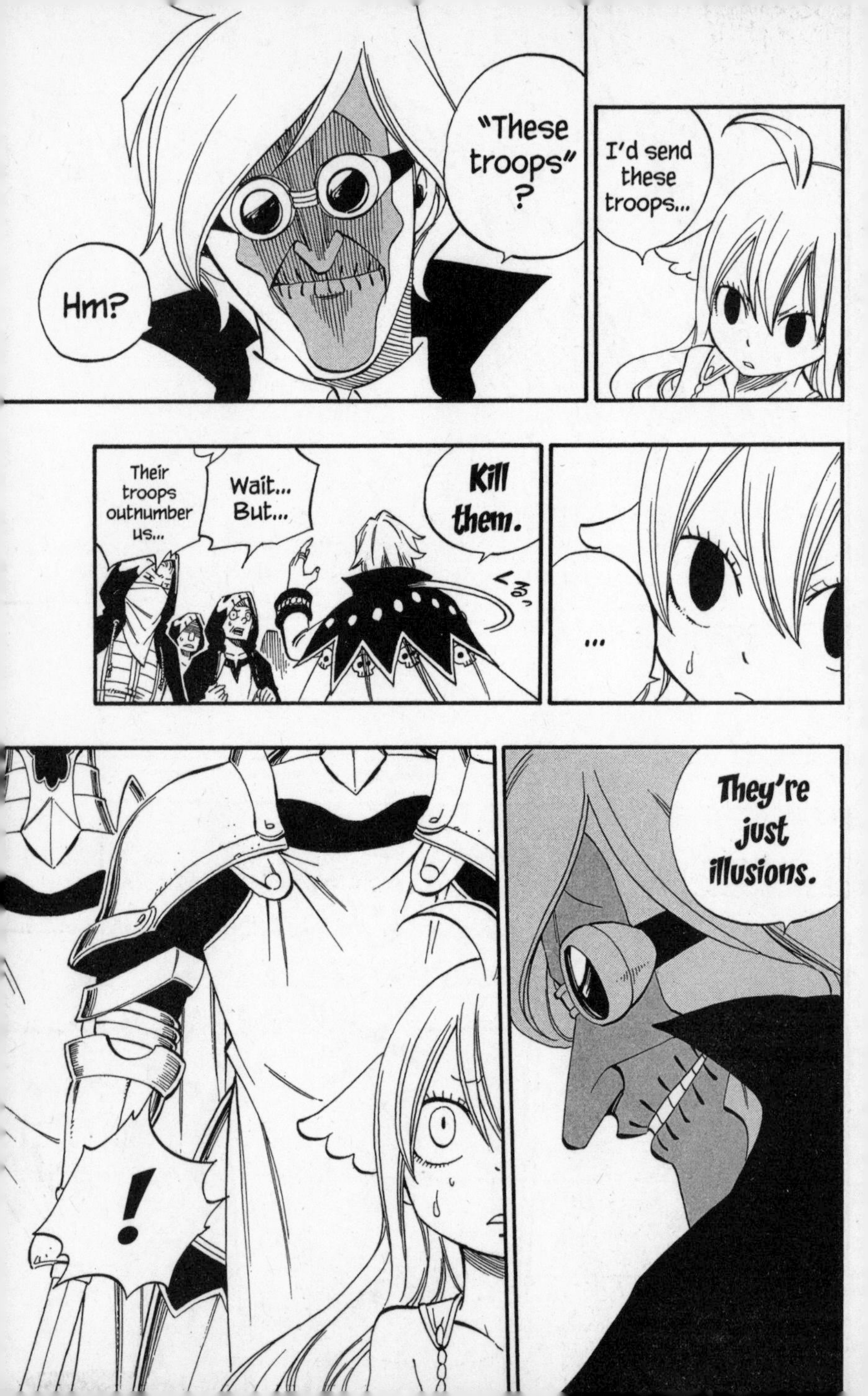
I'd send these troops...
"These troops"?
Hm?
...
Kill them.
Wait... But...
Their troops outnumber us...
They're just illusions.
!

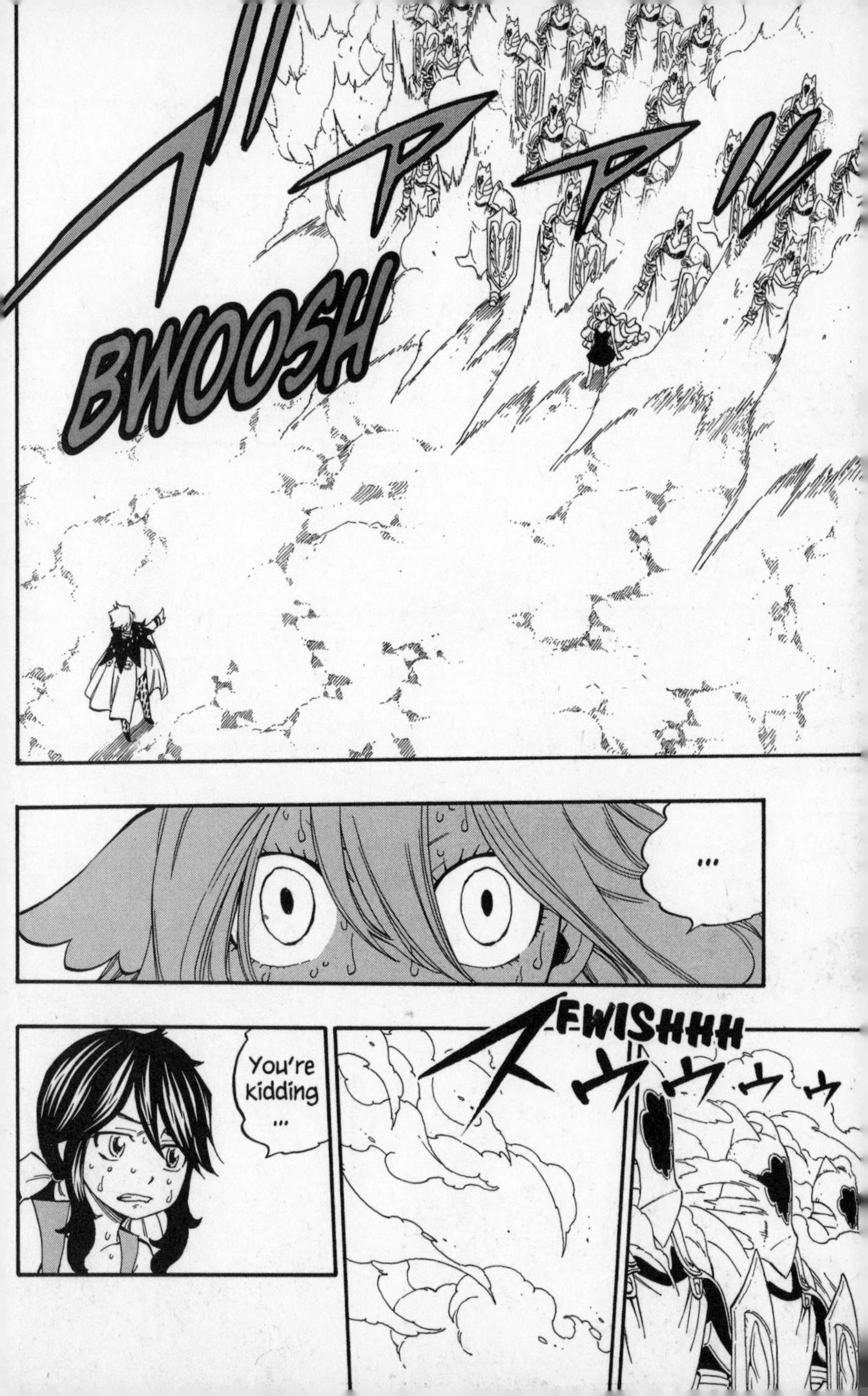
ゴ
ア
ア
ッ
BWOOSH
...
FWISHHH
ヴ
ウ
ウ
ゥ
You're kidding ...

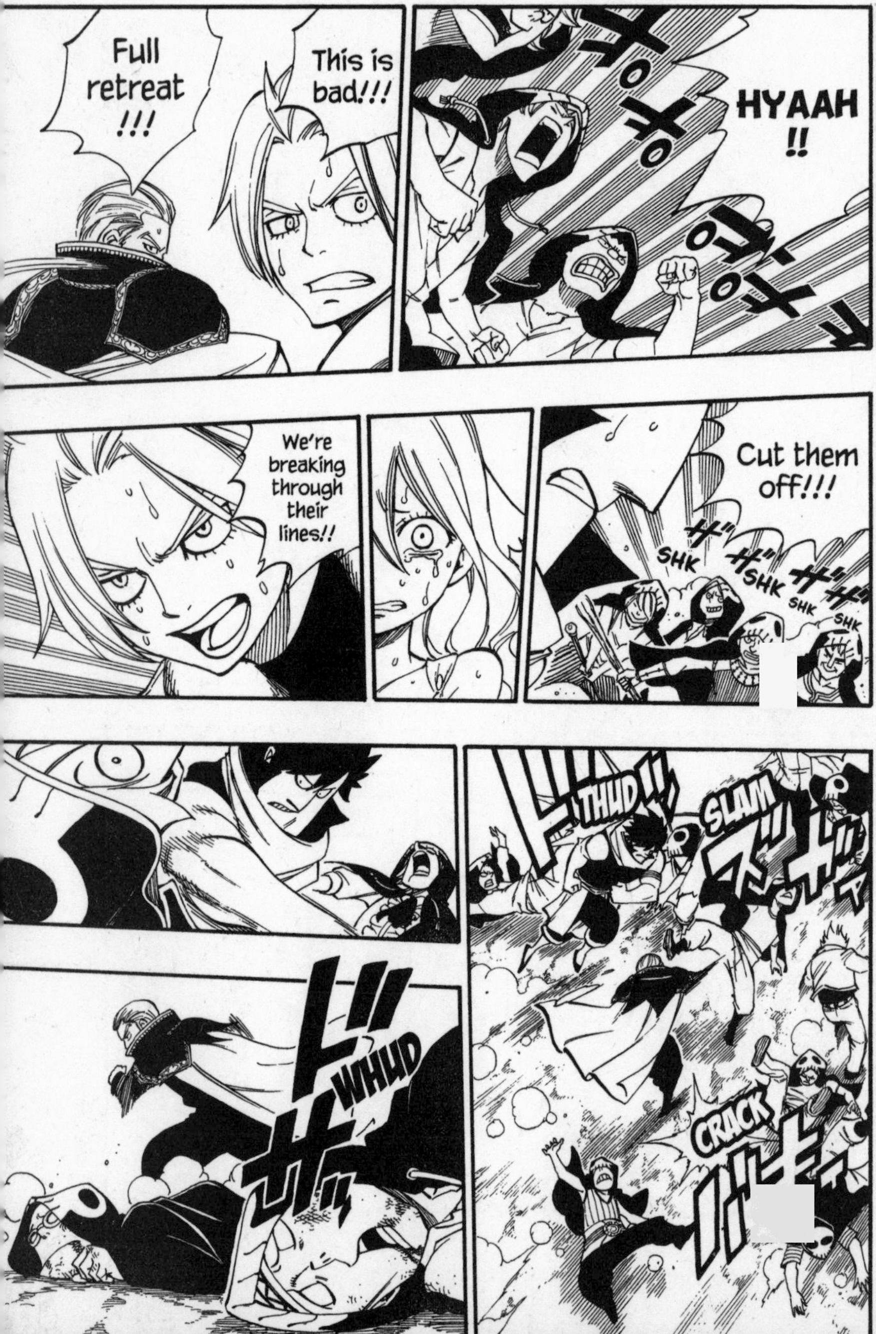
HYAAH!!
This is bad!!!
Full retreat!!!
Cut them off!!!
SHK
SHK
SHK
SHK
We're breaking through their lines!!
THUD!!
SLAM
CRACK
WHUD

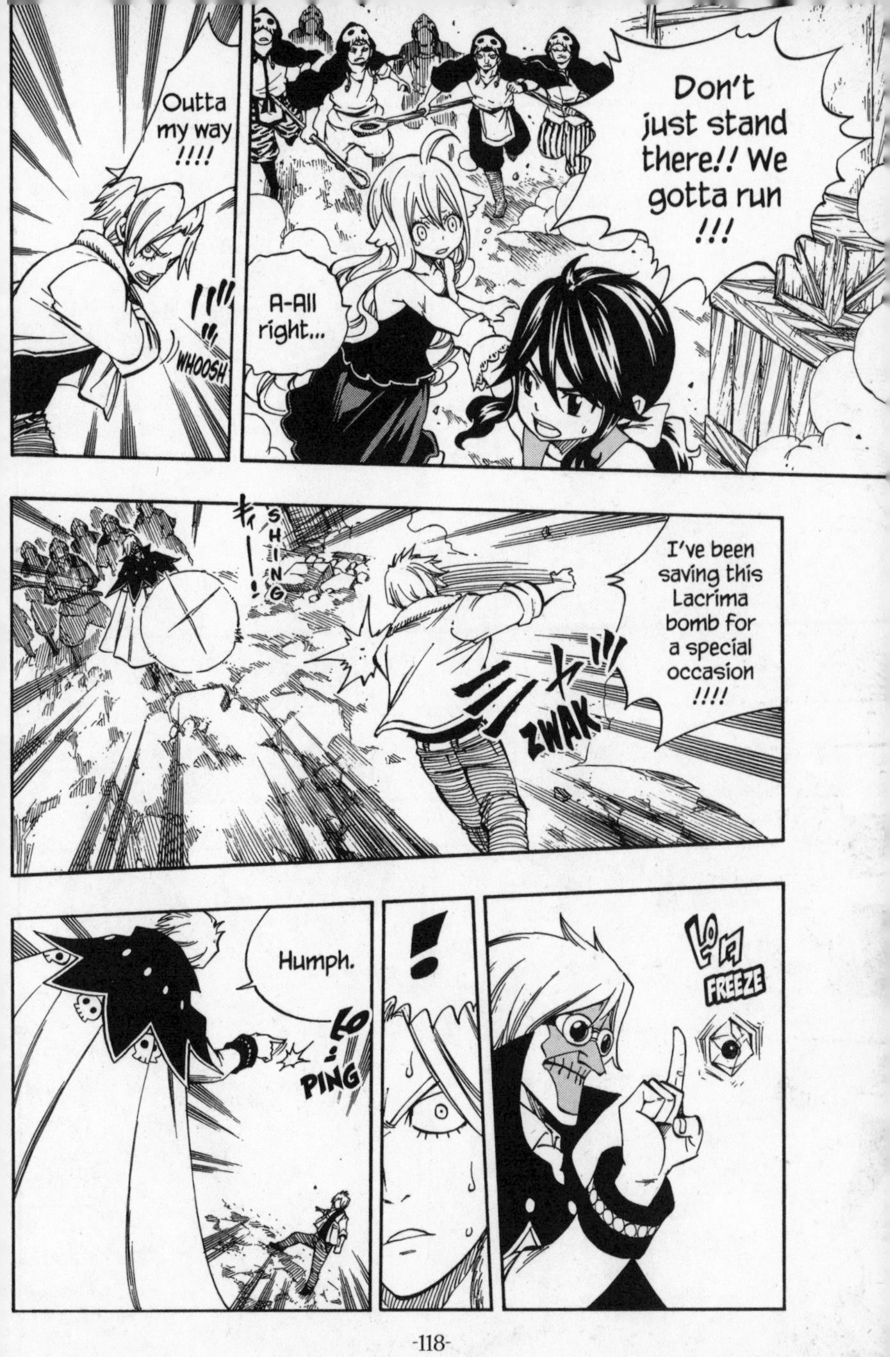
Don't just stand there!! We gotta run !!!
A-All right...
Outta my way !!!!
WHOOSH
I've been saving this Lacrima bomb for a special occasion !!!!
ZWAK
SHING
FREEZE
!
Humph.
PING

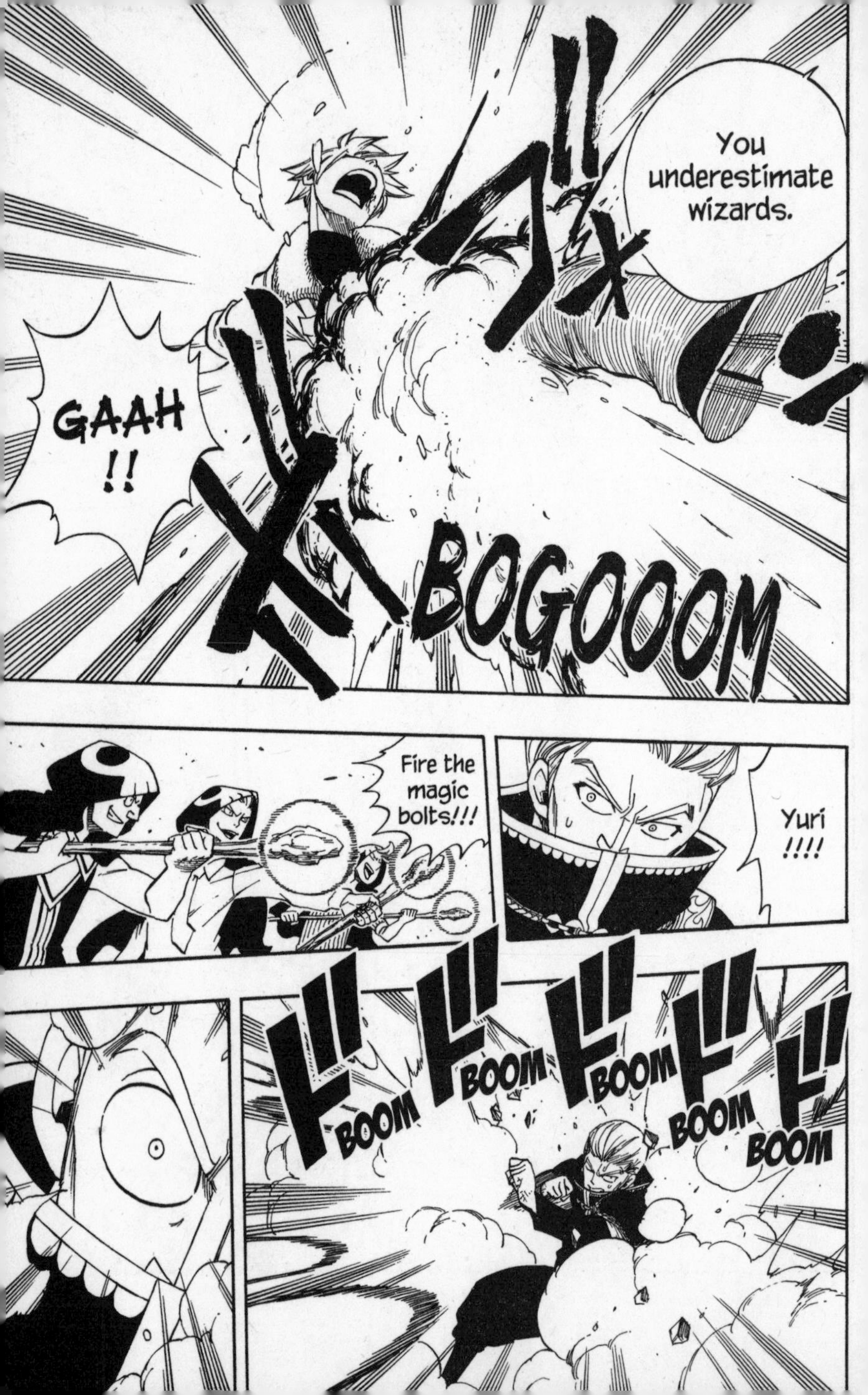

You underestimate wizards.
GAAH !!
BOGOOOM
Yuri !!!!
Fire the magic bolts!!!
BOOM
BOOM
BOOM
BOOM
BOOM

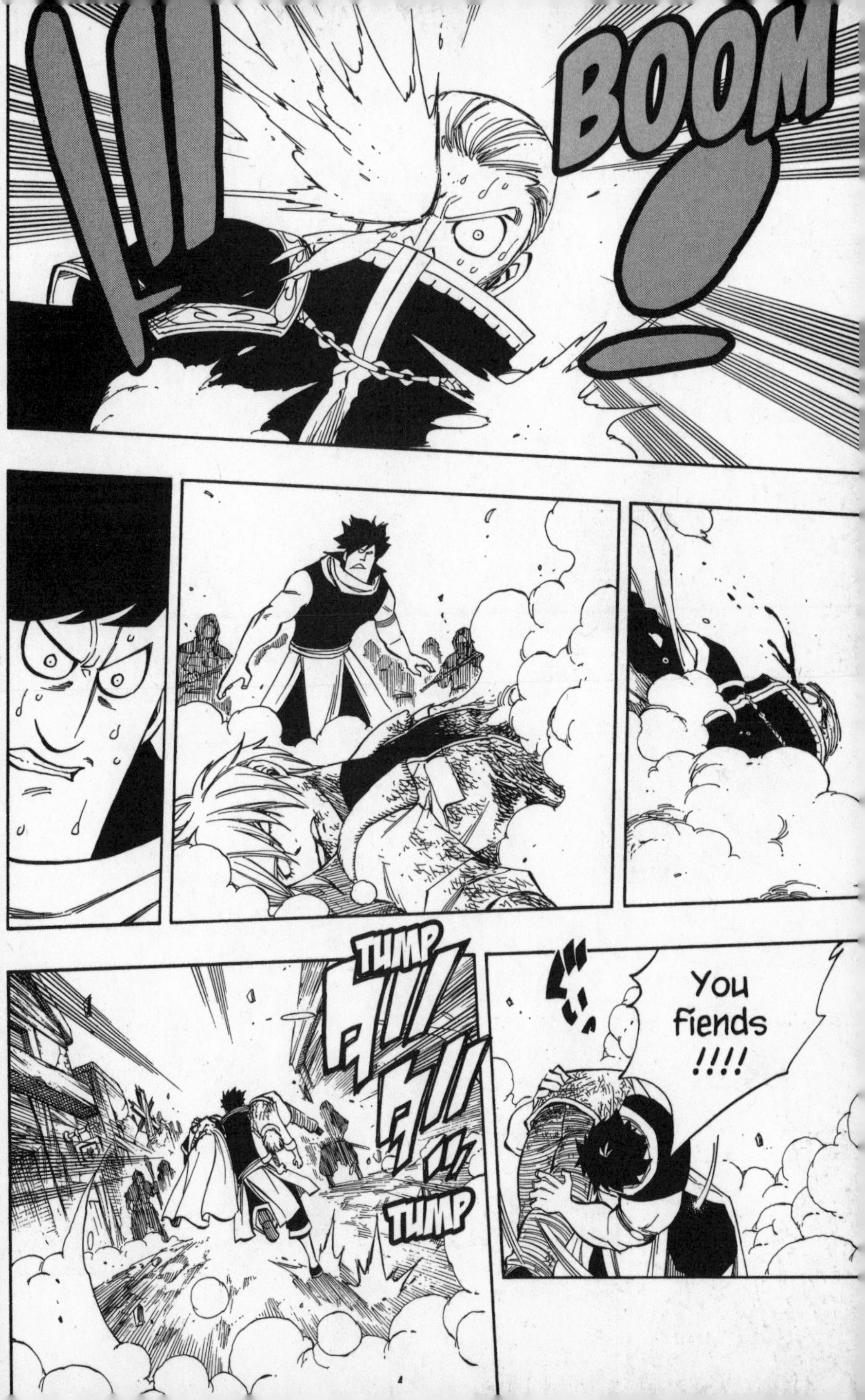
BOOM
You fiends !!!!
TUMP
TUMP

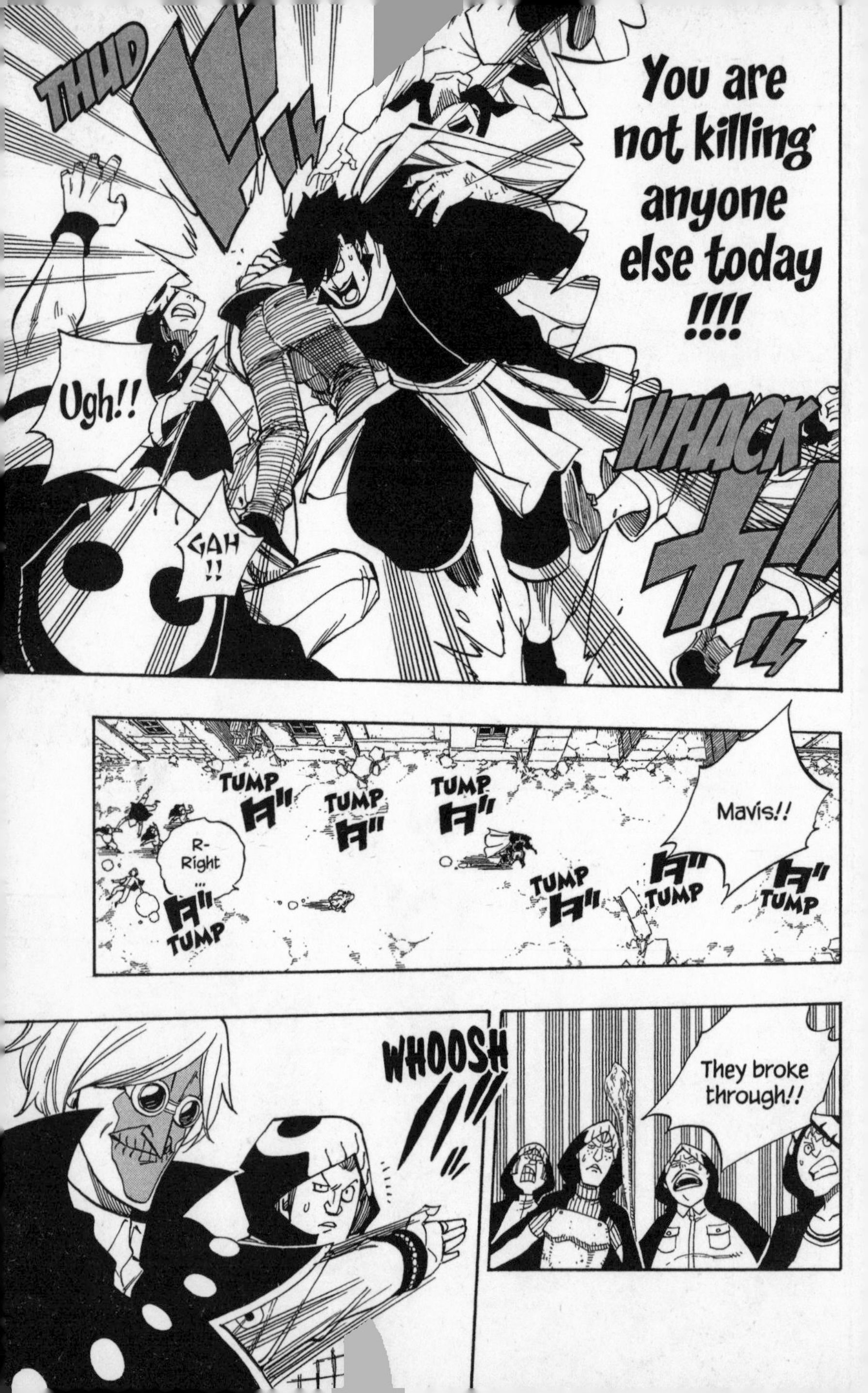
You are not killing anyone else today !!!!
THUD
WHACK
Ugh!!
GAH !!
Mavis!!
TUMP
TUMP
TUMP
TUMP
TUMP
TUMP
TUMP
R- Right ...
TUMP
They broke through!!
WHOOSH

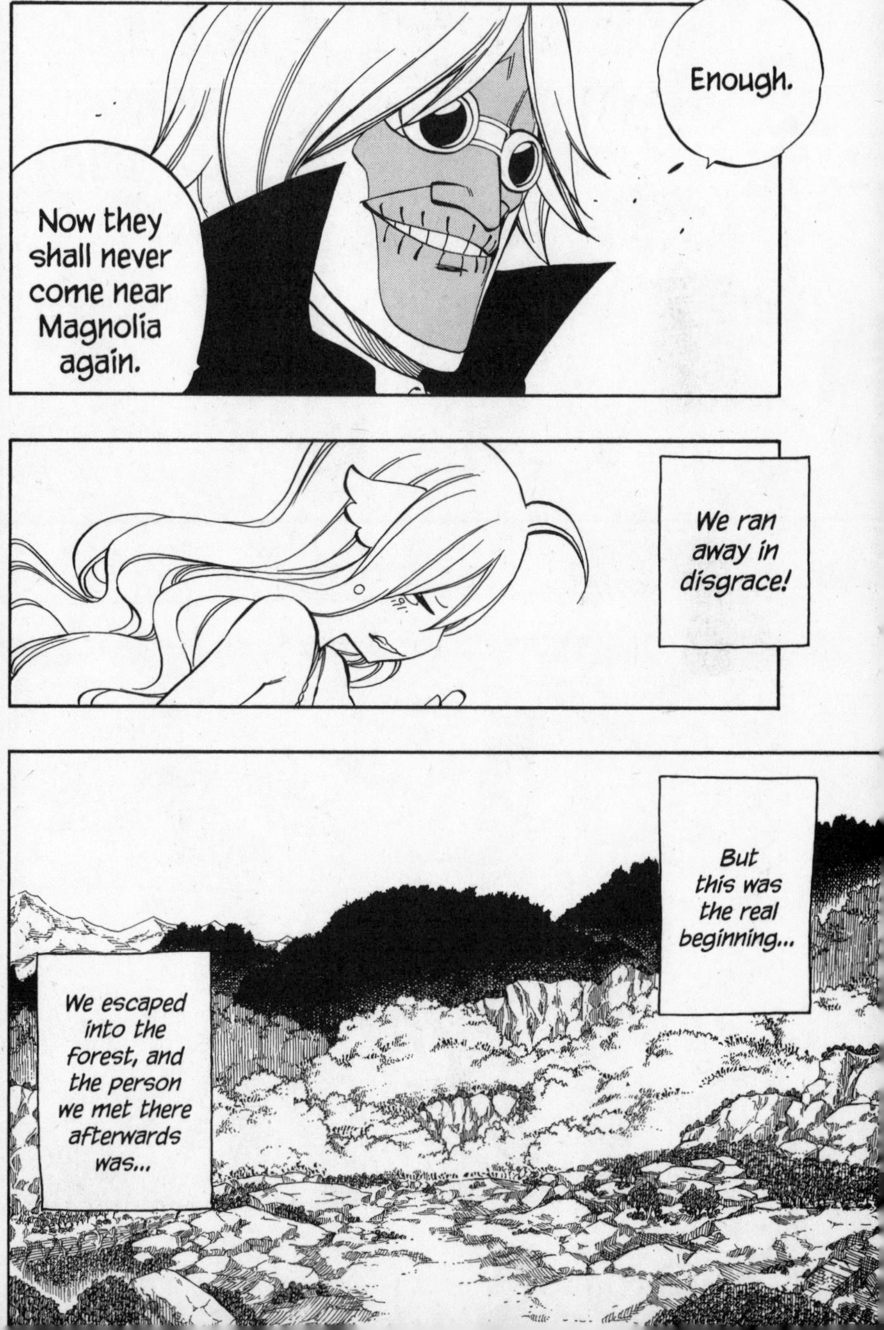
Enough.
Now they shall never come near Magnolia again.
We ran away in disgrace!
But this was the real beginning...
We escaped into the forest, and the person we met there afterwards was...

FAIRY TAIL ZERØ

Chapter 7: Black Wizard Mavis

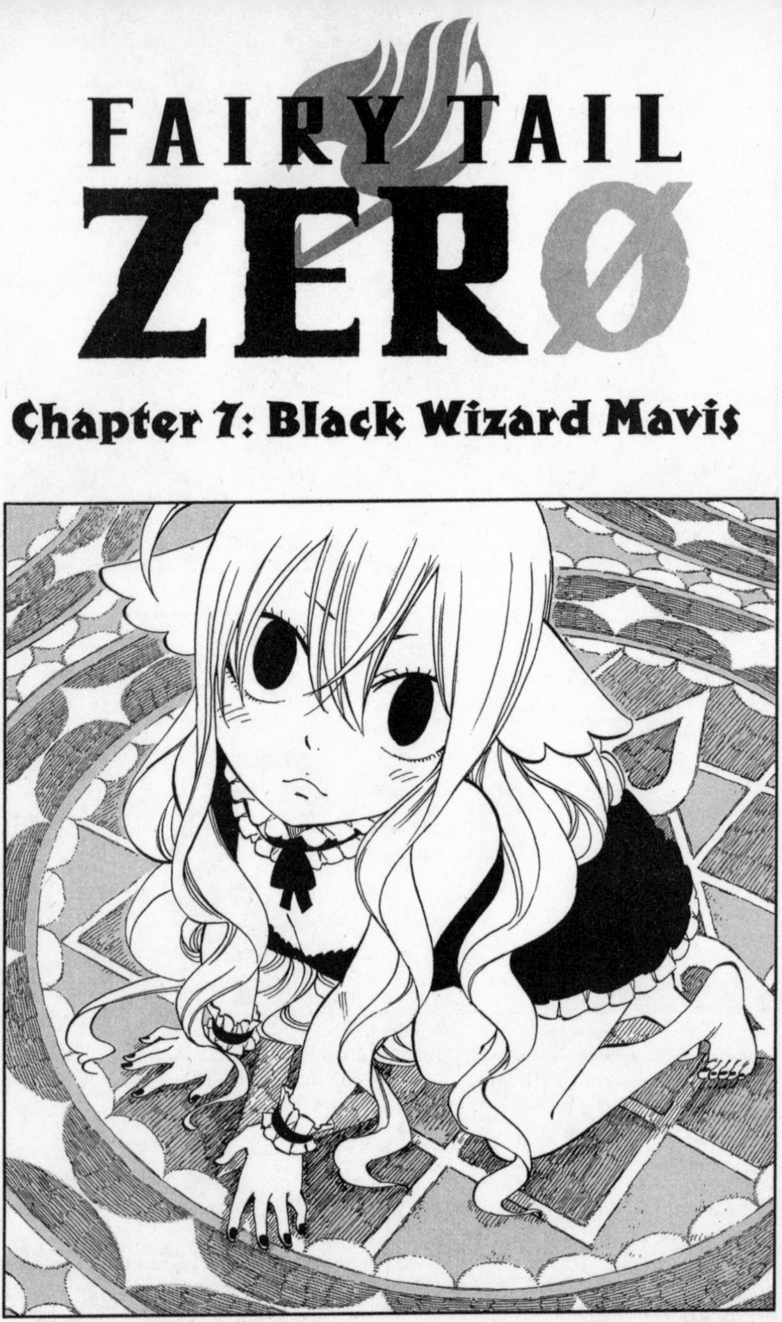

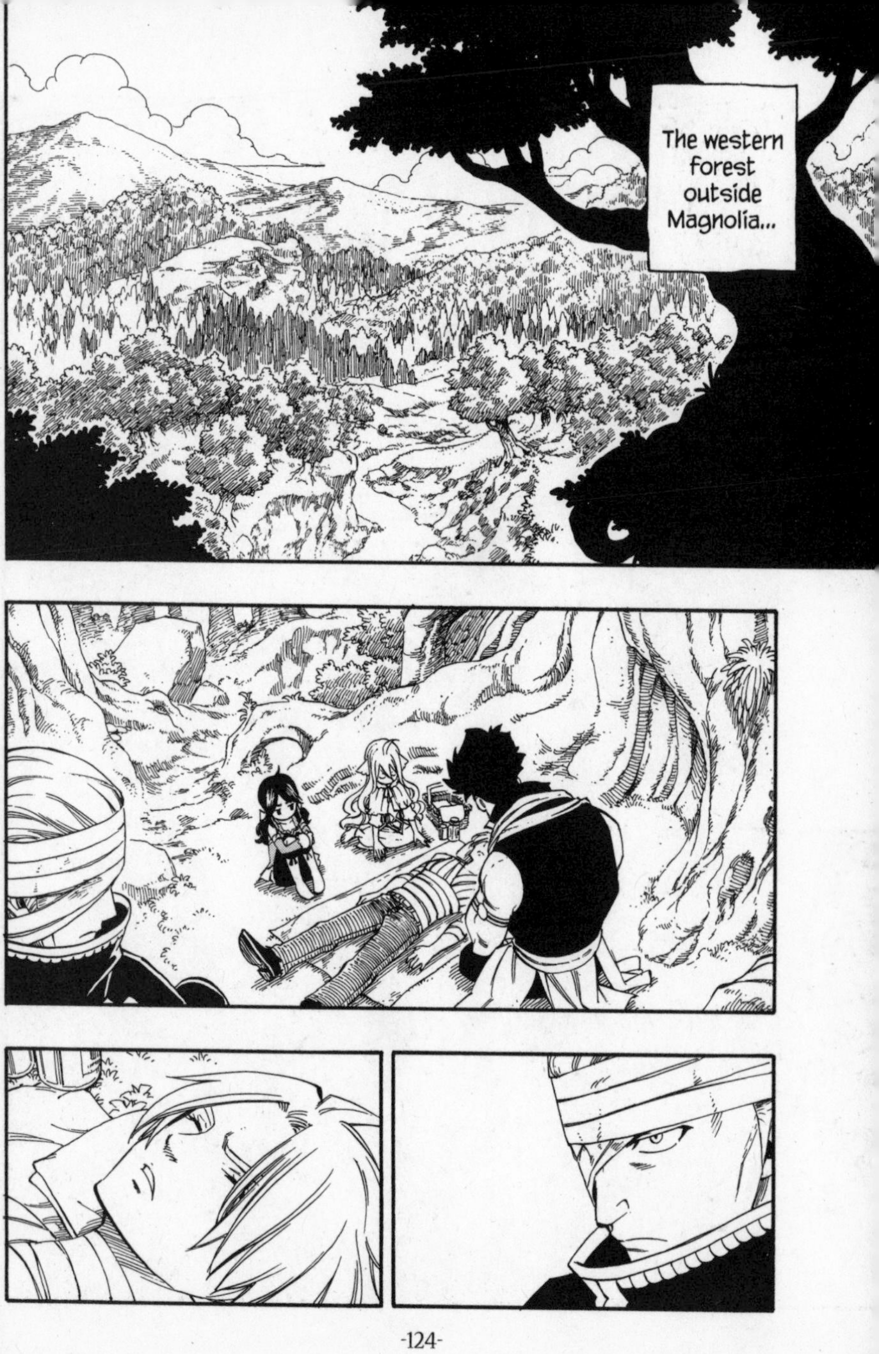
The western forest outside Magnolia...

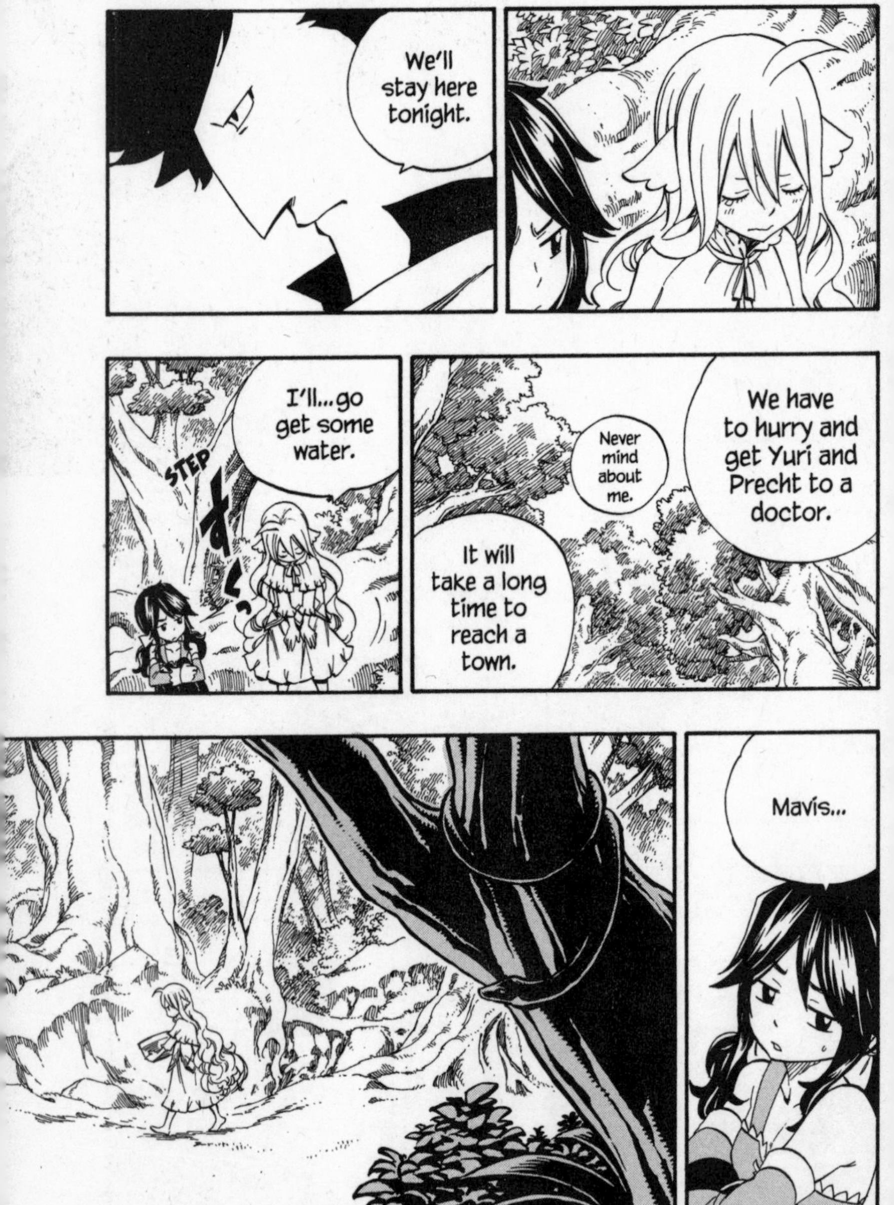
We'll stay here tonight.
We have to hurry and get Yuri and Precht to a doctor.
Never mind about me.
It will take a long time to reach a town.
I'll...go get some water.
STEP
Mavis...

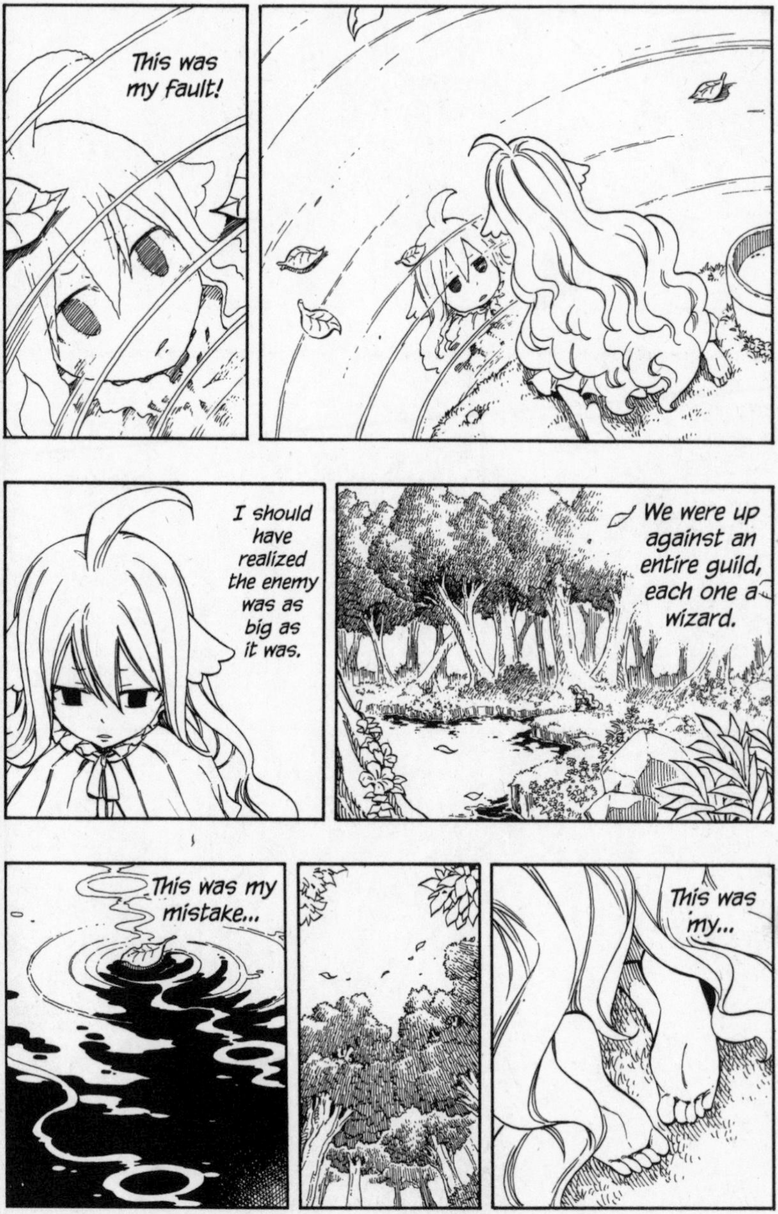
This was my fault!
We were up against an entire guild, each one a wizard.
I should have realized the enemy was as big as it was.
This was my...
This was my mistake...

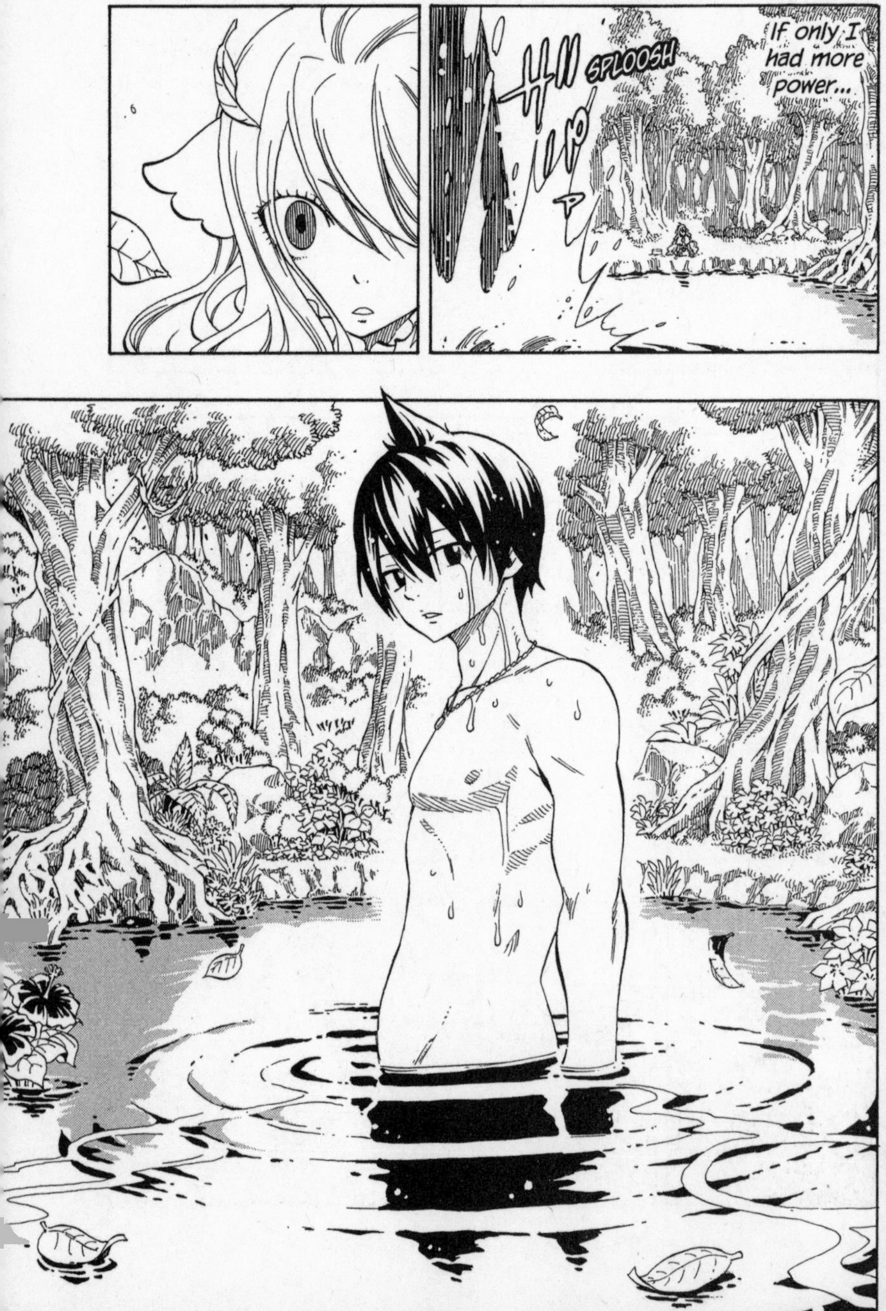
If only I had more power...
SPLOOSH

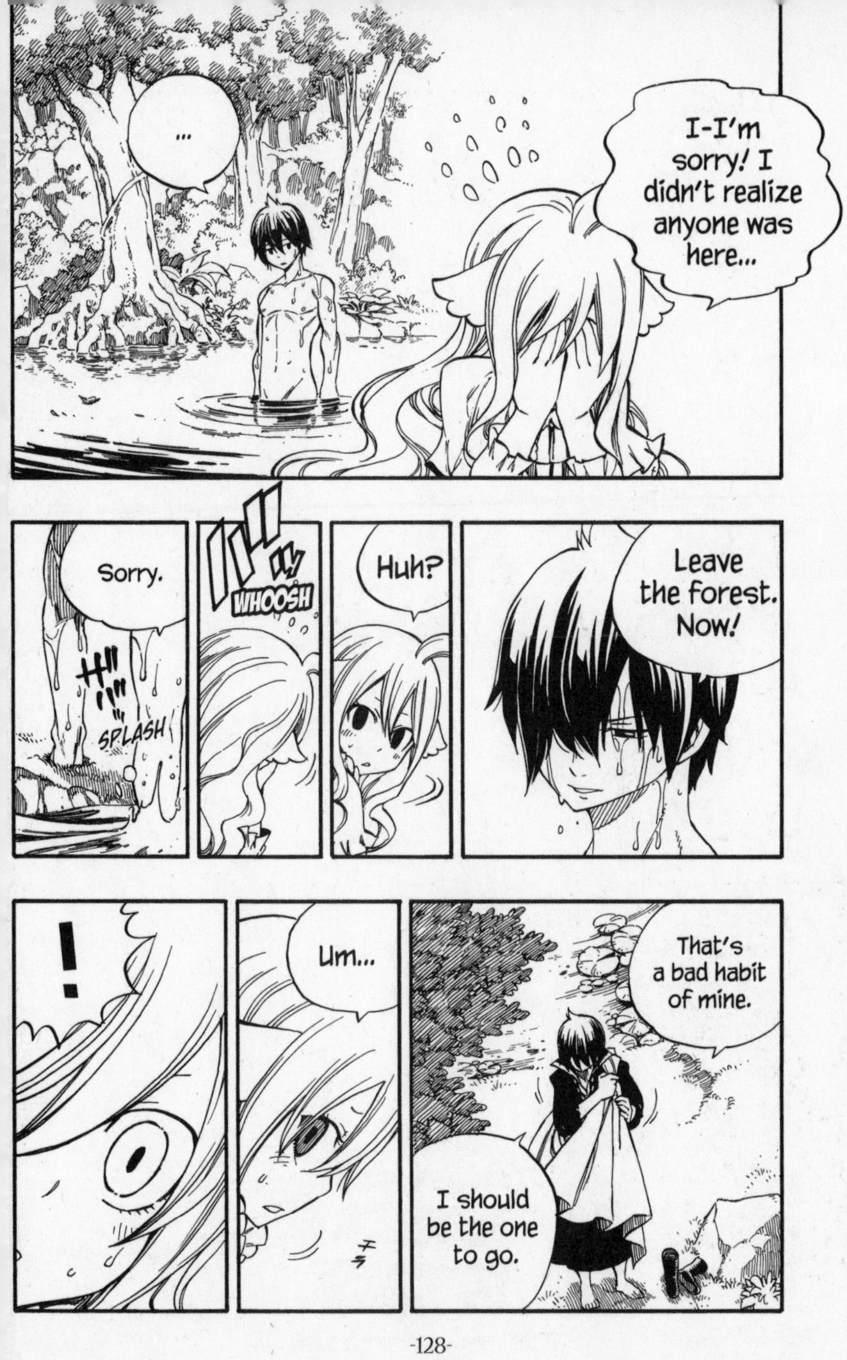
I-I'm sorry! I didn't realize anyone was here...
...
Leave the forest. Now!
Huh?
WHOOSH
Sorry.
SPLASH
That's a bad habit of mine.
I should be the one to go.
Um...
!

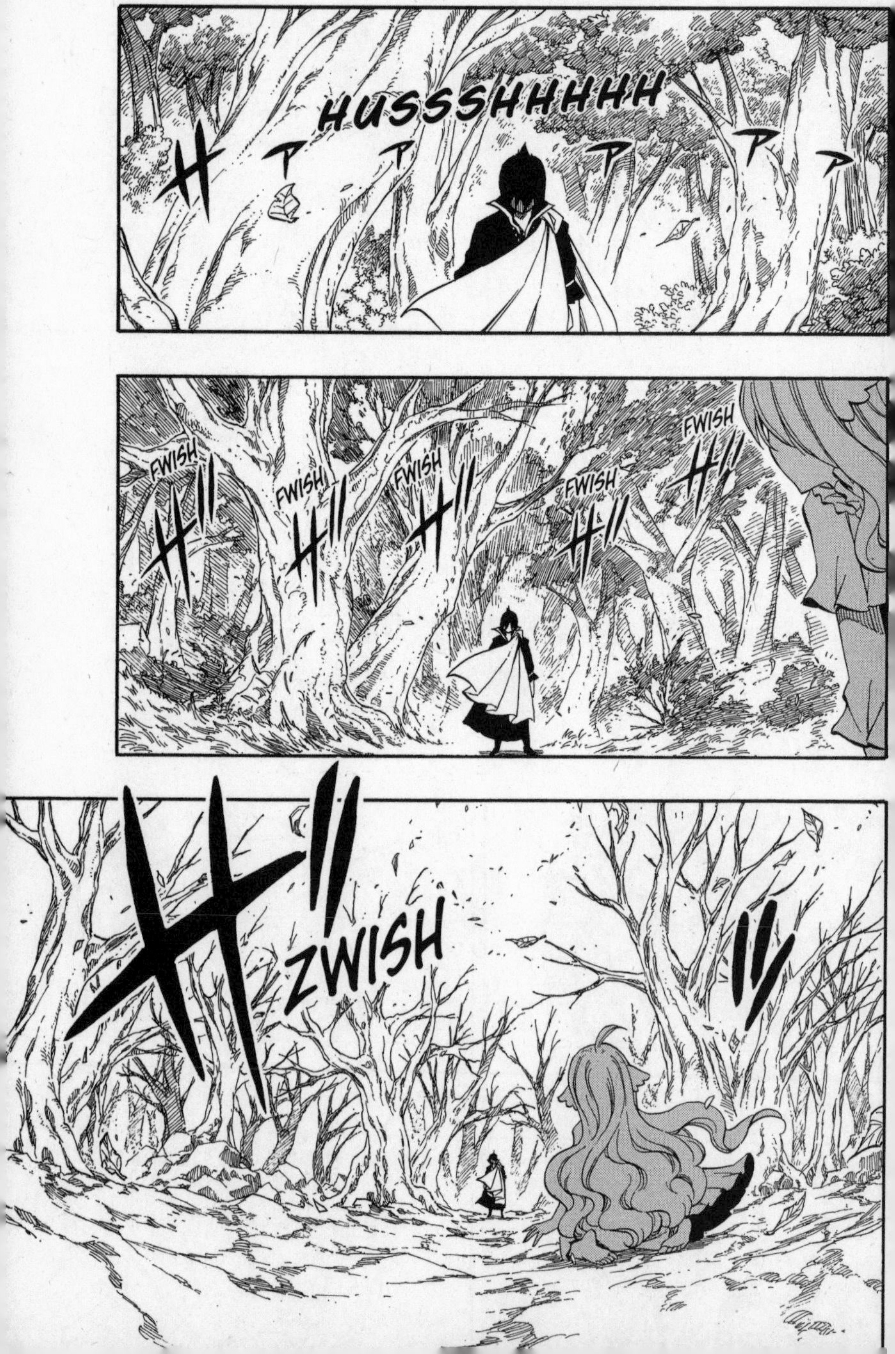
HUSSSHHHHH
FWISH
FWISH
FWISH
FWISH
FWISH
ZWISH

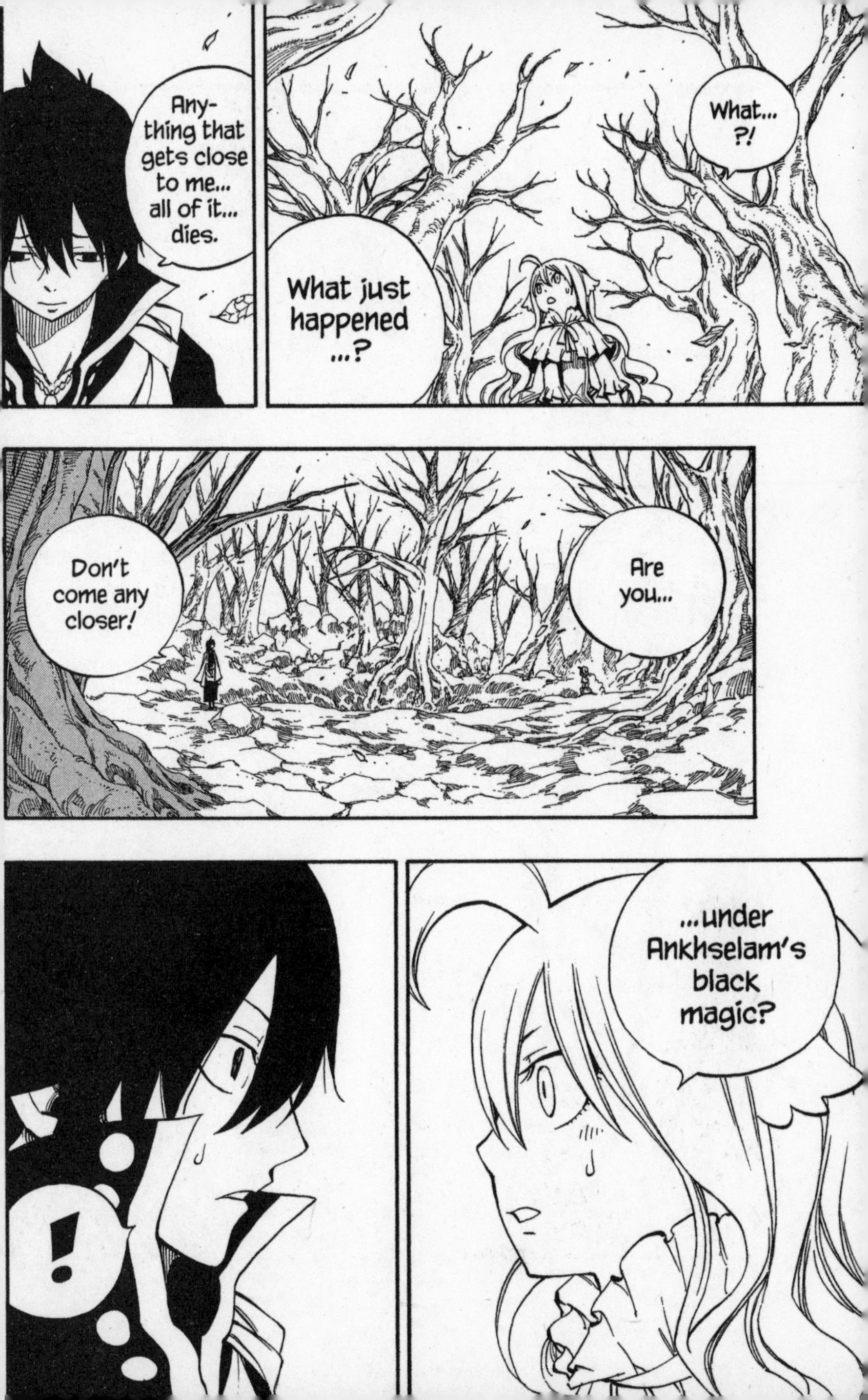
What... ?!
What just happened ...?
Any-thing that gets close to me... all of it... dies.
Are you...
Don't come any closer!
...under Ankhselam's black magic?
!

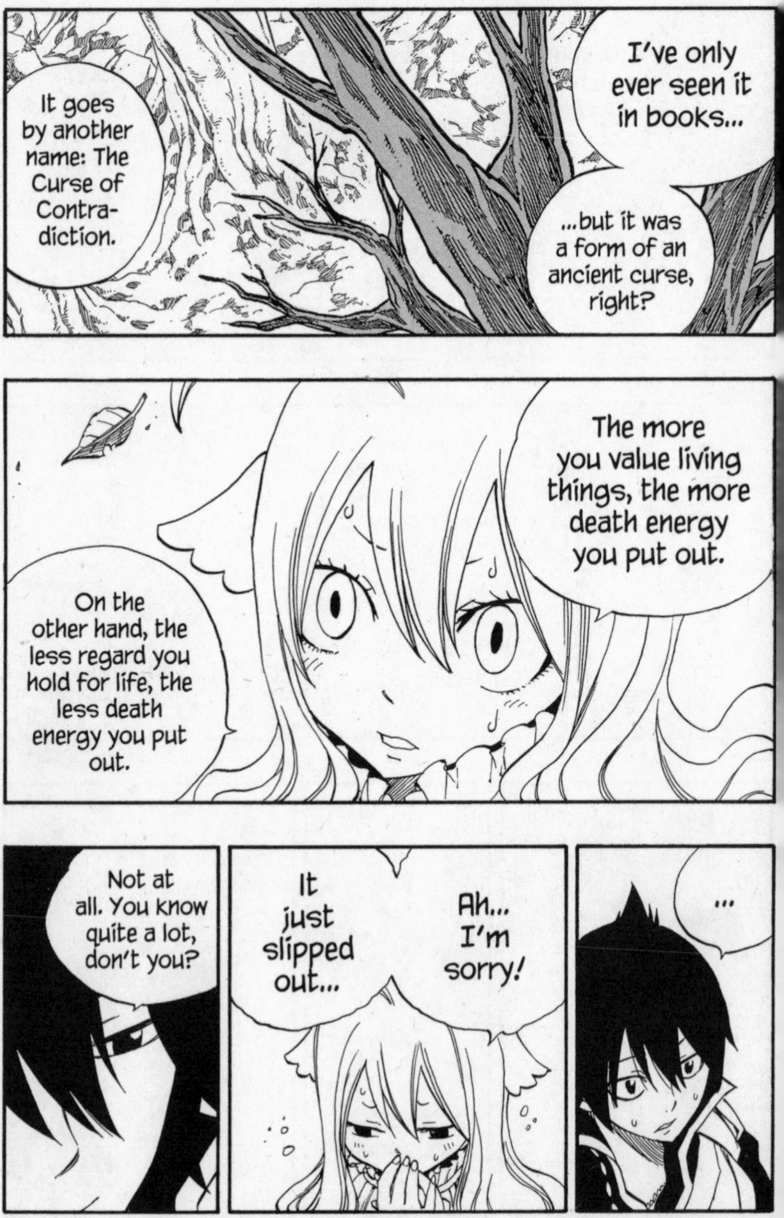
I've only ever seen it in books...
...but it was a form of an ancient curse, right?
It goes by another name: The Curse of Contradiction.
The more you value living things, the more death energy you put out.
On the other hand, the less regard you hold for life, the less death energy you put out.
...
Ah... I'm sorry!
It just slipped out...
Not at all. You know quite a lot, don't you?

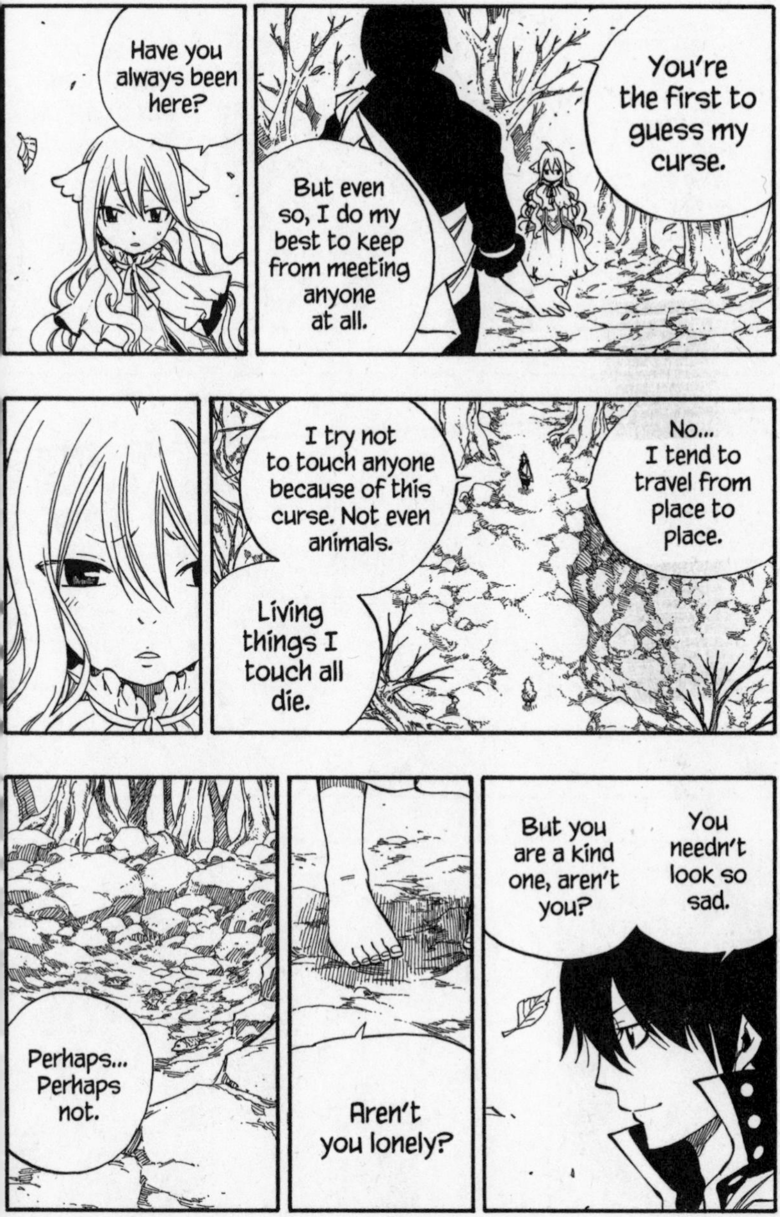
You're the first to guess my curse.
But even so, I do my best to keep from meeting anyone at all.
Have you always been here?
No... I tend to travel from place to place.
I try not to touch anyone because of this curse. Not even animals.
Living things I touch all die.
You needn't look so sad.
But you are a kind one, aren't you?
Aren't you lonely?
Perhaps... Perhaps not.

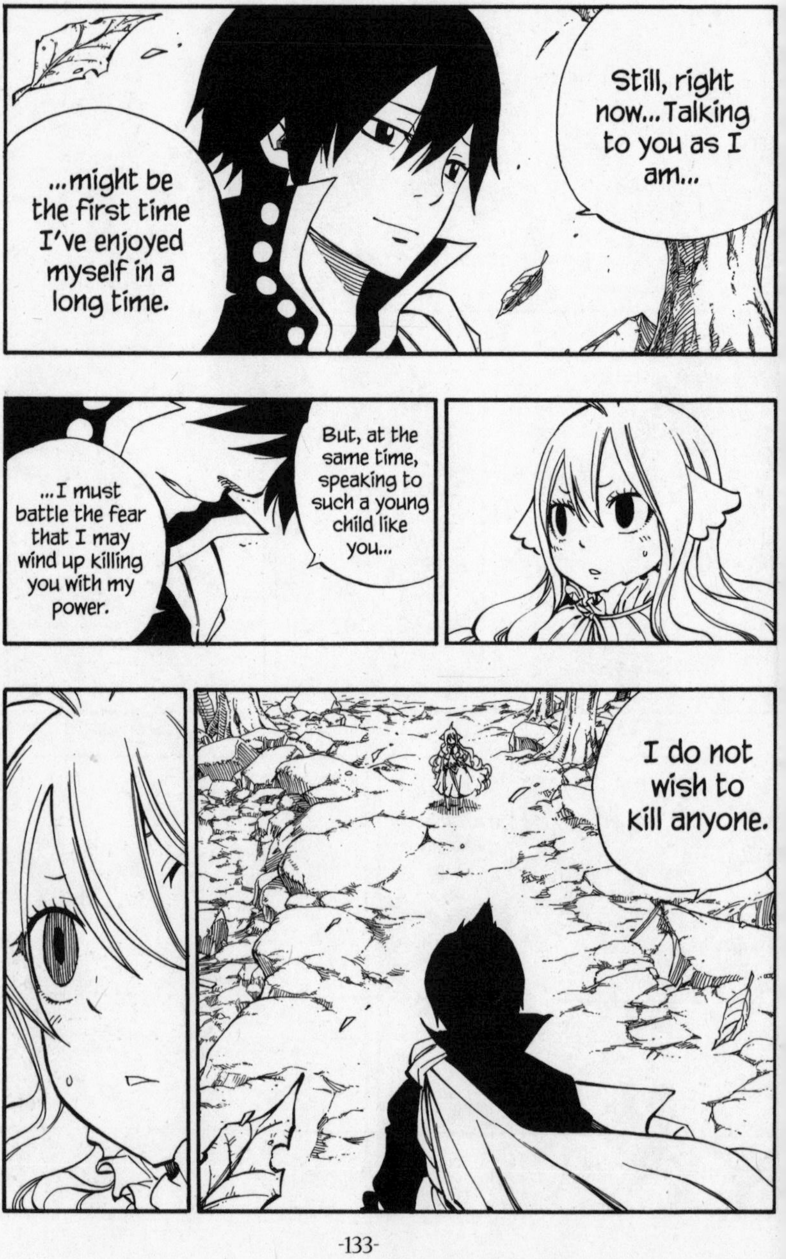
Still, right now... Talking to you as I am...
...might be the first time I've enjoyed myself in a long time.
But, at the same time, speaking to such a young child like you...
...I must battle the fear that I may wind up killing you with my power.
I do not wish to kill anyone.

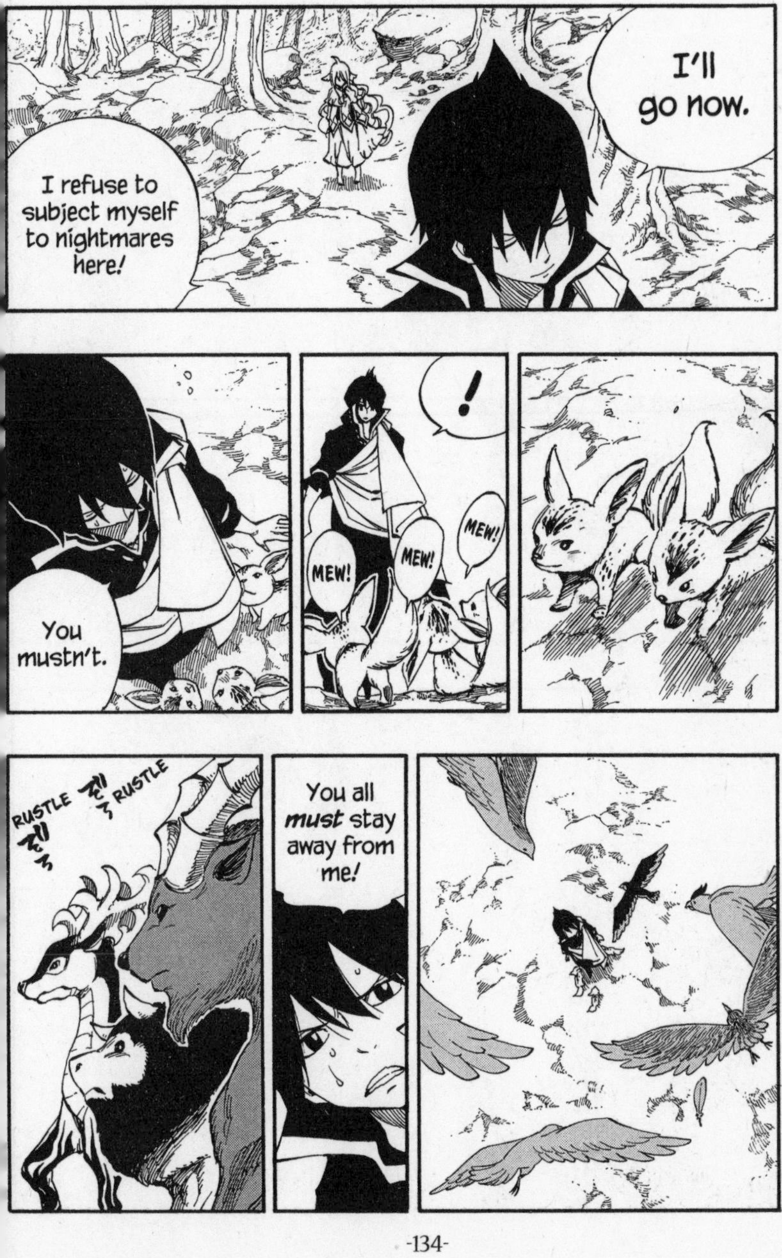
I'll go now.
I refuse to subject myself to nightmares here!
!
MEW!
MEW!
MEW!
You mustn't.
You all *must* stay away from me!
RUSTLE
RUSTLE

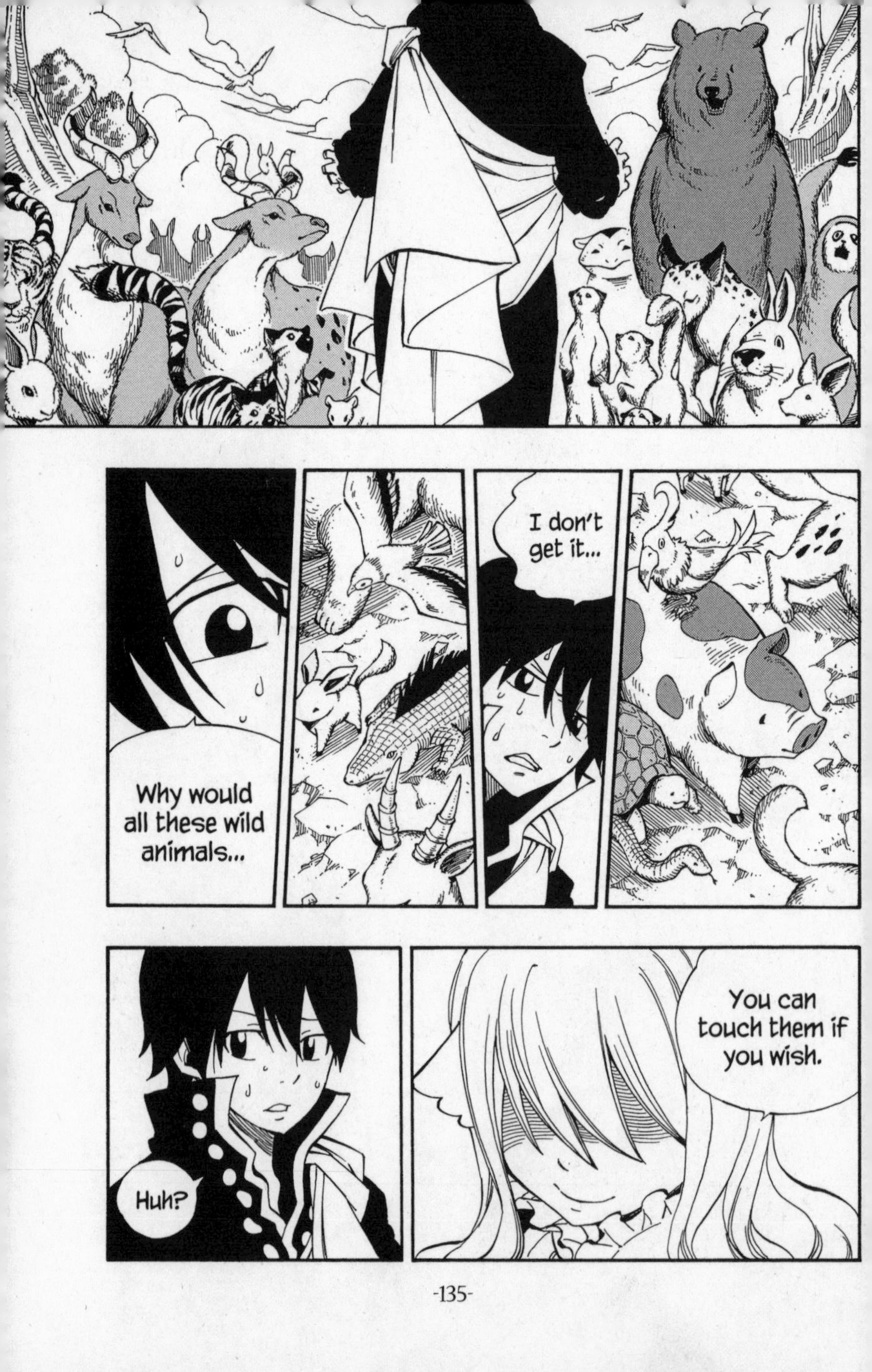
I don't get it...
Why would all these wild animals...
You can touch them if you wish.
Huh?

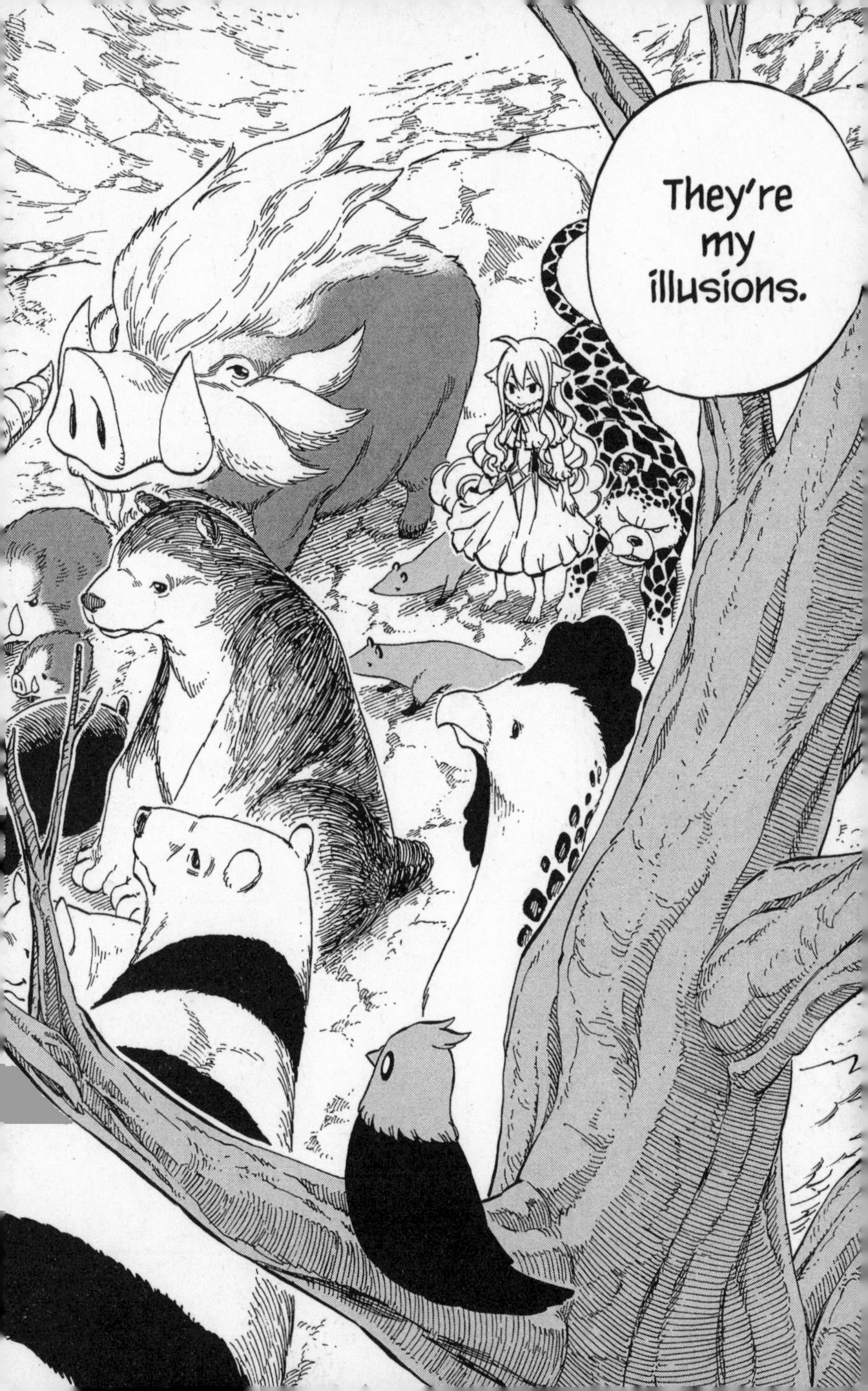
They're my illusions.

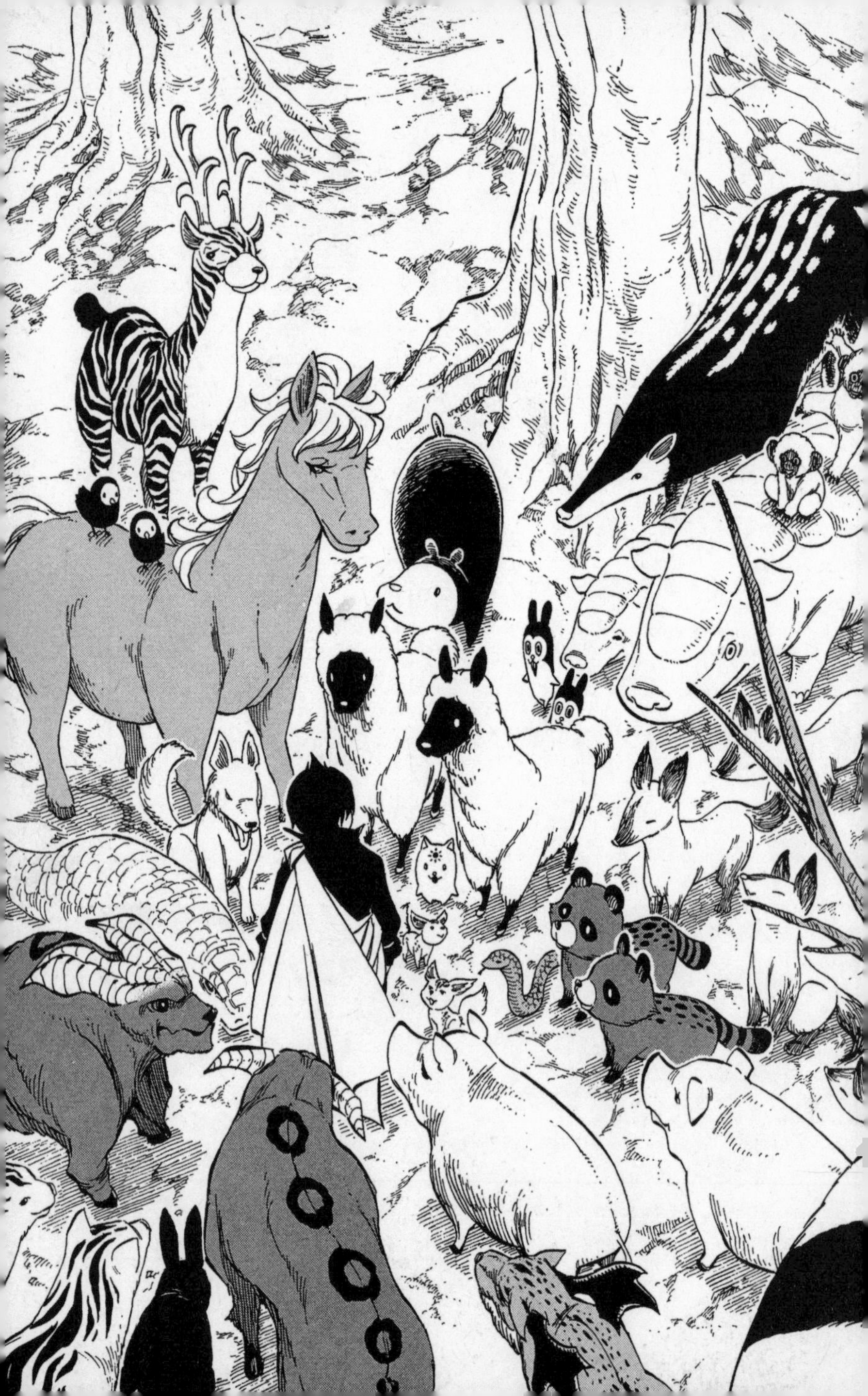

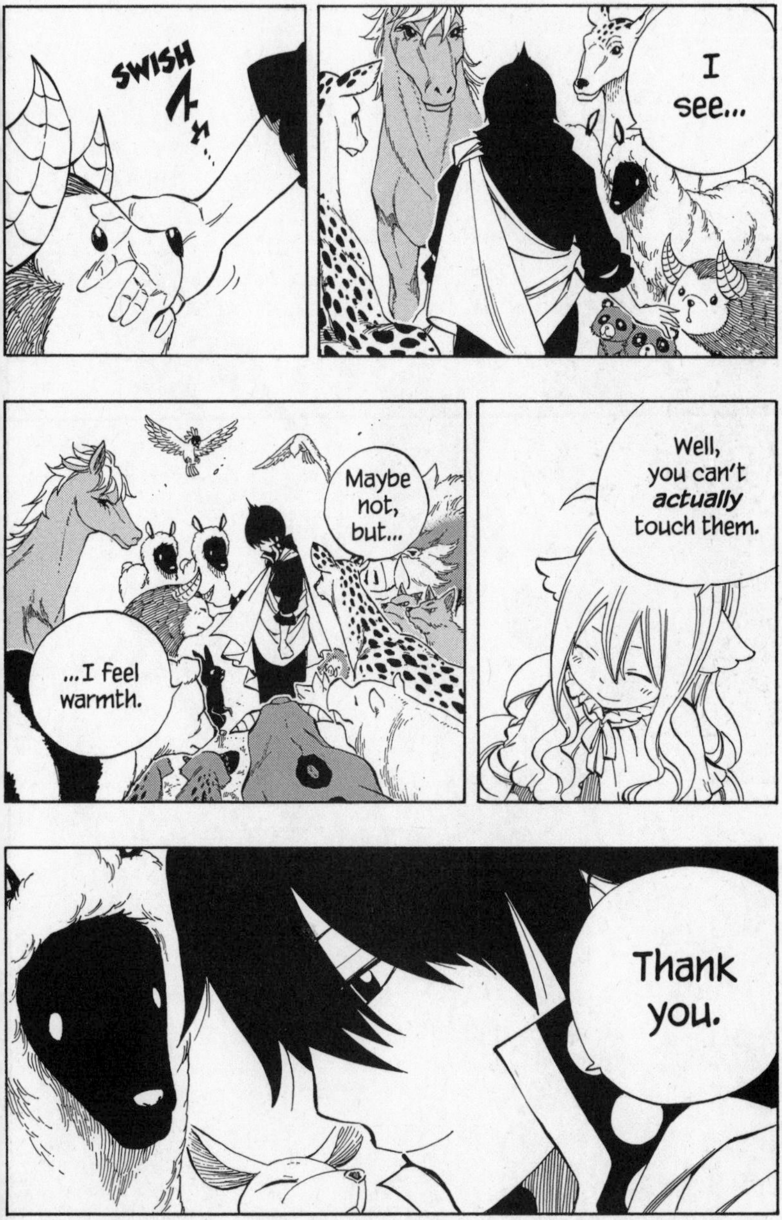
I see...
SWISH
Well, you can't *actually* touch them.
Maybe not, but...
...I feel warmth.
Thank you.

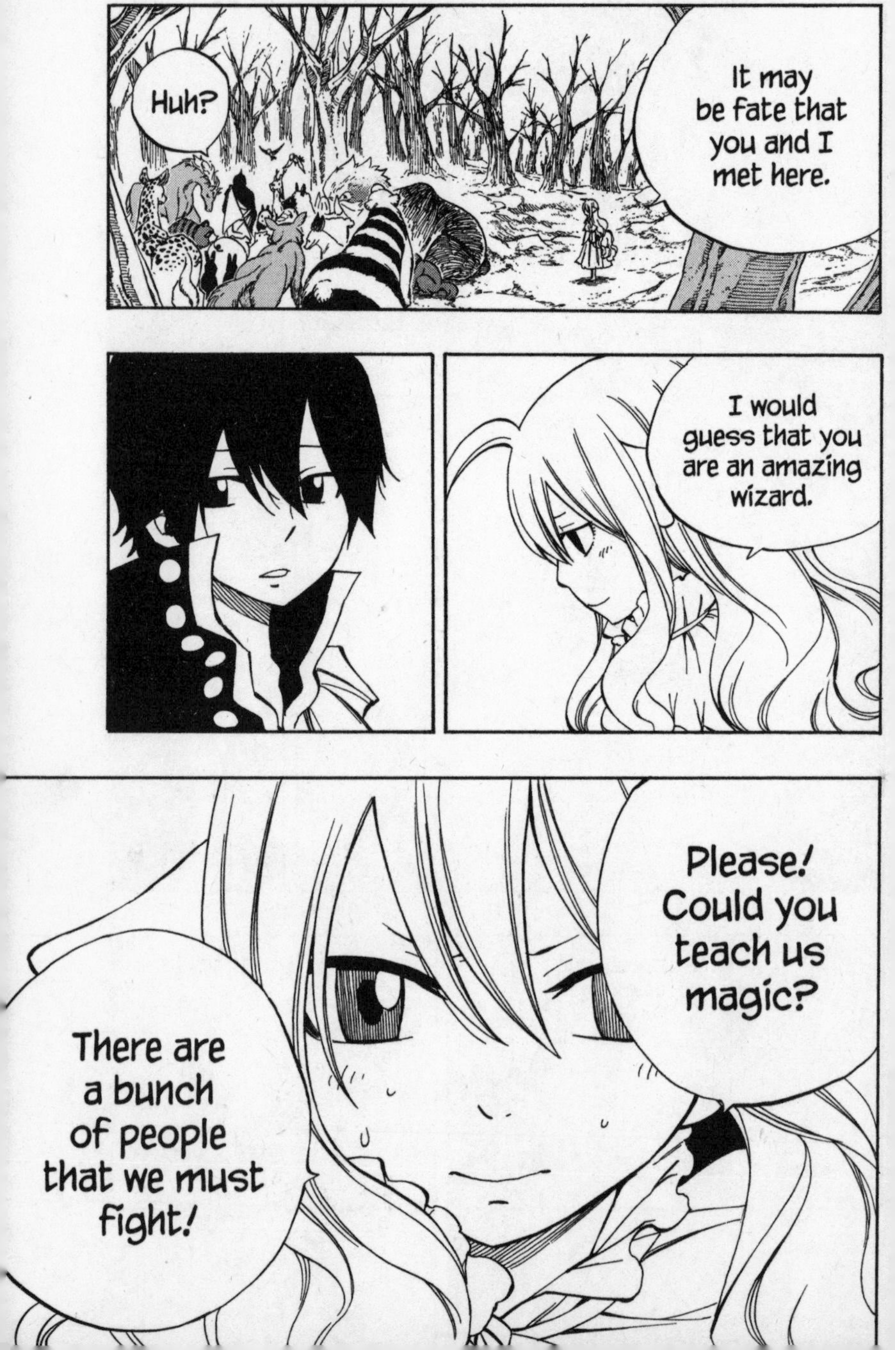
It may be fate that you and I met here.
Huh?
I would guess that you are an amazing wizard.
Please! Could you teach us magic?
There are a bunch of people that we must fight!

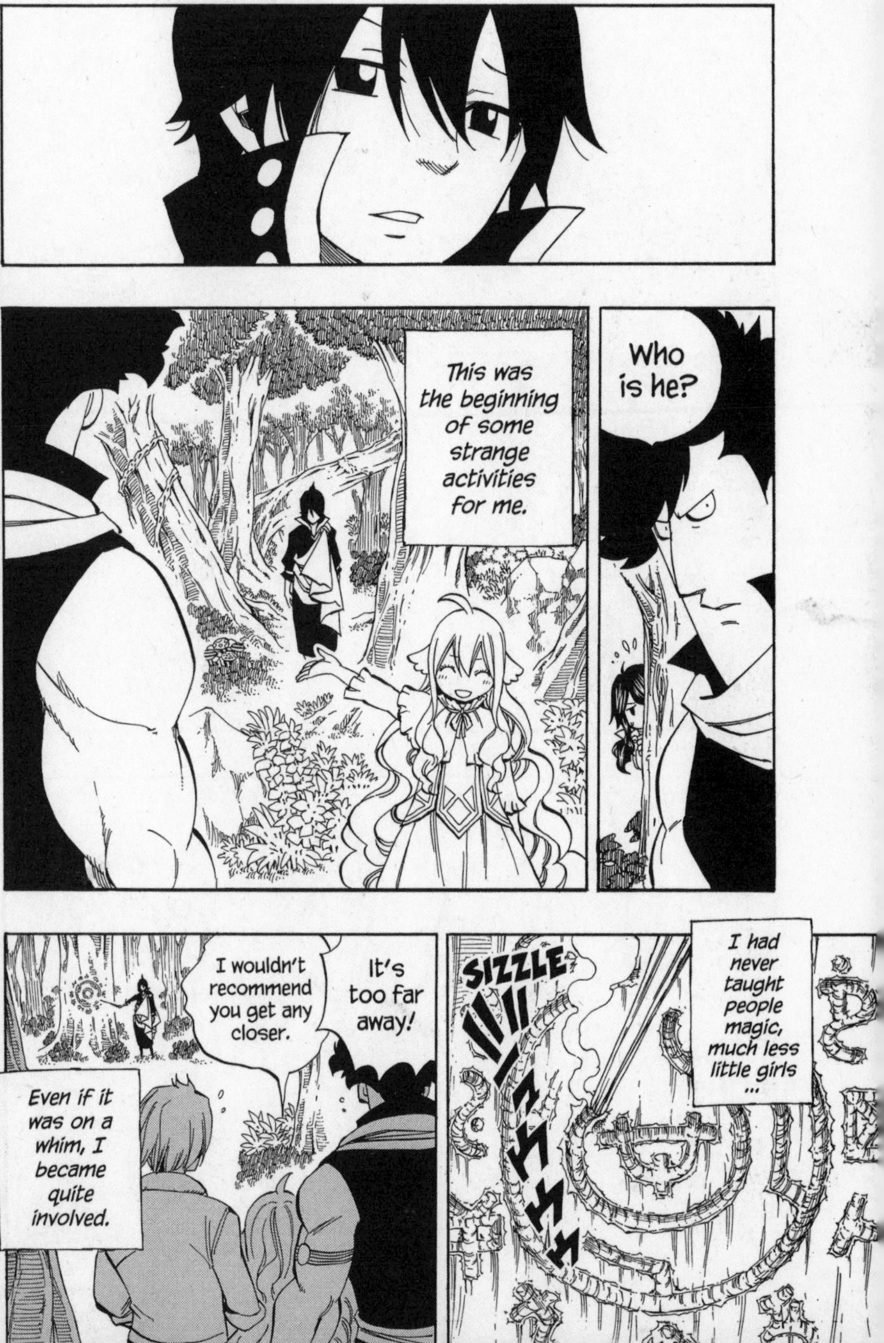
Who is he?
This was the beginning of some strange activities for me.
I had never taught people magic, much less little girls ...
SIZZLE
It's too far away!
I wouldn't recommend you get any closer.
Even if it was on a whim, I became quite involved.

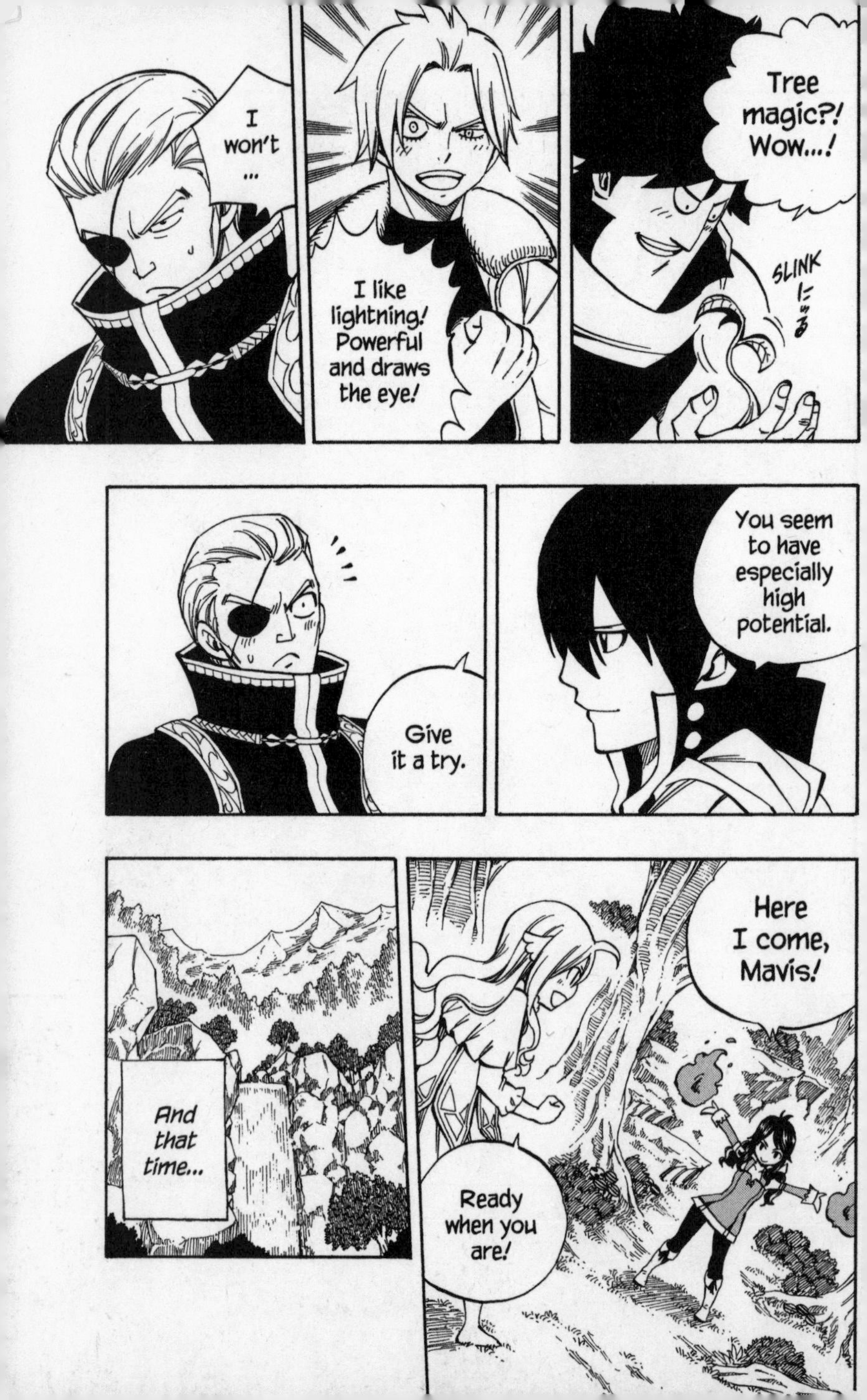
Tree magic?! Wow...!
SLINK
I like lightning! Powerful and draws the eye!
I won't ...
You seem to have especially high potential.
Give it a try.
Here I come, Mavis!
Ready when you are!
And that time...

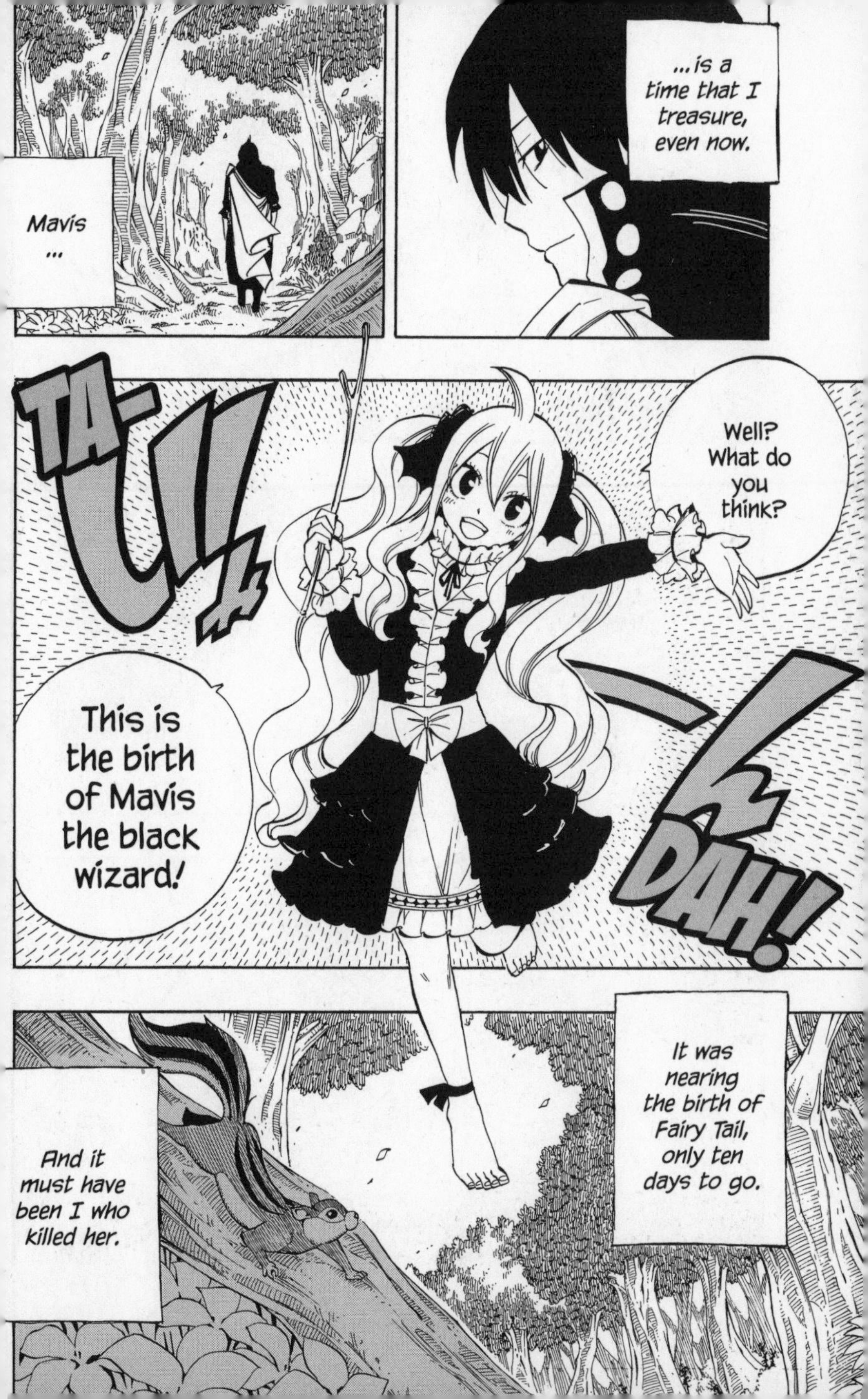
...is a time that I treasure, even now.
Mavis ...
Well? What do you think?
TA-
DAH!
This is the birth of Mavis the black wizard!
It was nearing the birth of Fairy Tail, only ten days to go.
And it must have been I who killed her.

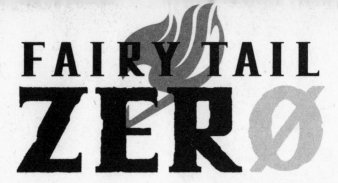

FAIRY TAIL ZERØ

Chapter 8: Is Magnolia Burning Down?

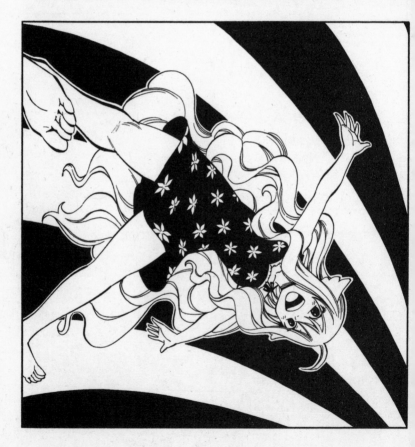

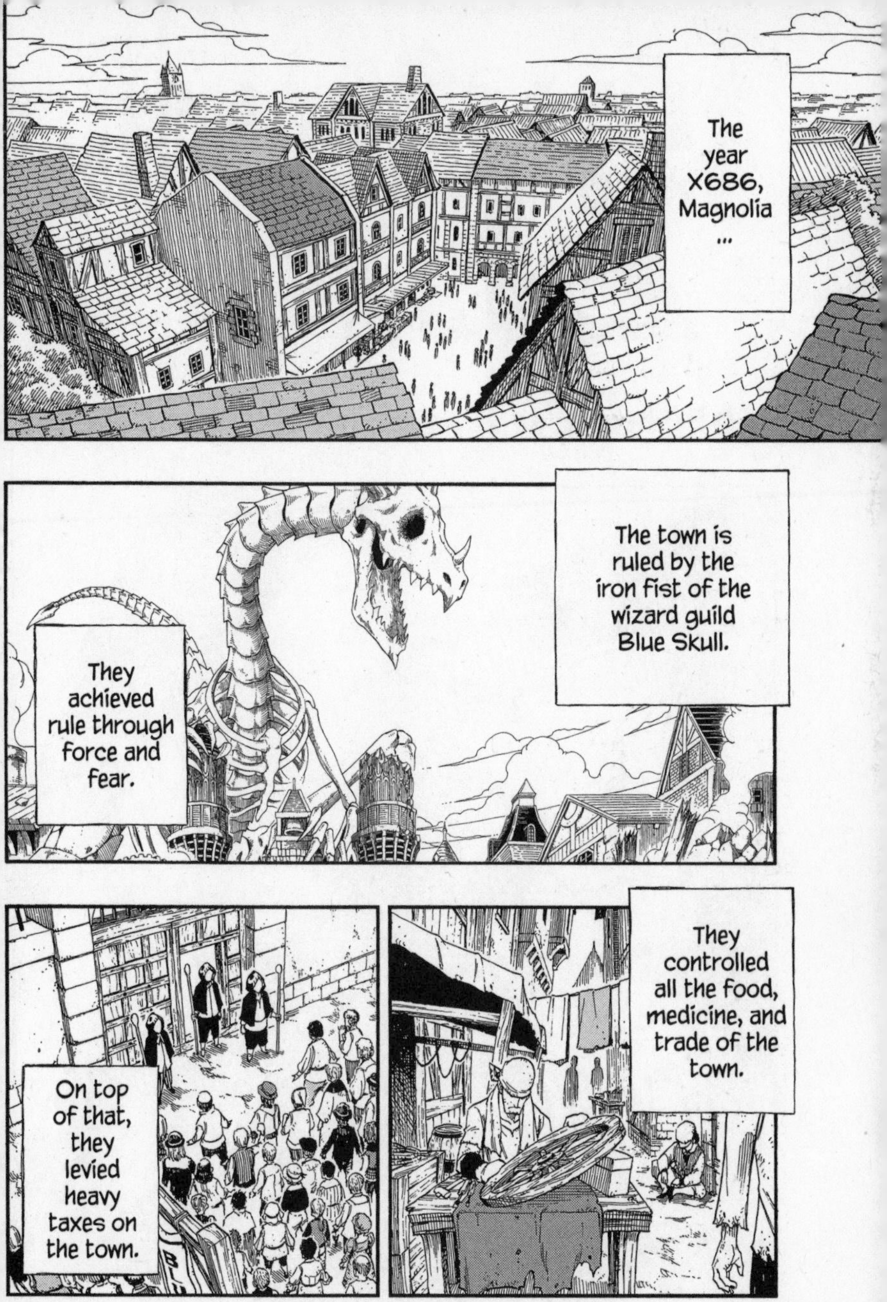
The year X686, Magnolia ...
The town is ruled by the iron fist of the wizard guild Blue Skull.
They achieved rule through force and fear.
They controlled all the food, medicine, and trade of the town.
On top of that, they levied heavy taxes on the town.

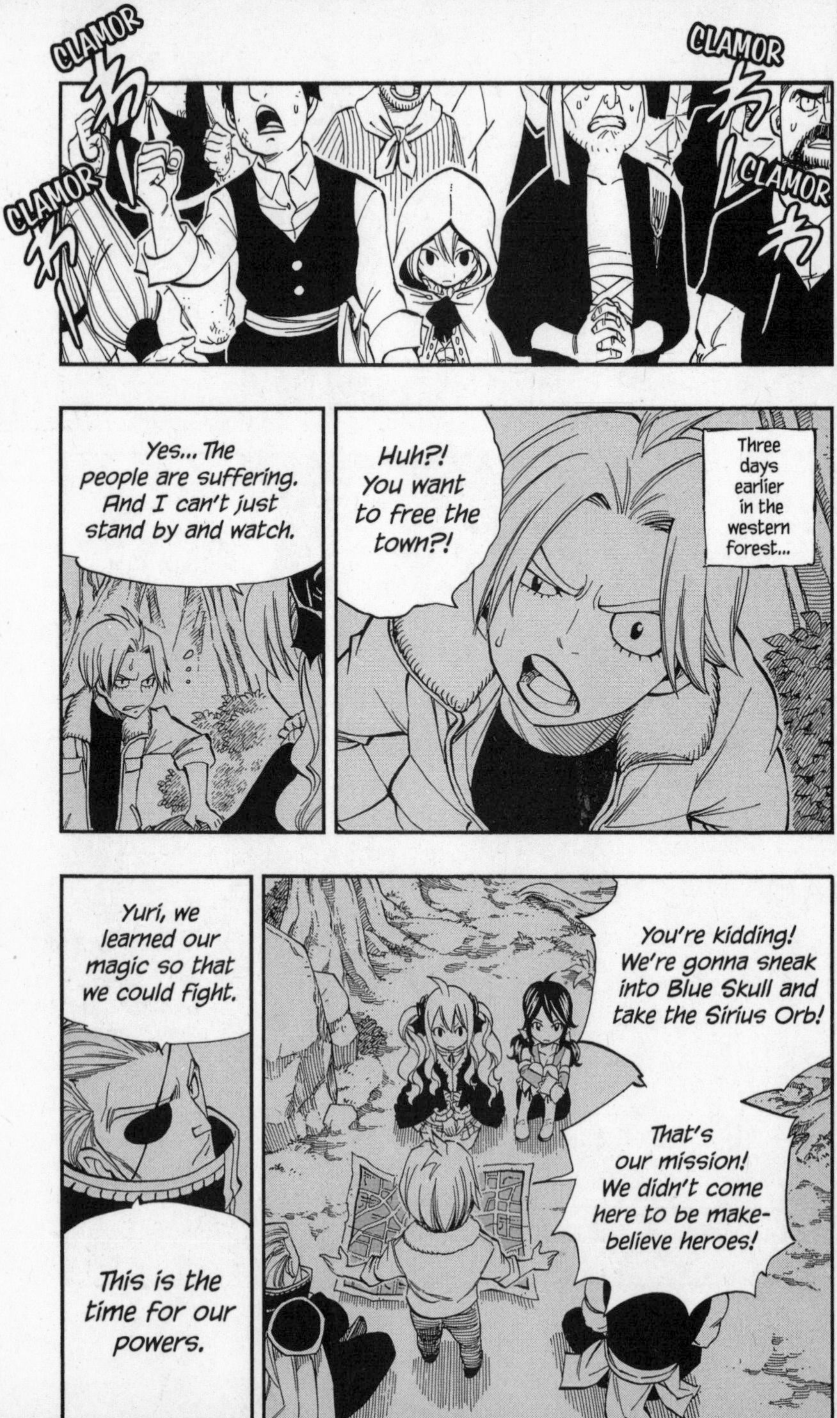
CLAMOR
CLAMOR
CLAMOR
CLAMOR
Three days earlier in the western forest...
Huh?! You want to free the town?!
Yes... The people are suffering. And I can't just stand by and watch.
You're kidding! We're gonna sneak into Blue Skull and take the Sirius Orb!
That's our mission! We didn't come here to be make-believe heroes!
Yuri, we learned our magic so that we could fight.
This is the time for our powers.

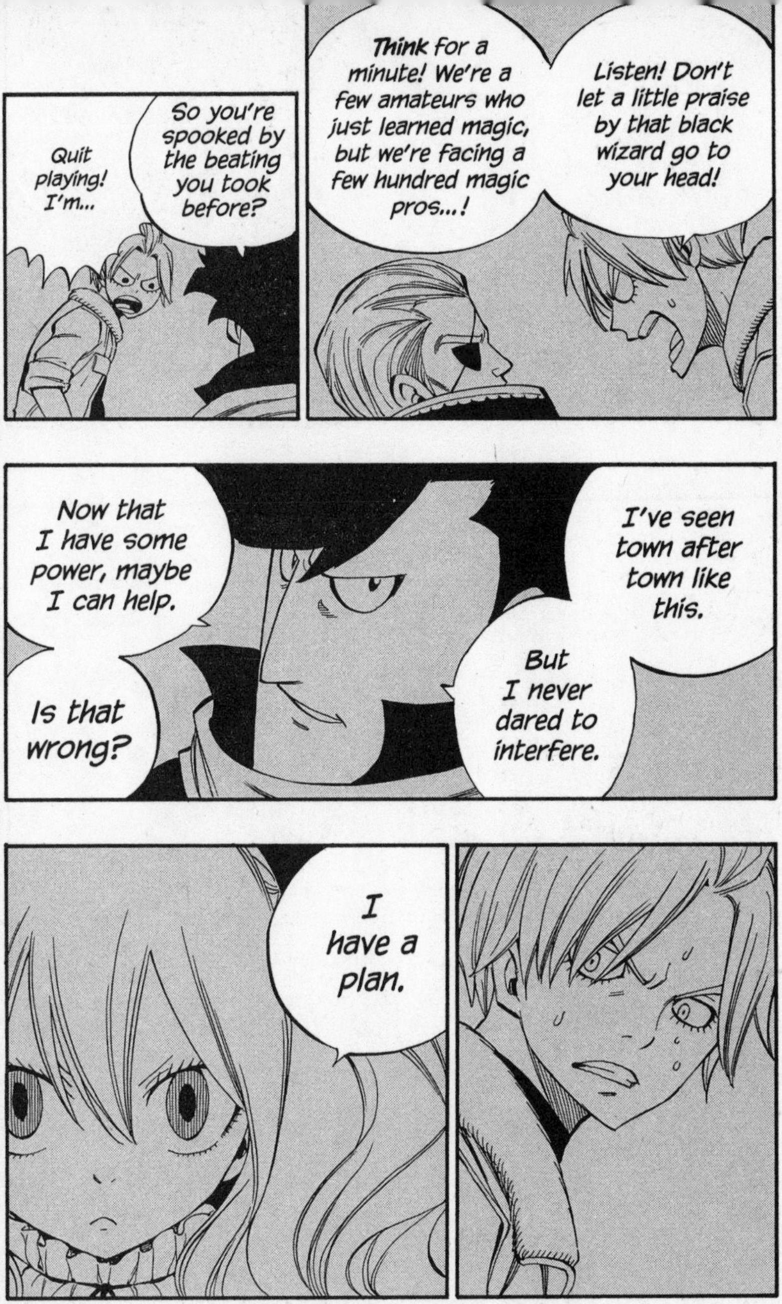
Listen! Don't let a little praise by that black wizard go to your head!
Think for a minute! We're a few amateurs who just learned magic, but we're facing a few hundred magic pros...!
So you're spooked by the beating you took before?
Quit playing! I'm...
I've seen town after town like this.
But I never dared to interfere.
Now that I have some power, maybe I can help.
Is that wrong?
I have a plan.

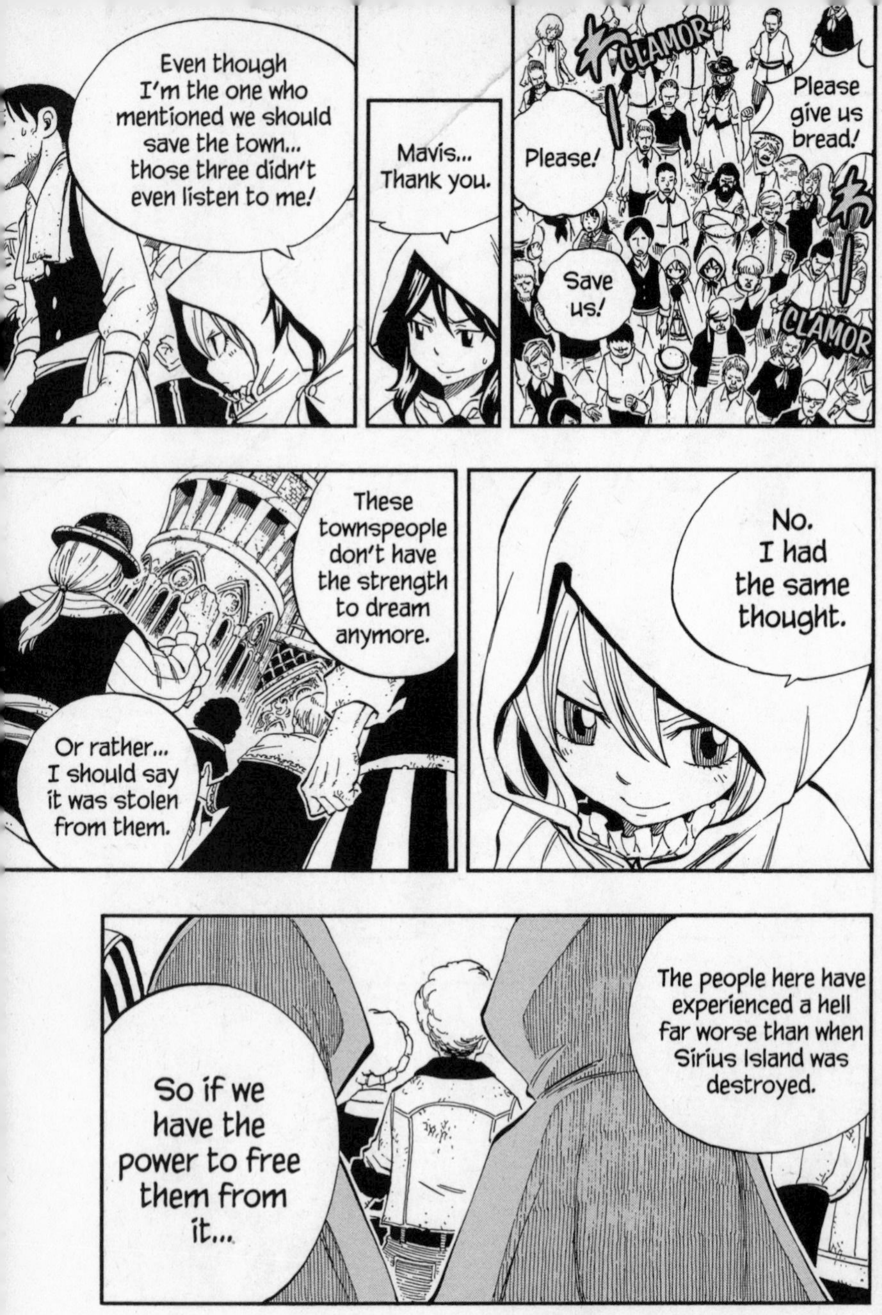
CLAMOR
Please give us bread!
Please!
Save us!
CLAMOR
Mavis... Thank you.
Even though I'm the one who mentioned we should save the town... those three didn't even listen to me!
No. I had the same thought.
These townspeople don't have the strength to dream anymore.
Or rather... I should say it was stolen from them.
The people here have experienced a hell far worse than when Sirius Island was destroyed.
So if we have the power to free them from it...

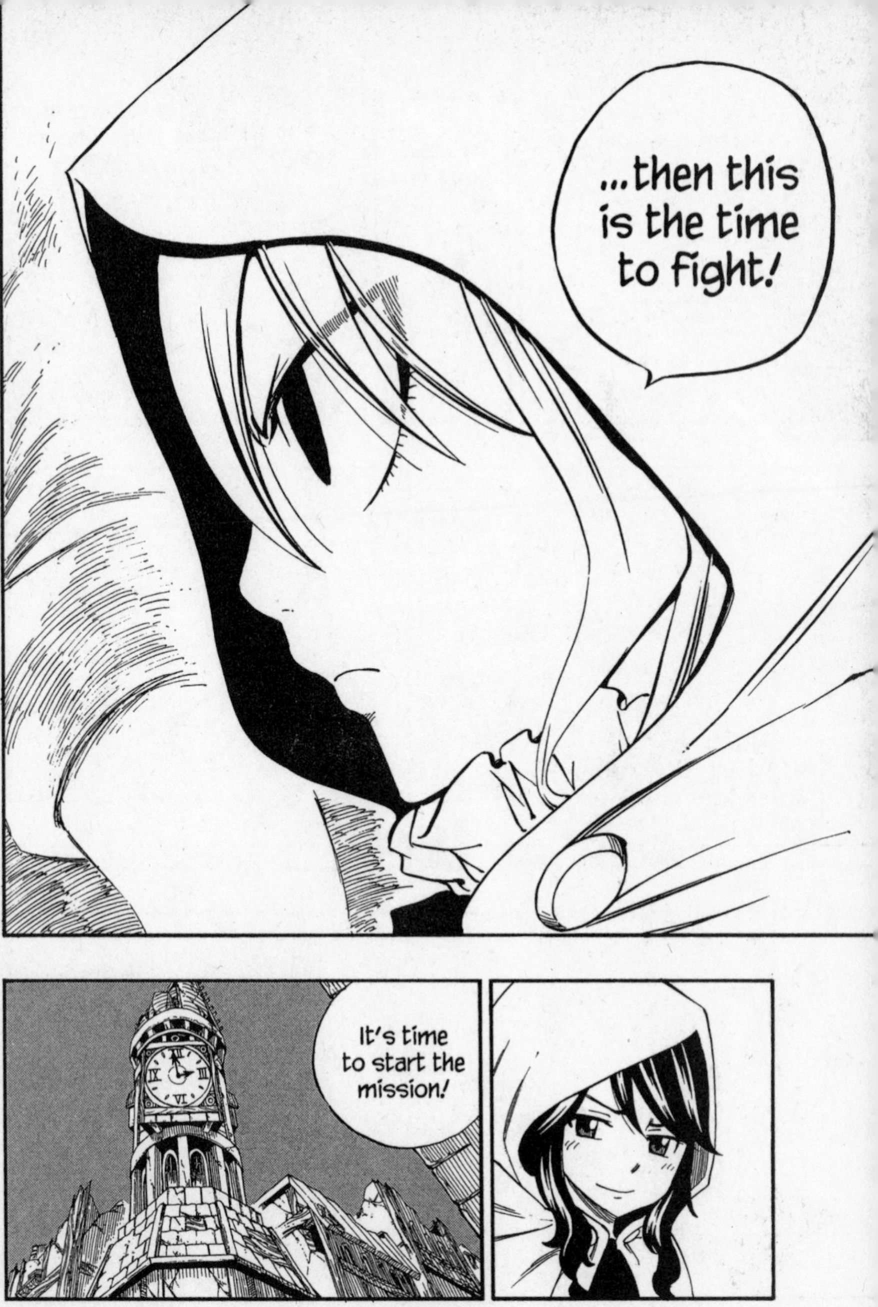
...then this is the time to fight!
It's time to start the mission!

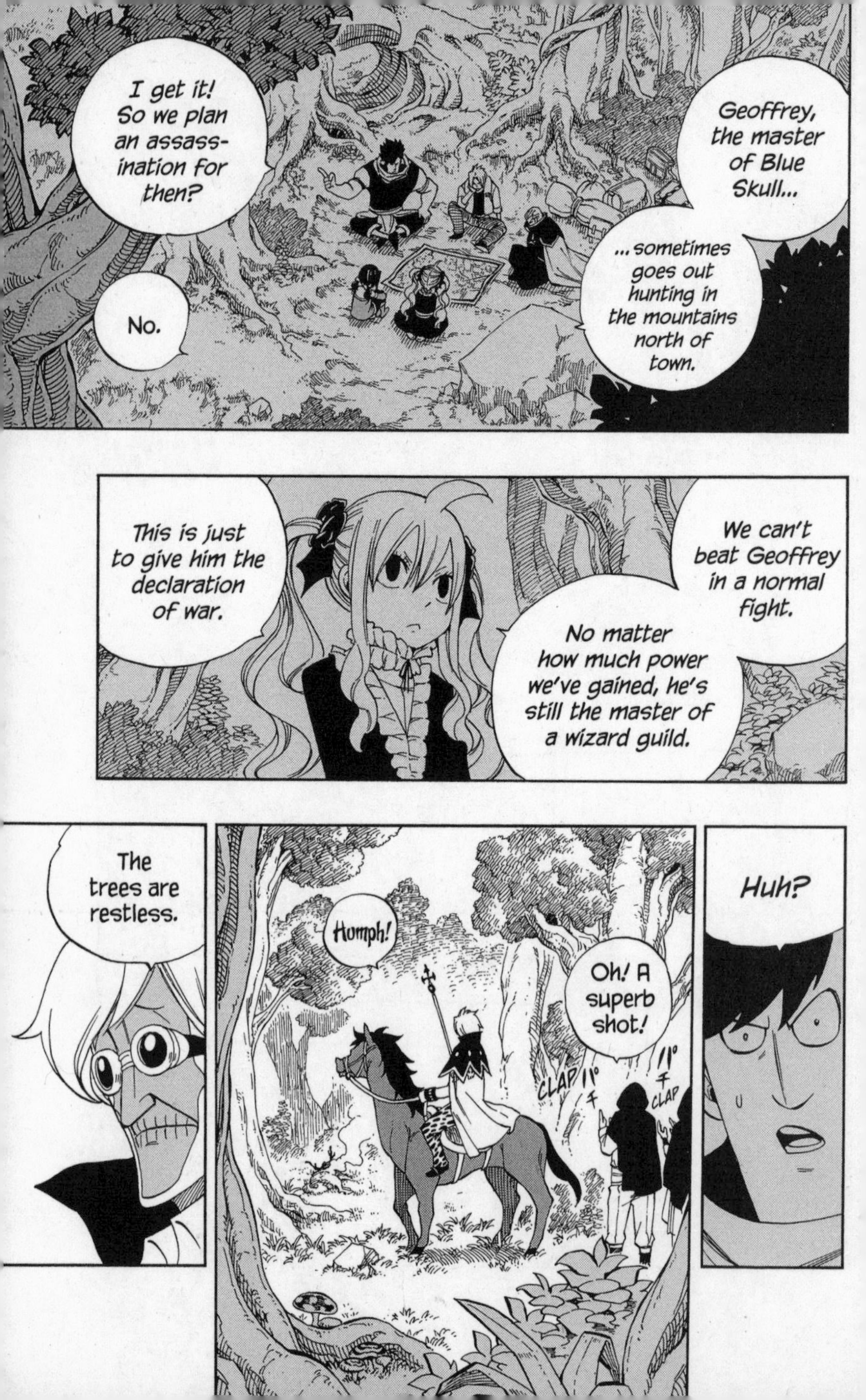
Geoffrey, the master of Blue Skull...
...sometimes goes out hunting in the mountains north of town.
I get it! So we plan an assassination for then?
No.
We can't beat Geoffrey in a normal fight.
No matter how much power we've gained, he's still the master of a wizard guild.
This is just to give him the declaration of war.
Huh?
Oh! A superb shot!
パチ CLAP
CLAP パチ
Humph!
The trees are restless.

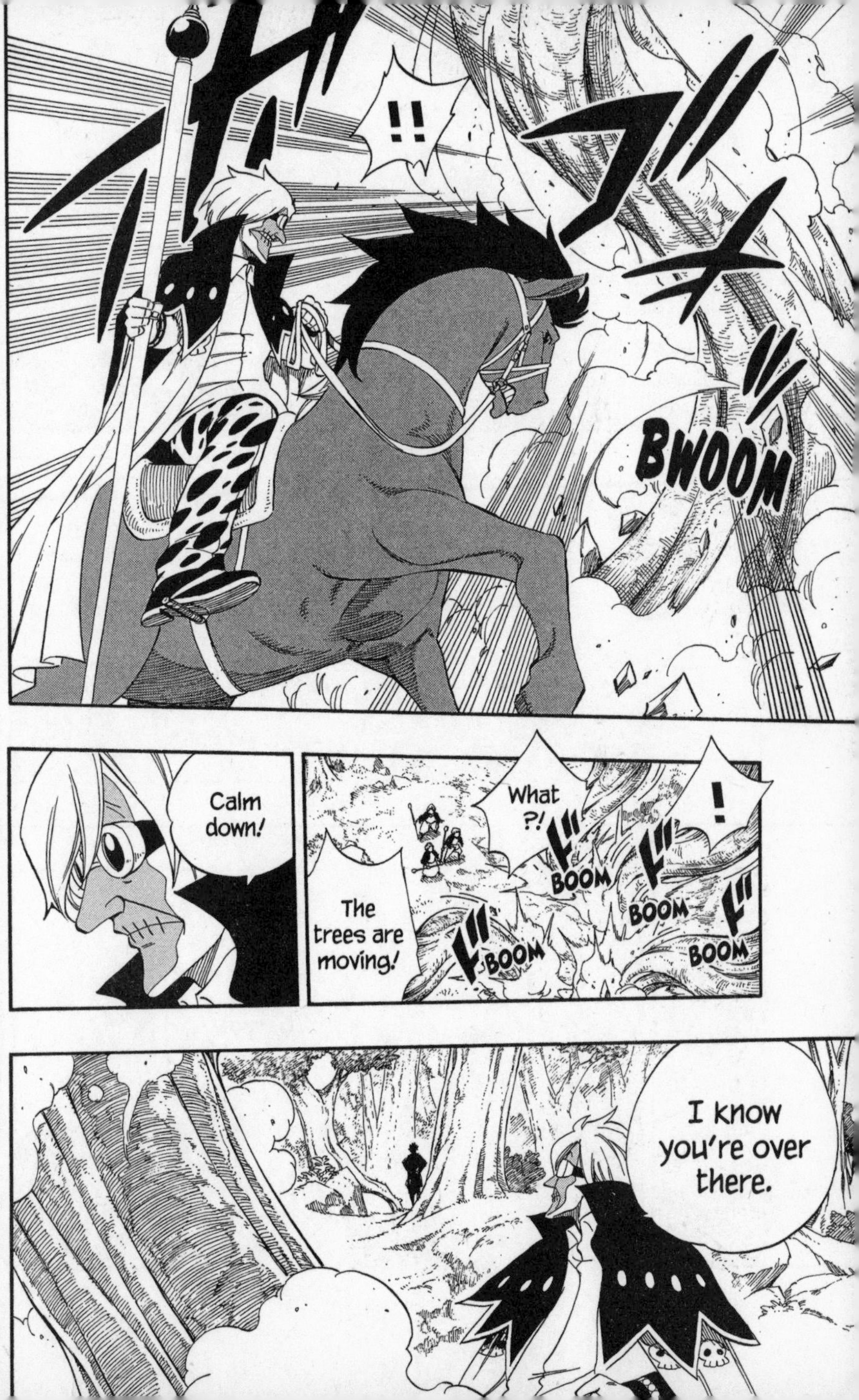
!!
BWOOM
!
What ?!
The trees are moving!
BOOM
BOOM
BOOM
BOOM
Calm down!
I know you're over there.

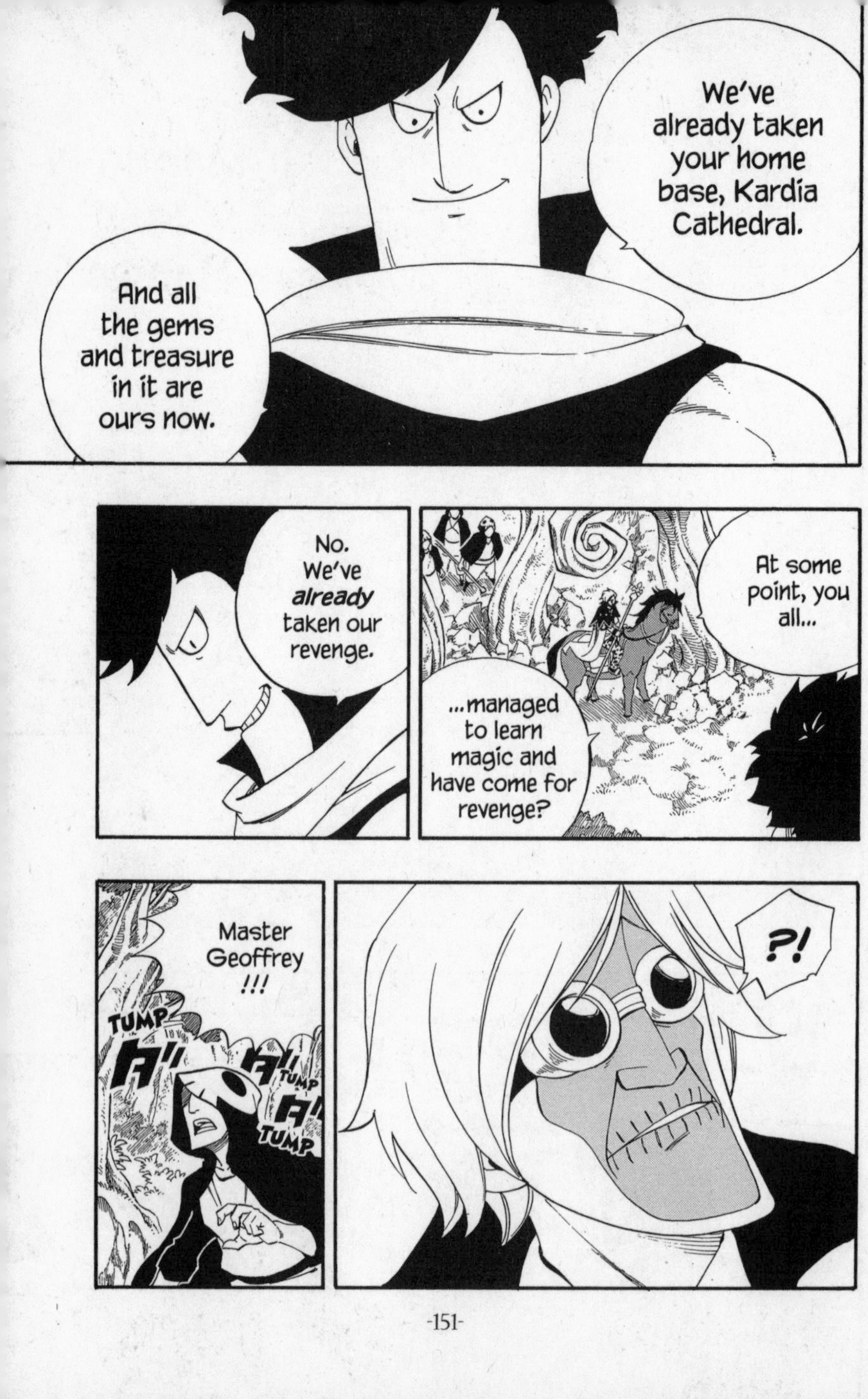
We've already taken your home base, Kardia Cathedral.
And all the gems and treasure in it are ours now.
At some point, you all...
...managed to learn magic and have come for revenge?
No. We've *already* taken our revenge.
?!
Master Geoffrey !!!
TUMP
TUMP
TUMP

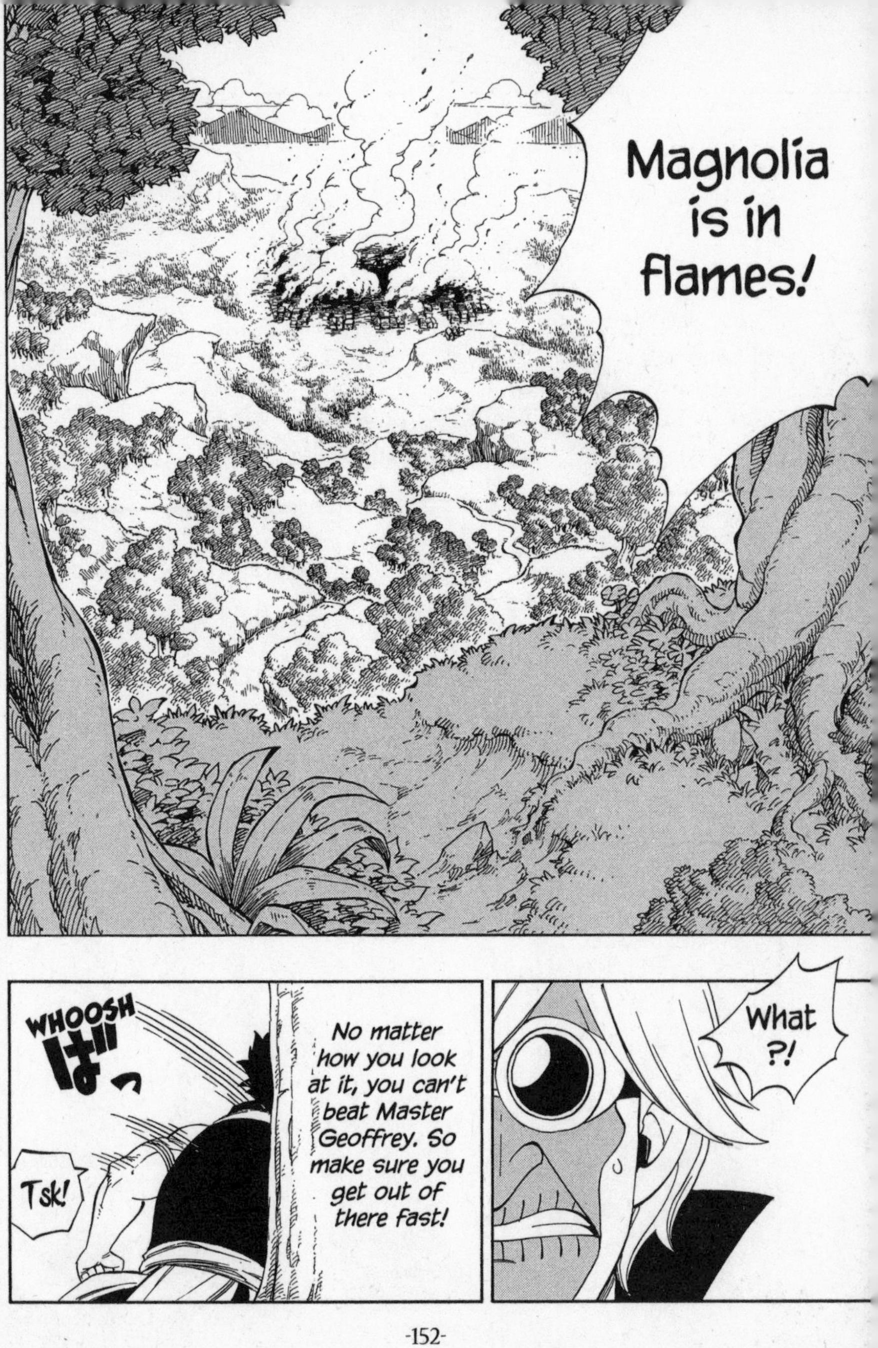
Magnolia is in flames!
What ?!
No matter how you look at it, you can't beat Master Geoffrey. So make sure you get out of there fast!
WHOOSH
はっ
Tsk!

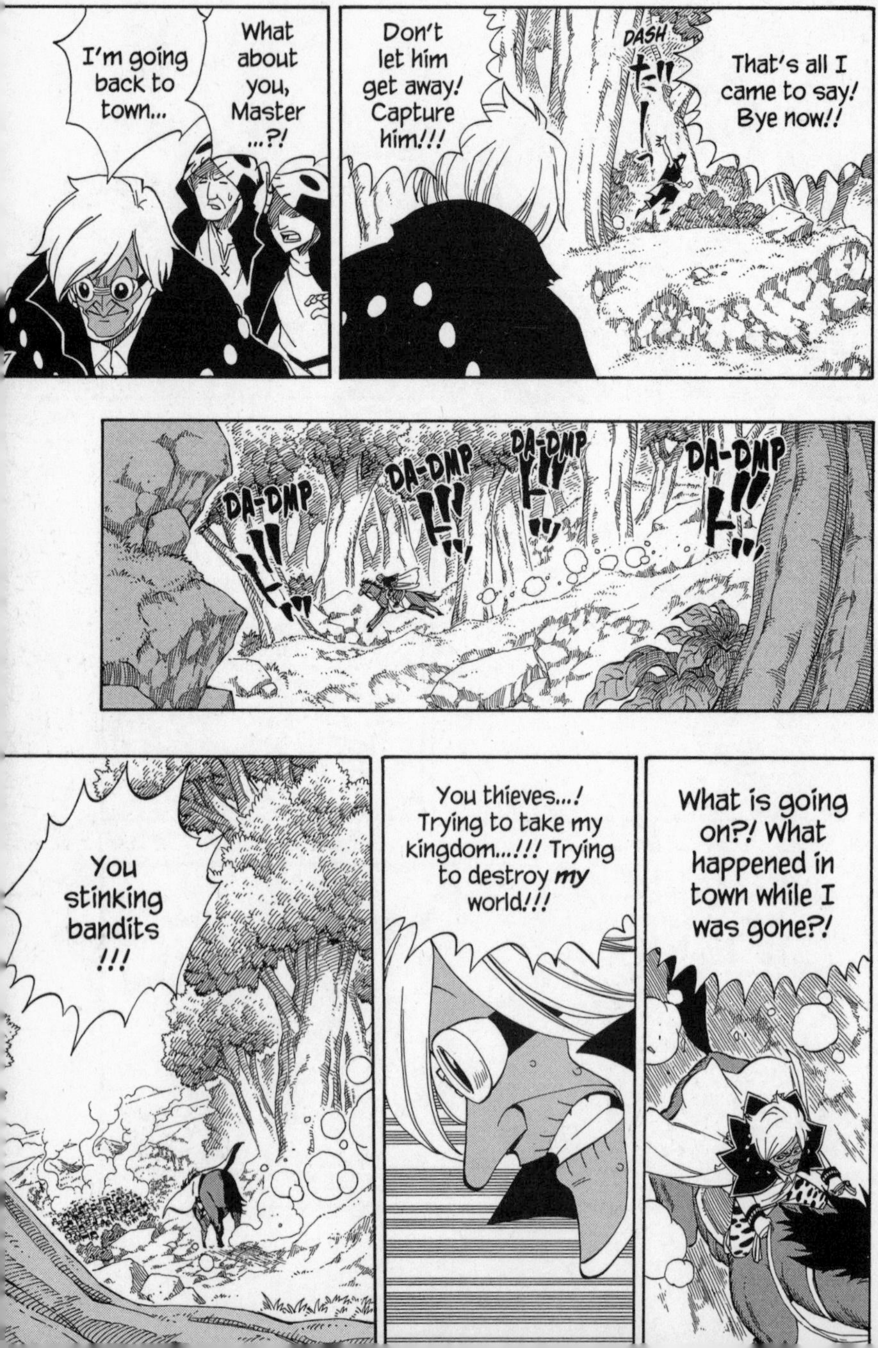

That's all I came to say! Bye now!!
DASH
Don't let him get away! Capture him!!!
What about you, Master ...?!
I'm going back to town...
DA-DMP
DA-DMP
DA-DMP
DA-DMP
What is going on?! What happened in town while I was gone?!
You thieves...! Trying to take my kingdom...!!! Trying to destroy *my* world!!!
You stinking bandits !!!

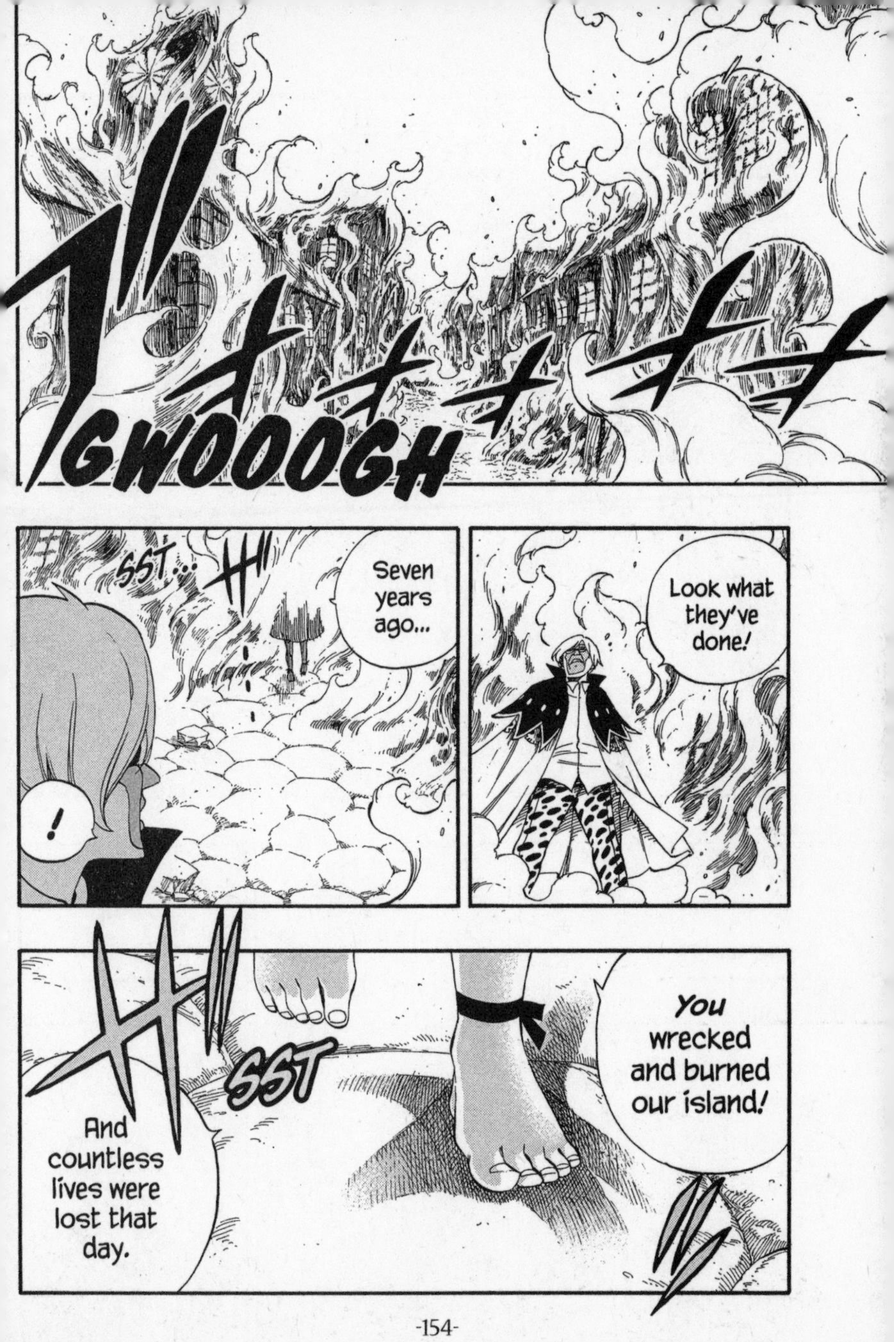
GWOOOGH
Look what they've done!
SST...
Seven years ago...
!
You wrecked and burned our island!
SST
And countless lives were lost that day.

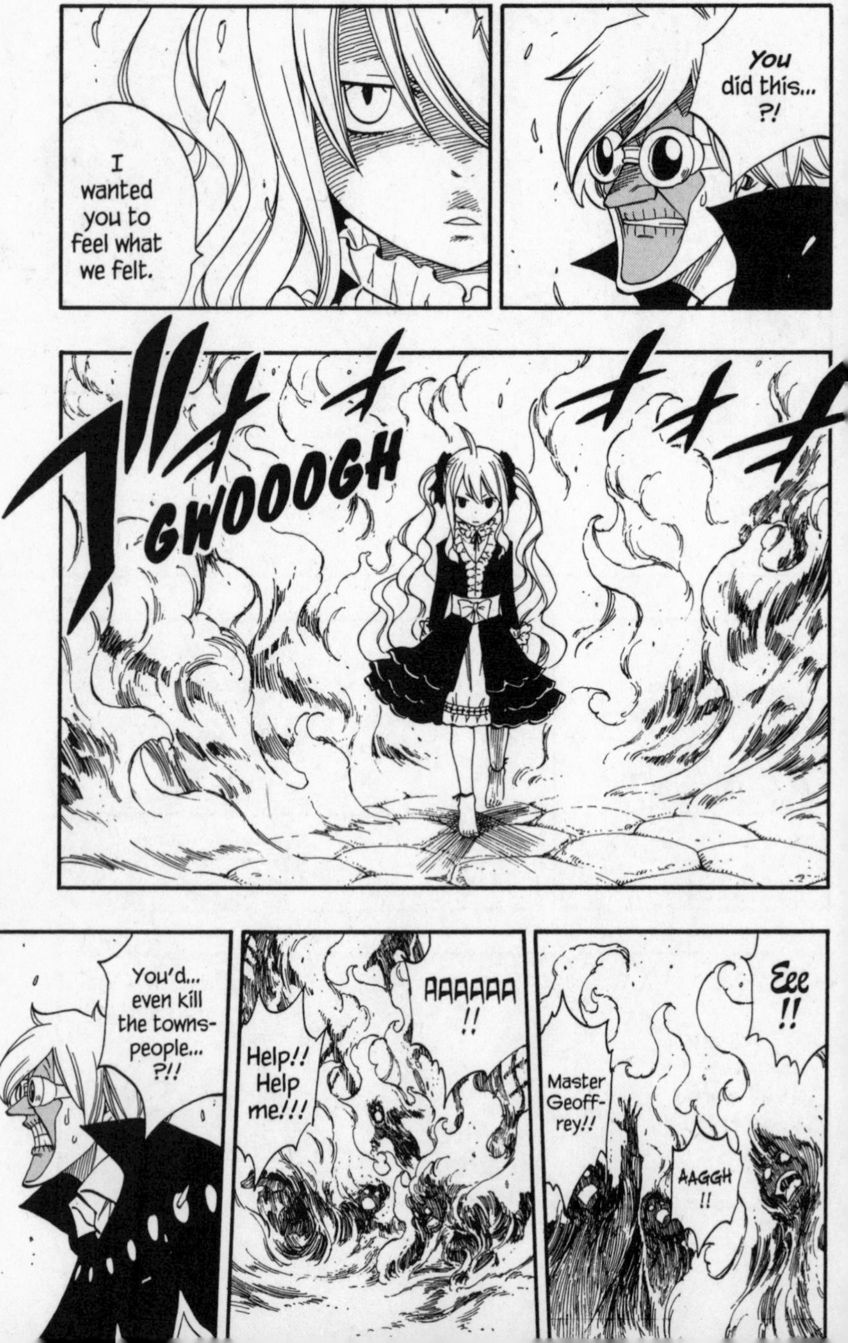
You did this... ?!
I wanted you to feel what we felt.
GWOOOGH
Eee !!
Master Geoffrey!!
AAGGH !!
AAAAAA !!
Help!! Help me!!!
You'd... even kill the townspeople... ?!!

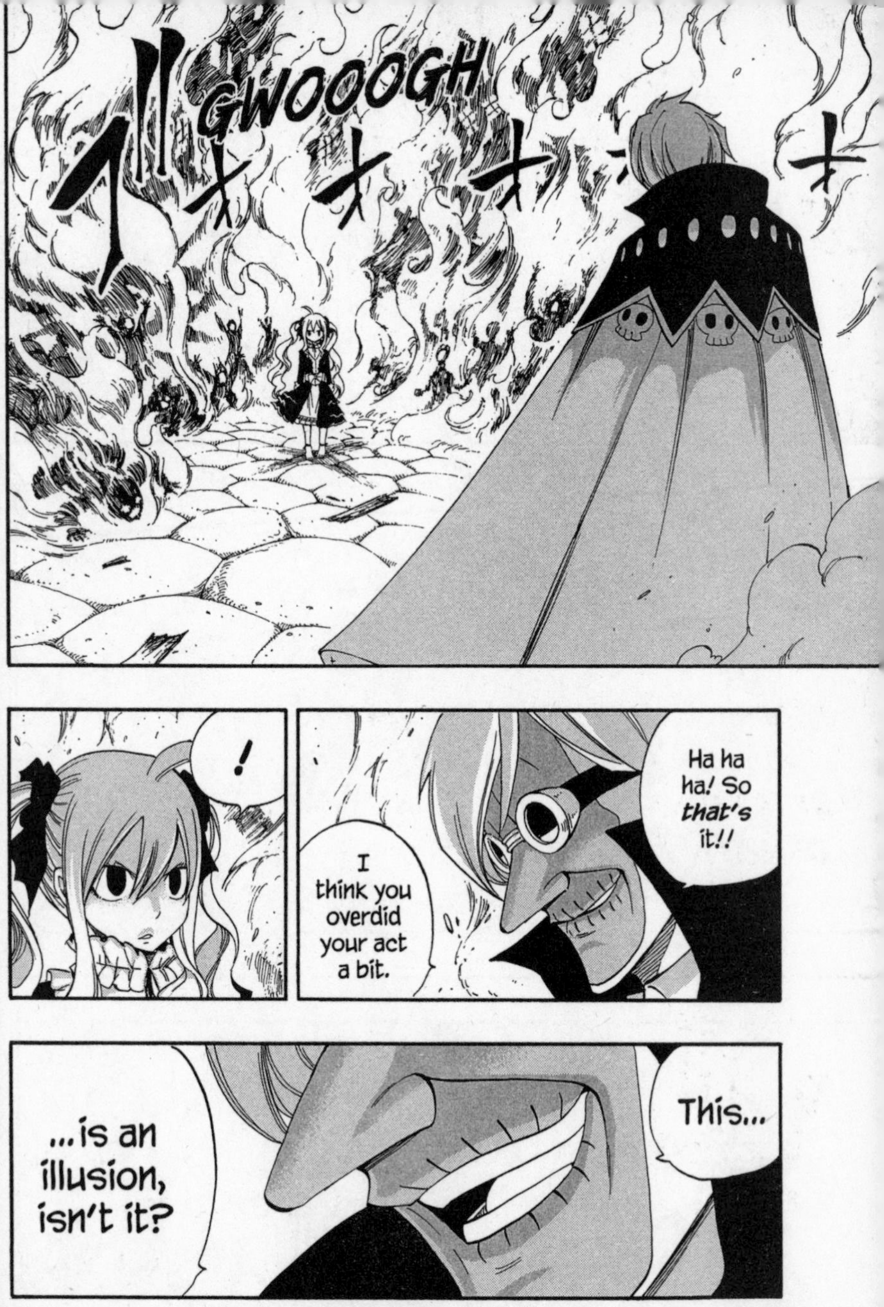
GWOOOGH
Ha ha ha! So *that's* it!!
I think you overdid your act a bit.
!
This...
...is an illusion, isn't it?

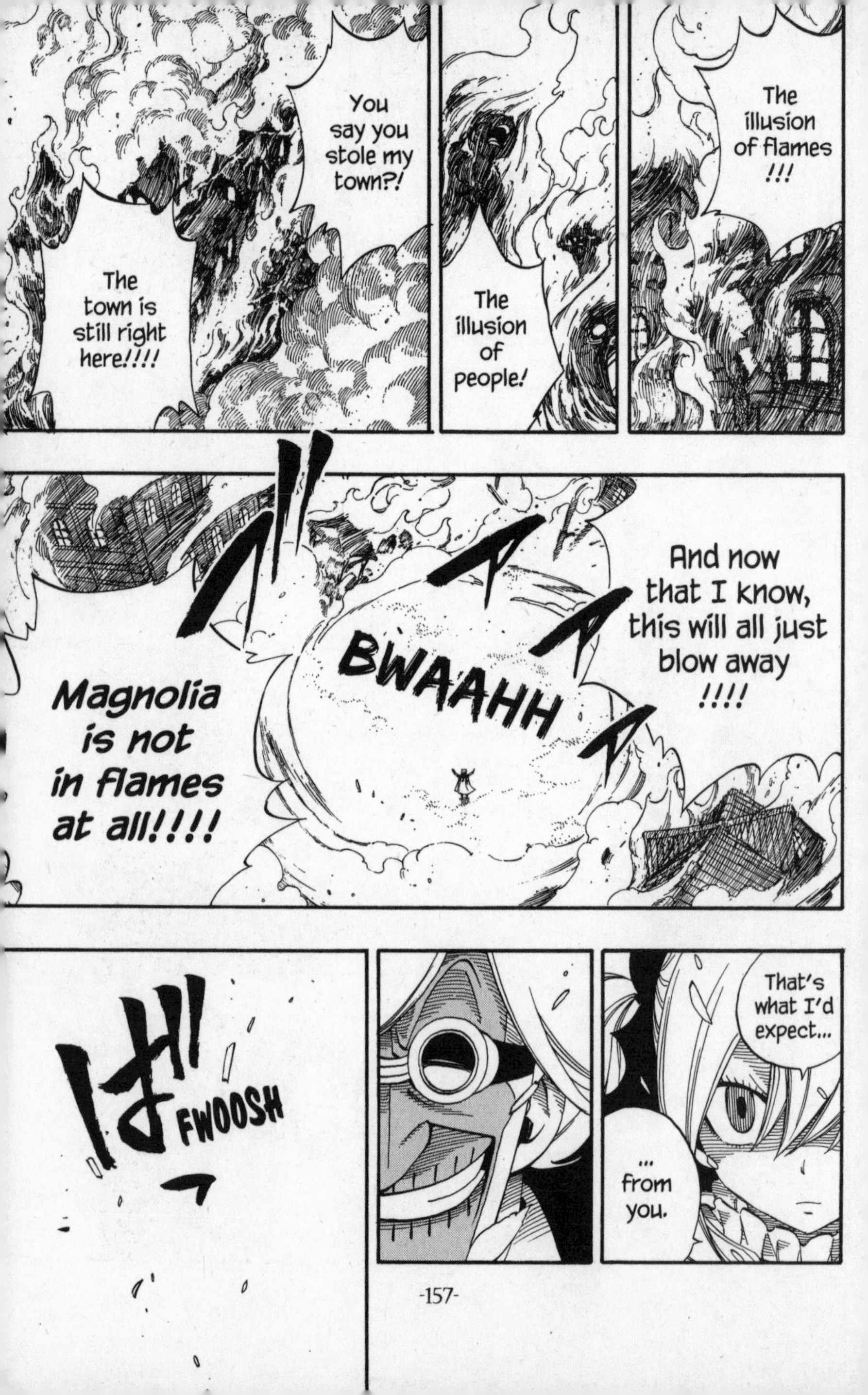
The illusion of flames!!!
The illusion of people!
You say you stole my town?!
The town is still right here!!!!
And now that I know, this will all just blow away!!!!
BWAAHH
Magnolia is not in flames at all!!!!
That's what I'd expect...
...from you.
FWOOSH

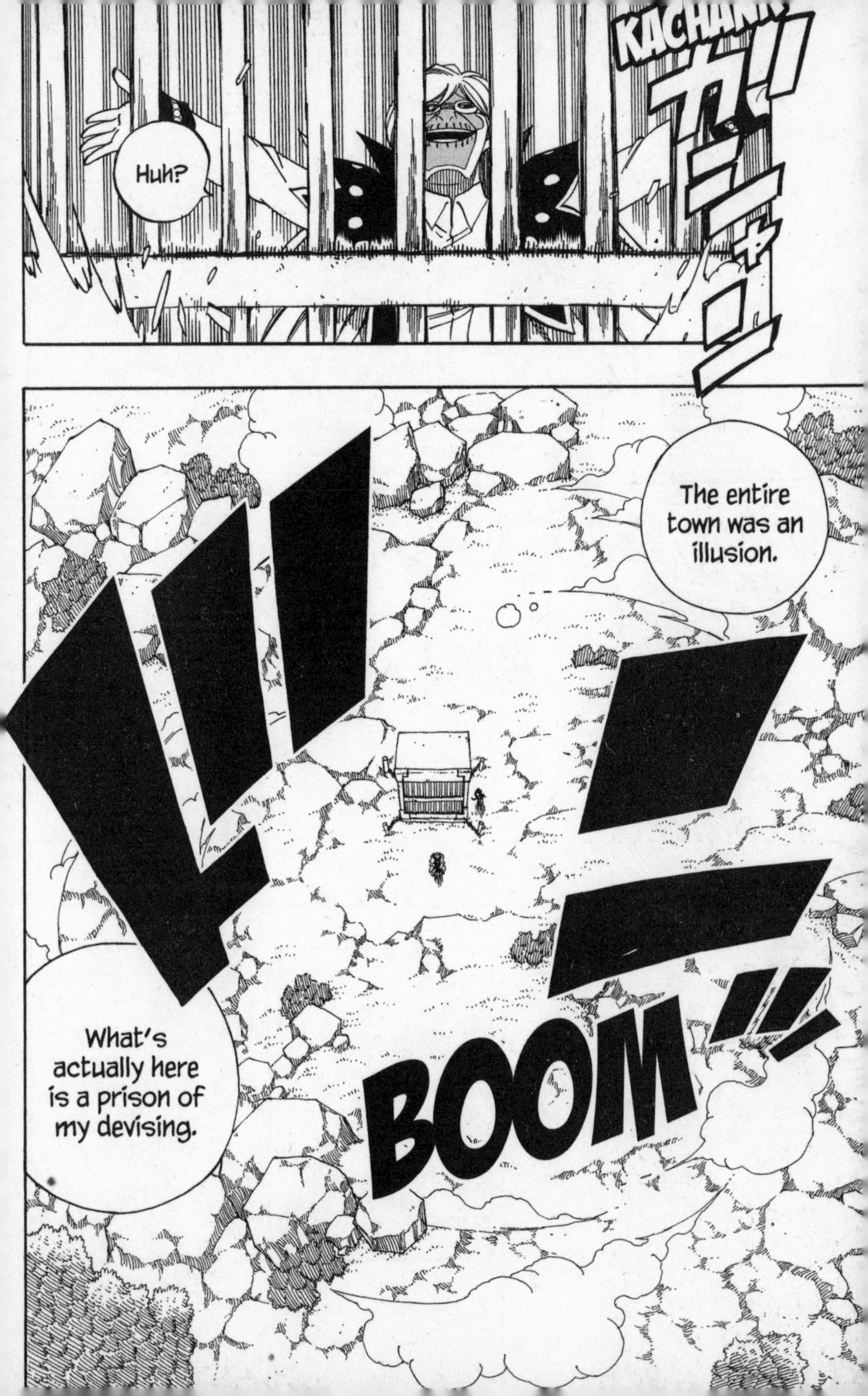
KACHANK
Huh?
The entire town was an illusion.
BOOM!!
What's actually here is a prison of my devising.

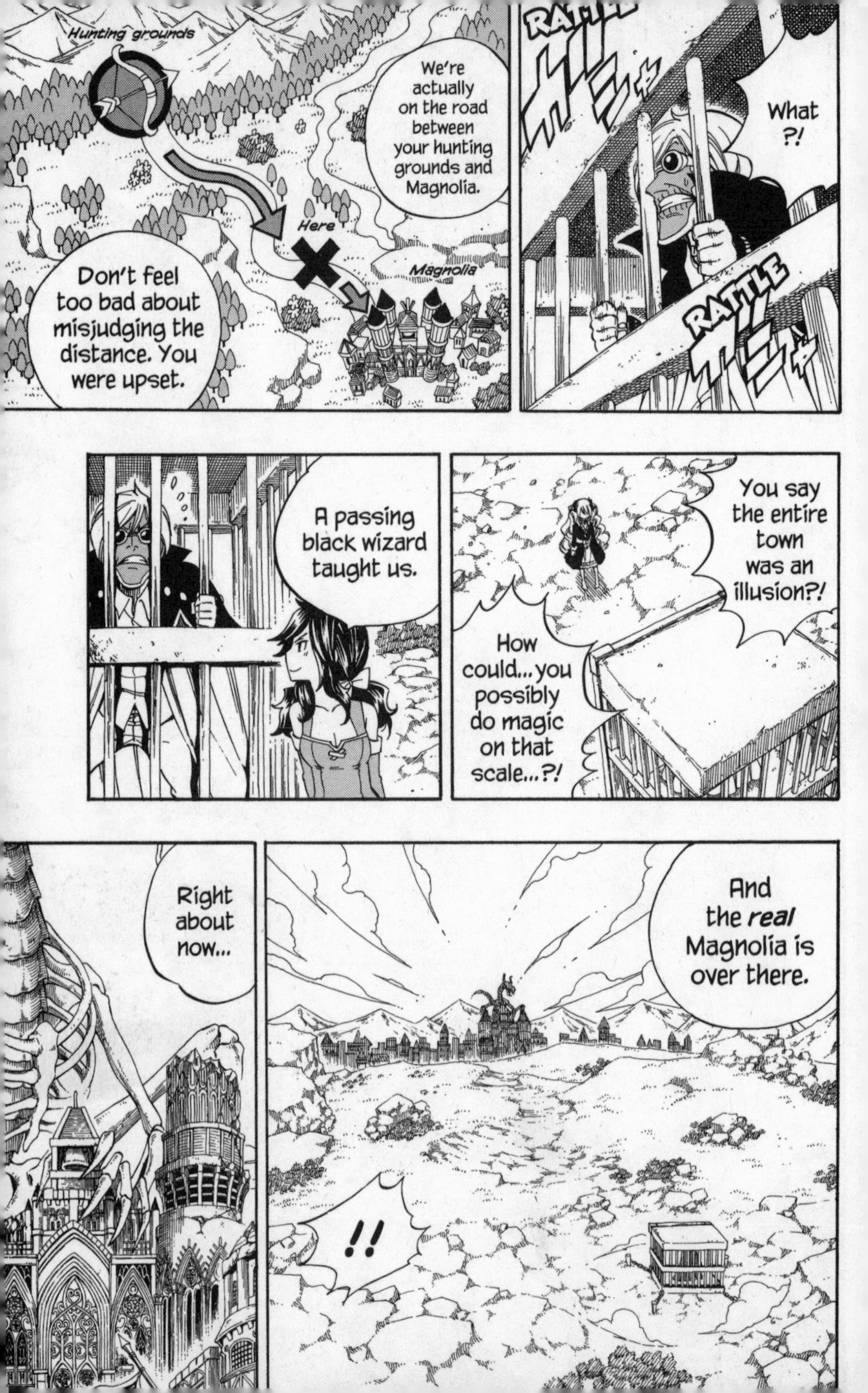
RATTLE
What ?!
RATTLE
We're actually on the road between your hunting grounds and Magnolia.
Hunting grounds
Here
Magnolia
Don't feel too bad about misjudging the distance. You were upset.
You say the entire town was an illusion?!
How could...you possibly do magic on that scale...?!
A passing black wizard taught us.
And the *real* Magnolia is over there.
!!
Right about now...

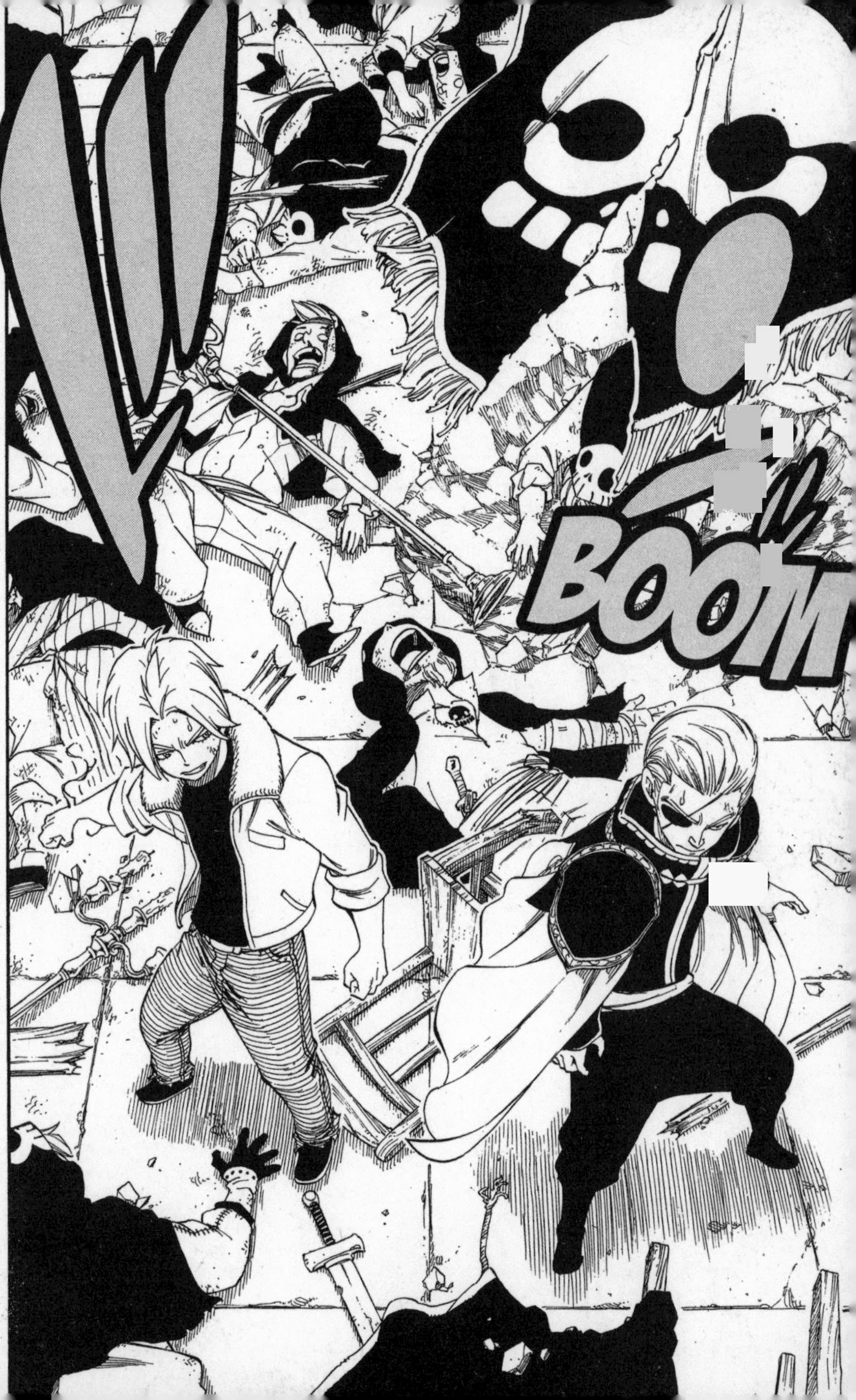
BOOM

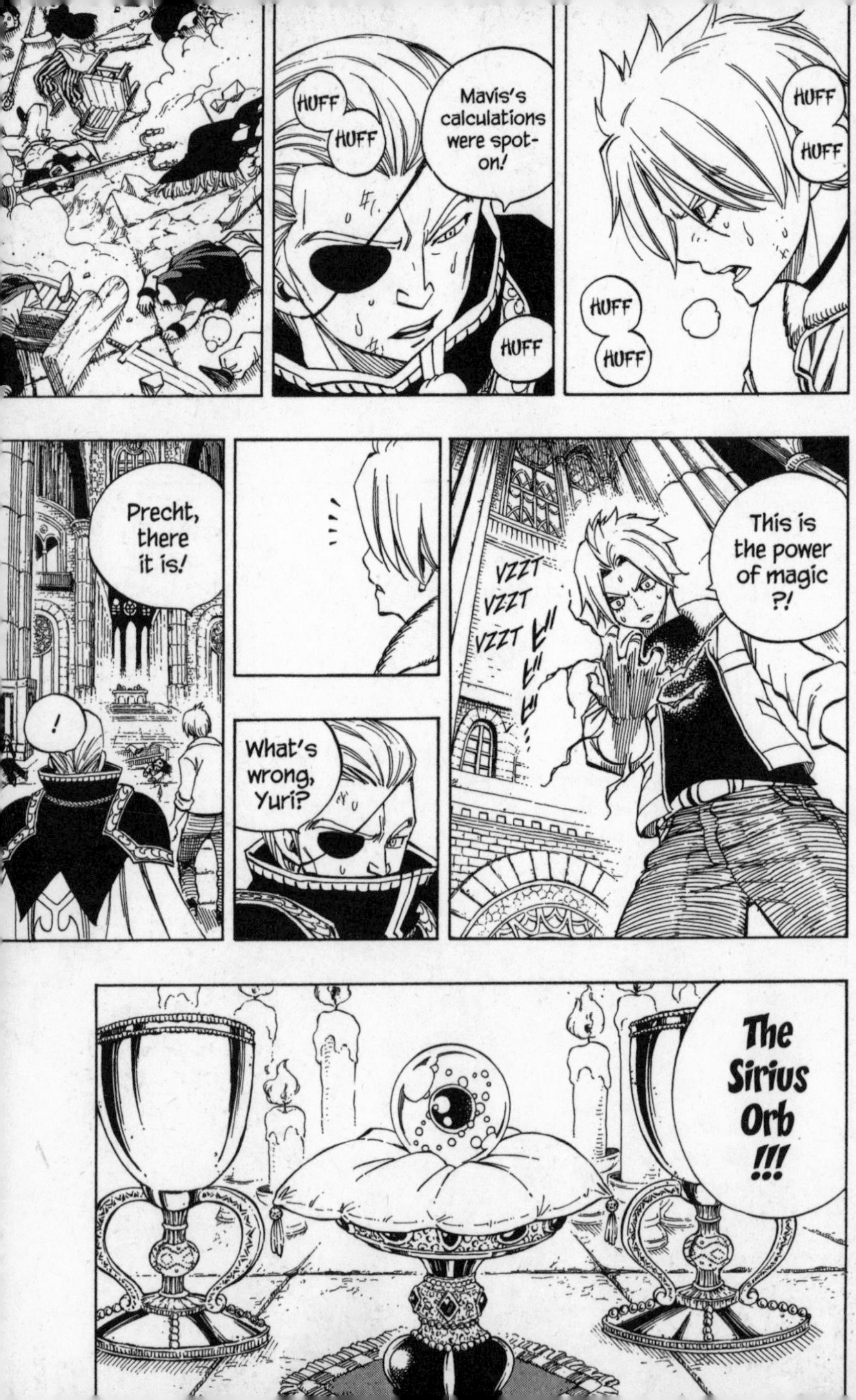
HUFF
HUFF
HUFF
HUFF
Mavis's calculations were spot-on!
HUFF
HUFF
HUFF
This is the power of magic ?!
VZZT
VZZT
VZZT
What's wrong, Yuri?
Precht, there it is!
!
The Sirius Orb!!!

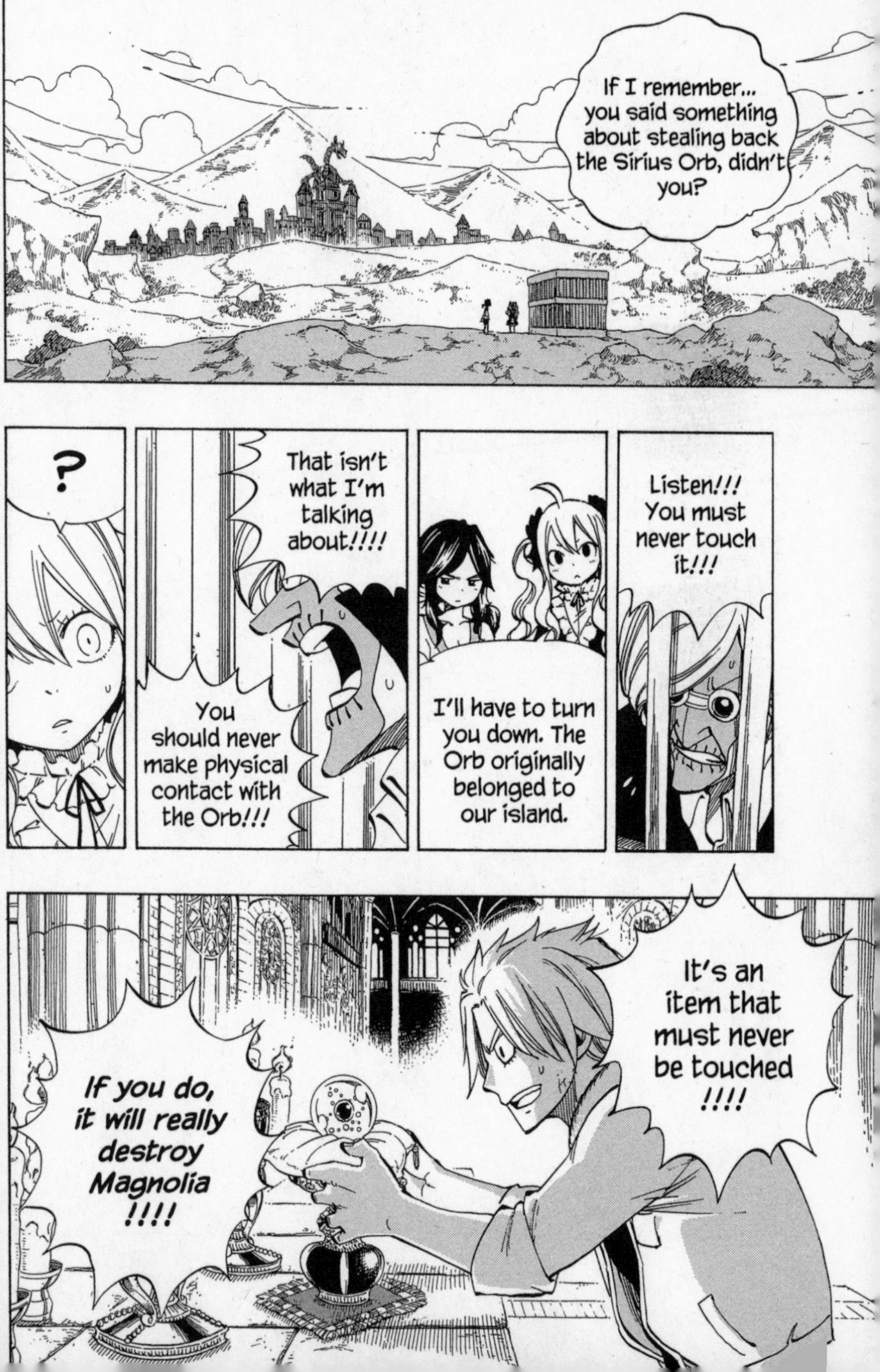
If I remember... you said something about stealing back the Sirius Orb, didn't you?
Listen!!! You must never touch it!!!
I'll have to turn you down. The Orb originally belonged to our island.
That isn't what I'm talking about!!!!
You should never make physical contact with the Orb!!!
?
It's an item that must never be touched !!!!
If you do, it will really destroy Magnolia !!!!

FAIRY TAIL ZERØ

Chapter 9: Treasure

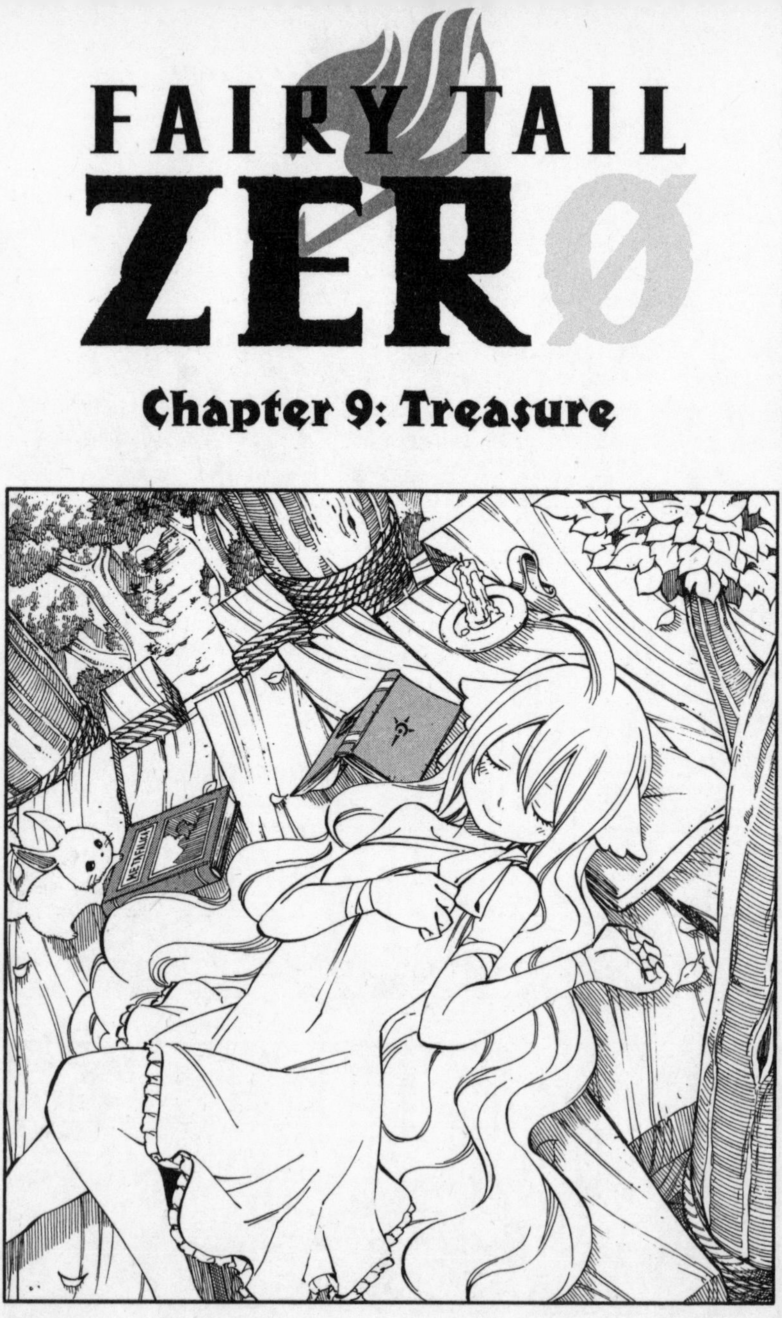

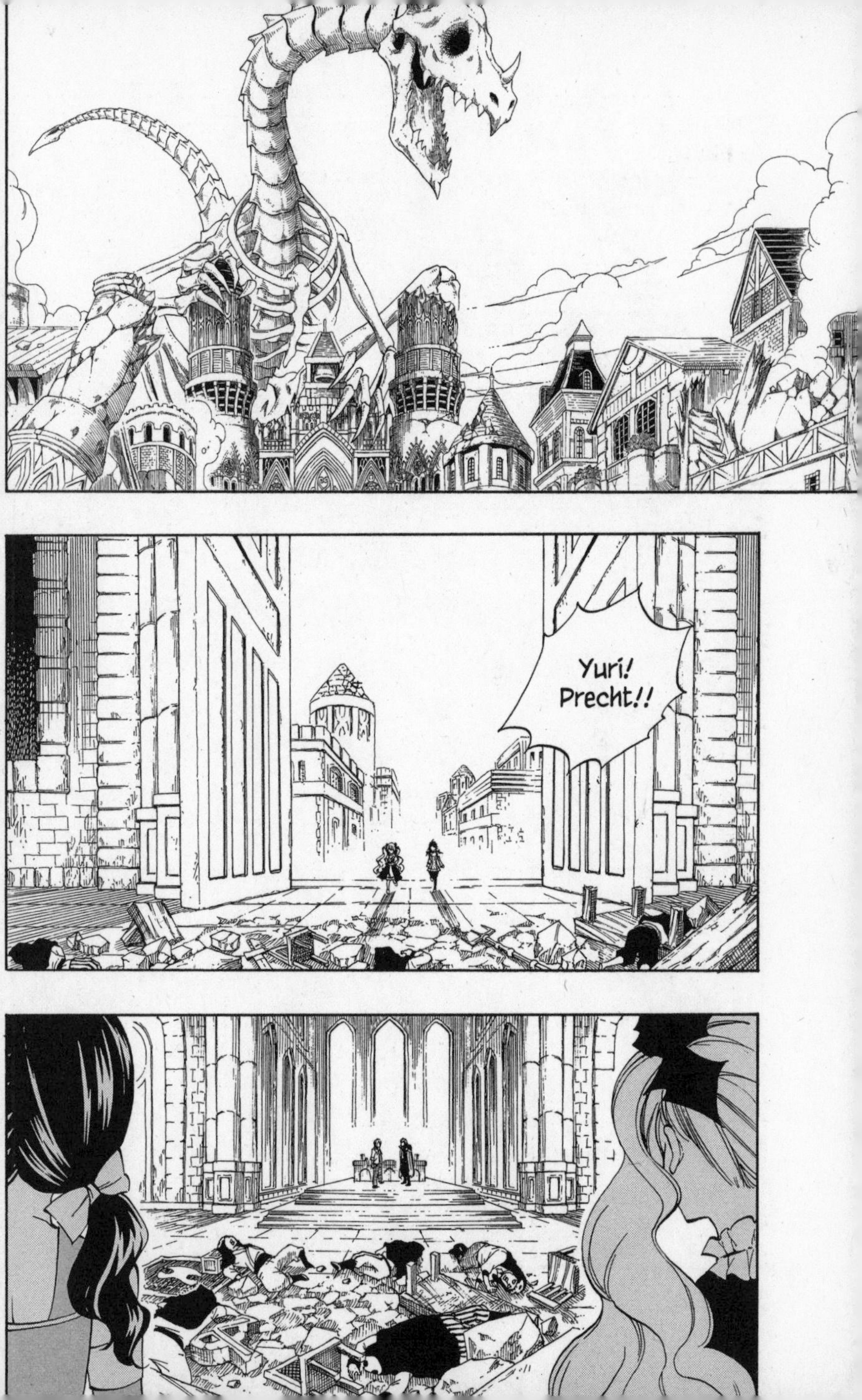
Yuri! Precht!!

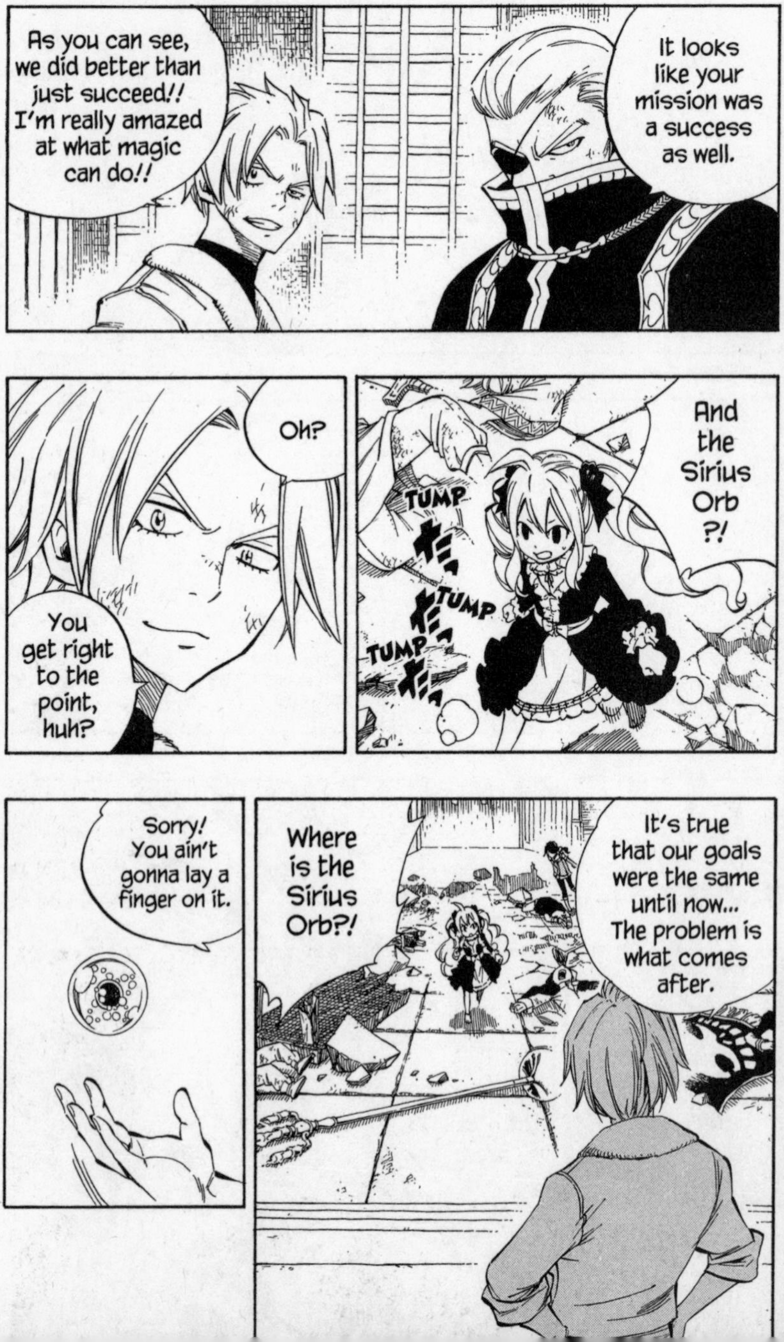
It looks like your mission was a success as well.
As you can see, we did better than just succeed!! I'm really amazed at what magic can do!!
And the Sirius Orb?!
TUMP
TUMP
TUMP
Oh?
You get right to the point, huh?
It's true that our goals were the same until now... The problem is what comes after.
Where is the Sirius Orb?!
Sorry! You ain't gonna lay a finger on it.

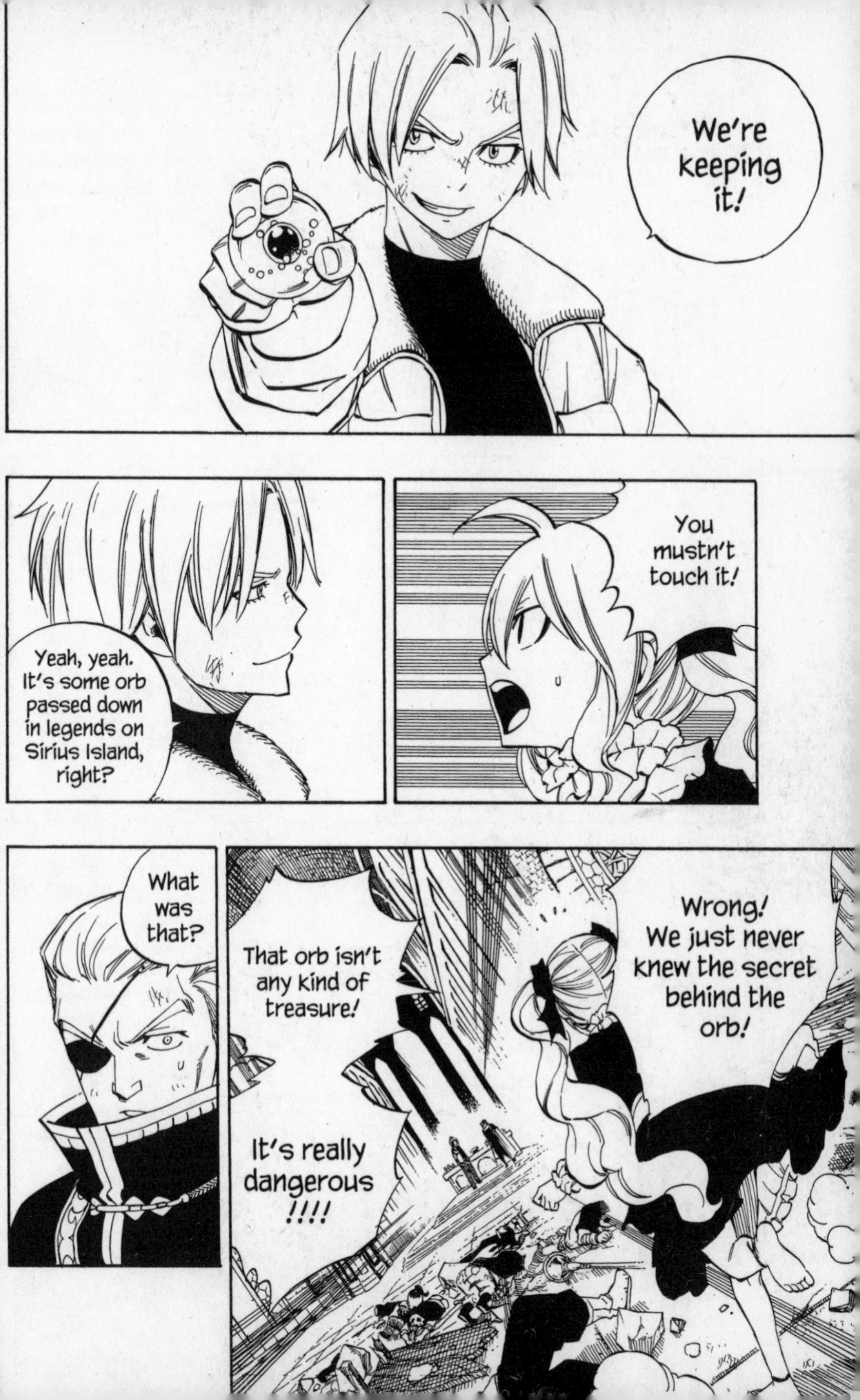
We're keeping it!
You mustn't touch it!
Yeah, yeah. It's some orb passed down in legends on Sirius Island, right?
Wrong! We just never knew the secret behind the orb!
That orb isn't any kind of treasure!
It's really dangerous !!!!
What was that?

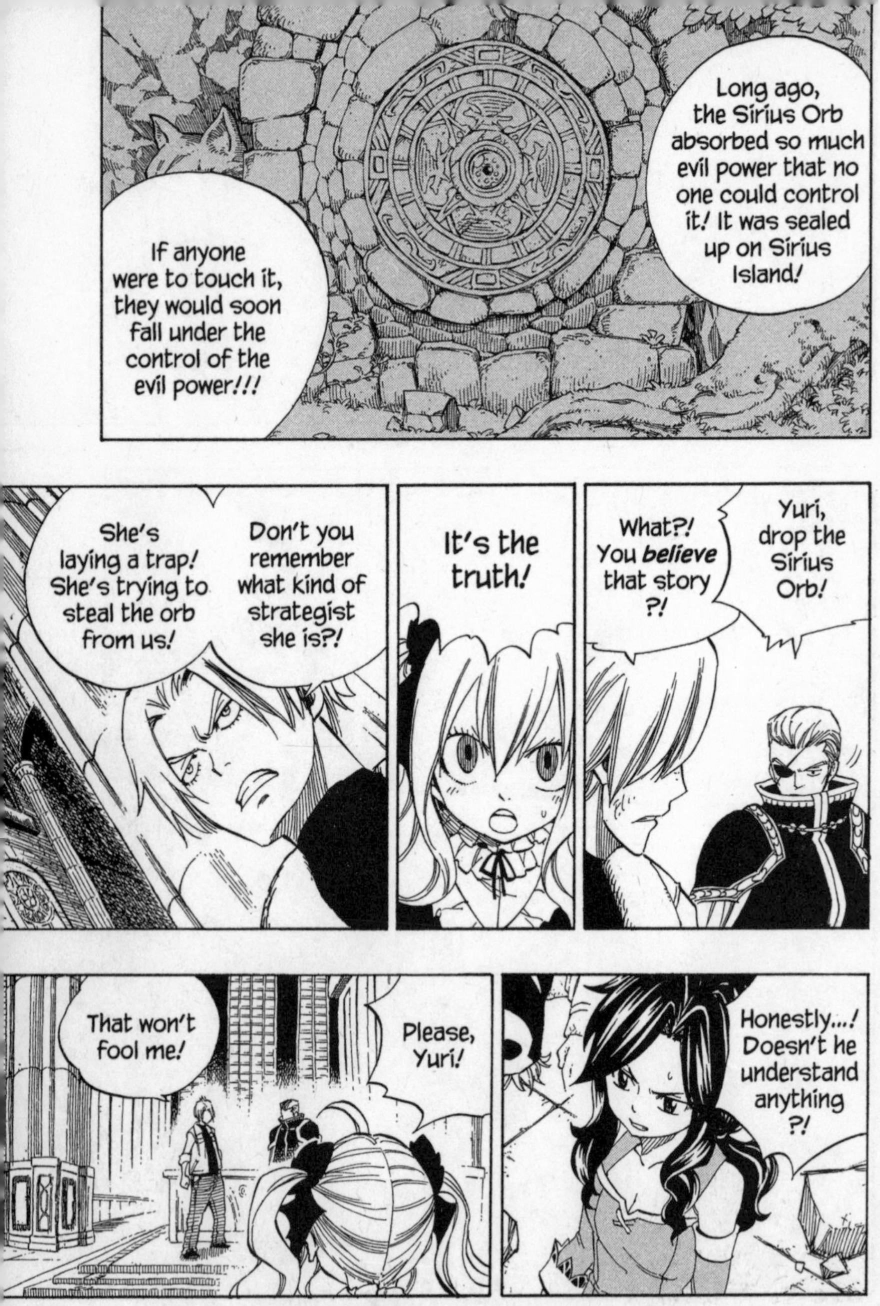
Long ago, the Sirius Orb absorbed so much evil power that no one could control it! It was sealed up on Sirius Island!
If anyone were to touch it, they would soon fall under the control of the evil power!!!
Yuri, drop the Sirius Orb!
What?! You *believe* that story?!
It's the truth!
Don't you remember what kind of strategist she is?!
She's laying a trap! She's trying to steal the orb from us!
Honestly...! Doesn't he understand anything?!
Please, Yuri!
That won't fool me!

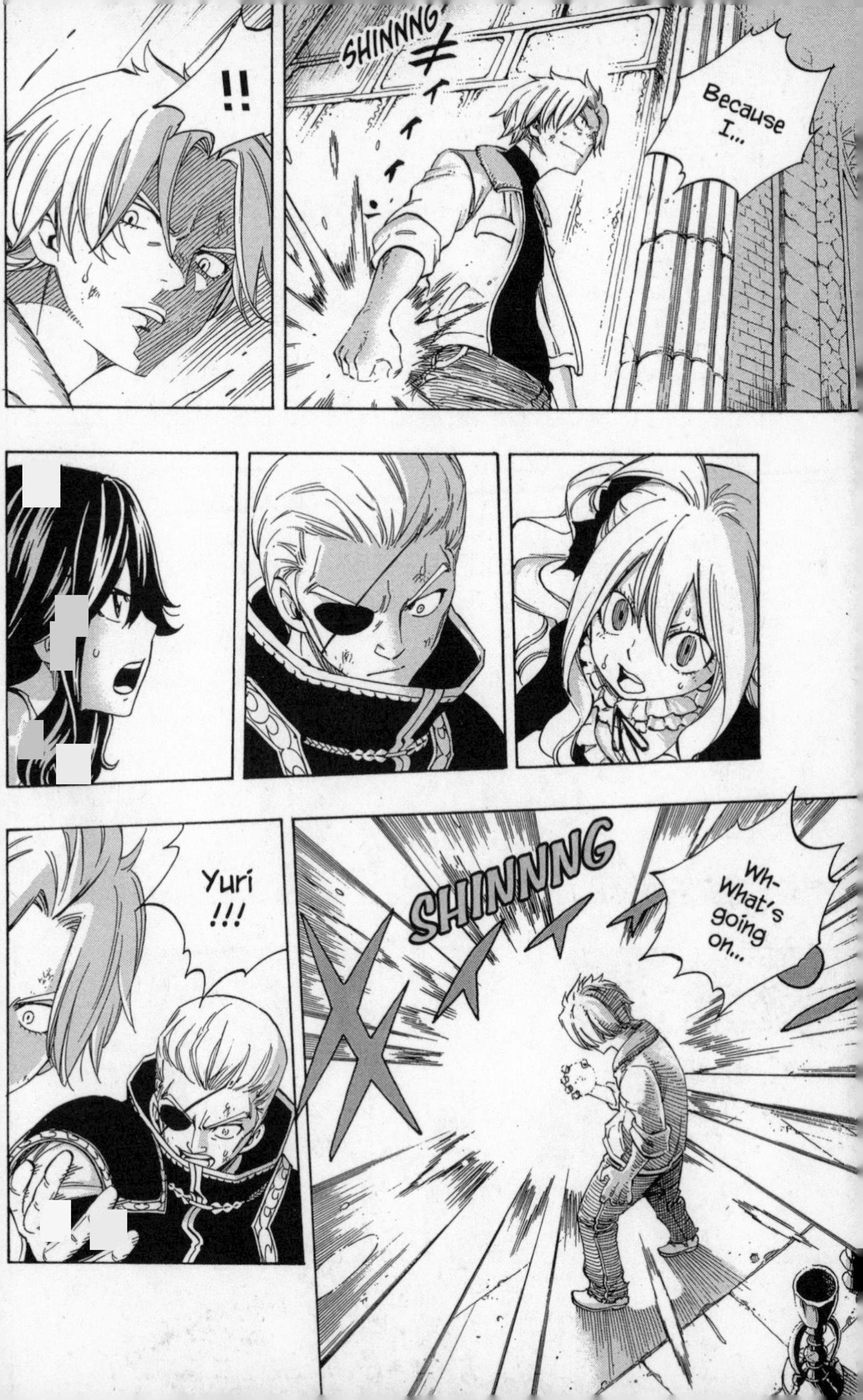
Because I...
SHINNNG
!!
Wh- What's going on...
SHINNNG
Yuri !!!

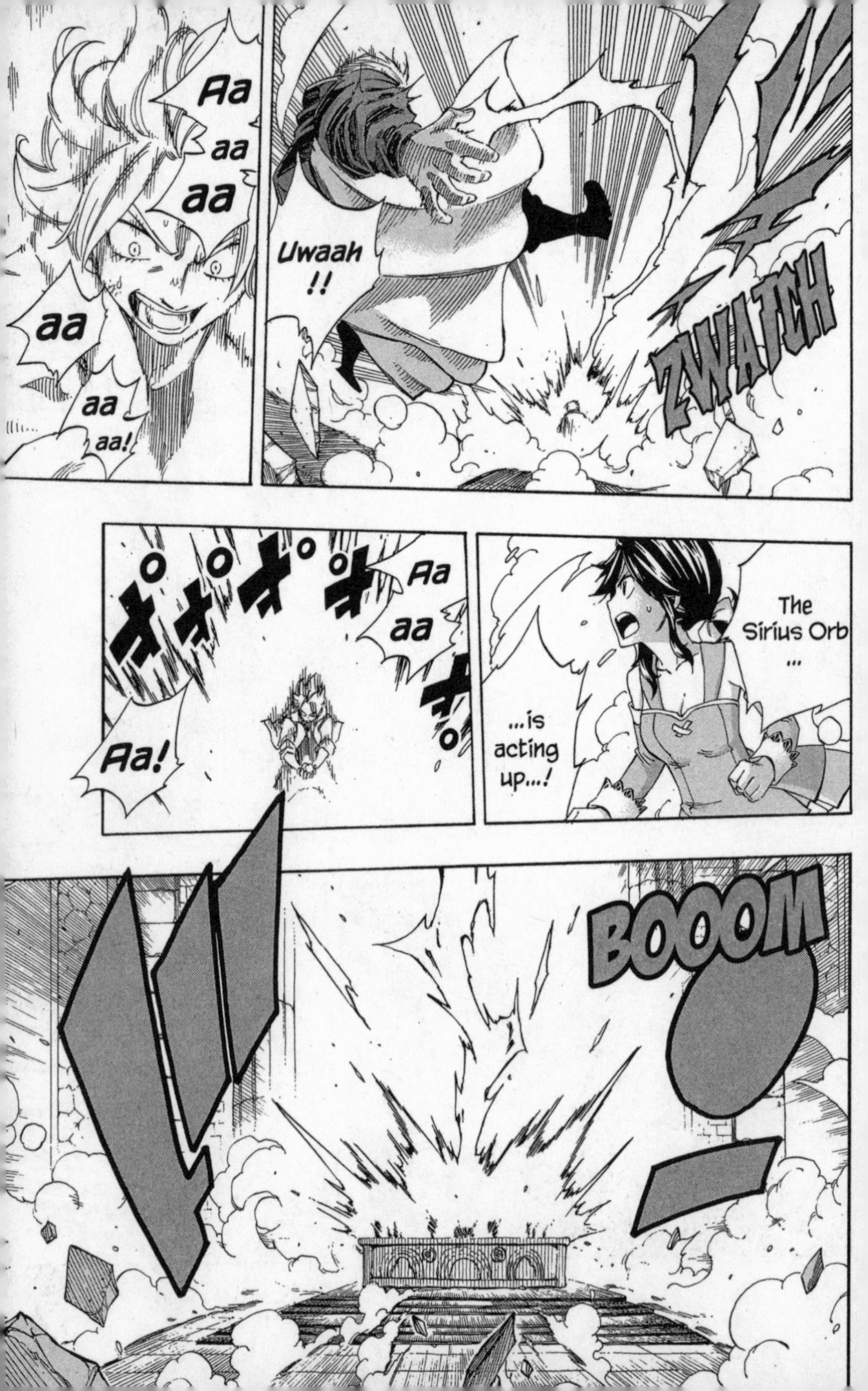
ZWATCH
Uwaah !!
Aa aa aa
aa
aa aa!
The Sirius Orb ...
...is acting up...!
Aa aa
Aa!
BOOOM

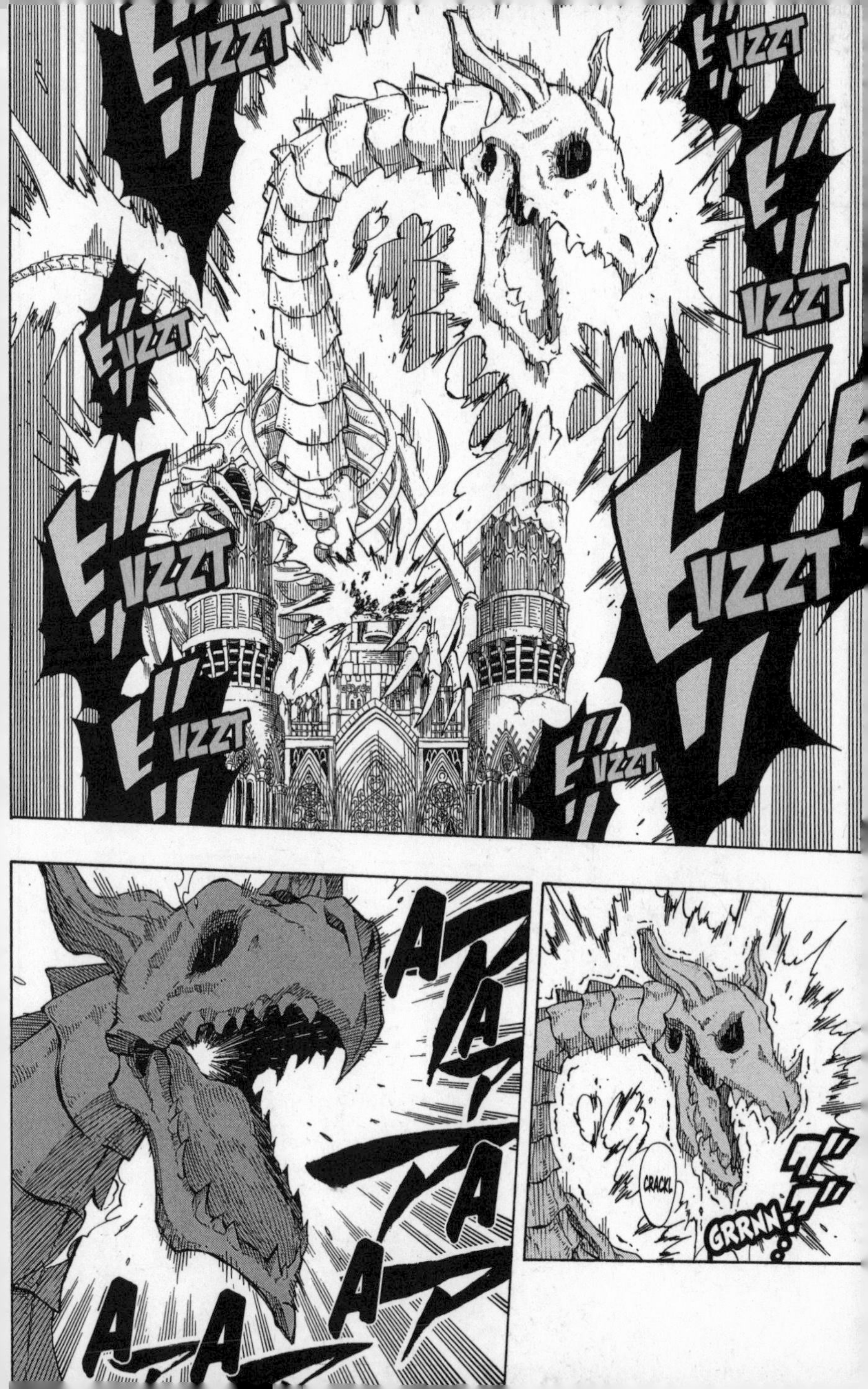

ビ VZZT
ビ VZZT
ビ VZZT
ビ VZZT
ビ VZZT
ビ VZZT
ビ VZZT
ビ VZZT
CRACKL
ゴゴ GRRNN
AAAAAAAA

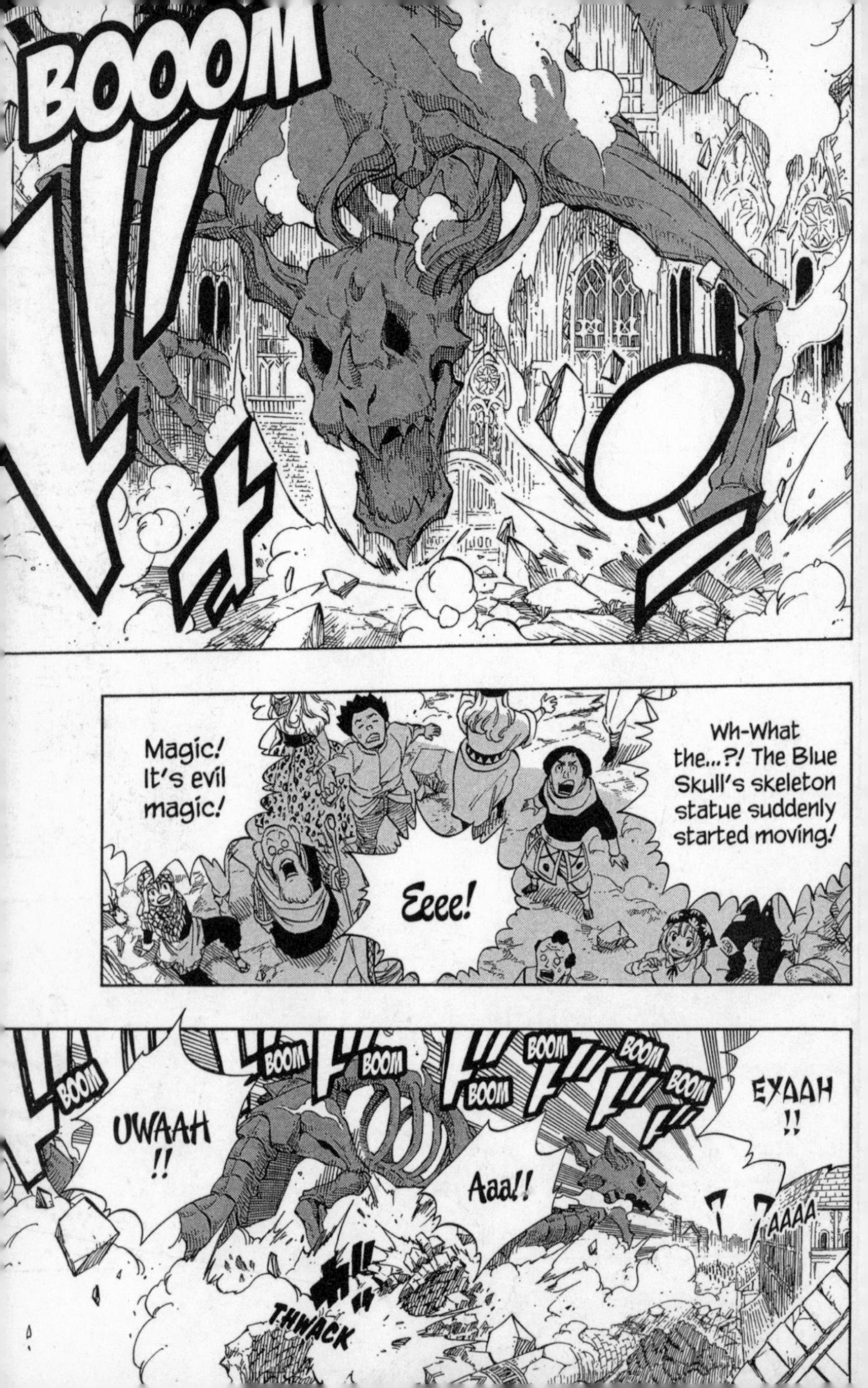
BOOOM
Wh-What the...?! The Blue Skull's skeleton statue suddenly started moving!
Magic! It's evil magic!
Eeee!
EYAAH !!
BOOM
BOOM
BOOM
BOOM
BOOM
BOOM
Aaa!!
UWAAH !!
AAAA
THWACK

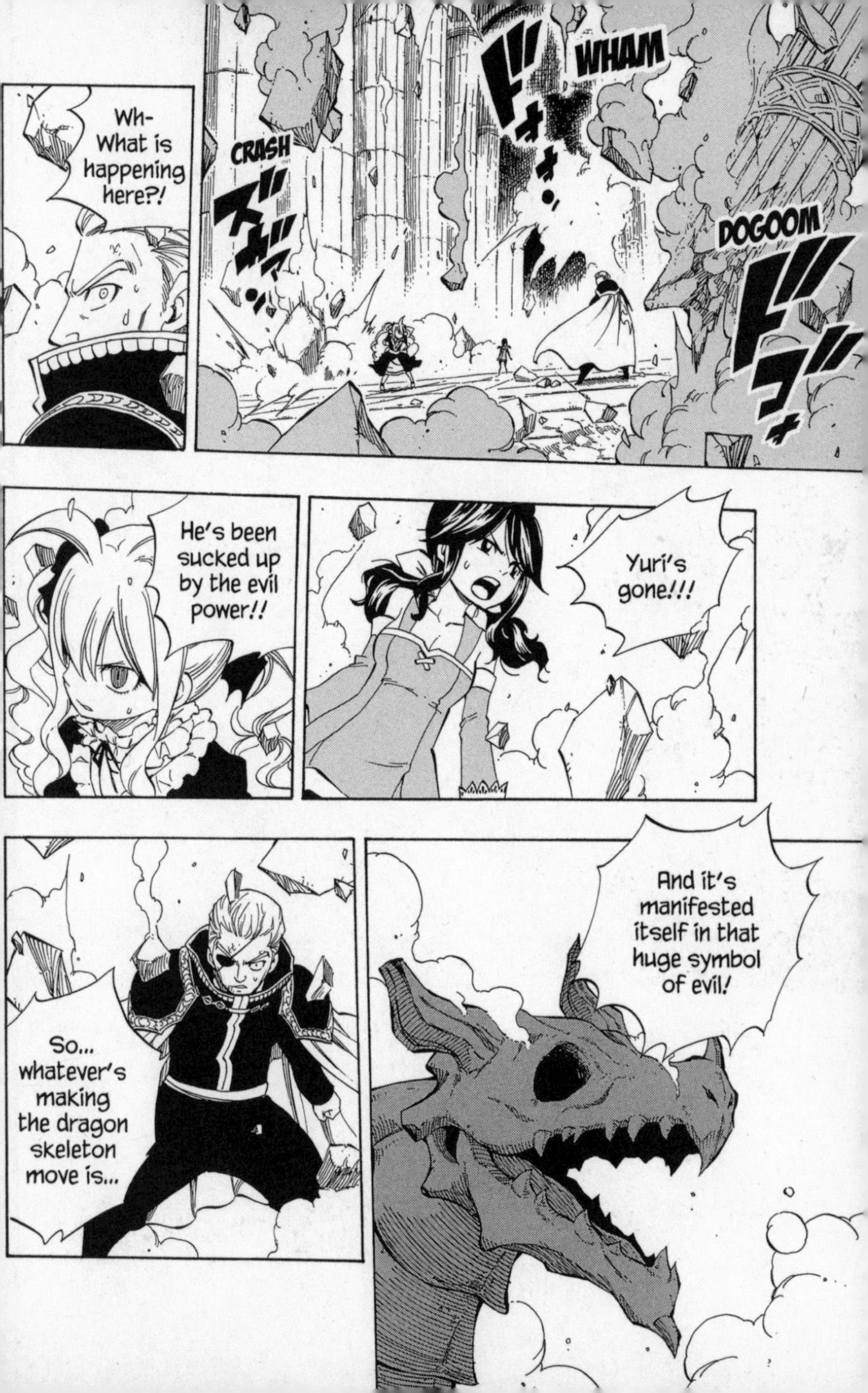
WHAM
DOGOOM
CRASH
Wh- What is happening here?!
Yuri's gone!!!
He's been sucked up by the evil power!!
And it's manifested itself in that huge symbol of evil!
So... whatever's making the dragon skeleton move is...

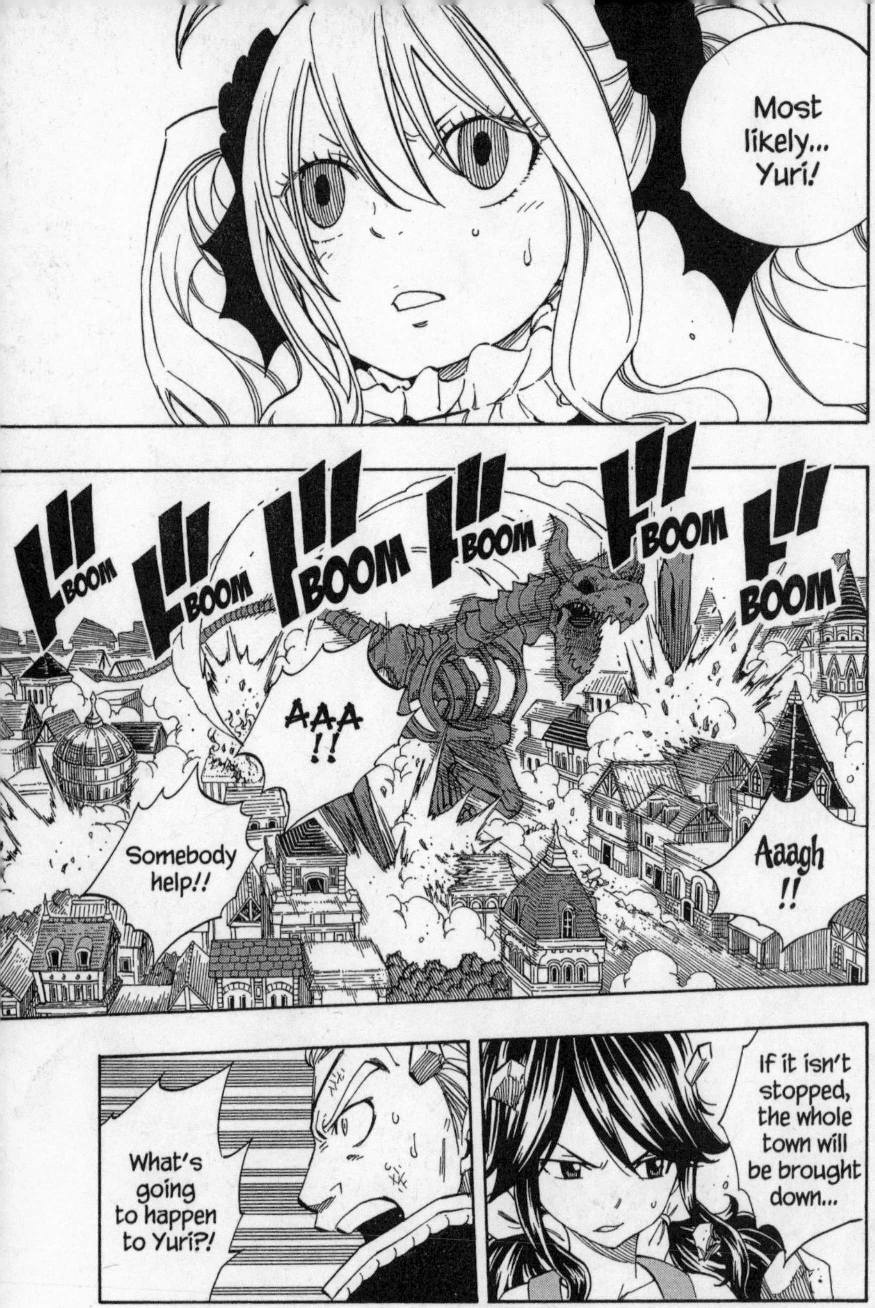
Most likely... Yuri!
BOOM
BOOM
BOOM
BOOM
BOOM
BOOM
AAA !!
Aaagh !!
Somebody help!!
If it isn't stopped, the whole town will be brought down...
What's going to happen to Yuri?!

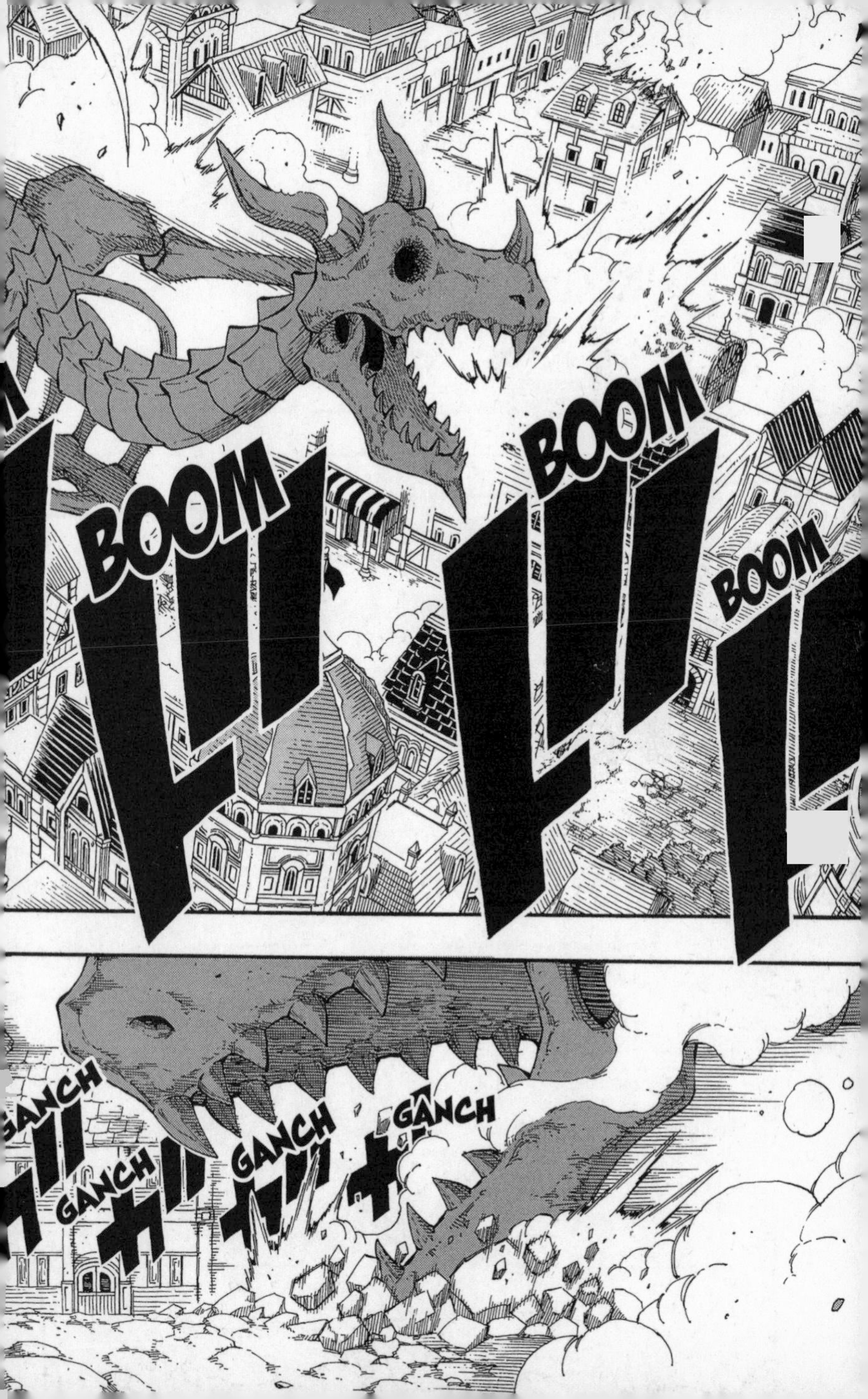
BOOM
BOOM
BOOM
GANCH
GANCH
GANCH
GANCH

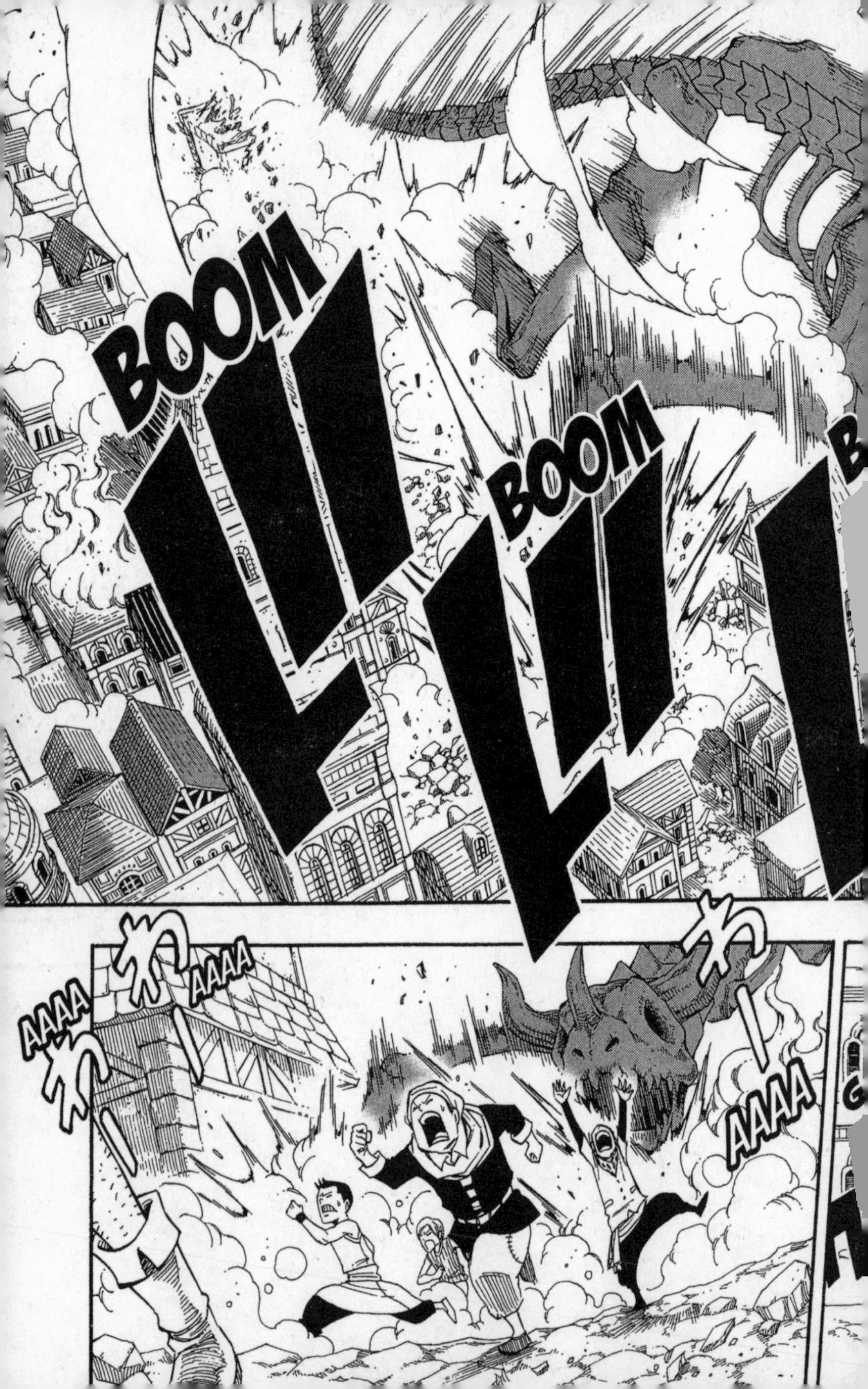
BOOM
BOOM
わー
AAAA
わー
AAAA
わー
AAAA

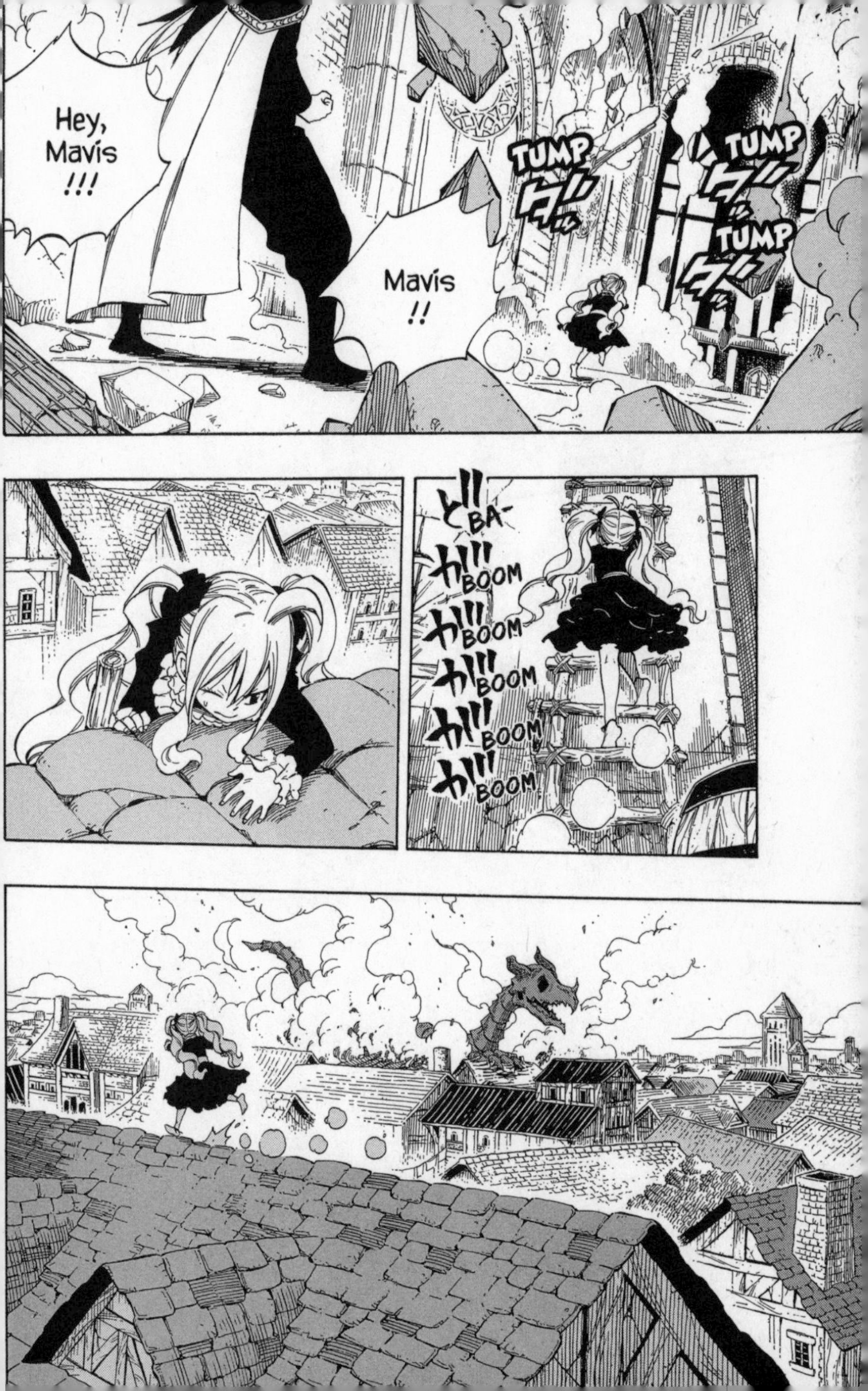

TUMP
TUMP
TUMP
Hey, Mavis!!!
Mavis!!
BA-
BOOM
BOOM
BOOM
BOOM
BOOM

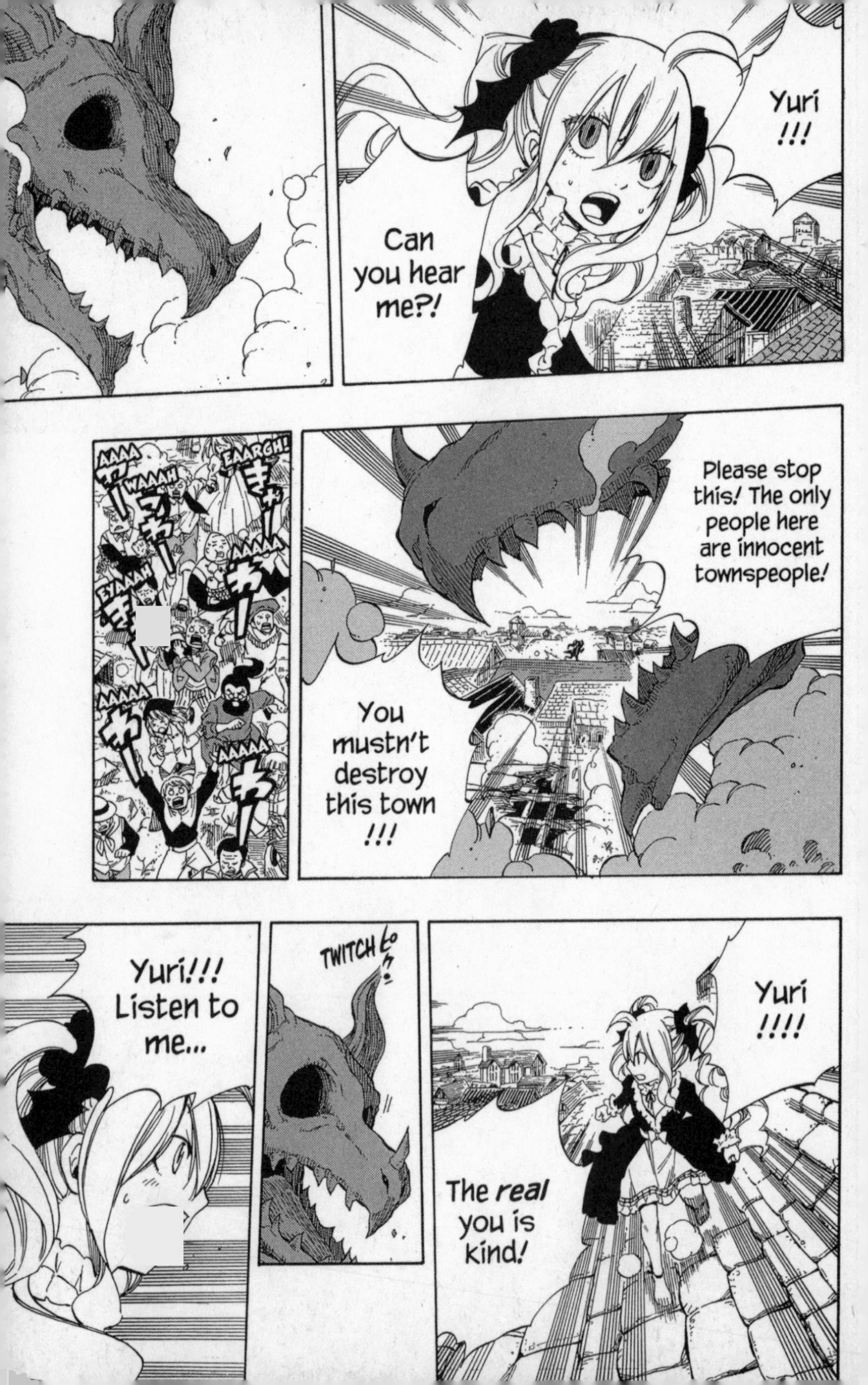
Yuri !!!
Can you hear me?!
Please stop this! The only people here are innocent townspeople!
You mustn't destroy this town !!!
EAARGH!
AAAA
WAAAH
AAAAA
EYAAAH
AAAAA
AAAAA
Yuri !!!!
The *real* you is kind!
TWITCH
Yuri!!! Listen to me...

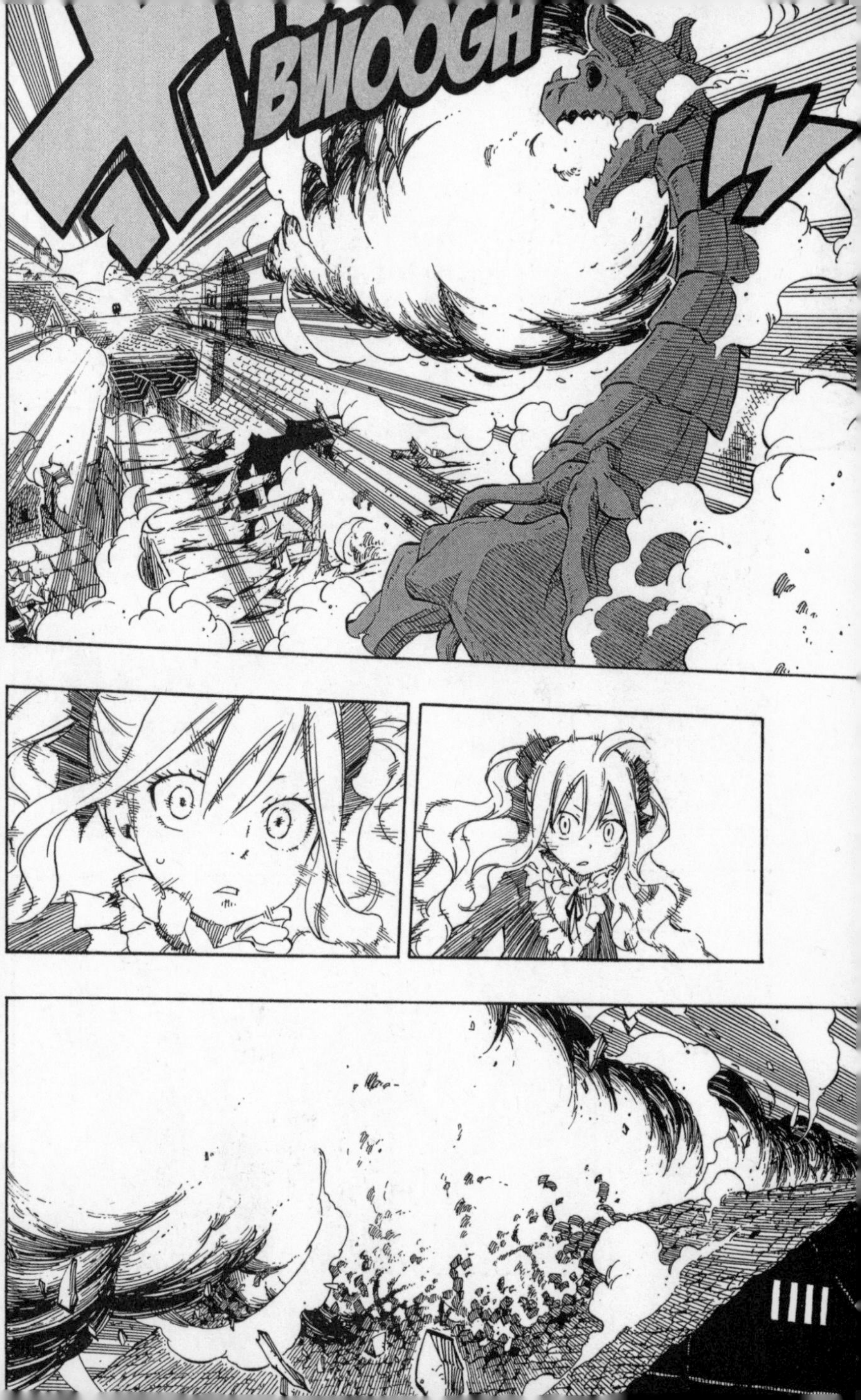
BWOOGH

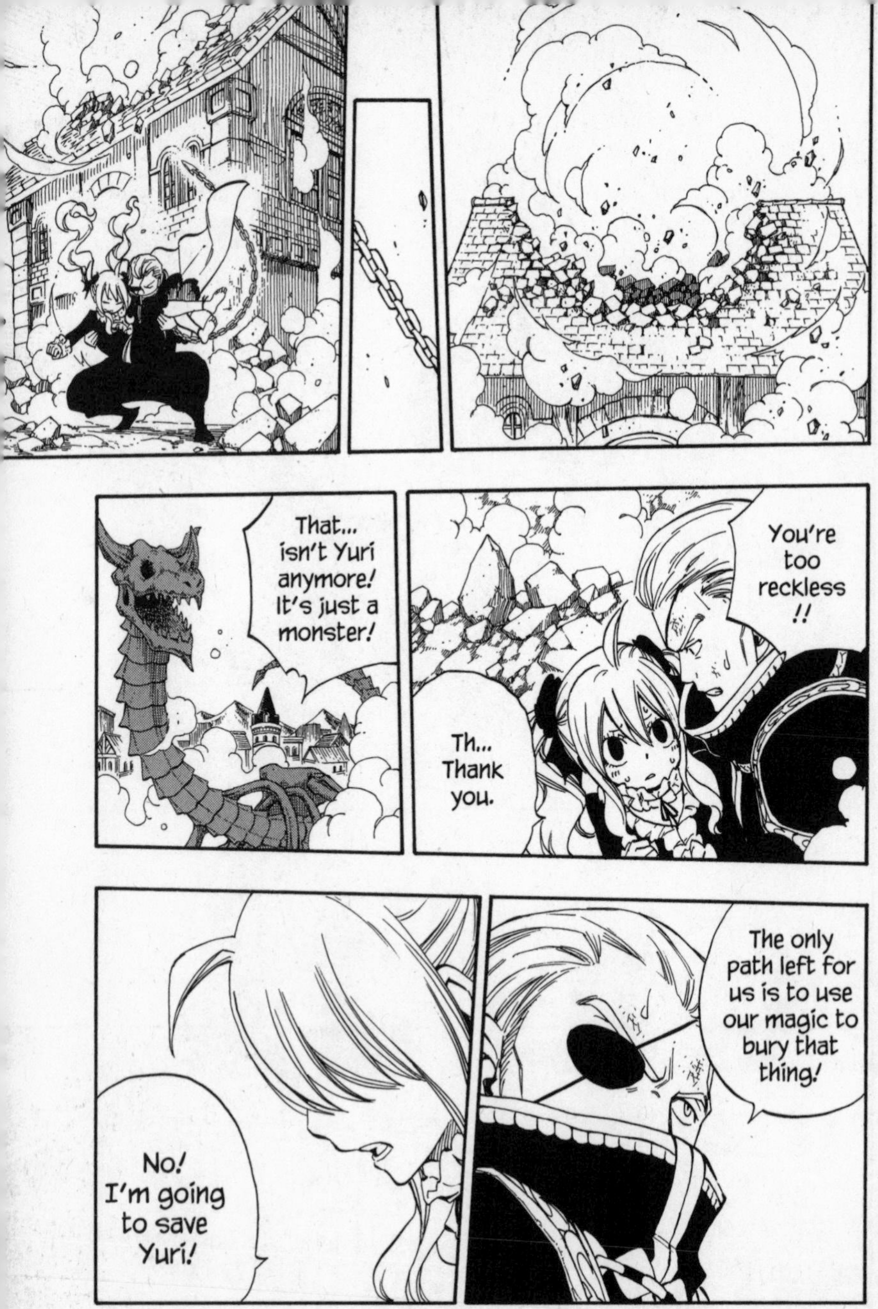
You're too reckless !!
Th... Thank you.
That... isn't Yuri anymore! It's just a monster!
The only path left for us is to use our magic to bury that thing!
No! I'm going to save Yuri!

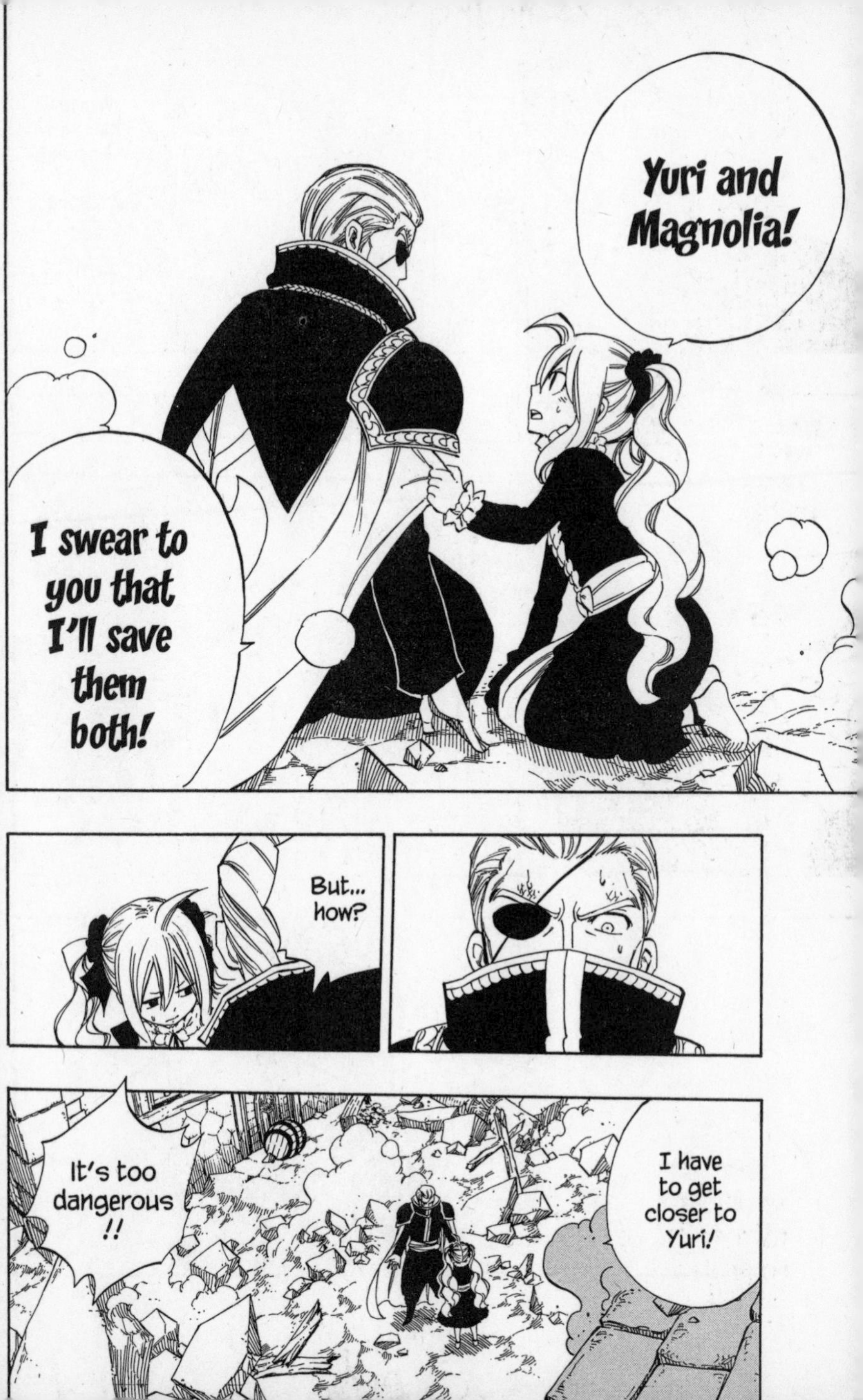
Yuri and Magnolia!
I swear to you that I'll save them both!
But... how?
I have to get closer to Yuri!
It's too dangerous!!

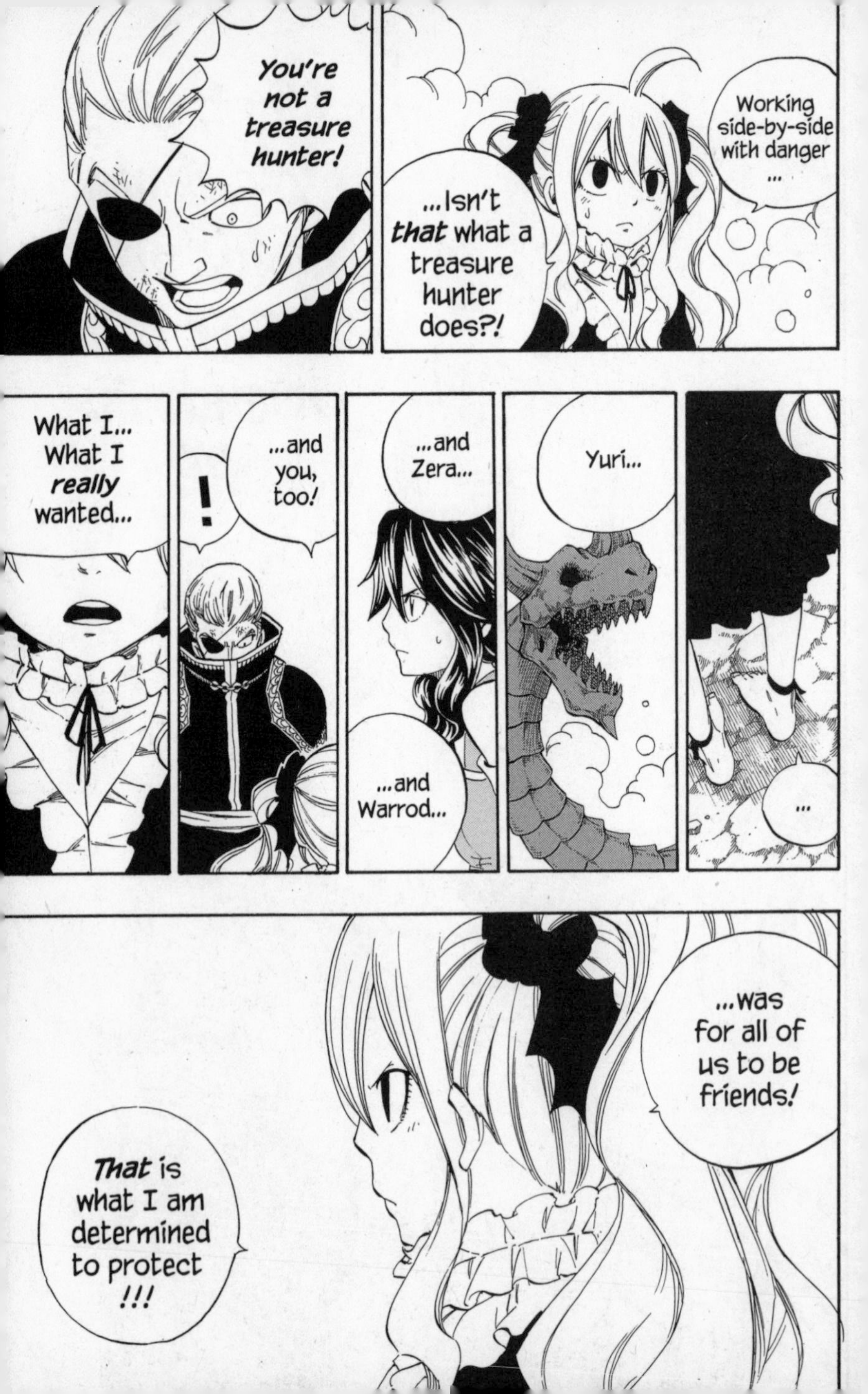
Working side-by-side with danger ...
...Isn't *that* what a treasure hunter does?!
You're not a treasure hunter!
...
Yuri...
...and Zera...
...and Warrod...
...and you, too!
!
What I... What I *really* wanted...
...was for all of us to be friends!
That is what I am determined to protect !!!

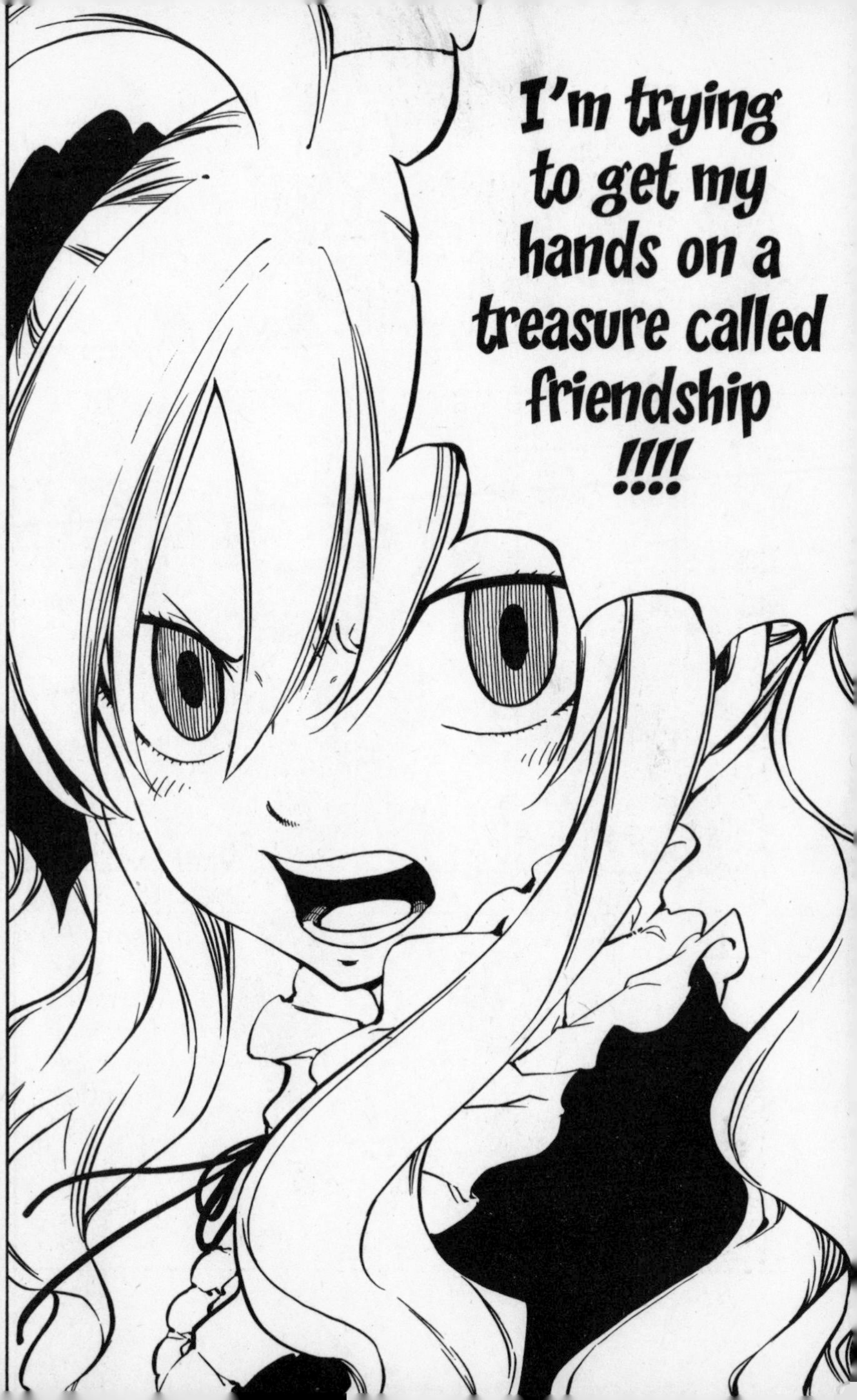
I'm trying to get my hands on a treasure called friendship!!!!

FAIRY TAIL ZERØ

Chapter 10: Law

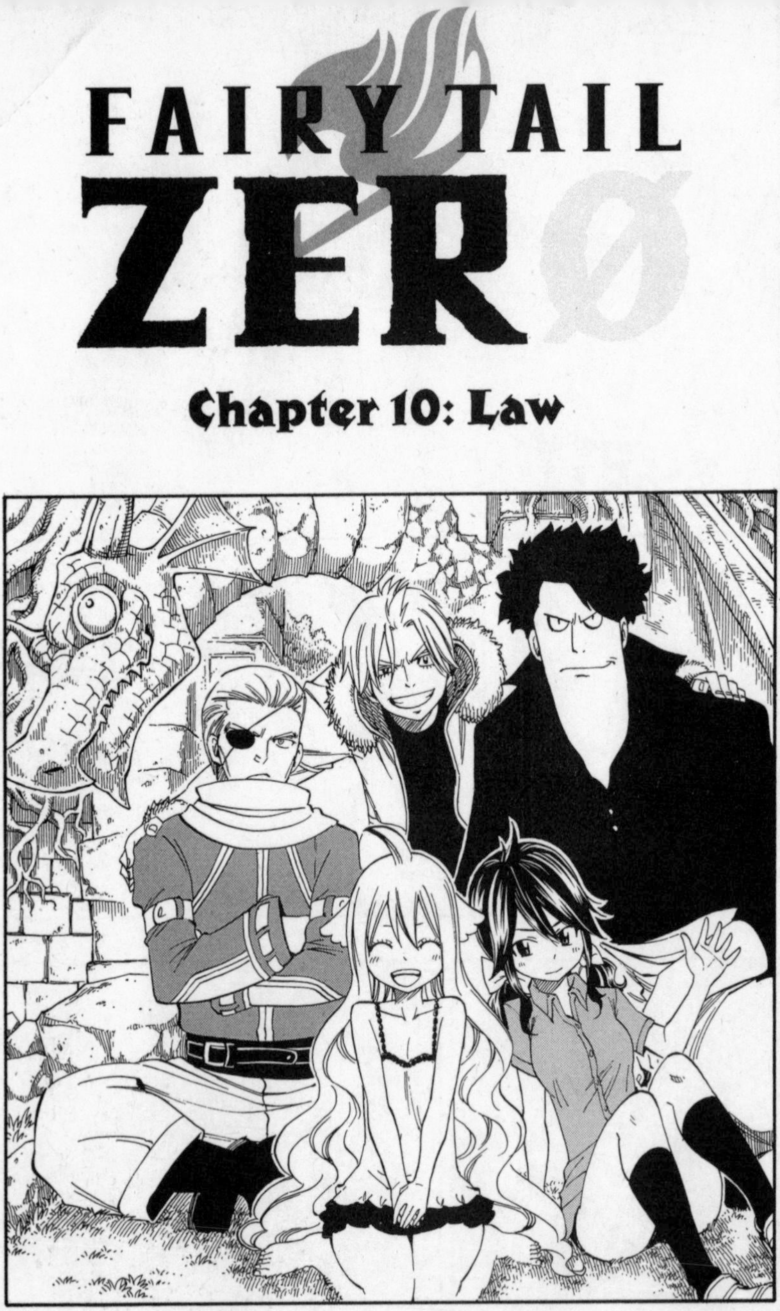

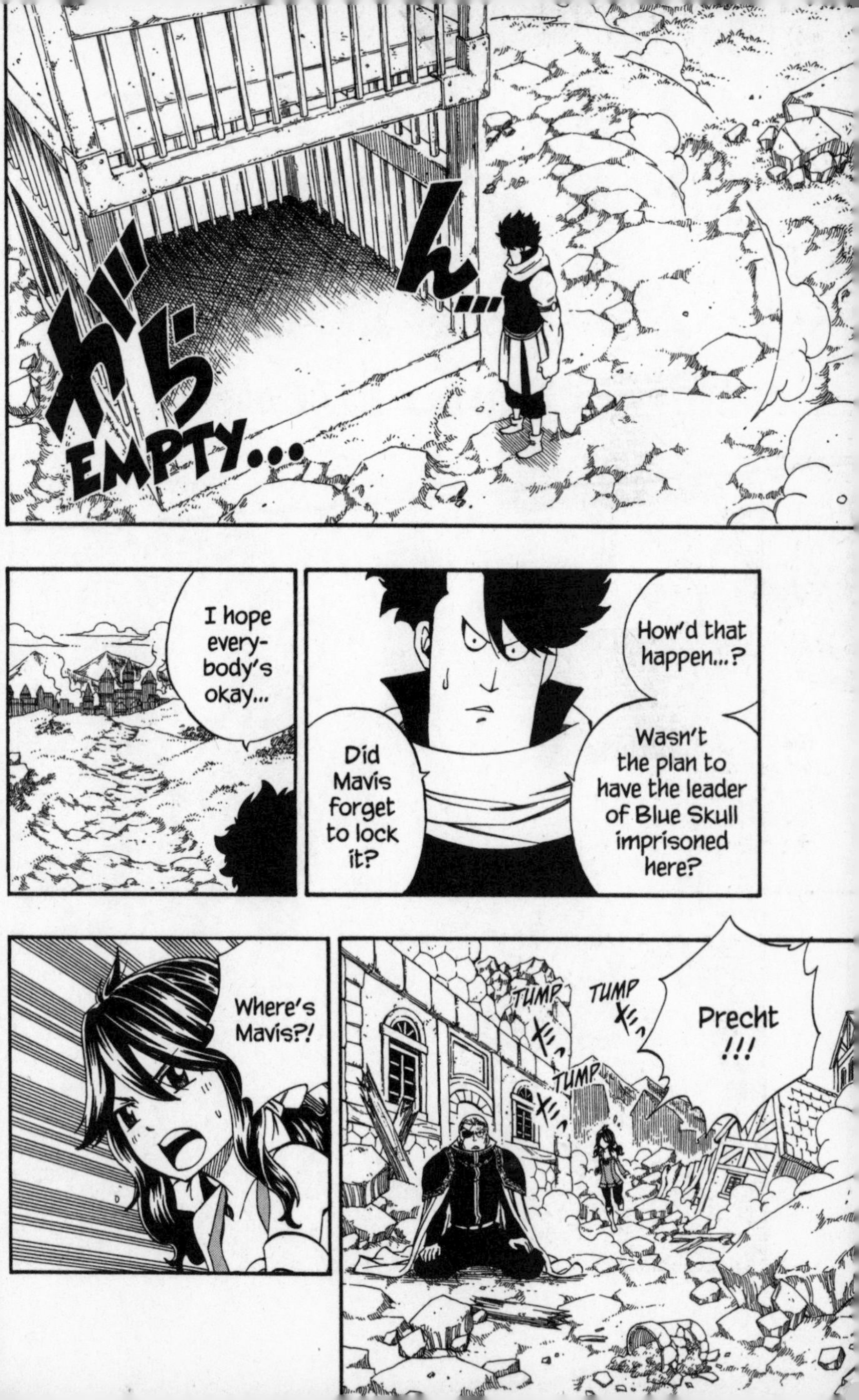
ん...
から
EMPTY...
How'd that happen...?
Wasn't the plan to have the leader of Blue Skull imprisoned here?
Did Mavis forget to lock it?
I hope everybody's okay...
Precht !!!
TUMP
TUMP
TUMP
Where's Mavis?!

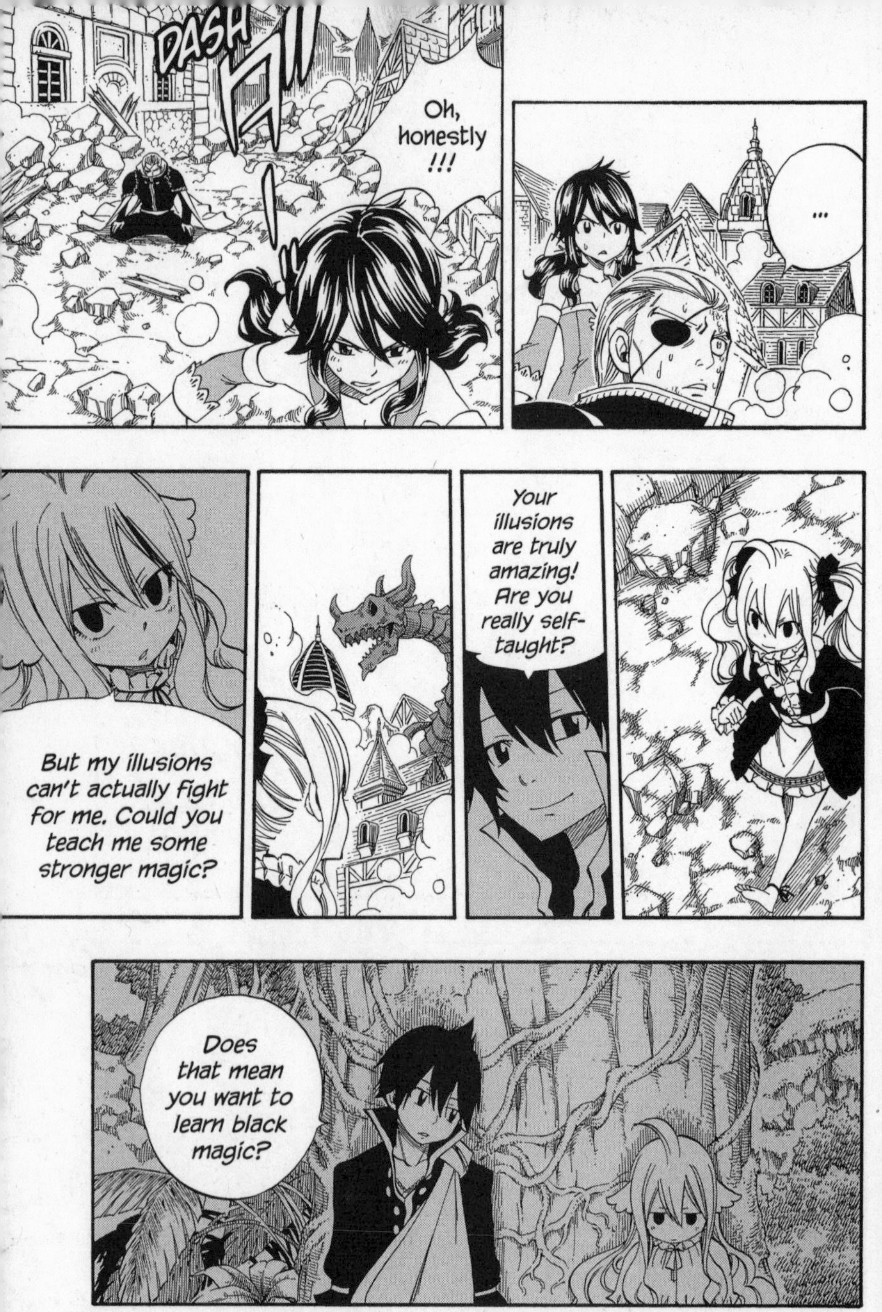

...
DASH
Oh, honestly!!!
Your illusions are truly amazing! Are you really self-taught?
But my illusions can't actually fight for me. Could you teach me some stronger magic?
Does that mean you want to learn black magic?

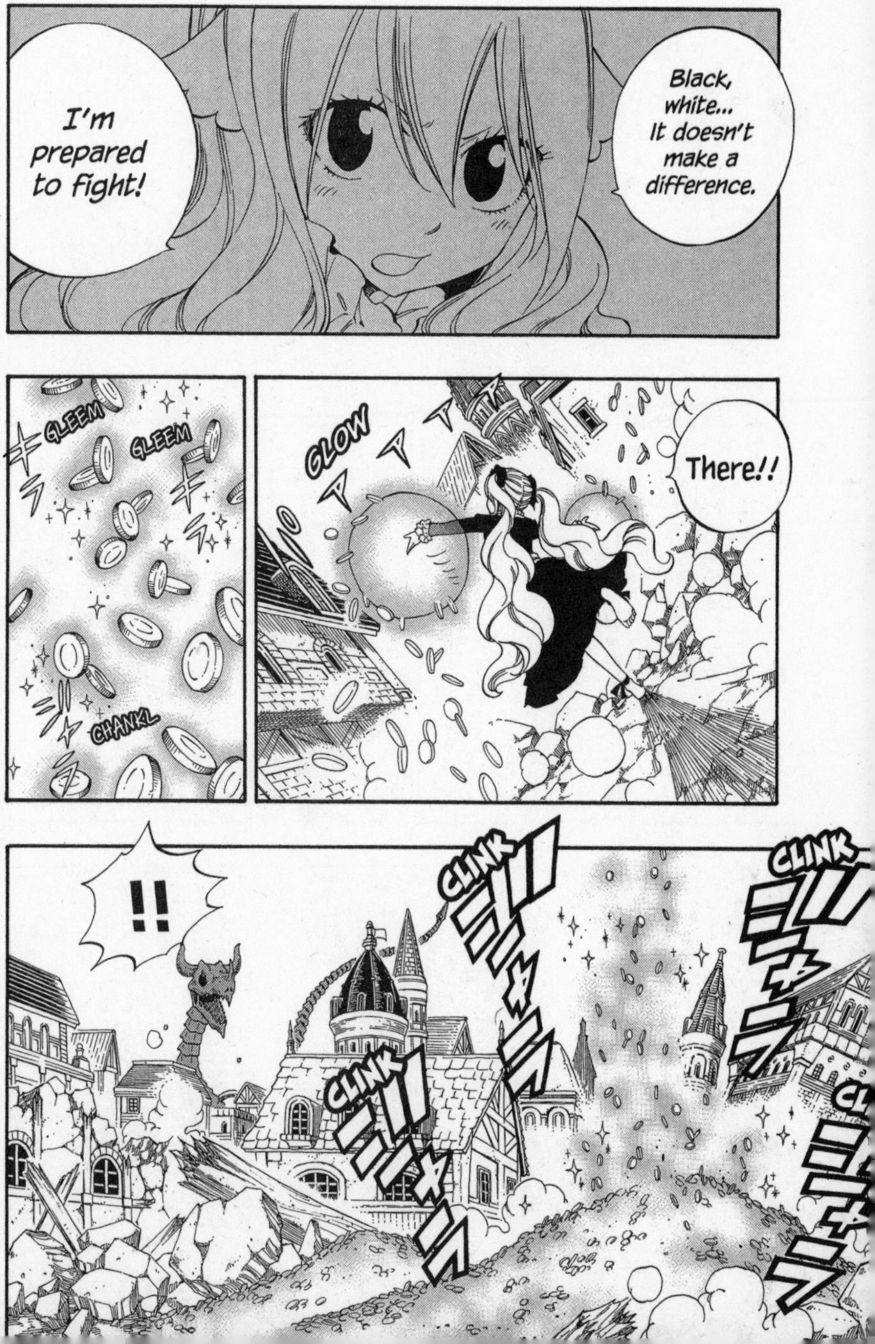
Black, white... It doesn't make a difference.
I'm prepared to fight!
GLOW
There!!
GLEEM
GLEEM
CHANKL
CLINK
CLINK
CLINK
!!

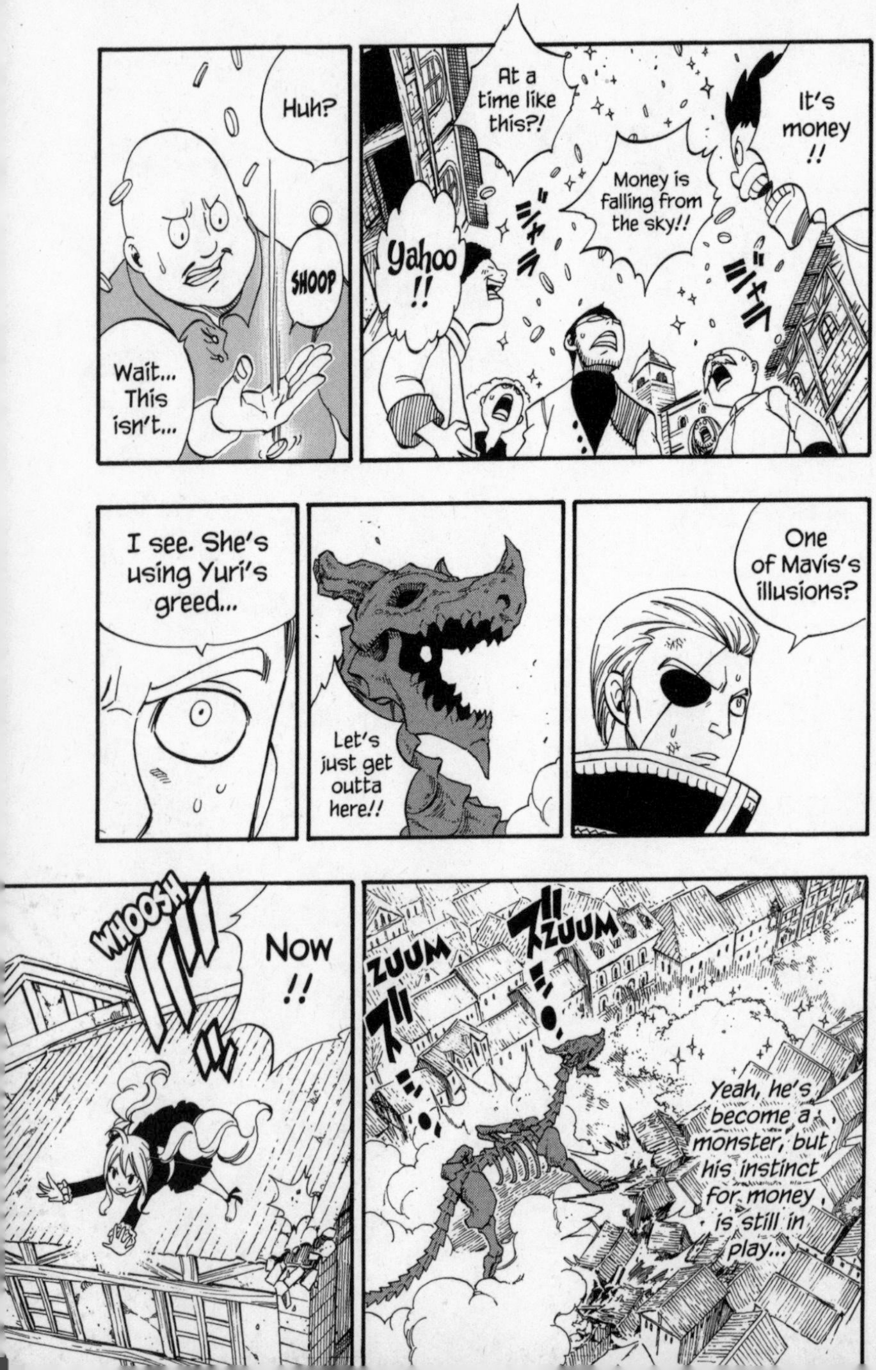
It's money!!
Money is falling from the sky!!
At a time like this?!
Yahoo!!
Huh?
SHOOP
Wait... This isn't...
One of Mavis's illusions?
Let's just get outta here!!
I see. She's using Yuri's greed...
ZUUM
ZUUM
Yeah, he's become a monster, but his instinct for money is still in play...
Now!!
WHOOSH

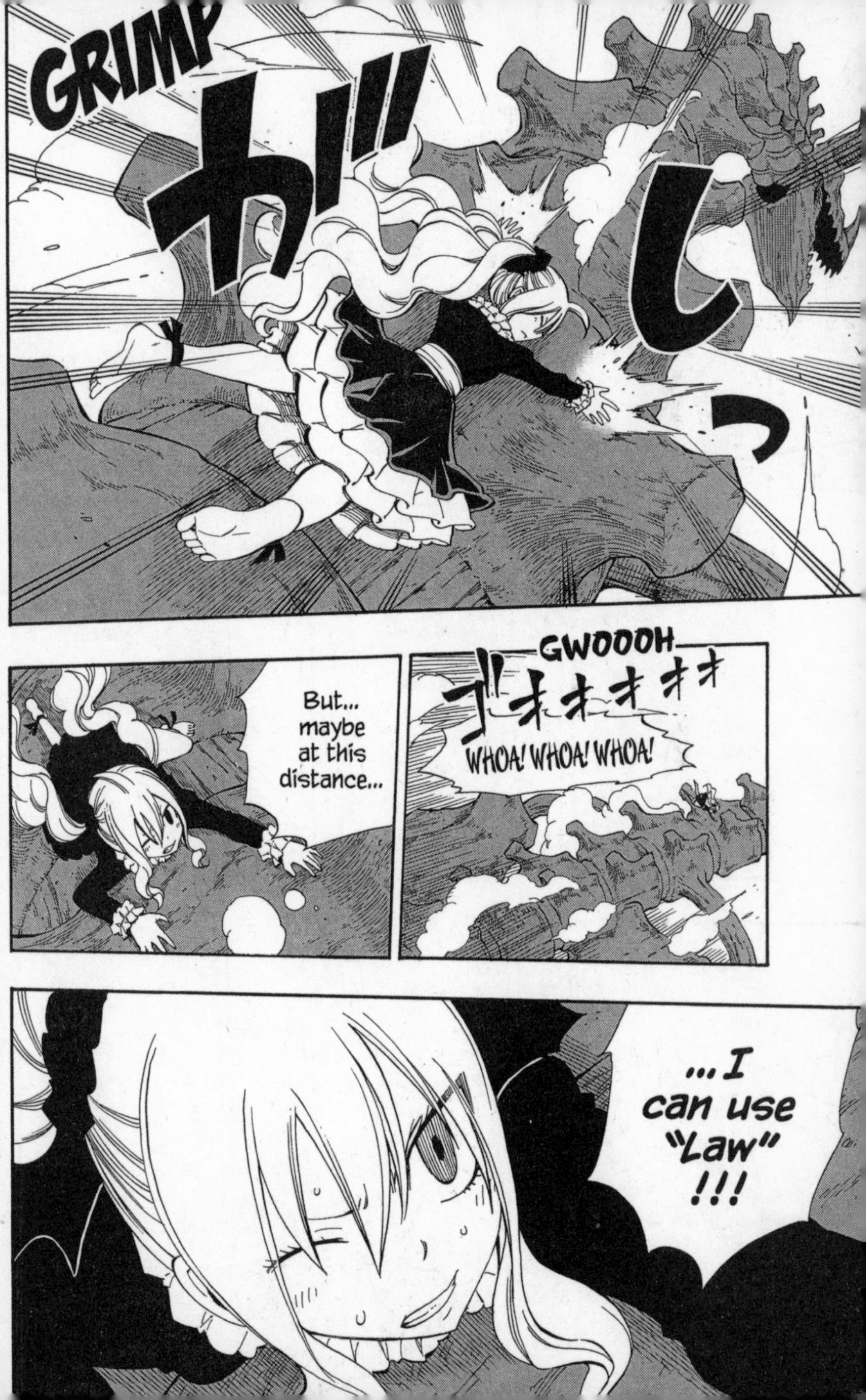
GRIMP
ガしっ
GWOOOH
ゴオオオオオ
WHOA! WHOA! WHOA!
But... maybe at this distance...
...I can use "Law" !!!

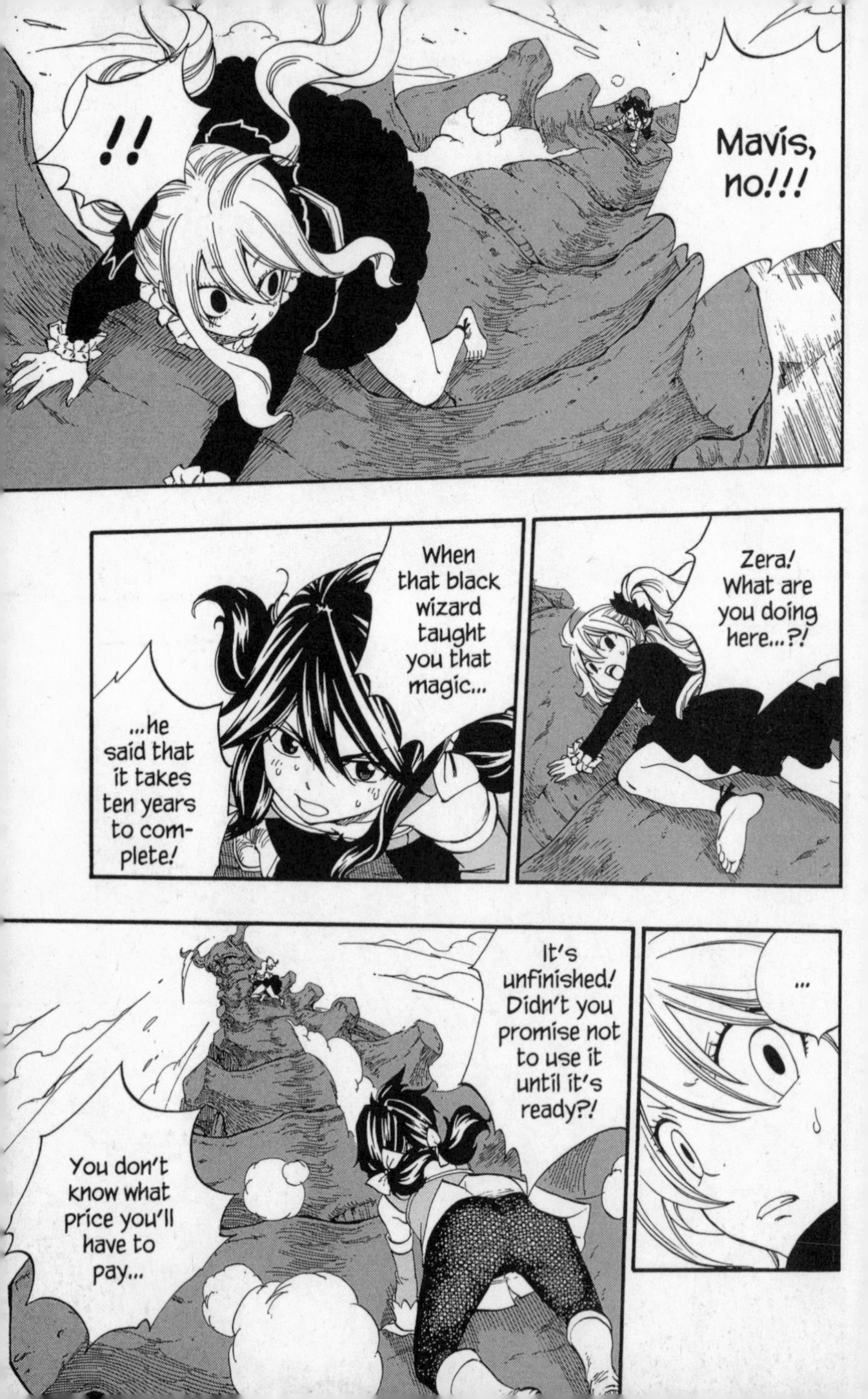
Mavis, no!!!
!!
Zera! What are you doing here...?!
When that black wizard taught you that magic...
...he said that it takes ten years to complete!
...
It's unfinished! Didn't you promise not to use it until it's ready?!
You don't know what price you'll have to pay...

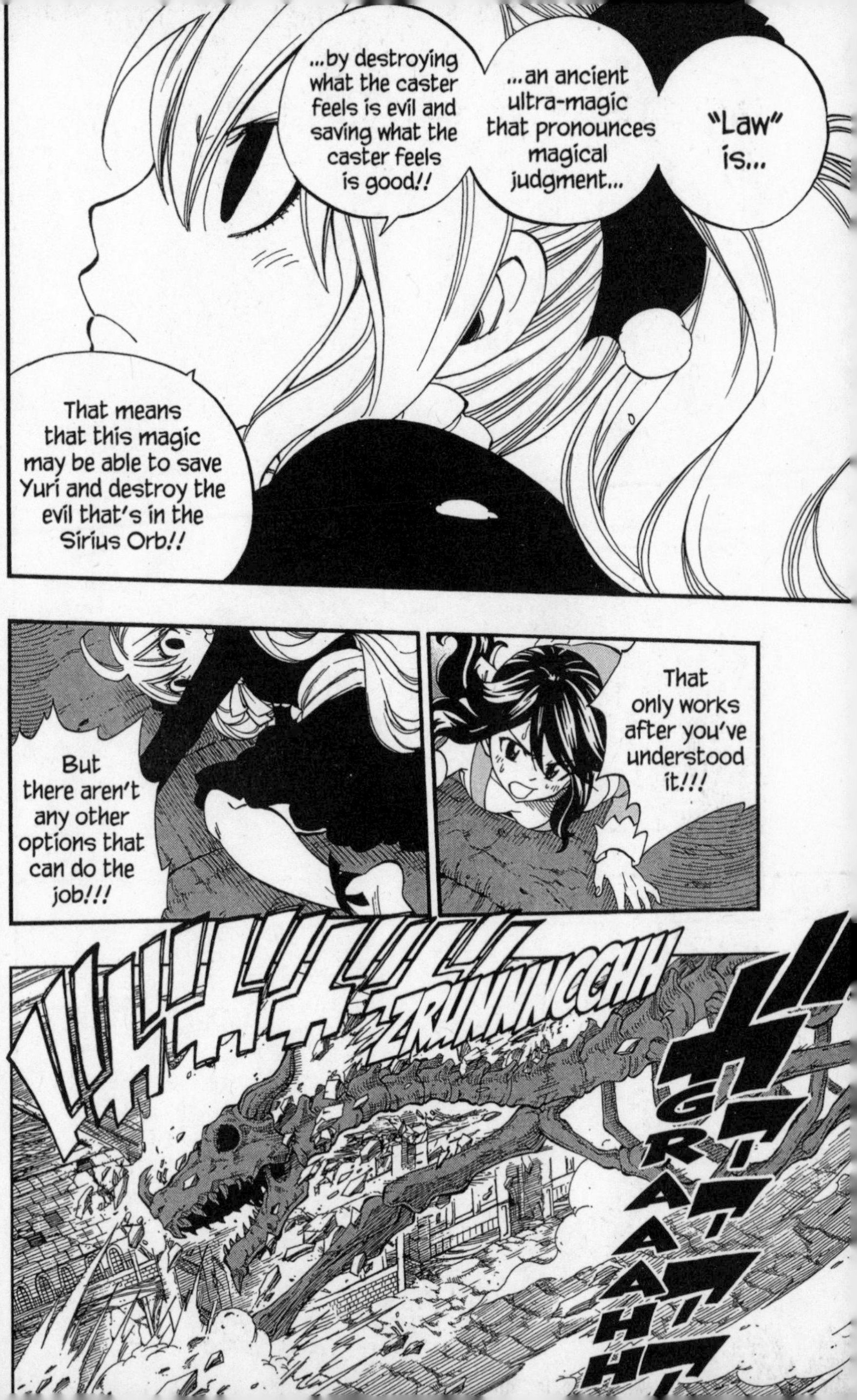
"Law" is...
...an ancient ultra-magic that pronounces magical judgment...
...by destroying what the caster feels is evil and saving what the caster feels is good!!
That means that this magic may be able to save Yuri and destroy the evil that's in the Sirius Orb!!
That only works after you've understood it!!!
But there aren't any other options that can do the job!!!
GRAAAH
ZRUNNNNCCHH

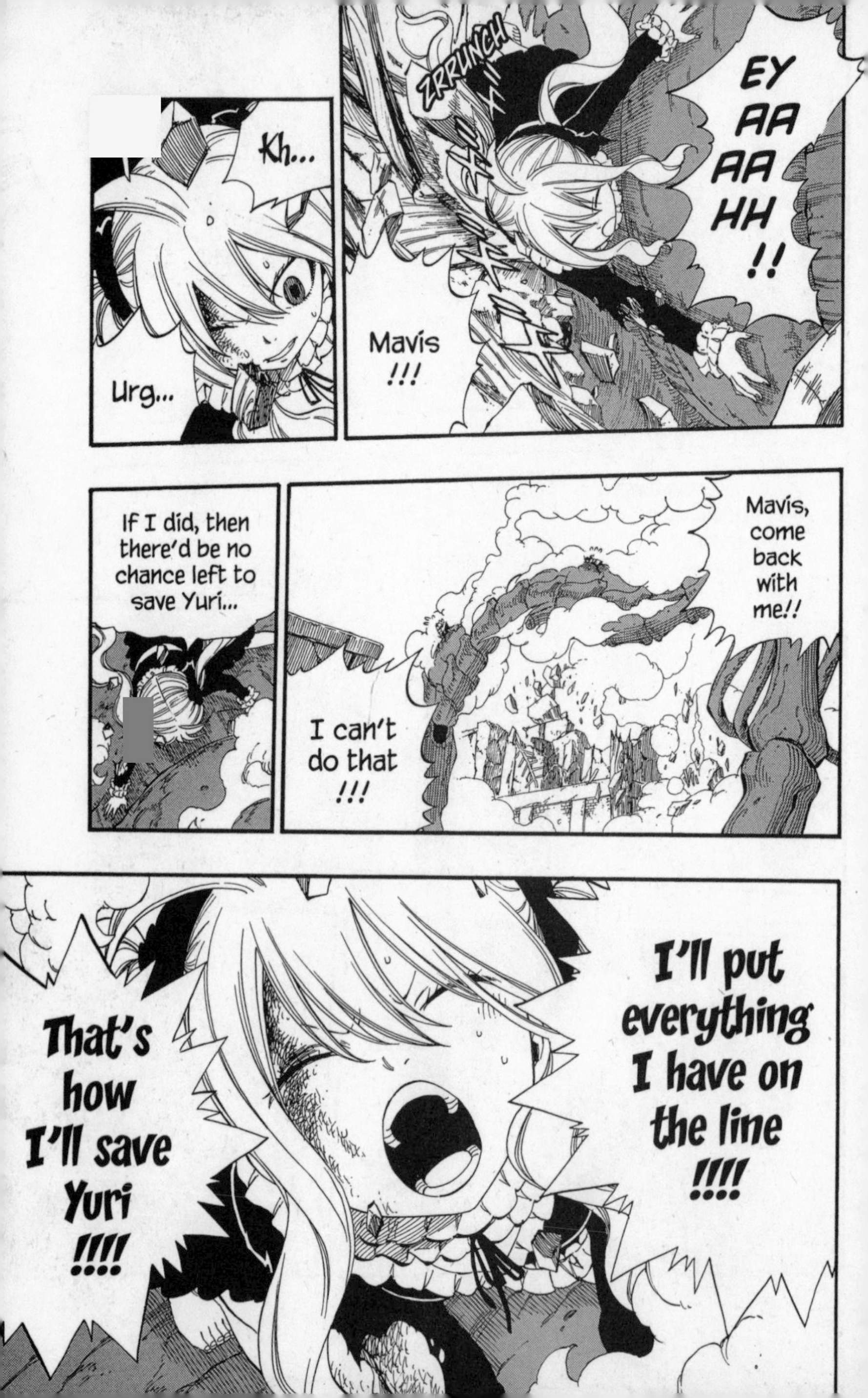
EY AAAAHH!!
ZRRUNCH
Mavis!!!
Kh...
Urg...
Mavis, come back with me!!
I can't do that!!!
If I did, then there'd be no chance left to save Yuri...
I'll put everything I have on the line!!!!
That's how I'll save Yuri!!!!

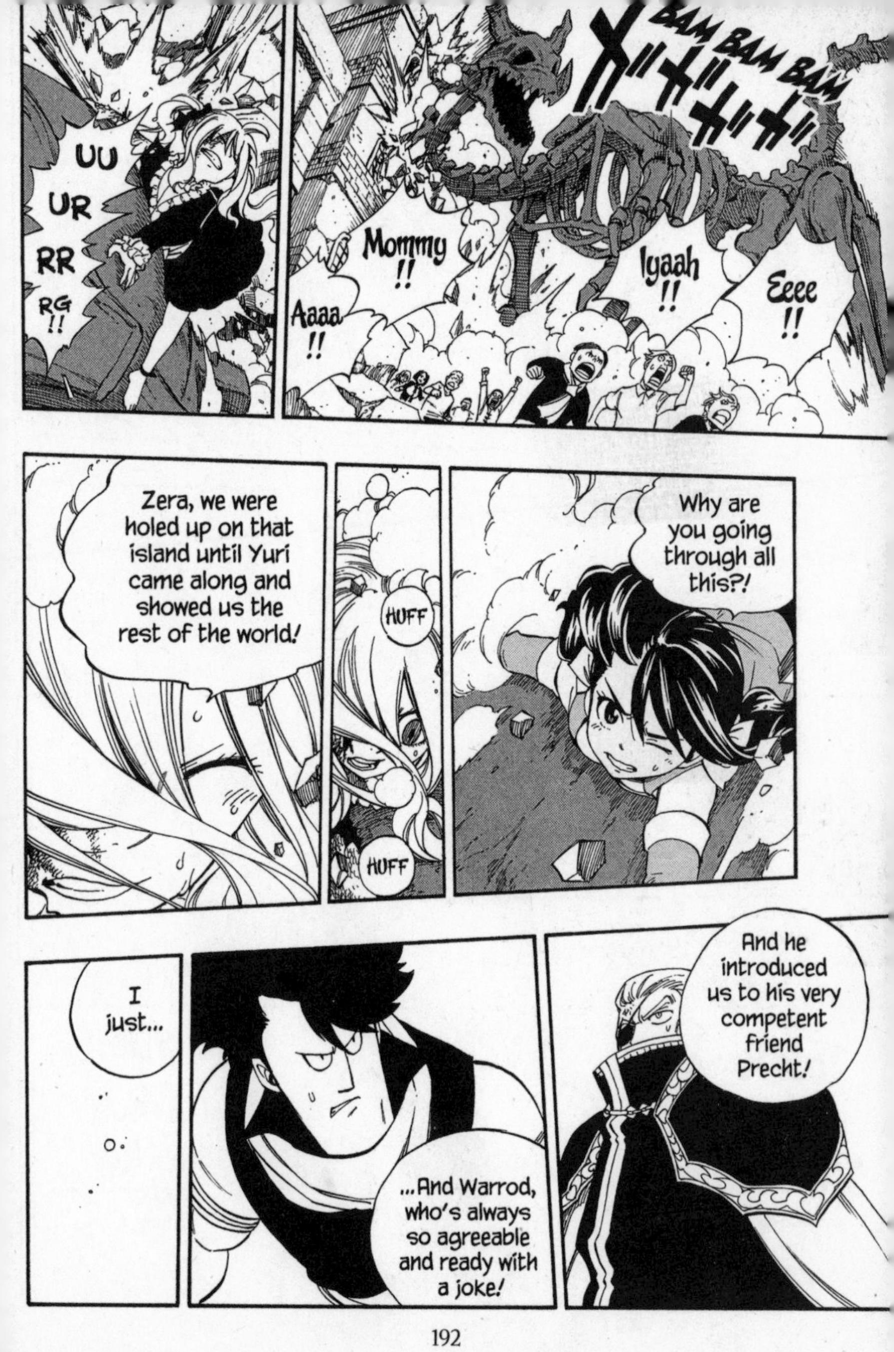
BAM BAM BAM
Eeee!!
Iyaah!!
Mommy!!
Aaaa!!
UU UR RR RG!!
Why are you going through all this?!
HUFF
HUFF
Zera, we were holed up on that island until Yuri came along and showed us the rest of the world!
And he introduced us to his very competent friend Precht!
...And Warrod, who's always so agreeable and ready with a joke!
I just...

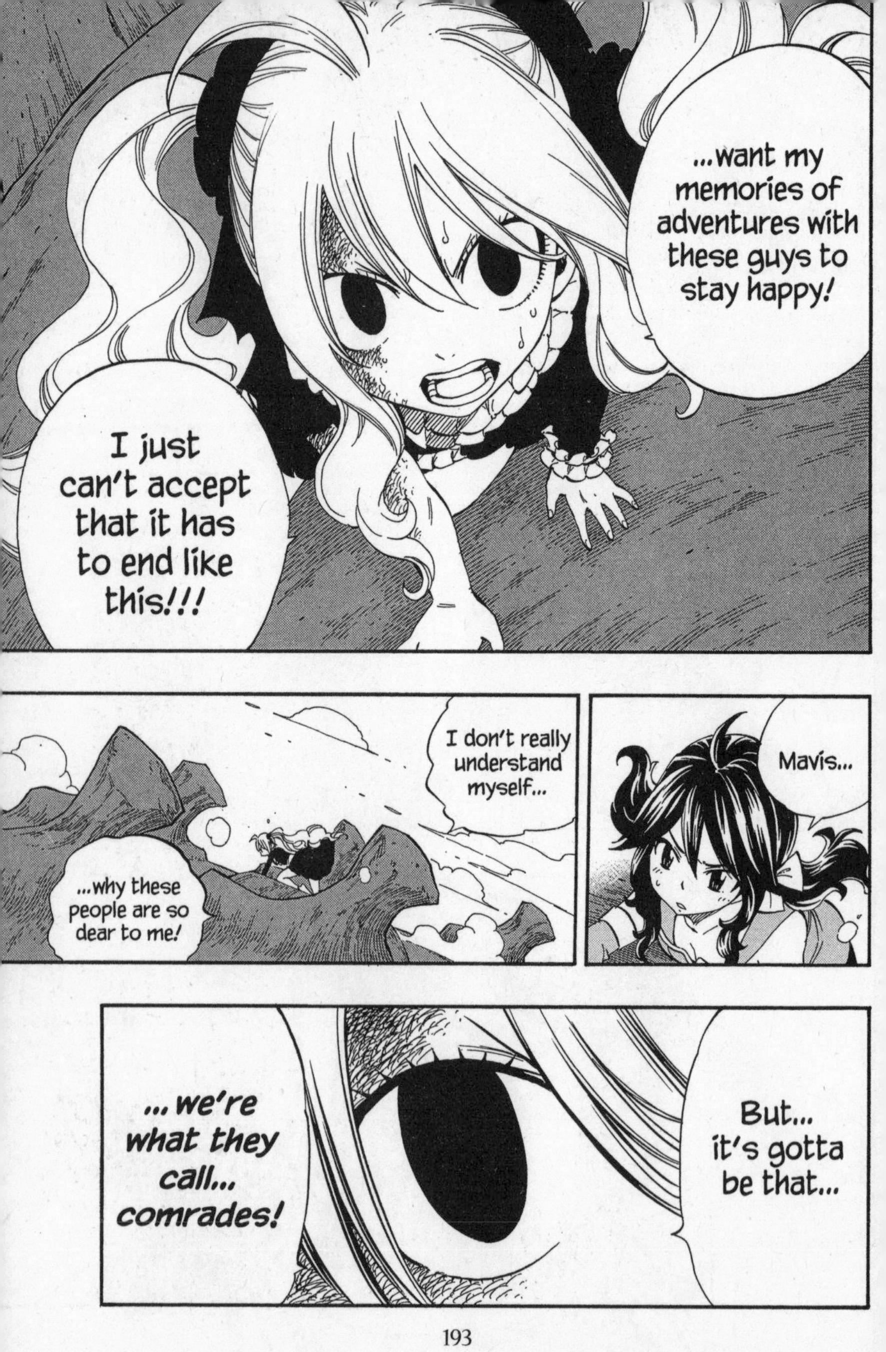
...want my memories of adventures with these guys to stay happy!
I just can't accept that it has to end like this!!!
Mavis...
I don't really understand myself...
...why these people are so dear to me!
But... it's gotta be that...
...we're what they call... comrades!

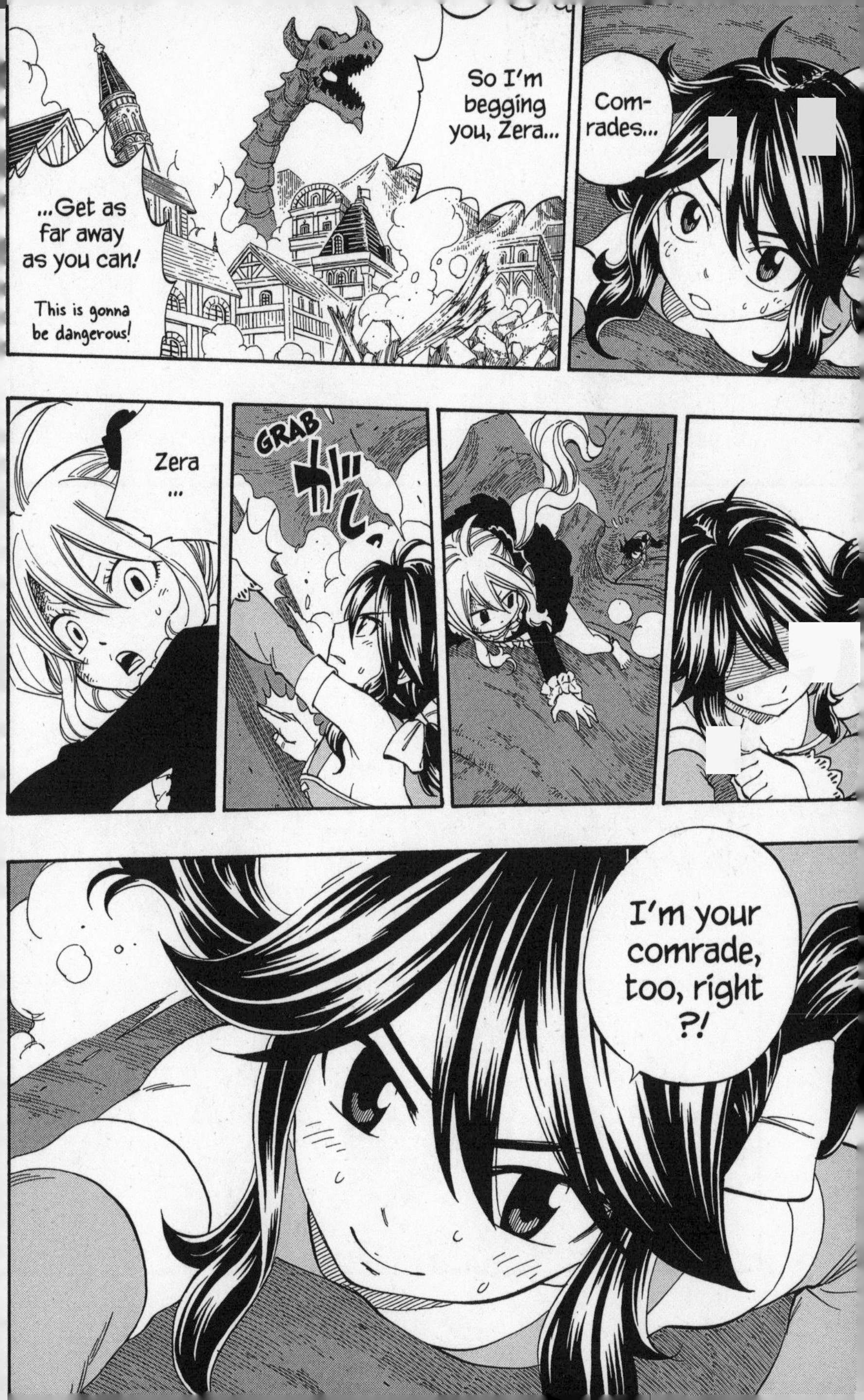
Com-rades...
So I'm begging you, Zera...
...Get as far away as you can!
This is gonna be dangerous!
GRAB
Zera ...
I'm your comrade, too, right?!

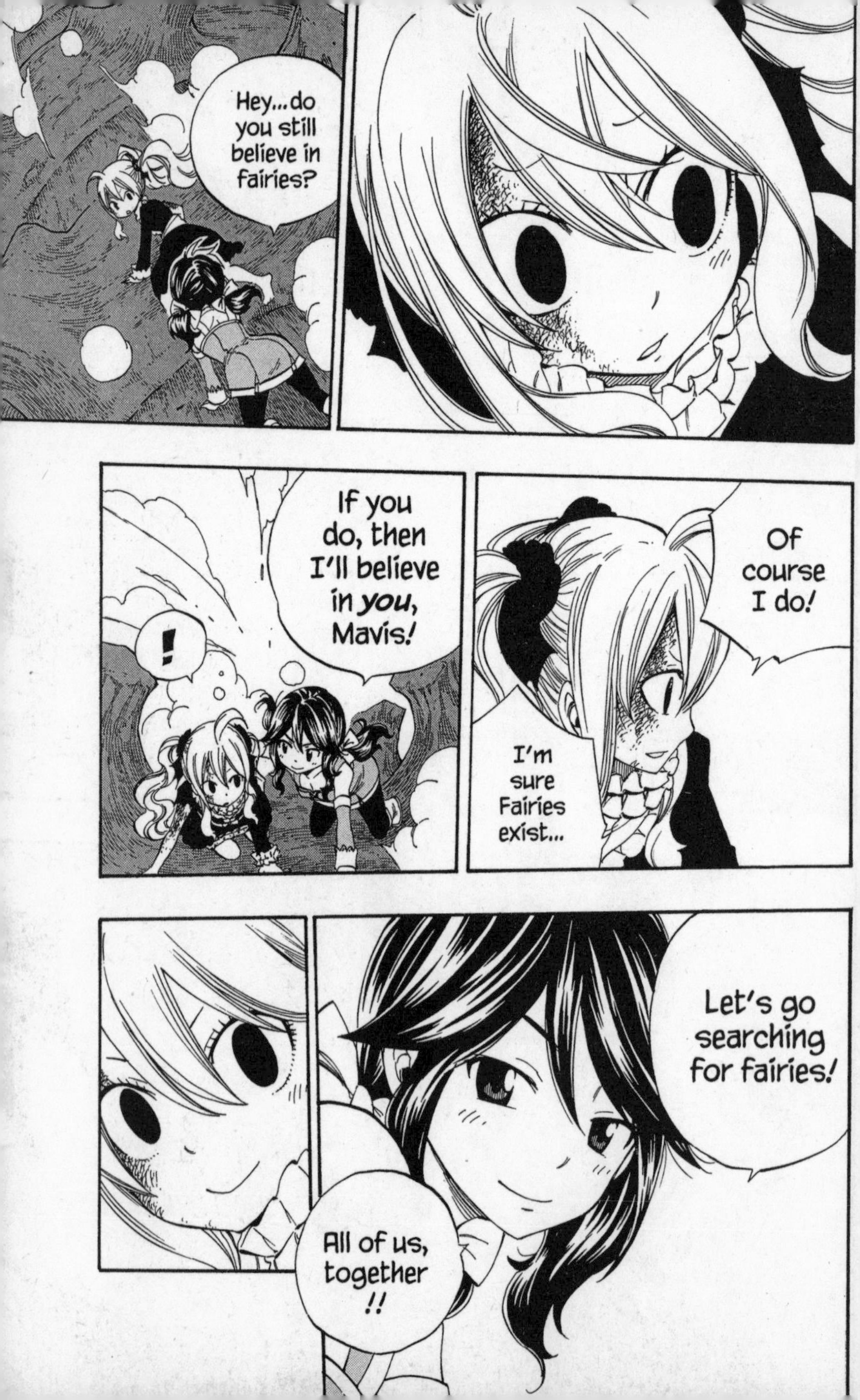
Hey...do you still believe in fairies?
Of course I do!
I'm sure Fairies exist...
If you do, then I'll believe in *you*, Mavis!
!
Let's go searching for fairies!
All of us, together!!

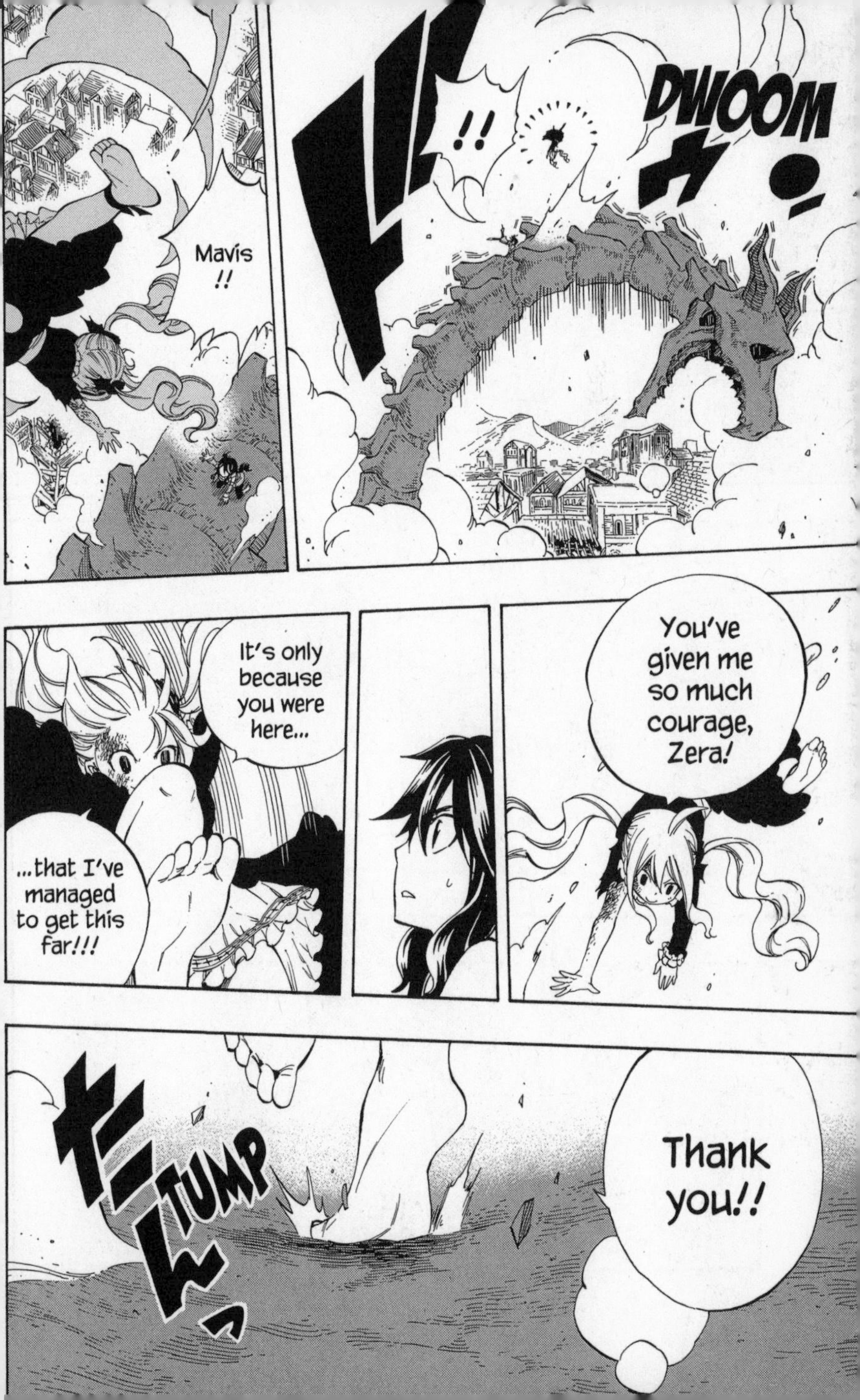
DWOOM
!!
Mavis !!
You've given me so much courage, Zera!
It's only because you were here...
...that I've managed to get this far!!!
Thank you!!
TUMP

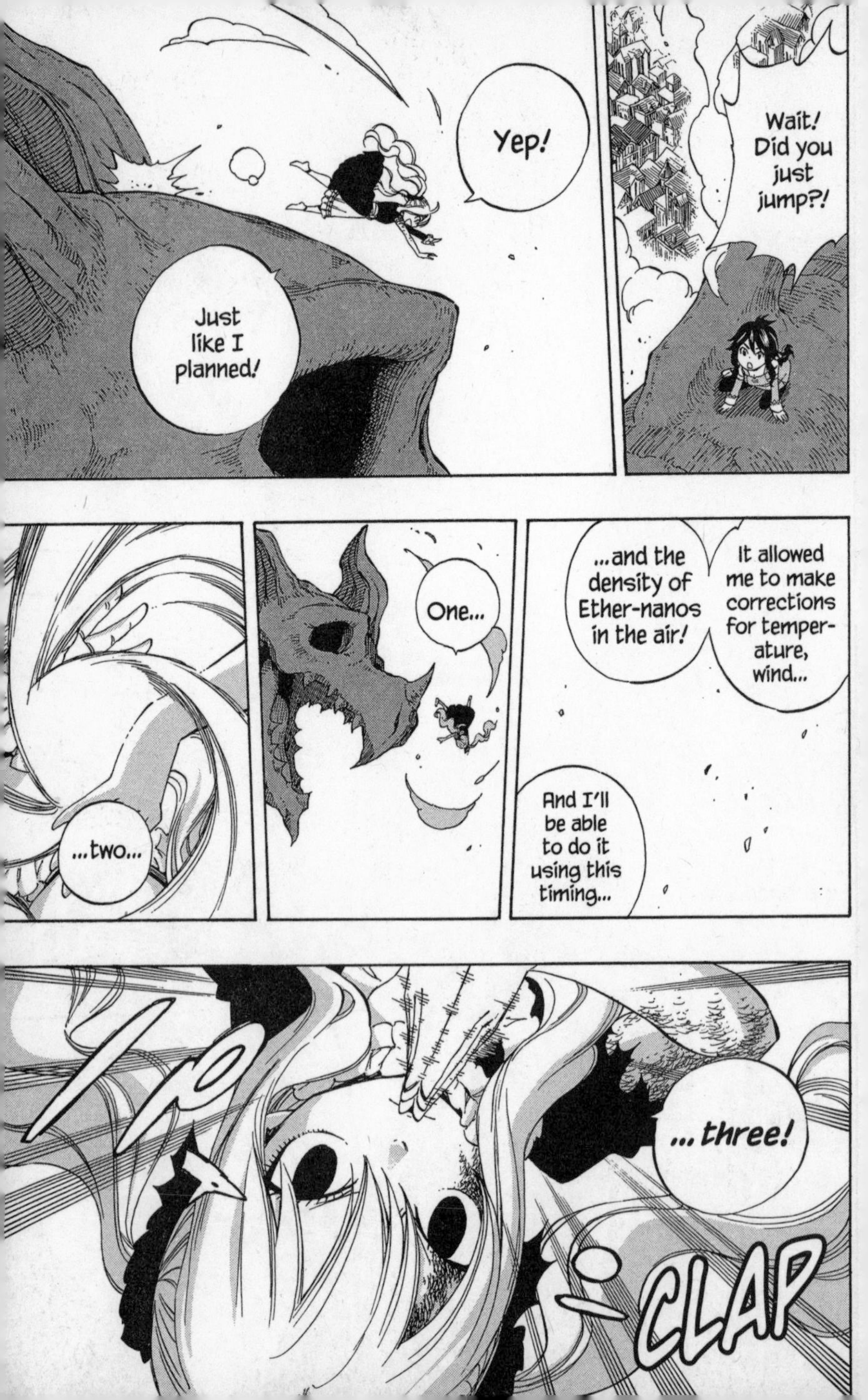
Wait! Did you just jump?!
Yep!
Just like I planned!
It allowed me to make corrections for temper-ature, wind...
...and the density of Ether-nanos in the air!
And I'll be able to do it using this timing...
One...
...two...
...three!
CLAP

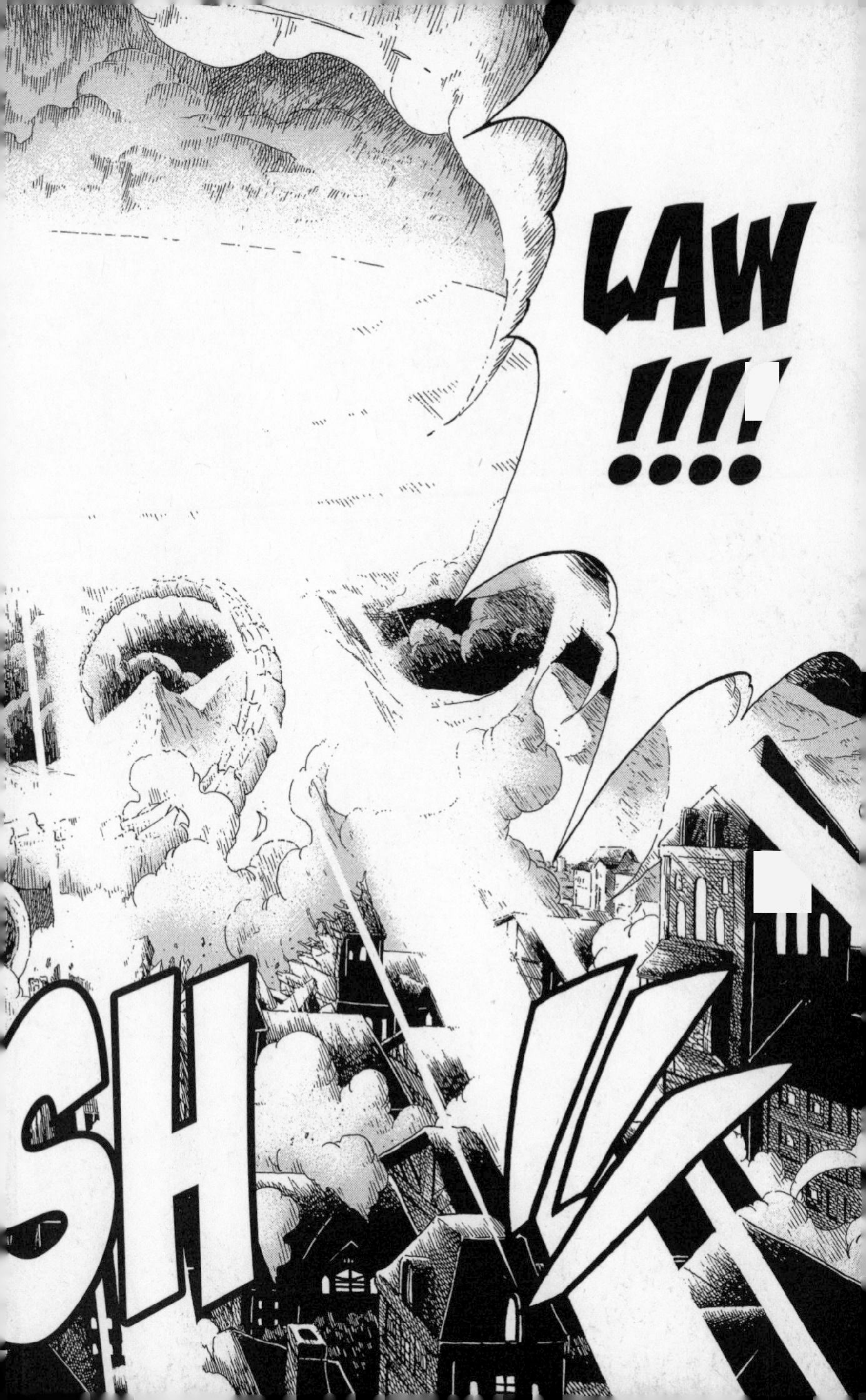
LAW!!!!

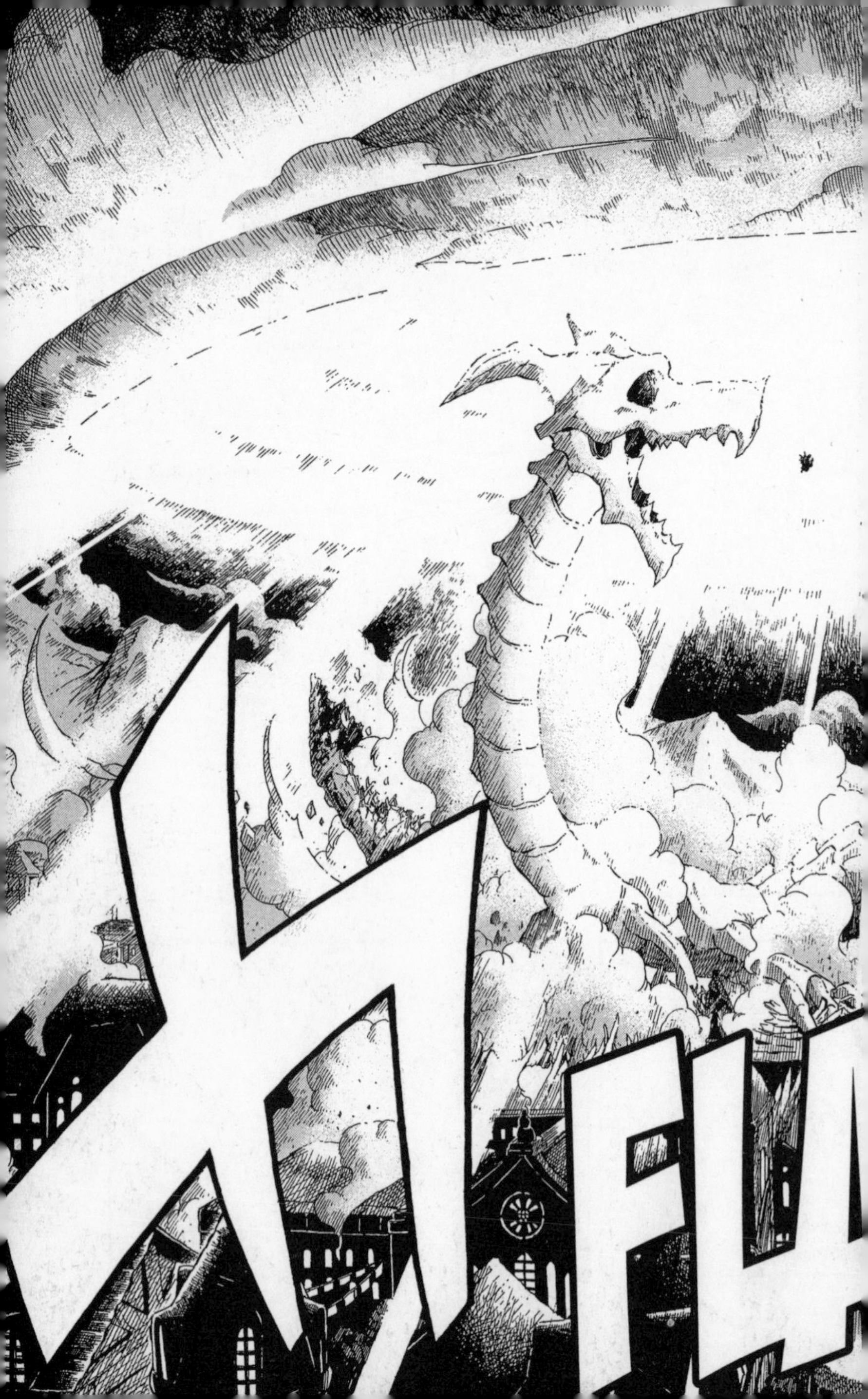

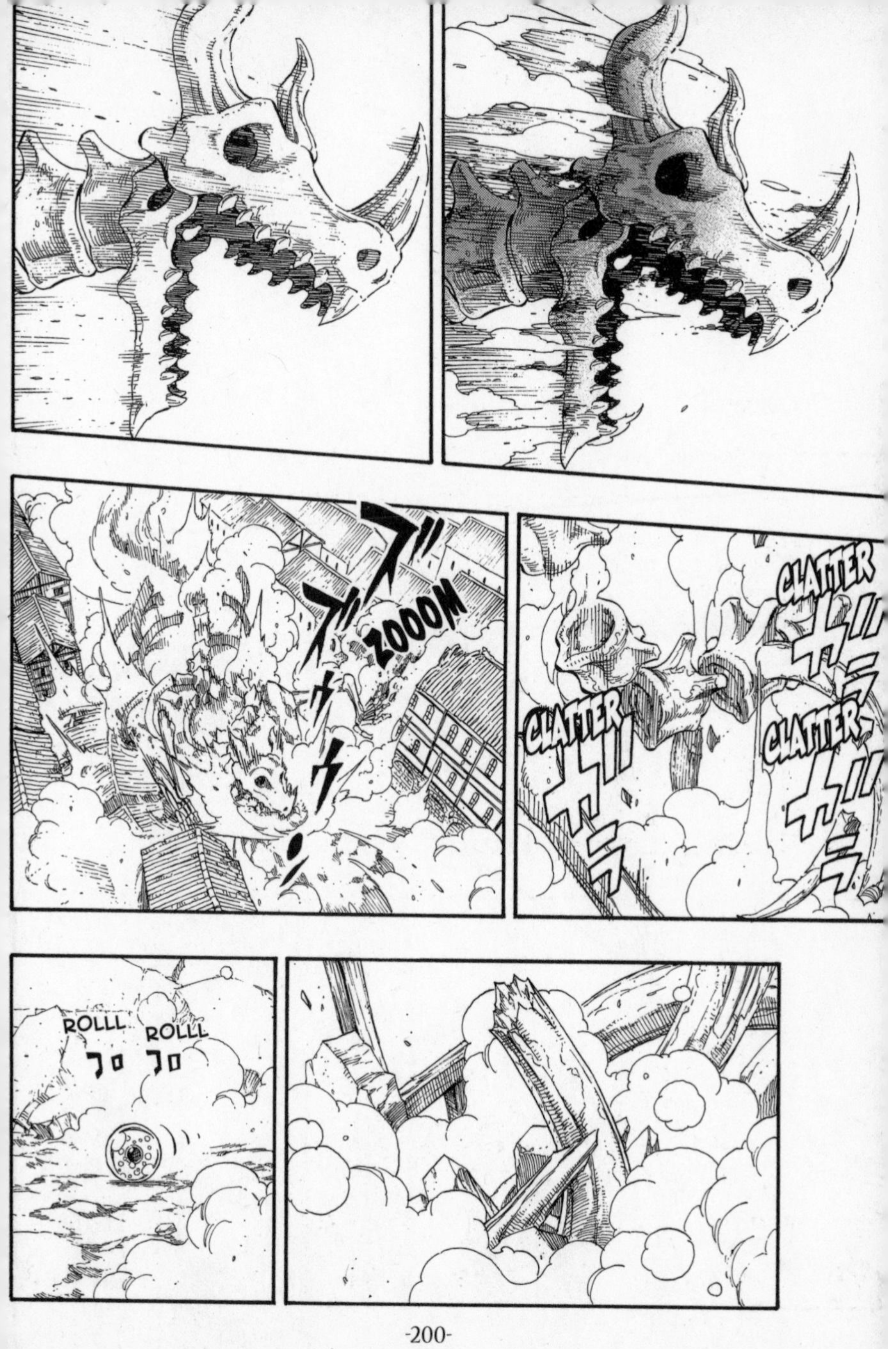

CLATTER
ガラ
CLATTER
ガラ
CLATTER
ガラ
ZOOOM
ROLLL
コロ
ROLLL
コロ

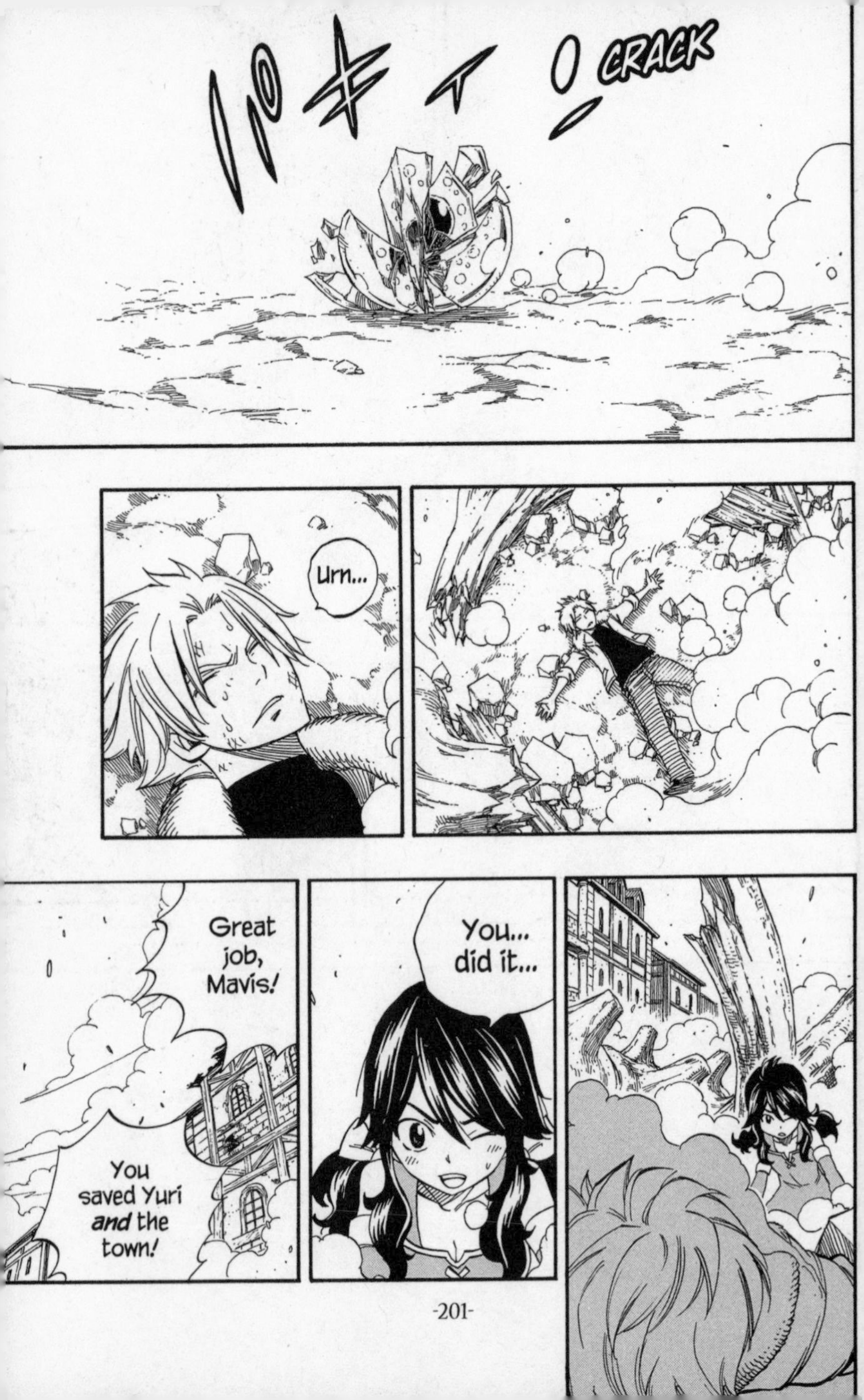
CRACK
Urn...
You... did it...
Great job, Mavis!
You saved Yuri *and* the town!

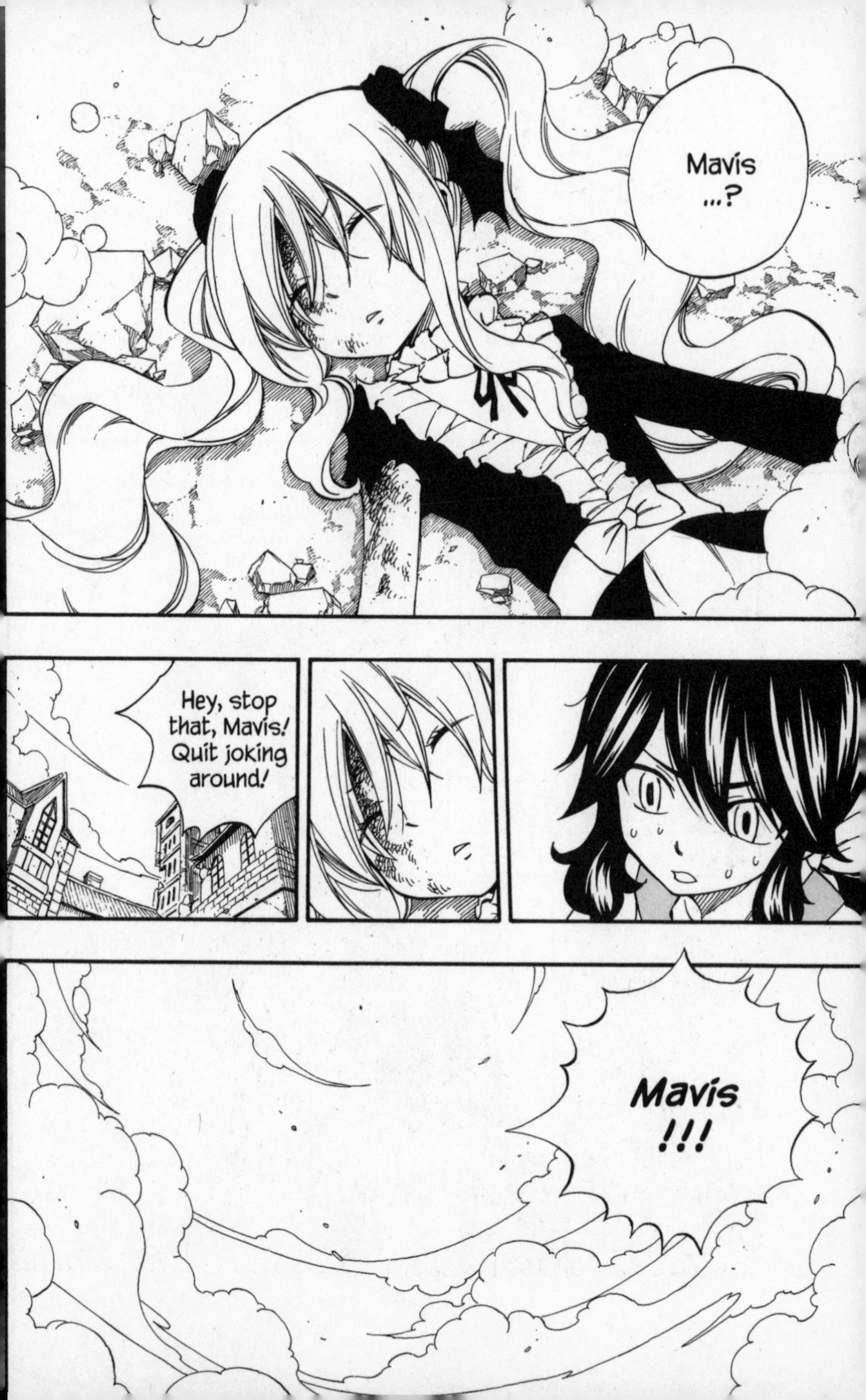
Mavis ...?
Hey, stop that, Mavis! Quit joking around!
Mavis !!!

FAIRY TAIL ZERO

Chapter 11: That Which Vanishes

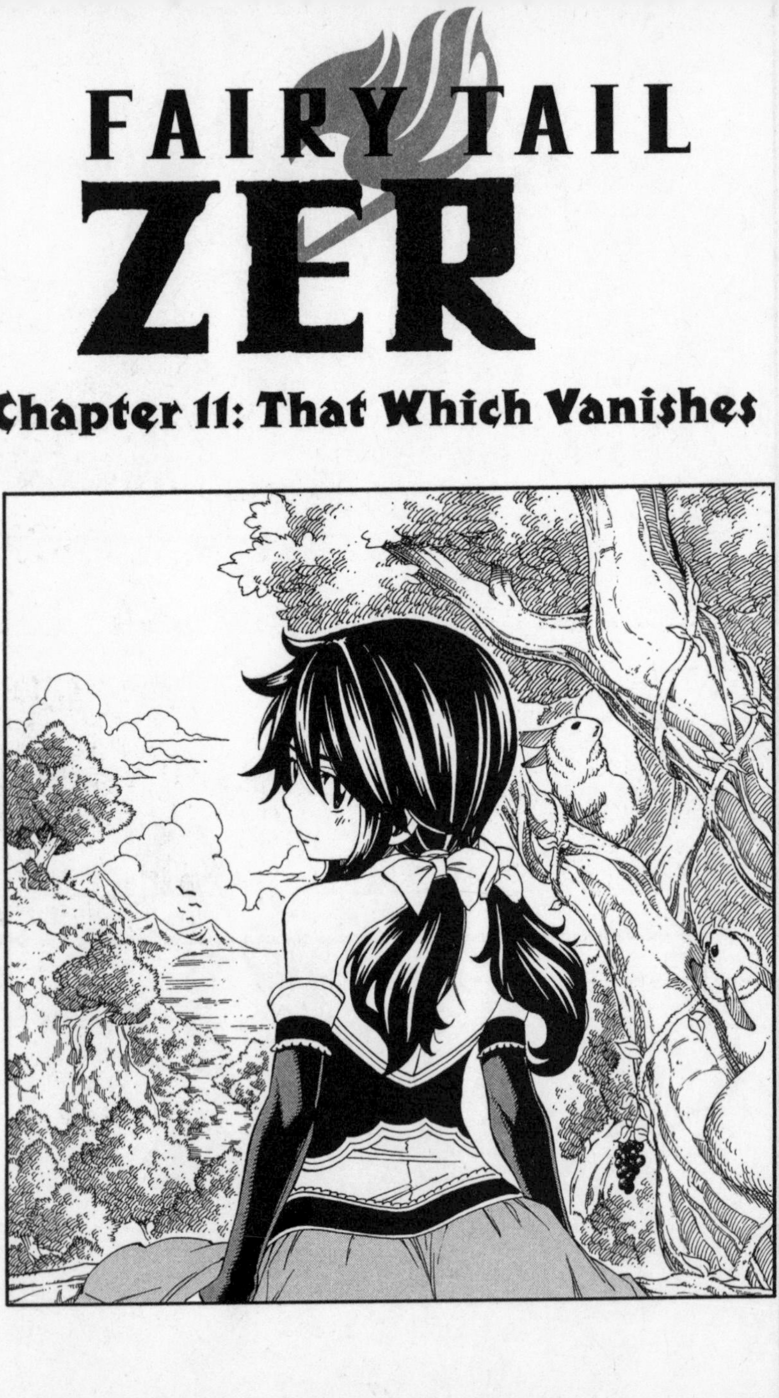

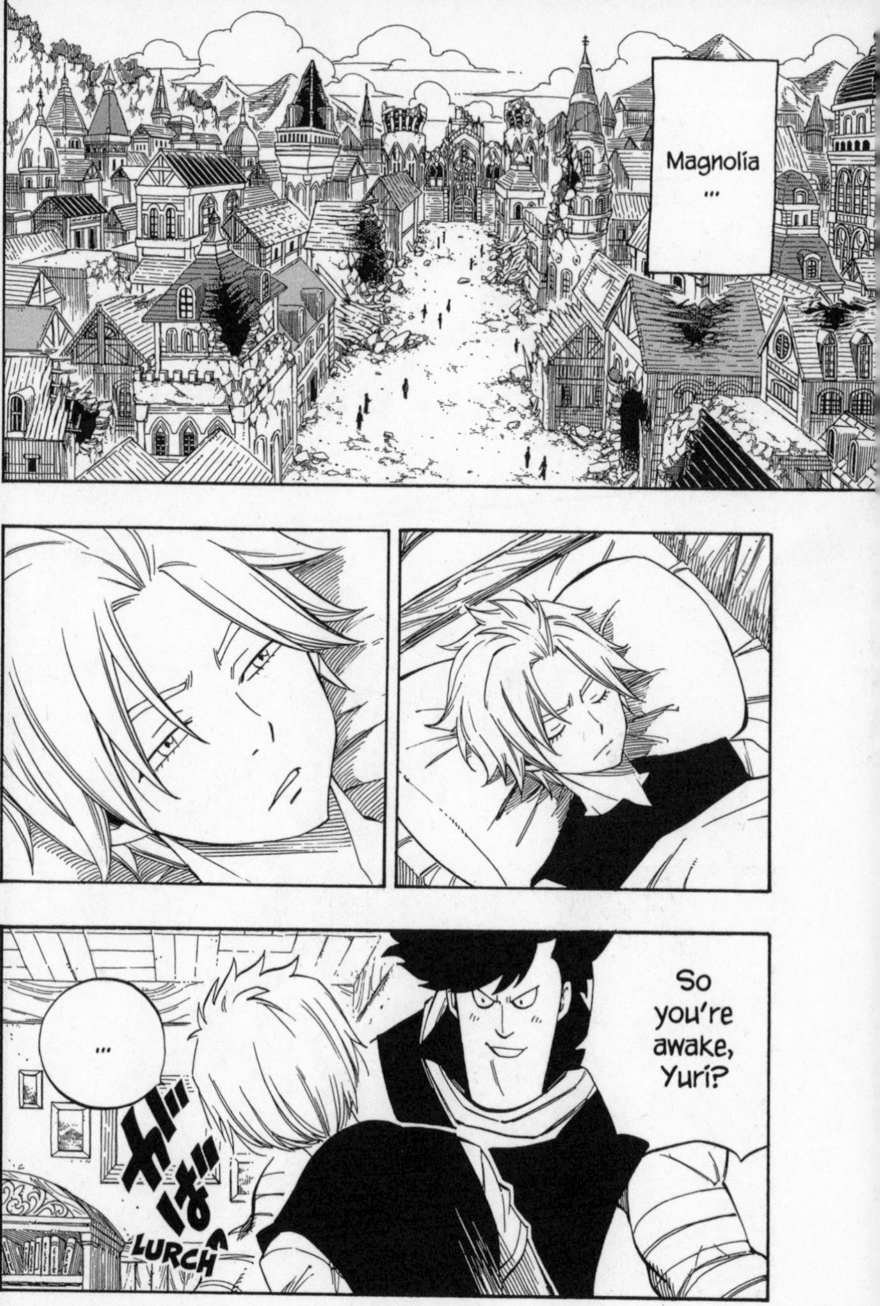
Magnolia
...
So you're awake, Yuri?
...
LURCH

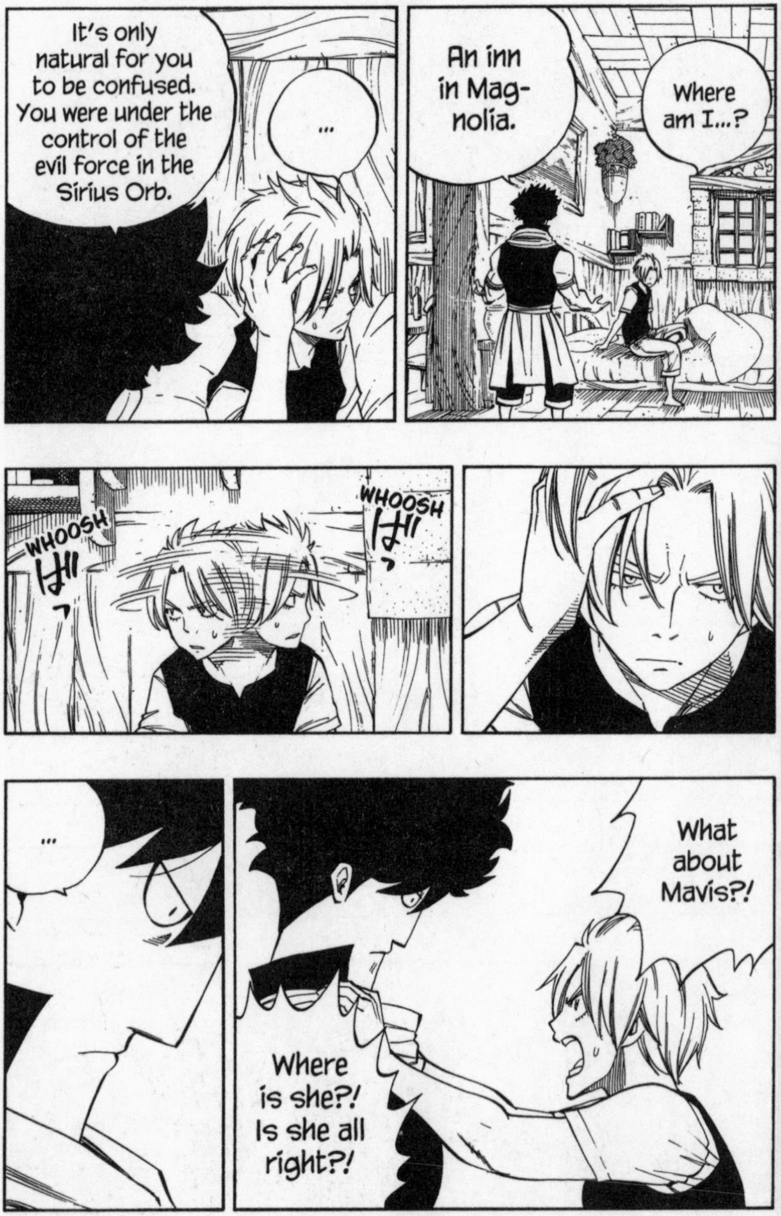
Where am I...?
An inn in Mag-nolia.
...
It's only natural for you to be confused. You were under the control of the evil force in the Sirius Orb.
WHOOSH
ばっ
WHOOSH
ばっ
What about Mavis?!
Where is she?! Is she all right?!
...

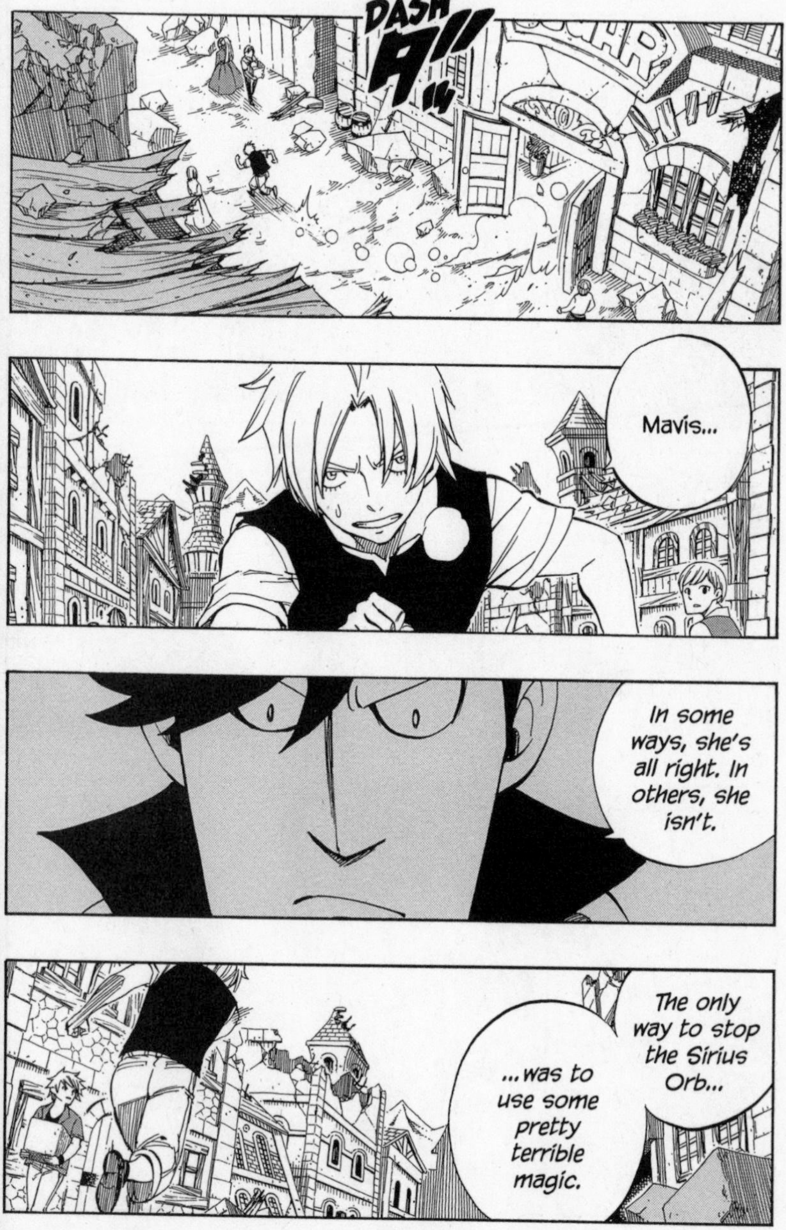
DASH
Mavis...
In some ways, she's all right. In others, she isn't.
The only way to stop the Sirius Orb...
...was to use some pretty terrible magic.

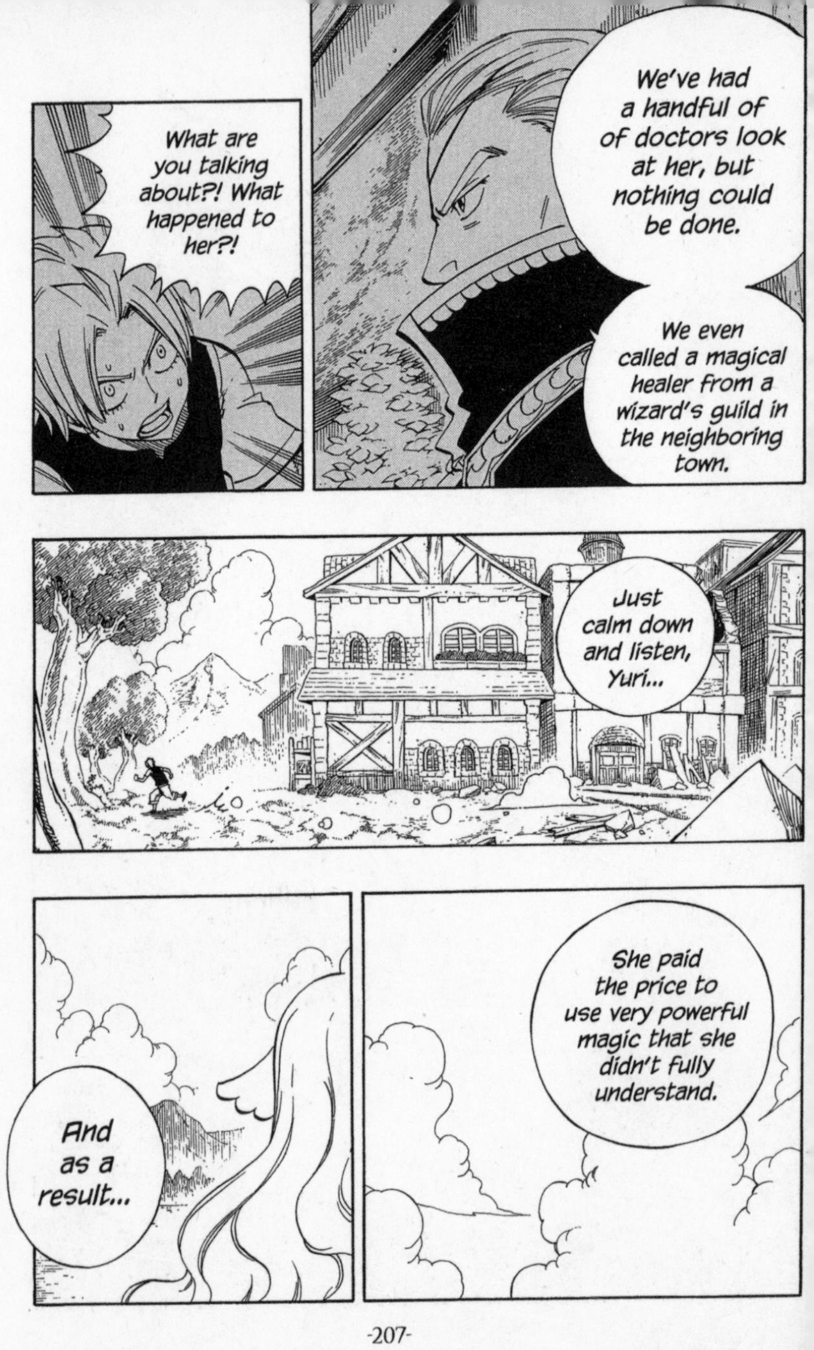
We've had a handful of of doctors look at her, but nothing could be done.
We even called a magical healer from a wizard's guild in the neighboring town.
What are you talking about?! What happened to her?!
Just calm down and listen, Yuri...
She paid the price to use very powerful magic that she didn't fully understand.
And as a result...

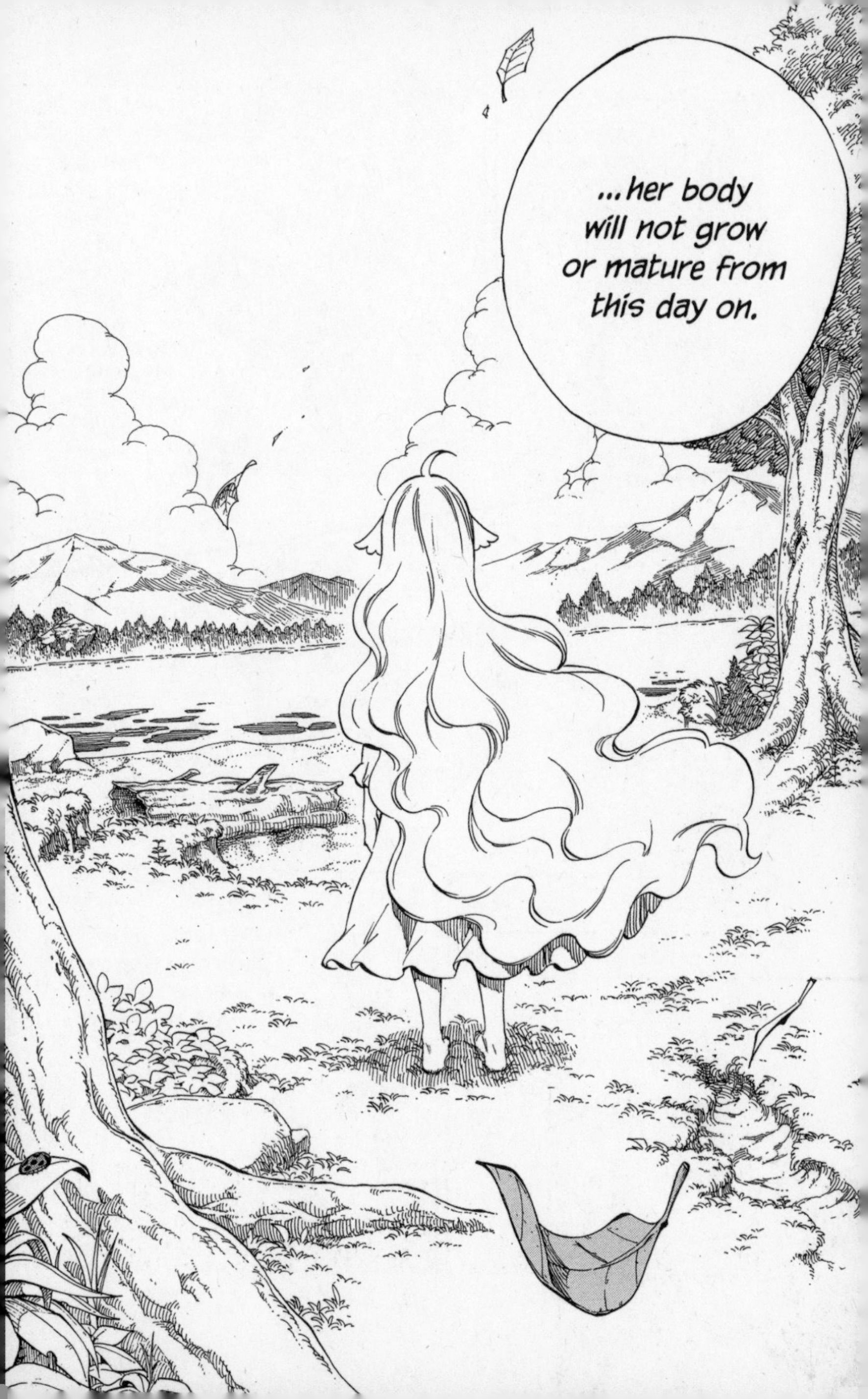
...her body will not grow or mature from this day on.

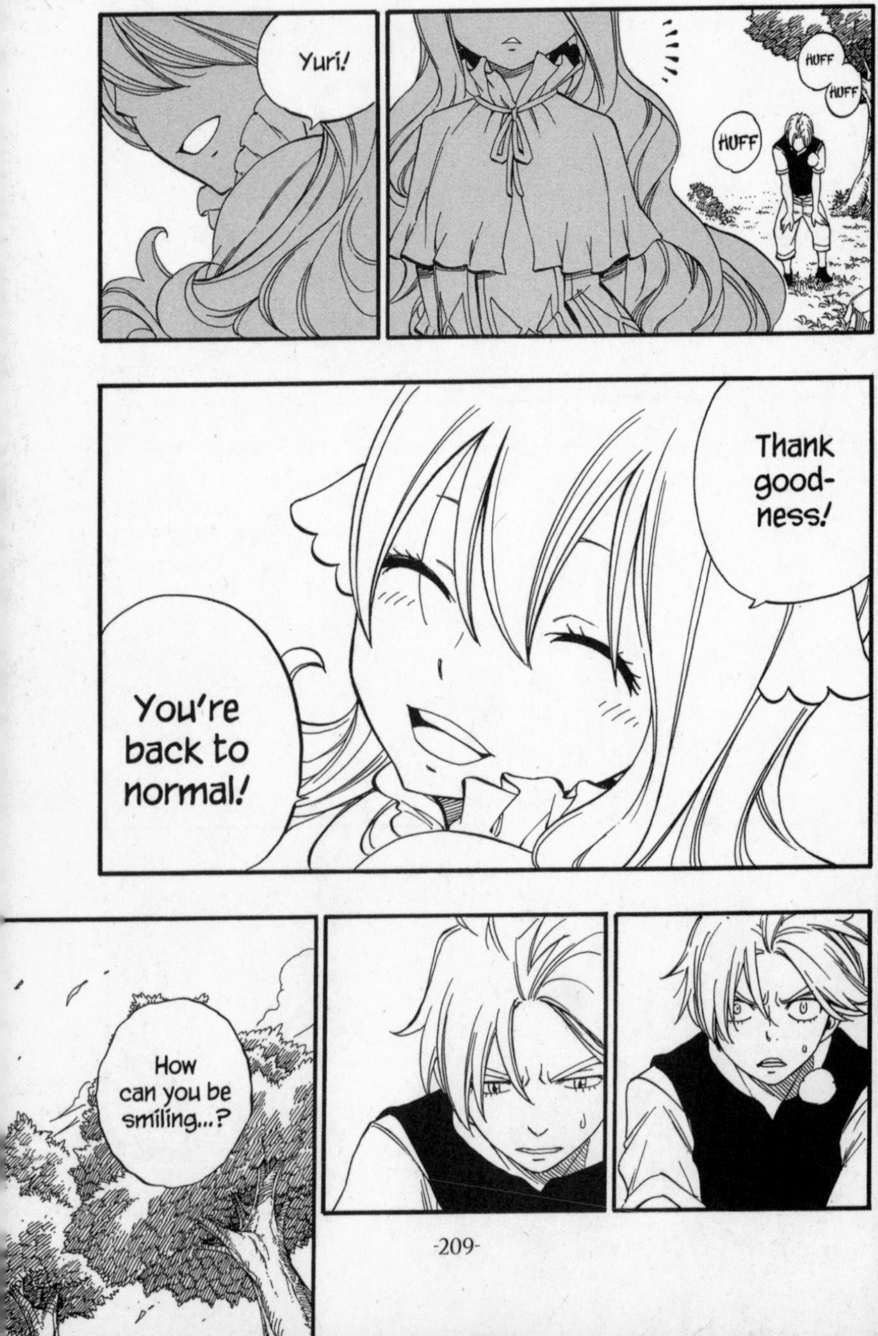
HUFF
HUFF
HUFF
Yuri!
Thank goodness!
You're back to normal!
How can you be smiling...?

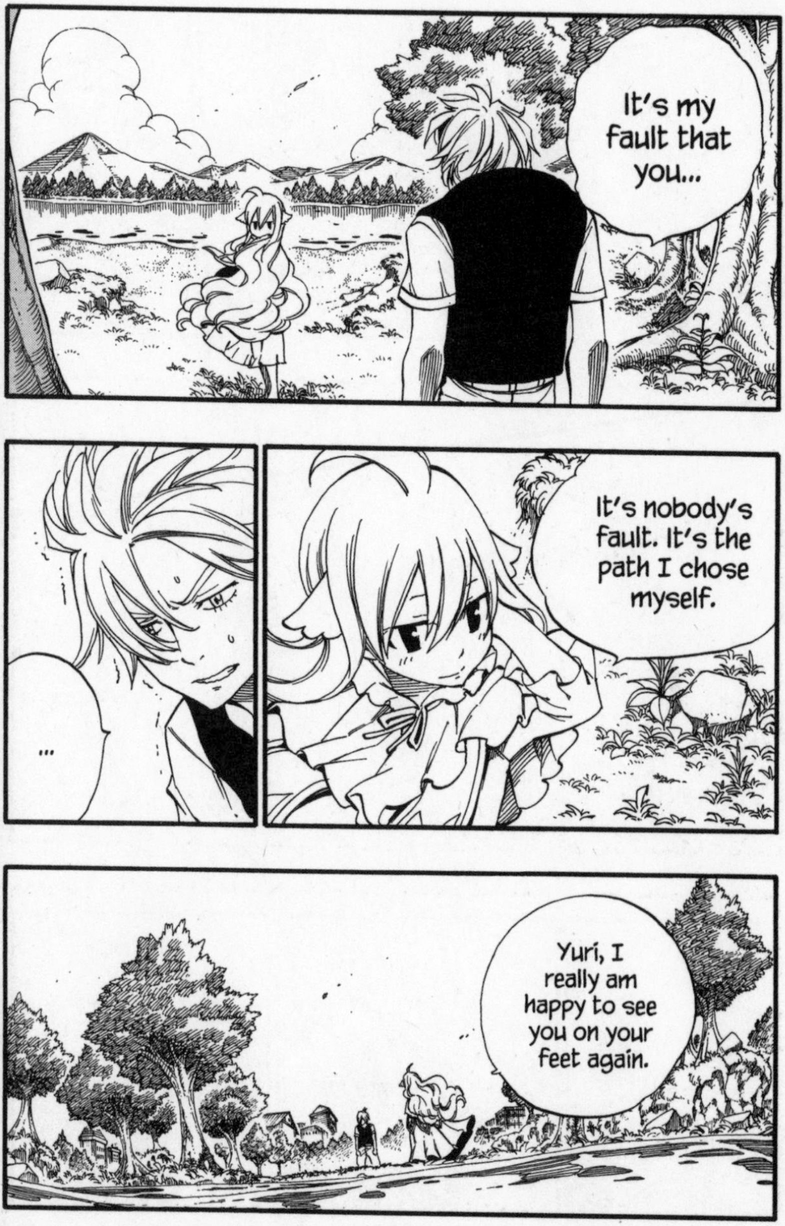
It's my fault that you...
It's nobody's fault. It's the path I chose myself.
...
Yuri, I really am happy to see you on your feet again.

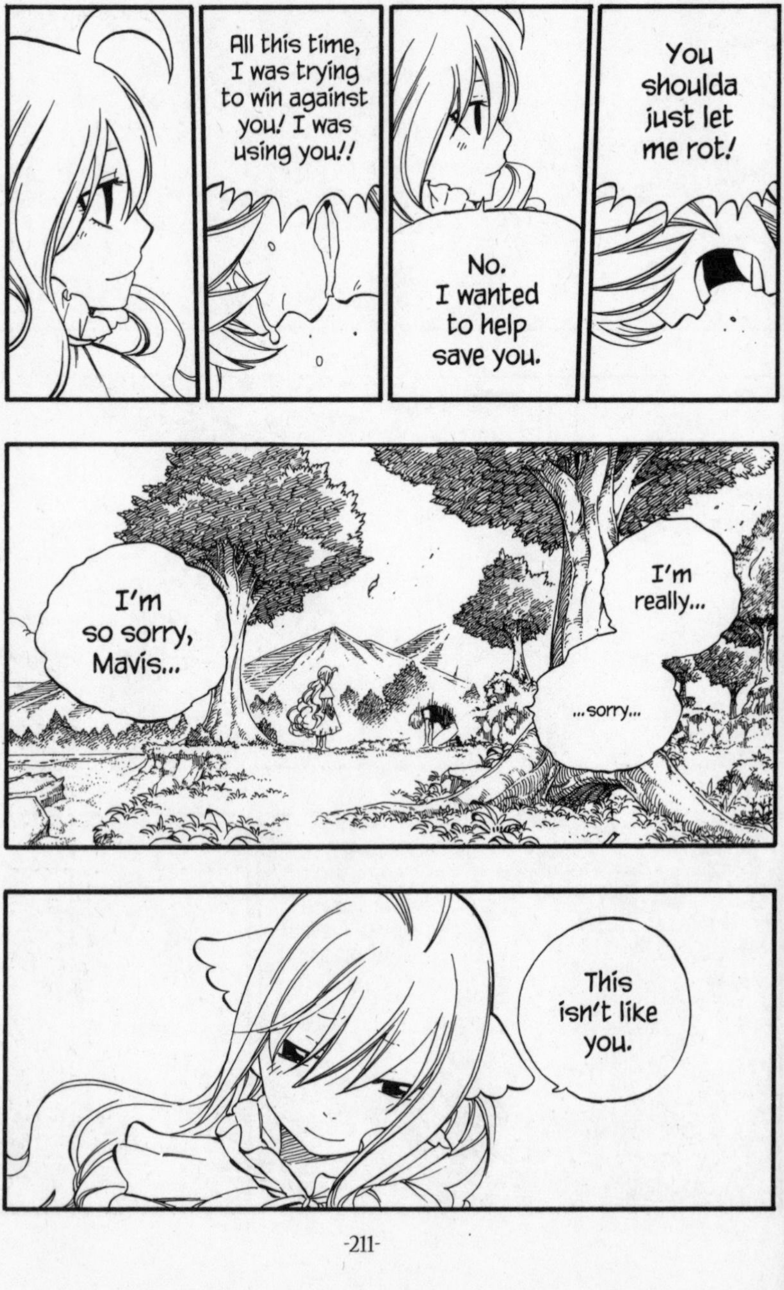
You shoulda just let me rot!
No. I wanted to help save you.
All this time, I was trying to win against you! I was using you!!
I'm really...
...sorry...
I'm so sorry, Mavis...
This isn't like you.

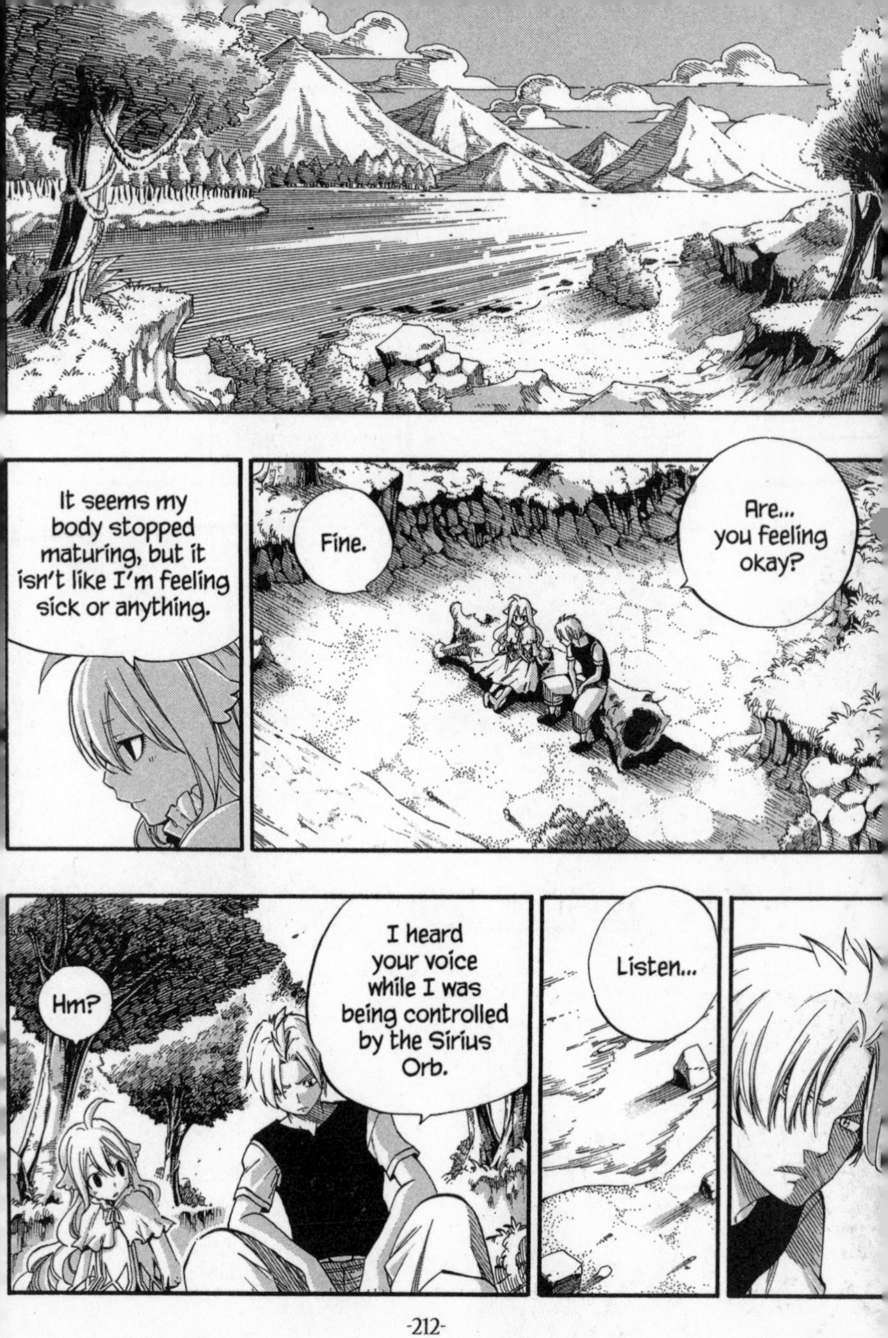
Are... you feeling okay?
Fine.
It seems my body stopped maturing, but it isn't like I'm feeling sick or anything.
Listen...
I heard your voice while I was being controlled by the Sirius Orb.
Hm?

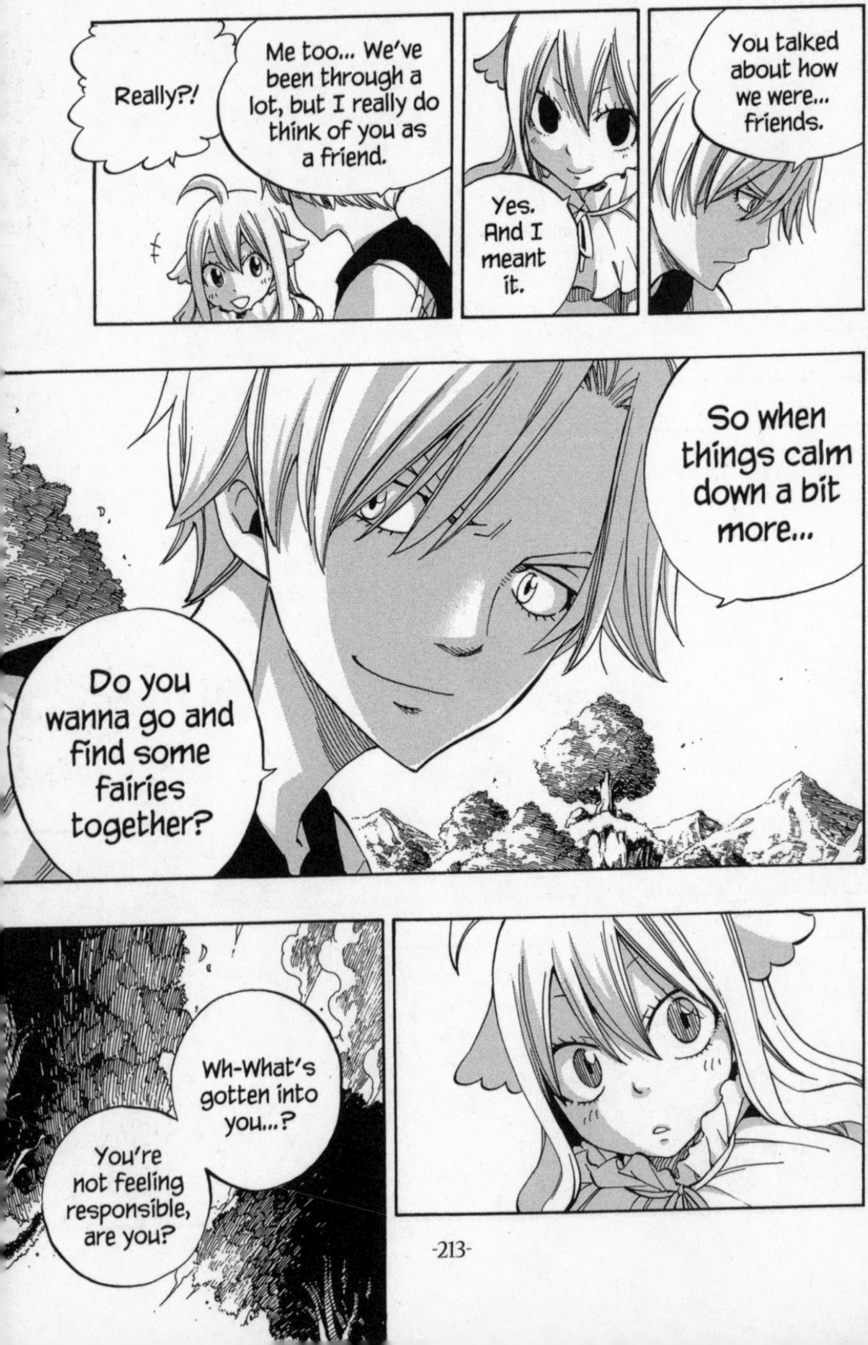
You talked about how we were... friends.
Yes. And I meant it.
Me too... We've been through a lot, but I really do think of you as a friend.
Really?!
So when things calm down a bit more...
Do you wanna go and find some fairies together?
Wh-What's gotten into you...?
You're not feeling responsible, are you?

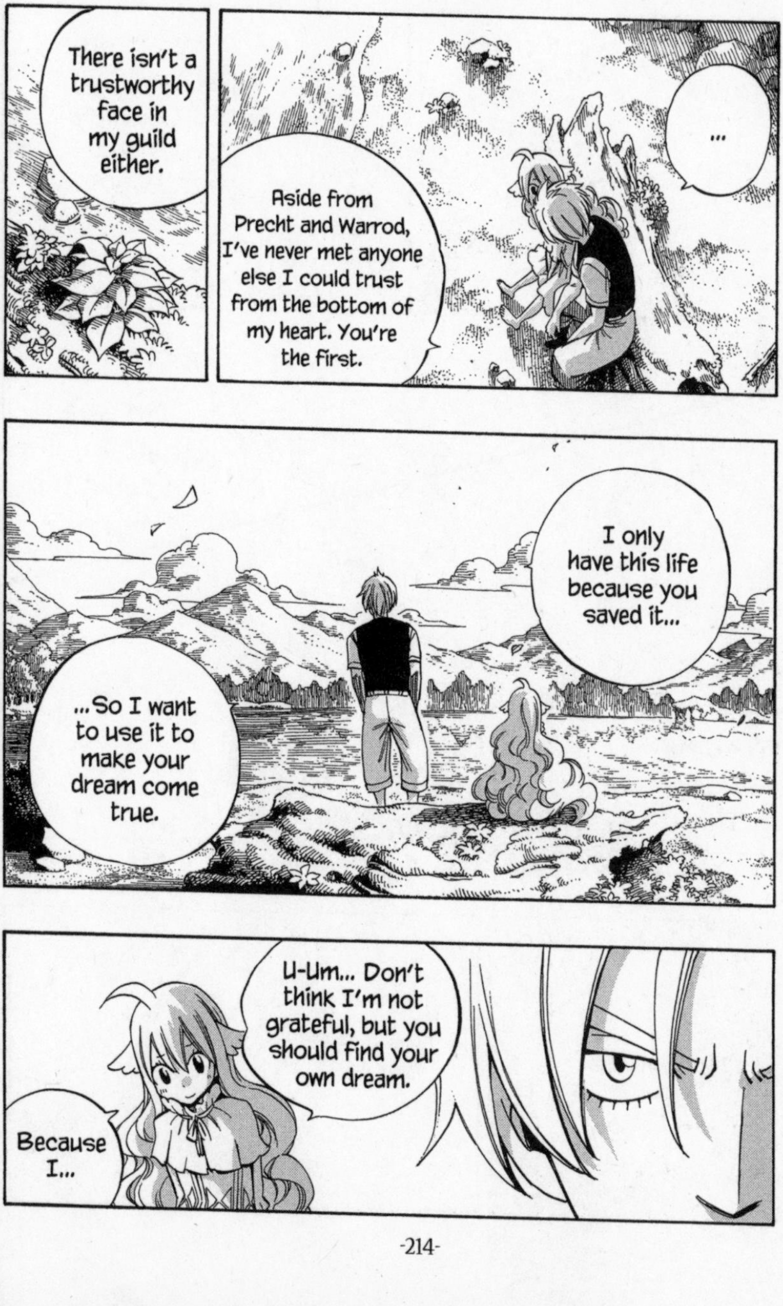
...
Aside from Precht and Warrod, I've never met anyone else I could trust from the bottom of my heart. You're the first.
There isn't a trustworthy face in my guild either.
I only have this life because you saved it...
...So I want to use it to make your dream come true.
U-Um... Don't think I'm not grateful, but you should find your own dream.
Because I...

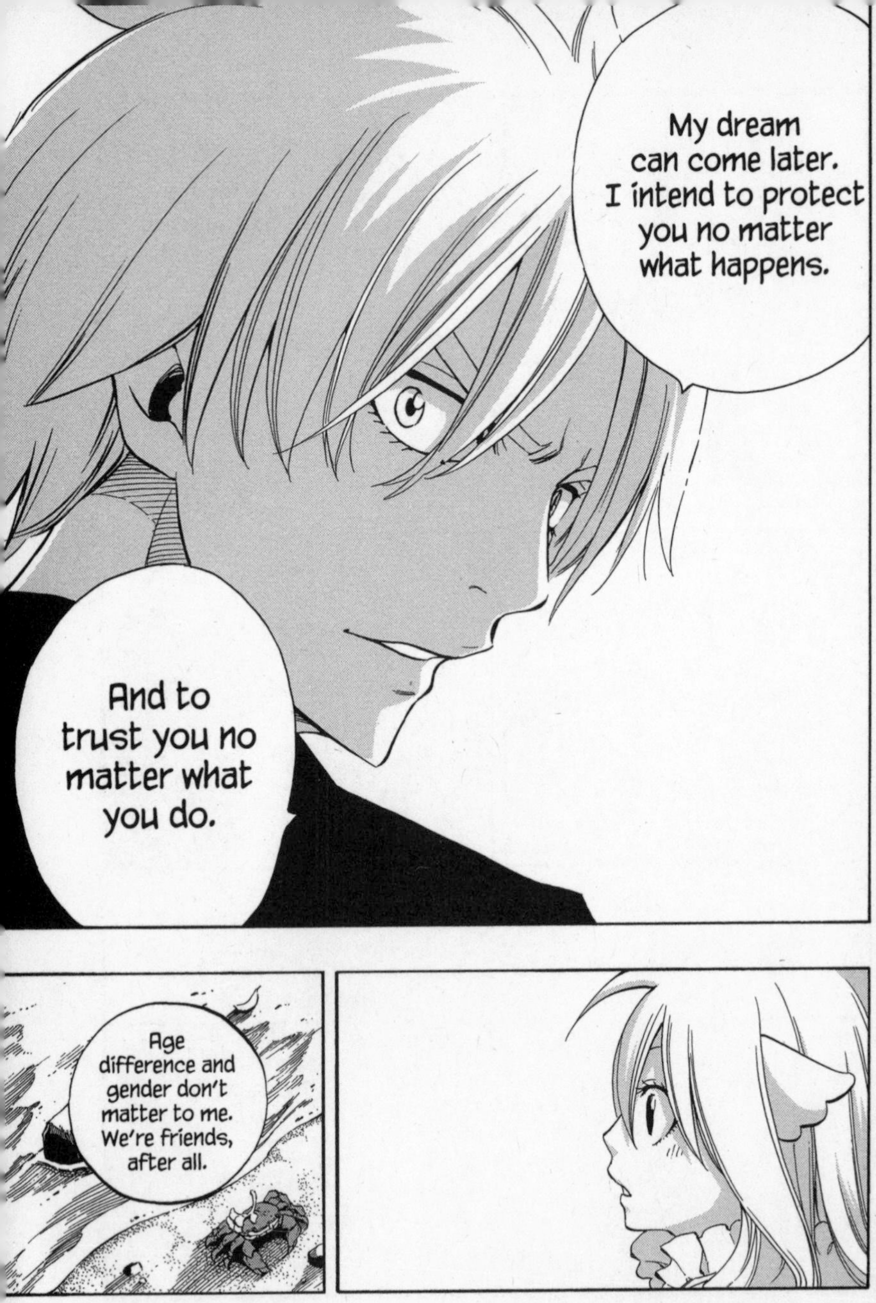
My dream can come later. I intend to protect you no matter what happens.
And to trust you no matter what you do.
Age difference and gender don't matter to me. We're friends, after all.

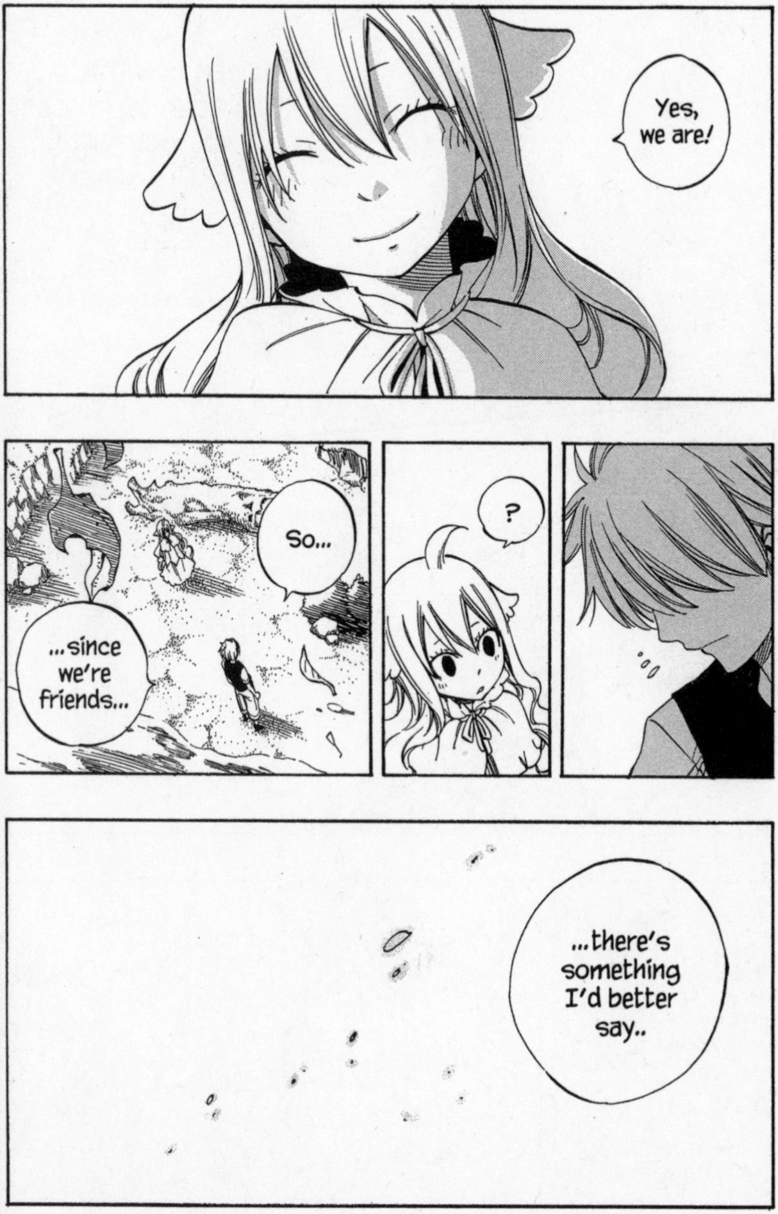
Yes, we are!
?
So...
...since we're friends...
...there's something I'd better say..

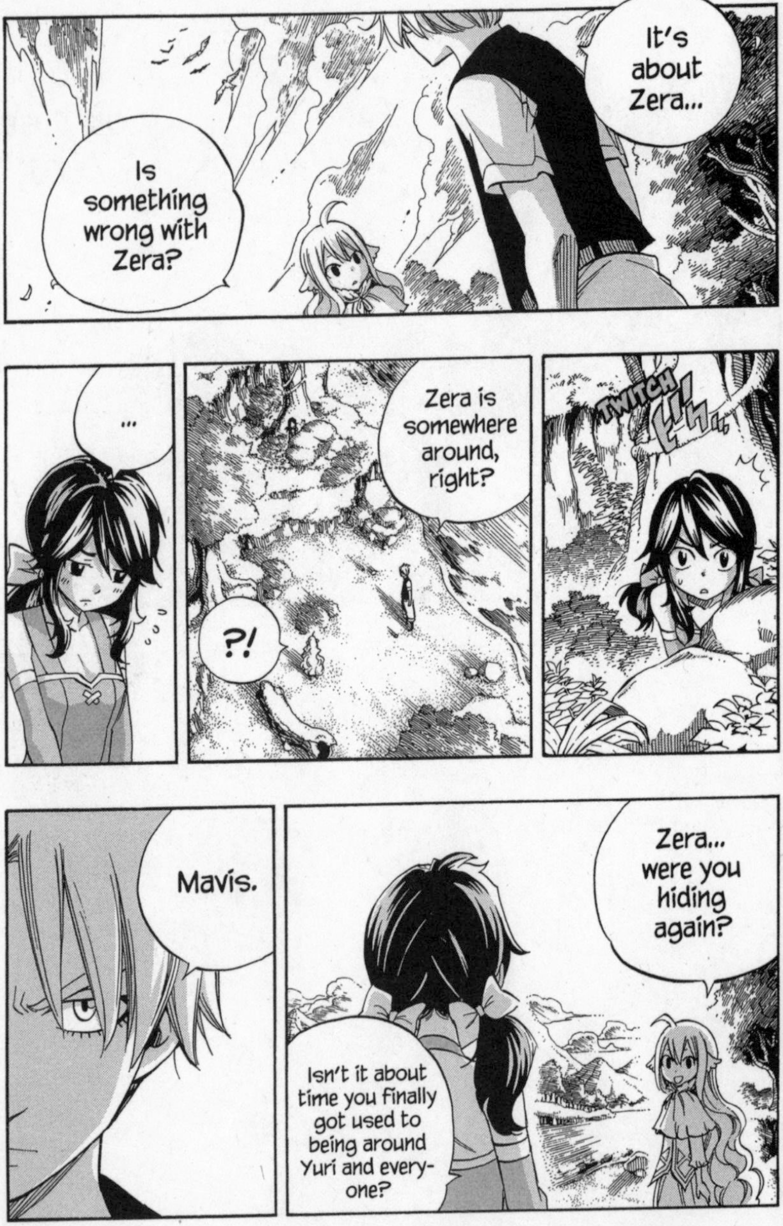
It's about Zera...
Is something wrong with Zera?
TWITCH
Zera is somewhere around, right?
?!
...
Zera... were you hiding again?
Isn't it about time you finally got used to being around Yuri and everyone?
Mavis.

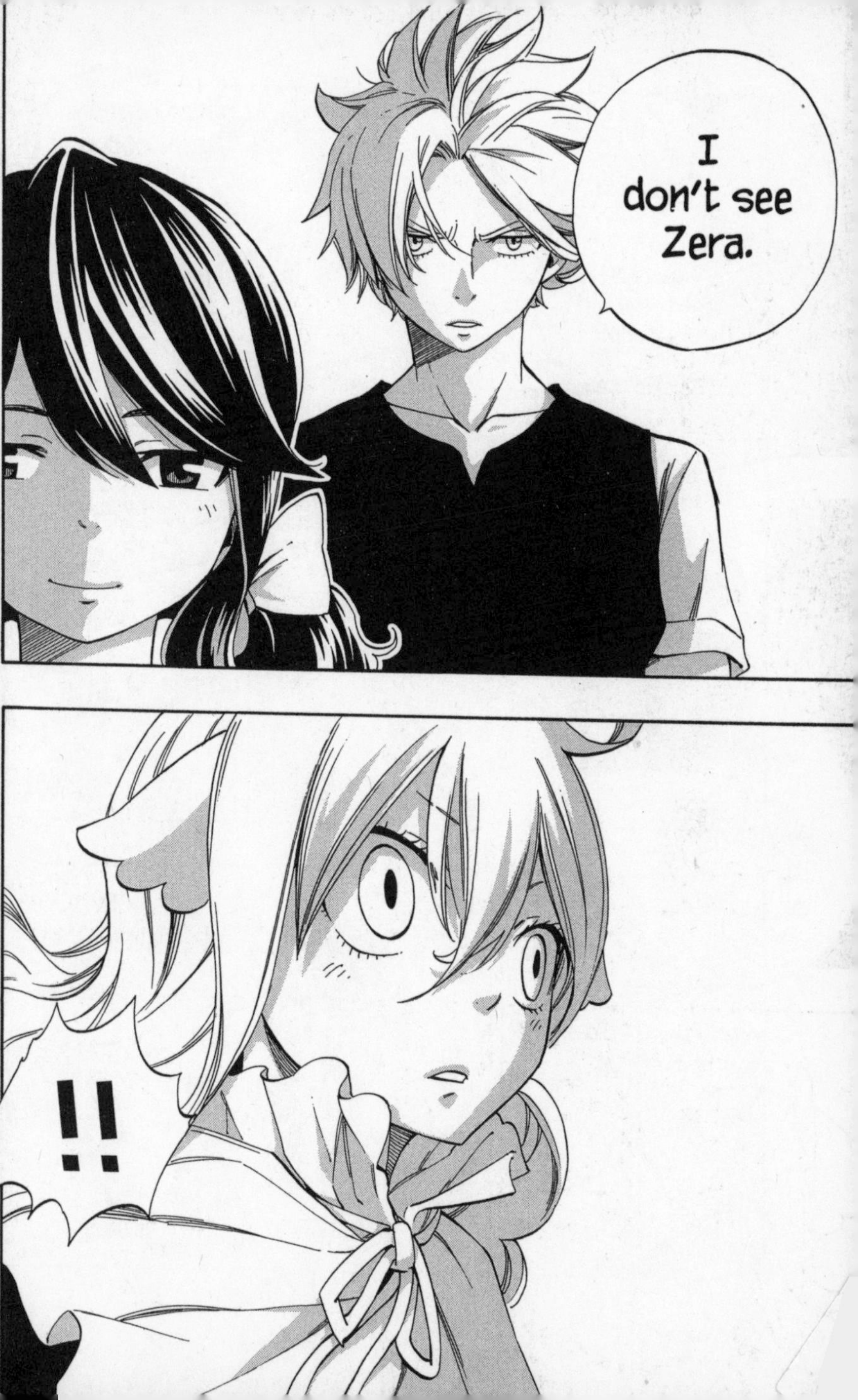
I don't see Zera.
!!

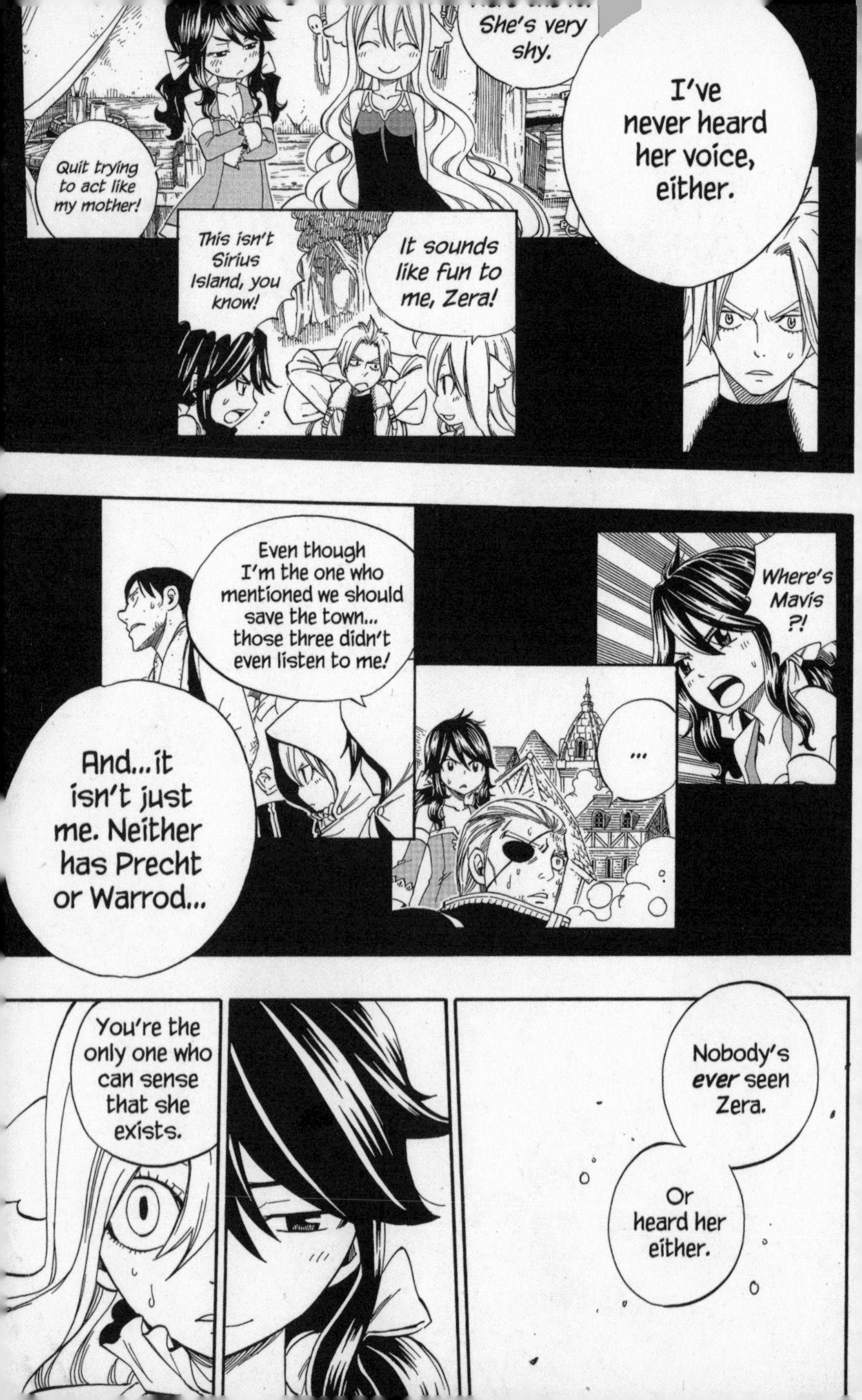

She's very shy.
Quit trying to act like my mother!
I've never heard her voice, either.
It sounds like fun to me, Zera!
This isn't Sirius Island, you know!
Where's Mavis ?!
...
Even though I'm the one who mentioned we should save the town... those three didn't even listen to me!
And...it isn't just me. Neither has Precht or Warrod...
Nobody's *ever* seen Zera.
Or heard her either.
You're the only one who can sense that she exists.

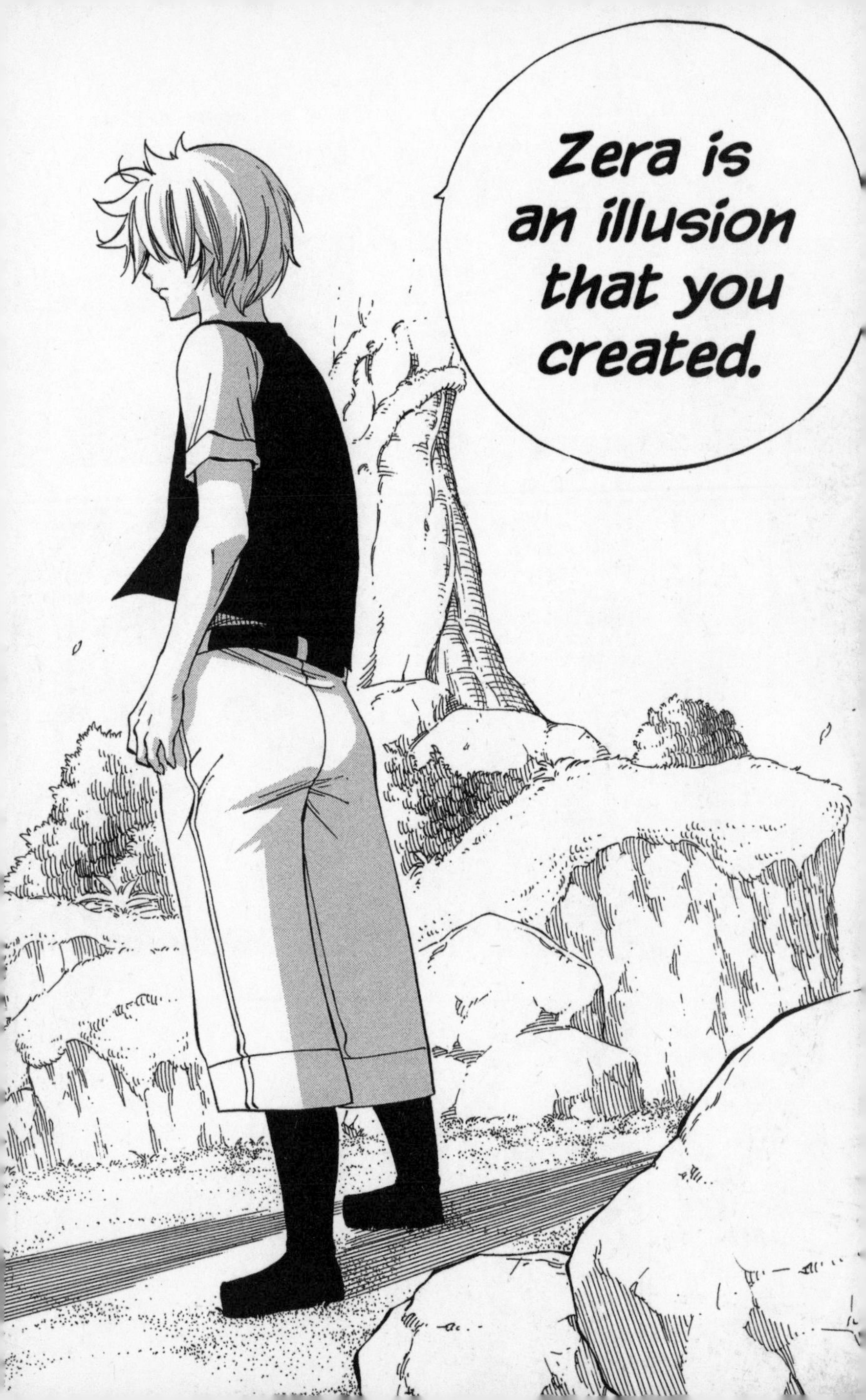
Zera is an illusion that you created.

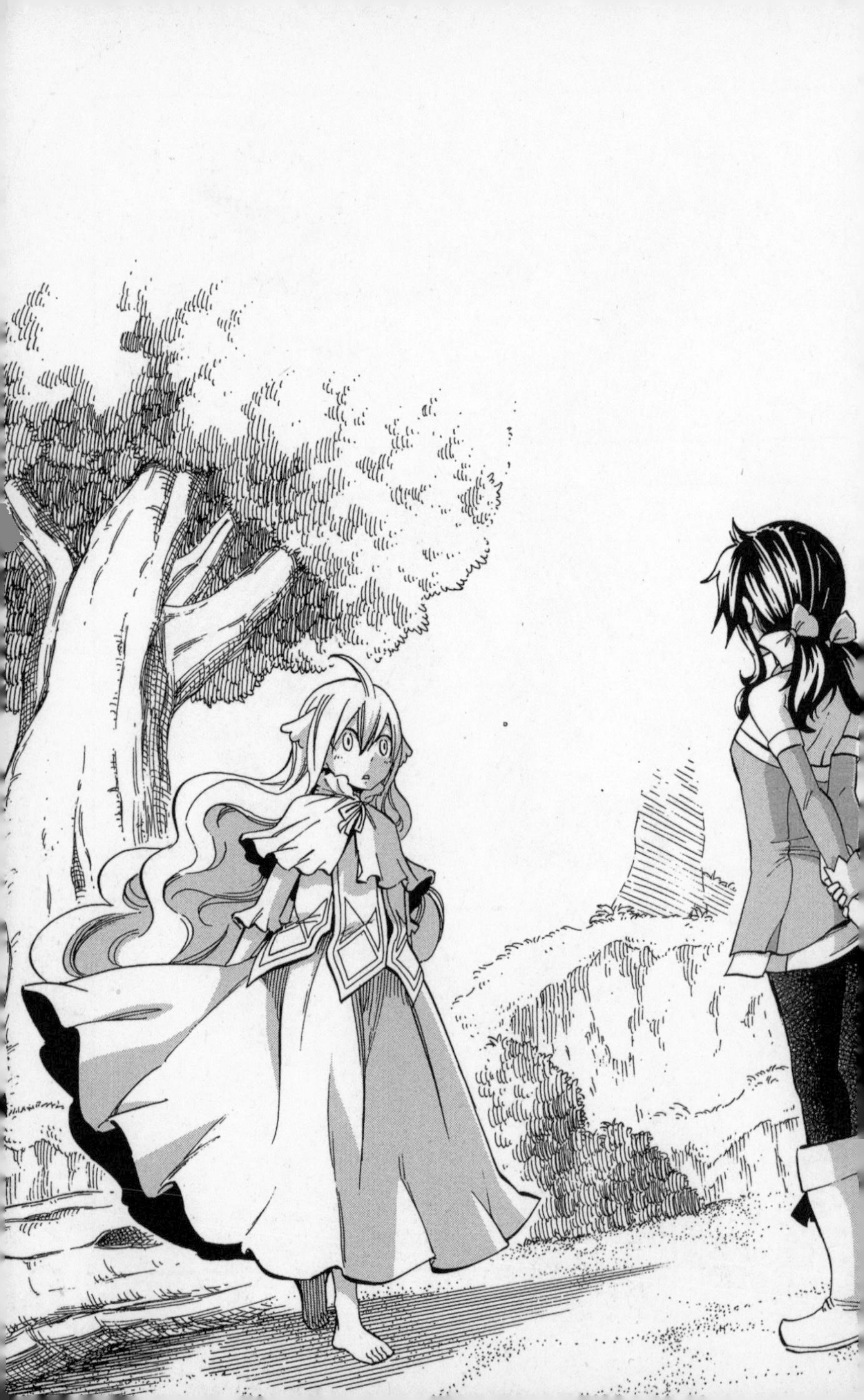

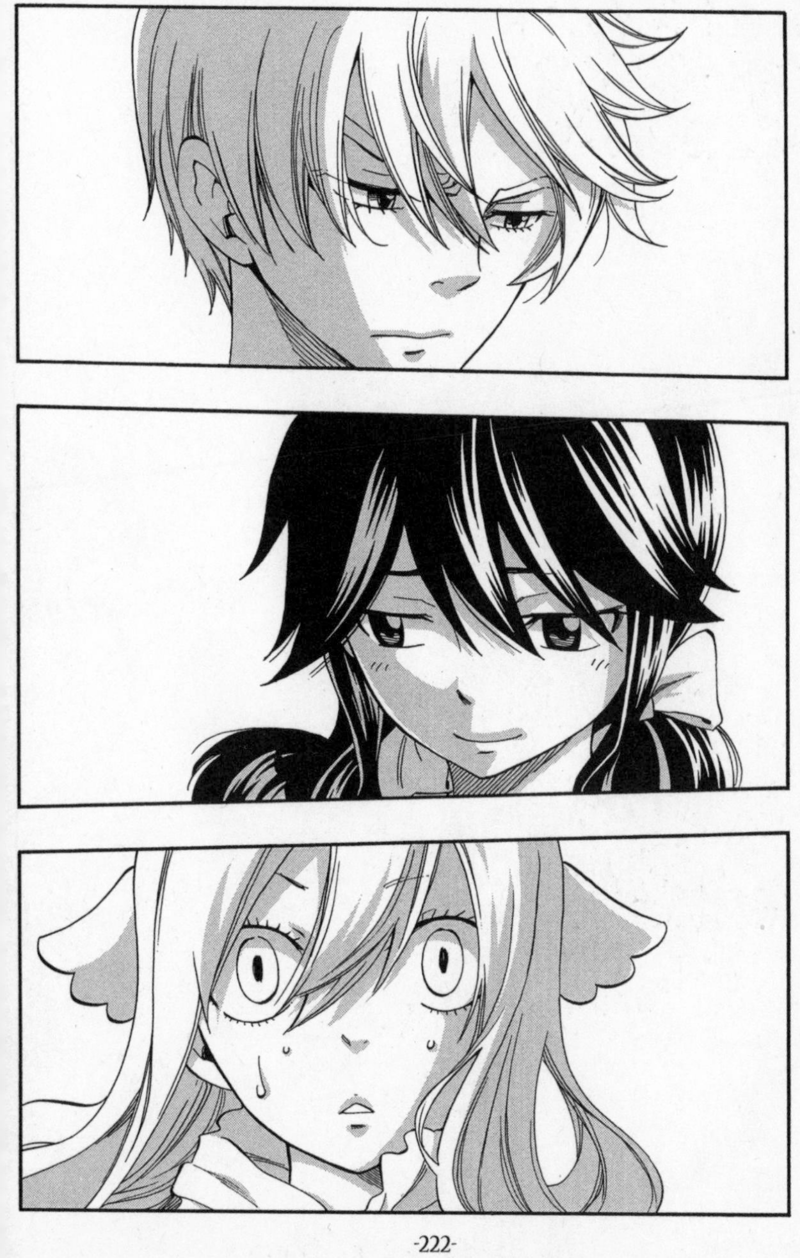

FAIRY TAIL ZERA

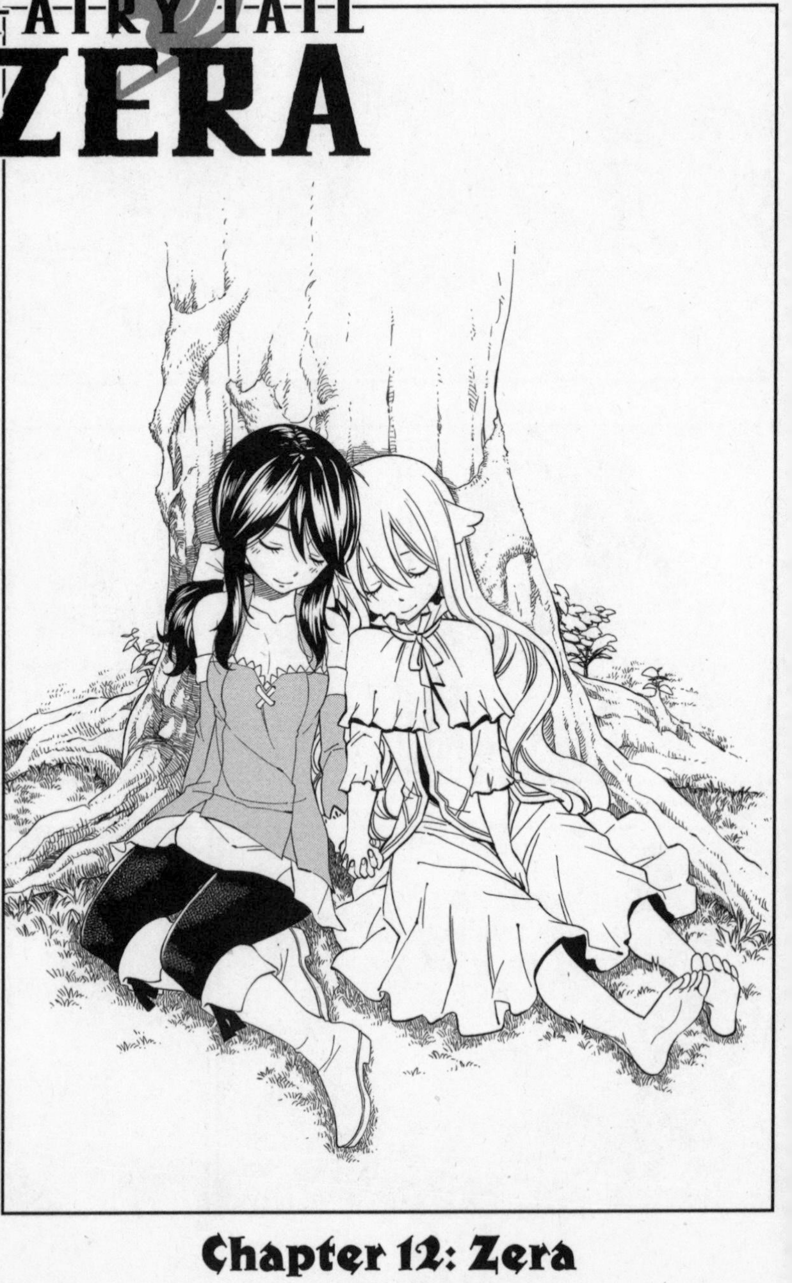

Chapter 12: Zera

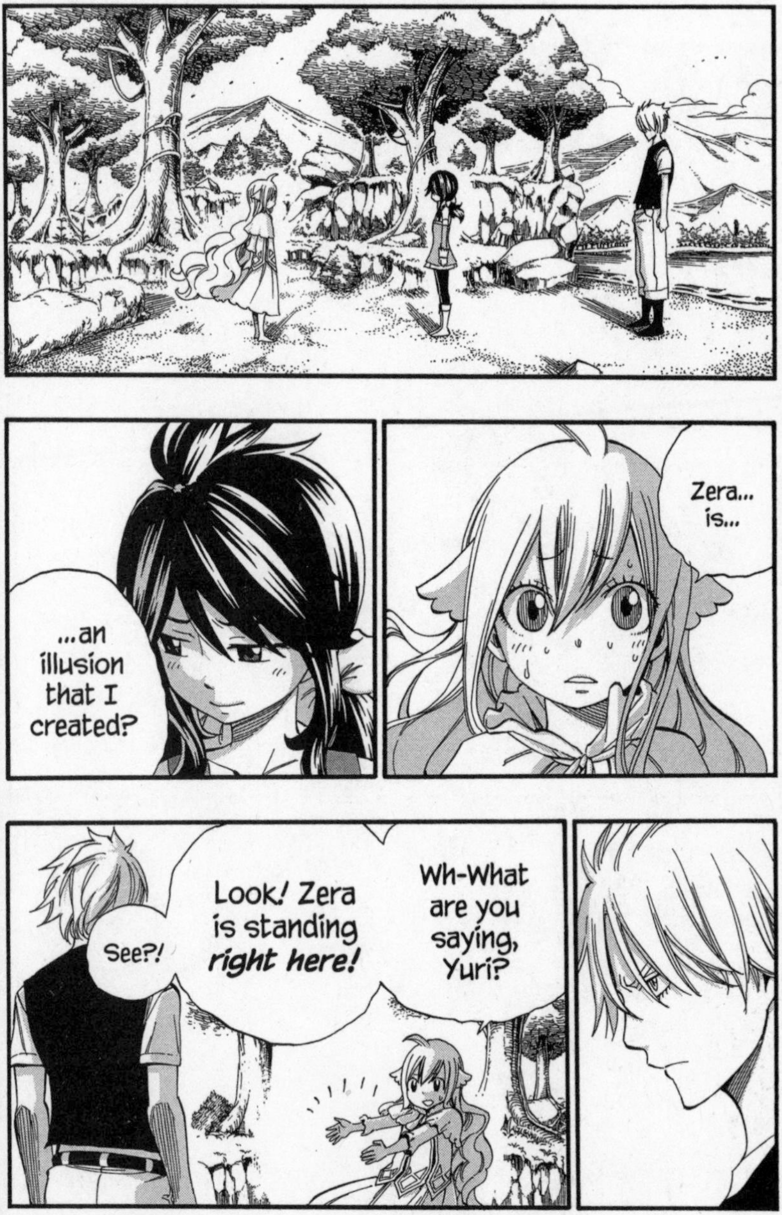
Zera... is...
...an illusion that I created?
Wh-What are you saying, Yuri?
Look! Zera is standing right here!
See?!

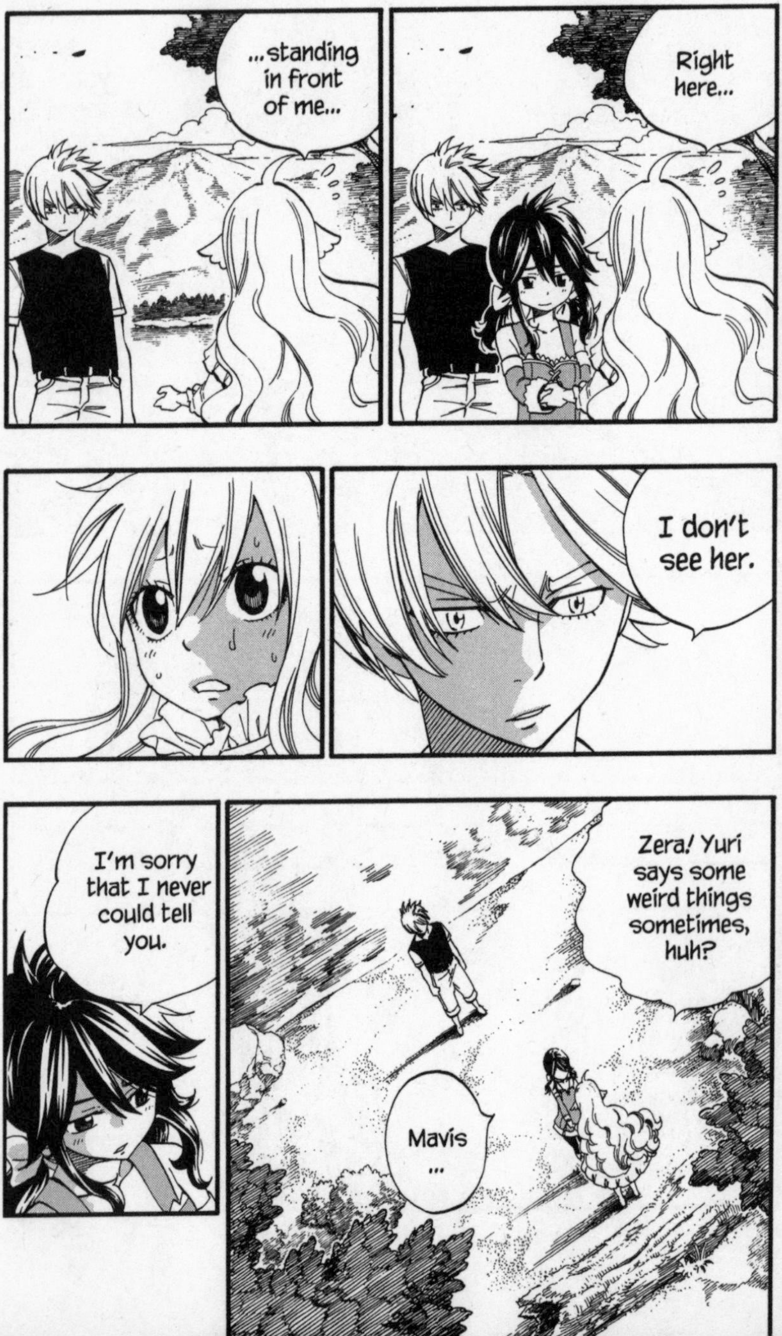
Right here...
...standing in front of me...
I don't see her.
Zera! Yuri says some weird things sometimes, huh?
Mavis ...
I'm sorry that I never could tell you.

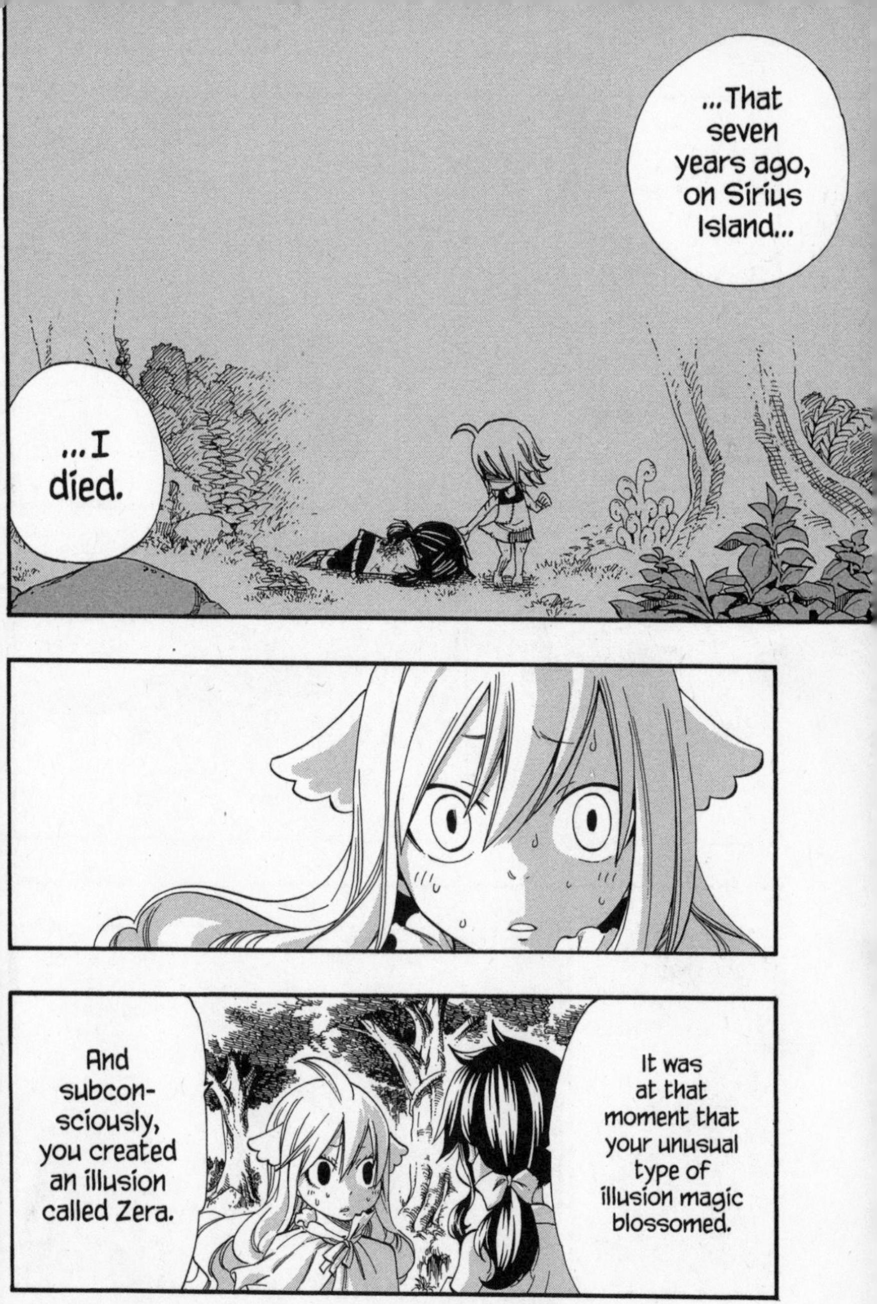
...That seven years ago, on Sirius Island...
...I died.
It was at that moment that your unusual type of illusion magic blossomed.
And subconsciously, you created an illusion called Zera.

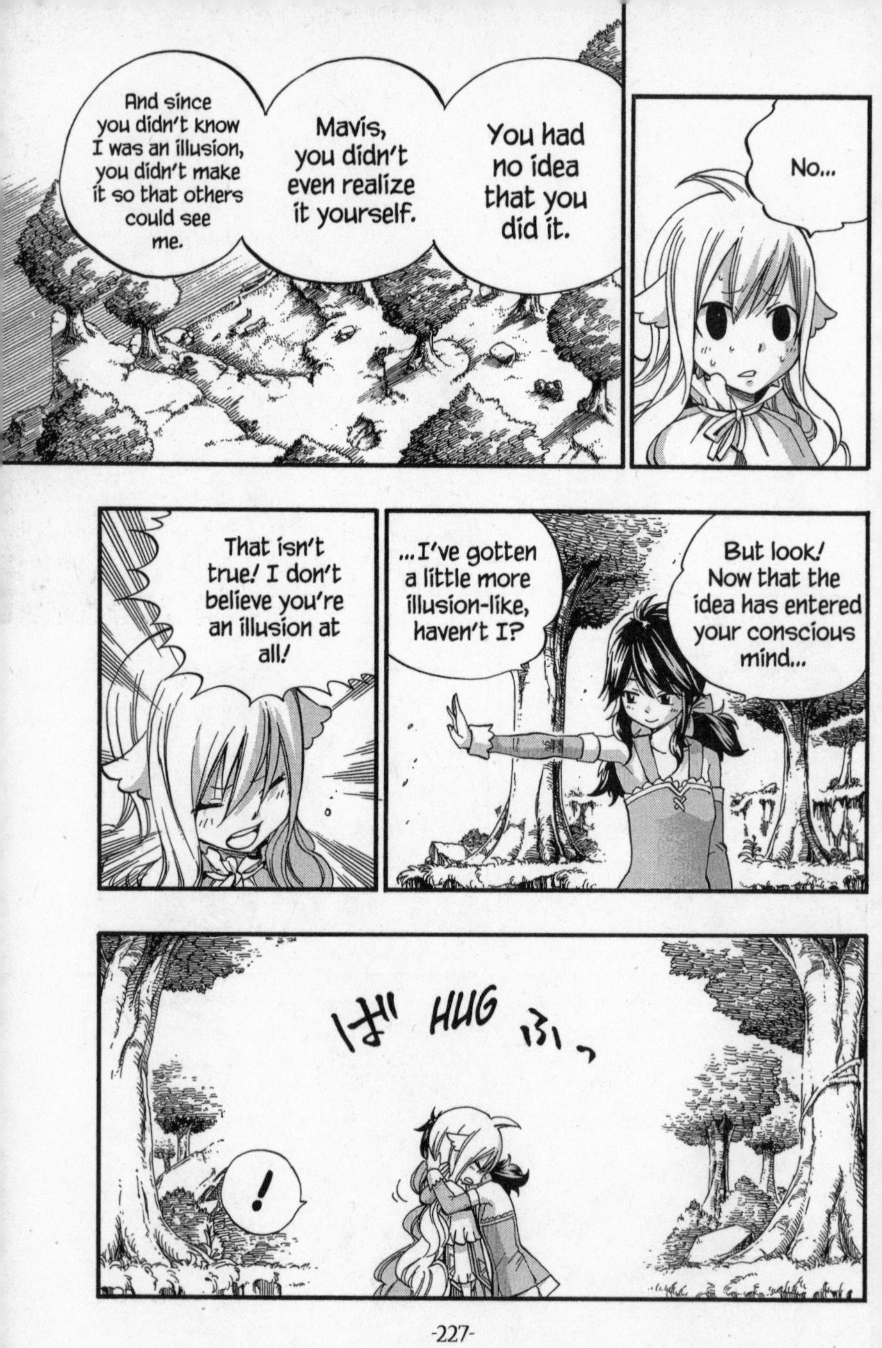
No...
You had no idea that you did it.
Mavis, you didn't even realize it yourself.
And since you didn't know I was an illusion, you didn't make it so that others could see me.
But look! Now that the idea has entered your conscious mind...
...I've gotten a little more illusion-like, haven't I?
That isn't true! I don't believe you're an illusion at all!
ば HUG ふっ
!

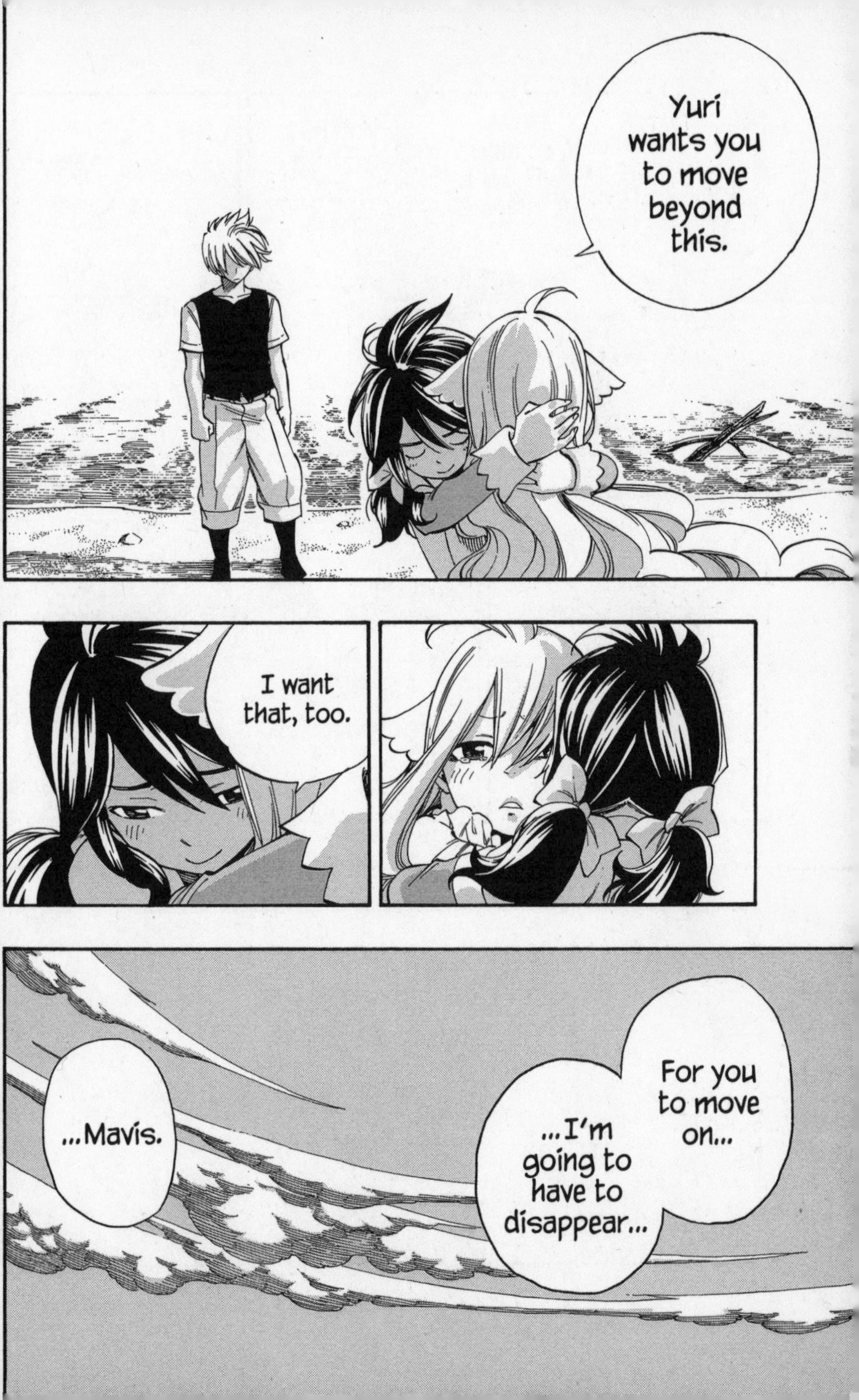
Yuri wants you to move beyond this.
I want that, too.
For you to move on...
...I'm going to have to disappear...
...Mavis.

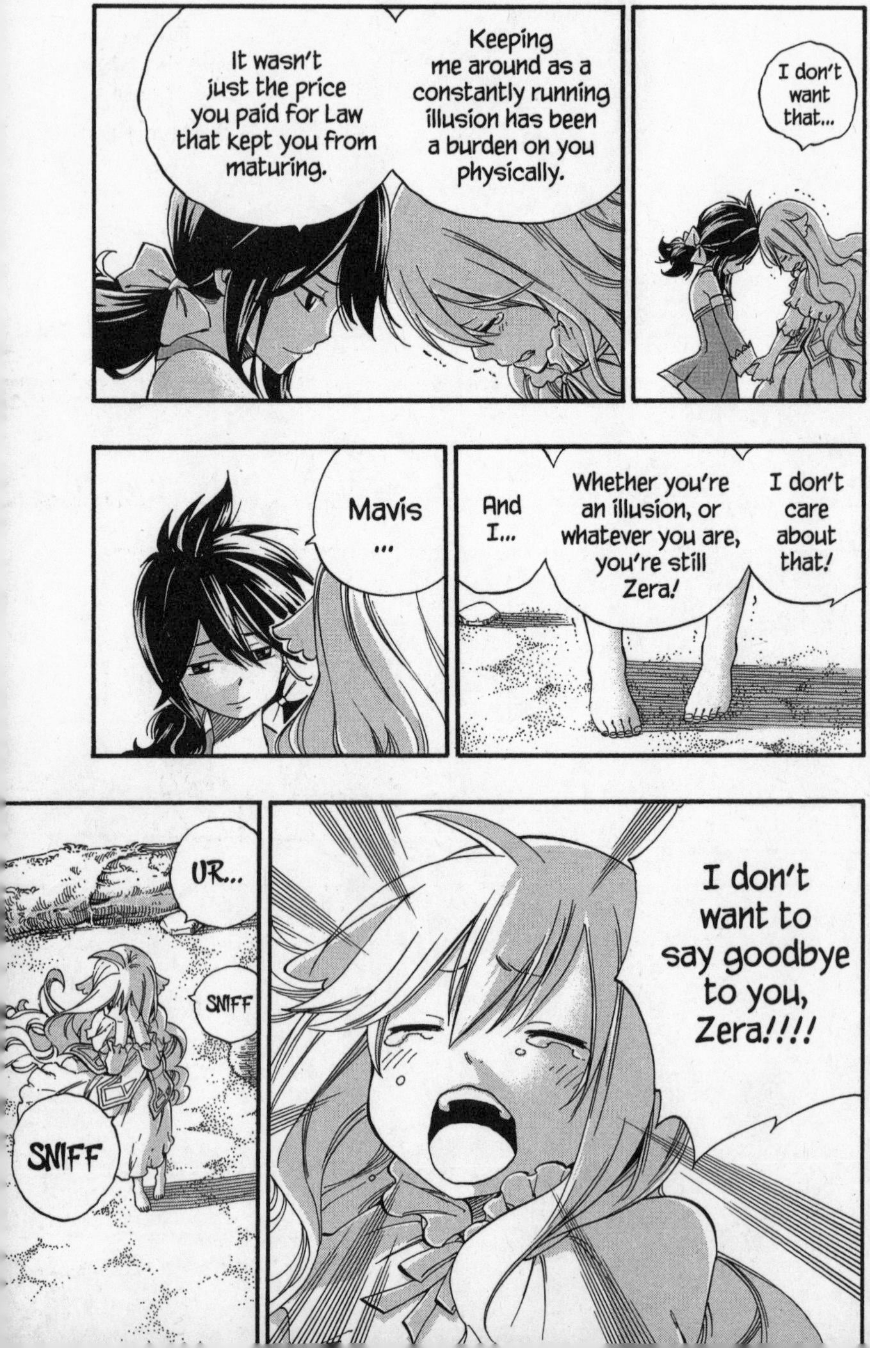
I don't want that...
Keeping me around as a constantly running illusion has been a burden on you physically.
It wasn't just the price you paid for Law that kept you from maturing.
I don't care about that!
Whether you're an illusion, or whatever you are, you're still Zera!
And I...
Mavis ...
I don't want to say goodbye to you, Zera!!!!
UR...
SNIFF
SNIFF

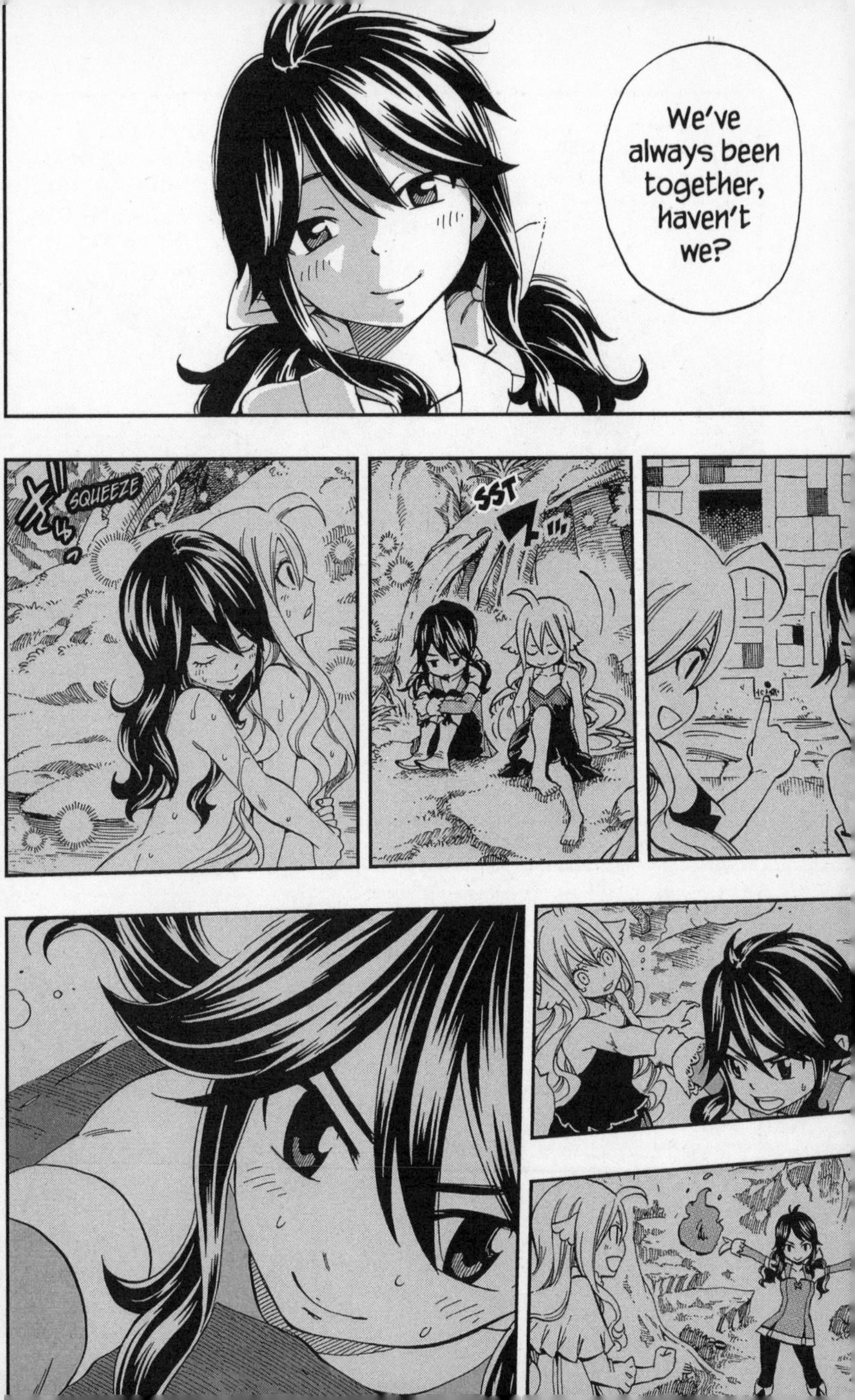
We've always been together, haven't we?
SST
SQUEEZE

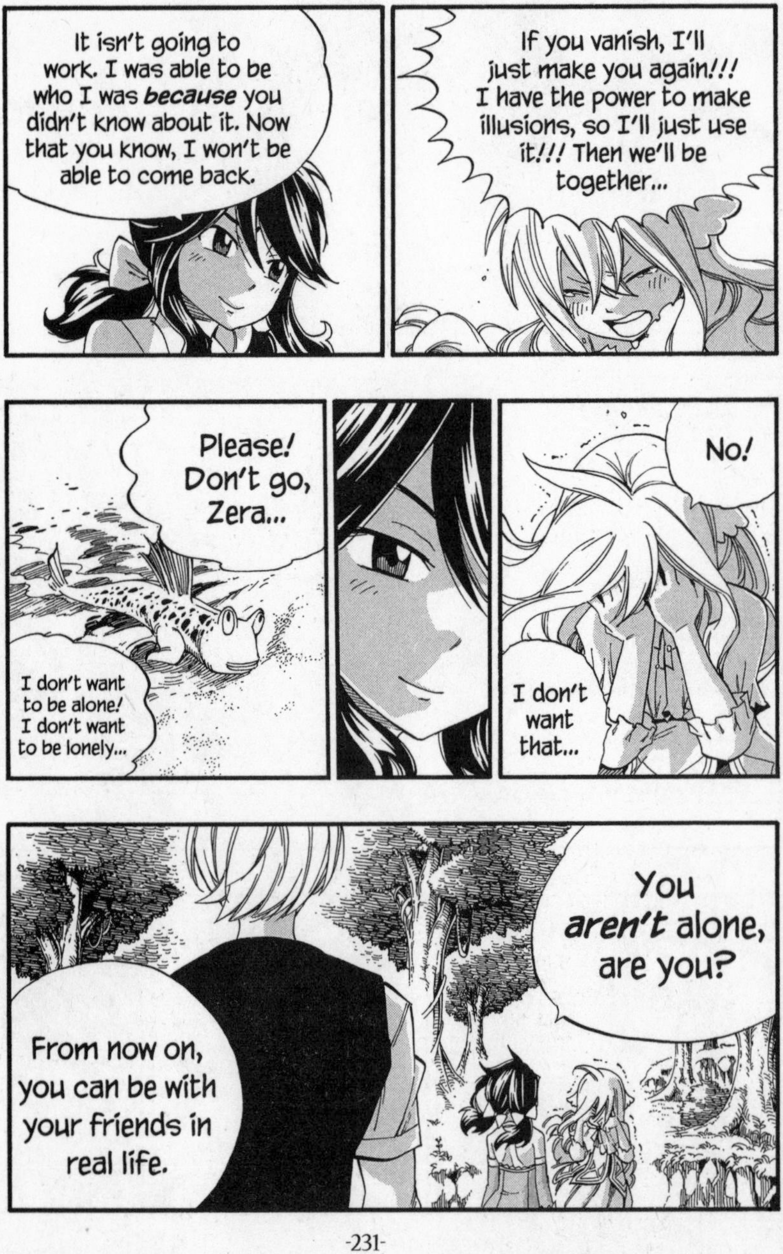
If you vanish, I'll just make you again!!! I have the power to make illusions, so I'll just use it!!! Then we'll be together...
It isn't going to work. I was able to be who I was *because* you didn't know about it. Now that you know, I won't be able to come back.
No!
I don't want that...
Please! Don't go, Zera...
I don't want to be alone! I don't want to be lonely...
You *aren't* alone, are you?
From now on, you can be with your friends in real life.

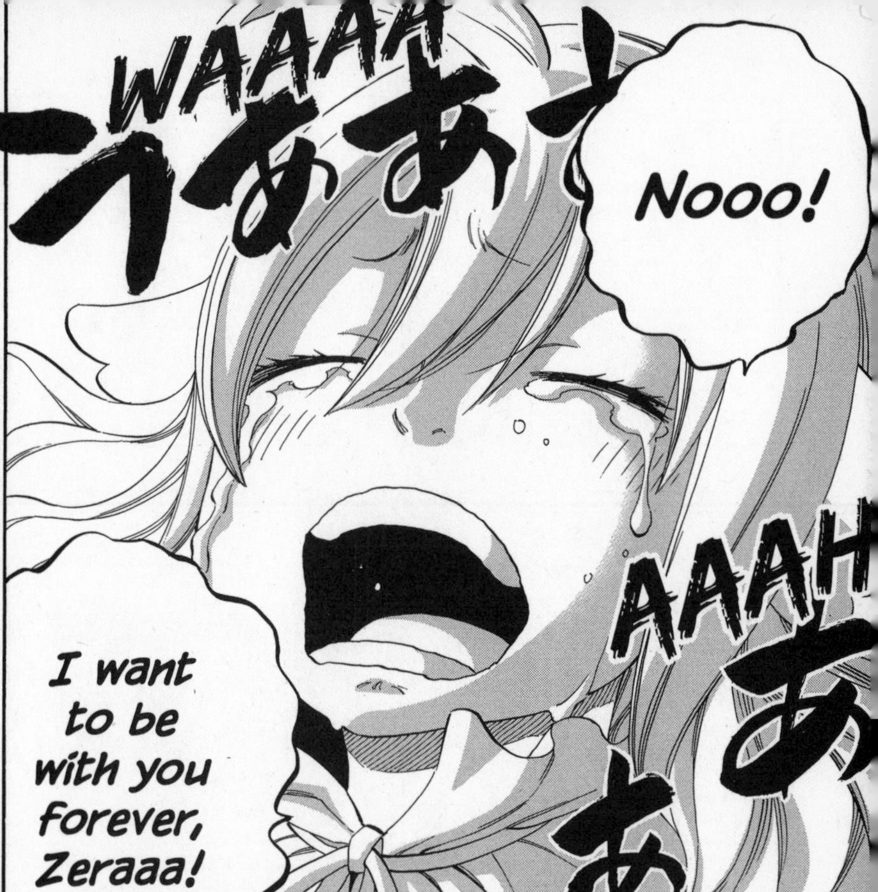
WAAAH
うああ
Nooo!
AAAH
ああ
I want to be with you forever, Zeraaa!

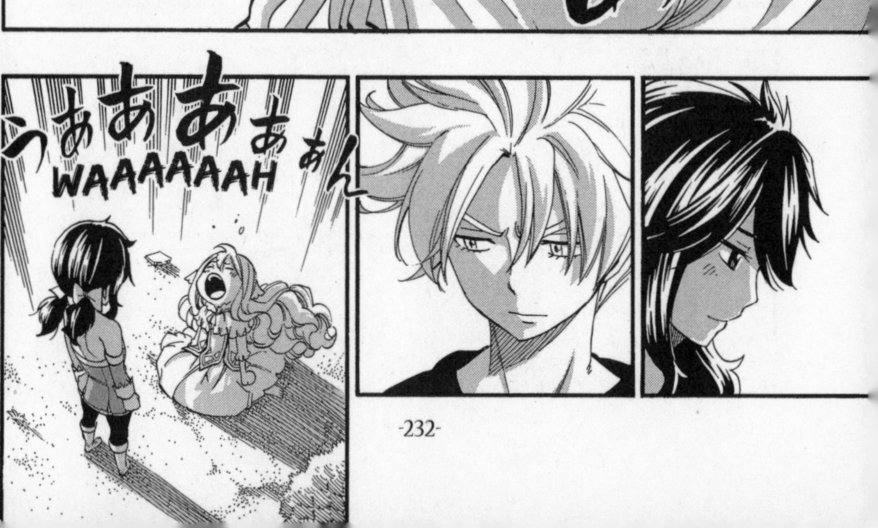
うあああぁぁん
WAAAAAAH

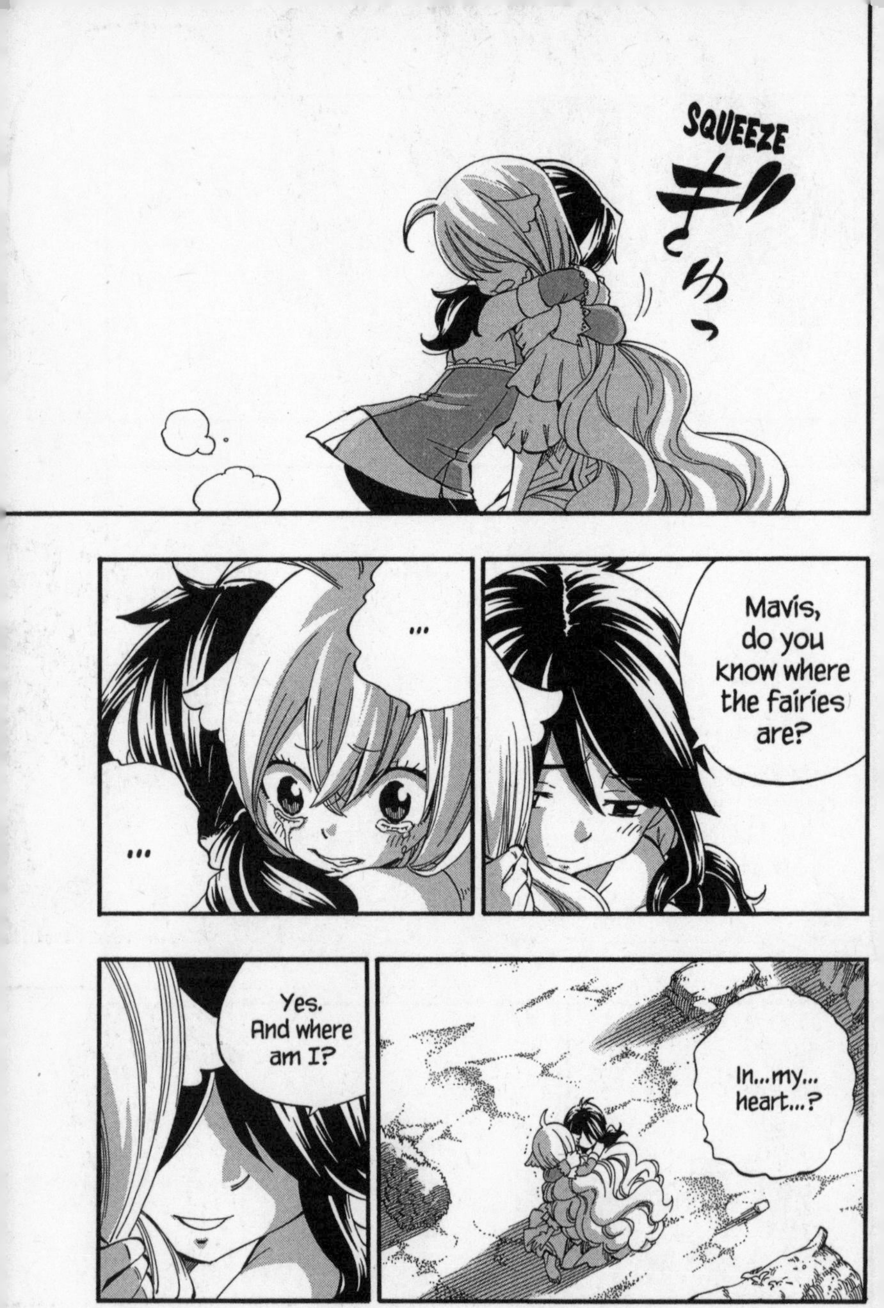
SQUEEZE
ぎゅっ
Mavis, do you know where the fairies are?
...
...
In...my... heart...?
Yes. And where am I?

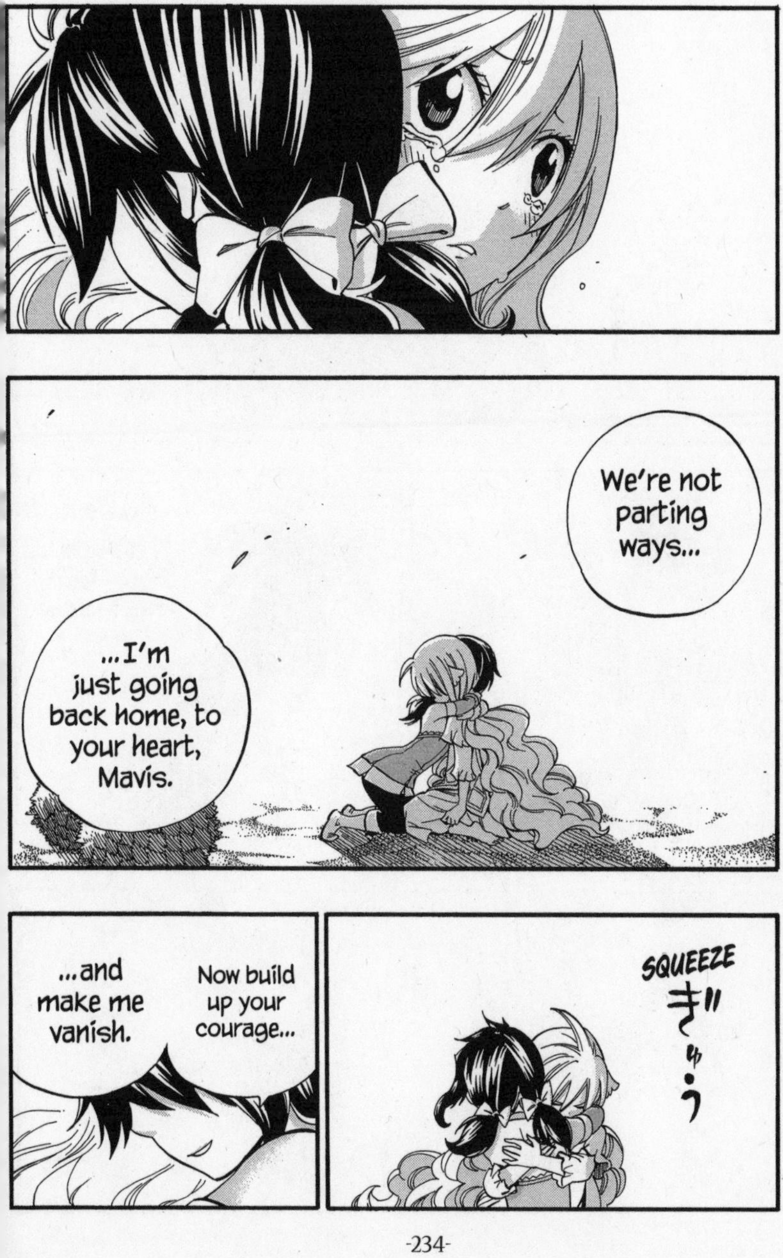
We're not parting ways...
...I'm just going back home, to your heart, Mavis.
SQUEEZE
ぎゅう
Now build up your courage...
...and make me vanish.

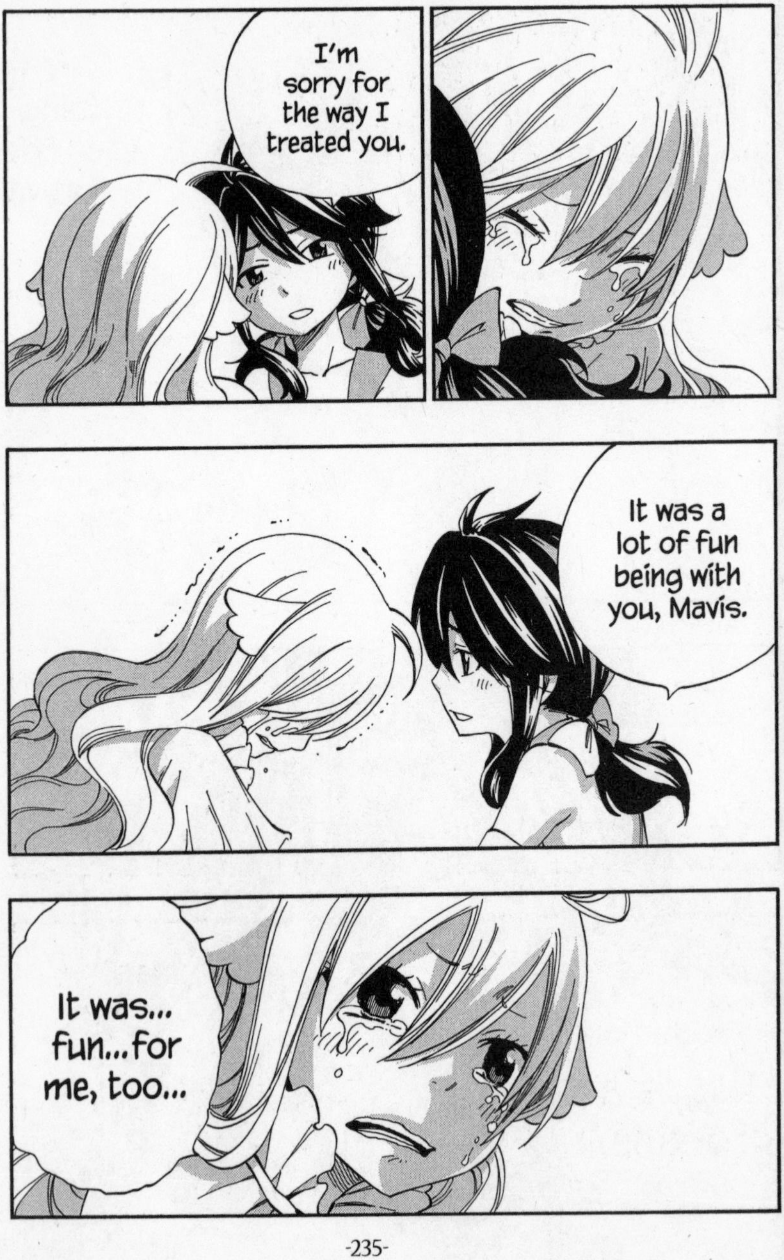
I'm sorry for the way I treated you.
It was a lot of fun being with you, Mavis.
It was... fun...for me, too...

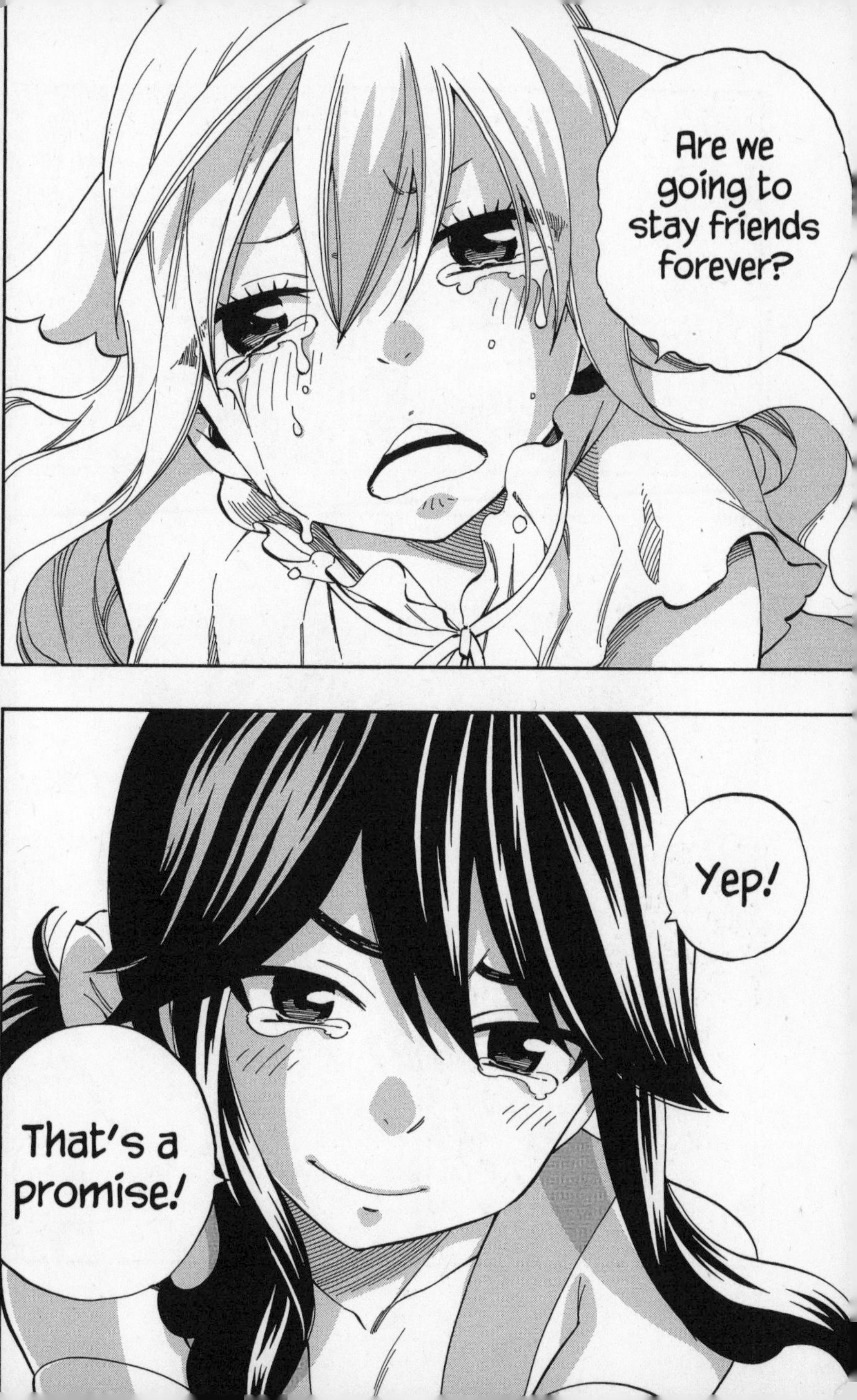
Are we going to stay friends forever?
Yep!
That's a promise!

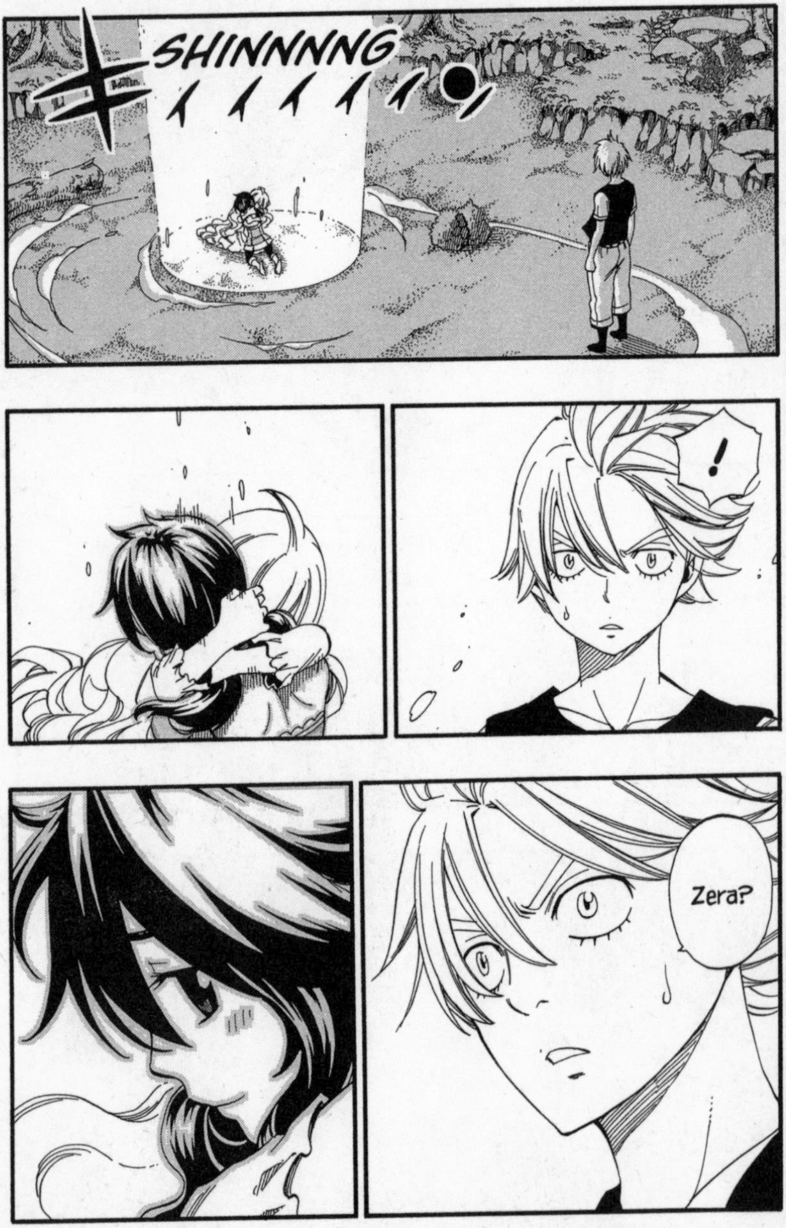
SHINNNNG
!
Zera?

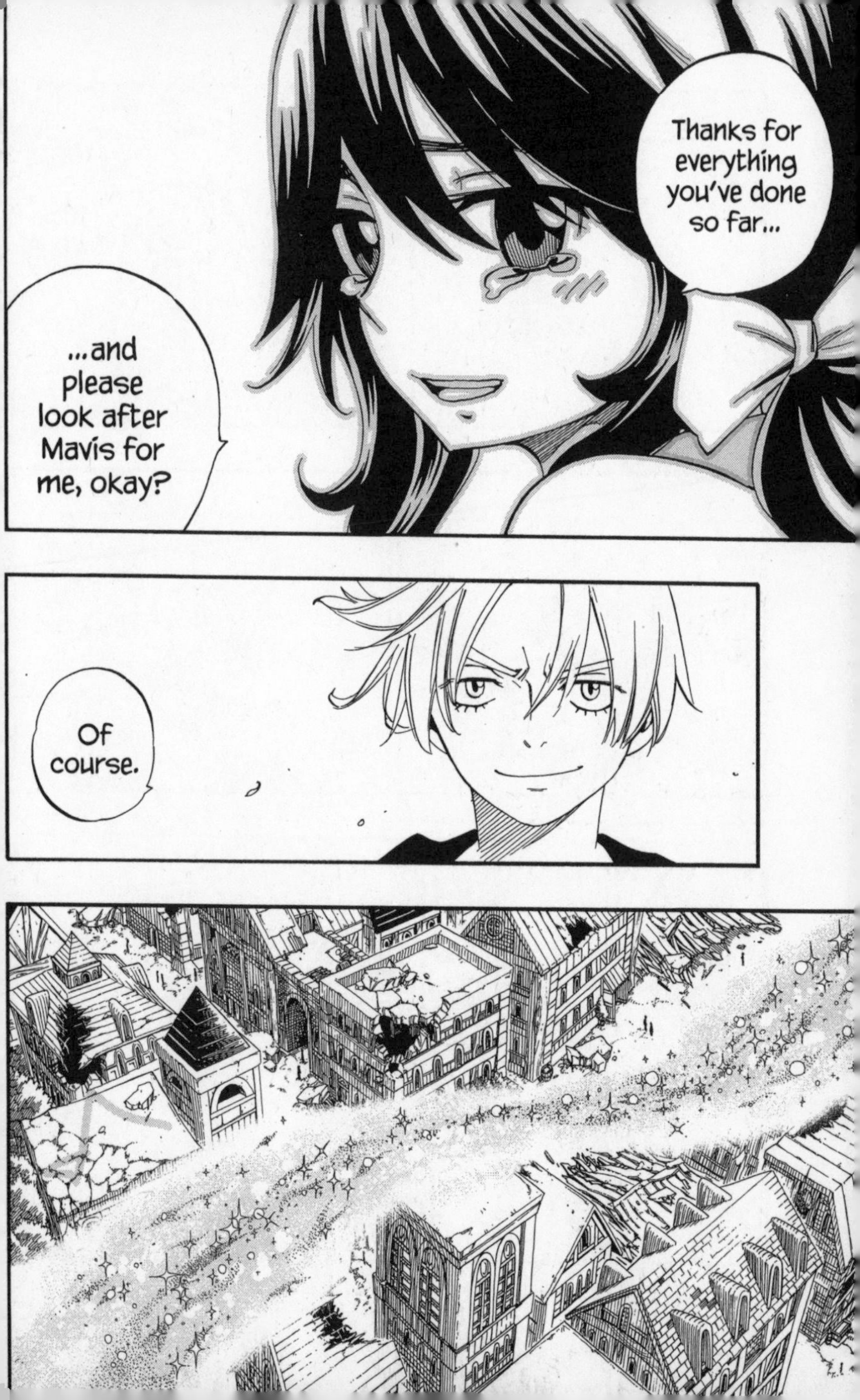
Thanks for everything you've done so far...
...and please look after Mavis for me, okay?
Of course.

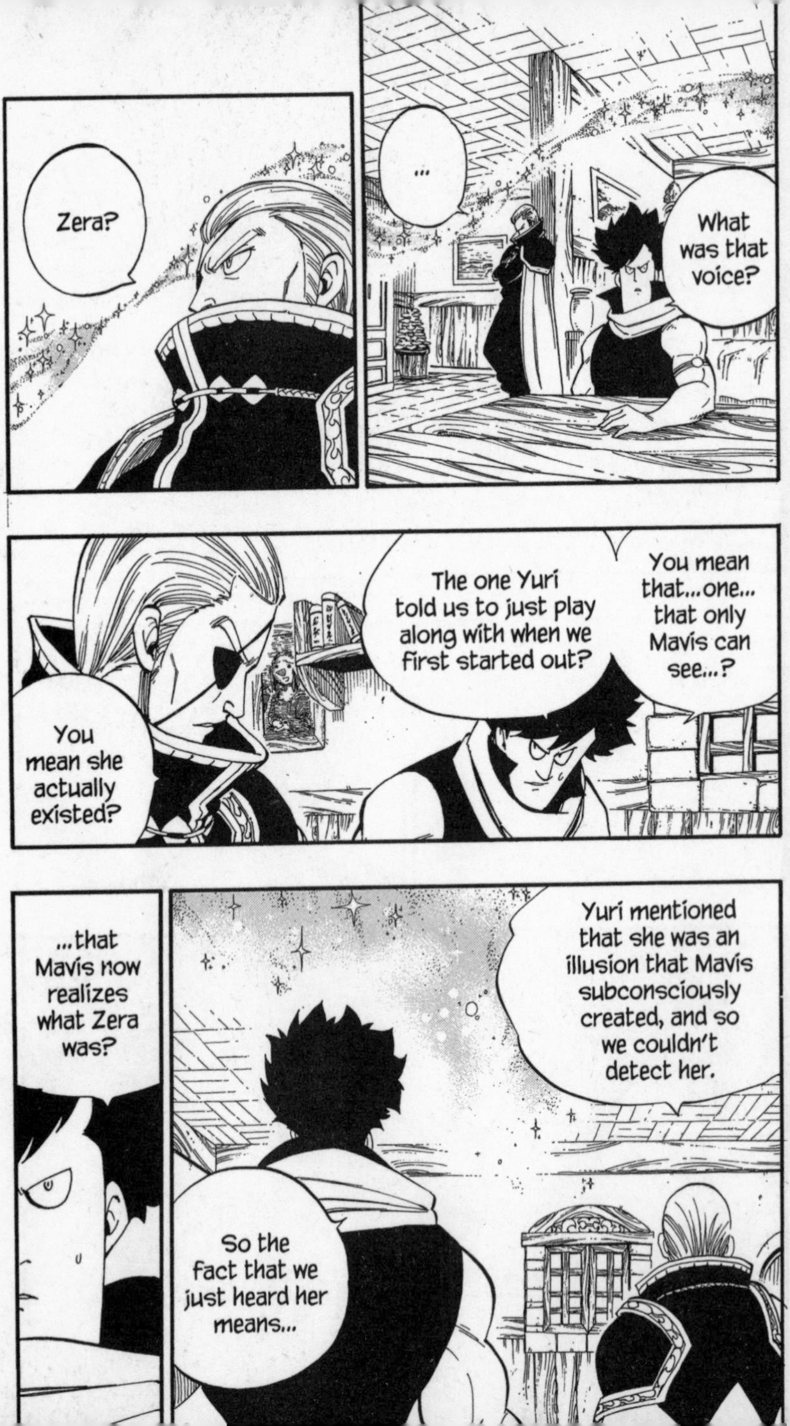
What was that voice?
...
Zera?
You mean that...one... that only Mavis can see...?
The one Yuri told us to just play along with when we first started out?
You mean she actually existed?
Yuri mentioned that she was an illusion that Mavis subconsciously created, and so we couldn't detect her.
So the fact that we just heard her means...
...that Mavis now realizes what Zera was?

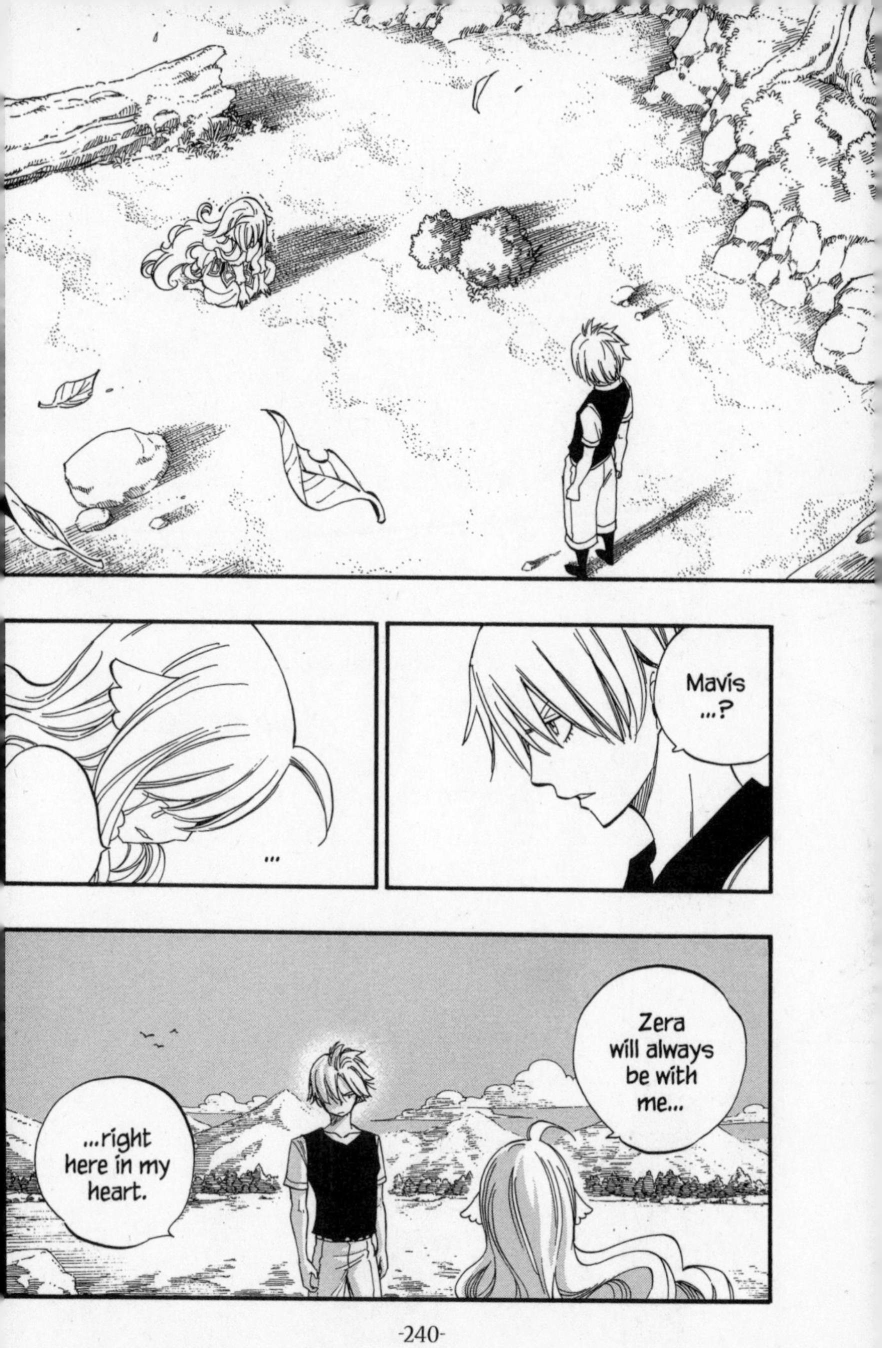
Mavis ...?
...
Zera will always be with me...
...right here in my heart.

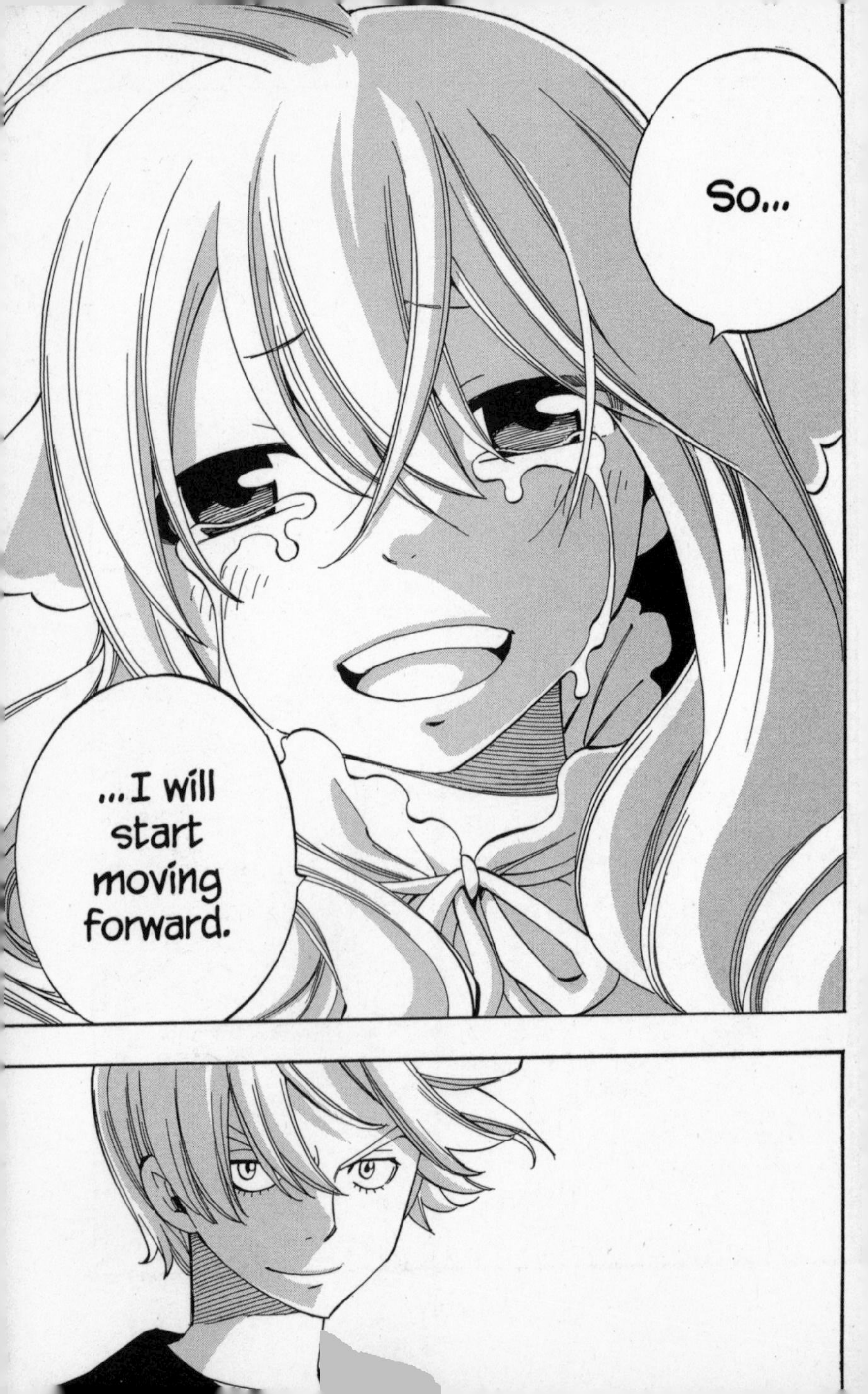
So...
...I will start moving forward.

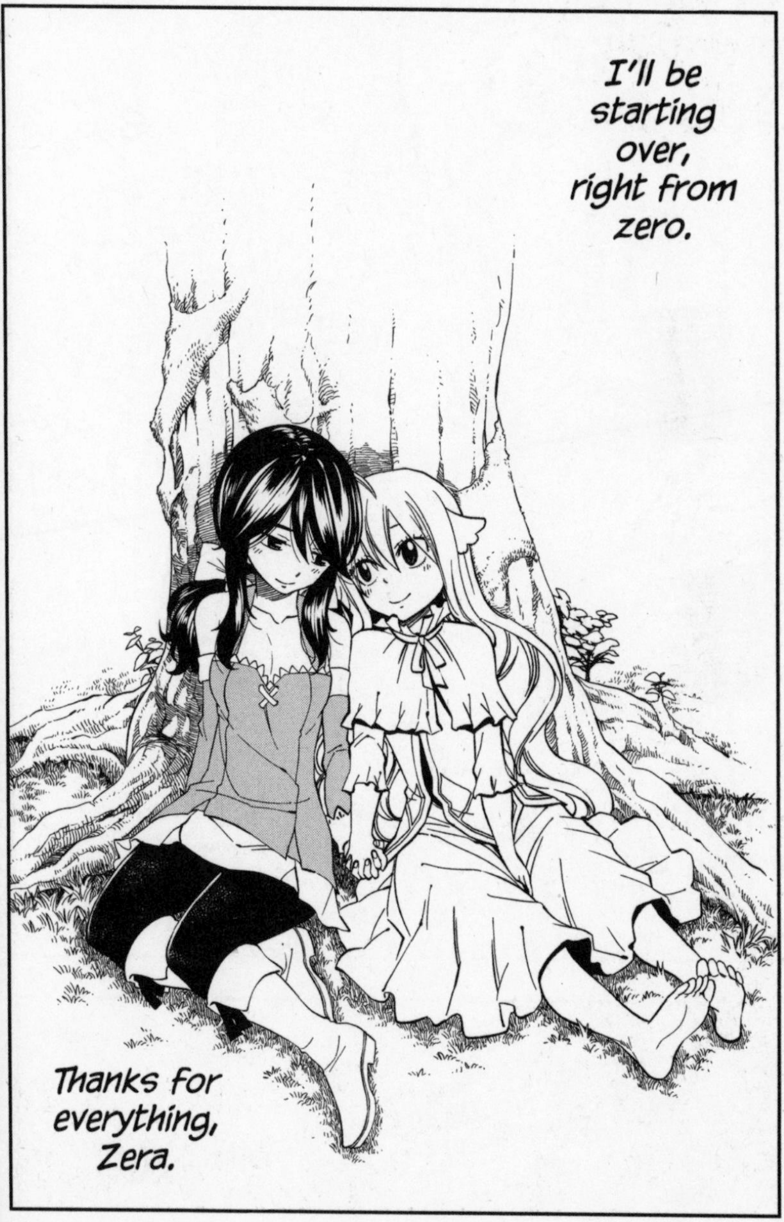
I'll be starting over, right from zero.
Thanks for everything, Zera.

FAIRY TAIL ZERO

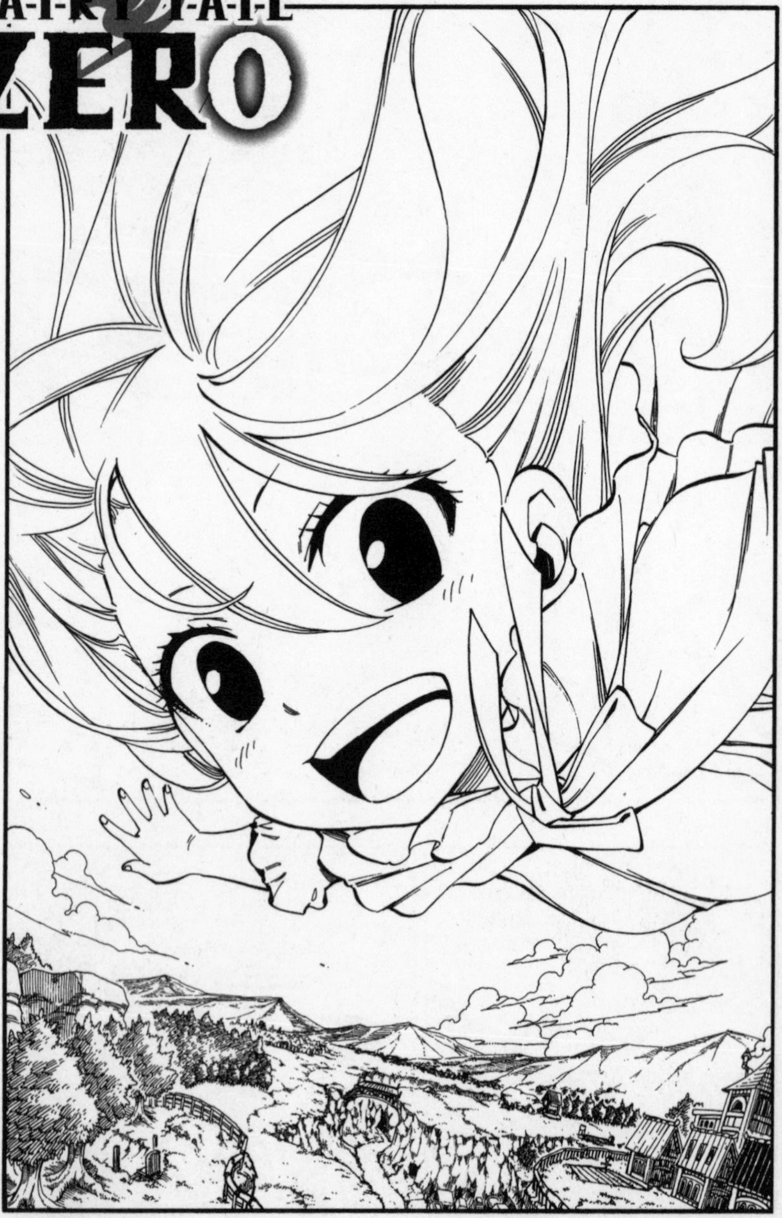

Chapter 13: Eternal Adventures

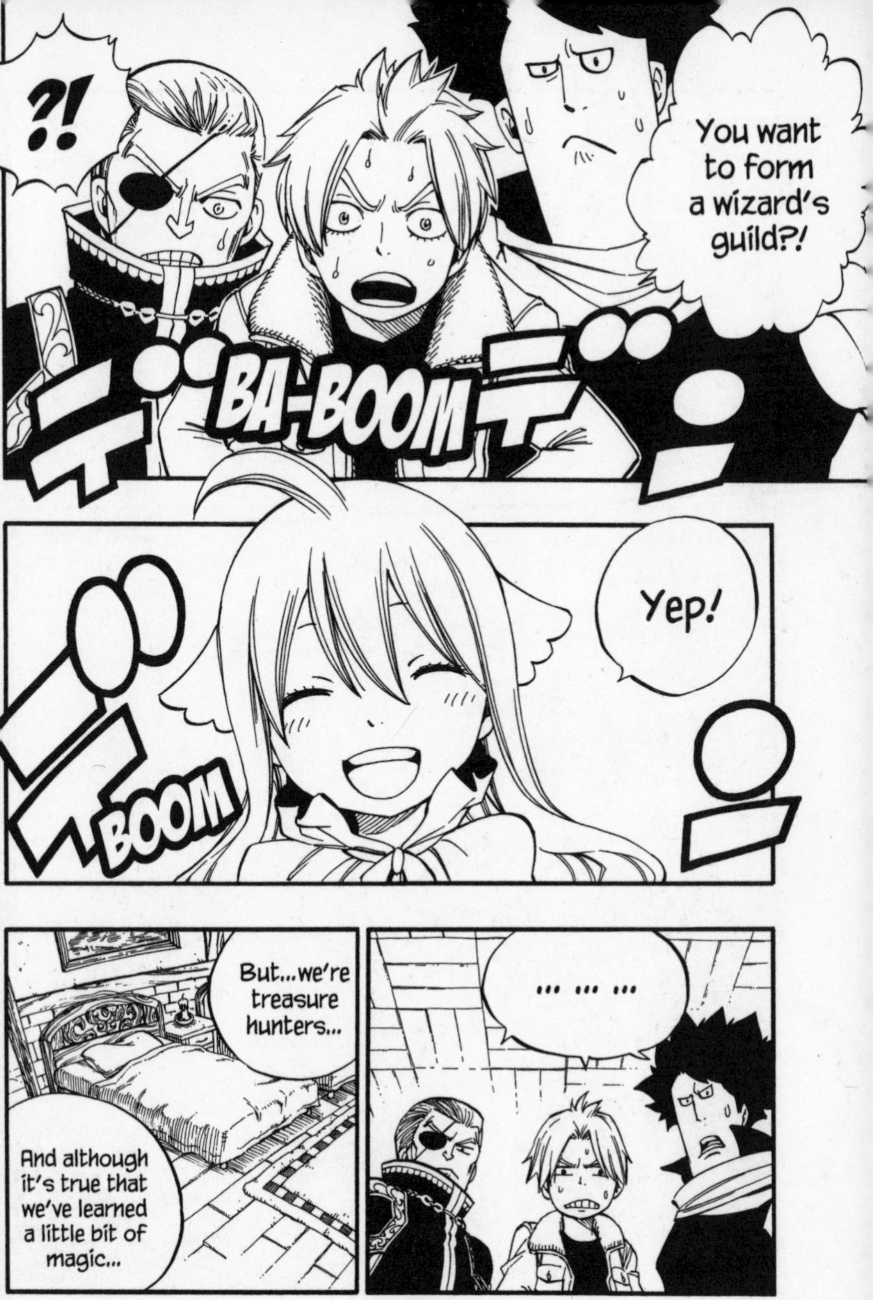
You want to form a wizard's guild?!
?!
BA-BOOM
Yep!
BOOM
... ...
But...we're treasure hunters...
And although it's true that we've learned a little bit of magic...

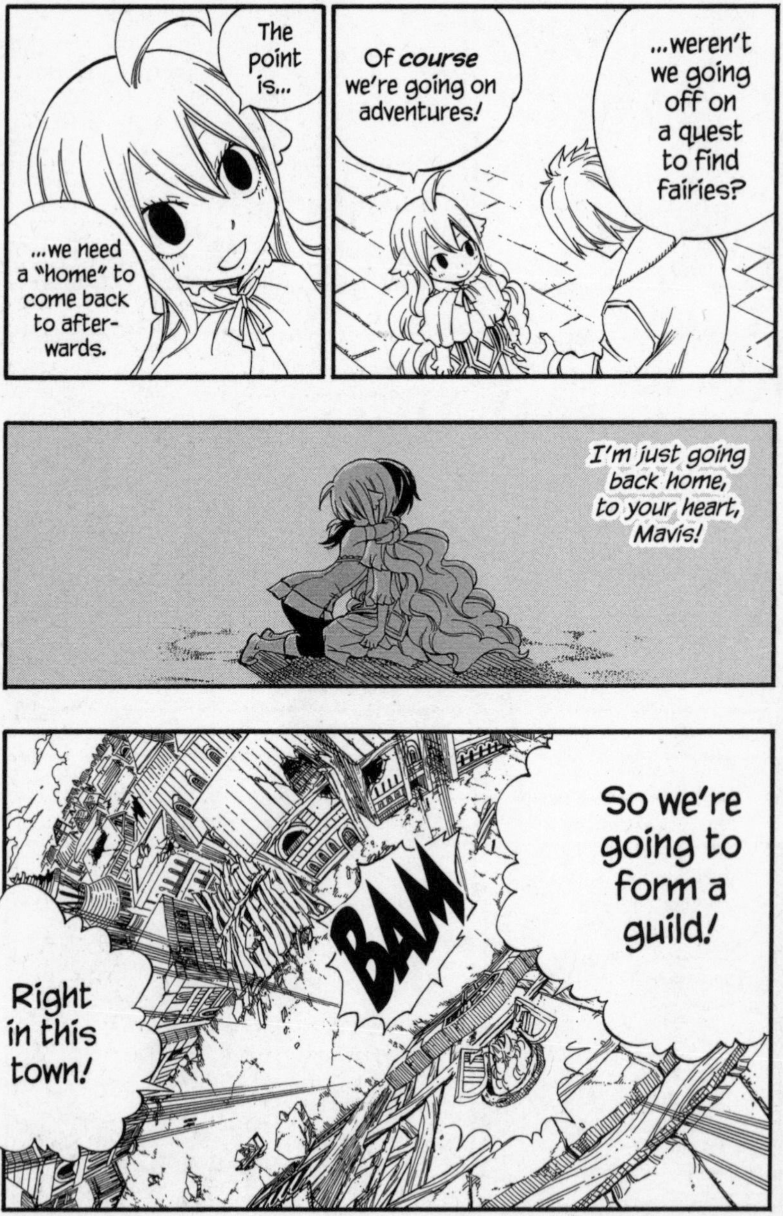
...weren't we going off on a quest to find fairies?
Of *course* we're going on adventures!
The point is...
...we need a "home" to come back to after-wards.
I'm just going back home, to your heart, Mavis!
So we're going to form a guild!
BAM
Right in this town!

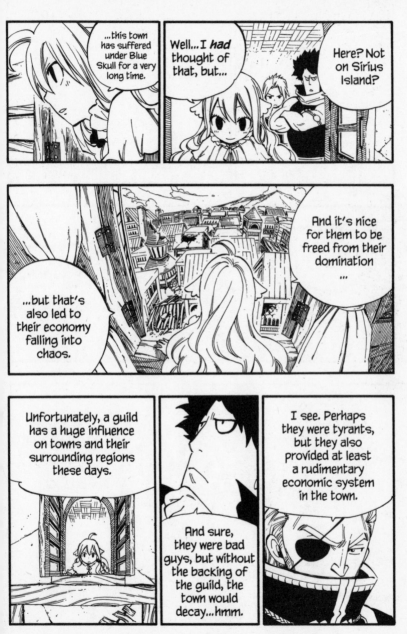

Here? Not on Sirius Island?
Well...I *had* thought of that, but...
...this town has suffered under Blue Skull for a very long time.
And it's nice for them to be freed from their domination ...
...but that's also led to their economy falling into chaos.
I see. Perhaps they were tyrants, but they also provided at least a rudimentary economic system in the town.
And sure, they were bad guys, but without the backing of the guild, the town would decay...hmm.
Unfortunately, a guild has a huge influence on towns and their surrounding regions these days.

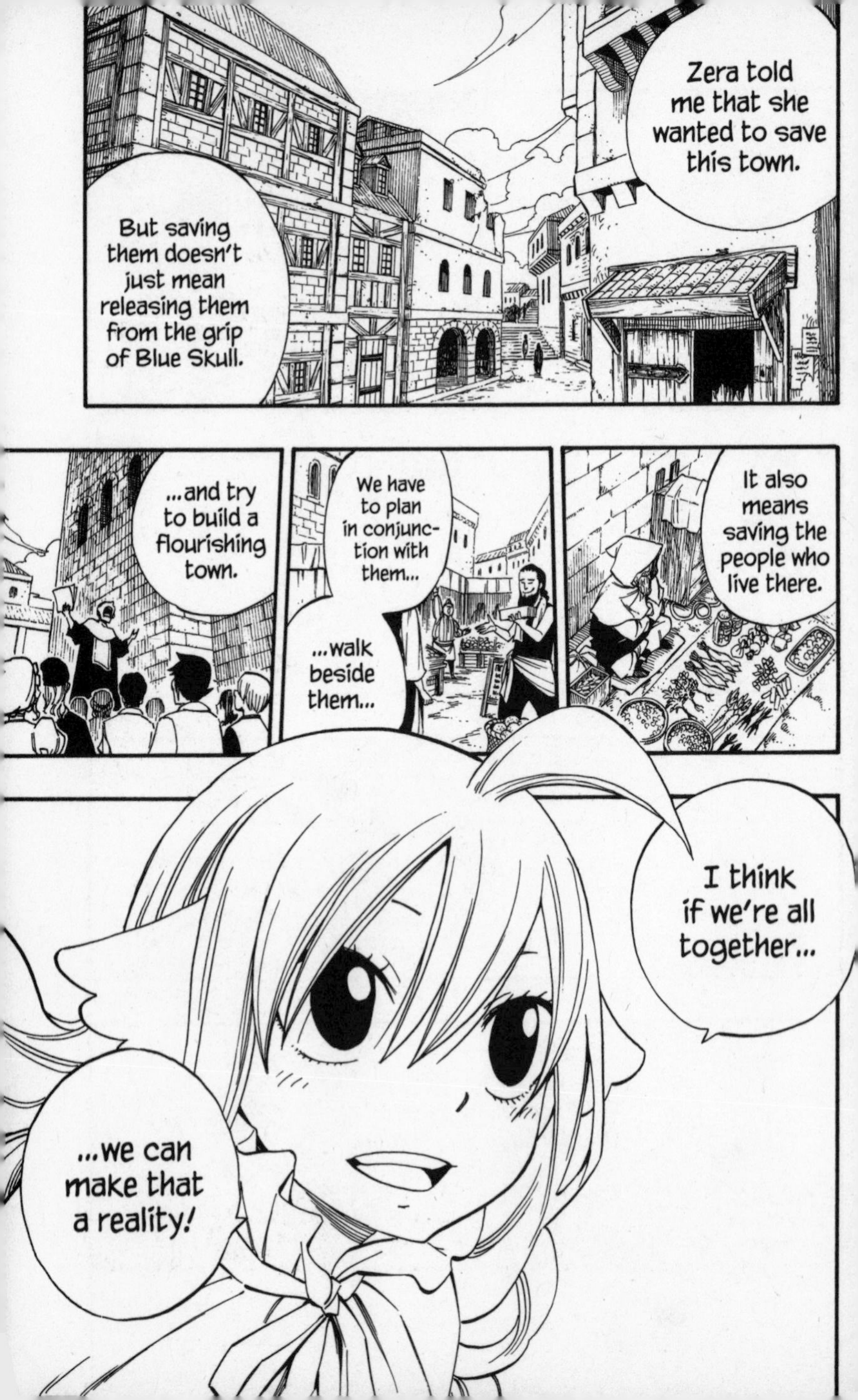
Zera told me that she wanted to save this town.
But saving them doesn't just mean releasing them from the grip of Blue Skull.
It also means saving the people who live there.
We have to plan in conjunction with them...
...walk beside them...
...and try to build a flourishing town.
I think if we're all together...
...we can make that a reality!

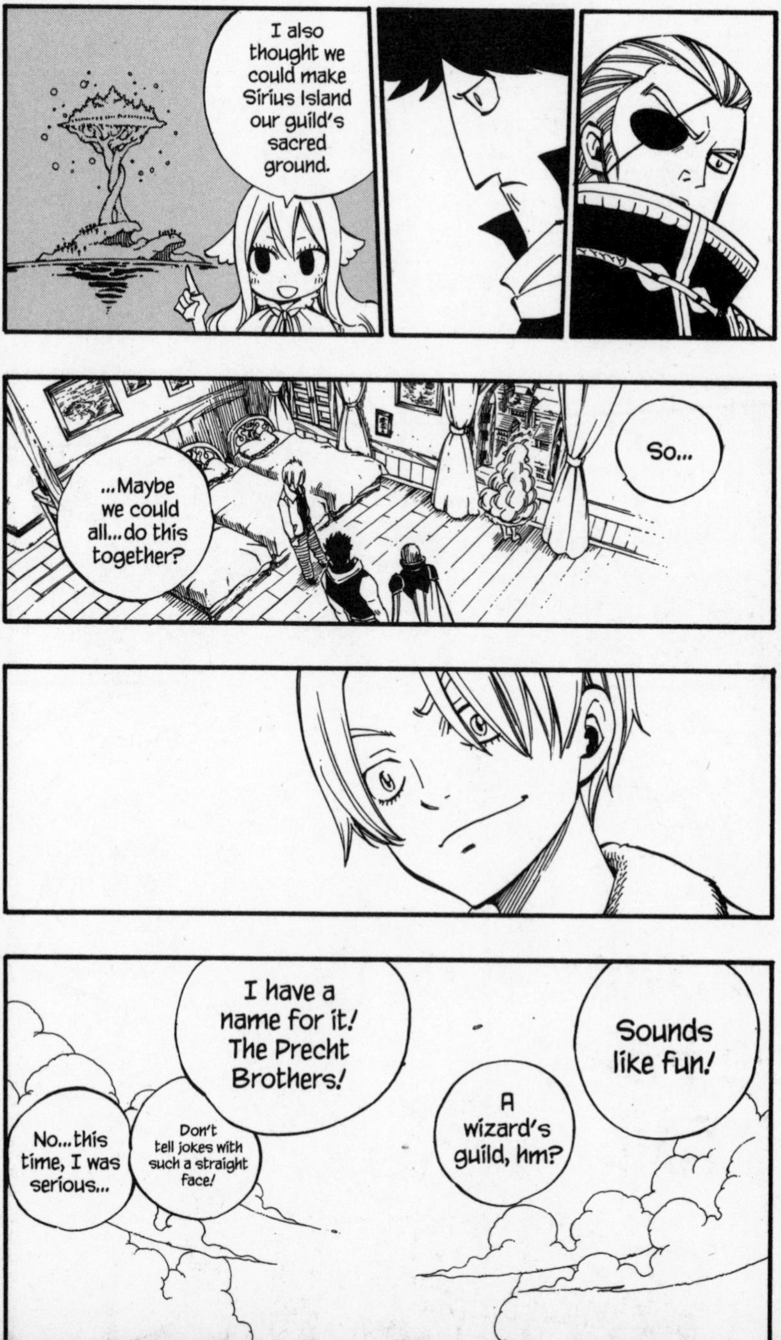
I also thought we could make Sirius Island our guild's sacred ground.
So...
...Maybe we could all...do this together?
Sounds like fun!
A wizard's guild, hm?
I have a name for it! The Precht Brothers!
Don't tell jokes with such a straight face!
No...this time, I was serious...

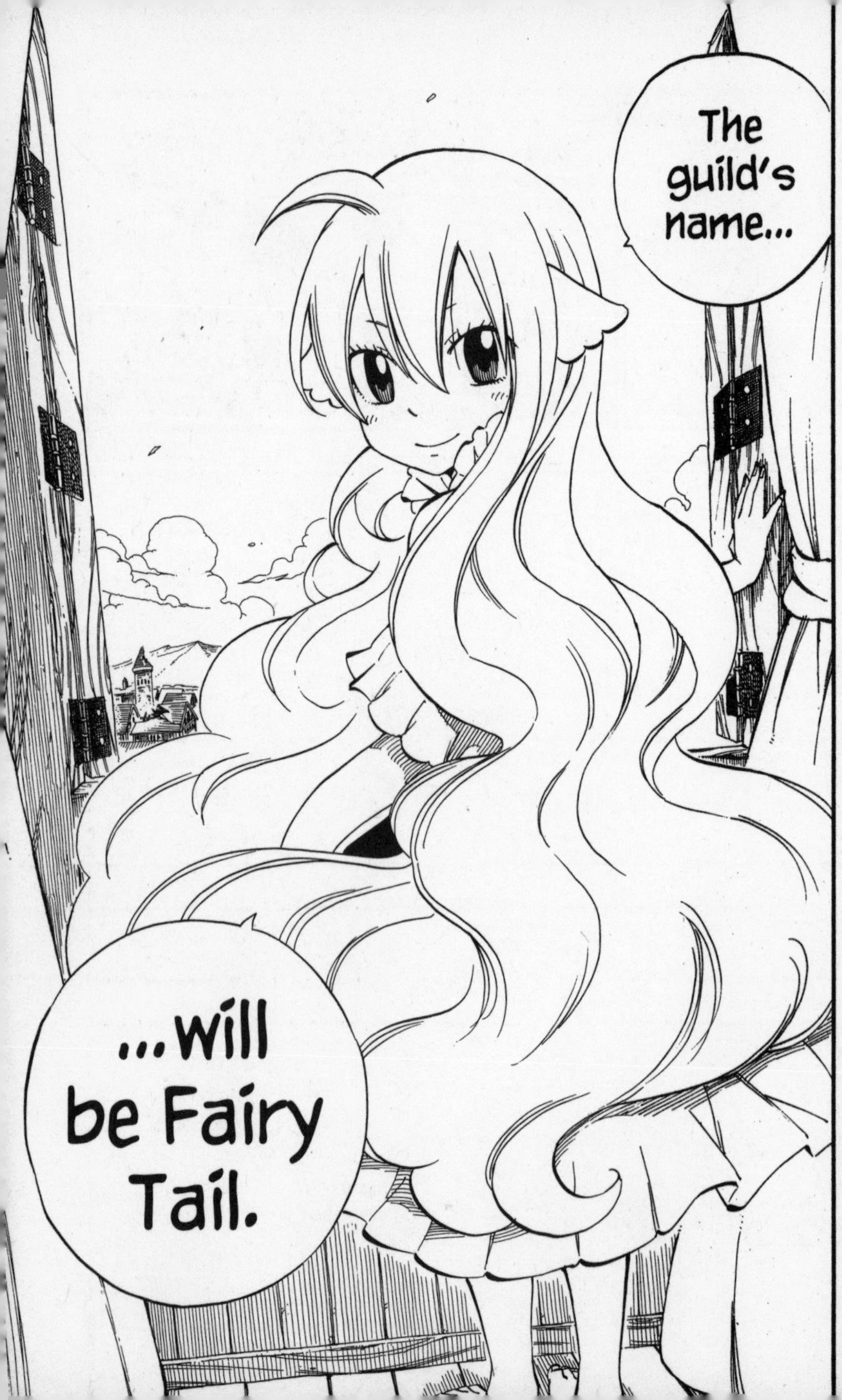
The guild's name...
...will be Fairy Tail.

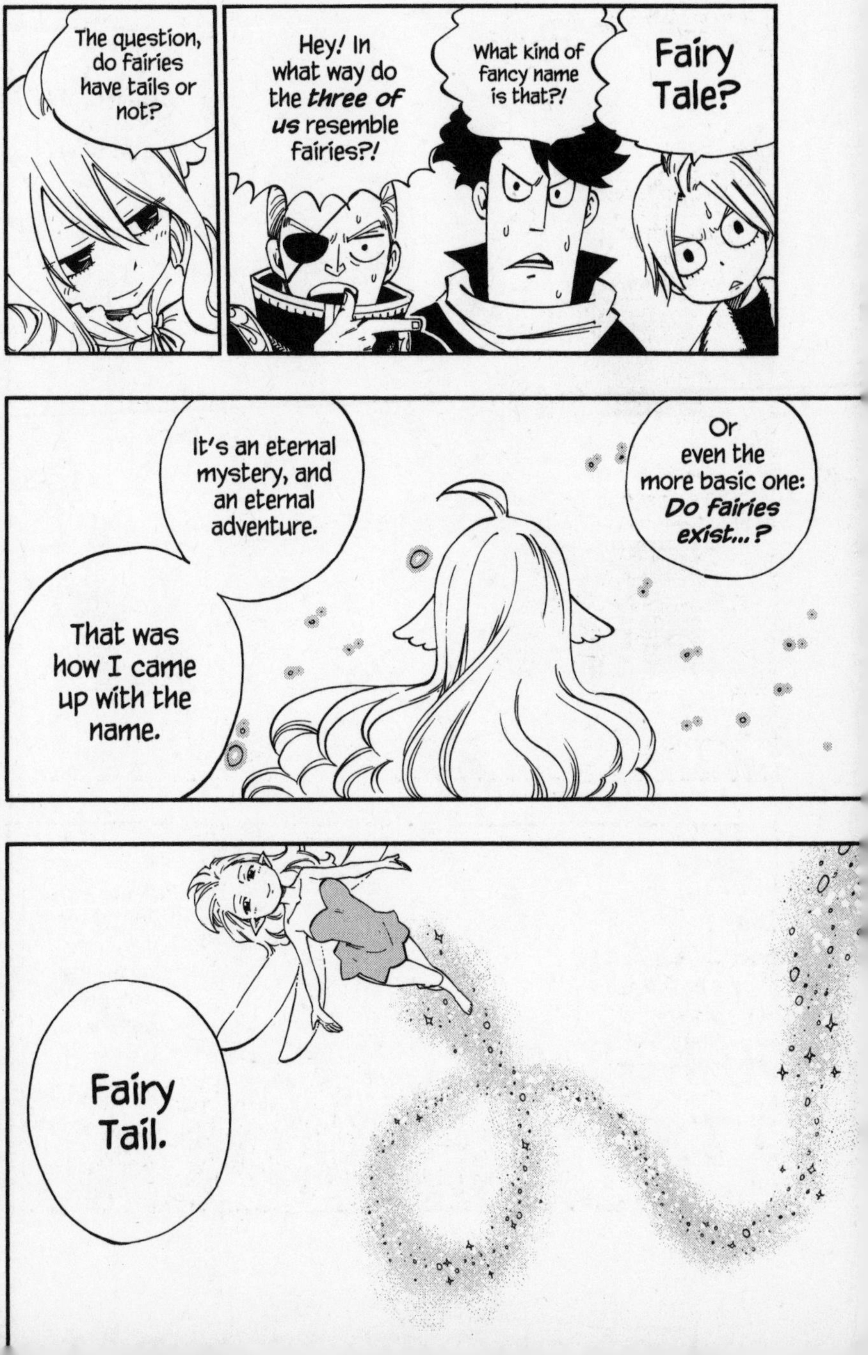
Fairy Tale?
What kind of fancy name is that?!
Hey! In what way do the *three of us* resemble fairies?!
The question, do fairies have tails or not?
Or even the more basic one: *Do fairies exist...?*
It's an eternal mystery, and an eternal adventure.
That was how I came up with the name.
Fairy Tail.

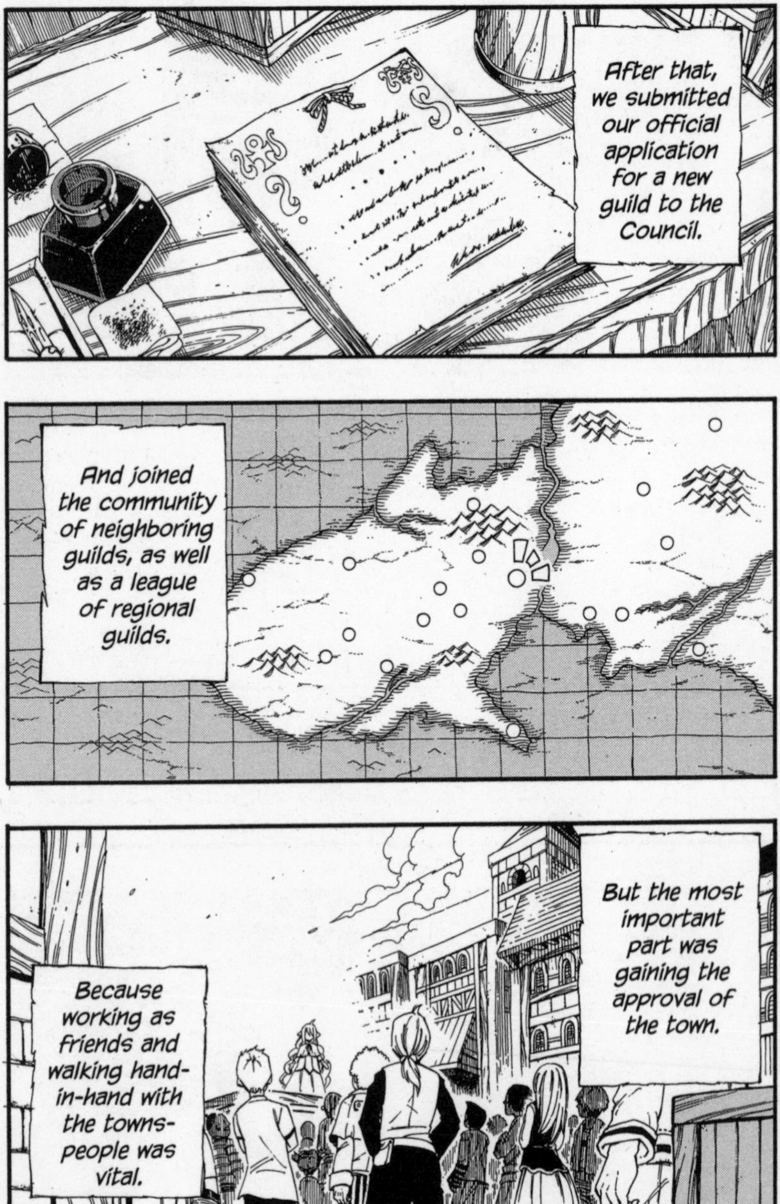
After that, we submitted our official application for a new guild to the Council.
And joined the community of neighboring guilds, as well as a league of regional guilds.
But the most important part was gaining the approval of the town.
Because working as friends and walking hand-in-hand with the towns-people was vital.

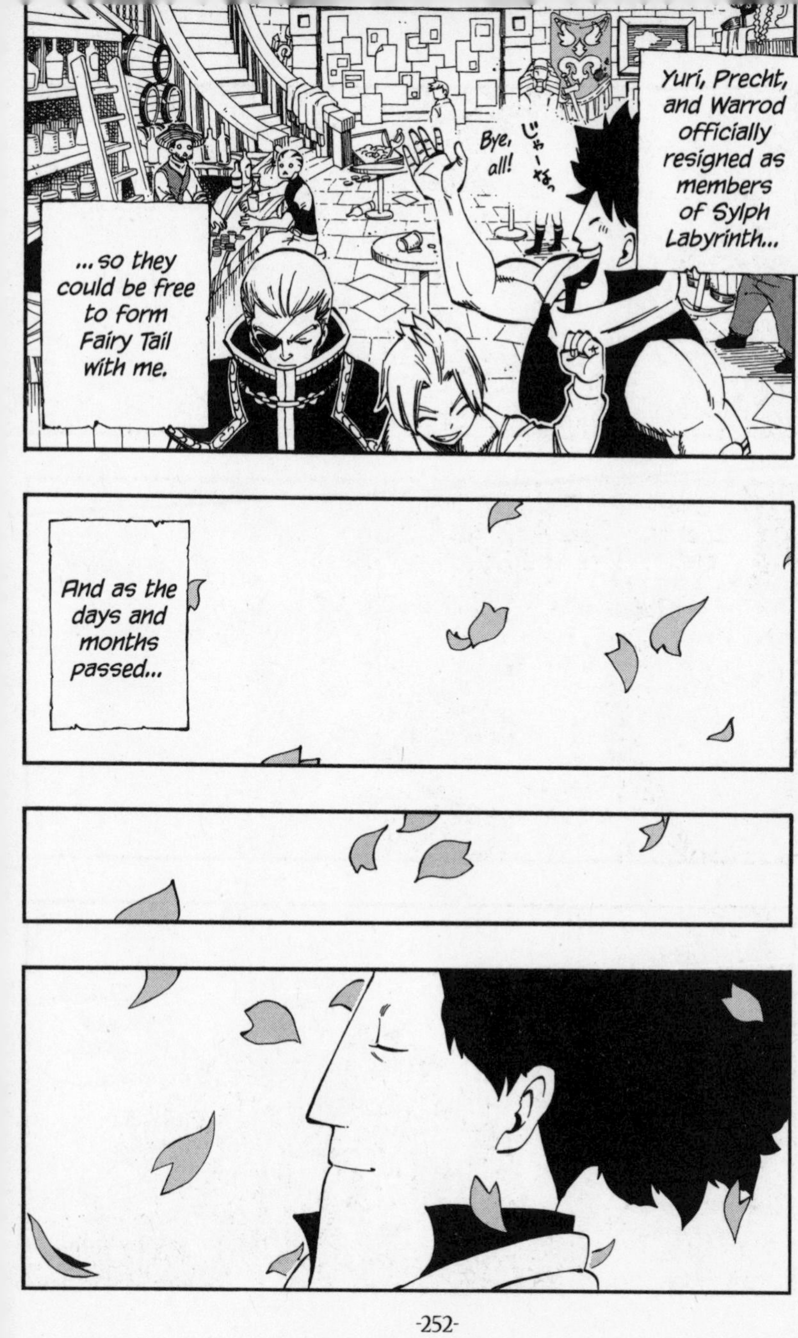
Yuri, Precht, and Warrod officially resigned as members of Sylph Labyrinth...
Bye, all!
じゃーなっ
...so they could be free to form Fairy Tail with me.
And as the days and months passed...

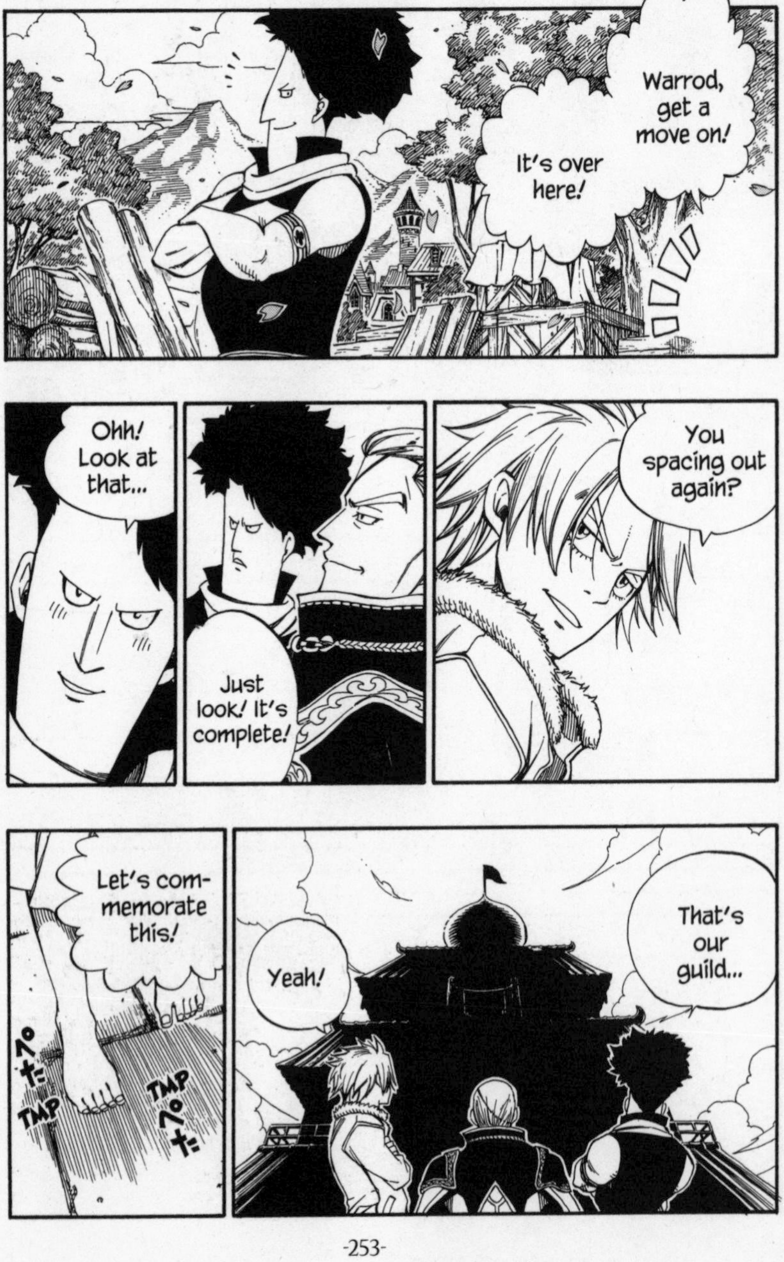
Warrod, get a move on!
It's over here!
You spacing out again?
Just look! It's complete!
Ohh! Look at that...
That's our guild...
Yeah!
Let's com-memorate this!
TMP
TMP

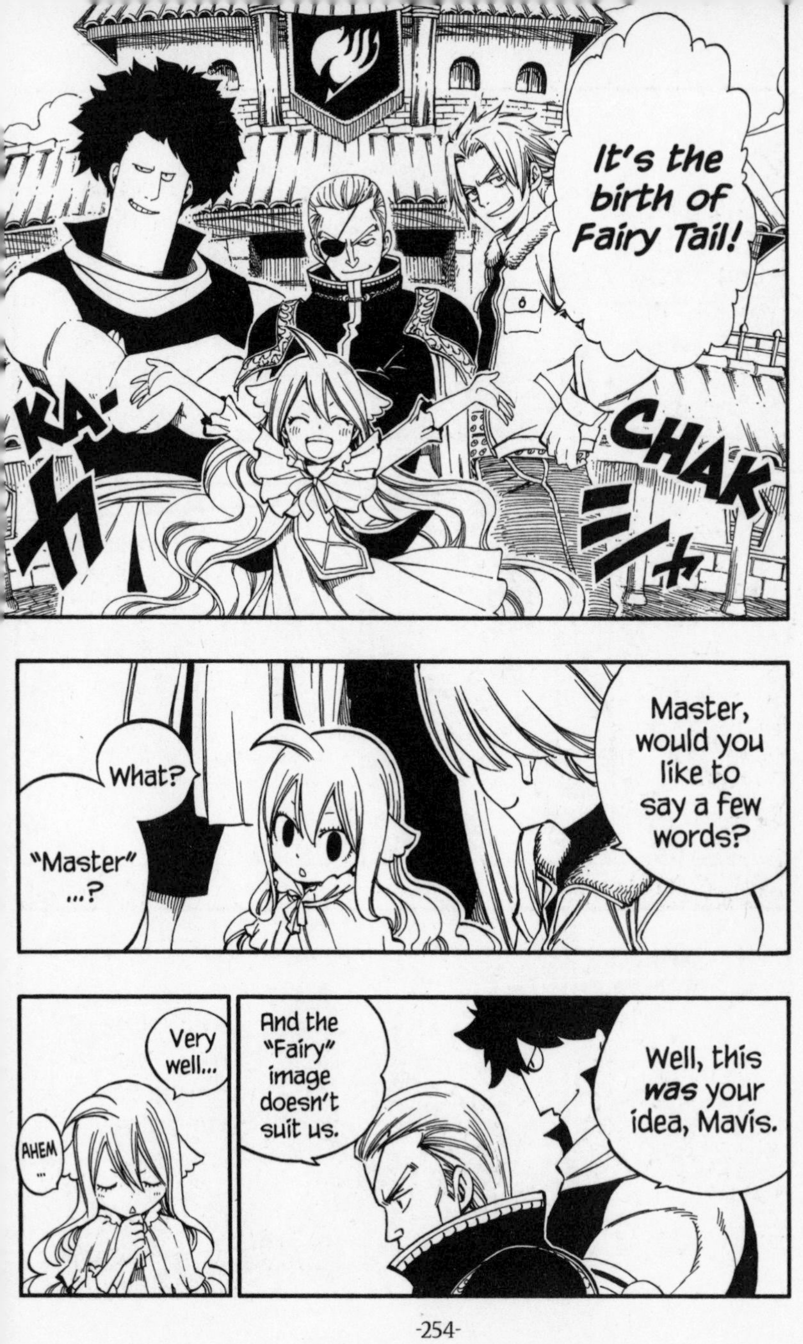
It's the birth of Fairy Tail!
KA-CHAK
Master, would you like to say a few words?
What?
"Master" ...?
Well, this *was* your idea, Mavis.
And the "Fairy" image doesn't suit us.
Very well...
AHEM ...

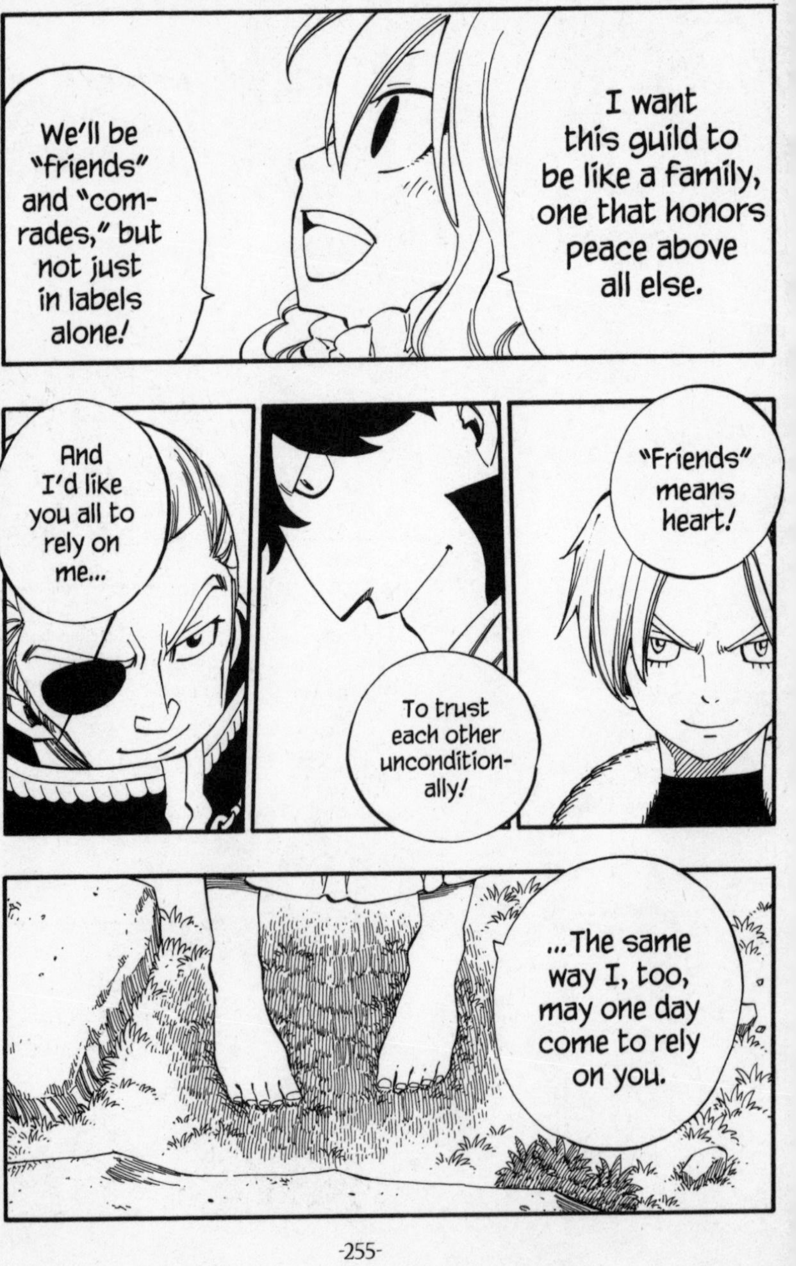
I want this guild to be like a family, one that honors peace above all else.
We'll be "friends" and "comrades," but not just in labels alone!
"Friends" means heart!
To trust each other unconditionally!
And I'd like you all to rely on me...
...The same way I, too, may one day come to rely on you.

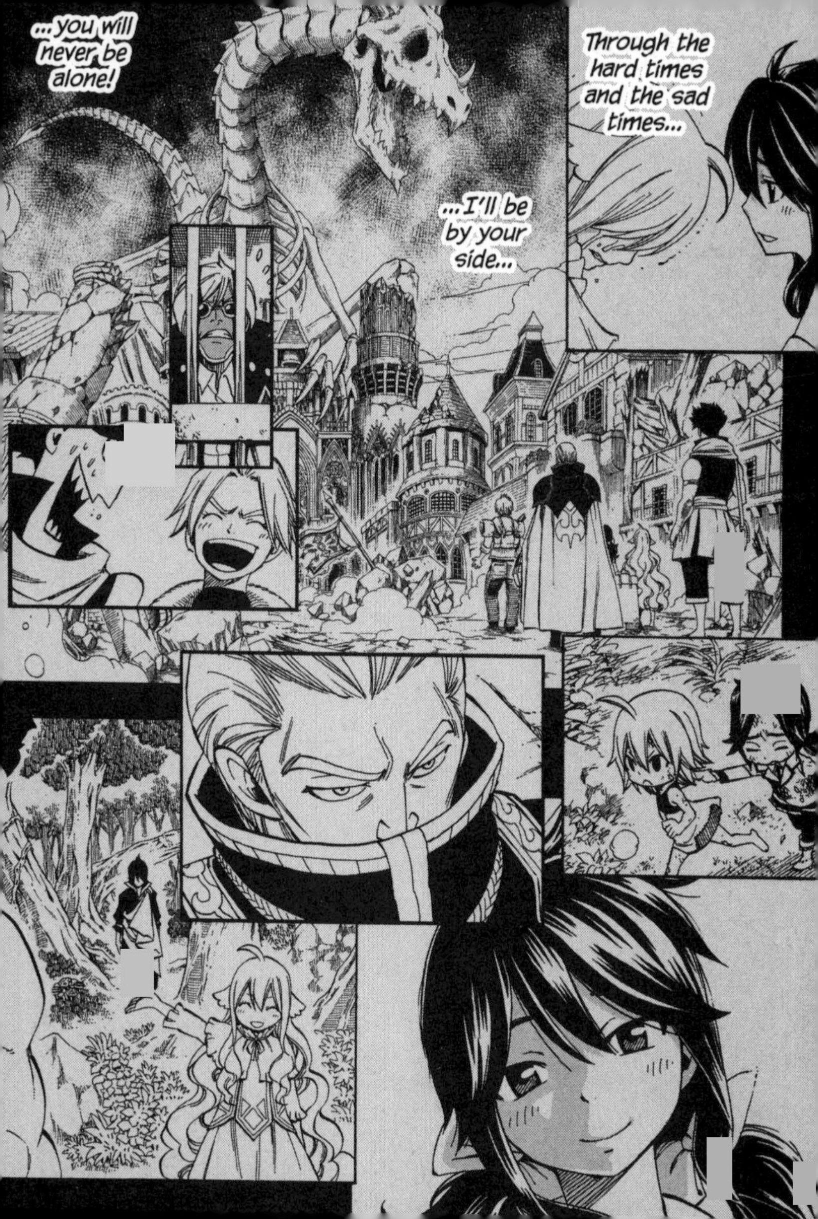
Through the hard times and the sad times...
...I'll be by your side...
...you will never be alone!

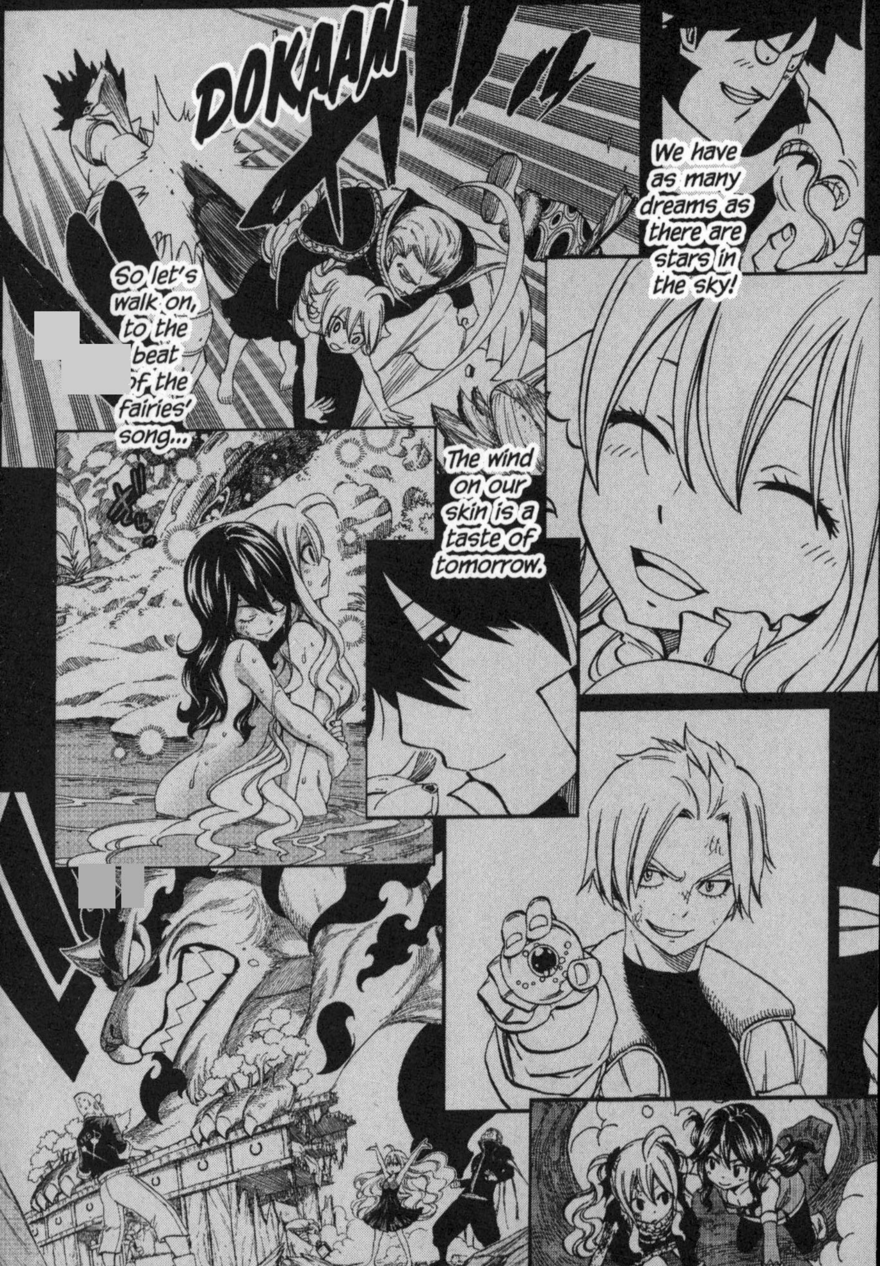
We have as many dreams as there are stars in the sky!
DOKAAM
So let's walk on, to the beat of the fairies' song...
The wind on our skin is a taste of tomorrow.

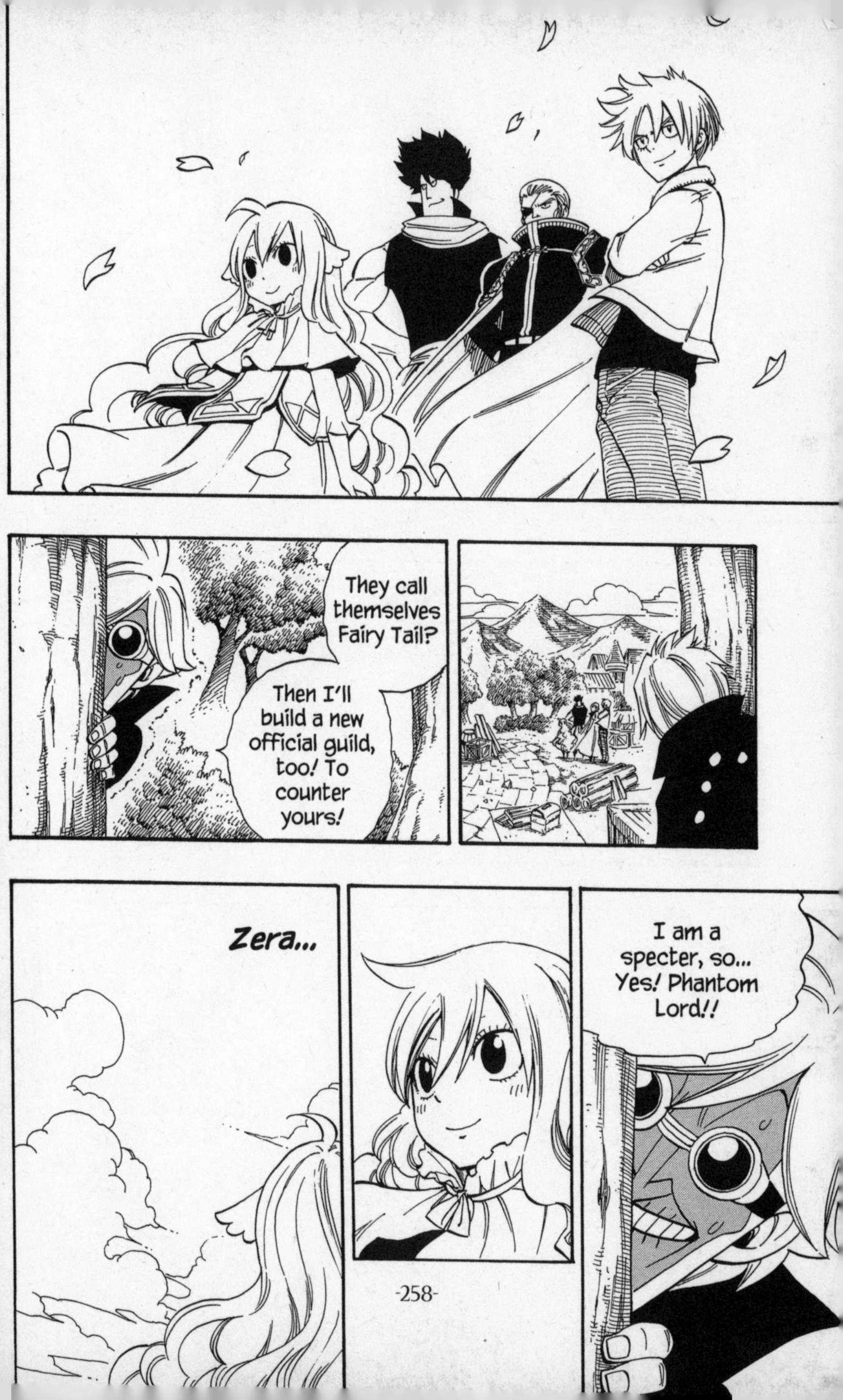
They call themselves Fairy Tail?
Then I'll build a new official guild, too! To counter yours!
I am a specter, so... Yes! Phantom Lord!!
Zera...

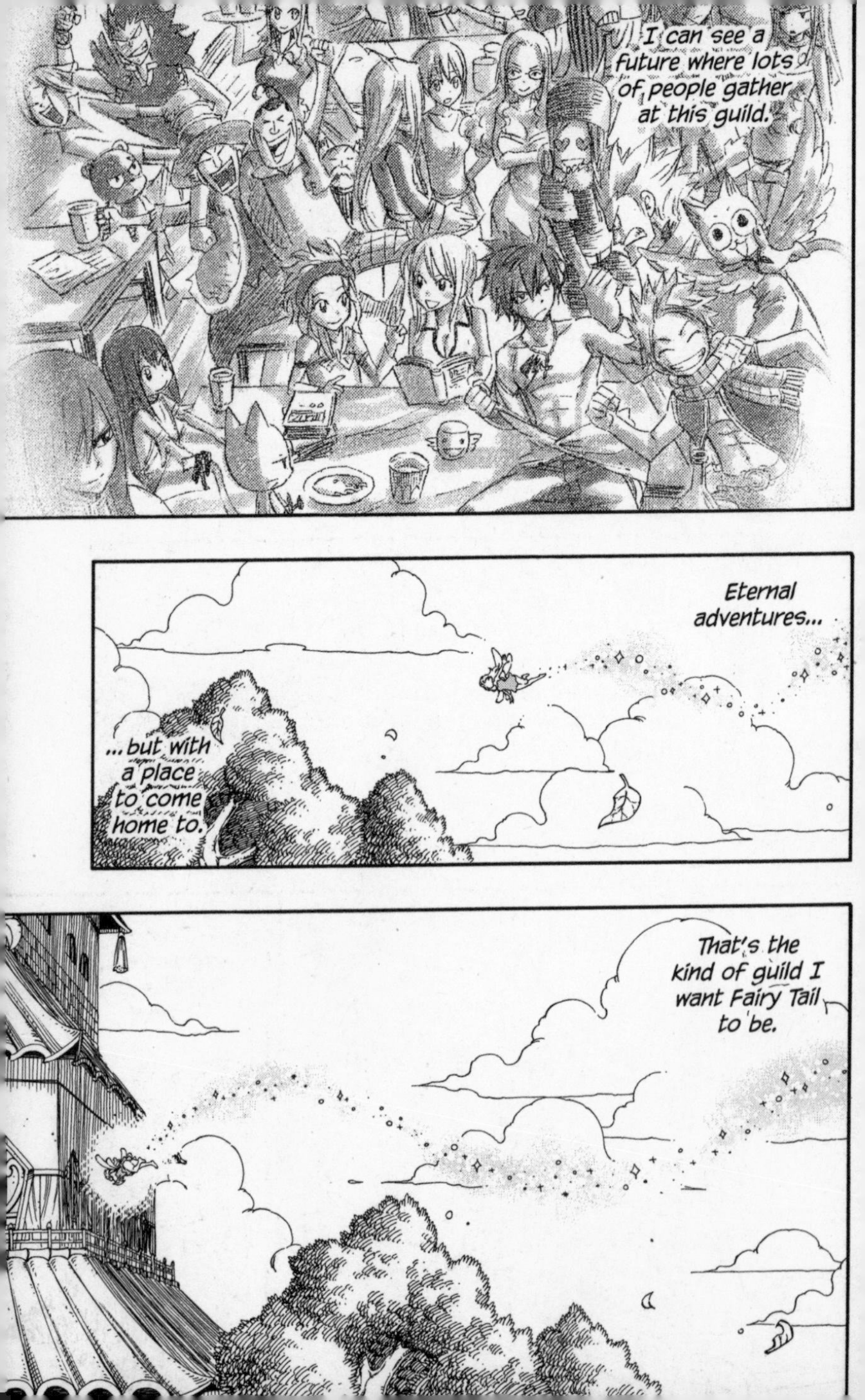
I can see a future where lots of people gather at this guild.
Eternal adventures...
...but with a place to come home to.
That's the kind of guild I want Fairy Tail to be.

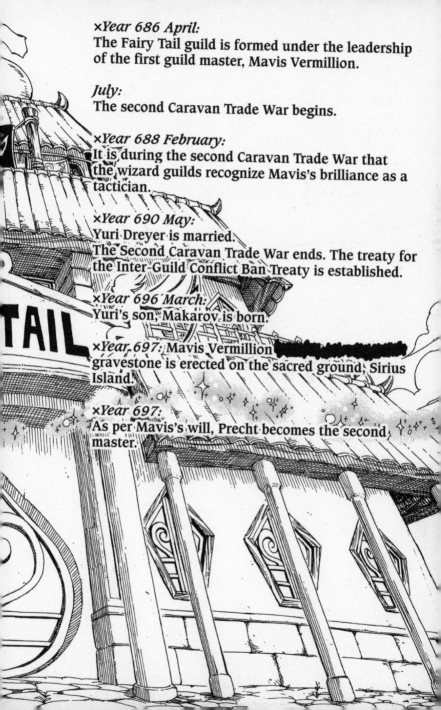

×*Year 686 April:*
The Fairy Tail guild is formed under the leadership of the first guild master, Mavis Vermillion.

July:
The second Caravan Trade War begins.

×*Year 688 February:*
It is during the second Caravan Trade War that the wizard guilds recognize Mavis's brilliance as a tactician.

×*Year 690 May:*
Yuri Dreyer is married.
The Second Caravan Trade War ends. The treaty for the Inter-Guild Conflict Ban Treaty is established.

×*Year 696 March:*
Yuri's son, Makarov is born.

×*Year 697:* Mavis Vermillion ▐▬▬▬▬▬▬▬▬▬▬ gravestone is erected on the sacred ground, Sirius Island.

×*Year 697:*
As per Mavis's will, Precht becomes the second master.

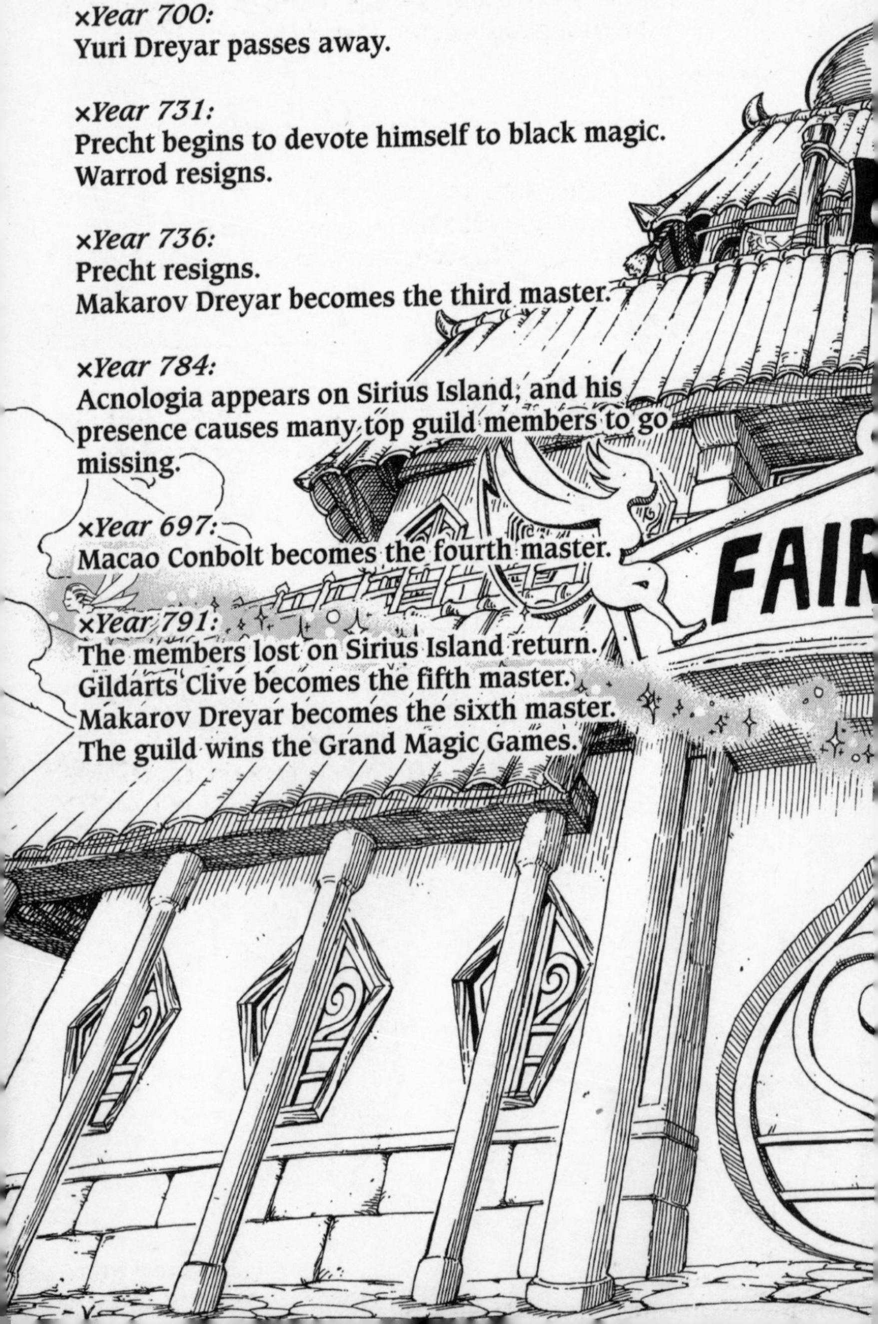

×Year 700:
Yuri Dreyar passes away.

×Year 731:
Precht begins to devote himself to black magic.
Warrod resigns.

×Year 736:
Precht resigns.
Makarov Dreyar becomes the third master.

×Year 784:
Acnologia appears on Sirius Island, and his presence causes many top guild members to go missing.

×Year 697:
Macao Conbolt becomes the fourth master.

×Year 791:
The members lost on Sirius Island return.
Gildarts Clive becomes the fifth master.
Makarov Dreyar becomes the sixth master.
The guild wins the Grand Magic Games.

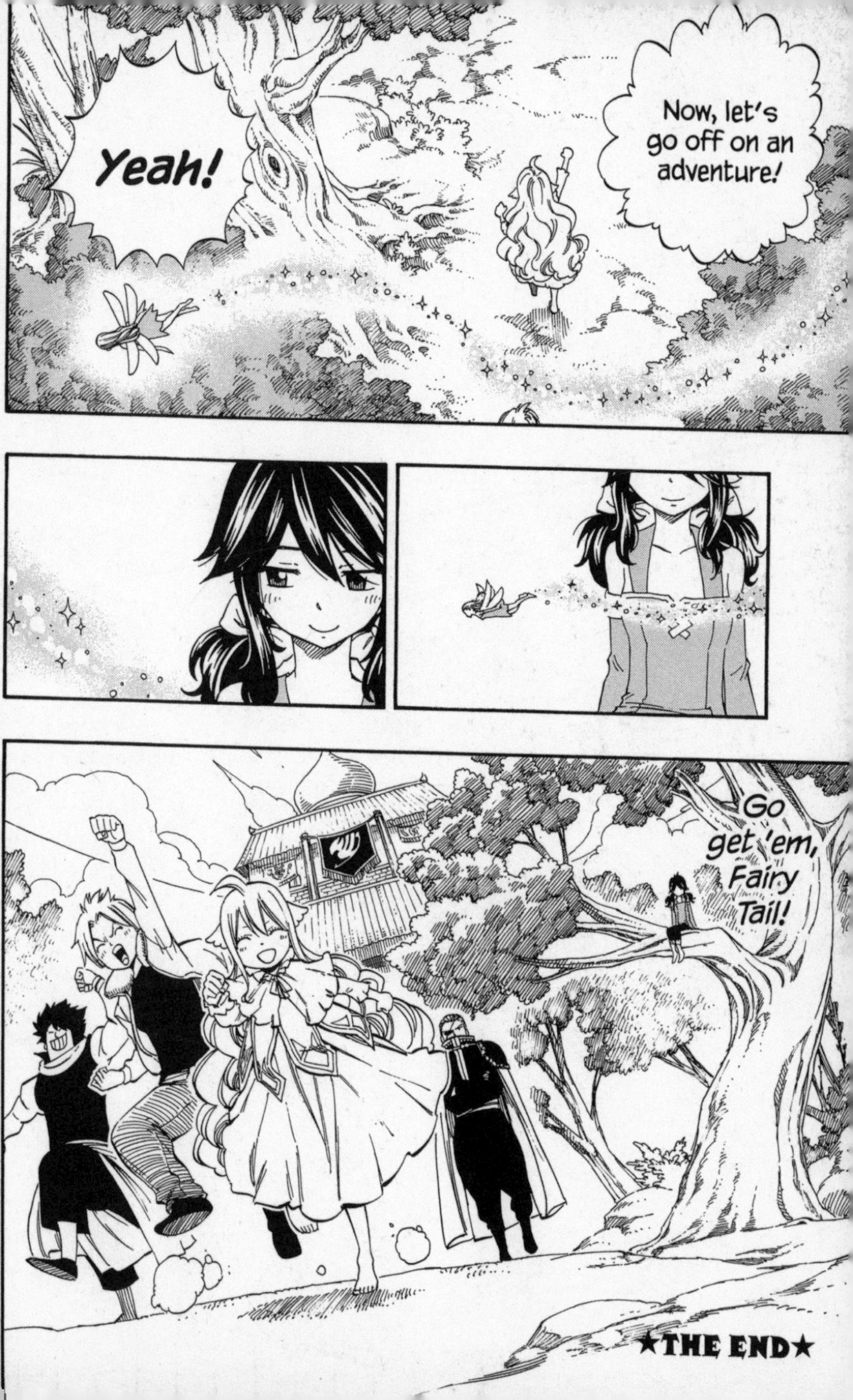
Now, let's go off on an adventure!
Yeah!
Go get 'em, Fairy Tail!
★THE END★

A Long-form Interview with HIRO MASHIMA

DETAILED EXPLANATIONS!!

FAIRY TAIL フェアリーテイル ZERØ ゼロ

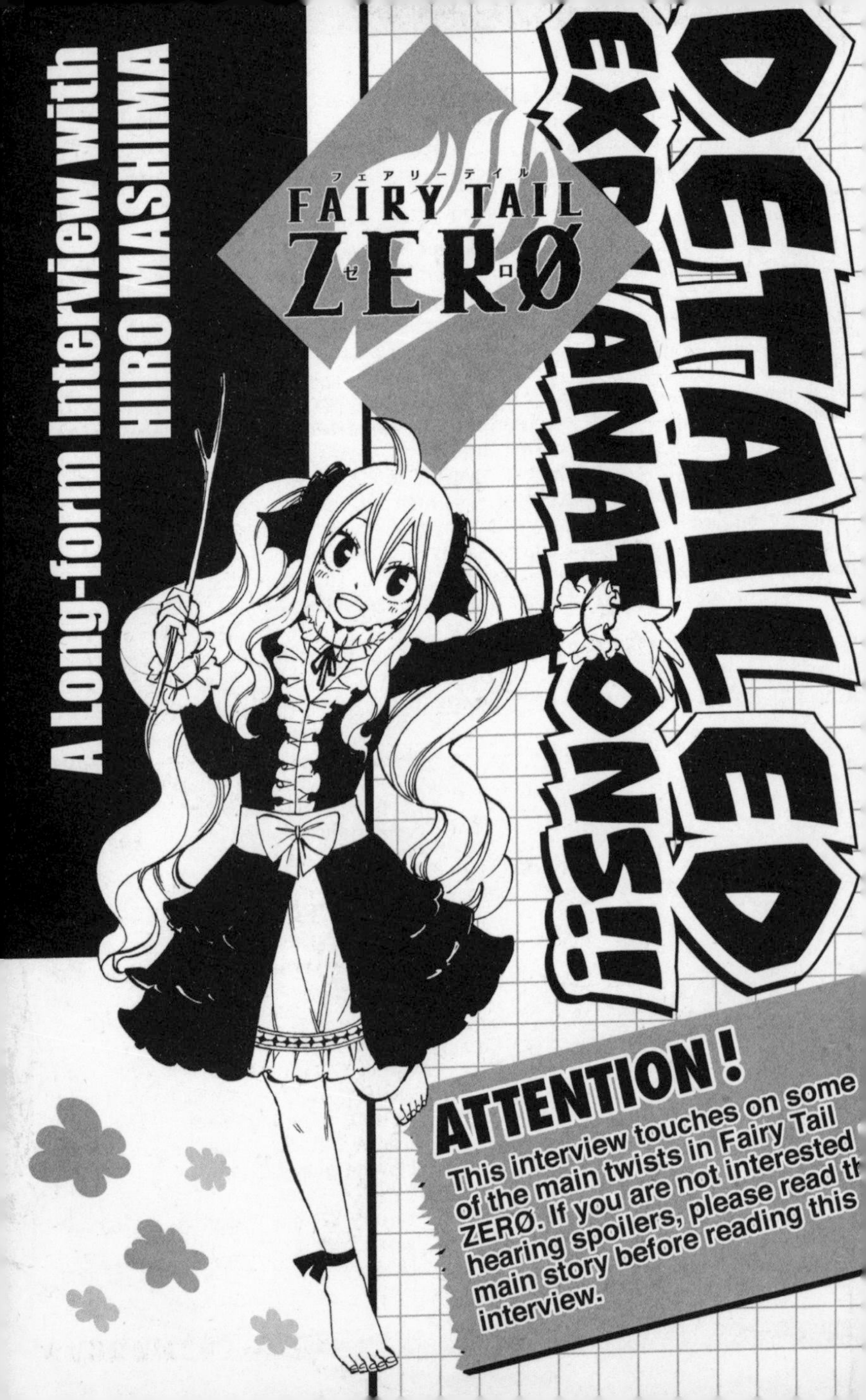

ATTENTION!

This interview touches on some of the main twists in Fairy Tail ZERØ. If you are not interested hearing spoilers, please read th main story before reading this interview.

A few days ago, you finished monthly serialization of Fairy Tail ZERØ. Well done! Now that you've finished it, how do you feel?
Mashima: Thank you very much. Well...my schedule has freed up! And, now that I've finished a story I really wanted to draw, I can report that it turned out pretty much how I wanted it to.

You looked forward to writing a story about the founding of Fairy Tail?
Mashima: Actually, it was supposed to be more important to the main story, but since FT ZERØ is a spinoff, it would have been a problem if you absolutely had to read it to understand the main Fairy Tail story. So I basically had to walk a fine line, making something that would inform the main story without actually being required reading.

Can you tell us the circumstances that led up to the serialization of FT ZERØ?
At the very beginning, there were no plans for me to draw a series in Monthly Fairy Tail Magazine. Back when they were sounding out ideas for the magazine, I was doing both the main weekly series and supervising the anime. I didn't even have a millimeter's room to stuff in a monthly manga series, so I rejected the idea at first. And it was just at that time that a dream job came along: doing character designs for a game!! Man, I was excited to do that job! But that was only one job—no follow-up work was on the horizon, and I realized that the work I really had to concentrate on was manga! So it was then that I decided to draw a manga series in Monthly Fairy Tail Magazine.

We all decided it would be a Fairy Tail spin-off manga, and during the early meetings, we also decided on Mavis as the main character, but I was worried about which era to draw it in. I thought that the area of her character that the fans would most want to know about was how she became a ghost. But I thought that story should be in the main series, so we altered the main story a bit so that a background story could appear in Weekly Magazine's Fairy Tail chapters.

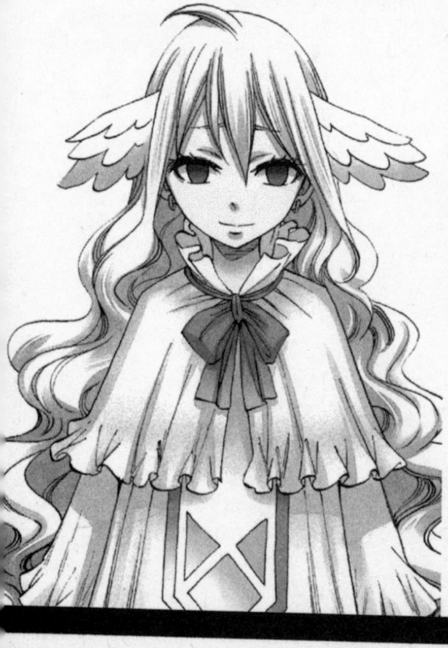

THE BIRTH OF MAVIS

How did Mavis come to be?
Mashima: When I came up with the name Mavis, I thought of an old grandpa-like character, but later, I realized "Mavis" was a girl's name. (Laughs.) This was when Mavis was only a name, and I had no visuals to go with it, so I thought, "Okay. She's female." And eventually her design became what it is now.

So how did she go from just "female" to a young girl?
Mashima: Hmm... That *is* surprising, huh? (Laughs.) I thought having the

first master of the guild be female was unexpected, but as it turned out, the only one who thought it was unexpected was me! Everyone else already knew from hearing the name, "Mavis," that she was female. So I thought I needed something else unexpected after that.

So you were hoping to shock your readers?
Mashima: That's right. Well, *surprise* them, anyway.

In the Vol. 32 afterword, you wrote that you brought Mavis back due to her unexpected popularity. You hadn't planned to include her in the Grand Magic Games?
Mashima: Yes, well, the enormously positive reader reaction to Mavis was a happy miscalculation on my part. There are some characters I draw expecting them to be popular, and when they aren't, it leaves me a little limp. (Laughs.) But, like in Mavis's case, when the opposite happens, it makes the author really happy, and I want to write stories with that character more. I suppose that also has to do with the fans saying that they want to see more of her, too. When they want to see more, you want to write more.

So when did you start thinking about Mavis's past?
I've had vague ideas about it for quite a while, which culminated with her appearance in the main story. Know what I mean? And starting about then, I started thinking, little by little, of how Fairy Tail was founded. That became the plot of FT ZERØ. That plan also included the point where Mavis met Zeref. But I've been digging ever more deeply into this past, so I'm very happy that the series allowed it to take a permanent form.

THERE ARE A LOT OF TWISTS TO FT ZERØ

In an interview that was printed in Vol. 12 of Monthly Fairy Tail Magazine, the voice actress who plays Mavis, Mamiko Noto, said she never once realized that Zera was an illusion. That she was cleanly fooled.
I'm delighted! Mainly because my staff figured it out when Zera died in the very first chapter. (Laughs.) Since they knew Zera was going to appear again in Chapter 2, my staff said, "Huh? Didn't she die in the first chapter?" And I tried to say, "She *seemed* to have, but..." (Laughs.) I still had trepidations about hiding the fact that Zera was an illusion until the end, and maybe that's why I never delved very deeply into Zera's character. But if I'd included her much more, it would've been more obvious that others couldn't see her, which would've been more suspicious. Some characters were purposely pretending as if they saw her, but... Really, I think it's great if people saw that twist coming, but I sense that those who were fooled had more fun reading it.

You also added some tricks in there in your foreshadowing.
Mashima: I really enjoy coming up with foreshadowing. Especially when I know how it's going to end, I tend to stuff in a lot of foreshadowing. Actually, I had thought up a lot more plot, but I had to cut out all the flab I could to fit each chapter into 20 pages.

In Chapter 3, when Mavis introduced Yuri to Zera, I thought Yuri was confused because he never expected a second young girl to be on this "deserted" island. But, actually, he was being introduced to a girl (Zera) whom he couldn't see, right?

Mashima: Actually, I had very detailed talks with my editor on what would give away the secret and what would keep it hidden. I came up with that based on those talks.

In Chapter 8, at the beginning of the operation to free Magnolia, Zera said, "Those three didn't even listen to me!" I thought they didn't listen because it was just the ravings of a little girl. But it was really because they couldn't hear her.
Mashima: Exactly! I liked that line, if I do say so myself. (Laughs.)

In Chapter 10, Warrod was wondering why Geoffrey wasn't in the empty cage...
Mashima: That was a place where I wanted a few more pages!! And it just isn't cool to supplement a story in an interview afterwards, but... Well in the story, it was supposed to have been Zera who locked the cage. But because she's an illusion, the cage was never actually locked, so Geoffrey was able to escape.

And a part of the foreshadowing was in the very logo of the series, right? How the logo seemed to slowly fade out of the logo?
Mashima: That idea came up when we were creating the first chapter. Since all the major plot twists in the story were set from the beginning, the logo was a way to play with it.

What really surprised me was the logo in Chapter 12. The final "Ø" of the logo vanished completely in Chapter 11, and become an "A," for "Zera."
Mashima: Actually, I wanted to do that just a little bit better. (laughs) Like going from a 0 (zero) to a 1 (one), or from an A to a B or something like that. I think something like that would have had a bit more impact. But it turned out to go from a "Ø" to an "A."

Where do such novel ideas come from?
Mashima: I'm always trying to come up with some new stuff every single day, and things like that just come up by accident. (Laughs.) Coming up with Chapter 1 was a slog. But when we figured out how to play with the logo, that was when we locked in Zera, and with that, the middle part of the story fell into place. But that took a lot of time. You wouldn't believe how long it took to finish the thumbnails for the first chapter.

Why was that?
Mashima: Well, when trying to pin down what life Mavis lived as a young girl, I just couldn't come up with anything good. I knew that the adventure had to start with Mavis on Sirius Island, but what kind of life she was living on that island was something I couldn't manage to figure out. I worried about that part forever!

The voice actress for Mavis, Mamiko Noto, said in the same interview that we mentioned before, "I had no idea that Mavis's past was so cruel."
Mashima: Actually, I wanted to go deeper into that aspect, too. I wanted to lay out exactly why Mavis wanted to build a guild of her own, but we just didn't have the pages. 20 pages per month is completely different from 20 pages per week. 20 pages a week is nearly the perfect length, but 20 pages per month is too short! A reader of a monthly magazine has to wait an entire month for the next chapter. So you absolutely have to put all the necessary plot elements within those 20 pages. In regular monthly comics, you need to put at least two pivotal scenes in every chapter, and because a monthly gives

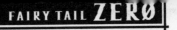

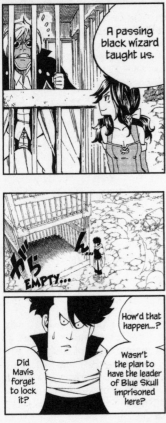

A passing black wizard taught us.
EMPTY...
How'd that happen...?
Wasn't the plan to have the leader of Blue Skull imprisoned here?
Did Mavis forget to lock it?

you about 30 to 40 pages, you can do it. Even if you can't do that with only 20 pages, I did my best to squeeze in at least 1.5 pivotal scenes. But it meant that I had to rush through some scenes...

When you talk about what you wanted to draw, what were you thinking of?
Mashima: At the very beginning, I thought Mavis would hate everything related to guilds, but gradually come to love them. I just didn't have the pages necessary to tell that story. Considering I had to tell the whole story over one year in 20-paged chapters, I had to change the structure midway and leave the foundation of the guild to somewhere around the very final episode. And in the end, that's pretty much how I drew it.

Well, I sort of figured the bonds of friendship and camaraderie you drew were the foundations of the guild. And that was fine for me.
Mashima: Really?! You know, that truly makes me happy when you say that! It was sort of a trial-and-error process, but I was hoping that was the form it would take.

WHAT TO LOOK FOR IN FT ZERØ

I'm sure FT ZERØ had a ton of highlights, but could you tell us which scenes or installments you tried to put extra effort into?
Mashima: I mentioned this earlier, but I'd say it was the hints foreshadowing Zera's real nature. Also, I put a lot of work into the scene where Mavis meets Zeref [in Chapter 7 where Zeref is bathing]. I hardly ever get a chance to draw that kind of scene... I mean, a fan-service scene with a guy! (Laughs.) Also, the way the story flows up until Mavis uses Law. Actually, I spent a lot of time wondering how Mavis was going to save Yuri. I had already decided that Mavis would use magic Zeref taught her, and, as a side effect, she would stop growing. But it was while I was drawing the thumbnails for the story that I thought, "What if she used Fairy Law?" Or at least, "Fairy Law would be based on a different magic called "Law" that, afterwards, Mavis refined to have no side effects. In the end, that was the idea that went into the manga. It's just that, with the name "Law," my editor and I argued back and forth an awful lot whether the readers would understand that Law and Fairy Law were different. I think those readers who could figure out that Fairy Law came originally from Law would look at this with a sense of, "that makes sense now."

Could you tell us a little about one of the key people in FT ZERØ, Zera?

Mashima: Yes. For better or for worse, Zera was a character made specifically for this story. Putting aside for the moment that she's an illusion, she was going to be a best friend for Mavis, and from that starting point, we created the rest of it. Visually, Mavis has short, thin eyebrows and an overall pale appearance, and so Zera has thick, black eyebrows. That was pretty much all I considered with her outward appearance. (Laughs.) Personally, I like stories where the bully grows up to be a good person. Think of the daughter of the innkeeper in *Les Misérables*. I imagined Zera as just that kind of character. I think if I had extra pages, I could have given her some more charm, but as things are, she's just one part of the system. I don't think I drew her quite as well as I would have liked to. Still, I knew from the very start that there were limits to what I could do. You know, I've been using those limits as an excuse this whole interview, huh? (Laughs.) I just wasn't able to go deeper into any of my characters. Back when I was writing Chapter 1, when my deadline was up and I had to start producing pages, I brought some thumbnail pages to my editors that were still completely blank. (Laughs.)

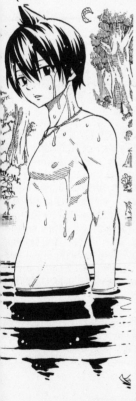

What happened?

Mashima: I really wasn't able to think up anything! In the end, I had to basically finish up the thumbnails that very day. I was completely out of time. And there was a part of Zera's character I was never able to get into. I often wish that I could have made the character a little more prominent.

I thought that chronology at the end of Chapter 13 was very interesting! There were lots of places where it would feed back into the main Fairy Tail story.

Mashima: There are some entries on there that I was only allowed to include because they had just been revealed a short time before. If this were the main story in Weekly Shonen Magazine, I would never have done it! (Laughs.) It's just a bunch of text, so I imagine a lot of readers would just skip it, but since this is Monthly Fairy Tail Magazine, I can get away with it. One of the assumptions was that the Fairy Tail Magazine was being read by Fairy Tail fans. Something like that would probably be forbidden in a regular manga magazine.

By the way, are there any events in the timeline that you have a specific episode in mind for?

Mashima: Yeah... The one that comes foremost in my mind is the Caravan Trade War portion. It's directly because of this war that Mavis came to be known as the Fairy General. At first, I thought I'd tell that story in FT ZERØ, so to a certain extent, I've more or less constructed that story in my mind. In fact, the treaty after the Second Caravan Trade War has come up in the main story in a

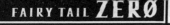

discussion between Council members.

Speaking of connections with the main story, you had a scene where we found out that the master of Blue Skull was Geoffrey, who later founded Phantom Lord!
Mashima: Yes. Geoffrey was the founder of Phantom Lord and an ancestor of the last master of Phantom Lord, Jose. Actually, in hindsight, it was a mistake to have never mentioned Jose's last name...

Now, to stray a bit from the discussion of FT ZERØ, including all of the types of magic we see from characters in all of Fairy Tail so far, if you were made a wizard, what would be the magic you'd most like to try?
Mashima: Well, I imagine that most of my readers could come up with an answer right off the bat, but... I don't really have one. (Laughs.) If you pried an answer out of me, it'd probably be...some kind of magic where I could play with time. (Laughs.) There are points where I'd really have loved to stop time, or have my own time run a bit slower than everybody else's. At the very least, a 48-hour day would be great! I'm sure everyone has thought of that, but...

How would you use that extra time?
Mashima: I'd work!! I'd work some, and play some... I guess...I'd do much the same things I do now, but instead, I'd have twice the amount of time to work and play than I do now. But if I did, my sleep time would be exactly the same as it is now. (Laughs.)

And finally, do you have a message for the readers of Monthly Fairy Tail Magazine?
Mashima: I want to thank you all for sticking with the magazine through all 13 issues! Monthly Fairy Tail Magazine was a first in a lot of ways for me. And with that large number of "firsts," it was a real challenge, but, at the same time, a joy to work on. I imagine it was a new experience for the people kind enough to pick up the magazine, too. And speaking for all of the people who worked hard to put out the magazine every

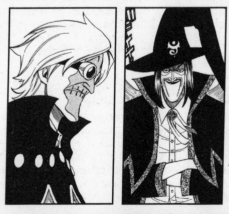

month, we would all like to express our gratitude to you! The main story of Fairy Tail still has a long way to go, so I hope you're still looking forward to the new adventures. And we also have a lot of DVDs yet to come, so please consider picking those up as well.

This interview was first published in Monthly Fairy Tail Magazine Volume 13, but portions of it have been re-recorded and corrected.

AFTERWORD

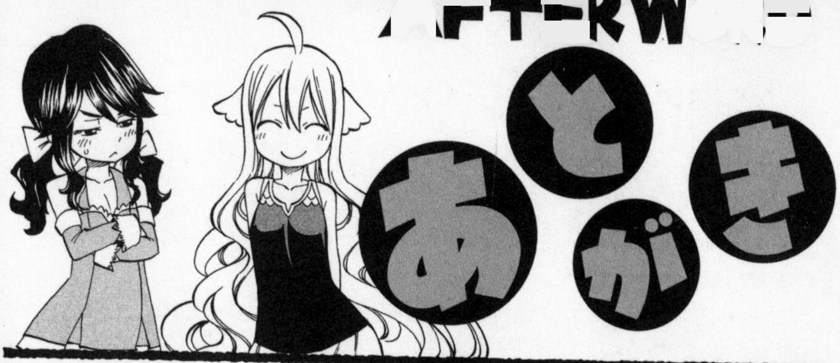
あとがき

I'm celebrating!! Fairy Tail ZERØ is now a graphic novel!! It's finally out! Originally, this was a manga exclusively for the people who bought Monthly Fairy Tail Magazine, but there were a lot of folks who asked for a graphic novel version, so we were able to gather the pages together into this volume. Nearly everything I'd say in an afterword like this is written in the interview, but the feeling that stayed with me when looking back was just how busy I was during this serialization. I was so busy that even I, the author, would forget what happened in the previous installment of the story as I was drawing the next one. I do a lot of thinking to come up with the plot of the main Fairy Tail story (even if it doesn't seem like it), and I suppose it's because I have so many characters, but I tend to confuse elements that have been decided on with elements that I'm still considering. I have to be really careful that elements that are still under consideration don't create inconsistencies with the established (or already decided) story. And there were a lot of under-consideration elements in Fairy Tail ZERØ, so I had to work pretty hard to make sure I wasn't contradicting the main Fairy Tail story. But being so busy, I often drew a blank when trying to recall the events of the previous episode. (Laughs.) Now, this isn't the end of Mavis's story. Much of what happened afterwards with Mavis is included in Volume 53 of Fairy Tail.

Translation Notes:

Japanese is tricky language for most Westerners, and translation is often more art than science. For your edification and reading pleasure, here are notes on some of the places where we could have gone in a different direction with our translation of the work, or where a Japanese cultural reference is used.

Page 19, Sirius

In Japanese, the name for the island on which Mavis and Zera lived is *Tenrô-jima*, which means literally, "Heaven Wolf Island." But it's worth noting that *tenrô* also refers to a star, the same star known as the "dog star," or Sirius in Western languages. Sirius is the brightest star in the night sky, and so it would follow that it is also the brightest star in its constellation, Canis Major. (And if you noticed the connection between Canis and "canine," it won't surprise you to learn that the constellation is "the great dog," or "Orion's dog," out of Greek mythology.) Japan gets its name for the star from Chinese, using characters that mean "celestial wolf." So, since the meanings of the Japanese and English names are the same, the translation uses the Western name of Sirius for both the island and the star.

Page 109, Jewels

In most fantasy, the currency used in the fantasy world is intuitively equivalent to the currency used by the intended reader. So if, for example, a horse in a fantasy universe written for American audiences costs four-hundred silver pieces, then the reader can automatically assume that the horse costs something around $400 USD. The same is true for Fairy Tail, but only with "jewels" being equivalent to "yen." And a quick-and-dirty conversion for yen is 100 yen to 1 US dollar. So 5,000 jewels would be about $50 USD.

Page 109, Lacrima

Lacrima is an Italian word with Latin origins that means "tear drop." But in the Fairy Tail world, it refers to a particular type of crystal that can hold and utilize magic energy, making it indispensible in crafting magical items. In the main Fairy Tail story, lacrima are used for everything from media players and cell phones to powering magical hyper-destructive cannons. But in the world of Fairy Tail ZERØ, apparently the use of lacrima isn't nearly as advanced or widespread yet.

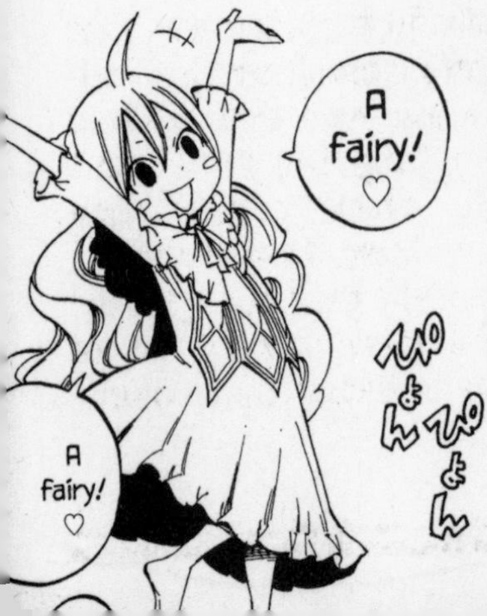
A fairy! ♡
A fairy! ♡
ぴょん
ぴょん
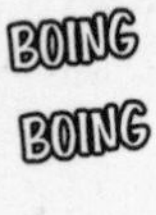
BOING
BOING

A Kodansha Comics Trade Paperback Original.

Fairy Tail ZERØ copyright © 2015 Hiro Mashima
English translation copyright © 2016 Hiro Mashima

Published in the United States by Kodansha Comics, an imprint of Kodansha USA Publishing, LLC, New York.

Publication rights for this English edition arranged through Kodansha Ltd., Tokyo.

First published in Japan in 2015 by Kodansha Ltd., Tokyo
ISBN 978-1-63236-284-1

Printed in the United States of America.

www.kodanshacomics.com

9 8 7 6 5 4 3 2 1

Translation: William Flanagan
Lettering: AndWorld Design
Editing: Haruko Hashimoto